FUTURE 2

English for Work, Life, and Academic Success

Second Edition

Series Consultants
Sarah Lynn
Ronna Magy
Federico Salas-Isnardi

 Pearson

Future 2
English for Work, Life, and Academic Success
Teacher's Edition
Second Edition

Pearson, 221 River Street, Hoboken, NJ 07030 USA

Staff credits: The people who made up the *Future* team, representing content development, design, manufacturing, marketing, multimedia, project management, publishing, rights management, and testing, are Pietro Alongi, Jennifer Castro, Dave Dickey, Gina DiLillo, Warren Fischbach, Pamela Fishman, Gosia Jaros-White, Joanna Konieczna, Michael Mone, Mary Perrotta Rich, Katarzyna Starzyńska-Kościuszko, Claire Van Poperin, Joseph Vella, Gabby Wu.

Text composition: Page Designs International
Cover design: EMC Design Ltd
Illustration credits: See credits page 282.
Photo credits: See credits page 282.
Development: Page Designs International

Library of Congress Cataloging-in-Publication Data
A catalog record for the print edition is available from the Library of Congress.

ISBN-13: 9780134547541 (Teacher's Edition)
ISBN-10: 0134547543 (Teacher's Edition)

Printed in the United States of America
1 2019

www.pearsoneltusa.com/future2e

CONTENTS

The instructional design of the second edition of *Future* has been carefully crafted and is aligned with the College and Career Readiness Standards (CCRS), the English Language Proficiency Standards (ELPS), and the National Reporting System (NRS) level descriptors and interpretive, productive, and interactive outcomes. It is also firmly grounded in the tried-and-true language teaching methods for which the first edition of *Future* was known.

In the second edition of Future, *the emphasis on rigor seen in the new standards is put into practice.* The comprehensive curriculum focuses on the academic skills needed for student success: the use of language in both oral and written communication, development of thinking skills, exposure to close reading skills, and frequent opportunities for writing. In each unit, language is developed in support of building increasingly complex content knowledge.

Future *helps students to both transition successfully into academic programs and to move along on-ramps leading to career pathways.* The levels of *Future* progressively introduce the level-appropriate language and skills needed for success in instruction and evaluation. This helps ensure that students feel empowered to continue their education. By advancing in the academic world and along chosen career pathways, students improve their chances of developing the knowledge, skills, and tools needed to be successful.

Future *has been designed to help students gain familiarity with the technological skills needed to succeed in today's world.* Students are exposed to technological terms and procedures in a variety of lessons. Hands-on opportunities for exposure to technology are afforded throughout the program in the *Go Online* activities. The Pearson Practice English App and the MyEnglishLab provide additional practical experience with technology.

Future *also helps students persist in their English studies.* The program motivates students to continue coming to class by providing ample opportunities for collaboration with classmates. In addition, the concrete strategies and study skills presented throughout the Student Book provide the clear-cut practicality that encourages students to persevere.

Future *is a rigorous integrated-skills course that employs coordinated instructional practices to promote student learning.* Listening, speaking, reading, and writing are integrated throughout the lessons, just as they are naturally woven together outside the classroom. In every lesson, scaffolded language activities and higher-order thinking challenge and engage students.

Key Academic Features of *Future*

Each type of lesson reflects sound pedagogy and offers a logical progression from unit to unit, as well as from one level to the next. This instructional design is tailored to meet the interests and needs of students at their language level and to fulfill key national standards.

Alignment with Critical Instructional Standards (CCRS, ELPS, NRS, WIOA)

The new English Language Proficiency Standards (ELPS) and the College and Career Readiness Standards (CCRS) are challenging educators to redefine ways of educating English language learners. These standards emphasize those skills that allow students to succeed in rigorous educational environments. The Workforce Innovation and Opportunity Act (WIOA) also places priority on academic readiness and requires a great emphasis on college and career preparation and technology integration. In addition, WIOA emphasizes workforce skills and civics knowledge in all sectors of instruction. Thus, English language programs are now challenged with integrating employability skills, academic language, and civics with basic English language instruction.

Future's second edition was designed to align with these standards. It clearly facilitates workplace proficiency and civic engagement. In addition, the high-leverage instruction prepares students to meet the rigorous demands of the standards. The lessons build vocabulary and content knowledge, while promoting critical thinking skills, in carefully sequenced activities that scaffold all learning.

Clear Evidence of Depth of Knowledge

Webb developed the Depth of Knowledge (DOK) framework to help educators align curriculum, standards, and assessment. The DOK framework mirrors the changes in the adult-education market and in the CCRS, ELPS, and WIOA standards.

The second edition of *Future* specifies cognitive skills in every lesson to ensure that students are engaging in different levels of thinking throughout the instruction. These purple highlighted verbs show teachers precisely which skills students will be practicing. A separate reference for teachers, *Language for Rigorous Tasks in* Future, clarifies what each verb means for a particular level and literacy strand.

Optimized Lesson Structure of *Future*

Unit Opener

- **Elicit and contextualize language.** A full-page photo introduces the unit theme and provides opportunities for teacher-guided interactive classroom discussion.

- **Scaffolded questions elicit background knowledge and unit vocabulary.** Preview questions help teachers assess how much students know about a particular unit theme.

- **Unit goals.** Unit goals introduce the competencies taught in a unit and allow students to set, track, and reflect on their own progress. Students revisit these goals to monitor their own progress.

Vocabulary

- **Emphasis on key vocabulary.** All vocabulary is contextualized and practiced in connection to the unit's theme. General vocabulary words, domain-specific vocabulary, and vocabulary from the Academic Word List are found throughout.

- **Picture-dictionary layout.** The presentation of key vocabulary through clear, colorful photos and illustrations scaffolds instruction and helps address diverse learner needs.

- **Elicitation before presentation.** New words are set to the side of the pictures. Teachers elicit what their students know by using the pictures first, and then focusing on the text. This activity allows formative assessment of how much students know and what they need to learn.

- **Recycling of new words.** After new vocabulary is introduced, it is contextualized throughout the course, giving students exposure to the words in a variety of situations. Research shows that the more encounters learners have with a target word, the more likely they are to retain that word.

- **Strategies for self-directed learning.** Study tips in the *Vocabulary* lessons introduce strategies students need to succeed in a variety of learning contexts.

- **Collaborative learning.** Students work in pairs and in teams while engaging in higher-order thinking skills such as identifying, categorizing, matching, and labeling.

Listening

- **Pre-listening activities.** Before students listen to each selection, they complete pre-listening activities, which pre-teach new vocabulary and help activate students' background knowledge. Students make predictions about what is to come. Predicting helps focus students on the social context, develops students' critical thinking, and is an important strategy for communicative competence.

- **Real conversations.** Students are provided multiple opportunities to listen to and engage in realistic conversations.

- **Interpretive listening.** A wide variety of comprehension exercises check students' ability to listen for general understanding (gist), for main idea, for detail, and to make connections to the language used in everyday life.

- **Multiple genres.** Throughout the program, students are exposed to a variety of listening types such as conversations, interviews, radio talk shows, and podcasts.

- **Problem-solving tasks.** In each unit, students discuss solutions to a particular problem related to the unit theme. These tasks engage students' critical thinking skills and develop the analytical fluency needed in academic and workplace settings.

- **Additional speaking practice.** Students wanting additional speaking practice may access MyEnglishLab.

Pronunciation

- **Systematic pronunciation syllabus.** Pronunciation presentations and practice exercises are included in all units. Students are taught to notice and attend to the natural patterns of English. Such instruction aids their comprehension as well as their production.

- **Focus on stress and intonation.** While some pronunciation lessons highlight specific sounds like *th*, most lessons focus on the stress, intonation, and rhythm of the English language. Such skills are critical to developing natural fluency.

- **Additional pronunciation practice.** Students wanting additional pronunciation practice may access the Pearson Practice English App and MyEnglishLab.

Grammar

- **Grammar naturally embedded in the spoken language.** Grammar is first presented for receptive learning in the preceding *Listening & Speaking* lesson. The *Grammar* lesson then begins with a grammar chart that explicitly showcases these target structures in easy-to-read chart form. Grammar Watch boxes follow to explain the structures and their uses.

- **Minimal metalanguage.** The Grammar Watch boxes use a limited amount of metalanguage in order to ensure that the forms and meaning of the target structures are accessible to all students.

- **Practice with both meaning and form.**
  Presentations focus on meaning as well as form.
  This practice helps learners incorporate more related
  structures into their own language use.

- **Progression from controlled to open practice.**
  Grammar practice activities progress from controlled
  to open, providing ample spoken and written practice
  in the target structure.

- **Contextualized activities.** Exercises are
  contextualized in meaningful situations that recycle
  themes and vocabulary from the unit, so that
  grammar practice is both authentic and meaningful.

- **Numerous pair and group activities.** Pair and
  small group activities allow students to practice
  new language structures in a safe, motivating
  environment. These interactions offer further
  collaborative opportunities for students to negotiate
  meaning in authentic dialogues.

- **Opportunities for students to apply what they
  know.** *Show what you know!* activities at the end of
  every *Grammar* lesson allow students to synthesize
  the vocabulary and grammatical structures in written
  outcomes. This allows students to extend their
  learning and allows teachers to formatively assess
  student progress.

- **Additional grammar practice.** Additional grammar
  practice is available in the *Grammar Review* at
  the back of the Student Book, in the Workbook,
  on the Pearson Practice English App, and
  through MyEnglishLab.

Reading

- **Alignment to CCR and ELP standards and NRS
  level descriptors.** The entirely new *Reading* lessons
  develop the content knowledge and domain-specific
  vocabulary needed to meet the requirements of
  today's standards and descriptors.

- **Pre-reading activities.** Drawing on students'
  background knowledge, pre-reading activities
  introduce reading-related vocabulary and phrases.
  These pre-reading activities give teachers an
  opportunity for formative assessment of students'
  text-related background knowledge.

- **Informational texts.** Content-rich informational texts
  build students' foundational knowledge and expose
  students to a variety of content-related vocabulary.
  All readings have been newly written to include the
  most current data and terms.

- **Academic Skills.** A specific, high-use academic
  skill is presented in each *Reading* lesson. Later in
  the lesson, students apply the skill to the reading
  and thus gain the practice needed to transfer the
  skill to other reading tasks in the classroom or
  the workplace.

- **High-leverage instructional practices.** A variety
  of critical thinking tasks are practiced in every
  lesson. The range of skills consistently includes
  predicting, citing evidence, making inferences,
  and summarizing.

- **Close-reading skills.** Close-reading activities are
  included for every reading. These activities require
  students to skim to find the general topic, to scan
  to locate specific facts, to return to the text to cite
  evidence, to summarize, and to make inferences.

- **Document literacy.** Students are exposed
  to formats such as websites, emails, and text
  messages. Students are introduced to standard print
  or online documents, such as school applications,
  health benefit forms, résumés, and leases. In this
  way, students gain familiarity with interpreting
  authentic information.

- **Numeracy.** The content-rich informational texts
  cultivate and refine students' numeracy skills.
  Students are required to demonstrate their numeric
  competence by interpreting information in charts
  and graphs.

- **Productive and interactive application.** The
  Show what you know! activity at the end of each
  Reading lesson provides opportunities for students
  to integrate and extend information. Working both
  individually and collaboratively, students reflect on,
  synthesize, and apply what they've learned.

- **Multi-modal practice.** Audio recordings of the
  readings in *Future* can be listened to and replayed.
  Listening while reading has been shown to have
  positive effects on reading fluency. Students can
  access the audio recordings using the Pearson
  Practice English App or MyEnglishLab.

Writing

- **Authenticity of purpose.** In *Future*'s second
  edition, students engage in meaningful academic
  and workplace-related writing tasks: Students write
  reports, fill out forms, write notes, and compose
  letters. In this way, students gain familiarity with
  presenting information in a variety of formats.
  Additional functional writing is often required in the
  Workplace, Life, and Community Skills lessons.

- **Contextualized Process Writing.** The *Writing*
  lessons in *Future*'s second edition follow a robust
  and scaffolded process-writing approach. This
  approach actively engages students in analyzing
  writing models, planning their own writing, and
  producing writing related to the unit theme.

- **Writing models.** At the beginning of each *Writing* lesson, questions guide students as they study and analyze a writing model. These questions help students attend to formal written elements, such as structure and purpose.

- **Focused questioning.** Specific questions on the writing topic focus students on the topic and ensure they engage with the subject matter.

- **Writing frames.** Sentence and paragraph frames scaffold lower-level students. These frames assist students in using new academic language, while helping them successfully complete the writing tasks.

- **Writing evaluation.** The *Writing Checklist* at the end of each *Writing* lesson reinforces the lesson's objective and provides an opportunity for students to review and revise their own work.

- **Integrated speaking and writing skills.** In every *Vocabulary, Reading,* and *Grammar* lesson, the *Show what you know!* feature now includes a writing step. Students first encounter key vocabulary, grammar structures, or reading-related topics in conversation with a partner. Subsequently, students integrate the language, structures, or topics in their own writing.

College and Career Readiness Standards (CCRS) Reading and Writing Lessons

- **Comprehensive development of academic skills.** The CCRS *Reading* and *Writing* lessons found in the Student Book are reinforced in the Workbook and in MyEnglishLab. The additional *CCRS Plus Reading* and *Writing* lessons in MyEnglishLab provide a boost for students by offering even more rigorous practice of academic reading and writing.

- **Specific academic learning outcomes.** A list of expected learning outcomes introduces each *CCRS Plus* lesson.

- **Student research.** In the *CCRS Plus Writing* lessons, students conduct research, draw evidence from relevant informational texts, and with the support of writing frames, compose topic-focused paragraphs. These lessons help students develop the research skills needed to succeed in today's ever-changing digital world.

Workplace, Life, and Community Skills

- **Exposure to real-life, functional skills.** The *Workplace, Life, and Community Skills* lessons ensure that students gain the knowledge and skills needed to succeed in the workplace and in the community. These important life skills are essential to students' ongoing success in relating to the world at large and clearly reflect the workplace focus required by the WIOA mandates.

- **Document literacy.** A variety of standard print or online documents used in the real world are presented: résumés, applications, maps, calendars, step-by-step instructions, safety guidelines, medicine labels, etc. Familiarity with these documents helps ensure students have the skills to interpret and use these important functional formats in their everyday lives.

- **Practical abilities.** Students are exposed to the practical skills needed to function in today's complex world. Students read and follow GPS directions, use money, and respond to help-wanted ads. Common protocols in banking, the postal system, and education are explained and clarified.

- **Knowledge building and vocabulary development.** Much of the content in the *Workplace, Life, and Community Skills* lessons requires background knowledge of the culture and bureaucratic systems. Scaffolded exposure to this information builds understanding. Students also come to understand key document-specific terms.

Soft Skills at Work

- **Real-life interpersonal problems that require critical thinking and collaborative problem solving.** A brief scenario introduces a common interpersonal problem in each *Soft Skills at Work* lesson. These problem-solving activities require sharing of ideas, opinions, and strategic critical thinking about effective behaviors in the workplace or other familiar environments. These lessons clearly reflect the current WIOA mandates.

- **Focused questioning.** Comprehension questions ensure students' understanding of and thoughtful responses to these engaging and challenging workplace situations.

- **Productive and interactive skills.** *Show what you know!* at the end of the lesson invites students to talk and write about the soft skills they bring to their own experiences.

- **Practical usage and transfer.** A *My Soft Skills Log* in the back of the Student Book is a personal reference for students as they reflect on their own interpersonal skills. This reference can serve as a resource when students apply for jobs and undergo performance reviews.

- **Contextualized workplace skills.** Every unit in *Future* contains a *Soft Skills at Work* lesson and a *Workplace, Life, and Community Skills* lesson related to the unit theme. In addition, every level of *Future* contains two units on employment and work-related topics. This ensures students receive ample exposure to the knowledge and communication skills needed to succeed in the workplace.

Review and Assessment

- **Checkpoints to track progress.** Every unit begins with a list of competencies to be covered. At the end of the unit, students reflect on their progress by reviewing the goals list and checking off the goals they have completed. Keeping track of completed goals motivates students and reinforces their sense of success and accomplishment.

- **Opportunities for ongoing assessment.** The *Show what you know!* activities at the end of most lessons can be used for formative assessment of language competencies. For teachers who want to do more formal assessments of what students have learned, the *Assessment Program* can be accessed in print or online. It contains a variety of interactive, printable tests and rubrics. A *Placement Test*, multilevel *Unit Tests*, as well as a *Midterm*, and a *Final Test* are included. A standardized test-prep exam is also provided. Computer-based *ExamView* generates many additional customizable tests.

Digital Components

- Pearson Practice English App provides easy mobile access to all the audio files, plus Grammar Coach videos, and Pronunciation Coach videos and activities. These activities allow students to listen and study on the go—anywhere, any time.

- MyEnglishLab allows online independent self-study and interactive practice in pronunciation, grammar, vocabulary, reading, writing, and listening. The MyEnglishLab includes the popular Grammar Coach videos and Pronunciation Coach videos with complete activities. It also contains the accompanying *CCRS Plus Reading and Writing* lessons and CASAS Test Prep Program. Teachers can also assign and monitor all the *Assessment Program* tests in MyEnglishLab.

SPEAKING AND WRITING ACTIVITIES

Future **provides students with multiple opportunities to build their speaking and writing skills.** Speaking tasks are integrated throughout the course. Writing activities build on the concepts students learn in a unit. If you wish to formally assess students' speaking or writing, you may use the rubrics provided on pages T-ix and T-x.

Speaking Activities

Speaking activities offer students an opportunity to practice their spoken fluency and to demonstrate their understanding of the vocabulary, grammar, and competencies from the unit and the course.

After students have worked together, allow some students to perform the activity in front of the class. If you wish to use this activity for evaluation purposes, use the Speaking Rubric to make notes about each student's performance. For each category listed in the rubric (Vocabulary, Grammar, Fluency, and Task completion), include comments about both *strong points* and *weak points*. You can then use those comments to give each student a rating of 1, 2, or 3 for each category.

The purpose of this kind of evaluation is to give fair and clear feedback to students and to give them specific points to work on so they can improve their fluency. It is important to use language that a student can understand and to give examples of what the student did or didn't say. For example, *You used a lot of vocabulary from the unit* or *You need to work on forms of be. Review the grammar charts in the unit.* Feedback should be given in a timely manner in order to be most effective and helpful.

Writing Activities

Each unit of *Future* includes a Writing lesson, which is thematically related to the unit. The writing task gives students an opportunity to apply their knowledge of the grammar and vocabulary they have learned, while also allowing them to build their writing skills and develop their writing fluency.

If you wish to give students a formal evaluation of their writing, use the Writing Rubric to make notes. For each category listed in the rubric (Vocabulary, Grammar, Mechanics and Format, and Task completion), include comments about both *strong points* and *weak points*. You can then use those comments to give each student a rating of 1, 2, or 3 for each category.

The purpose of this kind of evaluation is to give fair and clear feedback to students and to give them specific points to work on so they can improve their writing skills. It is important to use language that a student can understand and to give examples of what the student did or did not do. For example, you might say: *You used the simple present correctly* or *You need to work on punctuation. Remember to capitalize names.* Feedback should be given in a timely manner in order to be most effective and helpful.

SPEAKING RUBRIC

Name: _____

Class: _____ Date: _____

Activity: _____ Unit: _____ Page: _____

Vocabulary	Score	Comments
Uses a variety of vocabulary words and expressions from the unit	3	
Uses some vocabulary words and expressions from the unit	2	
Uses few vocabulary words or expressions from the unit	1	
Grammar	**Score**	**Comments**
Uses a variety of grammar points from the unit; uses grammar with control and accuracy	3	
Uses some grammar points from the unit; uses grammar with less control and accuracy	2	
Does not use grammar points from the unit; uses grammar with little control or accuracy	1	
Fluency	**Score**	**Comments**
Speech is authentic and fluent; there is authentic communication with partner	3	
Speech is overly rehearsed at points; not true communication	2	
Speech is not authentic; is not really listening to and communicating with partner	1	
Task completion	**Score**	**Comments**
Student completed the task successfully	3	
Student mostly completed the task; student went off topic at various points	2	
Student was not able to successfully complete the task: see comments	1	

Name: _____

Class: _____ Date: _____

Activity: _____ Unit: _____ Page: _____

Vocabulary	Score	Comments
Uses a variety of vocabulary words and expressions from the unit	3	
Uses some vocabulary words and expressions from the unit	2	
Uses few vocabulary words or expressions from the unit	1	

Grammar	Score	Comments
Uses a variety of grammar points from the unit; uses grammar with control and accuracy	3	
Uses some grammar points from the unit; uses grammar with less control and accuracy	2	
Does not use grammar points from the unit; uses grammar with little control or accuracy	1	

Mechanics (Spelling, Punctuation, Capitalization) and Format	Score	Comments
Very few or no mechanical errors; follows format of model	3	
Some mechanical errors that do not affect comprehensibility; follows format of model with some errors	2	
Many mechanical errors reduce comprehensibility; does not follow format of model	1	

Task completion	Score	Comments
Student completed the task successfully	3	
Student mostly completed the task; student went off topic at various points	2	
Student was not able to successfully complete the task: see comments	1	

LANGUAGE FOR RIGOROUS TASKS IN *FUTURE*

In order to highlight the rigor that has always been part of *Future*, a verb has been added to each exercise to capture the higher order thinking skill students perform. These verbs, highlighted in purple, appear in every lesson. They illuminate the variety and depth of rigorous thinking skills integrated in the instruction. With *Future*, students learn English and also how to think critically in English.

As students progress through the series, they learn the language for and application of an ever broadening body of critical thinking and problem solving skills. The lower levels of *Future* target and recycle an essential body of academic terms for higher order thinking skills and strategies (*summarize, cite evidence*) mixed in with more accessible terms (*work together, think about it*). The higher levels include more nuanced academic terms. For example, *work together* becomes *collaborate*; *think about it* becomes *analyze* or *recall* or *reflect,* depending on the specific higher order thinking skill.

The benefits of highlighting the thinking skills are multiple:

- Students are exposed to academic language in a practical way. Not only do students learn the terms, but they learn to apply the rigorous thinking skills in concrete and scaffolded tasks.

- Through varied application of a higher order thinking skill, students learn a repertoire of appropriate and transferable strategies.

For example, in *Future 2*, students employ the skill *Interpret* in a variety of contexts. Through these multiple contexts, students gain a robust and practical understanding of the meaning of the verb *interpret*.

In the *Grammar* Lesson, students apply information from graphics to demonstrate understanding of a grammar concept or rule. In the *Reading* Lesson, students complete sentences using information from charts and tables. In the *Workplace, Life, and Community Skills* Lesson, students apply information from graphics or what they hear or read to answer questions or to complete sentences.

This document, *Language for Rigorous Tasks in Future*, clarifies how students are learning higher order thinking skills in a particular level and literacy strand. Instructors can use this document to identify which lessons teach which higher order thinking skills and what academic language is introduced in each level.

ACT IT OUT
Workplace, Life, and Community Skills - students role-play a scenario based on content

ANALYZE
Vocabulary - students determine what items go under specific headings; students recognize words/phrases from different lists

APPLY
Grammar - students apply a grammar concept or rule to write, complete, or modify sentences (choose punctuation, create different forms of words)
Listening and Speaking - students listen to a word or sentence and then apply a pronunciation rule; students listen to and repeat sentences

BRAINSTORM
Listening and Speaking - students come up with ideas in response to a question or picture
Reading - students come up with ideas in response to a question or picture before reading
Workplace, Life, and Community Skills - students think about personal connections to lesson content

CATEGORIZE
Vocabulary - students consider items like words or pictures and then fill in a chart to sort them by heading

CHOOSE
Grammar - students choose the correct grammar form, word, or phrase to complete sentences; students choose an answer to match a question
Listening and Speaking - students choose the word, sound, or pronunciation they hear; students choose from a set of answers

CITE EVIDENCE
Reading - students record where they find text evidence to answer a question or complete a statement

COMPARE
Grammar - students discuss differences between two pictures, practicing a grammar concept
Workplace, Life, and Community Skills - students consider the differences between two graphics

COMPLETE
Grammar - students complete sentences by applying a grammar concept or rule

LANGUAGE FOR RIGOROUS TASKS IN *FUTURE*

Reading - students choose vocabulary words from the unit to complete sentences before reading

Vocabulary - students complete sentences based on what they see in a picture

CREATE

Listening and Speaking - students create new conversations based on provided information or graphics

DECIDE

Grammar - students complete sentences by applying a grammar concept or rule

Reading - students choose an answer based on considering options or provided information

Workplace, Life, and Community Skills - students make a decision based on provided information

DESCRIBE

Grammar - students talk about what they see in a picture(s)

Listening and Speaking - students answer questions about a picture

Workplace, Life, and Community Skills - students match elements of a picture with descriptions

DETERMINE

Workplace, Life, and Community Skills - students read a text and decide how it connects to unit content; students consider statements or answer questions based on a graphic

DISCUSS

Grammar - students talk about pictures using a grammar concept

Listening and Speaking - students answer questions in preparation for listening to a text

Reading - students answer questions before reading a text

Workplace, Life, and Community Skills - students answer questions about a topic before reading; students talk about a scenario related to lesson content

Vocabulary - students talk about lesson vocabulary

EVALUATE

Grammar - students read sentences and make grammar corrections

EXPAND

Listening and Speaking - students extend understanding by adding or selecting information or answering questions that add additional detail

GIVE EXAMPLES

Vocabulary - students complete a chart with information based on lesson content

GO ONLINE

Workplace, Life, and Community Skills - students use the Internet to locate information related to lesson content

IDENTIFY

Grammar - students cross off the incorrect word in a sentence

Listening and Speaking - students find words with specific pronunciation patterns

Reading - students answer topic and main idea questions about a text; students use pictures to answer questions based on lesson content before reading a text

Vocabulary - students write words or sentences to identify pictures/realia

Workplace, Life, and Community Skills - students connect words or ideas with pictures/realia; students answer questions by locating information in a text

INTERPRET

Grammar - students apply information from graphics to demonstrate understanding of grammar concept or rule

Listening and Speaking - students activate prior knowledge by answering questions about a picture

Reading - students complete sentences by applying information from graphics

Workplace, Life, and Community Skills - students apply information from graphics or what they hear or read to answer questions or to complete sentences

LABEL

Grammar - students write words or sentences to apply a grammar concept or rule

Listening and Speaking; Workplace, Life, and Community Skills - students write words or sentences to identify pictures/realia

Reading - students write words to identify pictures/realia

LISTEN

Grammar - students pay attention to what they hear to repeat, answer questions, or fill in missing information

Listening and Speaking - students listen to and read a text simultaneously before repeating it

Workplace, Life, and Community Skills - students pay attention to what they hear to repeat, answer questions, or fill in missing information

LISTEN AND POINT

Vocabulary - students listen and then point to what they hear on a picture or text based on what they hear

LISTEN AND READ
Listening and Speaking - students listen to and read a text simultaneously and may repeat
Reading - students listen to and read a text simultaneously

LISTEN FOR DETAILS
Listening and Speaking - students pay attention to what they hear for details needed to complete tasks

LISTEN FOR MAIN IDEA
Listening and Speaking - students listen to a text and identify the main idea

MAKE CONNECTIONS
Grammar - students make personal connections to lesson content using grammar concepts
Listening and Speaking - students answer questions to activate prior knowledge; students create conversations based on a model; students make personal connections to lesson content
Reading - students answer questions to activate prior knowledge
Vocabulary - students talk about connections they make to the lesson vocabulary

MATCH
Grammar - students match items a from two columns
Listening and Speaking - students match words and definitions from two columns; students match pictures with sentences;
Reading - students match vocabulary words and meanings from two columns
Workplace, Life, and Community Skills - students match items from two columns; students match pictures with words or phrases

PRACTICE
Listening and Speaking - students practice pronouncing words, phrases, and sentences

PREDICT
Listening and Speaking - students make guesses about what is depicted in a picture
Vocabulary - students answer questions to activate prior knowledge

PRESENT
Listening and Speaking - students report to the class on a topic

PRESENT IT
Grammar - students make short presentations connected to lesson content
Listening and Speaking - students present information connecting themselves to lesson content

Reading - students make short presentations connected to lesson content
Soft Skills at Work - students present information connecting themselves to lesson content
Vocabulary - students present information connecting themselves to lesson content

READ
Grammar - students read a text to answer a question
Listening and Speaking - students read a short text to activate prior knowledge; students read captions that accompany graphics to activate prior knowledge
Reading - students read and listen to a text simultaneously
Soft Skills at Work - students read and answer questions about a workplace scenario
Writing - students read and answer questions about a writing model

ROLE-PLAY
Grammar - students demonstrate understanding of a grammar concept by creating and performing a conversation
Listening and Speaking - students create and perform conversations based on a model
Soft Skills at Work - students create and perform pretend workplace conversations
Workplace, Life, and Community Skills - students create and perform conversations based on a model conversation

SELF-ASSESS
Grammar - students compare answers with others; students pay attention to what they hear to check their answers
Listening and Speaking - students pay attention to what they hear to check their answers
Workplace, Life, and Community Skills - students pay attention to what they hear to check their answers

TALK ABOUT IT
Grammar - students work with classmates to apply grammar concepts
Vocabulary - students use lesson vocabulary to ask classmates questions, tell classmates about themselves, or engage in discussion
Workplace, Life, and Community Skills - students talk about questions related to workplace content

THINK ABOUT IT
Grammar - students think about or write about lesson content in preparation for a discussion or a writing task that incorporates the grammar concept or rule

LANGUAGE FOR RIGOROUS TASKS IN *FUTURE*

Reading - students make personal connections to content in preparation for writing
Soft Skills at Work - students think about how they personally demonstrate a soft skill in preparation for discussion and writing
Vocabulary - students think about a question or prompt in preparation for discussion or a writing task

WRITE

Grammar - students write sentences about a picture prompt, create questions, complete sentences or other tasks to apply a grammar concept or rule
Reading - students write about a topic related to a text

WRITE ABOUT IT

Grammar - students write sentences applying a grammar concept or rule
Reading - students write about a topic related to a reading
Soft Skills at Work - students record examples in their skills log of how they demonstrate a soft skill
Vocabulary - students complete a guided writing task using lesson vocabulary

REFERENCES

General

Bitterlin, G., D. Price, and B. Parrish. *High-leverage Instructional Practices.* CATESOL, Anaheim, 2018.

Bloom, B.S. *Taxonomy of Educational Objectives, Handbook I: The Cognitive Domain.* New York: David McKay Co, Inc., 1956.

Egan, P. and B. Parrish. *Oral language as a bridge to academic writing.* In K. Schaetzel, J. K. Kreeft Peyton, J. and R. Fernandez, eds. *Teaching academic writing to adults learning English.* Ann Arbor: University of Michigan Press, 2019.

Neri, R., M. Lozano, S. Chang, and J. Herman. *High-leverage Principles of Effective Instruction for English Learners.* West Ed, Center for Standards and Assessment Implementation, 2016.

Parrish, B. *Meeting the Language Needs of Today's Adult English Language Learner: Issue Brief.* Washington, D. C.: American Institutes for Research. U.S. Department of Education, Office of Career, Technical, and Adult Education, 2016.

Pimentel, S. *College and Career Readiness Standards for Adult Education.* U.S. Department of Education, Office of Vocational and Adult Education, 2013.

Rost, M. *Teaching and Researching Listening.* Harlow, England: Pearson Education, 2002.

U.S. Department of Education, Office of Vocational and Adult Education. *English Language Proficiency Standards for Adult Education*, 2016. Retrieved from https://lincs.ed.gov/publications/pdf/elp-standards-adult-ed.pdf.

Vinogradov, P. *Meeting the language needs of today's adult English language learner: Companion Learning resource.* Washington, D.C.: U.S. Department of Education, Office of Career, Technical, and Adult Education, 2016.

Zwiers, J. *Building Academic Language: Meeting Common Core Standards Across Disciplines.* San Francisco: Jossey-Bass, 2014.

Close Reading

Fisher, D. *Close Reading and the CCSS, Parts 1 and 2.* McGraw-Hill Education. Retrieved October 3, 2017 from https://www.youtube.com/watch?v=5w9v6-zUg3Y.

Fisher, D. and N. Frey. *Text Dependent Questions.* Principal Leadership, 2012. Retrieved October 3, 2017 from http://fisherandfrey.com/uploads/posts/Text_Dependent.pdf.

Frey, N. and D. Fisher. *Close Reading.* Principal Leadership, 2013. Retrieved October 3, 2017 from http://fisherandfrey.com/uploads/posts/Close_read.pdf.

Kruidenier, J. *Research-based principles for adult basic education reading instruction.* Washington, D.C.: National Institute for Literacy, Partnership for Reading, 2002.

Shanahan, T. *Common Core: Close Reading.* Instructor Magazine, 2013. Retrieved October 3, 2017 from http://www.scholastic.com/teachers/article/common-core-close-reading-0.

Writing

Egan, P. and B. Parrish. *Oral language as a bridge to academic writing.* In K. Schaetzel, J. K. Kreeft Peyton, J. and R. Fernandez, eds. *Teaching academic writing to adults learning English.* Ann Arbor: University of Michigan Press, 2019.

Ferris. D. and J. Hedgcock, eds. *Teaching ESL composition: Purpose, process, and practice.* New Jersey: Lawrence Erlbaum Associates, Inc., 1998.

Folse, K., "The Effect of Type of Written Exercise on L2 Vocabulary Retention," *TESOL Quarterly*, 40, no. 2, (2006): 273–93.

Kroll, B., ed. *Exploring the dynamics of second language writing.* New York: Cambridge University Press, 2003.

Lane, J. and E. Lange. *Essential teaching techniques: Giving feedback, addressing grammar, and helping students edit their own writing.* Plenary Address at CATESOL Orange County Conference, Fullerton, 2005.

Leki, I. *Understanding ESL writers: A guide for teachers.* New Hampshire: Boynton/Cook Publishers, 1992.

Silva, T. and P. Matsuda, eds. *Practicing theory in second language writing.* West Lafayette: Parlor Press, 2010.

U.S. Department of Education, Office of Vocational and Adult Education, *TEAL Just Write! Guide.* Washington, D.C.: 2011. https://teal.ed.gov/documents/TEAL_JustWriteGuide.pdf.

Zwiers, J. *Developing academic thinking skills in grades 6–12: A handbook of multiple intelligence activities.* Delaware: International Reading Association, 2005.

Grammar

Ellis, R. and H. Basturkmen and S. Loewen. "Learner uptake in communicative ESL lessons." *Language Learning* 51 (2001): 281–318.

FUTURE 2

English for Work, Life, and Academic Success

Second Edition

Series Consultants
Sarah Lynn
Ronna Magy
Federico Salas-Isnardi

Authors
Sarah Lynn
Wendy Pratt Long

Welcome to *Future: English for Work, Life, and Academic Success*

Future is a six-level, standards-based English language course for adult and young adult students. *Future* provides students with the contextualized academic language, strategies, and critical thinking skills needed for success in workplace, life, and academic settings. *Future* is aligned with the requirements of the Workforce Innovation and Opportunity Act (WIOA), the English Language Proficiency (ELP) and College and Career Readiness (CCR) standards, and the National Reporting System (NRS) level descriptors. The 21st century curriculum in *Future*'s second edition helps students acquire the basic literacy, language, and employability skills needed to meet the requirements set by the standards.

Future develops students' academic and critical thinking, digital literacy and numeracy, workplace and civic skills, and prepares students for taking standardized tests. Competency and skills incorporating standards are in the curriculum at every level, providing a foundation for academic rigor, research-based teaching strategies, corpus-informed language, and the best of digital tools.

In revising the course, we listened to hundreds of *Future* teachers and learners and studied the standards for guidance. *Future* continues to be the most comprehensive English communication course for adults, with its signature scaffolded lessons and multiple practice activities throughout. *Future*'s second edition provides enhanced content, rigorous academic language practice, and cooperative learning through individual and collaborative practice. Every lesson teaches the interpretive, interactive, and productive skills highlighted in the standards.

Future's Instructional Design

Learner Centered and Outcome Oriented

The student is at the center of *Future*. Lessons start by connecting to student experience and knowledge, and then present targeted skills in meaningful contexts. Varied and dynamic skill practice progresses from controlled to independent in a meticulously scaffolded sequence.

Headers highlighting Depth of Knowledge (DOK) terms are used throughout *Future* to illuminate the skills being practiced. Every lesson culminates in an activity in which students apply their learning, demonstrate their knowledge, and express themselves orally or in writing. DOK reference materials for teachers, available in the TE, on the ActiveTeach, and from the Pearson

English Portal, include specific suggestions on how to help students activate these cognitive skills.

Varied Practice

Cognitive science has proven what *Future* always knew: Students learn new skills through varied practice over time. Content-rich units that contextualize academic and employability skills naturally recycle concepts, language, and targeted skills. Individual and collaborative practice activities engage learners and lead to lasting outcomes. Lessons support both student collaboration and individual self-mastery. Students develop the interpretative, productive, and interactive skills identified in the NRS guidelines, while using the four language skills of reading, writing, listening, and speaking.

Goal Setting and Learning Assessment

For optimal learning to take place, students need to be involved in setting goals and in monitoring their own progress. *Future* addresses goal setting in numerous ways. In the Student Book, Unit Goals are identified on the unit opener page. Checkboxes at the end of lessons invite students to evaluate their mastery of the material, and suggest additional online practice.

High-quality assessment aligned to the standards checks student progress and helps students prepare to take standardized tests. The course-based assessment program is available in print and digital formats and includes a bank of customizable test items. Digital tests are assigned by the teacher and reported back in the LMS online gradebook. All levels include a midterm and final test. Test items are aligned with unit learning objectives and standards. The course Placement Test is available in print and digital formats. Test-prep materials are also provided for specific standardized tests.

One Integrated Program

Future provides everything adult English language learners need in one integrated program using the latest digital tools and time-tested print resources.

Integrated Skills Contextualized with Rich Content

Future contextualizes grammar, listening, speaking, pronunciation, reading, writing, and vocabulary in meaningful activities that simulate real workplace, educational, and community settings. A special lesson at the end of each unit highlights soft skills at work. While providing relevant content, *Future* helps build learner knowledge and equips adults for their many roles.

Meeting Work, Life, and Education Goals

Future recognizes that every adult learner brings a unique set of work, life, and academic experiences, as well as a distinct skill set. With its diverse array of print and digital resources, *Future* provides learners with multiple opportunities to practice with contextualized materials to build skill mastery. Specialized lessons for academic and workplace skill development are part of *Future*'s broad array of print and digital resources.

In addition to two units on employment in each level, every unit contains a Workplace, Life, and Community Skills lesson as well as a Soft Skills at Work lesson.

Workplace, Life, and Community Skills Lessons

In the second edition, the Life Skills lesson has been revised to focus on workplace, life, and community skills and to develop the real-life language and civic literacy skills required today. Lessons integrate and contextualize workplace content. In addition, every lesson includes practice with digital skills on a mobile device.

Soft Skills at Work Lessons

Future has further enhanced its development of workplace skills by adding a Soft Skills at Work lesson to each unit. Soft skills are the critical interpersonal communication skills needed to succeed in any workplace. Students begin each lesson by discussing a common challenge in the workplace. Then, while applying the lesson-focused soft skill, they work collaboratively to find socially appropriate solutions to the problem. The log at the back of the Student Book encourages students to track their own application of the soft skill, which they can use in job interviews.

Academic Rigor

Rigor and respect for the ability and experiences of the adult learner have always been central to *Future*. The standards provide the foundation for academic rigor. The reading, writing, listening, and speaking practice require learners to analyze, use context clues, interpret, cite evidence, build knowledge, support a claim, and summarize from a variety of

text formats. Regular practice with complex and content-rich materials develop academic language and build knowledge. Interactive activities allow for collaboration and exchange of ideas in workplace and in academic contexts. *Future* emphasizes rigor by highlighting the critical thinking and problem solving skills required in each activity.

Writing Lessons

In addition to the increased focus on writing in Show What You Know! activities, *Future* has added a cumulative writing lesson to every unit, a lesson that requires students to synthesize and apply their learning in a written outcome. Through a highly scaffolded approach, students begin by analyzing writing models before planning, and finally producing written work of their own. Writing models, Writing Skills, and a checklist help guide students through the writing process.

Reading lessons

All reading lessons have new, information-rich texts and a revised pedagogical approach in line with the CCR and ELP standards and the NRS descriptors. These informational texts are level appropriate, use high-frequency vocabulary, and focus on interpretation of graphic information. The readings build students' knowledge and develop their higher-order reading skills by teaching citation of evidence, summarizing, and interpretation of complex information from a variety of text formats.

Future Grows with Your Student

Future takes learners from absolute beginner level through low-advanced English proficiency, addressing students' abilities and learning priorities at each level. As the levels progress, the curricular content and unit structure change accordingly, with the upper levels incorporating more advanced academic language and skills in the text and in the readings.

Future Intro	Future Level 1	Future Level 2	Future Level 3	Future Level 4	Future Advanced
NRS Beginning ESL Literacy	NRS Low Beginning ESL	NRS High Beginning ESL	NRS Low Intermediate ESL	NRS High Intermediate ESL	NRS Advanced ESL
ELPS Level 1	**ELPS** Level 1	**ELPS** Level 2	**ELPS** Level 3	**ELPS** Level 4	**ELPS** Level 5
CCRS Level A	**CCRS** Level A	**CCRS** Level A	**CCRS** Level B	**CCRS** Level C	**CCRS** Level D
CASAS 180 and below	**CASAS** 181–190	**CASAS** 191–200	**CASAS** 201–210	**CASAS** 211–220	**CASAS** 221–235

The **Pearson Practice English App** provides easy mobile access to all of the audio files, plus Grammar Coach videos and activities, and the new Pronunciation coach videos. Listen and study on the go—anywhere, any time!

Abundant Opportunities for Student Practice

Student

Student books are a complete student resource, including lessons in grammar, listening and speaking, pronunciation, reading, writing, vocabulary, and Soft Skills at Work, taught and practiced in contextual activities.

Workbook—with audio—provides additional practice for each lesson in the student book, with new readings, and practice in writing, grammar, listening and speaking, plus activities for new Soft Skills at Work lessons.

MyEnglishLab allows online independent self study and interactive practice in pronunciation, grammar, vocabulary, reading, writing, and listening. The MEL includes the popular Grammar Coach videos and new Pronunciation Coach videos and activities.

Outstanding Teacher Resources

Teacher

Teacher's Edition includes culture notes, teaching tips, and numerous optional and extension activities, with lesson-by-lesson correlations to CCR and ELP standards. Rubrics are provided for evaluation of students' written and oral communication.

ActiveTeach for front-of-classroom projection of the student book, includes audio at point of use and pop-up activities, including grammar examples, academic conversation stems, and reader's anticipation guide.

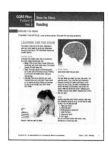

College and Career Readiness Plus Lessons supplement the student book with challenging reading and writing lessons for every level above Intro.

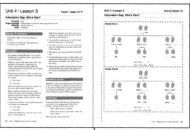

Assessment Program, accessed online with interactive and printable tests and rubrics, includes a Placement Test, multi-level unit, mid-term and final exams, and computer-based ExamView with additional tests ready-to-use and customizable. In addition, sample high-stakes test practice is included with CASAS test prep for listening and reading.

Multilevel Communicative Activities provide an array of reproducible communication activities and games that engage students through different modalities. Teachers' notes provide multilevel options for pre-level and above-level students, as well as extension activities for additional speaking and writing practice.

Go to the Teacher website for easy reference, correlations to federal and state standards, and course updates. www.pearsonelt.com/future2e

Preview questions activate student background knowledge and help the teacher assess how much students know about the unit theme.

All in the Family

2

PREVIEW

Look at the picture. What do you see? Who are these people?

A full-page photo introduces the **unit theme** and provides opportunities for interactive classroom discussion.

UNIT GOALS

☐ Identify family relationships
☐ Talk about family
☐ Talk about what people have in common
☐ Ask about mailing services
☐ Ask about people

☐ **Academic skill:** Retell information
☐ **Writing skill:** Use capital letters and commas in names of places
☐ **Workplace soft skill:** Separate work and home life

25

Unit goals introduce the competencies taught in the unit and allow students to track and reflect on their progress.

Key **vocabulary** is contextualized and practiced in connection to the unit theme.

Study tips introduce the learning skills and strategies students need to meet the rigor required by the CCRS.

Lesson 1 — Vocabulary

Family relationships

A PREDICT. Look at the pictures. Find Marta in each picture. Who are the other people in the pictures? What is their family relationship to Marta?

I think Paco is Marta's brother.

B ▶ LISTEN AND POINT. Then listen and repeat.

Paco Tina Manuel Ella Marta Lina Tony Delmar

Ben Marta Tina Eva Felix

Marta Ben Sandra Tom Ann

Tommy Liz Marta Ben

Liz Marta Ben Mary Tommy Sue Benny

26 Unit 2, Lesson 1

Vocabulary

Family relationships

1. brother	6. cousin	11. nephew	16. sister-in-law	21. grandmother
2. sister	7. uncle	12. wife	17. son	22. grandfather
3. father	8. fiancé	13. husband	18. daughter	23. granddaughter
4. mother	9. fiancée	14. mother-in-law	19. children	24. grandson
5. aunt	10. niece	15. father-in-law	20. parents	25. grandchildren

C WORK TOGETHER. Look at the pictures. Student A, ask a question about Marta's family. Student B, answer.

A: Who is Marta's sister?
B: Tina. Who are Marta's grandchildren?

D CATEGORIZE. Which family words are for females? Which are for males? Which are for both? Complete the chart.

Female — mother
Both — parents
Male — father

Study Tip

Make Connections

Write the names of five people in your family and their relationship to you.

Marie: niece
Pete: nephew

Show what you know!

1. **THINK ABOUT IT.** Make a list of your family members. Where do they live?

husband — New York	son — New York	parents — China
daughter — New York	brother — San Francisco	

2. **TALK ABOUT IT.** Talk about your family.

A: Is your family here?
B: My son and daughter are here. My mother and father are in China.

3. **WRITE ABOUT IT.** Write about your family.

My children are in New York. My parents are in China.

I can identify family relationships. ☐   I need more practice. ☐
For more practice, go to MyEnglishLab.

Unit 2, Lesson 1 27

In **Show what you know!**, students apply the target vocabulary in meaningful conversations and in writing.

Three **Listening and Speaking** lessons provide students opportunities for realistic conversations in work, community, and educational settings.

Pronunciation activities help students learn, practice, and internalize the patterns of spoken English and relate them to their own lives.

Listening and Speaking

Lesson 2 Talk about family

1 BEFORE YOU LISTEN

MAKE CONNECTIONS. How many family members live with you? Who are they?

2 LISTEN

Ⓐ ▶ PREDICT. Look at the picture of two new co-workers. What are they talking about? What do people talk about when they meet for the first time?

Ⓑ ▶ LISTEN FOR MAIN IDEA. Choose the correct word.

Amy and Sam are talking about _____.

a. work   b. families   c. cars

Ⓒ ▶ LISTEN FOR DETAILS. Choose the correct word.

1. Sam doesn't have a _____ family.
   a. big
   b. small

2. Sam has _____.
   a. one brother
   b. two brothers

3. Sam's _____ live in Senegal.
   a. brothers
   b. sisters

Multiple listening opportunities progress from listening for general understanding, to listening for details, to listening to an extended version of the conversation.

Ⓓ ▶ EXPAND. Listen to the whole conversation. Choose the correct word.

Sam's brother lives _____ Sam.
a. far from   b. with   c. near

28   Unit 2, Lesson 2

Listening and Speaking

3 PRONUNCIATION

Sentence stress
Some words in a sentence are **not stressed**. These words are very short and quiet. For example, *a, and, the.*

Ⓐ ▶ PRACTICE. Listen. Then listen again and repeat.

I have a brother and two sisters.
We live in the same apartment.
He works in a hospital.

Ⓑ ▶ APPLY. Listen. Circle the words that are not stressed.

1. I don't have a very big family.
2. My sisters live in Senegal.
3. He's a medical assistant.

4 CONVERSATION

Ⓐ ▶ LISTEN AND READ. Then listen and repeat.

A: Tell me about your family.
B: Well, I don't have a very big family. I have a brother and two sisters.
A: Do they live here?
B: My sisters live in Senegal, but my brother lives here.

Conversations carefully scaffold student learning and build language fluency.

Ⓑ WORK TOGETHER. Practice the conversation in Exercise A.

Ⓒ MAKE CONNECTIONS. Talk about your own family.

A. Tell me about your family.
B. I have a very big family. I have . . .

I can talk about family. ☐	I need more practice. ☐

For more practice, go to MyEnglishLab.

Unit 2, Lesson 2   29

Predict activities focus students on the social context of the conversation.

Checkpoints at the end of lessons provide students an opportunity to reflect on their progress and identify further resources for more practice.

Each unit presents three **Grammar** lessons in a systematic grammar progression. Every Grammar lesson focuses on language introduced in the preceding Listening and Speaking lesson. Additional grammar practice is available in the Grammar Review and online.

Images provide scaffolding for meaningful grammar practice.

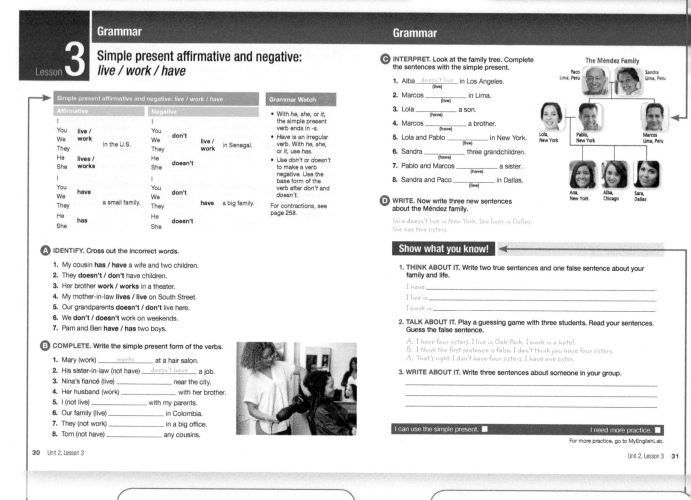

Grammar

Lesson 3
Simple present affirmative and negative: *live / work / have*

Simple present affirmative and negative: *live / work / have*

Affirmative			Negative			
I			I			
You	live /		You	don't		
We	work	in the U.S.	We		live /	in Senegal.
They			They		work	
He	lives /		He	doesn't		
She	works		She			
I			I			
You	have		You	don't		
We		a small family.	We		have	a big family.
They			They			
He	has		He	doesn't		
She			She			

Grammar Watch

- With *he, she, or it,* the simple present verb ends in -s.
- *Have* is an irregular verb. With *he, she, or it,* use has.
- Use *don't* or *doesn't* to make a verb negative. Use the base form of the verb after *don't* and *doesn't.*

For contractions, see page 258.

A IDENTIFY. Cross out the incorrect words.

1. My cousin **has / have** a wife and two children.
2. They **doesn't / don't** have children.
3. Her brother **work / works** in a theater.
4. My mother-in-law **lives / live** on South Street.
5. Our grandparents **doesn't / don't** live here.
6. We **don't / doesn't** work on weekends.
7. Pam and Ben **have / has** two boys.

B COMPLETE. Write the simple present form of the verbs.

1. Mary (work) _____works_____ at a hair salon.
2. His sister-in-law (not have) _____doesn't have_____ a job.
3. Nina's fiancé (live) _____ near the city.
4. Her husband (work) _____ with her brother.
5. I (not live) _____ with my parents.
6. Our family (live) _____ in Colombia.
7. They (not work) _____ in a big office.
8. Tom (not have) _____ any cousins.

Grammar

C INTERPRET. Look at the family tree. Complete the sentences with the simple present.

The Méndez Family

1. Alba _doesn't live_ in Los Angeles. (live)
2. Marcos _____ in Lima. (live)
3. Lola _____ a son. (have)
4. Marcos _____ a brother. (have)
5. Lola and Pablo _____ in New York. (live)
6. Sandra _____ three grandchildren. (have)
7. Pablo and Marcos _____ a sister. (have)
8. Sandra and Paco _____ in Dallas. (live)

D WRITE. Now write three new sentences about the Méndez family.

Sara doesn't live in New York. She lives in Dallas.
She has two sisters.

Show what you know!

1. **THINK ABOUT IT.** Write two true sentences and one false sentence about your family and life.

   I have _____ .
   I live in _____ .
   I work in _____ .

2. **TALK ABOUT IT.** Play a guessing game with three students. Read your sentences. Guess the false sentence.

   A: *I have four sisters. I live in Oak Park. I work in a hotel.*
   B: *I think the first sentence is false. I don't think you have four sisters.*
   A: *That's right. I don't have four sisters. I have one sister.*

3. **WRITE ABOUT IT.** Write three sentences about someone in your group.

   _____
   _____
   _____

I can use the simple present. ☐	I need more practice. ☐

For more practice, go to MyEnglishLab.

Grammar activities progress from controlled to open practice, leading students from understanding to mastery of the target grammar.

Every Show what you know! integrates an interactive exchange and a writing task so students demonstrate their mastery of the grammar point using a range of language skills.

Grammar charts present the target grammar point in a clear and simple format.

Workplace, Life, and Community Skills lessons develop real-life language and civic literacy while encouraging community participation.

Interactive activities develop real-life communication and collaboration skills.

Workplace, Life, and Community Skills

Lesson **4**

Help wanted ads and job requirements

1 READ HELP WANTED ADS

A IDENTIFY. Read the help wanted ads. Where can you find these ads? Where else can people find out about jobs?

CAR SERVICE DRIVERS NEEDED

Job description: Drivers for evening and weekend airport car service. Experience: 1 year of driving service. Part-time. Pay: $12/hr. For more information, and to apply, please send a letter of interest to Jonna Kern at jkern@carservice.org

Career.com

Office Assistant

Responsibilities: handle phone calls, greet visitors, and organize customer files. Preferred experience: 1 year of working in a busy office environment and formal training in computer application software. Class and hours: Full-time, M-F, 8 am-5 pm. Health benefits. Required materials: Cover letter, résumé, and list of references. Send to: erinhubs@hroffice.com. For full consideration, apply by 1/31.

B MATCH. Connect the sentence parts.

1. ____ A full-time employee works
2. ____ Responsibilities are
3. ____ A résumé includes
4. ____ A cover letter is
5. ____ Experience is
6. ____ References are
7. ____ Health benefits are

a. people who can describe you and your work.
b. a list of your job experiences and skills.
c. when your company pays some of your health insurance.
d. the activities and things you will do at a job.
e. a way to introduce yourself to your future employer.
f. your past work activities.
g. 40 hours a week.

C INTERPRET. Read the ads again. Answer the questions.

1. Which job is full-time? _____
2. What should someone do to apply for the car service driver position? _____
3. Which job requires evening and weekend work? _____
4. What is the pay for Car Service Drivers? _____
5. What are the responsibilities of an office assistant? _____
6. What kind of experience is preferred for the Office Assistant position? _____
7. When does the Office Assistant need to be able to work? _____

I can read help wanted ads. ■   I need more practice. ■

152 Unit 8, Lesson 4

Workplace, Life, and Community Skills

2 IDENTIFY JOB REQUIREMENTS

A WORK TOGETHER. Look at the résumés. Which job from 1A is each candidate applying for? Write your answers on the lines. How do you know?

B COMPARE. Look at the résumés. Answer the questions.

Which candidate is best qualified for the Car Service Driver job? Why?

Which candidate is best qualified for the Office Assistant job? Why?

C ROLE-PLAY. Act out a job interview. Choose a job from 1A. Student A, you are the interviewer. Student B, you are the applicant. Take turns.

D GO ONLINE. Search for a job posting website. Find a job you are interested in.

What are the job responsibilities? What experience do you need? How can you apply for the job?

Jin Mong
1234 New Moon Road, New Jersey 11112

Education: Jones Community College
Major: Hospitality
Work experience: OMBER Driver, June 2018-present,
Moon Gas, gas station attendant, June 2017-June 2018
Languages: English and Chinese
Skills: can operate a cash register

Ann Lopez
42 North Shore Road, Boynton Beach, FL
alopez@gmail.com

Education: Palm Beach High School, currently enrolled in Palm Beach State College, Office Technology
Work Experience: Starland Coffee Shop, server January 2018-present.
Relevant Experience: Work with customers, handle customer problems, train new staff
Languages: Spanish and English
Skills: Can type, order supplies, use a cash register

Kim Klaka
22 West Lane Street, #3A
Stockton, CA
kimklas@yippe.com

Education: Stockton High School, A.A in Office Systems and Technology.
Work Experience: Office Assistant, Gem Restaurant Supply, March 2017-present
Responsibilities: Handle phone calls, organize file room, work with customers; Office Clerk, Bel Blue Office Systems, October 2015-March 2017.
Responsibilities: Greet customers, enter new data in database
Languages: Polish, Russian, and English
Skills: Fluent in all Office Software Systems

Bin Fang
807 Kates Place, #21, Chicago, IL binfang@macro.com

Education: Jones Driving School, C-License
Work Experience: John's Taxi Service, September 2018-present;
Roberto's Car Service, December 2015-present
Skills: Can type, use a computer, operate a commercial vehicle

I can identify job requirements. ■   I need more practice. ■

For more practice, go to MyEnglishLab.

Unit 8, Lesson 4 153

In **Go Online** activities, students use their devices to practice concrete online tasks, such as researching information or inputting data.

All new informational **Reading** lessons develop academic language and build content knowledge to meet the rigorous requirements of the CCRS.

Close-reading activities require that students return to the reading to find textual evidence of detail, to summarize for general understanding, and to make inferences.

Students develop **numeracy** skills by interpreting numeric information in charts and graphs.

Lesson 7 — Reading

Read about jobs in the U.S.

1 BEFORE YOU READ

A LABEL. Label the pictures with the words in the box.

agriculture   health care   manufacturing   technology

1. _____ 2. _____ 3. _____ 4. _____

B MAKE CONNECTIONS. Think about the fields of employment in A. Which fields have the most jobs these days? What kinds of jobs are they?

2 READ

▶ LISTEN AND READ.

Academic Skill: Predict the topic
You can often guess what an article is about by looking at the title and pictures. This will prepare you to understand what you read.

Today's Hot Jobs

The U.S. job market is changing fast. At one time, most workers in the U.S. had jobs on farms. Now, less than 2 percent of workers have agricultural jobs. In 1960, 25 percent of workers had jobs in manufacturing. Now, only 10 percent of workers are making things in factories. So where are the jobs today?

Health Care
Many of the fastest-growing jobs are in health care. The U.S. population is getting older. These older Americans need medical care and help with daily living. The greatest need is for personal care aides. There may be more than 750 thousand new jobs of this kind by 2026. Personal care aides take care of people in their homes or in day programs. They sometimes work with people with disabilities or long-term illnesses. On average, they make about $22,000 a year. There are other

fast-growing jobs in health care, too. For example, by 2026, there may be a need for 437 thousand more registered nurses. On average, they make about $69,000 a year.

Computer and Information Technology
There are also many fast-growing jobs in computer and information technology. By 2026, there may be more than 546 thousand new jobs in this field. Almost 300 thousand of those jobs will be for software developers. Some software developers create programs for computers and cell phones. Others design computer networks (where many computers work together). On average, they make more than $100,000 a year.

Many of today's fastest-growing jobs are in these two fields. Where will tomorrow's jobs be?

Source: U.S. Department of Labor

Percentage of Growth in Jobs

Home health aides	47%
Physical therapist assistants	31%
Application software developers	31%
Occupational therapy assistants	29%

3 CLOSE READING

A IDENTIFY. What is the main idea?

The fastest-growing jobs in the United States _____.
a. are in health care and in computer and information technology
b. are some of the highest-paid jobs in the United States
c. are jobs creating programs for computers and cell phones

B CITE EVIDENCE. Answer the questions. Where is the information? Write the line numbers.

1. The number of jobs in manufacturing today is _____ it was in the past.   **Lines**
   a. higher than   b. lower than   c. the same as   _____
2. Personal care aides make about _____ on average.
   a. $2026 a month   b. $22,000 a year   c. $69,000 a year   _____
3. By 2026, there will probably be _____ new jobs for software developers.
   a. about 100,000   b. more than 546,000   c. almost 300,000   _____

C INTERPRET. Complete the sentences about the bar graph.

1. The bar graph shows _____.
   a. growing jobs in numbers   b. growing jobs in percentage   c. dying jobs in percentage   _____
2. The growth in jobs for application software developers _____.
   a. is higher than for home health aides   b. is lower than for occupational therapy assistants   c. is the same as for physical therapist assistants   _____

4 SUMMARIZE

Complete the summary with the words in the box.

employment   health care   job market   software   technology

The (1) _____ in the U.S. is changing. Two fields of (2) _____ are growing fast. There will be many new jobs in (3) _____, especially jobs for personal care aides. There will also be many new jobs in computer and information (4) _____, especially for (5) _____ developers.

Show what you know!

1. THINK ABOUT IT. What job do you want to have in five years? Why? What do you need to do to get that job?
2. TALK ABOUT IT. Talk about the jobs you want. Talk about how to get those jobs.
   In five years, I want to be a software developer. I need to learn about technology.
3. WRITE ABOUT IT. Now write about the job you want in five years.

I can predict the topic. ■   I need more practice. ■

To read more, go to MyEnglishLab.

Graphs and charts introduce students to information in a variety of formats, developing their visual literacy.

Academic tasks, such as summarizing, are introduced from the beginning and scaffolded to support low-level learners.

Informational readings containing level-appropriate complex text introduce academic language and build content knowledge.

Writing lessons follow a robust and scaffolded writing-process approach, engaging students in analyzing writing models, planning, and producing a final product.

A **Writing Skill** explains and models appropriate writing. Later in the lesson, students apply the skill to their own writing.

New **Soft Skills at Work** lessons engage students in real-life situations that develop the personal, social, and cultural skills critical for career success, and help students meet the WIOA requirements.

A brief scenario introduces a common workplace problem that can be solved using **critical thinking** and **soft skills**.

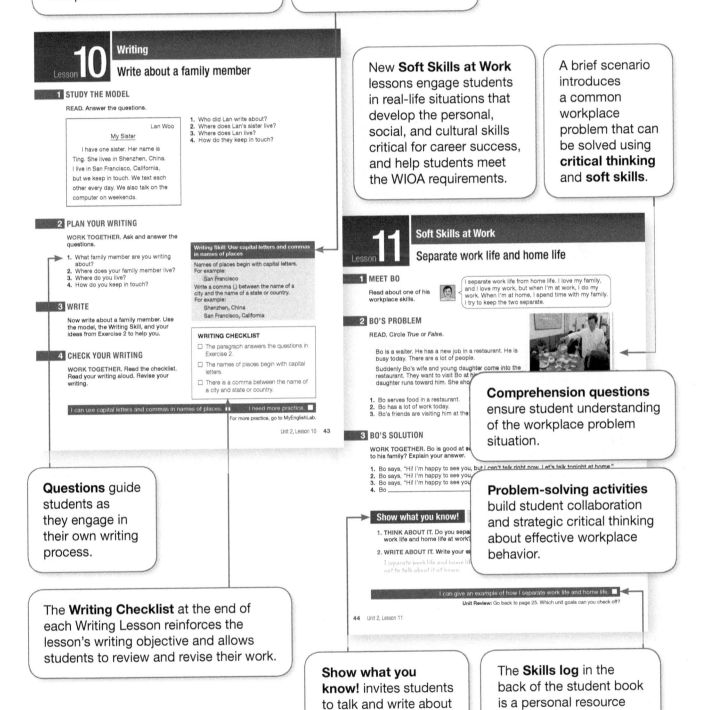

Lesson **10** Writing
Write about a family member

1 STUDY THE MODEL

READ. Answer the questions.

Lan Woo
My Sister
I have one sister. Her name is Ting. She lives in Shenzhen, China. I live in San Francisco, California, but we keep in touch. We text each other every day. We also talk on the computer on weekends.

1. Who did Lan write about?
2. Where does Lan's sister live?
3. Where does Lan live?
4. How do they keep in touch?

2 PLAN YOUR WRITING

WORK TOGETHER. Ask and answer the questions.

1. What family member are you writing about?
2. Where does your family member live?
3. Where do you live?
4. How do you keep in touch?

3 WRITE

Now write about a family member. Use the model, the Writing Skill, and your ideas from Exercise 2 to help you.

4 CHECK YOUR WRITING

WORK TOGETHER. Read the checklist. Read your writing aloud. Revise your writing.

Writing Skill: Use capital letters and commas in names of places

Names of places begin with capital letters. For example:
San Francisco

Write a comma (,) between the name of a city and the name of a state or country. For example:
Shenzhen, China
San Francisco, California

WRITING CHECKLIST
☐ The paragraph answers the questions in Exercise 2.
☐ The names of places begin with capital letters.
☐ There is a comma between the name of a city and state or country.

I can use capital letters and commas in names of places. ☐ I need more practice. ☐
For more practice, go to MyEnglishLab.

Unit 2, Lesson 10   43

Lesson **11** Soft Skills at Work
Separate work life and home life

1 MEET BO

Read about one of his workplace skills.

I separate work life from home life. I love my family, and I love my work, but when I'm at work, I do my work. When I'm at home, I spend time with my family. I try to keep the two separate.

2 BO'S PROBLEM

READ. Circle *True* or *False*.

Bo is a waiter. He has a new job in a restaurant. He is busy today. There are a lot of people.

Suddenly Bo's wife and young daughter come into the restaurant. They want to visit Bo at hi... daughter runs toward him. She sho...

1. Bo serves food in a restaurant.
2. Bo has a lot of work today.
3. Bo's friends are visiting him at the...

3 BO'S SOLUTION

WORK TOGETHER. Bo is good at s... to his family? Explain your answer.

1. Bo says, "Hi! I'm happy to see you, but I can't talk right now. Let's talk tonight at home."
2. Bo says, "Hi! I'm happy to see you...
3. Bo says, "Hi! I'm happy to see you...
4. Bo _____

Show what you know!

1. THINK ABOUT IT. Do you sepa... work life and home life at work?
2. WRITE ABOUT IT. Write your e...

I separate work life and home lif... not to talk about it at home.

I can give an example of how I separate work life and home life. ☐
Unit Review: Go back to page 25. Which unit goals can you check off?

44   Unit 2, Lesson 11

Comprehension questions ensure student understanding of the workplace problem situation.

Problem-solving activities build student collaboration and strategic critical thinking about effective workplace behavior.

Questions guide students as they engage in their own writing process.

The **Writing Checklist** at the end of each Writing Lesson reinforces the lesson's writing objective and allows students to review and revise their work.

Show what you know! invites students to talk and write about the soft skills they bring to the job.

The **Skills log** in the back of the student book is a personal resource for students as they apply for jobs or undergo performance reviews.

Unit	Vocabulary	Listening and Speaking	Reading	Grammar
Pre-Unit **Welcome to Class** *page 2*	Reasons for studying English	• Meet your classmates • Talk about your goals • Ask for help	• Locate information in your book	• Simple present: *be*
1 **Making Connections** *page 5*	Physical appearance	• Describe the way people look • Describe personalities • Get to know someone **Pronunciation skills:** • Word stress • Vowels in unstressed syllables • Sentence stress	• Read an article about group work in the classroom **Academic skill:** • Identify the topic and the main idea	• Simple present: *be* + adjective/*have* + adjective • *Be:* compound sentence with *and* and *but* • Simple present tense of *be: Yes/No* and information questions
2 **All in the Family** *page 25*	Family relationships	• Talk about family • Talk about what people have in common • Ask about people **Pronunciation skills:** • Sentence stress • Pronunciation of do	• Read an article about work/life balance **Academic skill:** • Retell information	• Simple present affirmative and negative: *live/work/have* • Simple present: *Yes/No* questions and short answers • Simple Present: Information questions and short answers
3 **Lots to Do** *page 45*	Clothing	• Describe your wants and needs • Talk about plans • Describe problems with purchases **Pronunciation skills:** • Pronunciation of *to* • Pronunciation of *going to*	• Read about ways to pay for things **Academic skill:** • Identify purpose	• Simple present: *Want/need* + infinitive • Future with *be going to* • Adverbs of degree: *very* and *too*
4 **Small Talk** *page 65*	Free-time activities	• Talk about free-time activities • Communicate likes and dislikes • Accept or decline an invitation **Pronunciation skills:** • Unpronounced syllables • *Have to* and *has to*	• Read about different writing styles **Academic skill:** • Predict the topic	• Adverbs of frequency • Simple present: *love/like/hate* + infinitive • Modal: *Have to*

Writing	Document Literacy Numeracy	Workplace, Life, and Community Skills	Soft Skills At Work
• Write questions to complete conversations	• Use unit and page numbers	• Introduce yourself • Greet people	
• Write about a study routine **Writing skill:** • Introduce and explain steps of a routine	• Read an application for an ID card • Interpret an ID card	• Read identification cards • Complete an application **Digital skill:** • Go online and search for an identification card application in your state	• Be inclusive
• Write about a family member **Writing skill:** • Use capital letters and commas in names of places	• Interpret a family tree • Complete a Venn Diagram • Interpret a chart	• Ask about mailing services **Digital skill:** • Go online and search for mailing services near you	• Separate work and home life
• Write about saving money **Writing skill:** • Use a topic sentence	• Compare cost • Calculate discount • Interpret an online order form • Understand a sales receipt • Compare ways to make big purchases	• Complete an online order and read a sales receipt **Digital skill:** • Go online and visit an online store.	• Listen actively
• Write about a free-time activity **Writing skill:** • Use details in your writing	• Complete a Venn Diagram • Interpret calendars • Interpret a bar graph • Understand emojis	• Understand a schedule of events **Digital skill:** • Go online and find a website of your local library. Add two events to a digital calendar. Invite a friend.	• Be professional

Unit	Vocabulary	Listening and Speaking	Reading	Grammar
5 **At Home** *page 85*	Household problems	• Describe problems in your home • Ask about an apartment • Get directions **Pronunciation skills:** • Stress in two-word nouns • Voiced and voiceless *th*	• Read an article about renters and homeowners **Academic skill:** • Skimming	• Present continuous • *There is/There are* • Imperatives
6 **In the Past** *page 105*	Events	• Talk about past activities • Talk about milestones • Talk about something that happened **Pronunciation skills:** • Extra syllable for *-ed* endings • Statements as questions	• Read an article about President Barack Obama **Academic skill:** • Scan for information	• Simple past: Regular verbs • Simple past: Irregular verbs • Simple past: Information questions
7 **Health Watch** *page 125*	Health problems	• Make a doctor's appointment • Talk about an injury • Call in when you have to miss work **Pronunciation skills:** • Linking sounds • *t* between two vowel sounds • Using pauses	• Read an article about stress **Academic skill:** • Use formatting cues	• Prepositions of time • Simple past: More irregular verbs • Ways to express reasons: *because, for*
8 **Job Hunting** *page 145*	Job titles and duties	• Talk about your skills • Answer questions about work history • Answer questions about availability **Pronunciation skills:** • Pronunciation of *can* and *can't* • Intonation of questions with *or*	• Read an article about jobs in the U.S. **Academic skill:** • Predict the topic	• *Can* to express ability • Time expressions with *ago, last, in,* and *later* • Ways to express alternatives: *or, and*

Writing	Document Literacy Numeracy	Workplace, Life, and Community Skills	Soft Skills At Work
• Write about your home **Writing skill:** • Structure paragraphs and use indents	• Compare cost on rent and utilities • Interpret a utility bill • Interpret a bar graph • Follow directions on a map • Understand signs	• Read apartment ads • Read a utility bill **Digital skill:** • Go online and search for an apartment in your town or city	• Take initiative
• Write a biography **Writing skill:** • Use commas with dates	• Interpret a to-do list • Identify holidays on a calendar • Create a timeline	• Recognize U.S. holidays **Digital skill:** • Go online and search for other U.S. holidays	• Be dependable
• Write about treating a health problem **Writing skill:** • Give a reason	• Interpret appointment cards • Identify dosage on medicine labels	• Read medicine labels **Digital skill:** • Go online and search for an online pharmacy. Find information on a medicine.	• Respect others
• Write about your job history **Writing skill:** • Use the correct tense	• Interpret a timeline • Interpret a bar graph	• Read help wanted ads • Identify job requirements **Digital skill:** • Go online and search for a job posting website	• Be honest

Unit	Vocabulary	Listening and Speaking	Reading	Grammar
9 **Parents and Children** *page 165*	School Subjects	• Make plans for school events • Talk about progress in school • Discuss your child's behavior in school **Pronunciation skills:** • Pronunciation of *will* • Extra syllables with *'s*	• Read an article about going to college **Academic skill:** • Use information in graphs and tables	• Future with *will* • Adverbs of manner • Object pronouns • Possessive nouns
10 **Let's Eat!** *page 185*	Food containers and quantities	• Ask for quantities of food • Make decisions when shopping for food • Order food in a restaurant **Pronunciation skills:** • Pronunciation of *to, the, a,* and *of*	• Read an article about the effects of coffee **Academic skill:** • Get meaning from context	• Count nouns/Non-count nouns and *How much/How many* • Comparative adjectives with *than* • Quantifiers with plural and non-count nouns
11 **Call 911!** *page 205*	Medical emergencies	• Call 911 to report a medical emergency • Describe an emergency • Respond to a police officer's instructions **Pronunciation skills:** • Stressed syllables • *H* sound	• Read an article about being safe at work **Academic skill:** • Identify supporting details	• Present continuous: Statements and questions • *There was/There were* • Compound imperatives
12 **The World of Work** *page 225*	Job Responsibilities	• Ask about policies at work • Ask a co-worker to cover your hours • Request a schedule change **Pronunciation skills:** • Intonation in *yes/no* questions • Intonation in information questions and statements	• Read an article about the Social Security program **Academic skill:** • Think about what you know	• Expressions of necessity and prohibition • Information questions with *Who/What/Which/When/Where* • *Can/Could* to ask permission

Writing	Document Literacy Numeracy	Workplace, Life, and Community Skills	Soft Skills At Work
• Write about school **Writing skill:** • Use commas between words in a list	• Interpret a bar graph • Compare cost of tuition	• Leave a phone message • Leave a voice message **Digital skill:** • Go online and search how to set up a personal voicemail greeting message on your mobile phone	• Plan well
• Write about nutrients in a dish **Writing skill:** • Use *like* and *such as* to introduce examples	• Identify food containers and quantities • Understand nutritional information on food labels • Compare food price in ads • Interpret a bar graph • Read a menu	• Read food labels **Digital skill:** • Go online and search for ingredients in a food you like	• Ask for help
• Write about an emergency **Writing skill:** • Answer *wh-* questions to give information	• Interpret a fire escape plan • Interpret a bar graph	• Identify fire hazards • Understand fire safety procedures **Digital skill:** • Go online and search for workplace fire-escape plans or your own workplace's fire-escape plan	• Follow safety procedures
• Write about job responsibilities **Writing skill:** • Give details to support an idea	• Calculate earnings from a pay stub • Understand types of deduction • Calculate overtime pay • Interpret a work schedule	• Read a pay stub • Understand payroll deductions and overtime hours **Digital skill:** • Go online and search for other common deductions that can appear on a pay stub	• Be a team player

Unit	CASAS Reading Standards (correlated to CASAS Reading Standards 2016)	CASAS Listening Standards (correlated to CASAS Listening Basic Skills Content Standard
1	**L1:** RDG 1.1, 2.2, 2.3; **L2:** RDG 1.7, 2.2, 2.3; **L3:** RDG 1.7, 2.1, 2.2, 2.3; **L4:** RDG 1.7, 2.2; **L5:** RDG 1.7; **L6:** RDG 1.7, 2.9; **L7:** RDG 1.7, 1.8, 2.2, 2.3, 3.2, 3.7, 3.11, 4.2; **L8:** RDG 1.7; **L9:** RDG 1.7, 2.1, 2.2, 2.6; **L10:** RDG 1.7, 1.8; **L11:** RDG 1.7, 1.8, 3.2;	**L1:** 2.1, 2.3, 2.9; **L2:** 1.3, 1.4, 1.6, 2.1, 2.3, 4.1, 4.2; **L3:** 1.3, 2.1, 2.3, 3.1, 3.3, 3.5, 4.1, 4.2; **L4:** 2.1, 2.3, 4.1, 4.2; **L5:** 1.4, 1.6, 2.1, 2.3, 4.1, 4.2, 6.1; **L6:** 2.1, 2.3, 3.13, 4.1, 4.2; **L7:** 2.1, 2.3, 4.2, 5.8, 6.1; **L8:** 1.4, 2.1, 2.3, 4.1, 4.2, 6.5; **L** 2.1, 2.3; **L11:** 2.1, 2.3, 4.1, 4.2;
2	**L1:** RDG 1.1, 2.2, 2.3; **L2:** RDG 1.7, 2.2, 2.3; **L3:** RDG 1.7, 2.1, 2.9; **L4:** RDG 1.7, 1.8, 2.2, 2.3, 3.2, 3.7, 3.11; **L5:** RDG 1.7, 2.2, 2.3; **L6:** RDG 1.7, 2.9; **L7:** RDG 1.7, 1.8, 2.2, 2.3, 3.2, 4.2, 4.9; **L8:** RDG 1.7, 2.2, 2.3; **L9:** RDG 1.7, 2.9; **L10:** RDG 1.7, 1.8, 2.1; **L11:** RDG 1.7, 1.8, 3.2;	**L1:** 2.1, 2.3, 2.9, 4.1, 4.2; **L2:** 1.4, 2.1, 2.3, 4.1, 4.2, 6.5; **L3:** 1.3, 2.1, 2.3, 3.1 3.3, 3.5, 4.1, 4.2; **L4:** 2.1, 2.3, 4.1, 4.2, 5.8, 6.1; **L5:** 1.4, 1.5, 2.1, 2.3, 4.1, 4.2 5.8, 6.1; **L6:** 2.1, 2.3, 3.6, 3.13, 4.1, 4.2; **L7:** 2.1, 2.3, 4.2; **L8:** 2.1, 2.3, 4.1, 4. 6.1, 6.2; **L10:** 2.1, 2.3; **L11:** 2.1, 2.3, 4.1, 4.2;
3	**L1:** RDG 1.7, 2.2, 2.3; **L2:** RDG 1.7, 2.2, 2.3; **L3:** RDG 1.7, 2.9; **L4:** RDG 1.7, 1.8, 2.2, 2.3, 3.2, 3.6; **L5:** RDG 1.7, 2.2, 2.3; **L6:** RDG 1.7, 2.9; **L7:** RDG 1.7, 1.8, 2.2, 2.3, 3.2, 3.11, 3.14, 4.2, 4.9; **L8:** RDG 1.7, 2.2, 2.3; **L9:** RDG 1.7; **L10:** RDG 1.7, 1.8, 2.1; **L11:** RDG 1.7, 1.8, 3.2;	**L1:** 2.1, 2.3, 2.9, 4.1, 4.2; **L2:** 1.4, 2.1, 2.3, 4.1, 4.2, 6.1, 6.2, 6.5; **L3:** 1.3, 2.1 2.3, 3.1, 4.1, 4.2; **L4:** 2.1, 2.3, 4.1, 4.2; **L5:** 1.5, 2.1, 2.3, 4.1, 4.2, 5.8, 6.1; **L6** 2.1, 2.3, 3.1, 3.3, 3.6, 4.1, 4.2; **L7:** 2.1, 2.3, 4.2, 5.8, 6.1; **L8:** 2.1, 2.3, 4.1, 4.2 6.1, 6.2; **L10:** 2.1, 2.3; **L11:** 2.1, 2.3, 4.1, 4.2;
4	**L1:** RDG 1.7, 2.2, 2.3; **L2:** RDG 1.7, 2.2, 2.3; **L3:** RDG 1.7, 2.9, 4.9; **L4:** RDG 1.7, 1.8, 2.2, 2.3, 3.2, 4.9; **L5:** RDG 1.7, 2.2, 2.3; **L6:** RDG 1.7, 2.9, 4.9; **L7:** RDG 1.7, 1.8, 2.2, 2.3, 3.2, 3.8, 3.11, 4.2, 4.9; **L8:** RDG 1.7, 2.2, 2.3; **L9:** RDG 1.7; **L10:** RDG 1.7, 1.8, 2.1; **L11:** RDG 1.7, 1.8, 3.2;	**L1:** 2.1, 2.3, 2.9, 4.1, 4.2; **L2:** 1.4, 2.01, 2.3, 4.1, 4.2, 6.1, 6.2; **L3:** 1.3, 2.1, 2. 3.1, 4.1, 4.2; **L4:** 2.1, 2.3, 4.1, 4.2; **L5:** 2.1, 2.3, 4.1, 4.2, 5.8, 6.1, 6.2, 6.5; **L6** 2.1, 2.3, 3.1, 4.1, 4.2; **L7:** 2.1, 2.3, 4.2, 5.8, 6.1, 6.2; **L8:** 1.5, 2.1, 2.3, 4.1, 4.2 6.1, 6.2, 6.5; **L9:** 3.1; **L10:** 2.1, 2.3; **L11:** 2.1, 2.3, 4.1, 4.2;
5	**L1:** RDG 1.7, 2.2, 2.3; **L2:** RDG 1.7, 2.2, 2.3; **L3:** RDG 1.7, 2.9, 4.9; **L4:** RDG 1.7, 1.8, 2.2, 2.3, 3.2, 3.6, 3.16, 4.9; **L5:** RDG 1.7, 2.2, 2.3; **L6:** RDG 1.7, 2.9; **L7:** RDG 1.7, 1.8, 2.3, 3.2, 3.4, 3.9, 3.11, 4.2, 4.9; **L8:** RDG 1.7, 2.2, 2.3, 3.4; **L9:** RDG 1.3, 1.7, 2.3, 3.6; **L10:** RDG 1.7, 1.8, 2.1; **L11:** RDG 1.7, 1.8, 3.2;	**L1:** 2.1, 2.3, 2.9, 4.2; **L2:** 2.1, 2.3, 4.1, 4.2, 6.1, 6.2, 6.5; **L3:** 1.3, 2.1, 2.3, 3.9 4.1, 4.2; **L4:** 2.1, 2.3, 4.2; **L5:** 2.1, 2.3, 4.2, 6.1, 6.2; **L6:** 2.1, 2.3, 3.1, 4.2; **L7:** 2.1, 2.3, 4.2, 5.8, 6.1, 6.2; **L8:** 2.1, 2.3, 4.1, 4.2, 5.4, 5.5, 6.1, 6.2; **L9:** 3.1, 3.4 **L10:** 2.1, 2.3; **L11:** 2.1, 2.3, 4.1, 4.2;
6	**L1:** RDG 1.7, 2.3; **L2:** RDG 1.7, 2.2, 2.3; **L3:** RDG 1.7, 2.9, 4.9; **L4:** RDG 1.7, 1.8, 2.3, 3.2, 4.9; **L5:** RDG 1.7, 2.2, 2.3; **L6:** RDG 1.7, 2.9; **L7:** RDG 1.7, 1.8, 2.3, 3.2, 3.10, 3.11, 4.2; **L8:** RDG 1.7, 2.2, 2.3; **L9:** RDG 1.7, 2.3, 2.6; **L10:** RDG 1.7, 1.8, 2.1; **L11:** RDG 1.7, 1.81, 3.2;	**L1:** 2.1, 2.3, 2.9, 4.2; **L2:** 2.1, 2.3, 4.1, 4.2, 6.1, 6.2, 6.5; **L3:** 1.3, 2.1, 2.3, 3.9 4.1, 4.2; **L4:** 2.1, 2.3, 4.2; **L5:** 1.4, 2.1, 2.3, 4.2, 6.1, 6.2, 6.5; **L6:** 2.1, 2.3, 3.6 3.9, 4.2; **L7:** 2.1, 2.3, 4.2, 5.8, 6.1, 6.2; **L8:** 2.1, 2.3, 4.1, 4.2, 6.1, 6.2, 6.5; **L9:** 3.1, 3.9, 4.1, 4.2; **L10:** 2.1, 2.3; **L11:** 2.1, 2.3, 4.1, 4.2;
7	**L1:** RDG 1.7, 2.3; **L2:** RDG 1.7, 2.2, 2.3; **L3:** RDG 1.7, 2.9, 4.9; **L4:** RDG 1.7, 1.8, 2.3, 3.2, 3.6, 4.9; **L5:** RDG 1.7, 2.3; **L6:** RDG 1.7, 2.9; **L7:** RDG 1.7, 1.8, 2.3, 3.2, 3.10, 3.11, 4.2, 4.9; **L8:** RDG 1.7, 2.3; **L9:** RDG 1.7, 2.3; **L10:** RDG 1.7, 1.8, 2.1; **L11:** RDG 1.7, 1.8, 3.2;	**L1:** 2.1, 2.3, 2.9, 4.2; **L2:** 1.2, 2.1, 2.3, 4.2, 6.1, 6.2, 6.5; **L3:** 1.3, 2.1, 2.3, 4.1 4.2; **L4:** 2.1, 2.3, 4.2, 5.4, 5.5; **L5:** 1.5, 2.1, 2.3, 4.2, 6.1, 6.2, 6.5; **L6:** 2.1, 2.3 3.9, 4.2; **L7:** 2.1, 2.3, 4.2, 5.8, 6.1, 6.2; **L8:** 1.4, 2.1, 2.3, 4.1, 4.2, 6.1, 6.2, 6.5 **L9:** 4.1, 4.2; **L10:** 2.1, 2.3; **L11:** 2.1, 2.3, 4.1, 4.2;
8	**L1:** RDG 1.7, 2.3; **L2:** RDG 1.7, 2.3; **L3:** RDG 1.7, 3.1; **L4:** RDG 1.7, 1.8, 2.2, 2.3, 3.2; **L5:** RDG 1.7, 2.3; **L6:** RDG 1.7, 2.9; **L7:** RDG 1.7, 1.8, 2.3, 3.2, 3.8, 3.11, 4.2; **L8:** RDG 1.7, 2.3, 3.8; **L9:** RDG 1.7, 2.3; **L10:** RDG 1.7, 1.8; **L11:** RDG 1.7, 1.8, 3.2;	**L1:** 2.1, 2.3, 2.9, 4.2, 5.8; **L2:** 1.4, 2.1, 2.3, 4.2, 6.1, 6.2, 6.5; **L3:** 1.3. 2.1. 2.3. 4.1. 4.2; **L4:** 2.1, 2.3, 4.2, 5.4, 5.5; **L5:** 2.1, 2.3, 4.2, 6.1, 6.2, 6.5; **L6:** 2.1, 2.3, 3.11, 4.2; **L7:** 2.1, 2.3, 4.2, 5.8, 6.1, 6.2; **L8:** 1.4, 2.1, 2.3, 4.1, 4.2, 6.1, 6.2, 6. **L9:** 3.5, 4.1, 5.2; **L10:** 2.1, 2.3, 3.9; **L11:** 2.1, 2.3, 4.1, 4.2;
9	**L1:** RDG 1.7, 2.3; **L2:** RDG 1.7, 2.3; **L3:** RDG 1.7, 3.1; **L4:** RDG 1.7, 1.8, 2.3, 3.2; **L5:** RDG 1.7, 2.3; **L6:** RDG 1.7, 2.9; **L7:** RDG 1.7, 1.8, 2.3, 3.2, 3.4, 3.8, 3.11, 4.2; **L8:** RDG 1.7, 2.3; **L9:** RDG 1.7; **L10:** RDG 1.7, 1.8, 2.1; **L11:** RDG 1.7, 1.8, 3.2;	**L1:** 2.1, 2.3, 2.9, 4.2, 5.8; **L2:** 1.4, 2.1, 2.3, 4.2, 6.1, 6.2, 6.5; **L3:** 1.3, 2.1, 2.3, 3.3, 4.1, 4.2; **L4:** 2.1, 2.3, 4.2, 6.5; **L5:** 2.1, 2.3, 4.2, 6.1, 6.2, 6.5; **L6:** 2.1, 2.3, 3.2, 4.2; **L7:** 2.1, 2.3, 4.2, 5.8, 6.1, 6.2; **L8:** 1.2, 2.1, 2.3, 4.1, 4.2, 6.1, 6.2, 6.5 **L9:** 4.1, 4.2, 3.8; **L10:** 2.1, 2.3, 3.9; **L11:** 2.1, 2.3, 4.1, 4.2;
10	**L1:** RDG 1.7, 2.3; **L2:** RDG 1.7, 2.3; **L3:** RDG 1.7, 2.6; **L4:** RDG 1.7, 1.8, 2.3, 3.2; **L5:** RDG 1.7, 2.3; **L6:** RDG 1.7, 2.2, 2.6, 2.9; **L7:** RDG 1.7, 1.8, 2.3, 3.2, 3.11, 4.2, 4.9; **L8:** RDG 1.7, 2.3; **L9:** RDG 1.7; **L10:** RDG 1.7, 1.8, 2.1; **L11:** RDG 1.7, 1.8, 3.2;	**L1:** 2.1, 2.3, 2.9, 4.2; **L2:** 1.4, 2.1, 2.3, 4.2, 6.1, 6.2, 6.5; **L3:** 1.3, 2.1, 2.3, 3.3, 4.1, 4.2; **L4:** 2.1, 2.3, 4.2; **L5:** 2.1, 2.3, 4.21, 6.1, 6.2, 6.5; **L6:** 2.1. 2.3. 3.10. 4 5.8; **L7:** 2.1, 2.3, 4.2, 5.8, 6.1, 6.2; **L8:** 1.4, 2.1, 2.3, 4.1, 4.2, 6.1, 6.2, 6.5; **L1** 2.1, 2.3, 3.11; **L11:** 2.1, 2.3, 4.1, 4.2
11	**L1:** RDG 1.7, 2.3; **L2:** RDG 1.7, 2.3; **L3:** RDG 1.7, 2.6; **L4:** RDG 1.7, 1.8, 2.3, 3.2, 3.4, 3.6; **L5:** RDG 1.7, 2.3; **L6:** RDG 1.7, 2.9; **L7:** RDG 1.7, 1.8, 2.3, 3.2, 3.11, 4.2, 4.9; **L8:** RDG 1.7, 2.3; **L9:** RDG 1.7, 2.9; **L10:** RDG 1.7, 1.8, 2.1; **L11:** RDG 1.7, 1.8, 3.2;	**L1:** 2.1, 2.3, 2.9, 4.2; **L2:** 1.4, 2.1, 2.3, 4.2, 6.1, 6.2, 6.5; **L3:** 1.3, 2.1, 2.3, 3.3, 3.9, 4.1, 4.2; **L4:** 2.1, 2.3, 4.2; **L5:** 1.1, 2.1, 2.3, 4.2, 6.1, 6.2, 6.5; **L6:** 2.1, 2.3, 3.5, 4.2, 5.8; **L7:** 2.1, 2.3, 4.2, 5.8, 6.1, 6.2; **L8:** 1.4, 2.1, 2.3, 4.1, 4.2, 6.1, 6.2 **L9:** 3.4; **L10:** 2.1, 2.3, 3.6; **L11:** 2.1, 2.3, 4.1, 4.2;
12	**L1:** RDG 1.7, 2.3; **L2:** RDG 1.7, 2.3; **L3:** RDG 1.7, 1.8, 2.3, 3.2; **L4:** RDG 1.7, 1.8, 2.3, 3.2, 3.4; **L5:** RDG 1.7, 2.3; **L6:** RDG 1.7, 2.9, 3.4; **L7:** RDG 1.7, 1.8, 2.3, 3.2, 3.7, 3.11, 4.2; **L8:** RDG 1.7, 2.3; **L9:** RDG 1.7, 2.9; **L10:** RDG 1.7, 1.8, 3.2; **L11:** RDG 1.7, 1.8, 3.2;	**L1:** 2.1, 2.3, 2.9, 4.2; **L2:** 1.4, 2.1, 2.3, 4.2, 6.1, 6.2, 6.5; **L3:** 1.3, 2.1, 2.3, 3.9, 4.1, 4.2; **L4:** 2.1, 2.3, 4.2; **L5:** 2.1, 2.3, 4.2, 6.1, 6.5; **L6:** 2.1, 2.3, 3.6; **L7:** 2.1, 2.3, 4.2, 5.8, 6.1, 6.2; **L8:** 1.4, 2.1, 2.3, 4.1, 4.2, 6.1, 6.2, 6.5; **L9:** 3.1; **L10** 2.1, 2.3, 3.11; **L11:** 2.1, 2.3, 4.1, 4.2;

CASAS: Comprehensive Adult Student Assessment System
CCRS: College and Career Readiness Standards (R=Reading; W=Writing; SL=Speaking/Listening; L=Language)
ELPS: English Language Proficiency Standards

SAS Competencies	CCRS Correlations, Level A	ELPS Correlations, Level 2
.1.2, 0.1.5, 0.2.1, 7.4.1; **L2:** 0.1.2, 0.1.4, 0.1.5, 0.2.1; **L3:** 0.1.2, .0.1.5, 0.1.6, 0.2.1; **L4:** 0.1.2, 0.1.5, 0.2.1, 4.1.1, 7.4.4, 7.7.3; .1.2, 0.1.4, 0.1.5, 0.1.6, 0.2.1; **L6:** 0.1.2, 0.1.4, 0.1.5; **L7:** 0.1.2, , 4.8.1, 4.8.2; **L8:** 0.1.2, 0.1.4, 0.1.5, 0.1.6, 0.2.1; **L9:** 0.1.2, , 0.1.5, 0.1.6, 0.2.1; **L10:** 0.1.2, 0.1.5, 0.1.6, 0.2.1, 0.2.4, 7.4.1; 0.1.2, 0.1.4, 0.1.5, 0.1.6, 0.2.1;	**L1:** SL.K.6, L.1.5a, L.1.5b, L.1.5c, L.1.6; **L3:** L.1.1c, L.1.1d, L.1.1e, L.1.1g; **L4:** W.1.7, W.1.8, SL.K.3; **L6:** L.1.1h; **L7:** RI/RL.1.1, RI.1.2, RI.1.4, SL.K.2, SL.1.4; **L8:** SL.1.1, SL.K.6; **L9:** L.1.1e, L.1.1g; **L10:** W.1.2, W.1.5, L.1.1l;	ELPS 1-3, 5, 7-10
.1.2, 0.1.5, 0.2.1, 7.4.1; **L2:** 0.1.2, 0.1.4, 0.1.5, 0.2.1; **L3:** 0.1.2, .0.1.5; **L4:** 0.1.2, 0.1.5, 0.2.1; **L5:** 0.1.2, 0.1.4, 0.1.5, 0.1.6, **L6:** 0.1.2, 0.1.5, 0.1.6, 0.2.1; **L7:** 0.1.2, 0.1.5, 2.4.2, 2.4.3, , 7.4.4, 7.7.3; **L8:** 0.1.2, 0.1.4, 0.1.5, 0.1.6, 0.2.1; **L9:** 0.1.2, ; **L10:** 0.1.2, 0.1.5, 0.1.6; **L11:** 0.1.2, 0.1.4, 0.1.5, 0.1.6, 0.2.1, , **L1:** SL.1.1, SL.K.6, L.1.5a, L.1.5b, L.1.5c, L.1.6;	**L3:** L.1.1c, L.1.1d, L.1.1e, L.1.1g; **L4:** RI/RL.1.1, RI.1.2, RI.1.4, SL.K.2, SL.1.4; **L5:** SL.K.3; **L6:** L.1.1e, L.1.1g; **L7:** W.1.7, W.1.8; **L8:** SL.1.1a, SL.1.1b, SL.1.1c, SL.K.6; **L9:** L.1.1c, L.1.1h, L.1.1k; **L10:** W.1.2, W.1.5, L.1.1l;	ELPS 1-3, 5-10
.1.2, 0.1.5, 1.2.9, 7.4.1; **L2:** 0.1.2, 0.1.5, 0.2.1; **L3:** 0.1.2, 0.1.5; .1.2, 0.1.5, 0.2.1, 1.6.4, 4.5.6, 7.4.4, 7.7.3; **L5:** 0.1.2, 0.1.5, , 0.2.1; **L6:** 0.1.2, 0.1.5, 0.1.6, 0.2.1; **L7:** 0.1.2, 0.1.5, 1.3.1; **L8:** , 0.1.4, 0.1.5, 0.1.6, 1.3.3; **L9:** 0.1.2; **L10:** 0.1.2, 0.1.5, 0.1.6; 0.1.2, 0.1.4, 0.1.5, 0.1.6, 0.2.1, 4.8.3;	**L1:** SL.1.1a, SL.1.1b, SL.1.1c, SL.K.6, L.1.1l, L.1.2g, L.1.5a, L.1.5b, L.1.5c, L.1.6; **L3:** SL.K.3, SL.1.4, L.1.1c, L.1.1d, L.1.1e, L.1.1g; **L4:** RI/RL.1.1, W.1.7, W.1.8; **L6:** L.1.1d, L.1.1e, L.1.1g; **L7:** RI/RL.1.1, RI.1.2, RI.1.4; **L8:** SL.1.1a, SL.1.1b, SL.1.1c, SL.K.6; **L10:** W.1.2, W.1.5, L.1.1l;	ELPS 1-3, 5, 7-10
.1.2, 0.1.5, 0.2.1, 0.2.4, 7.4.1; **L2:** 0.1.2, 0.1.5, 0.2.1, 0.2.4; **L3:** , 0.1.5, 0.2.1, 0.2.4, 7.1.4; **L4:** 0.1.2, 0.1.5, 2.8.3, 4.5.6, 7.4.4, ; **L5:** 0.1.2, 0.1.5, 0.1.6; **L6:** 0.1.2, 0.1.5, 0.1.6, 0.2.1, 0.2.4, ; **L7:** 0.1.2, 0.1.5, 7.7.4; **L8:** 0.1.2, 0.1.4, 0.1.5, 0.1.6, 0.2.3; **L9:** ; **L10:** 0.1.2, 0.1.5, 0.1.6, 0.2.4; **L11:** 0.1.2, 0.1.4, 0.1.5, 0.1.6, , 4.8.3, 4.8.4;	**L1:** SL.1.1a, SL.1.1b, SL.1.1c, SL.K.6, L.1.1l, L.1.5a, L.1.5b, L.1.5c, L.1.6; **L3:** L.1.1c, L.1.1d, L.1.1e, L.1.1g, L.1.1k; **L4:** RI.1.7, W.1.7, W.1.8, SL.K.3; **L5:** SL.1.4; **L7:** RI/RL.1.1, RI.1.2, RI.1.4, SL.K.2; **L8:** SL.1.1a, SL.1.1b, SL.1.1c, SL.K.6; **L10:** W.1.2, W.1.5, L.1.1l;	ELPS 1-3, 5-10
.1.2, 0.1.5, 7.4.1, 8.2.6; **L2:** 0.1.2, 0.1.5, 4.1.8, 8.2.6; **L3:** 0.1.2, , 8.2.6; **L4:** 0.1.2, 0.1.5, 1.4.2, 1.5.3, 4.5.6, 7.4.4, 7.7.3; **L5:** , 0.1.5, 0.1.6, 1.4.2; **L6:** 0.1.2, 0.1.5, 0.1.6, 1.4.2; **L7:** 0.1.2, , 1.5.2, 6.7.2, 7.2.3; **L8:** 0.1.2, 0.1.5, 0.1.6, 2.2.1, 2.2.5; **L9:** , 1.9.1; **L10:** 0.1.2, 0.1.5, 0.1.6, 0.2.4, 1.4.1; **L11:** 0.1.2, 0.1.4, , 0.1.6, 0.2.1, 4.8.3, 4.8.4;	**L1:** SL.1.1a, SL.1.1b, SL.1.1c, SL.K.6, L.1.5a, L.1.5b, L.1.5c, L.1.6; **L3:** L.1.1c, L.1.1d, L.1.1e, L.1.1g, L.1.2h; **L4:** RI.1.9, W.1.7, W.1.8; **L5:** SL.K.3; **L6:** SL.1.1a, SL.1.1b, SL.1.1c, SL.K.6; **L7:** RI/RL.1.1, RI.1.2, RI.1.4, RI.1.5, RI.1.7, SL.K.2, SL.1.4; **L10:** W.1.2, W.1.5, L.1.1l;	ELPS 1-5, 7-10
.1.2, 0.1.5, 0.2.4, 7.4.1; **L2:** 0.1.2, 0.1.5, 0.2.4; **L3:** 0.1.2, 0.1.5, ; **L4:** 0.1.2, 0.1.5, 2.7.1, 4.5.6, 7.7.3, 7.4.4; **L5:** 0.1.2, 0.1.5, , 0.2.1; **L6:** 0.1.2, 0.1.5, 0.1.6, 0.2.1; **L7:** 0.1.2, 0.1.5, 5.2.1; **L8:** , 0.1.5, 0.1.6, 0.1.8, 0.2.1; **L9:** 0.1.2, 0.1.5, 0.1.6, 0.2.1; **L10:** , 0.1.5, 0.1.6; **L11:** 0.1.2, 0.1.4, 0.1.5, 0.1.6, 0.2.1, 7.3.2;	**L1:** SL.1.1a, SL.1.1b, SL.1.1c, SL.K.6, L.1.1l, L.1.5a, L.1.6; **L3:** L.1.1c, L.1.1d, L.1.1e, L.1.1g; **L4:** RI/RL.1.1, RI.1.4, W.1.7, W.1.8; **L5:** SL.K.3, SL.1.4; **L6:** L.1.1c, L.1.1d, L.1.1e, L.1.1g; **L7:** RI/RL.1.1, RI.1.2, SL.K.2; **L8:** SL.1.1a, SL.1.1b, SL.1.1c, SL.K.6; **L9:** L.1.1c, L.1.1d, L.1.1e, L.1.1g, L.1.1k, L.1.1l; **L10:** W.1.2, W.1.5, L.1.1l;	ELPS 1-3, 5, 7-10
.1.2, 0.1.5, 3.6.3, 7.4.1; **L2:** 0.1.2, 0.1.5, 3.1.2; **L3:** 0.1.2, 0.1.5, , 3.1.2; **L4:** 0.1.2, 0.1.5, 3.3.2, 3.4.1, 4.5.6, 7.7.3, 7.4.4; **L5:** , 0.1.5, 0.1.6, 0.2.1, 3.6.2; **L6:** 0.1.2, 0.1.5, 0.1.6; **L7:** 0.1.2, , 0.2.1, 7.5.4; **L8:** 0.1.2, 0.1.4, 0.1.5, 0.1.6, 0.1.8, 0.2.1, 4.6.5; ▪.1.2; **L10:** 0.1.2, 0.1.5, 0.1.6, 3.6.3; **L11:** 0.1.2, 0.1.4, 0.1.5, ▪, 0.2.1, 4.8.5, 7.3.2;	**L1:** SL.1.1a, SL.1.1b, SL.1.1c, SL.K.6, L.1.5a, L.1.5b, L.1.5c, L.1.6; **L2:** SL.K.3; **L3:** L.1.1j; **L4:** W.1.7, W.1.8; **L5:** SL.K.3; **L6:** L.1.1c, L.1.1d, L.1.1e, L.1.1g; **L7:** RI/RL.1.1, RI.1.2, RI.1.4, RI.1.5, SL.K.2, SL.K.3, SL.1.4; **L8:** SL.1.1a, SL.1.1b, SL.1.1c, SL.K.6; **L9:** L.1.1h, L.1.1l; **L10:** W.1.2, W.1.5, L.1.1l;	ELPS 1-3, 5, 7-10
.1.2, 0.1.5, 4.4.4, 7.1.1, 7.4.1; **L2:** 0.1.2, 0.1.5, 4.1.5; **L3:** 0.1.2, , 0.2.1, 3.1.2; **L4:** 0.1.2, 0.1.5, 4.1.3, 4.1.5, 4.5.6, 7.4.4, 7.7.3; ▪.1.2, 0.1.5, 0.1.6, 0.2.1, 4.1.5; **L6:** 0.1.2, 0.1.5, 0.1.6, 0.2.1; **L7:** , 0.1.5, 0.2.1, 7.1.1; **L8:** 0.1.2, 0.1.4, 0.1.5, 0.1.6, 0.1.8, 0.2.1, ▪, 4.6.5; **L9:** 0.1.2; **L10:** 0.1.2, 0.1.5, 0.1.6; **L11:** 0.1.2, 0.1.4, ▪, 0.1.6, 0.2.1, 4.8.1, 4.8.5;	**L1:** SL.1.1a, SL.1.1b, SL.1.1c, SL.K.6, L.1.5a, L.1.5b, L.1.5c, L.1.6; **L2:** SL.K.3; **L4:** W.1.7, W.1.8; **L7:** RI/RL.1.1, RI.1.2, RI.1.4, SL.K.2; **L8:** RI.1.5, SL.1.1a, SL.1.1b, SL.1.1c, SL.K.3, SL.1.4, SL.K.6; **L9:** L.1.1h, L.1.1l; **L10:** W.1.2, W.1.5, L.1.1l;	ELPS 1-3, 5, 7-10
.1.2, 0.1.5, 7.4.1; **L2:** 0.1.2, 0.1.5; **L3:** 0.1.2, 0.1.5, 0.2.1, 3.1.2; ▪.1.2, 0.1.5, 2.1.7, 4.5.6, 7.4.4, 7.7.3; **L5:** 0.1.2, 0.1.4, 0.1.5, ▪, 2.8.6; **L6:** 0.1.2, 0.1.5, 0.1.6; **L7:** 0.1.2, 0.1.5, 0.2.1, 6.7.2, ; **L8:** 0.1.2, 0.1.4, 0.1.5, 0.1.6, 2.8.6; **L9:** 0.1.2; **L10:** 0.1.2, ▪, 0.1.6; **L11:** 0.1.2, 0.1.4, 0.1.5, 0.1.6, 0.2.1, 7.1.2;	**L1:** SL.1.1a, SL.1.1b, SL.1.1c, SL.1.4, SL.K.6, L.1.6; **L2:** SL.K.3; **L3:** L.1.1e, L.1.1g; **L4:** W.1.7, W.1.8; **L5:** SL.K.3; **L6:** L.1.1d, L.1.2h; **L7:** RI/RL.1.1, RI.1.2, RI.1.4, RI.1.7; **L8:** SL.1.1a, SL.1.1b, SL.1.1c, SL.K.3, SL.K.6, L.1.1b; **L9:** L.1.1b, L.1.1c, L.1.2h, L.1.2i; **L10:** W.1.2, W.1.5, L.1.1l, L.1.2e;	ELPS 1-3, 5, 7-10
.1.2, 0.1.5, 1.2.8, 7.4.1; **L2:** 0.1.2, 0.1.5, 1.2.8; **L3:** 0.1.2, 0.1.5, , 2.6.3; **L4:** 0.1.2, 0.1.5, 1.2.8, 1.6.1, 3.5.1, 3.5.2, 4.5.6, 7.4.4, ▪; **L5:** 0.1.2, 0.1.4, 0.1.5, 0.1.6, 1.2.8; **L6:** 0.1.2, 0.1.5, 0.1.6, ; **L7:** 0.1.2, 0.1.5, 0.2.1; **L8:** 0.1.2, 0.1.5, 0.1.6, 2.6.4; **L9:** 0.1.2; , 0.1.2, 0.1.5, 0.1.6; **L11:** 0.1.2, 0.1.4, 0.1.5, 0.1.6, 0.2.1, 4.6.5, ▪;	**L1:** SL.1.1a, SL.1.1b, SL.1.1c, SL.K.6, L.1.5a, L.1.5b, L.1.5c, L.1.6; **L2:** SL.K.3; **L3:** L.1.1c, L.1.1e, L.1.1f, L.1.1g, L.1.2h, L.1.2i; **L4:** W.1.7, W.1.8; **L5:** SL.K.3; **L6:** SL.1.4, L.1.1f, L.1.1l, L.1.2g, L.1.2i; **L7:** RI/RL.1.1, RI.1.2, RI.1.4, SL.K.2, L.1. 4; **L8:** SL.1.1a, SL.1.1b, SL.1.1c; **L9:** L.1.1c, L.1.1e, L.1.1g; **L10:** W.1.2, W.1.5, L.1.1l, L.1.2e;	ELPS 1-5, 7-10
.1.2, 0.1.5, 2.1.2, 7.4.1; **L2:** 0.1.2, 0.1.5, 2.1.2; **L3:** 0.1.2, 0.1.5; ▪.1.2, 0.1.5, 1.4.8, 3.4.1, 3.4.2, 4.3.1, 4.5.6, 7.4.4, 7.7.3; **L5:** ▪, 0.1.4, 0.1.5, 0.1.6; **L6:** 0.1.2, 0.1.5, 0.1.6; **L7:** 0.1.2, 0.1.5, , 4.3.1; **L8:** 0.1.2, 0.1.5, 0.1.6, 5.5.6; **L9:** 0.1.2; **L10:** 0.1.2, , 0.1.6; **L11:** 0.1.2, 0.1.5, 0.1.6, 0.2.1, 4.3.4;	**L1:** SL.1.1a, SL.1.1b, SL.1.1c, SL.K.6, L.1.5a, L.1.5b, L.1.5c, L.1.6; **L2:** SL.K.3; **L3:** L.1.1c, L.1.1e, L.1.2h; **L4:** W.1.7, W.1.8; **L5:** SL.K.3; **L6:** SL.1.4; **L7:** RI/RL.1.1, RI.1.2, RI.1.4, SL.K.2; **L8:** SL.1.1a, SL.1.1b, SL.1.1c, SL.K.3, SL.K.6; **L9:** L.1.1g, L.1.1h, L.1.1l; **L10:** W.1.2, W.1.5, L.1.1l;	ELPS 1-3, 5, 7-10
.1.2, 0.1.5, 4.4.4, 7.4.1; **L2:** 0.1.2, 0.1.4, 0.1.5, 4.2.4; **L3:** 0.1.2, , 4.4.4; **L4:** 0.1.2, 0.1.5, 4.2.1, 4.5.6, 7.4.4, 7.7.3; **L5:** 0.1.2, , 0.1.5, 0.1.6, 4.1.6, 4.6.5; **L6:** 0.1.2, 0.1.5, 0.1.6; **L7:** 0.1.2, , 2.5.2; **L8:** 0.1.2, 0.1.4, 0.1.5, 0.1.6, 4.1.6, 4.6.5; **L9:** 0.1.2; , 0.1.2, 0.1.5, 0.1.6, 4.4.4; **L11:** 0.1.2, 0.1.5, 0.1.6, 0.2.1, 4.6.4, ▪,	**L1:** SL.1.1a, SL.1.1b, SL.K.6, L.1.5a, L.1.5b, L.1.5c, L.1.6; **L2:** SL.K.3; **L4:** W.1.7, W.1.8; **L5:** SL.K.3; **L6:** L.1.1k, L.1.2a; **L7:** RI/RL.1.1, RI.1.2, RI.1.4; **L8:** SL.1.1a, SL.1.1b, SL.1.1c, SL.K.3, SL.K.6; **L9:** L.1.1l; **L10:** W.1.2, W.1.5, L.1.1l;	ELPS 1-3, 5, 7-10

▪nits of *Future* meet most of the **EFF Content Standards**. For details, as well as ▪orrelations to other state standards, go to www.pearsoneltusa.com/future2e.

ABOUT THE SERIES CONSULTANTS AND AUTHORS

AUTHOR, SERIES CONSULTANT, AND LEARNING EXPERT

Sarah Lynn is an ESOL teacher, trainer, author, and curriculum design specialist. She has taught adult learners in the U.S. and abroad for decades, most recently at Harvard University's Center for Workforce Development. As a teacher-trainer and frequent conference presenter throughout the United States and Latin America, Ms. Lynn has led sessions and workshops on topics such as: fostering student agency and resilience, brain-based teaching techniques, literacy and learning, and teaching in a multilevel classroom. Collaborating with program leaders, teachers, and students, she has developed numerous curricula for college and career readiness, reading and writing skill development, and contextualized content for adult English language learners. Ms. Lynn has co-authored several Pearson ELT publications, including *Business Across Cultures, Future, Future U.S. Citizens,* and *Project Success.* She holds a master's degree in TESOL from Teachers College, Columbia University.

SERIES CONSULTANTS

Ronna Magy has worked as an ESOL classroom teacher, author, teacher-trainer, and curriculum development specialist. She served as the ESL Teacher Adviser in charge of professional development for the Division of Adult and Career Education of the Los Angeles Unified School District. She is a frequent conference presenter on the College and Career Readiness Standards (CCRS), the English Language Proficiency Standards (ELPS), and on the language, literacy, and soft skills needed for academic and workplace success. Ms. Magy has authored/co-authored and trained teachers on modules for CALPRO, the California Adult Literacy Professional Development Project, including modules on integrating and contextualizing workforce skills in the ESOL classroom and evidence-based writing instruction. She is the author of adult ESL publications on English for the workplace, reading and writing, citizenship, and life skills and test preparation. Ms. Magy holds a master's degree in social welfare from the University of California at Berkeley.

Federico Salas-Isnardi has worked in adult education as a teacher, administrator, professional developer, materials writer, and consultant. He contributed to a number of state projects in Texas including the adoption of adult education content standards and the design of statewide professional development and accountability systems.

Over nearly 30 years he has conducted professional development seminars for thousands of teachers, law enforcement officers, social workers, and business people in the United States and abroad. His areas of concentration have been educational leadership, communicative competence, literacy, intercultural communication, citizenship, and diversity education. He has taught customized workplace ESOL and Spanish programs as well as high-school equivalence classes, citizenship and civics, labor market information seminars, and middle-school mathematics. Mr. Salas-Isnardi has been a contributing writer or series consultant for a number of ESL publications, and he has co-authored curriculum for site-based workforce ESL and Spanish classes.

Mr. Salas-Isnardi is a certified diversity trainer. He has a Masters Degree in Applied Linguistics and doctoral level coursework in adult education.

AUTHOR

Wendy Pratt Long has previously worked as an EFL teacher and administrator. She has taught English to children, adolescents, and adults at all language levels in Mexico and Canada. She earned a master's degree in applied linguistics from the Universidad de las Americas, in Puebla, Mexico. Now working in the field of educational publishing, she has authored and co-authored ancillary materials including *Center Stage 2 Teacher's Edition, Summit 2 Workbook, Top Notch 2 Workbook, Top Notch Copy & Go* (Fundamentals and Level 3), and *Top Notch Assessment Packages* (Fundamentals and Levels 2 and 3). She has collaborated with Pearson on numerous other projects, including the assessment programs for *Center Stage 2* and *Summit 2* and CD-ROMs for multiple levels of the *WorldView* and *Trends* series.

ACKNOWLEDGMENTS

The Publisher would like to acknowledge the teachers, students, and survey and focus-group participants for their valuable input. Thank you to the following reviewers and consultants who made suggestions, contributed to this *Future* revision, and helped make *Future: English for Work, Life, and Academic Success* even better in this second edition. There are many more who also shared their comments and experiences using *Future*—a big thank you to all.

Fuad Al-Daraweesh The University of Toledo, Toledo, OH

Denise Alexander Bucks County Community College, Newtown, PA

Isabel Alonso Bergen Community College, Hackensack, NJ

Veronica Avitia LeBarron Park, El Paso, TX

Maria Bazan-Myrick Houston Community College, Houston, TX

Sara M. Bulnes Miami Dade College, Miami, FL

Alexander Chakshiri Santa Maria High School, Santa Maria, CA

Scott C. Cohen, M.A.Ed. Bergen Community College, Paramus, NJ

Judit Criado Fiuza Mercy Center, Bronx, NY

Megan Ernst Glendale Community College, Glendale, CA

Rebecca Feit-Klein Essex County College Adult Learning Center, West Caldwell, NJ

Caitlin Floyd Nationalities Service Center, Philadelphia, PA

Becky Gould International Community High School, Bronx, NY

Ingrid Greenberg San Diego Continuing Education, San Diego Community College District, San Diego, CA

Steve Gwynne San Diego Continuing Education, San Diego, CA

Robin Hatfield, M.Ed. Learning Institute of Texas, Houston,TX

Coral Horton Miami Dade College, Kendall Campus, Miami, FL

Roxana Hurtado Miami-Dade County Public Schools, Miami, FL

Lisa Johnson City College of San Francisco, San Francisco, CA

Kristine R. Kelly ATLAS @ Hamline University, St. Paul, MN

Jennifer King Austin Community College, Austin, TX

Lia Lerner, Ed.D. Burbank Adult School, Burbank, CA

Ting Li The University of Toledo, Ottawa Hills, OH

Nichole M. Lucas University of Dayton, Dayton, OH

Ruth Luman Modesto Junior College, Modesto, CA

Josephine Majul El Monte-Rosemead adult School, El Monte, CA

Dr. June Ohrnberger Suffolk County Community College, Selden, NY

Sue Park The Learning Institute of Texas, Houston, TX

Dr. Sergei Paromchik Adult Education Department, Hillsborough County Public Schools, Tampa, FL

Patricia Patton Uniontown ESL, Uniontown, PA

Matthew Piech Amarillo College, Amarillo, TX

Guillermo Rocha Essex County College, NJ

Audrene Rowe Essex County School, Newark, NJ

Naomi Sato Glendale Community College, Glendale, CA

Alejandra Solis Lone Star College, Houston, TX

Geneva Tesh Houston Community College, Houston, TX

Karyna Tytar Lake Washington Institute of Technology, Kirkland, WA

Miguel Veloso Miami Springs Adult, Miami, FL

Minah Woo Howard Community College, Columbia, MD

Pre-Unit

Welcome to Class

1 MEET YOUR CLASSMATES

A ▶ Read and listen to the conversation.

Ayida: Hi. My name is Ayida.

Carmen: Hello, Ayida. I'm Carmen.

Ayida: Nice to meet you, Carmen.

Carmen: Nice to meet you, too.

Ayida: Where are you from?

Carmen: Peru. How about you?

Ayida: I'm from Haiti.

B WORK TOGETHER. Practice the conversation. Use your own names and information.

2 TALK ABOUT YOUR GOALS

A Why are you studying English? Check the boxes.

☐ to get a job or a better job

☐ to get United States citizenship

☐ to continue my education

☐ to help my children with schoolwork

☐ to get into a career program

☐ other goal: _____

B DISCUSS. Talk about your goals. Do you have any of the same goals?

1 MEET YOUR CLASSMATES

Classroom Communication

From the first class, encourage a supportive, friendly classroom by modeling supportive, friendly behavior yourself. Get to know your students' names and things about them. Make sure they know your name and things about you.

A ▶ Read and listen to the conversation.

1. Walk around the class. Stop in front of a student. Say: *Hi. My name is _____.* Hold your hand out to shake hands.
2. If the student says hello and says his or her name, continue the conversation. Say: *Nice to meet you.* If the student doesn't say anything, ask: *What's your name?* When he or she answers, say: *Nice to meet you.*
3. Talk to five or six more students in this way.
4. Read the directions. Tell students to read the conversation silently.
5. Play the audio. Students listen and read.
6. Play the audio again. Pause after each line and ask students to repeat.

B WORK TOGETHER. Practice the...

1. Read the directions.
2. Model the conversation with a volunteer. Hold your book up and encourage the class to follow in the book. Shake hands with your volunteer.
3. Pair students to take turns playing Ayida and Carmen.
4. Walk around and help with pronunciation as needed. Tell students to shake hands when they meet each other.
5. Call on students to perform their conversation for the class.

Classroom Communication

The custom of greeting and shaking hands is different around the world. In some cultures, a firm handshake is customary. In others, men and women do not shake each other's hands. Still others do not shake hands at all. Tell students: *Different countries have different ways to greet someone.* Allow students the option to nod instead of shaking hands with other students.

■ EXPANSION: Speaking practice for 1B

Have pairs walk around together and introduce themselves to other pairs.

Classroom Communication

Before leaving class on the first day, ask volunteers to say the name of a classmate they met. This way the students begin to learn each other's names from the beginning.

2 TALK ABOUT YOUR GOALS

A Why are you studying English? Check the...

1. Ask the class if anyone knows what *goals* are. Accept answers, then write: *goals = I want to do this.*
2. Ask: *Why do you want to learn English? What is your goal?* Elicit some answers and write them on the board.
3. Read the directions. Draw two square boxes on the board. Say: *Read. If your answer is yes, check the box.* Make a check mark in one box on the board.
4. Explain that students will work on their own and check the information about themselves.
5. Point to the words *other goal.* Tell students that if they have a different goal from the five in the book, they can write it there.
6. Walk around and help as needed. Model language students will use in Exercise 2B by looking at their information. Say, for example: *Oh, you're studying English because you want to get a better job?*

B DISCUSS. Talk about your goals. Do you...

1. Write the targeted language on the board. Write: *I am studying English because I want to _____.* Say a few examples, pointing out how you are filling in the blank with a goal.
2. Form groups of 3. Put students sitting near each other together.
3. Walk around and help as needed.
4. To review, ask questions about each item, asking for a show of hands. For example: *Who is studying English to get a better job?* You can ask volunteers to read the goal they wrote in the last item.

Culture Note

Students come from a variety of educational backgrounds. They may be uncomfortable working together and afraid to take risks. Conduct your classroom so that everyone feels safe to make mistakes. Lead students gently into working in pairs and in groups. As the weeks go on, they will become more and more comfortable with this.

Welcome to Class

3 ASK FOR HELP

Teaching Tip: Use a pencil

Ask students to use a pencil to write their answers. This allows them to erase an incorrect answer and clearly mark the correct answer.

Ⓐ Look at the pictures. Complete the...

1. Say: *Sometimes we don't understand something. Then we need to ask questions.*
2. Call on a volunteer to read the directions and the questions and phrases from the box.
3. Explain why *Can you speak more slowly?* is crossed out. (because it is the answer to number 1)
4. Call on a volunteer to role-play number 1 with you. You play the role of the student who asks *Where are you from?*
5. Check comprehension: *What was the student's problem?* (He didn't understand what his classmate said.) *How did he ask for help?* (He asked his classmate to speak more slowly.)
6. Do the second cartoon together with the class. Read aloud, ask for ideas and write the answer on the board. Call on two students to read the conversation. Remind students to cross off the phrase they used.
7. Give students time to complete the conversations.

Ⓑ ▶ SELF-ASSESS. Listen and check your...

1. Read the directions.
2. Play the audio. Students listen.
3. Play the audio again. Students check and correct their answers.
4. To confirm, play the audio one more time.
5. *Optional:* Form pairs. Have students read each cartoon box. Then have them switch roles.

Ⓒ ROLE-PLAY. Choose one conversation...

Teaching Tip: Role-plays

Introduce the activity of role-play. Explain to students what it is. Tell them that there are many role-plays in the book and that starting with Unit 1, you'll evaluate them when they do them. Tell them it is a great way to practice the language they learned. Explain to them that they will see themselves improve as they do more and more of them.

1. Read the directions.
2. Show a conversation from Exercise 3A on the board. Call on an above-level volunteer to model a conversation with you. Show students how to change the information. Then model the new conversation for the class.
3. Walk around and help as needed.
4. Call on pairs to role-play their conversations for the class.

■ MULTILEVEL INSTRUCTION for 3C

Pre-level scaffolding You may now have an idea which students need more support, guidance, and practice. Pair these students and have them change the information in cartoon 2 or 5.

Above-level expansion You may now have an idea which students learn quickly, participate willingly, and need to be challenged. Pair these students and have them change as many conversations as they can in the allotted time.

Welcome to Class

3 ASK FOR HELP

A Look at the pictures. Complete the conversations.

~~Can you speak more slowly?~~   Can you repeat that?
How do you pronounce this?   How do you spell that?
What does this word mean?   What's this called in English?

1.

- Where are you from?
- I'm sorry. *Can you speak more slowly?*
- Oh, sorry. Where are you from?
- I'm from Korea.

2.

- What's this called in English?
- It's a pencil sharpener.
- Thank you.

3.

- Excuse me. How do you pronounce this?
- Registration.
- New Student Registration
- Registration?
- Yes. That's right.

4.

- Can you help me?
- Sure.
- What does this word mean?
- Occupation? It means a job or career.

5.

- Please turn to page 45.
- I'm sorry. Can you repeat that?
- Sure. Please turn to page 45.

6.

- My name is Chiao.
- Chiao? How do you spell that?
- C-H-I-A-O.
- Thanks.

B ▶ SELF-ASSESS. Listen and check your answers.

C ROLE-PLAY. Choose one conversation from Exercise A. Make your own conversation. Use different information.

Welcome to Class

4 LEARN ABOUT *FUTURE*

A EXPLORE. Turn to page iii. Answer the questions.

1. What information is on this page?   The contents of the book
2. How many units are in this book?   12
3. Which unit is about food?   Unit 10
4. Which two units are about work?   Unit 8 and Unit 12

B Sometimes you will need to go to the back of the book to do activities. Look at the chart. Find the pages in the book and complete the chart.

Page	
245	My Soft Skills Log
247	Grammar Review

C There is additional information for you in the back of the book. Find each section. Write the page number.

Grammar Reference   258   Map of the U.S. and Canada   278
Audio Script   266   Map of the World   276
Word List   262   Index   279

Welcome to Class

4 LEARN ABOUT *FUTURE*

A EXPLORE. Turn to page iii. Answer the...

1. Read the directions. Call on students to read the questions aloud.
2. Form pairs by having students sitting next to each other work together. Ask them to work together.
3. Read the questions one by one and ask students to answer. Write the information as they say it so students can confirm their answers.

B Sometimes you will need to go to the back...

1. Read the directions.
2. Hold up your book. Say: *Look at page 245.* Point to the chart. Walk around and make sure students find it.
3. Tell students they can work together to complete the activity.
4. Call on students to say what is on page 247. Write it on the board.

C There is additional information for you in...

1. Holding up the book, leaf through the back pages. Say: *There is a lot of information in the back of your book. Let's find a few things.*
2. Do item 1 together. Read the title. Have students repeat. Tell students to look through the pages and raise their hands when they find it. This is another quick way to begin to identify pre- and above-level students.
3. Call on volunteers to come to the board and write the headings and the page numbers.
4. Say: *Let's check to be sure these pages are correct.* Have all students turn to the pages listed on the board. Make corrections as necessary.

Teaching Tip: Ending class

End every class by thanking students for coming and participating. Leave a few minutes at the end of every class to review with the class what you learned. For this class, review students' names and some information their classmates learned about each other.

1 Making Connections

Unit Overview

Goals
- See the list of goals on the facing page

Pronunciation
- Word stress
- Vowels in unstressed syllables
- Sentence stress

Reading
- Read about group work in the classroom
- Identify the topic and the main idea

Grammar
- Simple present: *be* + adjective; contractions
- Simple present: *have* + object; contractions
- *Be*: compound sentence with *and* and *but*
- *Yes/no* questions with *be* and short answers; contractions in negative short answers
- Information questions with *be* and short answers

Writing
- Write about a study routine
- Introduce and explain steps of a routine

Document Literacy and Numearcy
- Read an application for an ID card
- Interpret an ID card

Workplace, Life, and Community Skills
- Read identification cards
- Complete an application
- Digital Skills: Search for an identification card application in your state

Life Skills Writing
- Complete a driver's license application

Soft Skills at Work
- Be inclusive

Preview

1. Set the context of the unit by greeting the class and introducing yourself.
2. Show the Unit Opener. Ask: *What is the unit title?* (Making Connections) Ask the class to repeat.
3. Explain: Making connections *means finding how two things, people, or ideas are similar.*
4. Say: *Look at the picture.* Ask the Preview questions. (Possible answers: a family visiting another family, greeting each other, smiling, bringing food)
5. Write the answers. Ask the class to repeat.

Unit Goals

1. Point to the Unit Goals. Explain that this list shows what you will be studying in this unit.
2. Tell students to read the goals silently.
3. Say each goal. Ask the class to repeat. Explain unfamiliar vocabulary as needed.
4. Point to the ☐ next to the first goal. Say: *We will come back to this page again. You will write a checkmark next to the goals you learned in this unit.*

Oral Presentation

1. Tell students they will give a short presentation at the end of the unit.
2. Write the topics:
   Option 1: *Describe a good friend*
   Option 2: *Group work*
3. Assign the topics to two students.

Unit Wrap-Up

1. Review the Unit Goals with students.
2. Direct students to the Grammar Review.
3. If you assigned presentations, ask students to present.

 ActiveTeach for Wrap-Up: Team Projects

 ActiveTeach for Wrap-Up: Persistence Activities

Making Connections

1

PREVIEW

Look at the picture. What do you see?
Where are the people? What are they doing?

UNIT GOALS

- ☐ Describe physical appearance
- ☐ Describe the way people look
- ☐ Complete an application
- ☐ Read identification cards
- ☐ Describe personalities
- ☐ Get to know someone

- ☐ **Academic skill:** Identify the topic and the main idea
- ☐ **Writing skill:** Introduce and explain steps of a routine
- ☐ **Workplace soft skill:** Show how you are inclusive

Lesson 1

Words to describe physical appearance

A **PREDICT.** Look at the pictures. What words describe the people?

Taha: short, thin

B ► **LISTEN AND POINT.** Then listen and repeat.

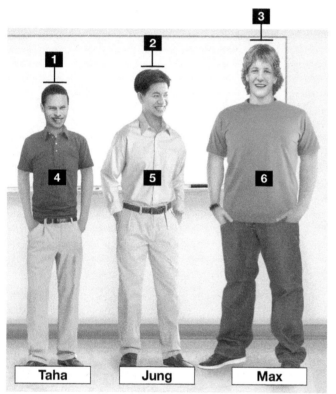

Taha   Jung   Max

Felix   Sara   Ana   Mai

Kwami   Yusef   David

Correlations

ELPS Level 2: 2, 7, 8
CCRS Level A: SL. 1.1, SL.K.6, L.1.5, L.1.6
CASAS Reading: RGD 1.7, 2.2, 2.3
CASAS Listening: L2.1, 2.3, 2.9
CASAS Competencies: 0.1.2, 0.1.5, 0.2.1, 7.4.1
Complete standards language available on the Pearson English Portal.

Self-Directed Learning

State the **lesson objective.** Say: *In this lesson, we will learn to describe people's height, weight, and hair.*

Ⓐ PREDICT. Look at the pictures. What words…

1. Read the directions. Tell students to cover the list on page 7.
2. Point to picture 1 and ask: *What are some words that describe Taha?* Say: *Look at the pictures. What are some words that describe the other people?*
3. Students call out answers. Help students pronounce physical descriptions if they have difficulty.
4. If a student calls out an incorrect description, ask a *yes/no* clarification question: *Does Kwami have a mustache?* (no) If nobody can identify the correct description (beard), tell students they will now listen and practice descriptions.

Ⓑ ▶ LISTEN AND POINT. Then listen and repeat.

1. Read the directions. Play the audio. Students listen and point to the appropriate picture.
2. While the audio is playing, walk around and check that students are pointing to the correct pictures. Pause the audio after item 16.
3. Say each physical description in random order and ask students to point to the appropriate picture.
4. Tell students to look at page 7. Resume the audio. Students listen, read, and repeat.

5. *Optional:* Say each description and use a gesture or action to indicate its meaning. For example, adjust the height of your hand to show *short, average height,* and *tall.* Ask students to repeat. Use the same gestures or actions in random order and tell students to call out the description.

 ActiveTeach for B: Vocabulary Flashcards

▬▬ **EXPANSION: Speaking practice for B**
Ask: *What words describe Max?* As students call out answers, list them on the board (for example, *tall, heavy, wavy hair, long hair*). Do this also for two other people in the pictures.

▬▬ **EXPANSION: Pronunciation practice for B**

1. Say words to describe physical appearance in random order and ask the class to repeat.
2. Ask an above-level student to come to the front of the room and lead this activity. Tell the student to say the word again if the class does not repeat it clearly.

▬▬ **EXPANSION: Writing practice for B**

1. Tell the class to close their books. Say a word and tell students to write it. Repeat for several words to describe physical appearance.
2. Students compare answers with a partner.
3. Walk around and spot-check students' answers. If many students have difficulty, tell them they will practice spelling later in the unit.

▬▬ **EXPANSION: Vocabulary practice for B**

1. Name a category (for example, hair type) and ask students to say a word or phrase in that category.
2. Ask: *What is a word for hair length?* If a student says a word or phrase not on the list, write it.
3. Repeat for other categories.

Vocabulary

C WORK TOGETHER. Look at the pictures...

1. Read the directions. Model the activity. Tell the class you are A and they are B.
2. Point to a picture and describe the person. Students name the person.
3. Pair students and tell them to take turns playing A and B.

■■ **MULTILEVEL INSTRUCTION for C**

Pre-level scaffolding Pair students. Perform the activity with them to make sure they understand what to do.

Above-level expansion Student A describes several people, and Student B points to them and names them.

D COMPLETE. Look at the people in the...

1. Write the sentence frame for item 1 on the board. Say: *Now let's describe people's hair. Look at Taha. What kind of hair does he have?* Elicit *short* and *curly*. Write the words to complete the sentence on the board.
2. Have students work individually to complete the activity.
3. Call on students to read the answers.

■■ **MULTILEVEL INSTRUCTION for D**

Cross-ability In multilevel classes, pair a higher level student with a lower level student to complete the activity.

Study Tip: Make connections

1. Say: *This tip can help you remember new words.*
2. Read the **Study Tip**. Model the activity. Say: *I'm thinking of my friend.* If possible, show a photo. List four vocabulary words to describe that person on the board.
3. Walk around as students write their words. If misspellings occur, tell students to check the list on the board or on page 7. Call on a few students to read their descriptions out loud.
4. Say: *You can remember new vocabulary when you connect the new word with things that are important to you.* Tell students they can use this tip to remember other new vocabulary.

■■ **EXPANSION: Graphic organizer and vocabulary practice for D**

1. Tell students to bring in a picture of a person from a magazine, or provide magazines for students to cut out pictures. Tell them that they will make a web diagram with their picture.

2. Model the activity. Paste a photo of a person from a magazine on a sheet of paper, and draw lines radiating from the photo. Say: *Look at the vocabulary list. Which words describe this person?* Write the physical descriptions you elicit on your web diagram.
3. Tell students to paste or tape their photo on a sheet of paper and write at least four physical descriptions on their web diagram.

Culture Note

1. Say: *In the U.S., it is not polite to draw attention to someone's weight if they are too thin or too heavy. Be careful with the word* heavy.
2. Ask: *In your native country, do you have to be careful when talking about a person's weight?*

Show what you know!

1. WRITE ABOUT IT. Look at the words to...

1. Read the directions and the example.
2. Model the activity. Ask: *What are four words that describe me?* Write the words on the board.
3. Say: *Write the words that describe you on a piece of paper. Be sure to write words describing your hair.*
4. Students put their words in a box.

2. TALK ABOUT IT. Take a piece of paper from...

1. Read the directions.
2. Model the activity. Draw a piece of paper from the box. Read the description. Ask the class: *Who is it?* The class guesses the person.
3. Pass the box to the student whom the class identified. Tell the student to take a piece of paper and repeat the activity. Continue until all the students have had a turn.
4. For incorrect guesses, point out or elicit something that doesn't match the description (for example, *David has curly hair, not straight hair*).

Self-Directed Learning

Point out the blue bar. Ask students if they can do the lesson learning objective or if they need more practice. Tell them to check one of the boxes. Assign Extra Practice as needed.

Extra Practice

  pp. 2–3

Vocabulary

Words to describe physical appearance

A. height
1. short
2. average height
3. tall

B. weight
4. thin/slim
5. average weight
6. heavy

C. hair type
7. bald
8. curly
9. wavy
10. straight

D. hair length
11. short
12. medium-length
13. long

E. facial hair
14. a beard
15. a mustache
16. a goatee

C **WORK TOGETHER.** Look at the pictures. Student A, point to a picture. Describe the person. Student B, name the person.

Student A points to picture 1.
A: Short. Thin.
B: Taha?
A: Yes!

D **COMPLETE.** Look at the people in the pictures. Complete the sentences.

	Length	Type
1. Taha has	*short*	*curly*	hair.
2. Ana has	medium-length	wavy	hair.
3. Mai has	long	straight	hair.
4. David has	short	curly	hair.

Study Tip

Make Connections
Think of a friend. Write four words to describe your friend.

Show what you know!

1. **WRITE ABOUT IT.** Look at the words to describe weight, height, and hair. Which words describe you? Write four words on a piece of paper. Put your paper in a box.

   thin, short, long wavy hair

2. **TALK ABOUT IT.** Take a piece of paper from the box. Read the words to the class. Ask the class, "Who is it?"

I can describe people's height, weight, and hair. ■   I need more practice. ■

For more practice, go to MyEnglishLab.

Describe the way people look

1 BEFORE YOU LISTEN

CATEGORIZE. Read the words. Complete the chart.

attractive   good-looking   ugly
beautiful   handsome   unattractive

Positive	Negative
attractive beautiful, good-looking, handsome	ugly, unattractive

2 LISTEN

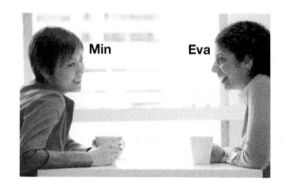

Min   Eva

A ▶ **LISTEN FOR MAIN IDEA. Look at the picture of two co-workers. Listen to the conversation. What does Min ask about?**

a. a party
b. Eva's friend
c. a supervisor

B ▶ **LISTEN FOR DETAILS. Answer the questions.**

1. Where is Min going tonight?

    a. to her class   **b.** to her job   **c.** to a party

2. What does Min say about Eva's friend?

    a. "He's unattractive."   **b.** "He's good-looking."   **c.** "He's handsome."

3. What does Eva's friend look like?

    a.    **b.**    **c.**

C ▶ **EXPAND. Listen to the whole conversation. Complete the sentence.**

Victor is Eva's _____.

    a. friend   **b.** brother

Correlations

ELPS Level 2: 2, 7
CASAS Reading: RDG 1.7, 2.2, 2.3
CASAS Listening: L1.3, 1.4, 1.6, 2.1, 2.3, 4.1, 4.2
CASAS Competencies: 0.1.2, 0.1.4, 0.1.5, 0.2.1
Complete standards language available on the Pearson English Portal.

Self-Directed Learning

State the **lesson objective**. Say: *In this lesson, we will learn to describe the way people look.*

1 BEFORE YOU LISTEN

CATEGORIZE. Read the words. Complete the...

1. Say: *Look at the words to describe how people look.* Read the words in the box.
2. Tell students to look at the example. Ask: *Is* attractive *positive or negative?* Students call out the answer.
3. Give students time to complete the chart.
4. Call on students to say each word and whether it is positive or negative. Write the answers on the board.

Culture Note

1. Say: *In the U.S., people use the word* beautiful *more often to describe women than men. They also use the word* handsome *more often to describe men than women.*
2. Ask: *In your native country, do people use different words to describe men and women?*

2 LISTEN

A ▶ LISTEN FOR MAIN IDEA. Look at the...

1. Tell students to look at the picture. Say: *This is Min and Eva. They are co-workers.* Ask: *What is a co-worker?* (someone you work with) *Where are they?* (workplace cafeteria or break room) *What are they doing?* (talking and drinking coffee/tea)
2. Ask: *What does Min ask about?* Read the answer choices.
3. Play the audio. Students listen and circle the letter of the correct answer.
4. Elicit the correct answer from the class.

▪ EXPANSION: Speaking practice for 2A

Have students work in pairs to describe Min and Eva's physical appearance.

B ▶ LISTEN FOR DETAILS. Answer the...

1. Tell students to read the questions and answer choices silently.
2. Play the audio. Students listen and circle the letter of the correct answer.
3. Students compare answers with a partner.
4. Call on volunteers to ask and answer the questions.
5. Say: *Min thinks Eva's friend is handsome. What does Eva's friend look like?* (He has short, black hair.)
6. Ask about **register**: *Do Min and Eva know each other well? How do you know?* (Yes. Eva is inviting Min to her party.)

Teaching Tip: Use the script

Optional: If students need additional support, tell them to read the Audio Script on page 266 as they listen to the conversations.

C ▶ EXPAND. Listen to the whole...

1. Read the directions and the sentence frame and answer choices.
2. Play the audio. Students listen and complete the sentence.
3. Ask: *Do you need to listen one more time?* If yes, play the audio again.
4. Ask: *Who does Min think is handsome?* (Victor) *Is Victor Eva's friend?* (No, he is Eva's brother.) Review the correct answer with the class.

▪ EXPANSION: Vocabulary and graphic organizer practice for 2C

1. On the board, draw a three-column chart. Label the columns *Min, Eva,* and *Victor.* Tell students to copy the chart.
2. Pair students and tell them to look again at the pictures, questions, and answers in Exercise 2A, 2B, and 2C. Tell pairs to complete the chart with physical descriptions of Min, Eva, and Victor and with what they know about each person.

Workplace Culture

1. Say: *Min and Eva are co-workers. Eva invites Min to her party. In the U.S., co-workers often socialize outside of work. They meet after work or on the weekends.*
2. Ask: *Do co-workers meet outside work in your native country? When is it OK? When is it not OK?*

Listening and Speaking

3 PRONUNCIATION

A ▶ PRACTICE. Listen. Then listen again and...

1. Tell students to close their books. Write the words they will hear. Pronounce each word and draw lines between syllables. Explain: *Each part of a word is a syllable.* Ask: *How many syllables does* party *have?* (2)

2. Tell students to open their books. Read the Pronunciation Note. Say *party* and make the first syllable long and loud. Ask: *How is a syllable stressed?* (It is long and loud.) *How many syllables do we stress in words of more than one syllable?* (one)

3. Say: *Listen. Pay attention to the syllables that are stressed.*

4. Play the audio. Clap your hands with the stressed syllables as the class listens. Pause the audio.

5. Say: *Now, listen and clap with the stressed syllables.* Play the audio again. Students clap their hands as they say the stressed syllables. Students listen and repeat.

 ActiveTeach for 3A: Pronunciation Coach

B ▶ APPLY. Listen. Mark (•) the stressed...

1. Read the directions. Write item 1. Pronounce *handsome.* Ask: *Which syllable is long and strong?* (the first syllable) Pronounce *handsome* as many times as needed. Mark the stressed syllable *hand-*.

2. Play the audio. Students listen and put a dot on the stressed syllable. If necessary, play the audio again.

3. Ask: *What syllables are stressed?* Review the correct answers with students.

4. Say the first word. Emphasize the stress pattern. Ask students to repeat the word. Repeat for the other words.

4 CONVERSATION

A ▶ LISTEN AND READ. Then listen and repeat.

1. Note: This conversation is the same one students heard in Exercise 2A on page 8.

2. Tell students to read the conversation silently and look for words that they practiced in Exercise 3A and 3B (*party, tonight, inviting,* and *handsome*). Tell them to underline the stressed syllable in these words.

3. Play the audio. Students listen.

4. Play the audio again. Students listen and repeat.

5. Walk around and help students with their pronunciation and stress placement as needed.

B WORK TOGETHER. Practice the...

1. Read the directions.

2. Model the conversation with an above-level student. Emphasize the syllable stress for words practiced in Exercise 4A.

3. Pair students. Walk around and check that students are using the correct stress patterns.

C CREATE. Make new conversations. Use...

1. Read the directions.

2. Tell students to look at the information in the boxes. Say each item and tell the class to repeat.

3. Write the conversation with blanks. Fill in the first two blanks with names from the class. When you come to the next blank, ask what color the blank is in the book. Point to the box that is the same color and fill in the blank with the first item.

4. Point out that students may change *he's* and *he* to *she's* and *she* in A's last line.

5. Ask a pair of on-level students to practice the conversation on the board for the class.

6. Erase the words in the blanks and ask two above-level students to make up a new conversation.

7. Tell pairs to take turns playing A and B and to use the vocabulary words to fill in the blanks.

8. Walk around during the activity and check students' syllable stress.

9. Tell students to stand, mingle, and practice the conversation with several new partners.

D ROLE-PLAY. Make your own conversations...

1. Read the directions.

2. Say: *Think of someone you want to know more about. Write three words to describe that person.*

3. Model the activity. Say: *I'm thinking of...* Write three words to describe the person. Play A and practice the conversation in Exercise 4C with an above-level student. Complete A's last line with the information you listed on the board.

4. Tell students to practice the conversation in Exercise 4C with a new partner.

Self-Directed Learning

Point out the blue bar. Ask students if they can do the lesson learning objective or if they need more practice. Tell them to check one of the boxes. Assign Extra Practice as needed.

Extra Practice
pp. 4–5

Listening and Speaking

3 PRONUNCIATION

A ▶ **PRACTICE. Listen. Then listen again and repeat.**

par·ty   to·**night**   **beau**·ti·ful   at·**trac**·tive

B ▶ **APPLY. Listen. Mark (•) the stressed syllable.**

1. hand·some

2. in·vit·ing

3. ug·ly

4. in·tro·duce

4 CONVERSATION

A ▶ **LISTEN AND READ. Then listen and repeat.**

A: Hi, Eva.
B: Hi, Min. Are you coming to my party tonight?
A: Of course. Are you inviting your friend?
B: Which friend?
A: You know—he's handsome and he has short, black hair.

B **WORK TOGETHER. Practice the conversation in Exercise A.**

C **CREATE. Make new conversations. Use the words in the boxes.**

A: Hi, _____.
B: Hi, _____. Are you coming to my party tonight?
A: Of course. Are you inviting your friend?
B: Which friend?
A: You know—he's _____ and he has _____, _____ hair.

thin
average height
average weight

wavy
long
curly

red
brown
black

D **ROLE-PLAY. Make your own conversations. Use different words to describe the friend.**

I can describe the way people look. ■

I need more practice. ■

For more practice, go to MyEnglishLab.

Grammar

Simple present: *be* + adjective / *have* + object

Simple present: *be* + adjective						
Affirmative			**Negative**			
I	am		I	am		
They	are	tall.	They	are	not	short.
He	is		He	is		

Simple present: *have* + object						
Affirmative			**Negative**			
I			I			
	have			do		
They		black hair.	They		not have	red hair.
He	has		He	does		

Grammar Watch

Contractions are short forms. Here are some examples:

- *he is not =* **he isn't**
- *he does not =* **he doesn't**
- *they are =* **they're**
- *they are not =* **they aren't**
- *they do not =* **they don't**

For more contractions, see page 258.

A IDENTIFY. Cross out the incorrect words.

My sister and brother ~~is~~ / **are** very good-looking, but they don't look alike. My sister ~~is~~ / **has** brown eyes, but my brother **has** / ~~isn't~~ blue eyes. My sister **has** / ~~have~~ long hair. It ~~has~~ / **is** curly. My brother's hair ~~are~~ / **is** short. And it **isn't** / ~~is~~ curly—it's straight. Also, my sister ~~has~~ / **is** tall, and my brother **has** / ~~is~~ average height. But my sister and brother ~~is~~ / **are** alike in one way: They **are** / ~~have~~ both slim.

B CHOOSE. Write the correct forms of *be* or *have*. Use contractions for the negative sentences.

1. Omar _____ *has* _____ brown hair.
2. Na (not) _____ *isn't* _____ thin.
3. Her co-workers _____ have _____ blond hair.
4. Josh and Jen _____ are _____ tall.
5. Amy's hair (not) _____ isn't _____ curly.
6. My supervisor's eyes _____ are _____ green.
7. Mike and Olga _____ are _____ very attractive.
8. Steve (not) _____ doesn't have _____ a beard.

Correlations

ELPS Level 2: 2, 3, 7, 10
CCRS Level A: L.1.1, W.1.2
CASAS Reading: RDG 1.7, 2.1, 2.2, 2.3
CASAS Listening: L1.3, 2.1, 2.3, 3.1, 3.3, 3.5, 4.1, 4.2
CASAS Competencies: 0.1.2, 0.1.4, 0.1.5, 0.1.6, 0.2.1
Complete standards language available on the Pearson English Portal.

Self-Directed Learning

State the **lesson objective.** Say: *In this lesson, we will learn to use the simple present with* be + *adjective and* have + *object.*

Simple present: *be* + adjective

 ActiveTeach: Grammar Discovery

1. Warm up. Say: *The conversation on page 9 used this grammar.* Turn back to page 9. Point to the sentence in Exercise 4A and then write: *He's handsome.*
2. Say: *Let's look at another example.* Write: *She is beautiful.*
3. Ask: *What are the adjectives?* Underline *handsome* and *beautiful.* Circle *is.* Ask: *What verb do we use with adjectives?* (be)
4. Tell students to look at the grammar charts.
5. Point to the top chart. Read the examples. Ask: *What are the adjectives?* Tell students to underline *tall* and *short.* Say: *Use* be *with adjectives.*
6. Point to the first sentence on the board and ask: *How do I make this sentence negative?* Elicit and write: *He is not handsome. / He isn't handsome.* Repeat with item 2.
7. Tell students to look at the vocabulary box on page 7. Ask: *What are the other adjectives that describe height?* (short, average height) *What are the adjectives that describe weight?* (thin/slim, average weight, heavy) *What's the adjective that describes a person with no hair?* (bald) Tell students to write *be + adjective* next to categories A, B, and item 7, *bald,* in C.

Simple present: *have* + object

 ActiveTeach: Grammar Discovery

1. Warm up. Write:
   • *He has curly hair.*
   • *He has brown eyes.*

2. Ask: *What are the objects?* Circle *hair* and *eyes.* Ask: *What verb do we use with objects?* (have) Say: *An object can be a noun. Sometimes an object also has an adjective.* Underline *curly* and *brown.*
3. Tell students to look at the bottom chart on page 10. Read the examples. Ask: *What are the objects?* Tell students to underline *hair* in both sentences. Say: *Use* have *with objects.*
4. Point to the first sentence on the board and ask: *How do I make this sentence negative?* Elicit and write: *He does not have curly hair. / He doesn't have curly hair.* Repeat with item 2.
5. Tell students to look at the vocabulary box on page 7. Ask: *What types of hair do people have?* (curly hair,...) *What lengths of hair do people have?* (short hair,...) *What facial hair do some men have?* (a beard,...) Tell students to write *have + object* next to items 8–10 in category C, and next to categories D and E.
6. Read the **Grammar Watch** note. Ask students to come to the board and rewrite the sentences in the grammar charts using contractions.

 ActiveTeach: Grammar Coach

Ⓐ IDENTIFY. Cross out the incorrect words.

1. Read the directions. Read the first sentence. Ask: *Why is the answer* are? (*Be* is used with adjectives. / *Good-looking* is an adjective.)
2. Walk around and make sure students use the correct form of the verbs.
3. Students compare answers with a partner.
4. Ask an above-level student to read the paragraph with the correct answers. Students check their answers.

EXPANSION: Graphic organizer practice for A

1. Tell students to write *Sister* and *Brother* at the top of a piece of paper.
2. Students list the adjectives for the siblings under each heading. Some adjectives are shared and go in both columns.

Ⓑ CHOOSE. Write the correct forms of *be* or...

1. Read the directions. Write item 1. Underline *brown hair* and ask: *Is this an adjective or an object?* Write *object.* Repeat for item 2. Tell students to look at the words after the blanks and decide if they are an adjective or object.
2. Students compare answers with a partner.
3. Call on students to read the completed sentences. For the negative items, write the contractions and tell students to check their spelling.

Grammar

C DESCRIBE. Look at the picture. Describe the...

1. Tell students to look at the picture but cover the names. Say: *They are famous people. Do you know who they are?* Elicit the names students know.

2. Tell students to look at the names in the book. Ask: *What do these famous people do? Where are they from?* Make statements and ask the class to identify the people (for example, *She's an actress* and elicit *Zhang Ziyi. She's from the U.S.* and elicit *Simone Biles.*). Use the following information: Zhou Qi—basketball player from China, Simone Biles—gymnast from the United States, Daddy Yankee—singer from Puerto Rico, Shakira—singer from Colombia, Zhang Ziyi—actress from China, Cristiano Ronaldo—soccer player from Portugal.

3. Read the directions and the example.

4. Elicit words to describe Zhou Qi and list them on the board (for example: *tall, black hair*). Point to *tall* and ask whether to use *be* or *have* (*be*). Elicit *Zhou Qi is tall* or *He's tall* and write it.

5. Pair students and tell them to take turns describing each person in the picture.

6. Walk around and check students' use of *be* and *have*.

■■■ MULTILEVEL INSTRUCTION for C

Pre-level scaffolding Tell students to write two physical descriptions next to the drawing of each person before they do the speaking activity.

Above-level expansion Students write several physical descriptions for each person.

D WRITE. Write two sentences to describe...

1. Write: *Shakira has long blond hair. Shakira has long wavy blond hair.* Point to the first sentence and ask: *How many adjectives?* Repeat for the second sentence. Write: *2 adjectives = no commas, 3 + adjectives = 1 comma.* Ask the class where to put the commas in the sentences.

2. Read the directions. Tell students to use *be* and *have*. Write another example with *be* (for example, *Shakira is slim.*). Remind students to start each sentence with a capital letter, end with a period, and use a comma where necessary.

3. Walk around and check that students are using correct punctuation.

4. Pair students and tell them to take turns reading their sentences to each other.

5. Ask for volunteers to read their sentences. Tell them to use *He, She,* or *This person* instead of the name. Ask the class to identify the people.

■■■ EXPANSION: Speaking practice for D

Students bring in magazines and take turns describing the celebrities pictured.

Show what you know!

1. THINK ABOUT IT. Describe someone in the...

1. Read the directions. Model the activity by asking the class to describe you. Elicit three sentences and write them.

2. Tell students to write three sentences about one person in the class, beginning each sentence with *This person is...* Tell them not to write the name of the person they're describing.

2. TALK ABOUT IT. Student A, read your...

1. Read the directions. Play B and model the activity with an above-level student. Direct A to read you one sentence at a time and wait for you to guess before reading the next sentence.

2. Pair students and tell them to practice the conversation.

■■■ MULTILEVEL INSTRUCTION for 2

Pre-level scaffolding Perform the activity with pairs to make sure they understand what to do.

Above-level expansion Pairs practice the conversation again. They describe a different person, but don't write sentences first.

3. WRITE ABOUT IT. Now write about three...

1. Read the directions. Say: *Begin each sentence with the person's name. Use at least three adjectives for each person.*

2. Ask students to check each other's sentences:
   - Sentences should begin with the person's name.
   - Sentences should use at least three adjectives.
   - Sentence should use *be* with adjectives and *have* with objects.

3. Have students volunteer to write their sentences on the board.

Self-Directed Learning

Point out the blue bar. Ask students if they can do the lesson learning objective or if they need more practice. Tell them to check one of the boxes. Assign Extra Practice as needed.

Extra Practice

  pp. 4–5

Grammar

C **DESCRIBE.** Look at the picture. Describe the people. Talk about their height, weight, and hair. There is more than one correct answer.

Shakira has long, wavy blond hair. She's short and thin.

D **WRITE.** Write two sentences to describe each person.

| Zhou Qi | Simone Biles | Daddy Yankee | Shakira | Zhang Ziyi | Cristiano Ronaldo |

Show what you know!

1. **THINK ABOUT IT.** Describe someone in the class. Write three sentences.

   This person is tall and slim.

2. **TALK ABOUT IT.** Student A, read your sentences. Student B, guess the person. Take turns.

   A: This person is tall and slim.
   B: Is it Bela?
   A: No, it isn't. This person has straight, blond hair.
   B: Is it Sofia?
   A: Yes!

3. **WRITE ABOUT IT.** Now write about three people in your class.

   Sofia is tall and slim and has straight, blond hair.

   _____

   _____

   _____

I can use the simple present with *be* + adjective and *have* + object. ☐   I need more practice. ☐

For more practice, go to MyEnglishLab.

Workplace, Life, and Community Skills

ID cards

---

1 READllAPPLICATION

A **INTERPRET.** Read the application for a state identification card. Answer the questions.

APPLICANT INFORMATION:

Last Name	First Name	Middle Name	Suffix
Jaylen	Isaiah	Caleb	Jr.

Address	Apt/Unit	City and State	Zip Code
3602 College Avenue	4B	Clarkston, Georgia	30021

Date of Birth	Social Security Number	U.S. Citizen	Gender
12 / 03 / 1990 MM DD YYYY	555 / 33 / 4444	○ Yes ● No	● Male ○ Female ○ Unspecified

Weight	Height	Eye Color	Hair Color
LBS. 178	FT. 5 IN. 10	green	brown

Telephone Number	E-mail Address	Do you need assistance in another language? Which One?
404-666-3333	icaleb@medinc.com	/

1. What is the applicant's full name? <u>Isaiah Caleb Jaylen, Jr</u>
2. When was he born? <u>12/03/1990</u>
3. What is his Social Security number? <u>555/33/4444</u>
4. How tall is he? <u>5' 10"</u>
5. How much does he weigh? <u>178 lbs.</u>
6. What color are his eyes? <u>Green</u>
7. What is his address? <u>3602 College Avenue; Apt 4B; Clarkston, Georgia 30021</u>
8. What is his e-mail address? <u>icaleb@medinc.com</u>

B **MATCH.** Look at the identification card.
Match the abbreviations and the words.

1. <u>e</u> F   **a.** brown
2. <u>d</u> DOB   **b.** weight
3. <u>a</u> BRN   **c.** height
4. <u>c</u> Ht.   **d.** date of birth
5. <u>b</u> Wt.   **e.** female
6. <u>f</u> BLK   **f.** black

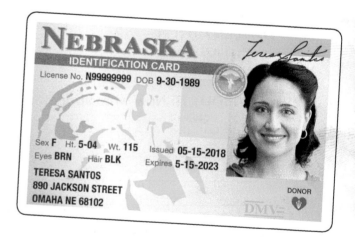

I can read identification cards. ■   I need more practice. ■

For more practice, go to MyEnglishLab.

Correlations

ELPS Level 2: 1, 2, 3, 4, 5, 6, 7, 8, 9, 10
CCRS Level A: W.1.7, W.1.8, SL.K.3
CASAS Reading: RDG 1.7, 2.2
CASAS Listening: L2.1, 2.3, 4.1, 4.2
CASAS Competencies: 0.1.2, 0.1.5, 0.2.1, 4.1.1, 7.4.4, 7.7.3
Complete standards language available on the Pearson English Portal.

Self-Directed Learning

State the **lesson objective**. Say: *In this lesson, we will learn to read identification cards and complete an application.*

1 READ AN APPLICATION

A INTERPRET. Read the application for...

Document Literacy: ID application

Context: ID applications are provided by the government
Purpose: Provide your personal information to apply for an ID
Key Words: *applicant, name, address, date of birth, gender, Social Security number, height*

1. Ask: *What is the lesson title?* (ID cards) Ask students to find the ID card on the page. Ask: *How do you get an ID card?* (fill out an application) Tell students to find the application on the page.
2. Orient students to the form. Ask about **context**: *Where do you get an application form for an ID card?* (at a state agency that issues ID cards) Ask about **purpose**: *Why do people fill out applications?* (to provide their personal information) Ask about **key words**: *What information is on an application form?* Elicit a few words (for example, *name, address, date of birth*).
3. *Optional:* Ask students about other kinds of applications (job, housing, credit card, loan).
4. Ask students to look at the application and find *Suffix*. Explain *Jr., Sr.,* and *III*. Write: *Father: Isaiah Caleb Jaylen, Son: Isaiah Caleb Jaylen.* Say: *The father and son have the same name, so the son is Isaiah Caleb Jaylen, Junior.* Add a comma and *Jr.* to the son's name. Say: *If Isaiah's grandfather also had the same name, Isaiah would be Isaiah Caleb Jaylen the Third.* Cross out *Jr.* and write *III.*
5. Tell students to find *Date of Birth* on the application. Write: *mm-dd-yyyy.* Label the abbreviations (*mm = month, dd = day, yyyy =*

year). Explain that the number of letters equals the number of digits to write (for example, not *9* for September but *09*, not *78* but *1978*). Tell students to write today's date in this format in their notebooks. Ask a volunteer to come to the board and write the date in this format. *then do birthdays on the board*

6. Read the directions. Pair students. Tell them to ask and answer the questions. *my birthday is...*
7. Read each question and call on volunteers to answer. Write the answers and, as needed, point to where the information is found in the application.

B MATCH. **Look at the identification card...**

Document Literacy: Identification card

Context: An ID card gives information about a person.
Purpose: You use an ID card to prove who you are. You need ID cards for air travel, some bus travel, job applications, rental applications, etc.
Key Words: *identification card, ID, sex, License No., DOB, Ht., Wt., issued, expires, signature*

1. Tell students to look at the identification card. Orient them to the ID card. Ask: *Where is this identification card from?* (Nebraska) Ask about **context**: *Whose identification card is this?* (Teresa Santos) *Where does she live?* (Omaha, NE) Ask about **purpose**: *What are identification cards for?* (to prove who you are) *When do you need an identification card?* (when you travel, apply for a job, apply for an apartment) Ask about **key words**: *What information is on an ID card?* (name, address, expiration date, issued date, sex, eye color, height, weight, etc.)
2. Read the directions.
3. Before students do the exercise, tell them to find and circle the abbreviations on the identification card. Tell them to use the card to figure out the meanings of the abbreviations. Say: *Point to F on the card. What's the word before F?* (sex) *So what do you think F means?* (female)
4. Students compare answers with a partner.
5. To check answers, write the abbreviations. Call on students to say the full words.

Self-Directed Learning

Point out the blue bar. Ask students if they can do the lesson learning objective or if they need more practice. Tell them to check one of the boxes. Assign Extra Practice as needed.

Workplace, Life, and Community Skills

2 COMPLETE AN APPLICATION

 A INTERPRET. Read the ID card. Use the...

1. As needed, review name order on applications. Write your full name. Label the parts *first, middle,* and *last*. Explain: *Your last name is your family name.* Ask students to point to *First Name* on the application, then *Middle Name* and *Last Name*. Tell students that application forms ask for information in a certain order, so they must read them carefully. Ask them to help you write your name in the order shown on the form.
2. Tell students to use Ana Martinez's ID card to complete the application as much as possible.
3. Students compare answers with a partner.
4. Ask: *What information about Ana Martinez is missing from her ID card?* (Middle Name, Suffix, Apt./Unit, Social Security Number, U.S. Citizenship status, Weight)

Numeracy: Math skills

Optional: You may wish to help students convert their height and weight to the U.S. system of measurement and give them the formulas to convert kilos to pounds and centimeters to feet + inches.

Weight: Multiply kilograms by 2.2 to convert to pounds.

Examples: 60 kilograms x 2.2 = 132 pounds
90 kilograms x 2.2 = 198 pounds

Height: Multiply centimeters by .3937 to convert to inches. Divide inches by 12 to change to feet; the remainder will be inches.

Examples: 163 centimeters x .3937 = 64 in.
64. in./12 = 5 ft. 4 in.
183 centimeters x .3937 = 72 in.
72 in./12 = 6 ft.

Language Note

Some application forms and ID cards use a middle initial, rather than a full middle name. This is the case for Ana Martinez's ID card. If this confuses students, point it out and say: *The first letter in a name is an* initial. *Ana's middle initial is M, but we do not know her middle name.* In the application form, students can leave that information blank.

 B WORK TOGETHER. Ask and answer...

1. Pair students. Say: *Now, look at Joseph Smith's identification card. Take turns asking each other questions about Joseph Smith.*
2. After students have finished, ask questions to check on comprehension. For example: *What is his zip code?*

> **ActiveTeach for 2B: Academic Conversation Support**

 C GO ONLINE. Search for an identification...

1. Read the directions. Ask students what they would search in English if they wanted to apply for an identification card.
2. Write the search string: *apply for identification card in [State].* Have students search the internet and find an identity card application. If the application is online and requires an account, tell students to look for a sample application form or search a nearby state.
3. Compare research as a class. Write a complete list of the information an application asks for.

Digital Skills for 2C

If necessary, explain that identification cards are issued by state government through the Department of Motor Vehicles (DMV), which also issues driver's licenses, or the Secretary of State office.

> **ActiveTeach: Review**

Self-Directed Learning

Point out the blue bar. Ask students if they can do the lesson learning objective or if they need more practice. Tell them to check one of the boxes. Assign Extra Practice as needed.

Extra Practice

 MyEnglishLab Workbook p. 6 Find an English Portal Life Skills Writing

---

Workplace, Life, and Community Skills

2 COMPLETE AN APPLICATION

A **INTERPRET.** Read the ID card. Use the information to complete the application. What information is missing?

APPLICANT INFORMATION:

Last Name	First Name	Middle Name	Suffix
Martinez	Ana	M	

Address	Apt/Unit	City and State	Zip Code
101 Chestnut St.		Yonkers, NY	10701

Date of Birth	Social Security Number	U.S. Citizen	Gender
05 / 07 / 1996 MM DD YYYY	/ /	○ Yes ○ No	○ Male ◉ Female ○ Unspecified

Weight	Height	Eye Color	Hair Color
LBS.	FT. 5 IN. 4	brown	brown

B **WORK TOGETHER.** Ask and answer questions about the identification card.

A: What's his last name?
B: Smith. What's his first name?
A: Joseph.

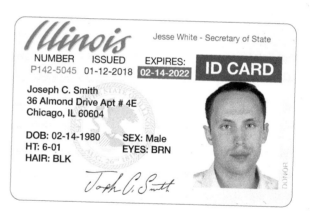

C GO ONLINE. Search for an identification card application in your state. Check the information it asks for.

☐ social security number
☐ last name
☐ first name
☐ middle name
☐ height
☐ weight
☐ eye color
☐ address
☐ mobile phone number
☐ e-mail address

I can complete an application. ☐   I need more practice. ☐

For more practice, go to MyEnglishLab.

Lesson 5

Describe personalities

1 BEFORE YOU LISTEN

MATCH. Write the words next to the definitions.

bossy	demanding	moody	shy	talkative
cheerful	laid-back	outgoing	supportive	

1. always tells other people what to do   _bossy_
2. is nervous when speaking to other people   shy
3. likes to talk a lot   talkative
4. changes feelings quickly and often   moody
5. is relaxed and not worried   laid-back
6. is happy and positive   cheerful
7. is helpful, caring, and giving   supportive
8. enjoys meeting new people   outgoing
9. expects good work   demanding

2 LISTEN

A ▶ **LISTEN FOR MAIN IDEA. Listen to two co-workers. What are they talking about?**

a. work   b. a friend   ⓒ a supervisor

B ▶ **LISTEN FOR DETAILS. What is the new supervisor like? Check the words.**

☑ outgoing   ☐ laid-back   ☐ bossy
☑ cheerful   ☑ demanding   ☑ supportive

C ▶ **EXPAND. Listen to the whole conversation.**

Kay is _____.

ⓐ quiet   b. loud   c. bossy

Correlations

ELPS Level 2: 2, 7
CASAS Reading: RDG 1.7
CASAS Listening: L1.4, 1.6, 2.1, 2.3, 4.1, 4.2, 6.1
CASAS Competencies: 0.1.2, 0.1.4, 0.1.5, 0.1.6, 0.2.1
Complete standards language available on the Pearson English Portal.

Self-Directed Learning

State the **lesson objective**. Say: *In this lesson, we will learn to describe personalities.*

1 BEFORE YOU LISTEN

MATCH. Write the words next to the definitions.

1. Say: *Look at the words to describe people.* Read the words in the box.
2. Ask students to read the definitions silently.
3. Tell students to look at the example. Say: *Someone who always tells other people what to do is... bossy.*
4. Form groups of 3. Together, students match the other words and definitions.
5. Ask a student to read each item and call on a classmate to answer.
6. *Optional:* Give students a couple of minutes to study the words and definitions. While students are studying, write the words. Pronounce each word and ask the class to repeat. Tell them to close their books. Read the definitions in random order and ask the class to call out the words.

■ **EXPANSION: Graphic organizer practice for 1**

1. Pair students and tell them to draw a chart with three columns. Tell them to label the columns *Positive, Negative,* and *Positive or Negative.* Explain: Positive *means* good *and* negative *means* bad.
2. Partners then decide whether each personality trait is positive or negative or could be either. They write each word in the appropriate place on the chart.

Teaching Tip: Matching strategy

When words that may be new are presented through a matching activity, teach students the following strategy: Tell students to do the items they're sure of first, cross out the words in the box, and then try to figure out the others.

2 LISTEN

A ▶ **LISTEN FOR MAIN IDEA. Listen to two...**

1. Read the directions and the answer choices. Play the audio. Students circle the letter of the correct answer.
2. Ask students to raise their hands if they checked a. Repeat for b and c.

B ▶ **LISTEN FOR DETAILS. What is the new...**

1. Read the directions and the words.
2. Play the audio. Students listen and check.
3. Check answers by asking a question for each word (for example, *Is the new supervisor outgoing? Is she cheerful?*).

C ▶ **EXPAND. Listen to the whole conversation.**

1. Call on a student to read the sentence and answer choices.
2. Play the audio. Students listen and circle the letter of the correct answer.
3. Ask: *Is Kay's supervisor quiet, too?* (no) Elicit: *She is talkative / outgoing.*

■ **EXPANSION: Vocabulary practice for 2C**

1. Ask students to look at the words in Exercise 1. Say: *Which personality traits do you like in a supervisor?* Students rank the words in order from *1* (best) to *9* (worst).
2. Pair students. Partners compare their lists.
3. Say each word and tell students to raise their hands if it's their number 1. Tally on the board.

Career Awareness: Food server

Food servers prepare and serve food. They also often greet customers, set and clear tables, stock supplies, and use a cash register. They work in many places including restaurants, cafés, food trucks, and work cafeterias. They don't usually need a certain level of education. They receive training on the job.

■ **EXPANSION: Career awareness for 2C**

Ask students about the job in this lesson: *What job do Erica and Kay have? What does a food server do? Where does a food server work? Do you need to study to be a food server? Do you want to be a food server?*

Listening and Speaking

3 PRONUNCIATION

A ▶ PRACTICE. Listen. Then listen again and...

1. Write: *a-bout*. Pronounce *about*. Ask: *How many syllables does* about *have?* (two) Pronounce *about* again. Ask: *Which syllable is stressed?* Underline *bout*.
2. Say: *The vowel sound in a stressed syllable is long and clear.* Mark the stress over the *ou* in *about*. Pronounce *about*, drawing out the *ou* sound.
3. Point to *a-bout* on the board. Say: *-bout is the stressed syllable. What is the unstressed syllable?* Circle *a-*.
4. Say: *Vowels in unstressed syllables often have a very short, quiet sound.* To demonstrate this sound, say "uh" several times and ask the class to repeat. Then pronounce *about* several times, modeling the "uh" sound of the unstressed syllable.
5. Tell students to open their books and read the **Pronunciation Note** silently.
6. Play the audio. Students listen. Then students listen and repeat.

 ActiveTeach for 3A: Pronunciation Coach

Language Note

Help students articulate difficult sounds by having them adjust the position of their tongue. Tell students to place their tongue low, in the middle, and then high in their mouth. Then tell them to place their tongue in the front, center, and back of their mouth. Explain: *To say the "uh" sound, place your tongue in the middle, center of your mouth. Make sure your tongue is relaxed.*

B ▶ APPLY. Listen. Circle the unstressed...

1. Read the directions.
2. Play the audio. Students listen and circle the unstressed syllables. If necessary, play the audio again and have students listen twice before answering.

4 CONVERSATION

A ▶ LISTEN AND READ. Then listen and repeat.

1. Note: This conversation is the same one students heard in Exercise 2A on page 14.
2. Tell students to read the conversation silently and look for words that they practiced in Exercise 2B (*outgoing, cheerful, demanding, supportive*). Tell them to circle the unstressed vowels in *about*.
3. Play the audio. Students listen and repeat.

B WORK TOGETHER. Practice the...

1. Pair students and tell them to practice the conversation in Exercise 4A.
2. Tell students to take turns playing A and B.

C CREATE. Make new conversations. Use the...

1. Tell students to look at the information in the boxes. Say each item and ask the class to repeat.
2. Show the conversation on the board with blanks and read it. When you come to a blank, fill it in with the first set of words in the boxes (*your new co-worker, talkative, funny, talkative but moody*).
3. Ask a pair of on-level students to practice the conversation on the board for the class.
4. Erase the words in the blanks and ask two above-level students to make up a new conversation.
5. Tell pairs to take turns playing A and B and to use the vocabulary lists to fill in the blanks.
6. Walk around and check students' pronunciation of the unstressed syllable in *about*.
7. Tell students to stand, mingle, and practice the conversation with several new partners.
8. Call on pairs to practice for the class.

D MAKE CONNECTIONS. Talk about the...

1. Using the vocabulary presented in this unit, students list personality traits for a friend, family member, or co-worker.
2. Play A and practice a conversation with an above-level student (for example, *My brother's name is Robert.*). Prompt the student to ask: *What's he like?* And then: *Yeah? What else?*
3. Pair students and tell them to take turns having this conversation.
4. Tell students to stand, mingle, and practice the conversation with several new partners.

■■■ MULTILEVEL INSTRUCTION for 4D

Pre-level scaffolding Pairs can write out the conversation and practice.

Above-level expansion Pairs can use vocabulary not presented in this unit and talk about several people.

Self-Directed Learning

Point out the blue bar. Ask students if they can do the lesson learning objective or if they need more practice. Tell them to check one of the boxes. Assign Extra Practice as needed.

Extra Practice

  p. 7

3 PRONUNCIATION

A ▶ **PRACTICE. Listen. Then listen again and repeat.**

about   quiet   talkative   beautiful   attractive

B ▶ **APPLY. Listen. Circle the unstressed syllables.**

1. cheer(ful)
2. (sup)por·tive
3. (de)mand(ing)
4. pro(blem)

> **Vowels in unstressed syllables**
>
> The vowel sound in a stressed syllable is long and clear. Vowels in unstressed syllables often have a very short, quiet sound. For example, ab**out**.

4 CONVERSATION

A ▶ **LISTEN AND READ. Then listen and repeat.**

A: Kay, tell me about your new supervisor. What's she like?
B: Well, she's outgoing and she's cheerful.
A: Yeah? What else?
B: She's demanding but she's supportive, too.

B **WORK TOGETHER. Practice the conversation in Exercise A.**

C **CREATE. Make new conversations. Use the words in the boxes.**

A: Tell me about _____. What's he like?
B: Well, he's _____ and he's _____.
A: Yeah? What else?
B: He's _____.

D **MAKE CONNECTIONS. Talk about the personalities of friends, family members, or co-workers.**

your new co-worker
your supervisor
a good friend

talkative
friendly
cheerful

funny
outgoing
interesting

talkative but moody
laid-back but supportive
cheerful but demanding

I can describe personalities. ■   I need more practice. ■

For more practice, go to MyEnglishLab.

Be: compound sentence with *and* and *but*

Be: compound sentence with *and* and *but*		
She's outgoing	and	she's cheerful.
She's demanding	but	she's supportive.

Grammar Watch

- Use *and* to join two sentences with similar ideas.
- Use *but* to join two sentences with opposite ideas.
- Use *but* when the second idea is surprising or unexpected.

A IDENTIFY. Cross out the incorrect word.

1. Karim is bald ~~and~~ / **but** Mac's hair is long.
2. Sara is my friend. She's funny **and** / ~~but~~ she's nice.
3. Amy isn't a supervisor **but** / ~~and~~ she is bossy.
4. I'm shy ~~and~~ / **but** my brother is outgoing. We're different.
5. Brad is happy at his job ~~but~~ / **and** he is a good worker.

Karim   Mac

B CHOOSE. Write *and* or *but*.

1. We have a nice break room at work. It isn't big ____*but*____ it is comfortable. We have a refrigerator ____*and*____ we have a microwave. We have a TV, too, ____*but*____ we don't have time to watch it.

2. Jim is a customer service representative ____*and*____ he is good at his job. He is outgoing ____*and*____ he is kind to customers. His co-workers like him. He is helpful ____*and*____ he is supportive.

3. I have a job in a medical office. A lot of people work there, ____*and*____ it's really busy. My supervisor is OK. She has good ideas ____*but*____ she is very bossy.

Correlations
ELPS Level 2: 2, 7, 10
CCRS Level A: L.1.1
CASAS Reading: RDG 1.7, 2.9
CASAS Listening: L2.1, 2.3, 3.13, 4.1, 4.2
CASAS Competencies: 0.1.2, 0.1.4, 0.1.5
Complete standards language available on the Pearson English Portal.

Self-Directed Learning

State the **lesson objective**. Say: *In this lesson, we will learn to make compound sentences with and / but.*

Be: compound sentence with *and* and *but*

 ActiveTeach: Grammar Discovery

1. Warm up. Say: *The conversation on page 15 used this grammar.* Turn back to page 15. Point to the sentences in Exercise 4A and then write:
   - *She's outgoing and she's cheerful.*
   - *She's demanding but she's supportive.*
2. Underline *and* and *but*.
3. Students close their books. Erase *and* and *but* from the sentences on the board. Add periods and capitalize *she's* to make sentences:
   - *She's outgoing. She's cheerful.*
   - *She's demanding. She's supportive.*
4. Read the first point of the **Grammar Watch** note. Ask: *Which two sentences have similar ideas?* Write *and* between the first pair of sentences.
5. Read the second and third points of the **Grammar Watch** note. Ask: *Which two sentences have opposite or surprising ideas?* Write *but* between the second pair of sentences.
6. Have students look at the sentences in the grammar chart on page 16. Point out that they are the same as the ones on page 15. Read each sentence. Students repeat.
7. Tell students that two sentences joined together with *and* or *but* are compound sentences.
8. Write: *My friend is funny and...*, *My friend is funny but...* Elicit possible ways to complete these sentences. Write a few student sentences on the board.

 ActiveTeach: Grammar Coach

A **IDENTIFY. Cross out the incorrect word.**

1. Read the directions. Write item 1 on the board. Tell students to look at the photos. Circle *is bald* and *hair is long*. Ask: *Are these similar ideas or opposite ideas?* (opposite) Cross out *and*.
2. Walk around and when you spot an incorrect answer, read the two sentences that make up the compound. Ask: *Are these similar ideas or opposite ideas? Should you use* and *or* but?
3. Call on students to read the sentences out loud.

■■ **EXPANSION: Writing practice for A**

1. Tell students to look back at the picture on page 11.
2. Tell students to write three sentences comparing the people. Each sentence should use either *and* or *but* (for example, *Simone Biles is short but Zhou Qi is tall.*).
3. Call on students to write their sentences on the board.
4. *Optional:* Use other pictures in the book to repeat this activity. Choose a picture with two or more people. If necessary, assign names to the people in the picture.

B **CHOOSE. Write *and* or *but*.**

1. Read the directions.
2. Read the first sentence in item 1. Ask: *What is a break room?* (a room at work where workers take a break, have coffee, lunch, etc.)
3. Write the second sentence in item 1: *It isn't big _____ it is comfortable.* Ask: *Are these similar ideas or opposite ideas?* (opposite) *Do I write* and *or* but? Write *but* to complete the compound sentence.
4. Write the third sentence in item 1: *We have a refrigerator _____ we have a microwave.* Ask: *Are these similar ideas or opposite ideas?* (similar) *Do I write* and *or* but? Write *and* to complete the compound sentence.
5. Tell students to complete the rest of the sentences. Walk around and check for the correct use of *and* and *but*. When you spot an incorrect answer, ask: *Are these similar ideas or opposite ideas?*
6. Call on students to read the sentences out loud.

Grammar

C APPLY. Make sentences. Use the words...

1. Read the directions.
2. Write the answer to item 1. Ask: *What form of the verb* be *is used in this sentence?* (is) *Why?* (because it agrees with *Nan* and *she*) *Why do we join the two sentences with* and*?* (because the two sentences are similar)
3. Students write the answers. Walk around and check that students start each sentence with a capital letter and end with a period.
4. Call on students to read the sentences out loud.

D WRITE. Now write two sentences about a...

1. Read the directions.
2. Read the first two sentences in the example. Ask: *Are* cheerful *and* supportive *similar ideas or opposite ideas?* (similar) Elicit the word you should use to combine them (*and*). Read the compound sentence in the example.
3. Model the activity. Write two sentences about someone you know. Elicit the word you should use to combine them (*and* or *but*).
4. Students compare answers with a partner.
5. Call on students to write their compound sentences on the board.

■■ MULTILEVEL INSTRUCTION for D

Pre-level scaffolding Provide sentence frames: *My _____ is _____. He/She is _____. My _____ is _____ and/but he/she is _____.* Assist students with completing the sentences.

Above-level expansion Have students write six sentences so they can practice combining with both *and* and *but*.

■■ EXPANSION: Speaking and listening practice for D

1. Play a game. Say: *You have to listen and remember your classmates' sentences. Then you will add a sentence about someone you know.*
2. The first student completes the sentence (for example, *My supervisor is cheerful and she's supportive.*).
3. The second student repeats the first student's sentence (*Musa's supervisor is cheerful and she's supportive.*) and then says his or her own sentence.
4. The third student repeats the information from the first and second student and then says a new sentence.
5. Continue until a student cannot repeat everyone else's descriptions. That student then starts over.
6. Continue until every student has had a turn.

Show what you know!

1. THINK ABOUT IT. Write four sentences about...

1. Read the directions.
2. Model the activity. Write sentences about the way you look or your personality. Write one with similar ideas and one with opposite ideas. Leave a blank where *and* or *but* should go. Ask: *Do I write* and *or* but*?* Complete the compound sentences.
3. Walk around and check that students are correctly joining sentences.

2. TALK ABOUT IT. Share your sentences. Are...

1. Read the directions.
2. Model the activity. Point to the compound sentences on the board about yourself. Read and underline one part of a sentence (for example, *I am shy.*). Tell students to look at their own sentences. Ask: *Who is similar? Who is opposite?* Students answer each question by raising their hands. Call on a volunteer to read a sentence about being similar or opposite (for example, *I am talkative.*). Write this sentence. Make a compound sentence that compares you and the student (for example, *I am shy but you are talkative.*).
3. Remind students to use the correct form of *be* when talking about their classmates.
4. Put students in groups of 3. Walk around and check that they are using the correct form of *be* and joining sentences appropriately.

3. WRITE ABOUT IT. Write four sentences about...

1. Read the directions. Still in groups of 3, tell students to write four sentences about the way they and their classmates are similar or different.
2. Ask students to check each other's sentences:
   • Sentences should use *and* to join similar ideas.
   • Sentence should use *but* to join opposite ideas.
   • Sentences should use the correct form of *be*.
3. Have students volunteer to write their sentences on the board.

Self-Directed Learning

Point out the blue bar. Ask students if they can do the lesson learning objective or if they need more practice. Tell them to check one of the boxes. Assign Extra Practice as needed.

Extra Practice

MyEnglishLab   Workbook p. 7

Grammar

C **APPLY.** Make sentences. Use the words and the correct form of *be*. Use *and* or *but*.

1. (Nan / cheerful / she / laid-back) _Nan is cheerful and she is laid-back._
2. (Ken / outgoing / he / moody) _Ken is outgoing but he is moody._
3. The cafeteria at my office is great. (The food / delicious / the workers / friendly)
   The food is delicious and the workers are friendly.
4. I have a good job. (My department head / interesting / my co-workers / funny)
   My department head is interesting and my co-workers are funny.
5. (Tina / shy / her sister / talkative) _Tina is shy but her sister is talkative._

D **WRITE.** Now write two sentences about a person you work or live with. Then write a new sentence with *and* or *but*.

My supervisor is cheerful. She is supportive.
My supervisor is cheerful and she is supportive.

_____

_____

_____

_____

Show what you know!

1. **THINK ABOUT IT.** Write four sentences about the way you look or your personality. Use a form of *be*. Write two sentences with *and*. Write two sentences with *but*.

   I am shy and I am quiet.
   I am slim but I am not tall.

2. **TALK ABOUT IT.** Share your sentences. Are you and your classmates similar? Make sentences with *and* or *but*.

3. **WRITE ABOUT IT.** Write four sentences about the way your classmates are similar or different. Write two sentences with *and*. Write two sentences with *but*.

   I am short but Dan is tall.
   Liz has blue eyes and so does Ian.

| I can make compound sentences with *and* / *but*. ■ | I need more practice. ■ |

For more practice, go to MyEnglishLab.

Read about group work in the classroom

1 BEFORE YOU READ

A **DECIDE.** Complete the sentences with the words in the box.

communication   discussion   participate   practice

1. I'm learning to play the guitar. I need to _____practice_____ every day.
2. We need to talk about the problem. Let's sit down and have a _____discussion_____.
3. All the children can join in the game. They can all _____participate_____.
4. Anna is a good speaker and a good listener. She has good _____communication_____ skills.

B **MAKE CONNECTIONS.** What's happening in the picture? Do you ever do this?

Academic Skill: Identify the Topic and the Main Idea

After you read, ask yourself, "What's the article about?" The answer is the topic of the article.

Then ask, "What does the writer say about the topic?" The answer is the main idea.

2 READ

▶ Listen and read.

Group Work in English Classes

1 English language teachers often ask students to work in small groups. The groups usually have three or four students. Working in small groups is good for language learning. Why? Here are a few reasons.

5 **1.** If someone wants to learn a new language, they have to practice it. In a small group, learners can get more practice speaking. They get practice listening to different speakers, too. Listening and speaking
10 improves communication skills.

2. Speaking in a small group is easier for many students. In the classroom, outgoing and talkative students often speak. Shy students
15 often don't. Small groups help shy students relax and participate more.

3. In small groups, students can help each other. When Student A helps Student B, Student A learns to explain something clearly. That's not easy. It's a
20 good skill to have.

What ideas from the article do you see in this picture?

Student B learns to ask questions. To ask a question, you have to think about what you know and what you don't. Both students are more active in their learning. Active learners learn and
25 remember more.

4. Small-group work helps students improve their interpersonal skills. Everyone needs to help the group to work well. Talkative students
30 have to listen. Quiet students can't be too laid-back. They have to share their ideas. Bossy students have to respect the other members of the group.

35 **5.** In many jobs, people have to work in teams. Employers want workers with good communication and interpersonal skills.

For these reasons, English language classes often have small-group work. It's an important part of
40 education in the United States.

Correlations

ELPS Level 2: 1, 2, 3, 7, 9
CCRS Level A: RI/RL.1.1, RI.1.2, RI.1.4, SL.K.2, SL.1.4
CASAS Reading: RDG 1.7, 1.8, 2.2, 2.3, 3.2, 3.7, 3.11, 4.2
CASAS Listening: L2.1, 2.3, 4.2, 5.8, 6.1
CASAS Competencies: 0.1.2, 0.1.5, 4.8.1, 4.8.2
Complete standards language available on the Pearson English Portal.

Self-Directed Learning

1. State the **lesson objective**. Say: *In this lesson, we will learn to identify the topic and main idea.*
2. Say: *We will read about group work in the classroom.*

1 BEFORE YOU READ

A DECIDE. **Complete the sentences with the...**

1. Read the directions. Say the words in the box.
2. Read the first sentence. Ask: *What helps you learn do something new?* (practice) Tell students to write *practice* to complete the sentence.
3. Tell students to complete the sentences.
4. Call on students to read the completed sentences aloud.

B MAKE CONNECTIONS. **What's happening in...**

1. **Scaffold:** With the class, brainstorm a list of words they can use to describe the photo (for example, *laptop, papers, diagram, group, talking, working*).
2. Ask: *What are they doing in the picture?* (group work) *Do you ever do this?* Elicit responses.

■ **EXPANSION: Graphic organizer practice for 1B**

1. Write two sentence stems: *I like group work because _____* and *I don't like group work because _____.*
2. Explain that people have different opinions about group work. Have students work individually to complete each sentence.
3. Make a T-chart with the headings *Positive* and *Negative*. Call on students to read their sentences. Write the things they like under *Positive* and the things they don't like under *Negative*.
4. Ask the class: *Do you think group work is helpful in learning English?*

Teaching Tip: Activate knowledge and experience

When students get to think about what they know about a topic before they read, they usually understand and remember the information better.

2 READ

▶ **Listen and read.**

1. Introduce the reading. Tell students to look at the article. Ask: *What is the title of the article?* (Group Work in English Classes)
2. Introduce the visual. Read the caption. Elicit descriptions of the picture. Point out that visuals often help students preview text or predict what the text will say.
3. Point to the **Academic Skill** and read it. Say: *A topic is what the article is about. The title often names the topic or gives clues about the topic.* Ask: *What do you think the topic is going to be?* (group work in English classes) *What do you think the main idea is going to be? What will the author say about group work in English classes?* Elicit ideas.

**ActiveTeach for 2: Anticipation Guide –
Before Reading exercise**

4. Read the text.
   a. Say: *Now we are going to read and listen to the article* Group Work in English Classes.
   b. Play the audio as students listen and read along silently.
   c. Call on an above-level student to read the first paragraph or read it yourself. Tell students to underline the main idea (*Working in small groups is good for language learning.*) Call on students to say what they underlined. Ask: *How many reasons for this does the article give?* (five) Ask: *How do you know?* (There are numbers.)
   d. Tell students that the key words or most important words in sentences are usually verbs, nouns, and sometimes adjectives. Point out that the key words are often repeated. Key words are almost never articles, prepositions, or helping verbs.
   e. Say: *The first sentence of each paragraph often tells you about the topic of the paragraph.* Tell students to read the first sentence of each numbered paragraph. Tell students to underline the key words and phrases and compare their ideas with a partner.
   f. Write numbers 1–5. Elicit the key words in the first sentences (1. practice; 2. speaking, easier; 3. help each other; 4. improve their interpersonal skills; 5. jobs, work in teams)

**ActiveTeach for 2: Anticipation Guide –
After Reading exercise**

Reading

3 CLOSE READING

A IDENTIFY. Answer the questions.

1. Say: *Now we are going to identify the topic and main idea.*
2. Read the directions. Have students circle the answers.
3. Elicit the answers from the class.
4. **Reinforce academic language:** Point to the word *identify*. Say: Identify *means recognize. This means we can say what something is. We can identify the topic and main idea.*

B CITE EVIDENCE. Answer the questions...

1. Say: *Now we are going to find information in the reading. We use line numbers to say where the information is. Let's practice. What line number talks about a communication skill?* (10). *Give other examples to clarify the idea of line numbers.*
2. Read the directions. Walk around as students work on the activity. If students are struggling, have them work in pairs or direct them to the text lines where they can find the information.
3. Call on students to read the sentence with the correct completion. Ask a different student: *Where is that information? What line number?*

4 SUMMARIZE

 ActiveTeach for 4: Vocabulary Practice

1. Read the directions. Ask students to read aloud the words in the box.
2. Tell students to complete the paragraph.
3. To check answers, call on students to read the sentences in the summary with the blanks filled in. Ask other students to read the completed summary silently.

▬▬ **EXPANSION: Speaking practice for 4**

1. Put students in pairs or small groups. Tell them to review the T-chart from Expansion Exercise for 1B. Ask: *Does the article talk about your ideas? Do you agree with the ideas in the article?*
2. Tell students to answer the questions with their classmates.

Culture Note
1. Say: *In the U.S., teachers often have students work in small groups because they want their students to speak in class and learn from each other.* 2. Ask: *In your native country, do you often do group work? In what kinds of classes?*

Show what you know!

1. WRITE ABOUT IT. Write about how...

1. Write the sentence frame. Read the directions. Point to the sentence frame.
2. Model the activity. Say and write a sentence about how small-group work helps you learn something (for example, *Small group work helps me learn to speak Spanish because I have to talk a lot.*). Underline *I have to talk a lot.* Tell students that their examples are about learning English.
3. Have students write their sentence(s) on a sheet of paper. Walk around and answer any questions.
4. Say: *Share your sentence with at least two people. Check their sentences. If the sentences are not correct, help your partner correct them.*
5. Collect the papers for review or put them in the students' writing portfolios.

2. PRESENT IT. Make a short presentation...

1. Write the categories: *students learning English, shy students, talkative students, bossy students, students with strong skills,* and *students who have questions.*
2. Read the directions.
3. Put students in five groups. Assign each group one of the categories. One student in each group takes notes on their ideas.
4. Walk around and answer any questions.
5. Call on volunteers to present on each topic to the class. Take notes on each category, or call on a student to do it.

 ActiveTeach for 2: Academic Conversation Support

Self-Directed Learning

Point out the blue bar. Ask students if they can do the lesson learning objective or if they need more practice. Tell them to check one of the boxes. Assign Extra Practice as needed.

▬▬ **EXPANSION: Self-directed learning**

Ask students to reflect: *What did you learn from this reading?* Call on students to share something they learned.

Extra Practice
MyEnglishLab CCRS Plus   Workbook pp. 8–9

Reading

3 CLOSE READING

A IDENTIFY. Answer the questions.

1. What is the article about?
   a. teachers of English   (b.) group work in ESL classes   c. education in the U.S.

2. What is the main idea?
   a. Employers want workers with good communication and interpersonal skills.   (b.) Small-group work in class is good for English language learners.   c. Small-group work is often part of education in the United States.

B CITE EVIDENCE. Answer the questions. Where is the information? Write the line numbers.

			Lines
1. What is an example of a communication skill? a. working b. reading (c.) speaking			9–10
2. Why are small groups good for shy students? a. They can just sit and listen. (b.) They can relax. c. They can be bossy.			15–16
3. Which statement is true about active learners? a. They talk too much in class. b. It's hard for them to sit for a long time. (c.) They do more thinking and learning.			21–25
4. When do people need to use interpersonal skills? (a.) to work well with other people b. to understand their own feelings c. to remember what they learn			35–37

4 SUMMARIZE

Complete the summary with the words in the box.

active   communication   practice   skills

Small group work is important in English language classes. It helps students be more
(1) ____active____ learners. They get more (2) ____practice____ speaking. They can develop
other (3) __communication__ skills, too. They can also develop interpersonal (4) ____skills____.
These are important in school and at work.

Show what you know!

1. WRITE ABOUT IT. Write about how small-group work helps you learn English.

   Small group work helps me learn English because _____.

2. PRESENT IT. Make a short presentation. How does small-group work help people learn English? How does it help shy students, talkative students, bossy students, students with strong skills, or students who have questions?

I can identify the topic and main idea. ■   I need more practice. ■

To read more, go to My English Lab.

Lesson 8 Listening and Speaking

Get to know someone

1 BEFORE YOU LISTEN

MAKE CONNECTIONS. In the U.S., which questions are OK to ask when you meet someone at work? Check the questions.

☑ What do you do?   ☑ Where are you from?

☐ Are you married?   ☐ Do you like your supervisor?

☐ How old are you?

2 LISTEN

A **PREDICT. Look at the picture.**
Where are they? They are at a party.

Ron
Kara
Pia

B ▶ **LISTEN FOR MAIN IDEA. Listen to the conversation. Answer the questions.**

1. What's happening?
   a. Ron is asking Pia's name.
   b. Ron and Pia are meeting for the first time.
   c. Pia and Ron are saying good-bye.

2. Where does Ron work?
   a. At a hospital.
   b. At a restaurant.
   c. At a school.

C ▶ **LISTEN FOR DETAILS. Listen again.**
Read the sentences. Circle *True* or *False*.

1. Ron is Kara's friend.   (True)   False
2. Kara is a nurse.   (True)   False
3. Ron is a cook.   (True)   False

D ▶ **EXPAND. Listen to the whole conversation.**
Read the sentences. Circle *True* or *False*.

1. Pia works at a hospital.   (True)   False
2. Pia is a nurse.   True   (False)

Correlations

ELPS Level 2: 2, 7
CCRS Level A: SL.1.1, SL.K.6
CASAS Reading: RDG 1.7
CASAS Listening: L1.4, 2.1, 2.3, 4.1, 4.2, 6.5
CASAS Competencies: 0.1.2, 0.1.4, 0.1.5, 0.1.6, 0.2.1
Complete standards language available on the Pearson English Portal.

Self-Directed Learning

State the **lesson objective**. Say: *In this lesson, we will learn to get to know someone.*

1 BEFORE YOU LISTEN

MAKE CONNECTIONS. In the U.S., which...

1. Read the directions. Students read and check the questions silently.
2. Read each question. Ask: *Is it OK to ask this in the U.S.?* Explain vocabulary as needed (for example, a supervisor is a boss).
3. Introduce yourself to several students. Ask each student one or two of the appropriate questions (for example, *Hi, I'm _____. What's your name? Nice to meet you, _____. Where are you from?*).

Culture Note

1. Write: *How old are you?* Reinforce that in the U.S. it is not polite to ask a person's age. Ask: *What other questions are not OK to ask when you meet someone for the first time in the U.S.?* Write questions, such as "How much money do you make?", under the heading *Not OK*. For emphasis, cross them out.
2. Ask: *In your native country, what questions are not OK to ask?* Have students discuss in pairs. Call on volunteers to read their questions to the class. Write the questions.

2 LISTEN

A PREDICT. **Look at the picture. Where are they?**

1. Tell students to look at the picture. Ask: *Where are they?* (at someone's house or apartment)
2. Ask: *How do you know?* Elicit: *food on the table, pictures on the wall, people sitting and talking, dressed casually*.
3. *Optional:* Reinforce vocabulary from Lesson 1: Have students describe the appearance of Kara, Ron, and Pia.

B ▶ LISTEN FOR MAIN IDEA. **Listen to the...**

1. Read the directions, the questions, and the answer choices.
2. Play the audio. Students listen and circle the letter of the correct answers.
3. Elicit the correct answers from the class.

C ▶ LISTEN FOR DETAILS. **Listen again. Read...**

1. Tell students to read the questions and answer choices silently.
2. Play the audio. Students circle the letter of the correct answer.
3. Students compare answers with a partner.
4. Call on volunteers to read a sentence and say if it is true or false.
5. Ask about **register**: *Which speakers know each other well? How can you tell?* (Pia and Kara are friends, and Pia says that. Kara and Ron know each other. Ron and Pia don't know each other— that is why Kara introduces them.)

Teaching Tip: Use the script

Optional: If students need additional support, tell them to read the Audio Script on page 266 as they listen to the conversations.

D ▶ EXPAND. **Listen to the whole...**

1. Read the directions and the sentences.
2. Play the audio. Students listen and circle *True* or *False*.
3. Ask: *Do you need to listen one more time?* If yes, play the audio again.
4. Ask: *Does Pia work at the hospital?* (yes) *Is Pia a nurse?* (no) Review the correct answers with the class.
5. *Optional:* Use the **Career Awareness** information to ask about the jobs in this lesson.

Career Awareness: Medical assistant

Medical assistants help physicians, or doctors, with medical and office tasks. For example, they run lab tests, take medical histories, and do paperwork. They work in hospitals and doctors' offices. Special certification is usually required.

Career Awareness: Cook

Cooks prepare and cook food, order supplies, and plan menus. They work in restaurants and kitchens. Most cooks receive training on the job and don't need a diploma or certificate.

Listening and Speaking

3 PRONUNCIATION

A ▶ PRACTICE. Listen. Then listen again...

1. Read the directions. Write: *Are you a nurse?* without the stress marks. Read the **Pronunciation Note.** Ask: *What are the important words?* Underline *you* and *nurse.* Ask: *Which words are not stressed?* (are, a)

2. Tell students to close their books. Say: *I'm going to read only the stressed words in the sentence. See if you can still understand the basic meaning.* Say: *work, cafeteria.*

3. Point to the sentence on the board. Pronounce each underlined word and ask: *How many syllables?* Draw a line separating the five syllables in *ca/fe/ter/i/a.* Say: *In words with more than one syllable, only one syllable is stressed.* Pronounce *cafeteria* and ask: *Which syllable is stressed?* Double underline *ter.*

4. Read the sentence on the board. Exaggerate the stress on *work* and *ter.*

5. Tell students to open their books and look at the stressed words in the sentences. Pronounce each stressed word and ask: *How many syllables?*

6. Play the audio. Students listen. Then students listen and repeat.

 ActiveTeach for 3A: Pronunciation Coach

B ▶ APPLY. Listen. Mark (•) the stressed...

1. Ask students to look at items 1–3. Ask: *What are the important words?*

2. Read the directions and play the audio.

3. Write items 1–3 on the board. Call on students to mark the stressed words on the board. Correct as needed.

4 CONVERSATION

A ▶ LISTEN AND READ. Then listen and repeat.

1. Note: This conversation is the same one students heard in Exercise 2B on page 20.

2. Tell students to find and underline the sentences in the conversation that they practiced in Exercise 3A and 3B. (Nice to meet you. Are you a nurse? No, I'm not. How about you?)

3. Write: *I want to introduce you to my friend.* Ask: *What are the important words in this sentence?* Identify *want, introduce,* and *friend.* Pronounce each word and ask: *How many syllables?* Draw a line separating the three syllables in *in/tro/duce.* Pronounce *introduce* and ask: *Which syllable is stressed?* Double-underline *duce.* Tell students

to underline the first sentence in the conversation and then mark the stress.

4. Play the audio. Students listen and read.

5. Play the audio again. Students listen and repeat after each sentence.

6. Walk around. Help with pronunciation as needed.

> **Teaching Tip: Provide context clues**
>
> For pre-level students or those with low first language literacy, have three above-level students perform the conversation so they can use body language and facial expressions to understand the conversation.

B WORK TOGETHER. Practice the...

1. Read the directions.

2. Model the conversation with two above-level students. Emphasize the stress patterns for sentences practiced in Exercise 4A.

3. Pair students. Walk around and check that students are using the correct stress patterns.

C ROLE-PLAY. Make your own conversations...

1. Read the directions.

2. Play A and model the activity with two above-level students. Prompt B to continue the conversation by asking a question from Exercise 1 on page 20. Prompt C to answer and ask another question.

3. Form groups of 3. Tell students take turns playing each person. Walk around and help as needed

▪▪ **MULTILEVEL INSTRUCTION for 4C**

Pre-level scaffolding Write questions students can use from Exercise 1 on page 20 or other ideas (*Where do you work? How do you like it?*) Students playing B and C ask one question each from the list. Before students role-play the conversation, tell them to write answers to each question.

Above-level expansion Students play B and C and ask several questions and ask partners to elaborate on their answers. They can ask, for example, *What's it like? What's your wife's/husband's name? Where do you go to school?*

Self-Directed Learning

Point out the blue bar. Ask students if they can do the lesson learning objective or if they need more practice. Tell them to check one of the boxes. Assign Extra Practice as needed.

> **Extra Practice**
>
> MyEnglishLab Workbook pp. 10–11

Listening and Speaking

3 PRONUNCIATION

A ▶ PRACTICE. Listen. Then listen again and repeat.

Are **you** a **nurse**?

No, I'm **not**.

I **work** in the **cafeteria**.

I'm a **cook**.

Sentence stress

In English, the important words in a sentence are stressed. They are usually long and loud. Some important words have more than one syllable. Only one of the syllables is stressed.

B ▶ APPLY. Listen. Mark (•) the stressed words.

1. Nice to meet you.
2. I'm a medical assistant.
3. How about you?

4 CONVERSATION

A ▶ LISTEN AND READ. Then listen and repeat.

A: Pia, I want to introduce you to my friend. Pia, this is Ron. Ron, this is Pia.
B: Nice to meet you, Ron.
C: Nice to meet you, too.
B: So, are you a nurse, like Kara?
C: No, I'm not. I work at the hospital, but I'm a cook in the cafeteria. How about you?

B WORK TOGETHER. Practice the conversation in Exercise A.

C ROLE-PLAY. Make your own conversations. Introduce your classmates and continue the conversation.

A: I want to introduce you to my classmate. _____, this is _____.
_____, this is _____.
B: Nice to meet you.
C: Nice to meet you, too.
B: So, _____ . . .

I can get to know someone. ■   I need more practice. ■

For more practice, go to MyEnglishLab.

Lesson 9

Simple present tense of *be*: *Yes / No* and information questions

Yes/no questions with *be*
Are you a nurse?

Short answers
Yes, I am. No, I am not.

Information questions with *be*
How is it?

Short answers
Good.

Grammar Watch

- You can use contractions in negative short answers to *Yes / No* questions.

  I am not. = *I'm not.*

  You are not. = *You're not.*

  You aren't.

- You can't use contractions in affirmative short answers.

- For more contractions, see page 258.

A **MATCH. Choose the correct answers to the questions.**

1. __d__ Is she talkative?
2. __g__ Who is your manager?
3. __e__ Am I bossy?
4. __b__ Where is your family from?
5 __c__ Are you from China?
6. __f__ Is he your co-worker?
7. __h__ What is your country like?
8. __a__ How old is your daughter?

a. She's four.
b. Brazil.
c. No, I'm not.
d. Yes, she is.
e. No, you're not.
f. Yes, he is.
g. Mr. Gómez.
h. It's beautiful.

B **WRITE. Read the answers. Write questions about the underlined information.**

1. **A:** What is your last name?
   B: My last name is Chow.

2. **A:** Are his sisters short?
   B: No, they aren't. His sisters are tall.

3. **A:** Where are they from?
   B: They're from Cuba.

4. **A:** How old is your son?
   B: My son is five years old.

5. **A:** Where is your office?
   B: My office is on Fifth Street.

6. **A:** Is he outgoing?
   B: No, he isn't. He's not outgoing. He's really shy!

7. **A:** What is her name?
   B: Her name is May.

8. **A:** Are Ted and Chris co-workers? / Are they co-workers?
   B: Yes, they are. Ted and Chris are co-workers.

I can use the simple present tense of *be* with *Yes / No* and information questions. ☐   I need more practice. ☐

For more practice, go to MyEnglishLab.

Correlations

ELPS Level 2: 10
CCRS Level A: L.1.1
CASAS Reading: RDG 1.7, 2.1, 2.2, 2.6
CASAS Competencies: 0.1.2, 0.1.4, 0.1.5, 0.1.6, 0.2.1
Complete standards language available on the Pearson English Portal.

Self-Directed Learning

State the **lesson objective**. Say: *In this lesson, we will learn to use the simple present tense of* be *with* yes/no *and information questions.*

Yes/no questions with *be*

 ActiveTeach: Grammar Discovery

1. Warm up. Say: *The conversation on page 21 used this grammar.* Turn back to page 21. Point to the sentence in Exercise 4A and then write:
   - *Are you a nurse?*
   - *No, I'm not.*
2. Underline *are* and *'m*. Ask: *What is* I'm *a contraction of?* (I am)
3. Tell students to look at the grammar charts.
4. Point to the top chart. Read the *yes/no* question and short answers. Ask a few students: *Are you a nurse?* Elicit: *Yes, I am* or *No, I am not.*
5. Write: *Kara is a nurse.* With the class, change the statement to a *yes/no* question. Draw arrows to indicate changing the order of the subject and verb. Write: *Is Kara a nurse?* Ask the question and elicit the short answer. Write: *Yes, she is.*
6. Read the **Grammar Watch** note. Write: *She is not.* Write the contractions: *She's not. She isn't.* Repeat with *you, we,* and *they.* Have students turn to page 258 for more on contractions.
7. Read the bottom question and answer in the grammar chart. Elicit other information question words such as *where, when,* and *what.* Write them on the board.

Information questions with *be*

1. Point to the bottom grammar chart. Read the information question and short answer.
2. Ask a few students: *Are you a student?* Elicit: *Yes, I am.* Then ask: *How is it?* Elicit a short answer.
3. Write: _____ *are you from?* Ask students what question word goes in the blank. (Where) Point out the order of the verb and the pronoun. Have students ask and answer the question with their classmates and you.

 ActiveTeach: Grammar Coach

A MATCH. **Choose the correct answers…**
1. Read the directions. Tell students to cross out the letter of the answers as they use them.
2. Read each question and call on a student to answer.

B WRITE. **Read the answers. Write questions…**
1. Tell students they will write information questions for A from B's answers. Help them understand the changes they need to make when they write questions from the answers, as follows:
   - Write item 1. Read B's answer. Point to A's question and ask: *Is this a yes/no question or an information question?* (information question) Read the answer again. Ask: *What is the question word?* Circle *What* in A's question. Circle *My last name* and *is* in B's answer and draw arrows to indicate students should change the order of the subject and verb.
   - Ask students to look at item 3. Read the answer. Ask: *What's the verb in this contraction?* Write: *They are from Cuba.* Draw arrows to indicate that students should change the order of the subject and verb.
2. Read each question and call on a student to answer.

■■ EXPANSION: Speaking practice for B
1. Pair students and tell them to take turns asking and answering questions from Exercises A and B.
2. Each partner should ask three different questions.

■■ MULTILEVEL INSTRUCTION for Expansion
Cross-ability Pre-level students ask questions first. Before switching roles, above-level students can help pre-level students write answers to three questions.

Self-Directed Learning

Point out the blue bar. Ask students if they can do the lesson learning objective or if they need more practice. Tell them to check one of the boxes. Assign Extra Practice as needed.

Extra Practice

  pp. 10–11

Correlations

ELPS Level 2: 3, 10
CCRS Level A: W.1.2, W.1.5, L.1.1
CASAS Reading: RDG 1.7, 1.8
CASAS Listening: L2.1, 2.3
CASAS Competencies: 0.1.2, 0.1.5, 0.1.6, 0.2.1, 0.2.4, 7.4.1
Complete standards language available on the Pearson English Portal.

Self-Directed Learning

1. State the **lesson objective**. Say: *In this lesson, we will learn to introduce and explain steps of a routine.*
2. Say: *You will write about your study routine.*

1 STUDY THE MODEL

1. Read the directions.
2. Point to the paragraph. Ask: *What is the title of the model?* (My Study Routine)
3. **Scaffold** the model. Write as a graphic organizer:

1	Study routine	
2	First	
3	Then	
4	After that	

4. Tell students to read the text and read the questions independently. Call on students to answer the questions. Write the information in the graphic organizer on the board.

2 PLAN YOUR WRITING

1. Erase the information in the right-hand column of the graphic organizer on the board.
2. Read the directions.
3. Model with a student. The student asks the teacher the questions.
4. Write the information into the graphic organizer.
5. Tell students to make their own graphic organizer on a piece of paper.
6. Have students work in pairs to ask and answer the questions and complete the graphic organizer with their own information.

3 WRITE

1. Read the directions aloud.
2. Use your information in the graphic organizer from Exercise 2 to write sentences in a paragraph. Include indentation. Leave out the step words.

3. Point to the **Writing Skill**. Read it aloud while students listen.
4. Ask: *What words can we add to my paragraph?* For example, you can add *first* to the first step in my routine. Ask: *Why should we do this?* (It helps the reader know the order of the steps.) Add the words to the sentences.
5. Tell students to write. Circulate to make sure students are writing in paragraph form and using words to introduce the steps.

 ActiveTeach for 3: Writing Support

4 CHECK YOUR WRITING

1. Read the directions aloud. Point to the **Writing Checklist**. Call on students to read the checklist items aloud.
2. Pair students to review their writings together. Say: *Read your sentences with a partner. Use the Writing Checklist.* For additional help, remind students that a correct sentence:
   - *begins with a capital letter*
   - *has a subject*
   - *has a verb*
   - *has a period*
   - *is a complete idea*
3. Walk around and verify that students are using the checklist. Collect the papers for review or put them in the students' writing portfolios.

Teaching Tip: Digital skills

Have students send their paragraph to you electronically. Apps such as WhatsApp or Remind work well for this, as well as email. Another option is to use a learning management system such as Google Classroom, CourseSites, Edmodo, Schoology, or Canvas and have students write their answers as a discussion-board post.

Self-Directed Learning

Point out the blue bar. Ask students if they can do the lesson learning objective or if they need more practice. Tell them to check one of the boxes. Assign Extra Practice as needed.

Extra Practice

 CCRS Plus   p. 12

Write about a study routine

1 STUDY THE MODEL

READ. Answer the questions.

Mona Jibril

My Study Routine

This is my routine to practice new words in English. First, I silently read a word from my list of new words. Then, I say the word aloud. After that, I close my notebook and write the word on a piece of paper.

1. What is Mona's routine for? It's for practicing new words.
2. What is the first step of her routine? Her first step is to silently read a word.
3. What does she do next? She says the word aloud.
4. What does she do after that? She writes the word.

2 PLAN YOUR WRITING

WORK TOGETHER. Ask and answer the questions.

1. What's one of your study routines?
2. What's the first step of your routine?
3. What do you do next?
4. What do you do after that?

3 WRITE

Now write about your study routine. Use the model, the Writing Skill, and your ideas from Exercise 2 to help you.

4 CHECK YOUR WRITING

WORK TOGETHER. Read the checklist. Read your writing aloud. Revise your writing.

Writing Skill: Introduce and explain steps of a routine

When you write about how to do something, explain each step. For each step, use words like *first, then,* and *after that.*

For example: First, I silently read a word from my list of new words. Then, I say the word aloud. After that, I close my notebook and write the word on a piece of paper.

WRITING CHECKLIST

☐ The paragraph answers the questions in Exercise 2.

☐ The paragraph uses the words *first, then,* and *after that.*

I can introduce and explains steps of a routine. ■   I need more practice. ■

For more practice, go to MyEnglishLab.

Be inclusive

1 MEET MEG

Read about one of her workplace skills.

I am inclusive. I work with many different people, and I am friendly to everyone. At work, everyone is included because we are all on the same team.

2 MEG'S PROBLEM

READ. Circle *True* or *False*.

Meg has a 15-minute break at work. She walks into the <u>break room</u>. She sees some of her friends. They are sitting at one table. They're telling stories and laughing. A new co-worker, Jana, is sitting at the table alone. She looks shy and a little lonely.

1. Meg and her co-workers are on a break.   (True)   False
2. Jana is talking to Meg's friends.   True   (False)
3. Jana is outgoing.   True   (False)

3 MEG'S SOLUTION

WORK TOGETHER. Meg is inclusive at work. What does she do next? Explain your answer.

1. Meg sits down with her friends and starts talking to them.
2. Meg says, "Hi, Jana," and then sits down with her friends.
(3.) Meg says, "Hi, Jana. Come sit with us over here."
4. Meg _____.

Show what you know!

1. **THINK ABOUT IT.** Are you inclusive and friendly to everyone? What ways are you inclusive to people in class? At work? At home? Give examples.

2. **WRITE ABOUT IT.** Write an example in your Skills Log.

   I am inclusive and friendly to everyone. For example, sometimes a new student joins the class. I always say hi and invite him or her to be my partner in pair work.

I can give an example of how I am inclusive. ☐

Unit Review: Go back to page 5. Which unit goals can you check off?

Correlations

CASAS Reading: RDG 1.7, 1.8, 3.2
CASAS Listening: L2.1, 2.3, 4.1, 4.2
CASAS Competencies: 0.1.2, 0.1.4, 0.1.5, 0.1.6, 0.2.1
Complete standards language available on the Pearson English Portal.

Self-Directed Learning

State the **lesson objective**. Say: *In this lesson, we will give an example of how we are inclusive.*

1 MEET MEG

1. Ask: *What is the title of this lesson?* (Be inclusive) Explain to students that *inclusive* comes from the verb *include*. Ask: *What does* inclusive *mean?* (to be someone who includes other people)
2. Ask: *Do you work?* If students say *yes*, ask: *Where do you work?* List their workplaces on the board in general terms. (store, restaurant, garage, etc.) Write: *Workplace Skill.* Say: Workplace *is where you work. Skills are things you can do.*
3. Read the directions. Say: *Listen as I read Meet Meg.*
4. Read the paragraph. Ask: *What is one of Meg's workplace skills?* (She is inclusive.) Next to *Workplace Skill,* write: *Be inclusive.*
5. Under *Workplace Skill,* write: *Examples.* Ask: *How is Meg inclusive? What examples does she give?* (She works with many different people. She is friendly to everyone.) Write the examples. Elicit other ways to be inclusive and write them under *Workplace Skill.*

2 MEG'S PROBLEM

1. Say: *Now we are going to read about Meg at work. Listen while I read.* Read the first three sentences. Use the photo to help students understand the situation. Say: *Look at the photo. What is Meg doing on her 15-minute break?* (She is going to the break room. She is visiting friends.)
2. Say: *Meg has a problem. Listen while I read.* Read the rest of the paragraph. Explain any unfamiliar vocabulary. For example, say: *Co-workers are people you work with.* As an example, name a co-worker in your program.
3. Read the directions. Call on students to answer. Ask them to **cite evidence:** *Where is that information?*
4. Ask: *What is Meg's problem?* (A new co-worker is not being included.)

3 MEG'S SOLUTION

1. Read the directions. Ask students to work together on the first three items. Walk around. Check that students understand that only one solution is correct.
2. Ask: *Is #1 inclusive?* (no) *Why not?* (She ignores Jana.) Ask: *Is #2 inclusive?* (no) *Why not?* (She greets Jana, but does not include her.) Ask: *Is #3 inclusive?* (yes) *Why?* (She invites Jana to join the group.)
3. Ask students if they have any other ideas. Call on students to share item 4 with the class. Write their responses. Ask: *Is this inclusive? Why?*

 ActiveTeach for 3: Academic Conversation Support

Workplace Culture

Say: *In the U.S., it is common to include co-workers from different cultures in your group conversations and activities.*

Show what you know!

1. THINK ABOUT IT. Are you inclusive and…

Read the directions. Have students think about their answers for a few minutes. Then ask them to share with a partner. Call on students to share with the class.

2. WRITE ABOUT IT. Write an example in your…

Read the directions and the example. Have students write their examples in their **Skills Log** at the back of the book. Circulate and assist students as necessary.

Self-Directed Learning

1. Point out the blue bar. Ask students if they can do the lesson learning objective or if they need more practice. Tell them to check one of the boxes. Assign Extra Practice as needed.
2. Ask students to turn to page 5. Go to the Unit Wrap-Up teaching notes on page T-5.

Extra Practice

 p. 13

2 All in the Family

Classroom Materials / Extra Practice

ActiveTeach

MyEnglishLab

Workbook

Find on English Portal

Life Skills Writing, MCA, Team Projects, Persistence Activities

Unit Overview

Goals
• See the list of goals on the facing page

Pronunciation
• Sentence stress
• Pronunciation of *do*

Reading
• Read about work/life balance
• Retell information

Grammar
• Simple present affirmative and negative: *live/work/have*
• Simple present: *Yes/no* questions and short answers
• Simple present: Information questions and short answers

Writing
• Write about a family member
• Use capital letters and commas in names of places

Document Literacy and Numearcy
• Interpret a family tree
• Complete a Venn Diagram
• Interpret a chart

Workplace, Life, and Community Skills
• Ask about mailing services
• Digital Skills: Search for mailing services near you

Life Skills Writing
• Complete a post office customs form

Soft Skills at Work
• Separate work and home life

Preview
1. Set the context of the unit by asking questions about family (for example, *Do you have a big family or a small family? Where do your family members live?*).
2. Show the Unit Opener. Ask: *What is the unit title?* (All in the Family)
3. Say: *Look at the picture.* Ask the Preview questions. (Possible answers: a family / a father, mother, son, and daughter)

Unit Goals
1. Point to the Unit Goals. Explain that this list shows what you will be studying in this unit.
2. Tell students to read the goals silently.
3. Say each goal. Explain unfamiliar vocabulary as needed.
4. Point to the ☐ next to the first goal. Say: *We will come back to this page again. You will write a checkmark next to the goals you learned in the unit.*

Oral Presentation
1. Tell students they will give a short presentation at the end of the unit.
2. Write the topics:
   Option 1: How to mail a package
   Option 2: A family member
3. Assign the topics to two students.

Unit Wrap-Up
1. Review the Unit Goals with students.
2. Direct students to the Grammar Review.
3. If you assigned presentations, ask students to present.

 ActiveTeach for Wrap-Up: Team Project

 ActiveTeach for Wrap-Up: Persistence Activities

2 All in the Family

PREVIEW

Look at the picture. What do you see?
Who are these people?

UNIT GOALS

- [ ] Identify family relationships
- [ ] Talk about family
- [ ] Talk about what people have in common
- [ ] Ask about mailing services
- [ ] Ask about people

- [ ] **Academic skill:** Retell information
- [ ] **Writing skill:** Use capital letters and commas in names of places
- [ ] **Workplace soft skill:** Separate work and home life

Family relationships

A **PREDICT.** Look at the pictures. Find Marta in each picture. Who are the other people in the pictures? What is their family relationship to Marta?

I think Paco is Marta's brother.

B ▶ **LISTEN AND POINT.** Then listen and repeat.

Paco Tina Manuel Ella Marta Lina Tony Delmar

Ben   Marta   Tina Eva Felix

Marta   Ben   Sandra Tom Ann

Tommy   Liz Marta   Ben

Liz   Marta   Ben Mary Tommy Sue Benny

Self-Directed Learning

State the **lesson objective**. Say: *In this lesson, we will learn to identify family relationships.*

A **PREDICT. Look at the pictures. Find Marta...**

1. Read the directions. Tell students to cover the list on page 27.
2. Point to the first family picture and ask: *Where is Marta? Who are the other family members in the picture? Which family relationships do you have?*
3. Students call out answers, using either numbers (*I think #1 is Marta's brother*) or names (*I think Paco is Marta's brother*). Help students with pronunciation if needed.
4. If a student calls out an incorrect family member, ask a *yes/no* clarification question: *Is #3 Marta's brother?* If nobody can identify the correct family relationship, tell students they will now listen to audio and practice the words for family members.

B ▶ **LISTEN AND POINT. Then listen and repeat.**

1. Read the directions. Play the audio. Students listen and point to the family members.
2. While the audio is playing, walk around and check that students are pointing to the correct pictures. Pause the audio after item 25.

3. When the audio finishes, say each family word in random order and ask students to point to the appropriate picture.
4. Tell students to look at page 27. Resume the audio. Students listen, read, and repeat.

 ActiveTeach for B: Vocabulary Flashcards

■ **EXPANSION: Vocabulary practice for B**

1. Say a family relationship and ask students to name that person.
2. Ask: *Who is Marta's son?* (Tommy) If necessary, point to a particular picture.
3. Repeat for five relationships.

■ **EXPANSION: Speaking and writing practice for B**

1. Tell students to write three sentences about people in the pictures (for example, *Liz is Marta's daughter.*).
2. Have students rewrite these sentences as questions (for example, *Who is Marta's daughter?*).
3. Form groups of 3. Students take turns asking each other their questions.

Language Note
Write: *Ben is Marta's fiancé. Marta is Ben's fiancée.* Underline *fiancé* and *fiancée*. Ask: *What is the difference in spelling?* (the word for a woman has an extra *e*)

Vocabulary

C WORK TOGETHER. Look at the pictures...

1. Read the directions. Play A and model the example with an above-level student.
2. Read each line in the example and ask the class to repeat. Model correct intonation.
3. Pair students and tell them to take turns asking and answering questions, using all the family words in the vocabulary box.

Classroom Communication

Show students how to correct each other's mistakes by modeling the activity again with an above-level student. Ask the student to play A and ask a new question. Play B and give an incorrect answer, as follows:

A: *Who are Marta's grandchildren?*
B: *Mary and Sue.*
A: *No.* [Points to Benny]
B: *Mary and Benny.*
A: *Yes. Good!*

D CATEGORIZE. Which family words are for...

1. Copy the diagram and examples onto the board. Say: Mother *is for females.* Father *is for males.* Parents *is for both females and males.*
2. Read the directions. Categorize the first five items on the vocabulary list as a class. Say each word and ask: *Is it female, male, or both?* Write each word in the appropriate place on the diagram.
3. Pair students. Tell them to draw their own diagrams and write all the vocabulary words in the appropriate place.
4. Tell students to switch partners and compare their charts with another classmate.

■ **EXPANSION: Vocabulary practice for D**

Tell students to look at their diagrams and underline the words that describe them.

Study Tip: Make connections

1. Point to the **Study Tip**. Read the directions and the examples.
2. Say: *To remember the words for family members, write the names of your family members and their relationship to you. Write the names of five people in your own family and their relationship to you.*
3. Walk around as students work. If misspellings occur, tell students to check the list on page 27.
4. Say: *You can remember new vocabulary when you apply it to your own life.* Remind students to use this strategy to remember other new vocabulary.

Show what you know!

1. THINK ABOUT IT. Make a list of your family...

1. Read the directions.
2. Model the activity. Write notes about your own family members. Tell students to use the list of family members they made in the **Study Tip** activity.

2. TALK ABOUT IT. Talk about your family.

1. Tell students to look at the lists they made in Step 1 and to circle the family members who live in this country.
2. Read the directions. Model the conversation with an above-level student. You play B and use the example answer. Then ask the question back to the student. Prompt him or her to answer from his or her list of family members.
3. Pair students and tell them to take turns asking and answering the question.
4. Tell students to switch partners and repeat several times.

3. WRITE ABOUT IT. Write about your family.

1. Read the directions and the example. Model the activity by writing sentences about your own family.
2. Share the checklist below. Then write a checkmark next to each as you point back to your sentences.
   • There are sentences about all the family members on your list.
   • Sentences begin with a capital letter and end with a period.
   • All family words should be spelled correctly.
3. Give students time to write their sentences.
4. Tell students to show their sentences to a partner and to use the checklist to review the sentences.
5. Walk around and verify that students are using the checklist. Collect the papers for review or put them in the students' writing portfolios.

Self-Directed Learning

Point out the blue bar. Ask students if they can do the lesson learning objective or if they need more practice. Tell them to check one of the boxes. Assign Extra Practice as needed.

Extra Practice

MyEnglishLab Workbook pp. 14–15

Vocabulary

Family relationships

1. brother	6. cousin	11. nephew	16. sister-in-law	21. grandmother
2. sister	7. uncle	12. wife	17. son	22. grandfather
3. father	8. fiancé	13. husband	18. daughter	23. granddaughter
4. mother	9. fiancée	14. mother-in-law	19. children	24. grandson
5. aunt	10. niece	15. father-in-law	20. parents	25. grandchildren

C WORK TOGETHER. Look at the pictures. Student A, ask a question about Marta's family. Student B, answer.

A: Who is Marta's sister?
B: Tina. Who are Marta's grandchildren?

D CATEGORIZE. Which family words are for females? Which are for males? Which are for both? Complete the chart.

Female	Both	Male
mother	parents	father
sister, aunt, fiancée, niece, wife, mother-in-law, sister-in-law, daughter, grandmother, granddaughter	cousin, children, grandchildren	brother, uncle, fiancé, nephew, husband, father-in-law, son, grandfather, grandson

> **Study Tip**
>
> **Make Connections**
> Write the names of five people in your family and their relationship to you.
>
> Marie: niece
> Pete: nephew

Show what you know!

1. THINK ABOUT IT. Make a list of your family members. Where do they live?

husband — New York   son — New York   parents — China
daughter — New York   brother — San Francisco

2. TALK ABOUT IT. Talk about your family.

A: Is your family here?
B: My son and daughter are here. My mother and father are in China.

3. WRITE ABOUT IT. Write about your family.

My children are in New York. My parents are in China.

I can identify family relationships. ☐   I need more practice. ☐

For more practice, go to MyEnglishLab.

Listening and Speaking

2 Talk about family

1 BEFORE YOU LISTEN

MAKE CONNECTIONS. How many family members live with you? Who are they?

2 LISTEN

A **PREDICT.** Look at the picture of two new co-workers. What are they talking about? What do people talk about when they meet for the first time?

B ▶ **LISTEN FOR MAIN IDEA.** Choose the correct word.

Amy and Sam are talking about _____.

a. work   **b.** families   **c.** cars

C ▶ **LISTEN FOR DETAILS.** Choose the correct word.

1. Sam doesn't have a _____ family.
   a. big
   b. small

2. Sam has _____.
   a. one brother
   b. two brothers

3. Sam's _____ live in Senegal.
   a. brothers
   b. sisters

D ▶ **EXPAND.** Listen to the whole conversation. Choose the correct word.

Sam's brother lives _____ Sam.

a. far from   **b.** with   **c.** near

Correlations

ELPS Level 2: 2, 7
CASAS Reading: RDG 1.7, 2.2, 2.3
CASAS Listening: L1.4, 2.1, 2.3, 4.1, 4.2, 6.5
CASAS Competencies: 0.1.2, 0.1.4, 0.1.5, 0.2.1
Complete standards language available on the Pearson English Portal.

Self-Directed Learning

State the **lesson objective**. Say: *In this lesson, we will learn to talk about family.*

1 BEFORE YOU LISTEN

MAKE CONNECTIONS. How many family…

1. Read the directions.
2. Have students list their family members on a sheet of paper, using the family words on page 27.
3. Call on students to answer.

Culture Note

1. Say: *In the U.S., parents and their children usually live together. In some families in the U.S., and in many other countries, parents, children, grandparents, aunts, uncles, and cousins may live together.*
2. Ask: *Who did you live with in your native country? Who do you live with in the U.S.?*

2 LISTEN

A PREDICT. Look at the picture of two new…

1. Tell students to read the directions silently and look at the picture. Ask: *What are Sam and Amy doing?* (eating, looking at their phones) *Where do you think they are?* (at lunch / in a cafeteria / in a restaurant) *What do you think they are looking at on their phones?* (pictures of their families)
2. Ask: *Are Sam and Amy old friends?* (No, they're new co-workers.) *What are they talking about?* Write students' ideas on the board. *What do people talk about when they meet for the first time?* (work, family, where they're from)

B ▶ LISTEN FOR MAIN IDEA. Choose the…

1. Read the directions. Play the audio. Students circle the letter of the correct answer.
2. Ask students to raise their hands if they checked *a*. Repeat for *b* and *c*.
3. Ask: *Was your guess in Exercise 2A correct?*

C ▶ LISTEN FOR DETAILS. Choose the…

1. Read the directions. Play the audio. Students listen and circle the letters for the correct answers.
2. Check answers by asking questions (for example, *Does Sam have a big or small family?*).
3. Ask about **register:** *Are they meeting for the first time?* (no) *How do you know?* (They don't introduce themselves.)
4. *Optional:* Ask the class: *How many sisters does Sam have?* (two) *Where does Sam's brother live?* (here)

Teaching Tip: Use the script

Optional: Remember that if students need additional support, tell them to read the Audio Script on page 266 as they listen to the conversation.

D ▶ EXPAND. Listen to the whole…

1. Read the directions. Play the audio. Students listen and circle the letter for the correct answer.
2. Explain *far from* and *with*. Draw two simple houses with one stick figure each on opposite sides of the board. Label the figures *Sam's brother* and *Sam*. Say: *Sam's brother lives <u>far from</u> Sam.* Then draw one simple house with two stick figures inside. Label the figures *Sam's brother* and *Sam*. Say: *Sam's brother lives <u>with</u> Sam.*
3. Ask a student to come to the board, read the completed sentence, and point to the correct picture.
4. *Optional:* Ask the class: *Do Sam and his brother live in a house or an apartment?* (an apartment) *Where does Sam's brother work?* (in a hospital)

■ EXPANSION: Graphic organizer practice for 2D

1. As a class, make a web diagram for Sam. Draw a circle with lines radiating out from it. Write *Sam* in the middle of the circle.
2. Ask: *What do we know about Sam?* Write information about him at the end of each line (for example, *from Senegal, small family, one brother, two sisters*). Circle *one brother* and *two sisters*.
3. Ask: *What do we know about Sam's brother and sisters?* Draw lines radiating out from these circles and write information about Sam's siblings at the end of the lines (for example, for *one brother: lives here, works in a hospital, lives with Sam*).

Listening and Speaking

3 PRONUNCIATION

A ▶ PRACTICE. Listen. Then listen again and...

1. Say: *Important words in a sentence are stressed.* Write: *I have a brother and two sisters.* Read it and ask: *What are the important words?* Underline *brother* and *two sisters*.

2. Say: *Short "grammar" words—for example* a, and, *and the—are usually short and weak.* Read the sentence again and ask: *What are the weak words?* Circle a and *and*.

3. Say: *Weak words often have the short, quiet vowel sound "uh."* Pronounce the "uh" sound several times. Read the sentences, modeling the "uh" pronunciation of the vowel sounds in the "grammar" words. Say: In *is also a weak word in these sentences.*

4. Tell students to read the Pronunciation Note silently.

5. Play the audio. Students listen. Then students listen and repeat.

 ActiveTeach for 3A: Pronunciation Coach

B ▶ APPLY. Listen. Circle the words that...

1. Read the directions.

2. Read the first sentence. Elicit the words that aren't stressed.

3. Play the audio. Students listen and circle the words that are not stressed.

4. Call on students to read a sentence and say which words are not stressed.

5. *Optional:* Play the audio again and have students repeat each sentence.

4 CONVERSATION

A ▶ LISTEN AND READ. Then listen and repeat.

1. Note: This conversation is the same one students heard in Exercise 2B on page 28.

2. Tell students to read the conversation silently and underline the words that aren't stressed.

3. Play the audio. Students listen and then listen and repeat.

B WORK TOGETHER. Practice the...

1. Read the directions.

2. Pair students and tell them to practice the conversation in Exercise 4A.

3. Tell students to take turns playing A and B.

4. Walk around and check that students are using correct stress patterns.

C MAKE CONNECTIONS. Talk about your own...

1. Tell students to look at the picture. Ask: *Is this a big family or a small family?* (a big family) *Do you have a big family or a small family?*

2. Read the directions.

3. Model the conversation with an above-level student. Play B and use real information.

4. Pair students and tell them to take turns playing A and B.

5. Walk around during the activity and provide help as needed.

6. *Optional:* Call on students to tell the class about their partner's family.

■ MULTILEVEL INSTRUCTION for 4C

Pre-level scaffolding Before they practice the conversation, tell students to write how they will finish B's response.

Above-level expansion Tell students to also talk about where their family members live.

Classroom Communication

When lessons involve discussing and describing family members, it is a great idea to have students share their family photos. Most students have photos of their family on their phones, so sharing photos is often easy to do. Sharing personal photos helps students learn more about each other's lives and builds classroom rapport.

■ EXPANSION: Speaking and listening practice for 4C

1. Have students share family photos to play a guessing game.

2. Have students work in pairs and show each other a photo of a group of family members.

3. Tell A to describe the physical characteristics and personality of a family member. Tell B to point to a photo to guess who it is.

4. Students switch roles and repeat.

Self-Directed Learning

Point out the blue bar. Ask students if they can do the lesson learning objective or if they need more practice. Tell them to check one of the boxes. Assign Extra Practice as needed.

Extra Practice

  pp. 16–17

Listening and Speaking

3 PRONUNCIATION

A ▶ **PRACTICE. Listen. Then listen again and repeat.**

I have a brother and two sisters.

We live in the same apartment.

He works in a hospital.

B ▶ **APPLY. Listen. Circle the words that are not stressed.**

1. I don't have (a) very big family.
2. My sisters live (in) Senegal.
3. He's (a) medical assistant.

4 CONVERSATION

A ▶ **LISTEN AND READ. Then listen and repeat.**

A: Tell me about your family.
B: Well, I don't have a very big family. I have a brother and two sisters.
A: Do they live here?
B: My sisters live in Senegal, but my brother lives here.

B **WORK TOGETHER. Practice the conversation in Exercise A.**

C **MAKE CONNECTIONS. Talk about your own family.**

A: Tell me about your family.
B: I have a very big family.
   I have . . .

I can talk about family. ■   I need more practice. ■

For more practice, go to MyEnglishLab.

Lesson 3

Simple present affirmative and negative: *live / work / have*

Simple present affirmative and negative: *live / work / have*				Grammar Watch
Affirmative		**Negative**		

Affirmative

I
You **live /**
We **work**   in the U.S.
They

He **lives /**
She **works**

I
You
We **have**   a small family.
They

He
She **has**

Negative

I
You
We **don't**   **live /**   in Senegal.
They   **work**

He
She **doesn't**

I
You
We **don't**
They   **have**   a big family.

He
She **doesn't**

Grammar Watch

- With *he, she,* or *it,* the simple present verb ends in *-s.*
- *Have* is an irregular verb. With *he, she,* or *it,* use *has.*
- Use *don't* or *doesn't* to make a verb negative. Use the base form of the verb after *don't* and *doesn't.*

For contractions, see page 258.

A IDENTIFY. Cross out the incorrect words.

1. My cousin **has / ~~have~~** a wife and two children.
2. They **~~doesn't~~ / don't** have children.
3. Her brother **~~work~~ / works** in a theater.
4. My mother-in-law **lives / ~~live~~** on South Street.
5. Our grandparents **~~doesn't~~ / don't** live here.
6. We **don't / ~~doesn't~~** work on weekends.
7. Pam and Ben **have / ~~has~~** two boys.

B COMPLETE. Write the simple present form of the verbs.

1. Mary (work) _____ works _____ at a hair salon.
2. His sister-in-law (not have) _____ doesn't have _____ a job.
3. Nina's fiancé (live) _____ lives _____ near the city.
4. Her husband (work) _____ works _____ with her brother.
5. I (not live) _____ don't live _____ with my parents.
6. Our family (live) _____ lives _____ in Colombia.
7. They (not work) _____ don't work _____ in a big office.
8. Tom (not have) _____ doesn't have _____ any cousins.

Correlations

ELPS Level 2: 2, 7, 10
CCRS Level A: L.1.1
CASAS Reading: RDG 1.7, 2.1, 2.9
CASAS Listening: L1.3, 2.1, 2.3, 3.1, 3.3, 3.5, 4.1, 4.2
CASAS Competencies: 0.1.2, 0.1.4, 0.1.5
Complete standards language available on the Pearson English Portal.

Self-Directed Learning

State the **lesson objective**. Say: *In this lesson, we will learn to use the simple present.*

Simple present of affirmative and negative: *live / work / have*

 ActiveTeach: Grammar Discovery

1. Warm up. Say: *The conversation and pronunciation practice on page 29 used this grammar.* Turn back to page 29. Point to the sentences in Exercises 3A, 3B, and 4A and then write:
   • *I don't have a very big family.*
   • *My sisters live in Senegal, but my brother lives here.*
   • *He works in a hospital.*
2. Underline *don't have, live, lives,* and *works*.
3. Tell students to look at the grammar charts. Point to the left chart and read the sentences aloud. Students repeat.
4. Ask: *When does the simple present verb end in -s?* (with *he, she,* and *it*) As students notice the pattern, tell them to underline the -s in *lives, works,* and *has*. Read the first point of the **Grammar Watch** note.
5. Point to the right chart and read the sentences out loud. Students repeat.
6. Ask: *How do you make a simple present sentence negative?* (*don't, doesn't*) Tell students to underline *don't* and *doesn't*. Read the second point of the **Grammar Watch** note.
7. Write: *I live in the United States. She lives in Senegal.* Ask the class to make the sentences negative. Elicit *don't* and *doesn't* and then draw a blank after each. Ask: *What verb form do I use with* don't? *What verb form do I use with* doesn't? Fill in the blanks and read the third point of the **Grammar Watch** note.
8. Read the negative sentences in the grammar chart and have students repeat.

9. **Reinforce:** Write: *I, we, they work / don't work* and *he, she, it works / doesn't work*.

 ActiveTeach: Grammar Coach

Ⓐ **IDENTIFY. Cross out the incorrect words.**

1. Read the directions. Read the example in item 1. Ask: *Why is the answer* has? (because *My cousin* is the same as *he,* and we say *he has*)
2. Walk around and check that students are using the correct form of the verb.
3. Students compare answers with a partner.
4. Call on students to read the completed sentences.

Ⓑ **COMPLETE. Write the simple present form...**

1. Tell students to look at the photo. Ask: *Where are they?* (hair salon) Read the directions.
2. Write item 1. Ask: *Why is the answer* works? (because *Mary* is the same as *she,* and we say *she works*)
3. Write item 2. Ask: *Why is the answer* doesn't have? (because *His sister-in-law* is the same as *she,* and we say *she doesn't have*)
4. Walk around and check that students are using the correct form of the verb.
5. Students compare answers with a partner.
6. Call on students to read the completed sentences.

▬ **EXPANSION: Speaking and writing practice for B**

Give pairs a photo of an anonymous (not famous) person. Tell pairs to make up information about their person. Tell them to write three affirmative and three negative sentences with *have, live,* and *work*. Write some examples.

Teaching Tip: Think-Pair-Share

Having students work individually, then compare in pairs before sharing with a larger group or class provides scaffolding that makes them more comfortable speaking in class.

Career Awareness: Hair stylist

Hair stylists work in hair salons. They wash, cut, and style hair. No formal education is required.

▬ **EXPANSION: Career awareness for B**

Ask students about the job in this lesson: *What does a hair stylist do? Where does a hair stylist work? Do you need to study to be a hair stylist? Do you want to be a hair stylist?*

Grammar

C INTERPRET. Look at the family tree...

1. Read the directions. Write item 1.
2. Read item 1. Tell students to point to Alba on the Méndez family tree. Ask: *Does Alba live in Los Angeles?* (no) Say: *So, the answer is* doesn't live.
3. Walk around and check that students are using the family tree to determine whether sentences are affirmative or negative.
4. Students compare answers with a partner.
5. Call on students to read the completed sentences.
6. *Optional:* As a class, change each negative sentence to an accurate affirmative sentence (for example, for item 1, *Alba lives in Chicago.*).

■ EXPANSION: Vocabulary practice for C

1. Tell students to choose one member of the Méndez family and to circle the family member on the family tree.
2. Then students write the names of all the other family members and their relationship to the person they chose (for example, a student who chose Sara would write *Paco: grandfather, Sandra: grandmother, Lola: mother,* etc.).

D WRITE. Now write three new sentences...

1. Read the directions and the examples.
2. Tell each student to write a sentence on the board for the class to read and correct.
3. Read each sentence. Ask the class: *Is this correct?* Circle any incorrect sentences and number them. Tell students to rewrite them in their notebooks.
4. Elicit the corrections and make them on the board. Reread the corrected sentences.

■ MULTILEVEL INSTRUCTION for D

Pre-level scaffolding Copy the example sentences. Underline *Sara, New York, She, Dallas, She, two sisters.* Tell students to replace the underlined information in their new sentences.

Above-level expansion Have students practice writing compound sentences with *and* and *but* like they did in Unit 1. For example, *Ana lives in New York, but Sara lives in Dallas.*

Show what you know!

1. THINK ABOUT IT. Write two true sentences...

1. Read the directions.
2. Model the activity. On the board, complete two sentences with real information about you and one sentence with made-up information. Don't tell the class which sentence is false.
3. Tell students that they shouldn't discuss their sentences with each other.

2. TALK ABOUT IT. Play a guessing game with...

1. Read the directions. Ask two above-level students to read the example out loud.
2. Play A and model the conversation by reading your sentences to the class. Prompt the class to play B and guess which of your sentences is false.
3. Put students in groups of 3. Tell students to take turns reading their sentences and guessing. Walk around and, as needed, help students guess.

3. WRITE ABOUT IT. Write three sentences...

1. Read the directions.
2. Give students time to write their sentences.
3. Ask pairs to check each other's sentences:
   • Sentences should use the correct form of the verb for *he, she,* and *it*.
   • Sentences with *have* should use the irregular forms (*has*).
   • Negative sentences should use *don't* or *doesn't* + base form of a verb.
4. Have students volunteer to write their sentences on the board.

Self-Directed Learning

Point out the blue bar. Ask students if they can do the lesson learning objective or if they need more practice. Tell them to check one of the boxes. Assign Extra Practice as needed.

Extra Practice

| MyEnglishLab | Workbook pp. 16–17 |

Grammar

C **INTERPRET. Look at the family tree. Complete the sentences with the simple present.**

1. Alba ___doesn't live___ in Los Angeles.
   (live)
2. Marcos ___lives___ in Lima.
   (live)
3. Lola ___doesn't have___ a son.
   (have)
4. Marcos ___has___ a brother.
   (have)
5. Lola and Pablo ___live___ in New York.
   (live)
6. Sandra ___has___ three grandchildren.
   (have)
7. Pablo and Marcos ___don't have___ a sister.
   (have)
8. Sandra and Paco ___don't live___ in Dallas.
   (live)

The Méndez Family

Paco
Lima, Peru

Sandra
Lima, Peru

Lola,
New York

Pablo,
New York

Marcos
Lima, Peru

Ana,
New York

Alba,
Chicago

Sara,
Dallas

D **WRITE. Now write three new sentences about the Méndez family.**

Sara doesn't live in New York. She lives in Dallas.
She has two sisters.

Show what you know!

1. **THINK ABOUT IT. Write two true sentences and one false sentence about your family and life.**

   I have _____.

   I live in _____.

   I work in _____.

2. **TALK ABOUT IT. Play a guessing game with three students. Read your sentences. Guess the false sentence.**

   A: I have four sisters. I live in Oak Park. I work in a hotel.
   B: I think the first sentence is false. I don't think you have four sisters.
   A: That's right. I don't have four sisters. I have one sister.

3. **WRITE ABOUT IT. Write three sentences about someone in your group.**

   _____
   _____
   _____

I can use the simple present. ☐   I need more practice. ☐

For more practice, go to MyEnglishLab.

Read about work / life balance

1 BEFORE YOU READ

A **DECIDE.** Complete the sentences with the words from the box.

> advice   expert   handle   responsibilities

1. The president has an important job with many ____responsibilities____.
2. I don't know what to do! Please give me some ____advice____.
3. I need some help with this job. One person cannot ____handle____ it all.
4. An ____expert____ is a person who knows a lot about a topic or has special skills.

B **BRAINSTORM.** Look at the picture. What do you think it means?

2 READ

▶ **Listen and read.**

> **Academic Skill: Retell information**
>
> *Retell* means to say in your own words what you read or hear. The words are different, but the meaning is the same.

Work / Life Balance

1 Today, it is hard for many adults in the United States to find enough time for both their work and their personal lives. Men and women have many responsibilities. Some are things they have
5 to do for their jobs. For example, they might have to travel for work, or they might have to work extra hours to finish a task. Others are things they need to do for themselves and their families. For example, they have to cook, clean,
10 and pay bills. People with children have to take care of them. How can busy adults handle all these responsibilities? Experts on work/life balance give this advice:

1. Prioritize. Ask yourself, "What is most
15 important?" You can't do everything. So write a list each day. Put a star ★ next to the most important thing to do. Only do the important things on your list.

2. Say no. You already have many responsibilities.
20 When people ask you to do something extra, tell them you can't. Say, "I'm sorry, but I don't have the time right now."

3. Take some time for yourself. Make sure you get a little time every day to do something you
25 like. Watch a TV program, take a bath, get some exercise, or read. Take care of yourself so you will have the energy to take care of your biggest responsibilities.

Correlations

ELPS Level 2: 1, 2, 3, 6, 7, 9
CCRS Level A: RI/RL.1., RI.1.2, RI.1.4, RI.1.8, W.1.2, SL.K.2, SL.1.4
CASAS Reading: RDG 1.7, 1.8, 2.2, 2.3, 3.2, 3.7, 3.11
CASAS Listening: L2.1, 2.3, 4.1, 4.2, 5.8, 6.1
CASAS Competencies: 0.1.2, 0.1.5, 0.2.1
Complete standards language available on the Pearson English Portal.

Self-Directed Learning

1. State the **lesson objective**. Say: *In this lesson, we will learn to retell information.*
2. Say: *We will read about work / life balance.*

1 BEFORE YOU READ

A DECIDE. Complete the sentences with the…

1. Read the directions. Say the words in the box.
2. Read the first sentence. Ask: *What is another word for the important things a leader does?* (responsibilities) Tell students to write *responsibilities* to complete the sentence.
3. Tell students to complete the sentences.
4. Call on students to read the completed sentences aloud.

B BRAINSTORM. Look at the picture. What do…

1. Tell the class to look at the picture. Ask: *What is the man doing?* Write: *juggling.* Ask: *How many balls is the man juggling?* (four)
2. Ask: *Can you juggle?*
3. Tell the class to look at the picture again. Ask: *What are the words on the balls?* (work, sleep, school, family) Explain that *juggling* also means trying to do two or more jobs or activities well at about the same time.
4. **Scaffold:** With the class, brainstorm a list of things that we juggle in our lives (for example, *fun, home, community, friends,* etc.).
5. Tell the class to look at the picture again. Ask: *How does he feel?* (tired, stressed) *Why?* (He has a lot of activities/responsibilities.) Ask: *Do you have a lot activities or responsibilities? Do you ever feel like the man in the picture?* Call on volunteers to answer.

Teaching Tip: Use comparisons

The picture is comparing similarities between two things: juggling balls and finding time for activities/responsibilities. Help students see the similarities between two things to understand an idea better.

2 READ

▶ Listen and read.

1. Introduce the reading. Point to the article and read the title: *Work/Life Balance.* Hold your right hand out in front of you, palm up, and say: *Work.* Then hold your left hand out and say: *Life.* Show the idea of *balance* by lifting one hand up as the other lowers a few times (as if your hands are a scale). Say: *Work/Life Balance.* Ask: *How do we find a balance between work and the other things we have to do in life?*
2. Introduce the visual. Tell the class to look at the picture. Say: *The woman is doing two things at the same time.* Ask: *What is she doing?* (holding a baby, working on a computer) *How does she feel?* (tired) Point out that visuals often help students preview text or predict what the text will say.

 ActiveTeach for 2: Anticipation Guide – *Before* Reading exercise

3. Read the text.
   a. Say: *Now we are going to read and listen to the article* Work/Life Balance. *It gives us advice about balancing work and personal life.*
   b. Play the audio as students listen and read along silently.
   c. Ask: *How many pieces of advice does the article give?* (three) *How do you know?* (there are numbers)
   d. Have students read the first sentence in red of each numbered paragraph. Tell students to underline these sentences. Say: Prioritize *means to decide what is most important.*
   e. Play the audio again. Students read and listen again.
4. Point to the **Academic Skill** and read it. Write the first sentence from the reading: *Today, it is hard for many adults in the U.S. to find enough time for both their work and their personal lives.* Ask: *How can we say this with different words?* Elicit ideas and write them.
5. Say: *Retell the advice about work/life balance. Use your own words.* Elicit ideas and write them (for example: *Make a list. Don't do extra things. Have fun.* etc.).

 ActiveTeach for 2: Anticipation Guide – *After* Reading exercise

Reading

3 CLOSE READING

A IDENTIFY. What is the main idea?

1. **Reinforce the Academic Skill** from page 18, Unit 1. Ask: *What is a main idea?* (what the writer has to say about a topic) Say: *Now we are going to identify the topic and main idea.*
2. Read the directions. Have students circle the answer.
3. Elicit the answer from the class.

B CITE EVIDENCE. Complete the sentences...

1. Say: *Now we are going to find information in the reading.* Remind students to look at line numbers when they find the information.
2. Read the directions. Walk around as students do the activity. If students are struggling, have them work in pairs or direct them to the text lines where they can find the information.
3. Call on students to read the sentence with the correct completion. Ask a different student: *Where is that information? What line number?*
4. **Reinforce academic language:** Point to the words *cite evidence*. Say: Cite evidence *means to show support. We cite evidence to show where the answer to a question is. This makes it clear that the answer is correct.*

4 SUMMARIZE

 ActiveTeach for 4: Vocabulary Practice

1. Read the directions. Ask students to read aloud the words in the box.
2. Tell students to complete the paragraph.
3. To check answers, call on students to read sentences in the summary with the blanks filled in. Ask other students to read the completed summary silently.

Show what you know!

1. THINK ABOUT IT. What are your family...

1. Tell students to draw a stick figure juggling three balls and write *family, school,* and *work* in the balls. Say: *This person is you. What are your family, school, and work responsibilities?* Tell students to draw lines from the balls and note their responsibilities.
2. Students put a star next to the most important responsibilities.

■ EXPANSION: Speaking practice for 1

1. Pair students. Pairs talk about their diagrams.
2. Ask: *Are you juggling too many responsibilities? Are you trying to do too much? Is the article's advice helpful to you?* Tell pairs to discuss. Tell each partner to note one of the article's suggestions that they want to try.

2. WRITE ABOUT IT. Write sentences about...

1. Read the directions and model. Say and write a sentence about your everyday responsibilities (for example: *At home, I am responsible for caring for my dog.*).
2. Tell students to use their diagrams from Step 1 and write sentences on a sheet of paper.
3. Walk around and answer any questions while students complete the activity.

3. PRESENT IT. Give a short presentation...

1. On separate lines, write the categories: *responsibilities at home, responsibilities at work, responsibilities at school, experts' advice,* and *good work/life balance.*
2. Read the directions. Tell students to take notes on their ideas next to each of the categories.
3. Pair students to practice their presentations. Walk around to provide help as needed.
4. Have students use feedback to improve their presentations.
5. Put students in small groups to give their presentations.
6. Collect the papers for review or put them in the students' writing portfolios.

 ActiveTeach for 3: Academic Conversation Support

Self-Directed Learning

Point out the blue bar. Ask students if they can do the lesson learning objective or if they need more practice. Tell them to check one of the boxes. Assign Extra Practice as needed.

■ **EXPANSION: Self-directed learning**

Ask students to reflect: *What did you learn from this reading?* Call on students to share something they learned.

Extra Practice		
CCRS Plus		Workbook pp. 18–19

Reading

3 CLOSE READING

A IDENTIFY. What is the main idea?

To have a good work/life balance, you need to _____.
a. have a job, be married, and have children
b. find time for both your responsibilities and the things you enjoy
c. always say no when people ask for your help

B CITE EVIDENCE. Complete the sentences. Where is the information? Write the line numbers.

Lines

1. It's hard for many adults to find a good work/life balance because they _____.   1–4
   a. don't know how to work hard
   b. spend too much time watching TV
   c. have a lot of responsibilities

2. Experts say to write a to-do list and _____.   15–18
   a. put the things you like to do on it
   b. do the most important things on it
   c. finish everything on it every day

3. The experts explain how to _____ when people ask you to do something extra.   19–22
   a. say no
   b. write a list
   c. get enough sleep

4. Taking a bath is an example of _____.   25–29
   a. a way to take care of yourself
   b. a responsibility
   c. a way to get exercise

5. The experts say that _____ will give you more energy.   26–29
   a. spending time with children
   b. handling responsibilities
   c. taking care of yourself

4 SUMMARIZE

Complete the summary with the words in the box.

| advice | responsibilities |
| balance | take care of |

When you have a lot of (1) __responsibilities__, both at work and at home, it's hard to have a good work/life (2) __balance__. Experts give this (3) __advice__: Write a to-do list every day, say no when people ask you to do extra things at work or at home, and (4) __take care of__ yourself.

Show what you know!

1. **THINK ABOUT IT.** What are your family, school, and work responsibilities? Make a list. Put a star next to the most important responsibilities.

2. **WRITE ABOUT IT.** Write sentences about your everyday responsibilities. Prioritize them.

   At work, I am responsible for sending and delivering mail.

3. **PRESENT IT.** Give a short presentation about your responsibilities at home, at work, and at school. What do you think about the experts' advice? What do you need to do to have a good work/life balance?

I can retell information. ■   I need more practice. ■

To read more, go to My English Lab.

Talk about what people have in common

1 BEFORE YOU LISTEN

DESCRIBE. Look at the picture of three brothers. How are they alike? What are some things that family members have in common? *(Answers will vary.)*

They have red hair. They are short. They like soccer.

2 LISTEN

A **PREDICT.** Look at the picture of two co-workers. What are they talking about?

(Answers will vary.)

a. a problem at work
b. their families
c. the latest smartphone

B ▶ **LISTEN FOR MAIN IDEA.** Listen to the conversation. Complete the sentence.

Tina and Lili _____.

a. don't have a lot in common
b. have a little in common
c. have a lot in common

Tina   Ming

C ▶ **LISTEN FOR DETAILS.** Listen again. Choose the answer.

1. Lili is Tina's _____.

a. sister   **b.** mother   **c.** grandmother

2. Tina looks like her _____.

a. father   **b.** sister   **c.** mother

3. Tina works in a _____.

a. hospital   **b.** store   **c.** bank

D ▶ **EXPAND.** Listen to the whole conversation. Answer the questions.

1. Does Tina have any sisters? _____ Yes. _____

2. Does Ming have any brothers? _____ No. _____

Correlations

ELPS Level 2: 2, 7
CCRS Level A: SL.K.3
CASAS Reading: RDG 1.7, 2.2, 2.3
CASAS Listening: L1.4, 1.5, 2.1, 2.3, 4.1, 4.2, 5.8, 6.1
CASAS Competencies: 0.1.2, 0.1.4, 0.1.5, 0.1.6, 0.2.1
Complete standards language available on the Pearson English Portal.

Self-Directed Learning

State the **lesson objective**. Say: *In this lesson, we will learn to talk about what people have in common.*

1 BEFORE YOU LISTEN

DESCRIBE. Look at the picture of three...

1. Tell students to look at the picture. Review the meaning of the expression *in common* that you discussed in the Unit Opener (something is the same for a group of people) Ask: *What can family members have in common?* As needed, explain: *Some things that people can have in common are interests, appearance, and personalities.*
2. Ask: *What do the three brothers have in common?* Write students' responses on the board. For example, *They have the same hair color. They like soccer.*

■ EXPANSION: Speaking practice for 1

1. Show the class photos of various groups of people engaged in activities. Choose photos of families, teams, work groups, and friends.
2. Put students in pairs or small groups to identify things the people in the photo have in common.
3. Elicit and write the ideas.

2 LISTEN

A PREDICT. Look at the picture of two...

1. Read the directions.
2. Call on students to read the answer choices. Tell students to look at the picture. Ask: *Where are they?* (at work) *What are they looking at?* (a phone/photos) *What do you think they are talking about?* Write students' answers on the board.

■ EXPANSION: Writing practice for 2A

1. Review vocabulary for physical appearance from Unit 1.
2. Tell students to write sentences to describe Tina and Ming. Ask: *What do they have in common?*

3. Put students in pairs to share sentences.
4. Call on students to share sentences with the class.

B ▶ LISTEN FOR MAIN IDEA. Listen to the...

1. Tell students to read the directions and the answer choices silently.
2. Play the audio. Ask: *Whose family are they talking about—Tina's or Ming's?* (Tina's family) Play the audio again as needed.
3. Ask: *Which answer is correct to complete the sentence?*
4. Finally, ask: *Was your guess in Exercise 2A correct?*

Teaching Tip: Use the script

Optional: If students need additional support, tell them to read the Audio Script on page 266 as they listen to the conversations.

C ▶ LISTEN FOR DETAILS. Listen again...

1. Read the directions. Call on students to read the items and answer choices.
2. Play the audio. Students choose the correct answers.
3. Tell students to compare answers with a partner.
4. Call on students for answers.
5. *Optional:* Ask: *What do Tina and her sister Lili have in common?* Elicit and write: *They look alike. They work in a bank. They are talkative.*
6. Ask about **register**: *Do you think Ming and Tina are friends?* (yes) *How do you know?* (They talk about their families. They joke.)

D ▶ EXPAND. Listen to the whole...

1. Say: *Now Tina is asking about Ming's family.* Read the directions. Call on students to read the questions.
2. Play the audio. Students listen and write the answers.
3. Students compare answers with a partner. Walk around and look at students' answers. Play the audio again if needed.
4. Call on students to answer the questions.
5. Ask: *How many sisters does Ming have? What do Ming and her sisters have in common?* Elicit and write: *They have two sisters. They don't have any brothers.*
6. *Optional:* Ask: *Do you think what Ming says is funny? Why?* (Possible answer: Yes, because the things they have in common is their family.)

Listening and Speaking

3 PRONUNCIATION

A ▶ PRACTICE. Listen. Then listen and repeat.

1. Tell students to look at the examples and underline each *do*.
2. Say: *Do has two pronunciations—a weak one and a strong one.* Write *do* on the board. Draw two lines branching out from *do* and write *weak* and *strong*.
3. Read the directions. Then read the **Pronunciation Note**.
4. Say: *Listen. Pay attention. In the three questions, does* do *have a strong or a weak pronunciation?*
5. Play the audio. Students listen and then listen and repeat.
6. Ask: *Is* do *strong or weak in the questions?*

 ActiveTeach for 3A: Pronunciation Coach

B ▶ APPLY. Listen. Circle *do* with a short,...

1. Read the directions. Say: *In these sentences,* do *sometimes has a strong pronunciation and it sometimes has a weak one.*
2. Play the audio. Students listen and circle *do* with a short, weak pronunciation.
3. Review the correct answers with students.
4. Put students in pairs to practice the conversations.
5. Call on students to say the conversations for the class.

4 CONVERSATION

A ▶ LISTEN AND READ. Then listen and repeat.

1. Note: This conversation is the same one students heard in Exercise 2B on page 34.
2. Play the audio. Students listen and read along silently. Ask: *Which examples of* do *are strong?* (Actually, we <u>do</u>. She works in a bank, and I <u>do</u>, too.) *Which are weak?* (<u>Do</u> you have a lot in common?)
3. Resume the audio. Students listen and repeat.

B WORK TOGETHER. Practice the...

1. Read the directions.
2. Model the conversation with an above-level student. Emphasize the pronunciations of *do* practiced in Exercise 3A and 3B.
3. Pair students to take turns playing A and B. Walk around and check that students are using the correct pronunciation of *do*.

> **Teaching Tip: Formative assessment**
>
> Model the conversation with multiple students to check pronunciation. Formative assessment can inform instructional choices around additional practice.

C CREATE. Make new conversations. Use the...

1. Read the directions. Remind students that the color of the boxes matches the color of the fill-in blanks.
2. Write the conversation on the board. Fill in the blanks with information from the boxes. Ask a pair of on-level students to read the conversation.
3. Erase the words in the blanks and ask two above-level students to make up a new conversation.
4. Tell pairs to take turns playing A and B and to use the vocabulary words to fill in the blanks.
5. Walk around during the activity and check students' pronunciation of *do*.
6. Tell students to stand, mingle, and practice the conversation with several new partners.

■■ MULTILEVEL INSTRUCTION for 4C

Pre-level scaffolding Ask pairs to write in their information before they practice.

Above-level expansion Tell pairs to practice without looking at the conversation.

D MAKE CONNECTIONS. Talk about your...

1. Ask two on-level students to read the example.
2. Read the directions. Tell students that A asks questions and B answers them with true information.
3. Play B and model the conversation with an above-level student.
4. Tell students to stand, mingle, and practice the conversation with several partners for five minutes.
5. Walk around and participate in the activity. Model clear pronunciation.
6. After five minutes, tell students to return to their seats. Call on students to tell the class about someone they talked to.

Self-Directed Learning

Point out the blue bar. Ask students if they can do the lesson learning objective or if they need more practice. Tell them to check one of the boxes. Assign Extra Practice as needed.

> **Extra Practice**
>
>   p. 20

Listening and Speaking

3 PRONUNCIATION

A ▶ PRACTICE. Listen. Then listen and repeat.

Do you have a lot in common?
Do you have brothers or sisters?
Do you work in a bank?

Pronunciation of *do*

Do often has a short, weak pronunciation before *you*. *Do you* often sounds like "d'ya."

B ▶ APPLY. Listen. Circle *do* with a short, weak pronunciation.

1. (Do) you have any brothers?
   Yes, I do.

2. (Do) we look alike?
   Yes, you do.

3. (Do) you look like your sister?
   Yes, I do.

4 CONVERSATION

A ▶ LISTEN AND READ. Then listen and repeat.

A: Tina, is that your sister?
B: Yes, it is. That's my sister, Lili. Do we look alike?
A: Yes, you do. You look a lot alike. Do you have a lot in common?
B: Actually, we do. She works in a bank, and I work in a bank, too. She's really talkative, and I'm really talkative.

B WORK TOGETHER. Practice the conversation in Exercise A.

C CREATE. Make new conversations. Use the words in the boxes.

A: Tina, is that your _____?
B: Yes, it is. That's my _____. Do we look alike?
A: Yes, you do. You look a lot alike. Do you have a lot in common?
B: Actually, we do. She works in a _____, and I work in a _____, too. She's really _____, and I'm really _____.

niece
aunt
cousin

restaurant
clothing store
hospital

outgoing
shy
laid-back

D MAKE CONNECTIONS. Talk about your family. Do you have a lot in common?

A: Do you have any brothers or sisters?
B: Yes, I do. I have two brothers.
A: Do you have a lot in common?

I can talk about what people have in common. ■   I need more practice. ■

For more practice, go to MyEnglishLab.

6 Lesson

Simple Present: *Yes / No* questions and short answers

start here

| Simple present: *Yes / No* questions and short answers | | | | | | |

| **Do** | you
they | **have** a lot in common? | **Yes,** | I
they | **do.** | No, | I
they | **don't.** |
| **Does** | she
he | | | she
he | **does.** | | she
he | **doesn't.** |

A MATCH. **Choose the correct answers to the questions.**

1. _c_ Do you have a big family?
2. _a_ Do they work in a bank?
3. _f_ Does he work in an office?
4. _e_ Do I work more than Dan?
5. _d_ Does she have a lot in common with you?
6. _b_ Do we look alike?

a. Yes, they do.
b. Yes, we do.
c. No, I don't.
d. Yes, she does.
e. No, you don't.
f. Yes, he does.

Grammar Watch

- Use *do / does* + subject + the base form of the verb in questions.
- Use *do / does* or *don't / doesn't* in short answers. Don't use the main verb.

B IDENTIFY. **Cross out the incorrect words.**

1. **A: Do / ~~Does~~** you have any sisters?
   B: Yes, I **do / ~~does~~**.

2. **A: ~~Do~~ / Does** he visit his family often?
   B: No, he ~~does~~ / **doesn't**.

3. **A: Do / ~~Does~~** they work for a big company?
   B: No, they ~~do~~ / **don't**. It's a small business.

4. **A: Do / ~~Does~~** your parents work?
   B: Yes, they **do** / ~~does~~.

5. **A: ~~Do~~ / Does** your niece have children?
   B: Yes, she **does** / ~~doesn't~~.

6. **A: ~~Do~~ / Does** your son live in Dallas?
   B: Yes, he **does** / ~~doesn't~~.

Self-Directed Learning

State the **lesson objective**. Say: *In this lesson, we will learn to ask and answer* Yes/No *questions in simple present.*

Simple present: *Yes/no* questions and short answers

 ActiveTeach: Grammar Discovery

1. Warm up. Say: *The conversation on page 35 used this grammar.* Turn back to page 35. Point to the sentences in exercise 4A and then write:
   - *Do we look alike?*
   - *Yes, you do.*
2. Say: *Let's look at another example.* Write: *Does she work in a bank?*
3. Ask: *How do these questions begin?* (*Do / Does*) Underline *Do* and *Does* as students notice the pattern.
4. Tell students to look at the grammar charts.
5. Read the example with *they*: *Do they have a lot in common. / Yes, they do.*
6. Have students read questions from the chart using different subjects. Have different students answer the questions using short answers.
7. Read the **Grammar Watch** note.
8. Say: *Use the base form of the main verb in questions.* Point to the base forms on the board. Say: *Don't use the main verb in the short answers.* Read a few answers to make this point.

 ActiveTeach: Grammar Coach

Ⓐ **MATCH. Choose the correct answers to the…**

1. Read the directions and model the example.
2. Students write the letter of the answer on the line next to the question.
3. Students compare answers with a partner.
4. Call on students to read the answers.

▰▰ **EXPANSION: Speaking practice for A**
Students repeat the exercise in pairs, with one student asking the question and the other student providing the correct answers.

Ⓑ **IDENTIFY. Cross out the incorrect words.**

1. Read the directions. Write item 1. Ask: *For A, do we use* Do *or* Does? (*Do*) *Why?* (the subject is *you*). Ask: *For B, do we use* Do *or* Does? (*Do*) *Why?* (the subject is *I*).
2. Tell students to circle the subjects in each sentence.
3. Tell students to compare their answers in pairs.
4. As they work, walk around and ask students how they know which word to use.
5. Call on students to give answers. Ask: *What information helps you decide which word is correct?*

Grammar

C **APPLY. Write the questions. Then look at...**

1. Read the directions. Tell students to look at the picture. Ask: *Who has a green shirt?* (Brad) *Who has a red dress?* (Meg) Point to the city names. Ask: *Who lives in Vancouver?* (Emily and Todd)

2. Write item 1 on the board. Ask: *Do we use do or does?* (do) Ask: *What information helps you decide which word is correct?* (*Sarah and Brad* is the same as *they*.)

3. Walk around and remind students to use contractions when the answer is *no*.

4. Tell students to compare their answers in pairs.

5. Check answers by playing A and calling on students to answer.

6. *Optional:* Pair students to take turns playing each role.

■ MULTILEVEL INSTRUCTION for C

Above-level expansion Students complete the activity in pairs. Student B covers the questions and uses the picture to answer the questions. Students take turns playing each role.

Show what you know!

1. THINK ABOUT IT. Complete the questions to...

1. Elicit information about places where students and their family members live and work. This can be done as a class. Write the places on the board.

2. Read the directions. Tell students to pick one place and use it to complete all three questions in Step 1.

2. TALK ABOUT IT. Student A, read your...

1. Read the directions. Tell students to take notes about their partner's answers.

2. Play A and model with an above-level student.

3. Pair students. Walk around and check that questions begin with *Do*.

■ EXPANSION: Grammar and Speaking for 2

1. Students do the same activities, but in groups of 3, using *he* and *she*.

2. On a piece of paper, students write the following sentences about themselves:
   I have family in _____.
   I live in _____.
   I work in _____.

3. Form groups of 3. Students read their sentences and take notes about their partners (for example, *Nina—family in New York*).

4. Tell students to take turns asking and answering questions about members of their group, using *he* and *she*. One student is the subject of the sentences, and the other two students ask and answer questions about him or her. For example:
   A: *Does she have family in Chicago?*
   B: *No, she doesn't.*

5. Walk around and check for the correct forms of *do*.

6. Have a few groups volunteer to ask and answer their sentences in front of the class.

3. WRITE ABOUT IT. Now write about your...

1. Read the directions and the example. Tell students to write four sentences.

2. Ask students to check each other's sentences:
   • Sentences should begin with a capital letter and end with an end mark.
   • Sentences should use the correct form of verbs for *he* and *she*.
   • Negative sentences should use *doesn't* + base form of a verb.

3. Have students volunteer to write their sentences on the board.

Self-Directed Learning

Point out the blue bar. Ask students if they can do the lesson learning objective or if they need more practice. Tell them to check one of the boxes. Assign Extra Practice as needed.

Extra Practice		
MyEnglishLab	Workbook	p. 20

Grammar

Start here to seven

C **APPLY.** Write the questions. Then look at the picture and write short answers.

1. **A:** ___Do___ Sarah and Brad ___have___ a daughter? (have)

   B: _Yes, they do._

2. **A:** ___Does___ Meg ___live___ in Tampa? (live)

   B: _Yes, she does._

3. **A:** ___Do___ Brian and Katie ___have___ two sons? (have)

   B: _No, they don't._

4. **A:** ___Does___ Emily ___have___ brown hair? (have)

   B: _No, she doesn't._

5. **A:** ___Do___ Brian and Todd ___have___ glasses? (have)

   B: _Yes, they do._

6. **A:** ___Does___ James ___have___ a brother? (have)

   B: _No, he doesn't._

7. **A:** ___Do___ Emily and Todd ___live___ in Seattle? (live)

   B: _No, they don't._

8. **A:** ___Does___ Sarah ___have___ blond hair? (have)

   B: _Yes, she does._

Show what you know!

1. **THINK ABOUT IT.** Complete the questions to ask a partner.

   Do you have any family in _____?

   Do you live in _____? Do you work in _____?

2. **TALK ABOUT IT.** Student A, read your questions. Student B, answer the questions. Take turns.

   A: Do you have any family in Chicago?
   B: Yes, I do. My brother lives in Chicago.
   A: Do you live in Chicago?
   B: No, I don't.

3. **WRITE ABOUT IT.** Now write about your partner.

   Jan has a brother. He lives in Chicago. Jan doesn't live in Chicago. She lives . . .

I can ask and answer *Yes / No* questions in simple present. ☐   I need more practice. ☐

For more practice, go to MyEnglishLab.

Lesson 7

Workplace, Life, and Community Skills

Mailing services

A **MATCH.** Label the pictures with the words from the box.

book of stamps   letter   tracking receipt
large envelope   package

1. _____large envelope_____   4. _____tracking receipt_____
2. _____book of stamps_____   5. _____package_____
3. _____letter_____

B **INTERPRET.** Read the chart. Circle *True* or *False*.

Service	Package or letter	Speed	Service	Package or letter	Speed
Priority Mail Express	70 pounds or less	1 day	First-Class Mail	3.5 ounces or less for standard-sized envelopes; 13 ounces or less for large envelopes and small packages	1-3 business days
Priority Mail	70 pounds or less	1–3 business days	Retail Ground	70 pounds or less	2-8 business days

1. It takes three days for a Priority Mail Express package to arrive.   True   **False**
2. You can send a 30-pound package by First-Class Mail.   True   **False**
3. You can send a letter by Priority Mail Express.   **True**   False
4. You can send a 2-pound package by Priority Mail.   **True**   False
5. It takes 1-3 days for a Retail Ground package to arrive.   True   **False**
6. Retail Ground is the fastest way to mail a package.   True   **False**

Correlations

ELPS Level 2: 1, 2, 3, 4, 5, 6, 7, 8, 9, 10
CCRS Level A: W.1.7, W.1.8
CASAS Reading: RDG 1.7, 1.8, 2.2, 2.3, 3.2, 4.2, 4.9
CASAS Listening: L2.1, 2.3, 4.2
CASAS Competencies: 0.1.2, 0.1.5, 2.4.2, 2.4.3, 4.5.6, 7.4.4, 7.7.3
Complete standards language available on the Pearson English Portal.

Self-Directed Learning

State the **lesson objective**. Say: *In this lesson, we will learn to ask about mailing services.*

A MATCH. Label the pictures with the words...

1. Write *mail*. Ask: *Do you write letters to friends and family in your country? Do you send them packages? Where do you go to mail packages?* (to the post office or other parcel service) *What does the clerk do with the package before he or she tells you the cost to mail it?* (weighs it)
2. Read the directions. Say the words in the box and have students repeat.
3. Students work individually to complete the task and then compare answers with a partner.
4. Call on students to give the answers.

B INTERPRET. Read the chart. Circle *True* or...

1. Say: *Look at the chart of mailing services.* Ask: *How many different ways are there to send a letter or package?* (four)
2. Tell students to look at the information in the chart under *Speed*. Draw a continuum from *slow* to *fast* on the board. Make three marks on the continuum. Point to each mark and ask the class to say the name of the service and the number of days it takes. Label the marks: *Retail ground: 2–8 days; Priority Mail / First-Class Mail: 1–3 days; Priority Mail Express: 1 day.*
3. Tell students to look at the information under *Package or letter.* Ask: *What weights do you see?* Elicit and write: *70 pounds, 3.5 ounces,* and *13 ounces.*
4. If possible, bring in a cereal box. Point out the weight and say: *This box of cereal is a little more / less than 13 ounces.* Ask: *What else weighs about 13 ounces?* List students' ideas on the board.
5. Point to something in the class that weighs about 70 pounds. Ask: *What else weighs about 70 pounds?* List students' ideas on the board.

6. Read the directions. Students circle *True* or *False* for each statement.
7. Call on students to read the statements and say if they are true or false. For each false sentence, elicit a sentences with correct information from the class.

Numeracy: Math skills

In this section, students learn about weights in the U.S.

Weight	Abbreviation	Equivalent (=)
1 pound	1 lb	16 ounces (oz) .45 kilograms (kg)
1 ounce	1 oz	28.35 grams .028 kg
1 kilogram	1 kg	2.2 pounds (lb)

■ EXPANSION: Numeracy practice for B

1. Write the Numeracy chart. Tell students to copy it.
2. Ask: *In your native country, what units of weight do you use?* (probably grams and kilograms)
3. Point to the equivalent information in the chart. Say: *To convert something from pounds to kilograms, multiply by 0.45. To convert something from ounces to grams, multiply by 28.35.*
4. Have students use calculators and convert 70 pounds to kilograms and 13 ounces to grams. Elicit and write: 70 pounds = 32 kilograms; 13 ounces = about 369 grams.

Language Note

Abbreviations for U.S. weights are not used in the lesson. However, point out the abbreviations for ounces (oz) and pounds (lb) when presenting the chart. These abbreviations are commonly used in the U.S.

■ EXPANSION: Speaking practice for B

1. Put students in pairs to take turns asking and answering *yes/no* questions about the chart and the statements (for example, *Does it take three days for a Priority Mail Express package to arrive? No, it doesn't. It takes one day to arrive.*).
2. Walk around and provide help as needed.
3. Call on students to ask a classmate a question.

Workplace, Life, and Community Skills

C DECIDE. Look at the list of mailing services...

1. Read the directions.
2. Say: *First, you decide how to send your letter or package, for example, by Priority Mail Express or Priority Mail, and you tell the clerk. Then the clerk might ask if you want any extra services. You pay extra for these.*
3. Tell students to look at the chart. Ask: *How many different services are there?* (six) Say the name of each service and ask the class to repeat.
4. Tell students to read the descriptions of each service silently and to underline the most important words in the descriptions.
5. Read the description of Certified Mail and explain *signed for.* Say: *With Certified Mail, the mail carrier won't leave a letter or package unless someone signs their name to show they received it.*
6. Read the description of Insurance and explain *lost* and *damaged.* Say: *With Insurance, you get your money back if something bad happens to your package—if it doesn't arrive or it arrives broken.*
7. Pair students. Say: *Student A, read what the first customer wants. Student B, say which mailing service is the best for the customer. Switch roles and repeat with the second customer.*
8. Call on two pairs of students—one to read what each customer wants, the other to suggest a mailing service (for the man: Certificate of Mailing and Delivery Confirmation or Certified Mail; for the woman: Insurance).

Teaching Tip: Authentic materials

Enhance the activities on pages 38 and 39 with authentic materials. Bring in shipping labels for express mail, priority mail, first-class mail, and parcel post and forms for extra mailing services.

D **LISTEN. Write the missing words.**

1. Read the directions.
2. Direct students' attention to the icons. Ask: *What do these mean?* (nothing explosive, nothing that can catch fire, nothing toxic) Point out that these things are *hazardous materials.*
3. Play the audio. Students listen.
4. Play the audio again. Students listen and fill in the blanks. If necessary, pause audio to allow students more time.
5. Now tell students to listen again and check their answers. Tell students to capitalize the names of mailing services. Play the audio again.
6. Ask one pair to role-play the completed conversation for the class. Correct as needed.

E ROLE-PLAY. Create another conversation...

1. Read the directions. Write: *package or letter, service,* and *speed.* Tell students to replace these details in the conversation.
2. Put students in pairs to role-play the new conversation, and then switch roles.
3. Call on volunteers to perform their role-play for the class.

 ActiveTeach for E: Role-Play Support

F GO ONLINE. **Search for mailing services...**

1. Read the directions. Ask students what they would search in English if they wanted to find nearby mailing services.
2. Write the search string: *mailing services near me.* Have students search the internet and write the names in the space provided.
3. Compare research as a class. Write a complete list of nearby mailing services that students discovered.

Digital Skills for F

Tell students that they can also find neighborhood services from maps, such as Google Maps. They can put the search term in the search box, and the map will show where the services are.

 ActiveTeach: Review

Self-Directed Learning

Point out the blue bar. Ask students if they can do the lesson learning objective or if they need more practice. Tell them to check one of the boxes. Assign Extra Practice as needed.

Extra Practice

| MyEnglishLab | Workbook pp. 21–22 | English Portal | Life Skills Writing |

Workplace, Life, and Community Skills

C **DECIDE.** Look at the list of mailing services. Then read what each customer wants. Which mailing service is best for each customer?

Extra Mailing Services

Certificate of Mailing
You get a receipt to show you mailed the item on a certain date.

Delivery Confirmation
You can find out when your package is delivered.

Certified Mail
You get a receipt to show you mailed the item. You can find out when the item is delivered and who signed for it.

Insurance
If your package is lost or damaged, you get money back.

Registered Mail
You get a receipt to show you mailed the item. Your item is both certified and insured.

COD (Collect on Delivery)
The person who receives the item pays for the cost of mailing.

I need to show my manager a receipt that says I mailed this letter today. I want to know when it arrives, but I don't need insurance.

I'm sending a gift to my brother. I want my money back if the package gets lost. I don't need the package certified.

D ▶ **LISTEN.** Write the missing words.

Customer: Hello. I'd like to mail this _____package_____.

Clerk: How do you want to send it?

Customer: How long does _____Retail Ground_____ take?

Clerk: Two to eight days.

Customer: Okay. I'll send it _____Priority Mail_____.

Clerk: Do you want _____Delivery Confirmation_____ or insurance?

Customer: Yes. _____Insurance_____, please.

Clerk: Does it contain any hazardous materials?

Customer: No.

E **ROLE-PLAY.** Create another conversation about mailing services.

F GO ONLINE. Search for mailing services near you. Write the address of the mailing service nearest you. What kind of packages can you send with this service?

I can ask about mailing services. ▪   I need more practice. ▪

For more practice, go to MyEnglishLab.

Lesson 8 — Ask about people

1 BEFORE YOU LISTEN

MAKE CONNECTIONS. What are game shows? Do you watch or listen to game shows on TV or on podcasts? Which shows do you watch?

2 LISTEN

A **PREDICT. Look at the picture. What is the podcast about?** *(Answers will vary.)*

a. a person's job
b. a person's family

B ▶ **LISTEN FOR MAIN IDEA. Complete the sentence.**

The name of the podcast is _____.
a. Oliver Marley and Family
b. The Rules of the Game
c. They're Your Family Now!

C ▶ **LISTEN FOR DETAILS. Who are the questions about?**

a. Trevor's wife
b. Trevor's in-laws
c. Marley's family

D ▶ **EXPAND. Listen to the whole conversation. Answer the questions.**

1. Where do Trevor's wife's grandparents live?
   a. with Trevor
   b. in San Antonio
   c. in a big house

2. How many sisters does Trevor's mother-in-law have?
   a. two
   b. three
   c. five

3. What does Trevor's brother-in-law do?
   a. He's an artist.
   b. He's an engineer.
   c. He's an accountant.

4. When does Ella work?
   a. at night
   b. during the day
   c. on weekends

Correlations

ELPS Level 2: 2, 7
CCRS Level A: SL.1.1, SL.K.6
CASAS Reading: RDG 1.7, 2.2, 2.3
CASAS Listening: L2.1, 2.3, 4.1, 4.2, 6.1, 6.2
CASAS Competencies: 0.1.2, 0.1.4, 0.1.5, 0.1.6, 0.2.1
Complete standards language available on the Pearson English Portal.

Self-Directed Learning

State the **lesson objective**. Say: *In this lesson, we will learn to ask about people.*

1 BEFORE YOU LISTEN

MAKE CONNECTIONS. What are game shows?...

1. Read the directions. As needed, explain: *A game show is a television program. People play games or answer questions to win money and prizes.* Say: *Raise your hand if you watch or listen to game shows.* Ask several students: *Which show do you watch?* Write the names.
2. Ask: *Do you know these game shows? What do people do? Play games? Answer questions?* Elicit simple descriptions of a few of the shows.

2 LISTEN

A PREDICT. Look at the picture. What is the...

1. Read the directions. Say: *On this podcast, people answer questions. What do you think they answer questions about?*
2. Students circle the letter of the answer.
3. Elicit the correct answer. Ask: *Why do you think so?* (The show is called *They're Your Family Now!*)
4. Tell students to point to the man with the microphone. Say: *He is the host. He asks the questions.* Tell students to point to Trevor. Say: *He is the contestant. He answers the questions.* Write *host* and *contestant* and tell students to label their pictures.

B ▶ LISTEN FOR MAIN IDEA. Complete the...

1. Read the directions.
2. Play the audio. Ask: *What's the name of this podcast?* Elicit the answer.
3. Ask: *What do contestants on* They're Your Family Now! *answer questions about?* Write the ideas on the board. Circle any that are correct. As needed, add *their in-laws* or *their wife's or husband's family.*

Teaching Tip: Use the script

Optional: Remember that if students need additional support, tell them to read the Audio Script on page 267 as they listen to the conversations.

C ▶ LISTEN FOR DETAILS. Who are the...

1. Tell students to read the directions and the answer choices silently.
2. Play the audio. Students listen and circle the letter of the correct answer.
3. Students compare answers with a partner. Elicit the correct answer.

D ▶ EXPAND. Listen to the whole...

1. Read the directions. Tell students to read the questions and answer choices silently.
2. Ask: *Where is San Antonio?* (in Texas) If possible, point out the location of San Antonio on a U.S. map.
3. Tell students to look at item 3. Say *artist, engineer,* and *accountant* and ask the class to repeat. Say a description of each job and ask the class to call out the job. Say: *designs roads, bridges, machines, etc.* (an engineer); *paints, draws, or sculpts* (an artist); and *keeps records of the money spent or received by a person or company* (an accountant).
4. Play the audio. Students listen and circle the letter of the correct answers.
5. Students compare answers with a partner. Tell them to take turns asking and answering the questions.
6. Call on students to ask one question each and then choose a classmate to answer.
7. *Optional:* Ask: *Which question did Trevor not answer correctly?* (item 3) *How much money has Trevor won so far?* ($300)

Career Awareness: Accountant

Accountants keep records of money spent or received by a person or company. Accountants work in offices of all kinds. They usually have a bachelor's degree in accounting. They need to be good at math.

■ EXPANSION: Career awareness for 2D

Ask students about the job in this lesson: *What do accountants do? Where do accountants work? Do you need to study to be an accountant? Do you want to be an accountant?*

Listening and Speaking

3 CONVERSATION

A ▶ LISTEN AND READ. Then listen and repeat.

1. Read the directions.
2. Play the audio. Students listen and read along silently.
3. Tell students to find and underline the questions.
4. Ask: *What does* Really? *mean? Say: Really? shows surprise or interest. It usually does not require an answer.*
5. Resume the audio. Students listen and repeat.

B WORK TOGETHER. Practice the...

1. Read the directions.
2. Pair students to take turns playing each role.
3. Call on volunteers to read the conversation aloud.

C CREATE. Make new conversations...

1. Read the directions. Remind students that the color of the boxes matches the color of the fill-in blanks.
2. Model the conversation with two above-level students. Use information from the boxes.
3. Pair students to take turns playing each role. Walk around during the activity and provide help as needed.
4. Call on volunteers to practice the conversation in front of the class.

> **Career Awareness: Engineer**
>
> There are many kinds of **engineers**. They use science and math and work on designing projects like roads, bridges, and buildings. Engineers need at least a bachelor's degree in their field.

> **Career Awareness: Hospital technician**
>
> **Hospital technicians** work in laboratories and help doctors test and treat patients. A college degree is usually required.

> **Career Awareness: Security guard**
>
> **Security guards** monitor buildings and sites to keep them safe and prevent vandalism, fire, and other harmful situations. A high school diploma is usually required.

■ EXPANSION: Career awareness for 3C

Ask students about the jobs in this lesson: *What do engineers do? Where do they work? Do you need to study to be an engineer? Do you want to be an engineer?* Repeat these questions for hospital technician and security guard.

D MAKE CONNECTIONS. Talk about your...

1. **Scaffold:** Demonstrate that students should each draw three circles on their own paper and write the name of a family member within each circle. Tell students to draw lines radiating out from the circles and list facts about each person: their relation, what they do, where they live, and any other information.
2. Read the directions.
3. Pair students and tell them to take turns telling each other about their family.
4. Tell students to stand, mingle, and practice with several new partners.

Self-Directed Learning

Point out the blue bar. Ask students if they can do the lesson learning objective or if they need more practice. Tell them to check one of the boxes. Assign Extra Practice as needed.

> **Extra Practice**
>
>   p. 23

Listening and Speaking

3 CONVERSATION

A ▶ **LISTEN AND READ. Then listen and repeat.**

A: Where does your son live?
B: He lives in San Antonio.
A: How many children does he have?
B: Well, he has two sons and two daughters.
A: Really? What does he do?
B: He works in an office. He's an engineer.

B **WORK TOGETHER. Practice the conversation in Exercise A.**

C **CREATE. Make new conversations. Use the words in the boxes.**

A: Where does your _____ live?
B: He lives in San Antonio.
A: How many _____ does he have?
B: Well, he has two _____ and
   two _____ .
A: Really? What does he do?
B: He works in _____ .
   He's _____ .

> cousin
> father-in-law
> son-in-law

> sons
> daughters
> brothers
> sisters

> an office, an accountant
> a hospital, a technician
> a school, a security guard

D **MAKE CONNECTIONS. Talk about your family. What do they do? Where do they live?**

I have a little brother. He is in school. He lives with my parents in Oklahoma.

I can ask about people. ■   I need more practice. ■

For more practice, go to MyEnglishLab.

Grammar

Simple Present: Information questions and short answers

Simple present: Information questions and answers

When	do does	you they he she	**work**?	At night.
Where	do does	you they he she	**live**?	In San Antonio.
How many brothers	do does	you they he she	**have**?	Two.

Grammar Watch

Other question words:
What does she do?
How often do you see them?

A IDENTIFY. Cross out the incorrect words. Then match the questions and answers.

1. __b__ How many days **do / does** you work?
2. __e__ What **do / does** your husband do?
3. __d__ When **do / does** they work?
4. __c__ How many grandchildren **do / does** they have?
5. __a__ Where **do / does** your parents live?
6. __f__ What **do / does** his co-workers have in common?

a. On Green Street.
b. I work six days a week.
c. Two.
d. On Monday, Thursday, and Friday.
e. He is an electrician.
f. They're cheerful.

B COMPLETE. Write the questions.

1. What _____do_____ your brothers _____do_____? (do)
2. How often _____do_____ your cousins _____visit_____? (visit)
3. When _____does_____ your husband _____go_____ to work? (go)
4. Where _____does_____ he _____live_____? (live)
5. How many children _____does_____ she _____have_____? (have)

I can use simple present information questions and answers. ■   I need more practice. ■

For more practice, go to MyEnglishLab.

Correlations

ELPS Level 2: 2, 7, 10
CCRS Level A: L.1.1
CASAS Reading: RDG 1.7, 2.9
CASAS Competencies: 0.1.2, 0.1.5
Complete standards language available on the Pearson English Portal.

Self-Directed Learning

State the **lesson objective**. Say: *In this lesson, we will learn to use simple present information questions and answers.*

Simple present: Information questions and answers

 ActiveTeach: Grammar Discovery

1. Warm up. Say: *The conversation on page 41 used this grammar.* Turn back to page 41. Point to the sentences in Exercise 3A and then write:
   - *Where does your son live?*
   - *He lives in San Antonio.*
   - *How many children does he have?*
2. Ask: *What words begin the questions? (Where, How many)* As students notice the pattern, circle the question words.
3. Tell students to look at the grammar charts. Read one sentence for each question word and have students repeat. Read the **Grammar Watch** note and have students repeat the questions.
4. Write a list of the question words in this unit (*when, where, how many, what, how often*). Say: *We use different question words for different information. For time, what word do I use? (when) For place, what word do I use? (where) For number, what word do I use? (how many)*
5. Tell students to cover the information questions in the grammar chart and look only at the answers. Read the information questions in random order. Ask the class to call out the answers.

 ActiveTeach: Grammar Coach

Teaching tip: Color code to teach structures

Copy grammar charts using different colors for different structures (question words, *do/does*, pronouns). This helps students see patterns.

A **IDENTIFY. Cross out the incorrect words...**
1. Read the directions.
2. Write item 1. Ask: *Why is the word* do? (because the subject is *you*) Circle *you*. Then read the question and elicit the answer.
3. Tell students to circle the subject in each question before completing the item.
4. Tell students to match the questions and answers.
5. Call on students and ask the questions in order. Elicit the correct answer.
6. Have students practice asking and answering the questions in pairs.

EXPANSION: Speaking practice for A

Have students work in pairs to take turns asking the questions and providing different answers.

B **COMPLETE. Write the questions.**
1. Read the directions.
2. Write item 1. Point to *do* in the first blank. Ask: *Why is the answer* do? (because the subject is *your brothers*) Point to *do* in the second blank and the *do* in parenthesis. Ask: *Why does this* do *not change?* (it is the base form) Circle *your*. Then read the question and elicit the answer.
3. Students complete and compare answers with a partner.
4. Call on students to read the questions aloud. Ask them to justify their answers.

EXPANSION: Speaking and writing practice for B
1. Write: *Every Saturday, At 9 p.m., In a store, Three,* and *She's a nurse.*
2. Put students in pairs to write questions for each answer (for example, *How often do you play soccer? When does she go to bed?*).
3. Call on students to read their questions aloud.
4. Have students find new partners and take turns asking and answering their questions.

Self-Directed Learning

Point out the blue bar. Ask students if they can do the lesson learning objective or if they need more practice. Tell them to check one of the boxes. Assign Extra Practice as needed.

Extra Practice

  p. 23

Writing

Correlations

ELPS Level 2: 3, 10
CCRS Level A: W.1.2, W.1.5, L.1.1
CASAS Reading: RDG 1.7, 1.8, 2.1
CASAS Listening: L2.1, 2.3
CASAS Competencies: 0.1.2, 0.1.5, 0.1.6
Complete standards language available on the Pearson English Portal.

Self-Directed Learning

1. State the **lesson objective**. Say: *In this lesson, we will learn to use capital letters and commas in names of places.*
2. Say: *You will write about a family member.*

1 STUDY THE MODEL

1. Read the directions.
2. Point to the paragraph. Ask: *What is the title of the model?* (My Sister)
3. **Scaffold** the model. Write as a graphic organizer:

1	Family member	
2	Family member's city	
3	Writer's city	
4	Ways to keep in touch	

4. Tell students to read the text and read the questions independently. Call on students to answer the questions. Write the information in the graphic organizer on the board.

2 PLAN YOUR WRITING

1. Erase the information in the right-hand column of the graphic organizer on the board.
2. Read the directions.
3. Model with a student. The student asks the teacher the questions.
4. Write the information into the graphic organizer.
5. Tell students to make their own graphic organizer on a piece of paper.
6. Have students work in pairs to ask and answer the questions and complete the graphic organizers with their own information.

3 WRITE

1. Read the directions aloud.
2. Point to the **Writing Skill**. Read it aloud while students listen.
3. Write: *I live in miami florida.*

4. Ask: *What words need to be capitalized?* (Miami, Florida) *Why?* (We capitalize the names of places.) Make the corrections.
5. Ask: *What is missing between Miami and Florida?* (a comma) Add the comma to the sentence. *Why?* (We write a comma between the name of a city and the name of a state or country.)
6. Point to the writing model. Ask: *What cities are capitalized?* (Shenzhen and San Francisco)
7. Use your information in the graphic organizer from Exercise 2 to write sentences in a paragraph. Include indentation. Leave out the capitalization and comma between place names.
8. Ask: *What do I need to capitalize? Where do I need a comma?* Add to your paragraph.
9. Tell students to write. Circulate to make sure students are writing in paragraph form.

 ActiveTeach for 3: Writing Support

4 CHECK YOUR WRITING

1. Read the directions aloud. Point to the **Writing Checklist**. Call on students to read the checklist items aloud.
2. Pair students to review their writings together. Say: *Read your sentences with a partner. Use the Writing Checklist.* For additional help, remind students that a correct sentence:
   - *begins with a capital letter*
   - *has a subject*
   - *has a verb*
   - *has a period*
   - *is a complete idea*
3. Walk around and verify that students are using the checklist. Collect the papers for review or put them in the students' writing portfolios.

Teaching Tip: Digital skills

Use the digital literacy resources on MEL to help students learn to use the keyboard to make uppercase letters, hard returns, and indents.

Self-Directed Learning

Point out the blue bar. Ask students if they can do the lesson learning objective or if they need more practice. Tell them to check one of the boxes. Assign Extra Practice as needed.

Extra Practice

 CCRS Plus   p. 24

Writing

Write about a family member

1 STUDY THE MODEL

READ. Answer the questions.

> Lan Woo
>
> My Sister
>
> I have one sister. Her name is
> Ting. She lives in Shenzhen, China.
> I live in San Francisco, California,
> but we keep in touch. We text each
> other every day. We also talk on the
> computer on weekends.

1. Who did Lan write about? Ting, her sister.
2. Where does Lan's sister live? Shenzhen, China.
3. Where does Lan live? San Francisco, California.
4. How do they keep in touch? They text each other every day. They also talk on the computer on weekends.

2 PLAN YOUR WRITING

WORK TOGETHER. Ask and answer the questions.

1. What family member are you writing about?
2. Where does your family member live?
3. Where do you live?
4. How do you keep in touch?

Writing Skill: Use capital letters and commas in names of places

Names of places begin with capital letters. For example:

San Francisco

Write a comma (,) between the name of a city and the name of a state or country. For example:

Shenzhen, China

San Francisco, California

3 WRITE

Now write about a family member. Use the model, the Writing Skill, and your ideas from Exercise 2 to help you.

4 CHECK YOUR WRITING

WORK TOGETHER. Read the checklist. Read your writing aloud. Revise your writing.

WRITING CHECKLIST

☐ The paragraph answers the questions in Exercise 2.

☐ The names of places begin with capital letters.

☐ There is a comma between the name of a city and state or country.

I can use capital letters and commas in names of places. ■   I need more practice. ■

For more practice, go to MyEnglishLab.

Soft Skills at Work

Separate work life and home life

1 MEET BO

Read about one of his workplace skills.

> I separate work life from home life. I love my family, and I love my work, but when I'm at work, I do my work. When I'm at home, I spend time with my family. I try to keep the two separate.

2 BO'S PROBLEM

READ. Circle *True* or *False*.

Bo is a waiter. He has a new job in a restaurant. He is busy today. There are a lot of people.

Suddenly Bo's wife and young daughter come into the restaurant. They want to visit Bo at his new job. Bo's daughter runs toward him. She shouts, "Hi, Daddy!"

1. Bo serves food in a restaurant.   (True)   False
2. Bo has a lot of work today.   (True)   False
3. Bo's friends are visiting him at the restaurant.   True   (False)

3 BO'S SOLUTION

WORK TOGETHER. Bo is good at separating work life and home life. What does he say to his family? Explain your answer.

1. Bo says, "Hi! I'm happy to see you, but I can't talk right now. Let's talk tonight at home."
2. Bo says, "Hi! I'm happy to see you. Come see the kitchen! I'll get you something to eat!"
3. Bo says, "Hi! I'm happy to see you. I'll talk to you after I help these customers."
4. Bo _____ .

Show what you know!

1. **THINK ABOUT IT.** Do you separate work life and home life? How do you separate work life and home life at work? At home? Give examples.

2. **WRITE ABOUT IT.** Write your example in your Skills Log.

I separate work life and home life. Sometimes I have a hard day at work, but I try not to talk about it at home.

I can give an example of how I separate work life and home life. ☐

Unit Review: Go back to page 25. Which unit goals can you check off?

Lesson **11** | Soft Skills at Work

Correlations

CASAS Reading: RDG 1.7, 1.8, 3.2
CASAS Listening: L2.1, L.2.3, L.4.1, L.4.2
CASAS Competencies: 0.1.2, 0.1.4, 0.1.5, 0.1.6, 0.2.1, 7.5.5
Complete standards language available on the Pearson English Portal.

Self-Directed Learning

State the **lesson objective**. Say: *In this lesson, we will give an example of how we separate work life and home life.*

1 MEET BO

1. Ask: *What is the title of this lesson?* (Separate work life and home life) Ask: *What does* separate *mean?* (to put two things in different places)
2. Write: *Workplace Skill*. Read the directions. Say: *Listen as I read* Meet Bo. Read the paragraph.
3. Ask: *What is one of Bo's workplace skills?* (He separates his work life and home life.) Next to *Workplace Skill*, write: *Separate work life and home life.*
4. Under *Workplace Skill*, write: *Examples*. Ask: *How does Bo separate work life and home life? Give me some examples.* (He works at work; he spends time with this family at home.)
5. Write the examples. Then elicit other ways to separate work life and home life and write them under *Workplace Skill*.

2 BO'S PROBLEM

1. Say: *Now we are going to read about Bo at work. Listen while I read.* Read the first paragraph. Use the photo and the **Career Awareness** information to help students understand Bo's job.
2. Say: *Look at the photo and talk about Bo's job.* (He's a waiter. He works hard. He is serving a lot of people in a busy restaurant.)
3. Say: *Bo has a problem at work. Listen while I read.* Read the second paragraph.
4. Read the directions. Call on students to answer. Ask them to **cite evidence**: *Where is that information?*
5. Ask: *What is Bo's problem?* (Bo's family visits the restaurant when he is busy at work.)

Career Awareness: Waiter

Waiters serve food to customers in restaurants. They are also called *servers*. A female server may be called a *waitress*. No formal education is required.

3 BO'S SOLUTION

1. Read the directions. Ask students to work together on the first three items.
2. Ask: *Is #1 a good way to separate work life and home life?* (yes) *Why?* (He explains his problem and says he will talk to them at home.) Ask: *Is #2 a good way to separate work life and home life?* (no) *Why not?* (Families of waiters shouldn't eat in the kitchen.) Ask: *Is #3 a good way to separate work life and home life?* (no) *Why not?* (Waiters need to be ready to serve customers, not talk to family.)
3. Ask students if they have any other ideas. Call on students to share item 4 with the class. Write their responses. Ask: *Is this a good way to separate work life and home life? Why?*

 ActiveTeach for 3: Academic Conversation Support

Show what you know!

1. THINK ABOUT IT. Do you separate work life...

Read the directions. Have students think about their answers for a few minutes. Then ask them to share with a partner. Call on students to share with the class.

2. WRITE ABOUT IT. Write your example in your...

Read the directions and the example. Have students write their examples in their **Skills Log** at the back of the book. Circulate and assist students as needed.

Self-Directed Learning

1. Point out the blue bar. Ask students if they can do the lesson learning objective or if they need more practice. Tell them to check one of the boxes. Assign Extra Practice as needed.
2. Ask students to turn to page 25. Go to the Unit Wrap-Up teaching notes on page T-25.

Extra Practice

 p. 25

3 Lots to Do

ActiveTeach

MyEnglishLab

Workbook

Find on English Portal

ActiveTeach MyEnglishLab Workbook Life Skills Writing, MCA, Team Projects, Persistence Activities

Unit Overview

Goals
- See the list of goals on the facing page

Pronunciation
- Pronunciation of *to*
- Pronunciation of *going to*

Reading
- Read about ways to pay for things
- Identify purpose

Grammar
- Simple present: *Want / need* + infinitive
- Future with *be going to*
- Adverbs of degree: *very* and *too*

Writing
- Write about saving money
- Use a topic sentence

Document Literacy and Numeracy
- Compare cost
- Calculate discount
- Interpret an online order form
- Understand a sales receipt
- Compare ways to make big purchases

Workplace, Life, and Community Skills
- Complete an online order and read a sales receipt
- Digital Skills: Visit an online store

Life Skills Writing
- Write a personal check

Soft Skills at Work
- Listen actively

Preview
1. Set the context of the unit by asking questions about errands and shopping (for example, *Do you always have a lot to do? Do you like to shop? What do you usually shop for?*).
2. Show the Unit Opener. Ask: *What is the unit title?* (Lots to Do)
3. Say: *Look at the picture.* Ask the Preview questions. (Possible answers: two men in a clothing store, looking at clothes, shopping)

Unit Goals
1. Point to the Unit Goals. Explain that this list shows what you will be studying in this unit.
2. Tell students to read the goals silently.
3. Say each goal. Explain unfamiliar vocabulary as needed.
4. Point to the ☐ next to the first goal. Say: *We will come back to this page again. You will write a checkmark next to the goals you learned in the unit.*

Oral Presentation
1. Tell students they will give a short presentation at the end of the unit.
2. Write the topics:
   Option 1: Clothes to wear in different types of weather
   Option 2: Making a big purchase, like a new TV
3. Assign the topics to two students.

Unit Wrap-Up
1. Review the Unit Goals with students.
2. Direct students to the Grammar Review.
3. If you assigned presentations, ask students to present.

 ActiveTeach for Wrap-Up: Team Project

 ActiveTeach for Wrap-Up: Persistence Activities

3 Lots to Do

PREVIEW
Look at the picture. What do you see? Where are the people? What are they doing?

UNIT GOALS

- [ ] Identify clothing
- [ ] Describe wants and needs
- [ ] Complete an online order and read store ads and sales receipts
- [ ] Talk about plans
- [ ] Describe problems with purchases
- [ ] **Academic skill:** Identify purpose
- [ ] **Writing skill:** Use a topic sentence
- [ ] **Workplace soft skills:** Show how you listen actively

A PREDICT. Look at the pictures. What do you see? What words for clothing do you know?

B ▶ LISTEN AND POINT. Listen again and repeat.

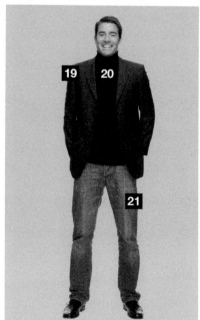

Correlations

ELPS Level 2: 2, 7, 8
CCRS Level A: SL.1.1, SL.K.6, L.1.2, L.1.5, L.1.6
CASAS Reading: RDG 1.7, 2.2, 2.3
CASAS Listening: L2.1, 2.3, 2.9, 4.1, 4.2
CASAS Competencies: 0.1.2, 0.1.5, 1.2.9, 7.4.1
Complete standards language available on the Pearson English Portal.

Self-Directed Learning

State the **lesson objective**. Say: *In this lesson, we will learn to identify clothing.*

A PREDICT. Look at the pictures. What do you...

1. Read the directions. Tell students to cover the list on page 47.
2. Point to #1 in the first picture. Ask: *What piece of clothing is this?* Say: *#1 is a coat.*
3. Say: *Look at the other numbers. What words for clothing do you know?* Students call out answers. Help students pronounce the clothing if they have difficulty.
4. If a student calls out an incorrect item, ask a *yes/no* clarification question: *Is #14 a coat?* If nobody can identify the correct clothing, tell students they will now listen to audio and practice the words for clothing.

B ▶ LISTEN AND POINT. Listen again and...

1. Read the directions. Play the audio. Students listen and point to the clothing.
2. While the audio is playing, walk around and check that students are pointing to the correct clothing. Pause the audio after item 21.
3. When the audio finishes, say clothing items in random order and ask students to point to the appropriate picture.
4. Tell students to look at page 47. Resume the audio. Students listen, read, and repeat.

 ActiveTeach for B: Vocabulary Flashcards

▊ EXPANSION: Vocabulary practice for B

1. Point to a piece of clothing that you are wearing.
2. Ask: *What clothing is this?* Students call out answers. If necessary, say: *It is the same as #7.*
3. Repeat for five pieces of clothing.

▊ EXPANSION: Speaking and writing practice for B

1. Tell students to write three sentences about people in the pictures (for example, *She is wearing a dress and high heels.*).
2. Have students rewrite these sentences as questions (for example, *Who is wearing a dress and high heels?*).
3. Pair students. Students take turns asking each other their questions. Their partners point to the person in the picture who fits the description.

Teaching Tip: Use word webs

A word web is useful to teach multiple words for the same object or idea. For example, a single type of clothing can have many different words associated with it. For example, write *shoes* or *pants* on the board and draw a big circle around the word. Draw lines from the circle and write related clothing words as they arise (for example, *high heels* and *sneakers*).

Teaching Tip: Use props

Use props to teach vocabulary for tangible objects. This personalizes the lesson and increases engagement. For example, when teaching clothing vocabulary, you can wear a variety of clothes to class (*a hat, gloves, a tie,* etc.). Or you can bring other clothing and keep it in a bag, to be pulled out as needed. You can also point out something that a student is wearing, even if it is new vocabulary (for example, *mittens* or *a skirt*). Write new words as they arise.

Vocabulary

C WORK TOGETHER. Look at the pictures...

1. Read the directions.
2. Play A and model the example with an above-level student.
3. Pair students and tell them to take turns pointing to a picture and naming the clothing shown. Use all of the pictures.
4. Walk around and help with pronunciation.

▄▄ MULTILEVEL INSTRUCTION for C

Pre-level scaffolding Before they practice, students write down a list of all the clothing words in each picture.

Above-level expansion Students can name the clothes by talking about the people. Tell them to use complete sentences (for example, *She is wearing a hat, gloves, a scarf, and a coat.*).

▄▄ EXPANSION: Learning strategy for C

1. Bring in (or ask students to bring in) clothing catalogs and fashion magazines.
2. Distribute the catalogs and magazines. Tell students to cut out five pictures that represent clothes or material from the vocabulary list.
3. Provide each student with tape and five index cards or tell students to cut up notebook paper. Tell students to tape the pictures onto the cards first and then write the words.
4. Walk around, and if misspellings occur, tell students to check the list on page 47. Students who finish early can quiz one another with their cards.
5. Say: *You can make cards with pictures to remember new words.* Remind students to use this strategy to remember other new vocabulary.

D CATEGORIZE. What do you wear for work,...

1. Read the directions.
2. Copy the chart and examples onto the board. Say: *A uniform is for work. A coat is for cold weather. A dress is for a party.*
3. Categorize the first five items on the vocabulary list as a class. Say each word and ask: *What do you wear it for?* Write each word in the appropriate column on the chart.
4. Pair students. Tell them to draw their own diagrams and write all the vocabulary words in the appropriate column.
5. Note: Some clothing can be worn for different occasions (for example, *a shirt*). Students can put these words in more than one column.
6. Tell students to switch partners and compare their charts with another classmate.

Study Tip: Test your spelling

1. Point to the **Study Tip**. Read the directions.
2. Say: *To practice spelling, try to spell words without looking at the book.*

Show what you know!

1. THINK ABOUT IT. Look at the clothing words...

Read the directions. If a lot of students are wearing the same type of clothing, tell them to add colors to their clothing words (for example, *blue sweater, red shirt*).

2. TALK ABOUT IT. Take a piece of paper from...

1. Read the directions.
2. Model the activity by taking the first piece of paper from the box. Read it to the class. Ask: *Who has that clothing on today?* Students call out answers until they guess correctly.
3. Students take turns drawing from the box and reading to the class.

▄▄ MULTILEVEL INSTRUCTION for 2

Pre-level scaffolding Write the vocabulary list. As students read the pieces of paper, underline the clothing words in the list. Give the class time to think about the clothing before calling out answers.

Above-level expansion When they read the pieces of paper, students make questions: *Who is wearing a sweater, a shirt, jeans, and boots?*

3. WRITE ABOUT IT. Now write a sentence...

1. Read the directions. Students write about the clothing that they are wearing.
2. Circulate and make sure that students use complete sentences.

Self-Directed Learning

Point out the blue bar. Ask students if they can do the lesson learning objective or if they need more practice. Tell them to check one of the boxes. Assign Extra Practice as needed.

Extra Practice

  p. 26

Vocabulary

Clothing

1. a coat	**6.** a suit	**11.** sweatpants	**16.** a raincoat	**19.** jacket
2. a hat	**7.** a tie	**12.** a cap	**17.** an umbrella	**20.** sweater
3. a scarf	**8.** high heels	**13.** sneakers	**18.** boots	**21.** jeans
4. gloves	**9.** dress	**14.** a uniform		
5. a shirt	**10.** a sweatshirt	**15.** a helmet		

C **WORK TOGETHER.** Look at the pictures. Student A, point to a picture. Student B, name the clothing in the picture.

Student A points to a picture.
B: A uniform, a helmet.
A: Right!

D **CATEGORIZE.** What do you wear for work, for cold weather, for a party? Write the words in the chart.

Clothing for Work	Clothing for Cold Weather	Clothing for a Party
uniform	coat	dress

Study Tip

Test Your Spelling
Read a word in the word list. Close your book. Write the word. Open your book and check your spelling. Continue with all the words in the list.

Show what you know!

1. **THINK ABOUT IT.** Look at the clothing words. On a piece of paper, write the name of 4 pieces of clothing you have on today. Put your paper in a box.

   sweater   jeans
   shirt   boots

2. **TALK ABOUT IT.** Take a piece of paper from the box. Read it to the class. Who has that clothing on today?

3. **WRITE ABOUT IT.** Now write a sentence about your clothing today.

   I have on a _____

I can identify clothing. ☐   I need more practice. ☐

Listening and Speaking

Describe your wants and needs

1 BEFORE YOU LISTEN

A LABEL. Write the words under the pictures.

clearance sale   pair of pants   receipt   shoppers

1. _____shoppers_____ **2.** _____receipt_____ **3.** ___clearance sale___ **4.** ___pair of pants___

B DISCUSS. Do you look for sales when you shop? Do you shop in stores, online, or both?

2 LISTEN

A PREDICT. Look at the picture. What is the woman doing? What is she listening to?

B ▶ LISTEN FOR MAIN IDEA. Listen to the podcast. Who is Lucy talking to?

a. people shopping at a clothing store
b. workers at a clothing store

C ▶ EXPAND. Listen to the whole conversation. What do the people talk about? Match.

1. __a__ Erica   **a.**    **b.**   **c.**

2. __c__ Karen

3. __b__ Nick

D ▶ LISTEN FOR DETAILS. Check (✓) the reason each person shops at Big Deals.

	Erica	Karen	Nick
It's convenient.			✓
They have great prices.	✓		
It's easy to return things.		✓	

Correlations

ELPS Level 2: 2, 7
CASAS Reading: RDG 1.7, 2.2, 2.3
CASAS Listening: L1.4, 2.1, 2.3, 4.1, 4.2, 6.1, 6.2, 6.5
CASAS Competencies: 0.1.2, 0.1.5, 0.2.1
Complete standards language available on the Pearson English Portal.

Self-Directed Learning

State the **lesson objective**. Say: *In this lesson, we will learn to describe our wants and needs.*

1 BEFORE YOU LISTEN

Ⓐ LABEL. Write the words under the pictures.

1. Read the directions. Say the words and phrases in the box.
2. Point to *sale* in *clearance sale*. Ask: *Are prices high or low during a sale?* (low) *What is a clearance sale?* (Stores are trying to sell last season's clothes because new clothes are coming.)
3. Give students time to label the pictures.
4. Ask: *Which picture is a* receipt? Students call out the number of the picture (2).
5. Repeat for the remaining words in the box.

Ⓑ DISCUSS. Do you look for sales when you…

1. Ask: *Do you look for sales when you shop?*
2. Ask for a show of hands.
3. Call on students to give reasons for their answers.

2 LISTEN

Ⓐ PREDICT. Look at the picture. What is the…

1. Tell students to look at the picture. Ask: *Where is she?* (outside, by a fence, on a deck or bridge) *What is she doing?* (sitting, listening to something, and looking at a tablet) *What do you think she is listening to?* (music, a podcast, an audio book)
2. Call on students to answer.

Ⓑ ▶ LISTEN FOR MAIN IDEA. Listen to the…

1. Students read the directions and the answer choices silently.
2. Write the title of the podcast, *Eye around Town*. Elicit or explain why the podcast has this title (the podcast is about taking a look at, or finding out about, things in the town).

3. Play the audio. Students circle the correct answer.
4. Ask: *Who is Lucy talking to?* Call on a student to answer.
5. Ask: *Was your prediction in Exercise 2A correct?* Ask for a show of hands.

Teaching Tip: Use the script

Optional: If students need additional support, tell them to read the Audio Script on page 267 as they listen to the conversations.

Ⓒ ▶ EXPAND. Listen to the whole…

1. Read the directions.
2. Tell students to look at the exercise. Read the names. Then say each letter and tell the class to call out the clothes.
3. Say: *You will hear three people talk about clothes. Match the item of clothing to the speaker.*
4. Play the audio. Students write the letter next to the name.
5. Students compare answers with a partner.

Ⓓ ▶ LISTEN FOR DETAILS. Check (✓) the…

1. Read the directions.
2. Call on students to read the sentences in the chart.
3. To make sure students understand the vocabulary in the chart, ask: *If something is convenient, does it make things easy or difficult for you?* (easy) *When you return something to a store, do you trade it for another item or get your money back?* (get my money back)
4. Play the audio. Students complete the chart.
5. Tell students to compare answers with a partner.
6. To check answers, ask: *Why does Erica shop at Big Deals?* Repeat with the other two shoppers.
7. Ask about **register**: *Does Lucy know the shoppers?* (no) *How do you know?* (She asks for their names and she uses *sir*.)

▬ EXPANSION: Graphic organizer practice for 2D

1. Tell students to make their own chart like the one in Exercise 2D. Instead of names of people, tell students to write the names of three stores.
2. Students rate each store by checking the boxes.
3. Write: *Where do you shop? Why?* Pair students. Tell them to take turns asking one another the questions and to use their charts to answer.

Listening and Speaking

3 PRONUNCIATION

Ⓐ ▶ PRACTICE. Listen. Then listen again and...

1. Read the **Pronunciation Note**. Have students repeat *wanna* after you.
2. Read the directions.
3. Have students read the example sentences silently.
4. Play the audio. Students listen and then listen and repeat.

 ActiveTeach for 3A: Pronunciation Coach

Ⓑ ▶ APPLY. Listen. Circle *to* with a short,...

1. Read the directions.
2. Play the audio. Students listen.
3. Play the audio again. Students listen and circle *to* with a short, weak pronunciation.
4. Ask: *What sentences have short, weak* to?
5. Say the first sentence. Emphasize the stress pattern and pronunciation of *to*. Ask students to repeat the sentence.
6. Repeat for the other sentences.

4 CONVERSATION

Ⓐ ▶ LISTEN AND READ. Then listen and repeat.

1. Tell students to look at the picture. Ask: *What are they doing?* (They are looking at clothes in a store window/window-shopping.)
2. Ask students to read the conversation silently and underline the *to*'s.
3. Ask: *Does* to *have a strong or a weak pronunciation?* (weak)
4. Play the audio. Students listen and then listen and repeat.

Teaching Tip: Set the context

Direct students' attention to the picture. Setting the context before they listen will help them understand the audio more easily.

Ⓑ WORK TOGETHER. Practice the...

1. Read the directions.
2. Pair students to take turns playing A and B. Walk around and check that students are using the correct pronunciation of *to*.

Ⓒ CREATE. Make new conversations. Use the...

1. Read the directions.
2. Tell students to look at the information in the boxes. Say each item and tell the class to repeat.
3. Show the conversation with blanks and read it. Elicit information from the boxes and fill in the blanks.
4. Ask a pair of on-level students to practice the conversation on the board for the class.
5. Erase the words in the blanks and ask two above-level students to make up a new conversation.
6. Tell pairs to take turns playing A and B and to use the vocabulary words to fill in the blanks.
7. Walk around during the activity and check students' pronunciation of *to*.
8. Tell students to stand, mingle, and practice the conversation with several new partners.

Ⓓ MAKE CONNECTIONS. Talk about the...

1. Read the directions.
2. Ask two on-level students to read the example conversation. Student A adds one thing he/she needs to buy.
3. Tell students to stand, mingle, and practice the conversation with several partners.
4. Walk around and participate in the activity. Model clear pronunciation.
5. Call on students to tell the class about one of the people that they talked to.

■■■ MULTILEVEL INSTRUCTION for 4D

Pre-level scaffolding Write: *Work, School,* and *Free Time*. Elicit examples of clothing students wear for each and list them. Tell students to use the lists in their conversations.

Teaching Tip: Formative assessment

Model the conversation with multiple students to check fluency in more open-ended production. Formative assessment can identify points you need to reteach or reinforce.

Self-Directed Learning

Point out the blue bar. Ask students if they can do the lesson learning objective or if they need more practice. Tell them to check one of the boxes. Assign Extra Practice as needed.

Extra Practice

  p. 27

Listening and Speaking

3 PRONUNCIATION

A ▶ PRACTICE. Listen. Then listen again and repeat.

need to	I need to buy a new uniform.
like to	I don't like to shop.
want to	I want to buy some jeans.

> **Pronunciation of to**
>
> The word *to* often has a short, weak pronunciation. It sounds like *ta*. In informal conversation, *want to* sounds like "wanna."

B ▶ APPLY. Listen. Circle *to* with a short, weak pronunciation.

1. I don't need ⟨to⟩ buy a suit.
2. I like ⟨to⟩ shop.
3. I want ⟨to⟩ get a new tie.
4. I need ⟨to⟩ buy a suit.

4 CONVERSATION

A ▶ LISTEN AND READ. Then listen and repeat.

A: What do you need to buy today?
B: Well, I don't need to buy anything, but I want to buy a new pair of pants for work.
C: And I want to look for a raincoat while I'm here.

B WORK TOGETHER. Practice the conversation in Exercise A.

C CREATE. Make new conversations. Use the words in the boxes.

A: What do you _____ buy today?
B: Well, I don't need to buy anything, but I want to buy _____.
A: And I want to look for _____ while I'm here.

need to	boots	a sweatshirt
want to	gloves	a scarf
have to	sweatpants	a jacket

D MAKE CONNECTIONS. Talk about the clothes that you need or want for work, for school, or for your free time.

A: What do you need?
B: I need a new uniform for work. How about you?

Simple present: *want / need* + infinitive	
Affirmative	**Negative**
I You We **want** They **to buy** a new pair of pants. He She **wants**	I You We **don't** They **need to** buy anything. He She **doesn't**

A COMPLETE. Write the correct form of the verbs.

1. A: I want ___to buy___ a few things after work today.
(buy)

Do you want ___to go___ to Shop Mart with me?
(go)

B: Sure. I need ___to return___ a cap there.
(return)

A: OK. What time do you want ___to leave___ here?
(leave)

2. A: Do you want ___to go___ shopping during lunch
(go)
today?

B: Maybe. I need ___to get___ a present for my co-worker. But I don't want
(get)

___to spend___ a lot of money. I need ___to check___ the sales online.
(spend)   (check)

A: I understand. I need ___to be___ careful with my money, too.
(be)

3. A: All my uniforms for work are old. I need ___to buy___ some new ones.
(buy)

B: Oh, really? I don't need ___to wear___ a uniform to work—regular clothes like
(wear)
jeans are OK.

B ▶ SELF-ASSESS. Listen and check your answers.

Grammar Watch

- Use *want* and *need* +
  an infinitive.
- An infinitive = *to* + the
  base form of the verb.
- You can also use
  want / need + a noun.
  I want a denim jacket.
  He needs sweatpants.

<table>
<tr><td colspan="2">Correlations</td></tr>
</table>

Correlations
ELPS Level 2: 2, 7, 10
CCRS Level A: SL.K.3, SL.1.4, L.1.1
CASAS Reading: RDG 1.7, 2.9
CASAS Listening: L1.3, 2.1, 2.3, 3.1, 4.1, 4.2
CASAS Competencies: 0.1.2, 0.1.5
Complete standards language available on the Pearson English Portal.

Self-Directed Learning

State the **lesson objective.** Say: *In this lesson, we will learn to use simple present:* want / need + *infinitive.*

Simple present: *want / need* + infinitive

 ActiveTeach: Grammar Discovery

1. Warm up. Say: *The pronunciation practice on page 51 used this grammar.* Turn back to page 51. Point to the sentences in Exercise 3A and then write:
   - *I need to buy a new uniform.*
   - *I want to buy some jeans.*
2. Read the sentences aloud and have students repeat. Ask: *What are the main verbs?* Underline *need* and *want*. Ask: *What's the infinitive?* Circle *to buy.*
3. Read the **Grammar Watch** note. Point to the sentences on the board. Say: *You can also say,* I need a new uniform. I want some jeans.
4. Ask: *How do you make a simple present sentence negative?* (don't, doesn't) Change the sentences to the negative with *don't need* and *don't want.*
5. Tell students to look at the grammar charts. Ask: *What is the infinitive?* (to buy) *Can you think of any other infinitives?* Elicit other infinitives and list them on the board, with new objects if necessary (for example: *to shop, to go, to eat something, to visit New York,* etc.).
6. Make sentences with the new infinitives, using both *want* and *need*, and ask the class to repeat. Remind students to use *wants* and *needs* with *he, she,* or *it*. Remind students to use the weak and quiet pronunciation of *to.*
7. Point to an infinitive and call on several students to make sentences on their own.

 ActiveTeach: Grammar Coach

Teaching Tip: Personalize activities

Personalization uses real information to help students learn. For example, personalize this grammar lesson by calling on a student who is wearing a piece of clothing listed in the vocabulary box on page 47. Ask: *Did you want to buy that jacket, or did you need to buy it?* Students take turns asking each other about their clothes.

Ⓐ COMPLETE. Write the correct form of the...

1. Read the directions and the verbs under the blanks. Ask: *What form are the verbs in?* (base form) *How do you make them infinitives?* (add *to*)
2. Write A's first line in item 1 and read it. Point to the second blank and write *go.* Underline *want* and ask: *What do we need to add?* Write *to* before *go.*
3. Walk around and check that students are using the infinitive.

■ **EXPANSION: Grammar and writing practice for A**

1. Tell students to give names to A and B in each conversation in Exercise A.
2. Then tell them to write a couple of sentences summarizing each conversation. For example, for Conversation 1: *Emma and Nicole want to go shopping later. Nicole needs to return something.* For Conversation 2: *David wants to go shopping during lunch. Justin does, too, but he doesn't want to spend a lot of money.*

Ⓑ ▶ SELF-ASSESS. Listen and check your...

1. Play the audio. Students listen and check their answers.
2. Tell students to look at their answers and double-check that each one includes *to.*

Grammar

C APPLY. Look at the pictures. Complete the...

1. Read the directions.
2. Write item 1. Tell students to look at the first picture. Ask: *What does Mary need to do?* Elicit possible answers with *go* and write them. (Mary needs to go to the shoe store. Mary needs to go shopping for shoes.)
3. Write item 2. Tell students to look at the first picture again. Ask: *Where does Jim want to go?* Elicit possible answers with *go* and write them.
4. Walk around and check that students are using the third-person singular -*s* and *to*.

Teaching Tip: Mini-review

If you notice that students are omitting the third-person singular -*s*, do a mini-review by using examples from the grammar chart on the board.

■■ **EXPANSION: Grammar and speaking practice for C**

Tell pairs to play the roles of the people in the pictures and say what they need or want to do in the first person (for example, Mary: *I need to go to the shoe store.* Jim: *I want to go to the bookstore.*).

D WORK TOGETHER. Compare your answers.

1. Pair students and tell them to take turns reading the sentences. Remind them that there may be more than one right answer.
2. To check answers, call on students to read sentences.

Show what you know!

1. THINK ABOUT IT. Make a list of three things...

1. Read the directions.
2. Write sentences about your own clothes' shopping needs and wants as examples.
3. Review the difference between *return* and *exchange*.
4. Students write their lists.

2. TALK ABOUT IT. Play the memory game...

1. Read the directions.
2. Ask three students seated in a row to role-play the example.
3. Ask three above-level students to model the game with you. Read one of your sentences from the board. Prompt the first student to change your sentence to the third person and then add his or her own sentence. Continue in this manner with the second and third students. If a student has difficulty, elicit help from the class.

4. Form groups. Remind students to say *needs* and *wants* when they talk about each group member.
5. If time permits, form new groups and play the game again.

■■ **MULTILEVEL INSTRUCTION for 2**

Cross-ability Ask one of the above-level students who helped model the game to lead each group. This student should take the last turn and say all group members' clothes shopping needs and wants. You may also want to ask this student to report the group's needs and wants to the class. Pre-level students can write a sentence using their list from Step 1 and take the first turn.

■■ **EXPANSION: Grammar and writing practice for 2**

Ask: *Do you remember your classmates' clothes shopping needs and wants?* As a class, tell students to call out as many sentences as they can. As an example, point to one of your own shopping needs or wants. Elicit a sentence and write it.

3. WRITE ABOUT IT. Now write three sentences...

1. Read the directions.
2. Ask students to check each other's sentences:
   • Sentences should include the verbs *want* or *need*.
   • Sentences should use the correct form of the verb.
   • Sentences should correctly use the infinitive.
3. Have students volunteer to write their sentences on the board.

Self-Directed Learning

Point out the blue bar. Ask students if they can do the lesson learning objective or if they need more practice. Tell them to check one of the boxes. Assign Extra Practice as needed.

Extra Practice

  p. 27

Grammar

C APPLY. Look at the pictures. Complete the sentences. Use the correct form of the verbs.

Mary   **Jim**

1. Mary _____*needs to go to the shoe store*_____.
   (need + go)

2. Jim _____*wants to go to the bookstore*_____.
   (want + go)

Larry   **Ray**

3. Larry _____*needs to buy a coat*_____.
   (need + buy)

4. Ray _____*wants to get an umbrella*_____.
   (want + get)

RETURNS

Hector   **Mariko**

5. Hector _____*needs to return pants*_____.
   (need + return)

6. Mariko _____*wants to exchange a shirt*_____.
   (want + exchange)

D WORK TOGETHER. Compare your answers.

Show what you know!

1. **THINK ABOUT IT.** Make a list of three things you want and three things you need to buy, exchange, or return.

2. **TALK ABOUT IT.** Play the memory game. Use your lists.

   Ravi: *I want to buy new gloves.*
   Marc: *Ravi wants to buy new gloves. I need to return a wool sweater.*
   Silvia: *Ravi wants to buy new gloves. Marc needs to return a wool sweater. I need to get a new umbrella.*

3. **WRITE ABOUT IT.** Now write three sentences about your needs and wants. Then write three sentences about your classmates.

   I want to return . . .
   I need to exchange . . .
   They want to buy . . .

I can use simple present: *want / need* + infinitive. ☐   I need more practice. ☐

For more practice, go to MyEnglishLab.

1 READ A STORE AD

WORK TOGETHER. Talk about the online ad. Answer the questions.

ZIP⚡
Superstore

WOMEN | MEN | HOME | BED & BATH | SHOES | BEAUTY | KIDS | JUNIORS | JEWELRY | WATCHES | ACTIVE   🔍 Search

DAILY DEALS for Tuesday, April 22nd

Designer raincoats
regular price: $89.00
daily deal: $24.98
You save over 70%

Men's gloves
$36.55
daily deal: $18.55
You save over 40%

Women's leather boots
regular price: $99.00
daily deal: $45.00
You save over 50%

Men's wool scarves
regular price: $30.00
Daily Deal
Discount 50%

1. What's on sale? Designer raincoats, men's gloves, women's leather boots, and men's wool scarves are on sale.
2. How much is the discount on each item? Over 70% on designer raincoats, over 40% on men's gloves, over on women's leather boots, and 50% on men's wool scarves.
3. Which item saves the most money? Designer raincoats; they have the highest discount.
4. Which item do you want to buy? Why? *(Answers will vary.)*
5. What is the sale price of wool scarves? $15.

2 COMPLETE AN ONLINE ORDER

A **INTERPRET.** Read the online order form. Circle *True* or *False*.

🛒 Items in Your Cart

		Quantity	Price
Item 1:	Designer Raincoat	1	$24.98
Item 2:	Women's Leather Boots	1	$45.00
	Subtotal:		$69.98
	Shipping:		FREE
	Tax:		$4.19
	Total		$74.17

Payment Method
Secure credit card payment
*Credit card number   *Expiration date *Security code
   11122233355668899   01 / 22   001

I can read a store ad. ■   I need more practice. ■

For more practice, go to MyEnglishLab.

Lesson 4 | Workplace, Life, and Community Skills

Correlations

ELPS Level 2: 1, 2, 3, 4, 5, 6, 7, 8, 9, 10
CCRS Level A: RI/RL.1., W.1.7, W.1.8
CASAS Reading: RDG 1.7, 1.8, 2.2, 2.3, 3.2, 3.6
CASAS Listening: L2.1, 2.3, 4.1, 4.2
CASAS Competencies: 0.1.2, 0.1.5, 0.2.1, 1.6.4, 4.5.6, 7.4.4, 7.7.3
Complete standards language available on the Pearson English Portal.

Numeracy: Math skills

Show students how to calculate *savings* on an item.

original price	x	(% discount)	=	savings
$90	x	.70 (70%)	=	$63

Show students how to calculate the *sale price*.

original price	–	savings		=	sale price
$90	–	$63		=	$27

Self-Directed Learning

State the **lesson objective**. Say: *In this lesson, we will learn to read a store ad, complete an online order, and read a sales receipt.*

Self-Directed Learning

Point out the blue bar at the bottom of page 52. Ask students if they can do the lesson learning objective or if they need more practice. Tell them to check one of the boxes. Assign Extra Practice as needed.

1 READ A STORE AD

WORK TOGETHER. Talk about the online ad...

Document Literacy: Store ad

Context: Store ads are found online and in magazines and newspapers.
Purpose: They advertise products and sales.
Key Words: *regular price, deal, save, sale price, discount*

1. Tell students to look at the store ad. Orient them to the document. Ask: *What are the products in this store ad?* (raincoats, gloves, boots, scarves) Ask about **context**: *Where is this store ad from?* (a clothing website / Zip Superstore) *Where else do you find store ads?* (magazines and newspapers) Ask about **purpose**: *What are store ads for?* (to advertise products and sales) *When is this sale?* (Tuesday, April 22nd) Ask about **key words**: *What information is in this store ad?* (products, regular prices, daily deals, savings)
2. Model the activity. Point to the first item in the ad and ask an above-level student: *What's on sale?* (designer raincoats) *What is the regular price?* ($89) *What is the discount?* (over 70%) *What is the daily deal or the sale price?* ($24.98)
3. For questions 1 and 2, tell students to underline the answers in the ad for each of the daily deals. For questions 3–5, tell students to circle the answers in the ad. Note: For question 5, students will have to calculate the sale price. Use the Numeracy box to show students how to calculate the sale price.

2 COMPLETE AN ONLINE ORDER

INTERPRET. Read the online order form...

Docment Literacy: Online order form

Context: Online order forms are found at online stores on websites like Amazon and eBay.
Purpose: You use online order forms to buy products online.
Key Words: *cart, quantity, price, subtotal, shipping, tax, total, payment method*

1. Tell students to look at the online order form. Orient them to the form. Ask: *What kind of form is this?* (online order form) Ask about **context**: *Where do you find online order forms?* (at online stores, on websites) Ask about **purpose**: What are online orders for? (buy products online) Ask about **key words**: *What information is on an online order form?* (quantity, price, subtotal, shipping tax, payment)
2. Read the directions. Tell students to read the online order form and the sentences on page 53 silently. Explain that *shipping* is the cost to send the product to you.
3. Review the correct answers with the class. Ask students to read the sentences and call on classmates to say *True* or *False*.
4. *Optional:* Tell students to rewrite the false sentences to make them true. (2. Shipping is free. 5. The shopper's credit card expires in January 2022. 6. Sales tax cost $4.19.)

Digital Skills for 2

Remind students that they should never use a credit card online unless they know they can trust the website.

Workplace, Life, and Community Skills

3 READ A SALES RECEIPT

A INTERPRET. Read the sales receipt. Answer...

Document Literacy: Sales receipt

Context: You get sales receipts at stores after making a purchase.
Purpose: Sales receipts show the price you paid for something you purchased.
Key Words: *discount, subtotal, sales tax, total, purchase, cash, change, returns*

1. Tell students to look at the sales receipts. Orient them to the receipts. Ask: *What kind of document is this?* (sales receipt) Ask about **context**: *When and where do you get sales receipts?* (at stores) *Where are these sales receipts from?* (Mayfield Department Store) Ask about **purpose**: *What are sales receipts for?* (show that you paid) Ask about **key words**: *What information is on a sales receipt?* (items, total, change, return policy)
2. Tell students to read the questions and circle the answers on the receipt.
3. Point out that the discount is 30% and the savings is $17.99. Explain that *subtotal* is the purchase amount before tax.
4. Pair students and tell them to take turns asking and answering the questions.
5. Tell students to write the answers next to the questions.
6. Ask: *How much is the sales tax?* (6%) *What state is Mayfield Department Store in?* (Florida—see the abbreviation *FL* next to sales tax)

■ **EXPANSION: Speaking practice for 3A**
1. Ask students to bring in receipts—for clothes, if possible.
2. Give them a list of things to find: the name of the store, the date of the purchase, the item(s) purchased, the discount(s), the purchase cost before tax, the tax, the amount paid, the change.

B EXAMINE. Read the store ad. Then, look at...
1. Read the directions. Say: *There are two mistakes on the receipts. What are they?* (The dates are different—if it is a one-day sale, then one receipt must be wrong. Also, on neither receipt is the discount 30% as advertised.)
2. Pair students. Tell them to look for the mistakes together.
3. Ask: *What are the mistakes?* Students call out answers.

■ **MULTILEVEL INSTRUCTION for 3B**
Pre-level scaffolding Help students identify possible mistakes by asking questions about the store ad. Ask: *How long is the sale?* (one day) *What is the discount?* (30% off)

C LISTEN. Then listen and repeat.
1. Play the audio. Students read along silently. Pause the audio after the conversation plays once.
2. Ask: *Which receipt goes with this conversation?* (receipt 1) *What's the mistake?* (ad says all swimwear is 30 percent, the receipt says 20 percent off)
3. Resume the audio. Students listen and repeat.

D ROLE-PLAY. Make a similar conversation...
1. Pair students and tell them to practice the conversation from Exercise 3C and to take turns playing each role.
2. Ask two on-level students to practice the conversation in front of the class.
3. Read the directions.
4. Say: *Make a new conversation about the receipts.* Students should work in pairs and use mistakes in the sales receipts.
5. Tell pairs to take turns playing each role.
6. Call on pairs to perform for the class.

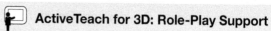 **ActiveTeach for 3D: Role-Play Support**

E GO ONLINE. Visit an online store. Find a...
1. Read the directions. Brainstorm the names of stores that students could visit.
2. Tell students to search for one of these stores online. Have students find a sale ad.
3. Compare research as a class. Write a list of the online sales that students discovered.

Digital Skills for 3E

It is a good idea to go to several online stores to see how you can get the best deal.

ActiveTeach: Review

Self-Directed Learning
Point out the blue bar. Ask students if they can do the lesson learning objective or if they need more practice. Tell them to check one of the boxes. Assign Extra Practice as needed.

Extra Practice

  Workbook pp. 28–29 Life Skills Writing

Workplace, Life, and Community Skills

1. The shopper orders two items.	(True)	False
2. Shipping costs $4.37.	True	(False)
3. The shopper pays with a credit card.	(True)	False
4. The site is a safe site to enter your credit card.	(True)	False
5. The shopper's credit card expires in February.	True	(False)
6. The shopper doesn't need to pay sales tax.	True	(False)

3 READ A SALES RECEIPT

A INTERPRET. Read the sales receipt. Answer the questions.

1. What is the date of purchase? 2/28/2018
2. What is the discount on the swimsuit? 30% / $17.99
3. How much does the swimsuit cost before tax? $42.00
4. How much is it after tax? $44.52
5. How much change does the customer get? $5.48
6. What is the return policy? Returns must be made within 30 days of purchase.

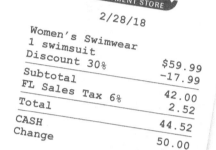

```
◆ MAYFIELD ◆
  DEPARTMENT STORE

      2/28/18
Women's Swimwear
1 swimsuit
Discount 30%           $59.99
                       -17.99
Subtotal
FL Sales Tax 6%         42.00
Total                    2.52
CASH                   44.52
Change                 50.00
                        5.48
Returns must be made within
30 days of purchase.
```

B EXAMINE. Read the store ad. Then, look at the sales receipts. Identify the two mistakes.

```
◆ MAYFIELD ◆
DEPARTMENT STORE

    7/25/2018
Men's swimwear       $25.00
1 swimsuit            -5.00
Discount 20%
                     $20.00
Subtotal              1.20
FL Sales Tax 6%      21.20
Total                21.20
CASH                  0.00
Change
```

```
◆ MAYFIELD ◆
DEPARTMENT STORE

    7/26/2018
Children's swimwear
1 swimsuit           $32.00
Discount 50%         -16.00
Subtotal             $16.00
FL Sales Tax 6%        .96
Total                16.96
CASH                 20.00
Change                3.04
```

C ▶ LISTEN. Then listen and repeat.

A: Excuse me. I think there's a mistake. The ad says all swimwear is 30 percent off.
B: Yes, that's right.
A: But my receipt says 20 percent off.
B: Oh, I'm sorry. I'll take care of that.

D ROLE-PLAY. Make a similar conversation about the incorrect sales receipt.

E GO ONLINE. Visit an online store. Find a sale ad.

What's on sale? How much can you save?

I can complete an online order and read a sales receipt. ■   I need more practice. ■

For more practice, go to MyEnglishLab.

Talk about plans

1 BEFORE YOU LISTEN

A **LABEL.** Look at the pictures. Where does the man go? Write the words under the pictures.

bank   hardware store   laundromat   supermarket

1. _____supermarket_____
2. _____bank_____
3. _____Laundromat_____
4. _____hardware store_____

B **BRAINSTORM.** What kinds of errands do people often run?

2 LISTEN

A ▶ **LISTEN FOR MAIN IDEA.** Complete the sentences.

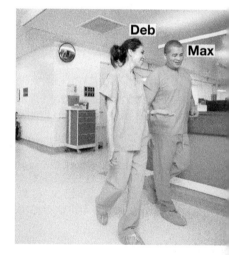

Deb

Max

1. They are talking about _____.
   a. plans   **b.** relaxing

2. _____ needs to go to the supermarket.
   a. Max   **b.** Deb

3. _____ is going to be busy.
   a. Max   **b.** Deb

B ▶ **LISTEN FOR DETAILS.** Number Deb's errands in order.

  _3_ go to the supermarket

  _1_ go to the ATM

  _2_ go to the hardware store

C ▶ **EXPAND.** Listen to the whole conversation. Complete the sentence.

Max wants to _____.
   a. take a nap   **b.** go to the ATM   **c.** stop at the supermarket

Correlations

ELPS Level 2: 2, 7
CASAS Reading: RDG 1.7, 2.2, 2.3
CASAS Listening: L1.5, 2.1, 2.3, 4.1, 4.2, 5.8, 6.1
CASAS Competencies: 0.1.2, 0.1.5, 0.1.6, 0.2.1
Complete standards language available on the Pearson English Portal.

Self-Directed Learning

State the **lesson objective**. Say: *In this lesson, we will learn to talk about plans.*

1 BEFORE YOU LISTEN

A LABEL. Look at the pictures. Where does...

1. Read the directions. Say the words and phrases in the box and have students repeat.
2. Ask: *Which picture is a* supermarket? Students call out the number of the picture.
3. Give students time to label the pictures.
4. Say: *Look at the pictures again. Where does the man go to buy meat and cheese?* (deli/supermarket) *Where does he go to get money?* (bank/ATM) *Where does he go to wash clothes?* (laundromat) *Where does he go to buy paint and a ladder?* (hardware store)

B BRAINSTORM. What kinds of errands do...

1. Read the question. Elicit a definition of *run errands* (for example, *go to places in town and do things you need to do*).
2. Write students' ideas on the board (for example, *go to the supermarket, go to the post office, go to the bank*).
3. *Optional:* Ask: *What errands do you like to run? What errands do you not like to run?*

2 LISTEN

A ▶ LISTEN FOR MAIN IDEA. Complete the...

1. Say: *Point to Deb. Point to Max.* Ask: *Where are they?* (at work/at the hospital)
2. Read the directions. Tell students to read the sentences and answer choices silently.
3. Play the audio. Students circle the correct answers.
4. Call on students to read the completed sentences.
5. Ask: *Who needs to run a lot of errands tomorrow?* (Deb)

B ▶ LISTEN FOR DETAILS. Number Deb's...

1. Read the directions. Call on students to read the list of errands.
2. Play the audio. Students number the errands in order.
3. Tell students to compare answers with a partner.
4. Say: *First, she needs to... Then she needs to... Then she's going to...* and tell the class to call out the errands.
5. Ask about **register**: *What is the relationship between Deb and Max?* (co-workers and friends) *How do you know?* (the photo shows them working together at the hospital; Max jokes with Deb)

C ▶ EXPAND. Listen to the whole...

1. Read the directions. Students read the sentence and the answer choices silently.
2. Play the audio. Students choose the correct answer.
3. Call on a student to read the completed sentence.
4. *Optional:* Ask: *Why?* (He got tired just thinking about tomorrow.) *Do you think Max's answer is funny?*

■ EXPANSION: Listening and writing practice for 2C

1. Play the audio again.
2. Tell students to write a list of errands for Max (1. Go to the laundromat; 2. Go to the deli; 3. Go to the bank)
3. Have students compare lists with a partner.

Culture Note

1. Say: *In the U.S., there are very large stores called* superstores. *These superstores often include clothing, groceries, hardware, books and electronics, toys and garden supplies. They may even have a restaurant and an ATM.*
2. Ask: *In your home country, are there a lot of superstores like these?*

Listening and Speaking

3 PRONUNCIATION

A ▶ PRACTICE. Listen. Then listen again and...

1. Read the **Pronunciation Note**.
2. Tell students to look at the first pair of examples. Ask: *Does* going to *come before another verb?* (yes) Tell students to circle *relax* and *stop*. Say each sentence twice, once with *going to* and once with *"gonna."* Tell students that both are correct.
3. Tell students to look at the second pair of examples. Ask: *Does* going to *come before another verb?* (no) Say the sentence twice, once with *going to* and once with *"gonna."* Write and then cross out: *I'm "gonna" the post office.*
4. Say *"gonna"* several times and ask the class to repeat. Tell them to use *"gonna"* when they repeat the first pair of examples and *going to* when they repeat the second pair of examples.
5. Play the audio. Students listen and then listen and repeat.

 ActiveTeach for 3A: Pronunciation Coach

B ▶ APPLY. Listen to the sentences. Circle...

1. Read the directions.
2. Play the audio. Students listen and circle *going to* when it sounds like *gonna*.
3. Play the audio again. Elicit the sentences with *gonna*.
4. Say the first sentence. Emphasize the stress pattern and pronunciation of *going to* (gonna). Ask students to repeat sentence.
5. Repeat for the other sentences.

4 CONVERSATION

A ▶ LISTEN AND READ. Then listen and repeat.

1. Note: This conversation is the same one students heard in Exercise 2A on page 54.
2. Tell students to read the conversation silently and underline *going to*, and then tell them to look at the words after *going to* and circle any verbs.
3. Check that students circled *relax* and *stop*. Ask: *Can these sentences use the pronunciation* "gonna"? (yes) Tell students to write *"gonna"* in parentheses above the two sentences.
4. Play the audio. Students listen and then listen and repeat.

B WORK TOGETHER. Practice the conversation.

1. Read the directions.
2. Pair students. Tell them to practice the conversation. Tell them to take turns playing A and B.

3. Walk around and check that students are using the correct pronunciation of *going to*.

C CREATE. Make new conversations. Use the...

1. Read the directions.
2. Tell students to look at the information in the boxes. Say each word or expression and ask the class to repeat. Ask: *What do you see in the blue box?* (actions) *What do you see in the yellow and green boxes?* (places)
3. Show the conversation on the board and complete it with words from the boxes.
4. Play A and model with a student. Switch roles.
5. Tell pairs to take turns playing each role and to use the boxes to fill in the blanks.
6. Walk around and help with students' pronunciation of *"gonna" relax* and *"gonna" stop*.
7. Tell students to stand, mingle, and practice the conversation with several new partners.
8. Call on pairs to perform for the class.

D MAKE CONNECTIONS. Talk about errands.

1. Read the directions.
2. Tell students to write a list of errands they need to run this week. Write your own list on the board as an example. Remind students that they can use the places in the pictures in Exercise 1A on page 54 and in the boxes in Exercise 4C.
3. At the top of your list on the board, write: *I need to go to...* Play B and model the conversation with an above-level student. Point to the errands on your list as you answer. Then switch roles and ask the student: *What errands do you need to run?*
4. Tell students to stand, mingle, and practice the conversation with several partners.
5. Walk around and participate in the activity.
6. Call on students to tell the class about one of the people that they talked to.

■ **MULTILEVEL INSTRUCTION for 4D**
Cross Ability The above-level student plays B first. After both partners have practiced both roles, the above-level student closes his or her book and the pre-level student asks A's question again.

Self-Directed Learning
Point out the blue bar. Ask students if they can do the lesson learning objective or if they need more practice. Tell them to check one of the boxes. Assign Extra Practice as needed.

Extra Practice
pp. 30–31

Listening and Speaking

3 PRONUNCIATION

A ▶ **PRACTICE. Listen. Then listen again and repeat.**

going to   I'm going to relax.
             She's going to stop at the bank.

going to   I'm going to the post office.
             You're going to the store with me.

Pronunciation of *going to*

In informal conversation, *going to* often has the pronunciation "gonna" before another verb. It does not have this pronunciation before a noun.

B ▶ **APPLY. Listen to the sentences. Circle *going to* when it sounds like *gonna*.**

1. I'm (going to) stop at the deli.
2. I'm (going to) go to the bank.
3. We're going to the ATM.
4. She's (going to) run errands.

4 CONVERSATION

A ▶ **LISTEN AND READ. Then listen and repeat.**

A: So, what are your plans for tomorrow?
B: Nothing. I'm going to relax.
A: Well, I have a lot to do. First, I need to go to the ATM. Then I need to go to the hardware store. Then I'm going to stop at the deli at the supermarket.
B: Wow. You're going to be busy.

B **WORK TOGETHER. Practice the conversation.**

C **CREATE. Make new conversations. Use the words in the boxes.**

A: So, what are your plans for tomorrow?
B: Nothing. I'm going to   .
A: Well, I have a lot to do. First, I need to go to the   .
Then I need to go to the   . Then I'm going to stop
at the   .
B: Wow. You're going to be busy.

stay home
sleep late
watch TV

grocery store
deli
post office

bakery
gas station
laundromat

D **MAKE CONNECTIONS. Talk about errands.**

A: What are you going to do tomorrow?
B: First, I need to go to the gas station and then . . .

I can talk about plans. ■	I need more practice. ■

For more practice, go to MyEnglishLab.

Future with *be going to*

Future with *be going to*

Affirmative			Negative		
I	**am**		I	**am**	
You			You		
We	**are**	**going to** relax tomorrow.	We	**are**	**not going to** run errands.
They			They		
He	**is**		He	**is**	
She			She		

A **COMPLETE.** Write sentences with *be going to*. Use contractions.

1. She _'s going to_ take the package to the mail room.
2. I _'m going to_ cash my check after work.
3. They _'re going to_ return the files to their supervisor.
4. He _'s going to_ talk to his team leader.
5. We _'re going to_ prepare for the meeting.
6. You _'re going to_ check your schedule online.

Grammar Watch

I am = **I'm**
I am not = **I'm not**

he is = **he's**
he is not = **he isn't**

we are = **we're**
we are not = **we aren't**

For more contractions, see page 258.

B **APPLY.** Complete the sentences with *be going to* and the words in parentheses.

1. Hector and Maria ___are going to get___ on-the-job training.
   (get)

   They _'re going to do_ it during the day at work.
   (do)

2. My uniform is dirty. I'm ___going to take___ my clothes to the
   (take)

   laundromat.

3. Tomorrow is a holiday, so a lot of people ___aren't going to come___
   (not come)

   to work. You're ___going to be___ almost alone in the office.
   (be)

4. We need to run a lot of errands. We ___aren't going to have___ time
   (not have)

   to relax.

5. Sally ___is going to work___ late. She ___isn't going to leave___ on time.
   (work) (not leave)

6. I _'m going to drive_ to work with a friend tomorrow.
   (drive)

   I _'m not going to take_ the bus.
   (not take)

Self-Directed Learning

State the **lesson objective**. Say: *In this lesson, we will learn to use the future with* be going to.

Future with *be going to*

 ActiveTeach: Grammar Discovery

1. Warm up. Say: *The conversation on page 55 used this grammar.* Turn back to page 55. Point to the sentences in Exercise 4A and then write:
   - *I'm going to relax.*
   - *I'm going to stop at the supermarket.*
2. Underline *'m going to relax* and *'m going to stop.* Say: *This is future with* be going to.
3. Tell students to look at the grammar charts. Read sentences and ask the class to repeat.
4. Write: be going to + *base form of a verb.* Say: *Use* be going to *to talk about the future.*
5. Circle *be* in *be going to* on the board. Ask: *What are the forms of* be? Elicit and write *am, is,* and *are.*
6. Tell students to read the **Grammar Watch** note silently.
7. Write: *I + am = _____, he + is = _____, we + are = _____.* Elicit and write: *I'm, he's, we're.*
8. Read sentences in the affirmative chart, using contractions, and ask the class to repeat.
9. Write: *I am not = _____, he Is not = _____, we are not = _____.* Elicit and write: *I'm not, he's not / he isn't, we're not / we aren't.*
10. Say: *You can review all of the contractions with* be *on page 258.*
11. Read the sentences in the negative chart, using contractions, and ask the class to repeat.

 ActiveTeach: Grammar Coach

Teaching Tip: Use a calendar

Any time that you need to communicate time expressions and tenses, you can use a calendar. Bring one to class (or keep one handy) or draw a basic calendar on the board. Begin by defining today (for example: *Today is Tuesday.*) and marking it with an X.

Ⓐ COMPLETE. Write sentences with *be going*…
1. Read the directions.
2. Walk around and remind students to use contractions with pronouns.
3. Tell students to compare their answers in pairs.
4. Call on students to read the sentences out loud.

■ **EXPANSION: Grammar practice for A**
1. Tell students to rewrite the sentences in Exercise A in the negative, adding *not* (for example, *She's not going to take the package…*).
2. Then tell students to rewrite the sentences in the negative again, making contractions with *not* (for example, *She isn't going to take the package…*). Point out that there is only one way to make item 2 negative (*I'm not going to…*).

Ⓑ APPLY. Complete the sentences with *be*…
1. Read the directions.
2. Write item 1, including the answer and the word in parentheses. Point to *get* in the answer and in parentheses and ask: *Does the verb after* to *change?* (no)
3. Remind students to use contractions when the subject is a pronoun.
4. To check answers, write the numbers from 2 to 6 on the board. Ask students to write only the answers on the board, and ask the class to check them. Make and discuss any necessary corrections.

Grammar

C INTERPRET. Look at the pictures. What are...

1. Tell students to look at the pictures. Say each place and ask the class to repeat.
2. Read the directions. Pair students and tell them to brainstorm ideas for each picture (for example, for Ali's Grocery Store: *buy milk, shop for food, pick up something for dinner*).
3. Ask an above-level student to read the example. Continue to model the activity by saying another sentence about picture 1 (for example, *He's going to buy stamps.*).
4. Form new pairs. Tell partners to take turns saying sentences about each picture and to say as many sentences as they can.
5. For each picture, call on a pair to say their sentences.

▆▆ MULTILEVEL INSTRUCTION for C

Pre-level scaffolding Tell students to look at the example and underline the words they need to change to talk about the other pictures. Check that they underline: *1, man, send a package.* (In picture 3, *is* also changes to *are.*)

Above-level expansion Tell students to say where the person is going (*The woman is going to the ATM.*) and what the person is going to do (*She's going to get cash.*). Tell students to say *going to* in the first sentence and *"gonna"* in the second.

D WRITE. Now write a sentence for each...

1. Read the directions.
2. Point to picture 2 in Exercise C. Elicit a sentence from the class and write it.
3. Walk around and check for the correct form of *be going to* + the base form of a verb.
4. Ask students to write any one of their sentences on the board. Read each sentence and ask the class to make any necessary corrections. Then the class guesses the picture by calling out the place.

Show what you know!

1. THINK ABOUT IT. Make a list of errands you...

1. Read the directions.
2. Brainstorm errands and write them. For ideas, tell students to look at Exercise C on page 51, Exercise 1A on page 54, Exercise 4A on page 55, and Exercise C on page 57. Begin each errand with the base form of a verb.
3. Say the errands on the board and ask the class to repeat.
4. Tell students to choose an errand from the board and think about how to act it out.

2. TALK ABOUT IT. Play charades. Take turns...

1. Choose an errand from the board to act out (not *stop at the bank*). Act out the errand and then read the example. Play A. Ask an on-level student to play B and an above-level student to play C and make a guess by completing C's line.
2. Tell students to highlight or underline *You're going to...* in the conversation.
3. Form groups of 5. Tell students to take turns acting out an errand. Tell them to use *You're going to...* to make guesses and to play three rounds.
4. Ask each group to act out an errand for the class to guess.

▆▆ EXPANSION: Speaking practice for 2
After Step 2, call on students to report what a group member is going to do (for example, *Amir is going to take the car to the car wash.*).

3. WRITE ABOUT IT. Write sentences about...

1. Read the directions. Tell students to write five sentences.
2. Ask students to check each other's sentences:
   • Sentences should use contractions with pronouns.
   • Sentences should use the correct form of *be going to* + the base form of a verb.
   • Sentences should begin with a capital letter and end with an end mark.
3. Circulate and assist students as necessary.
4. Call on each student to read one of his or her sentences.

▆▆ EXPANSION: Speaking practice for 3

1. Ask: *Do you remember what your classmates are going to do?*
2. Call on students to say what one of their classmates said that they were going to do in Step 3.
3. Continue until students have remembered what each student is going to do.

Self-Directed Learning

Point out the blue bar. Ask students if they can do the lesson learning objective or if they need more practice. Tell them to check one of the boxes. Assign Extra Practice as needed.

Extra Practice		
	pp. 30–31	

Grammar

C **INTERPRET.** Look at the pictures. What are the people going to do? There is more than one correct answer.

In picture 1, the man is going to send a package.

(Answers will vary.)

1

The family is going to shop for food.

2

The boys are going to buy books.

3

4

She is going to get money.

5

He is going to eat.

6

The man is going to borrow some books.

D **WRITE.** Now write a sentence for each picture in Exercise C.

Show what you know!

1. **THINK ABOUT IT.** Make a list of errands you are going to run this week.

2. **TALK ABOUT IT.** Play charades. Take turns acting out an errand. Other students, guess the errand.

   A: What am I going to do?
   B: You're going to stop at the bank.
   A: No.
   C: You're going to . . .

You're going to . . .

3. **WRITE ABOUT IT.** Write sentences about what your classmates are going to do.

I can use future with *be going to*. ■ I need more practice. ■

For more practice, go to MyEnglishLab.

Read about ways to pay for things

1 BEFORE YOU READ

A DECIDE. Complete the sentences with the words in the box.

cash   comparing   minimum   purchase

1. She's making a
_____purchase_____.
She's paying with
_____cash_____.

2. You don't have to pay
the whole bill, but
you have to pay the
_____minimum_____.

3. He's _____comparing_____
TVs. Which one is best?

B MAKE CONNECTIONS. How do you pay when you go shopping?
Do you use cash, a credit card, or another way to pay?

2 READ

▶ LISTEN AND READ.

Academic Skill: Identify Purpose

Authors write articles for different reasons. This is
the author's purpose. Knowing the author's purpose
helps you understand the main idea.

How Would You Like to Pay for That?

1 Are you thinking of making a big purchase soon, like a
TV or a computer? What is the best way to pay for it?
We interviewed three shoppers who just bought a
new $475 Sonpanic TV. Read how each shopper
5 paid for the TV. Then compare how much it really
cost them. You may be surprised!

Brian

Credit Card "I paid with my credit card. I use my credit card
because it gives me time. I get a month to pay the bill. I always
pay the total amount. That way I don't pay the credit card
10 company any interest. Credit card interest rates are too high.
Like 20%!"

Sonpanic TV	$475.00
Sales tax	+ 23.75
Total cost	**$498.75**
(Sales tax = 5% in Brian's state)	

Cindy

Credit Card "I paid with my credit card. I like to use my credit
card because it gives me time to pay. I never have enough
cash for big purchases. So I pay just the minimum every
15 month. The problem is, it can take years to pay off the whole
bill! So I pay a lot of interest."

Sonpanic TV	$475.00
Minimum monthly payment	$25.00
Number of months*	× 24
Cost of TV (including 20% interest)	$600.00
Sales tax	+ $30.40
Total cost	**$630.40**
(Sales tax = 6.4% in Cindy's state)	

Craig

Rent-to-Own "I bought my TV at the rent-to-own store because
I don't have enough cash right now, and I don't have a credit
card. At a rent-to-own store, I can get a new TV and bring it
20 home the same day. Every week, I pay $24 to the store for the
TV. If I don't have the money, I return the TV to the store. But if I
keep paying, at the end of the year, the TV will belong to me."

Sonpanic TV	$475.00
Weekly payment	$24.00
Number of weeks	× 52
Total cost of the TV	**$1,248.00**
(There's no sales tax in Craig's state.)	

*Source: http://www.bankrate.com

Correlations

ELPS Level 2: 1, 2, 3, 4, 5, 6, 7, 8, 9, 10
CCRS Level A: RI/RL.1., RI.1.2, RI.1.3, RI.1.4,
RI.1.8, SL.K.2
CASAS Reading: RDG 1.7, 1.8, 2.2, 2.3, 3.2, 3.11,
3.14, 4.2, 4.9
CASAS Listening: L2.1, 2.3, 4.2, 5.8, 6.1
CASAS Competencies: 0.1.2, 0.1.5, 1.3.1
**Complete standards language available on the
Pearson English Portal.**

Self-Directed Learning

1. State the **lesson objective**. Say: *In this lesson, we
will learn to identify purpose.*
2. Say: *We will read about ways to pay for things.*

1 BEFORE YOU READ

A DECIDE. **Complete the sentences with the...**

1. Read the directions. Say the words in the box.
2. Read the first sentence. Ask: *What phrase
means the same as* to buy? (make a purchase)
Tell students to write *purchase* to complete
the sentence.
3. Tell students to complete the sentences.
4. Call on students to read the completed
sentences aloud.

B MAKE CONNECTIONS. **How do you pay...**

1. **Scaffold:** Ask: *What are the different ways to
pay for big purchases, such as a TV or furniture?*
Brainstorm different ways to pay (for example,
*cash, credit card, debit card, check, gift card,
store credit, financing/rent-to-own*).
2. Explain terms as needed. For example, *financing*
means the store or another company, such as a
bank, lends you money and charges you interest.
3. Ask: *What are some other big purchases?* Write
students' ideas on the board—for example,
appliances (refrigerator, washer and dryer, etc.), *a
computer, a cell phone.* As needed, point out that
big refers to the cost, not the size of the product.
4. Ask: *How do you pay when you go shopping?*
Elicit responses.

2 READ

▶ **LISTEN AND READ.**

1. Point to the **Academic Skill** and read it. Ask:
*What are some reasons that an author writes
something?* Elicit ideas and write them (for
example, *to give information, to express an
opinion, to tell a story*).

2. Introduce the reading. Ask: *What is the title of this
article? What do you think the topic is going to be?*
(different ways to pay for purchases) *Who usually
asks the question in the title?* (a sales clerk)
3. Introduce the visuals. Tell students to look at the
photos. Ask: *Who are these people?* (customers,
people buying something) *What other visuals or
graphics do you see?* (some figures, amounts of
money) *What do they show?* (costs of different
kinds of payment)

 ActiveTeach for 2: Anticipation Guide –
Before **Reading exercise**

4. Read the text.
   a. Say: *Now we are going to read and listen to the
   article* How Would You Like to Pay for That? *As
   you read, think about the author's purpose in
   writing it.*
   b. Play the audio as students listen and read
   along silently.
   c. Have an above-level student read the first
   paragraph aloud or read it aloud yourself. Ask:
   How many shoppers did they interview? (three)
   What did the shoppers buy? (a new TV) *What
   was the price of the TV in each case before tax
   and the other extra costs?* ($475.00)
   d. Have students read the green paragraph
   headings. Ask: *What ways did the shoppers pay?*
   (credit card and rent-to-own) *Which shoppers
   used a credit card?* (Brian and Cindy) *Why do
   they use credit cards?* (It gives them time to pay.)
   Which one pays the total amount every month?
   (Brian) *Who used rent-to-own?* (Craig) *Why?* (He
   doesn't have cash or a credit card.) Tell students
   to underline the reasons.
   e. Tell students to circle the total cost for each
   purchase. Ask: *Who paid the least?*
   f. Tell students that the introduction and
   conclusion of a text often provide clues to the
   author's purpose. Tell students to read the
   introduction again and underline clues to the
   writer's purpose (for example, *the best way to
   pay, compare how much*).
   g. Ask: *Why did the author write this article?* (to
   compare different ways to pay)

 ActiveTeach for 2: Anticipation Guide –
After **Reading exercise**

Reading

3 CLOSE READING

A IDENTIFY. What is the main idea?

1. Say: *Now we are going to identify the main idea.*
2. Read the directions. Have students circle the answer.
3. Elicit the answer from the class.

B CITE EVIDENCE. Complete the statements...

1. Say: *Now we are going to find information in the reading.*
2. Read the directions. Walk around as students work on the activity. If students are struggling, have them work in pairs or direct them to the text lines where they can find the information.
3. Call on students to read the sentence with the correct completion. Ask a different student to **cite evidence**: *Where is that information? What is the line number?*

■ **EXPANSION: Graphic organizer practice for 3B**

1. Have students make a chart with these column headings: *Way to Pay, Reason, Total Cost*. Write the names of the shoppers on each row.
2. Tell students to take notes in the chart as they read.
3. Call on students to share their ideas.
4. Ask the class: *What is the best way to pay?*

C INTERPRET. Complete the sentences...

1. Read the directions. Tell students to look at the chart in the reading on page 58.
2. Walk around and check that students are using the chart to determine the answers.
3. Call on students to read the completed sentences.
4. **Reinforce academic language:** Point to the word *interpret*. Say: Interpret *means to decide what something means.*

Numeracy: Interpret data

Ask additional questions:

1. *How much did Brian pay in total?* ($498.75)
2. *How many months did Cindy make the minimum payment?* (24)
3. *How often did Craig have to make a payment?* (every week)
4. *How many payments did Craig make?* (52)
5. *How much more did Craig pay than Brian?* ($750)

4 SUMMARIZE

 ActiveTeach for 4: Vocabulary Practice

1. Read the directions. Ask students to read aloud the words in the box.
2. Tell students to complete the paragraph.
3. To check answers, call on students to read sentences in the summary with the blanks filled in. Ask other students to read the completed summary silently.

Show what you know!

1. THINK ABOUT IT. Make a list of big...

1. Read the directions.
2. Model the activity. Tell students about some big purchases you want to make someday.
3. Tell students to make a list of big purchases they want to make.

2. TALK ABOUT IT. Work with a partner...

1. Read the directions.
2. Pair students to compare their lists.
3. Call on students to share one of the things on their lists and the best way to pay for it.

 ActiveTeach for 2: Academic Conversation Support

3. WRITE ABOUT IT. Write about a big purchase...

1. Read the directions. Write sentence frames: *I want to buy _____. I will pay for it with _____.*
2. Model the activity. Say and complete the sentence frames about a purchase you want to make.
3. Have students write their sentence(s) on a sheet of paper. Walk around and answer any questions.
4. Collect the papers for review or put them in the students' writing portfolios.

Self-Directed Learning

Point out the blue bar. Ask students if they can do the lesson learning objective or if they need more practice. Tell them to check one of the boxes. Assign Extra Practice as needed.

■ **EXPANSION: Self-directed learning**

Ask students to reflect: *What did you learn from this reading?* Call on students to share something they learned.

Extra Practice

 CCRS Plus   Workbook pp. 32–33

Reading

3 CLOSE READING

A IDENTIFY. What is the main idea?

When you make a big purchase, _____.
- **a.** *how much* you pay depends on *how* you pay ✓
- **b.** it's best to pay for it in cash
- **c.** you always have to pay sales tax

B CITE EVIDENCE. Complete the statements. Where is the information? Write the line numbers.

Lines

1. Brian doesn't like to _____.
   - **a.** shop with a credit card
   - **b.** pay the total amount of his credit card bill
   - **c.** pay interest to his credit card company ✓   9–10

2. Cindy doesn't _____.
   - **a.** have a credit card
   - **b.** make big purchases with cash ✓
   - **c.** pay interest to her credit card company   13–14

3. Cindy is unhappy because she _____.
   - **a.** doesn't have a good TV
   - **b.** pays a lot of interest on big purchases ✓
   - **c.** has only a little cash   15–16

C INTERPRET. Complete the sentences about the chart.

1. The person who paid the most for the TV is _____.
   - **a.** Brian
   - **b.** Cindy
   - **c.** Craig ✓

2. The sales tax in Cindy's state is _____.
   - **a.** 0%
   - **b.** 6.4% ✓
   - **c.** 5%

4 SUMMARIZE

Complete the summary with the words in the box.

amount   interest   minimum   whole

Three shoppers all bought the same TV, but paid in different ways. Brian used a credit card and paid the (1) ____whole____ bill at the end of the month: $475 plus sales tax. Cindy used a credit card, too. She made only the (2) ____minimum____ monthly payment, so she'll pay a lot of (3) ____interest____. Her TV will cost $600 plus sales tax. Craig is renting a TV from a rent-to-own store. He'll pay the greatest (4) ____amount____: $1,248.

Show what you know!

1. **THINK ABOUT IT.** Make a list of big purchases you want to make someday.

2. **TALK ABOUT IT.** Work with a partner. Compare your list of purchases. What is the best way to pay for them?

3. **WRITE ABOUT IT.** Write about a big purchase and the way to pay for it.

I can identify purpose. ■   I need more practice. ■

To read more, go to MyEnglishLab.

Describe problems with purchases

1 ❘ BEFORE YOU LISTEN

MATCH. Look at the pictures. Match the pictures to the problems with the clothes.

There's a hole in it.   It's too tight.   A button is missing.
They're too loose.   ~~The zipper is broken.~~   A seam is ripped.

1

The zipper is broken.

2

They're too loose.

3

A button is missing.

4

There's a hole in it.

5

A seam is ripped.

6

It's too tight.

2 ❘ LISTEN

Ⓐ PREDICT. Look at the picture of two co-workers on a break. What are they talking about?

Ⓑ ▶ LISTEN FOR MAIN IDEA. Listen to the conversation. Complete the sentence.

Anna and Bessy are going to _____.
a. buy clothes   **b.** return clothes

Anna   Bessy

Ⓒ ▶ LISTEN FOR DETAILS. Listen again. Read the sentences. Circle *True* or *False*.

1. Bessy needs to buy a jacket.   True   (False)
2. There is a problem with Bessy's jacket.   (True)   False
3. Anna wants to buy a dress.   True   (False)

Ⓓ ▶ EXPAND. Listen to the whole conversation. Complete the sentence.

Anna's dress is really a _____ shirt _____.

Correlations

ELPS Level 2: 2, 7
CCRS Level A: SL.1.1, SL.K.6
CASAS Reading: RDG 1.7, 2.2, 2.3
CASAS Listening: L2.1, 2.3, 4.1, 4.2, 6.1, 6.2
CASAS Competencies: 0.1.2, 0.1.4, 0.1.5, 0.1.6, 1.3.3
Complete standards language available on the Pearson English Portal.

Self-Directed Learning

State the **lesson objective**. Say: *In this lesson, we will learn to describe problems with purchases.*

1 BEFORE YOU LISTEN

MATCH. Look at the pictures. Match the…

1. Tell the class to look at the photos. Elicit the name of each item of clothing (*a jacket, pants, a shirt, a scarf, a sweater, a dress*).
2. Read the directions.
3. Read the list of problems with the clothes and ask the class to repeat.
4. Tell students to look at picture 1. Ask: *What's the problem?* (The zipper is broken.)
5. Students match pictures to problems.
6. Students compare answers with a partner.
7. Ask: *What's the problem with each piece of clothing?* Call on students to say the problem in each picture.
8. Say: *People often return clothes to the store when they have these problems. They can get their money back or get another one.*
9. *Optional:* Elicit other reasons that people return clothes and write them (for example, *It's / They're too big. It's / They're too small. The hem is ripped. There's a spot on it / them.*).

2 LISTEN

Ⓐ **PREDICT. Look at the picture of two…**

1. Tell students to look at the picture. Ask: *Where are they?* (in a mall) *What are Anna and Bessy carrying?* (shopping bags) *What do you think they are talking about? Guess.* (shopping, clothes, a sale, a problem with something)
2. Elicit ideas from the class and list them on the board.

Ⓑ ▶ **LISTEN FOR MAIN IDEA. Listen to the…**

1. Tell students to read the directions and the answer choices silently.
2. Play the audio. Students circle the correct answer.
3. Elicit the correct answer. Ask: *Was your guess in Exercise 2A correct?* Circle the correct answer in the list on the board.

Teaching Tip: Use the script

Optional: If students need additional support, tell them to read the Audio Script on page 268 as they listen to the conversations.

Culture Note

1. Ask: *Do you sometimes return clothes or other purchases? Do you feel comfortable taking something back to the store where you bought it?*
2. Explain: *In the U.S., it's usually not a problem for customers to return purchases. Most stores have a return policy, or rules for returning purchases, posted near the cash registers.*
3. Ask: *What kinds of rules about returns do stores have?* Write: *You need to…*
4. Brainstorm and list students' ideas. Then read the sentences out loud (for example, *You need to have a receipt / return items in a certain amount of time / keep tags on the item / keep the item, like food, sealed.*).
5. Ask: *Is it easy to return purchases in your native country? Do stores have similar rules?*

Ⓒ ▶ **LISTEN FOR DETAILS. Listen again. Read…**

1. Read the directions. Tell students to read the sentences silently.
2. Play the audio. Students listen and circle *True* or *False*. Play the audio again as needed.
3. Review the correct answers with the class. Ask students to read the sentences and call on classmates to say *True* or *False*.
4. *Optional:* Tell students to rewrite the false sentences to make them true. (1. Bessy needs to <u>return</u> a jacket 3. Anna wants to <u>return</u> a dress.)
5. Ask: *What's the problem with Bessy's jacket?* (The zipper is broken.) As needed, play the audio again.

Ⓓ ▶ **EXPAND. Listen to the whole…**

1. Read the directions and the sentence frame.
2. Play the audio. Students complete the sentence.
3. Call on a student to read the completed sentence.
4. *Optional:* Ask: *Do you think people often make mistakes like this?*

Listening and Speaking

3 CONVERSATION

Ⓐ ▶ LISTEN AND READ. Then listen and repeat.

1. Note: This conversation is the same one students heard in Exercise 2B on page 60.
2. Tell students to read the conversation silently.
3. Play the audio. Students listen. Then students listen and repeat.

> **Teaching Tip: Choral reading**
>
> Before pairs practice the conversation, lead the class in a choral reading to build confidence. Divide the class in half. Stand in front of one half and have them read A's lines aloud with you. Then move to the other half and have them read B's lines aloud with you.

Ⓑ WORK TOGETHER. Practice the...

1. Pair students and tell them to practice the conversation in Exercise 3A.
2. Tell them to take turns playing A and B.

Ⓒ CREATE. Make new conversations. Use the...

1. Read the directions.
2. Tell students to look at the information in the boxes. Say each item and tell the class to repeat. Ask: *Which boxes have items of clothing?* (blue and green) *Which box has adjectives?* (yellow)
3. Show the conversation with blanks. Read through the conversation. When you come to a blank, fill it in with a student's name or information from the boxes. As you fill in each blank, say the color of the answer space and point to the same-color word or phrase you choose from the boxes.
4. Ask the student whose name you used and another on-level student to read the conversation on the board.
5. Erase the words in the blanks and ask two above-level students to make up a new conversation.
6. Pair students and tell them to take turns playing A and B and to use the information in the boxes to fill in the blanks.
7. Tell students to stand, mingle, and practice the conversation with several new partners.
8. Circulate and make sure students are completing the conversation correctly.
9. Call on pairs to perform for the class.

■ MULTILEVEL INSTRUCTION for 3C

Pre-level scaffolding Before practicing each part, students write words in the conversation. If the clothing word is plural, they also make any necessary changes to other words in the conversation.

Above-level expansion After practicing both parts, each partner thinks of a clothing item and a reason to return it. Then partners close their books and practice the role-play again.

Ⓓ ROLE-PLAY. Student A, talk about returning...

1. Read the directions.
2. Write the first two lines of the example conversation and continue it:
   A: *I need to return these pants.*
   B: *What's the problem?*
   A: *They're too tight.*
   B: *That's annoying. I need to return some shorts.*
   A: *What's wrong with them?*
   B: *There's a hole in them.*
3. Elicit other plural words for clothes (for example, *shoes, jeans, slacks, pajamas, gloves, underpants*).
4. Read the conversation with an above-level student. Point out the underlined words and phrases. Say: *Because the returned clothes are plural, other changes are made to the verbs and the pronouns.*
5. Pair students and tell them to take turns playing A and B and to only use plural clothes from the board. Tell them they can make up their own reasons for returning them.
6. Tell students to stand, mingle, and practice the conversation with several new partners.
7. Circulate and make sure students are completing the conversation correctly.
8. Call on pairs to perform for the class.

■ MULTI-LEVEL INSTRUCTION for 3D

Cross-ability Tell above-level students to talk about problems with plural clothing words. Pre-level students talk about problems with singular clothing words.

Self-Directed Learning

Point out the blue bar. Ask students if they can do the lesson learning objective or if they need more practice. Tell them to check one of the boxes. Assign Extra Practice as needed.

> **Extra Practice**
>
> MyEnglishLab   Workbook pp. 34–35

Listening and Speaking

3 CONVERSATION

A ▶ **LISTEN AND READ. Then listen and repeat.**

A: Hi, Bessy. Are you going out at lunchtime?
B: Yeah, I need to run an errand. I'm going to Kohn's. I need to return this jacket.
A: How come?
B: The zipper is broken.
A: That's very annoying. . . . Actually, I need to go to Kohn's, too. I need to return a dress.
B: Really? What's wrong with it?
A: It's too short.

B **WORK TOGETHER. Practice the conversation in Exercise A.**

C **CREATE. Make new conversations. Use the words in the boxes.**

A: Hi, _____. Are you going out at lunchtime?
B: Yeah, I need to run an errand. I'm going to Kohn's to return
   this _____.
A: What's the problem?
B: _____
A: That's very annoying. . . . Actually, I need to go to Kohn's,
   too. I need to return a _____.
B: Really? What's wrong with it?
A: It's too _____.

cap
shirt
sweater

A button is missing.
A seam is ripped.
There's a hole in it.

sweatshirt
raincoat
jacket

tight
long
big

D **ROLE-PLAY. Student A, talk about returning some clothes.
Student B, ask about the problem.**

A: I need to return these pants.
B: What's the problem?

I can describe problems with purchases. ■	I need more practice. ■

For more practice, go to MyEnglishLab.

Grammar

Adverbs of degree: *very* and *too*

<table>
<tr><td>**Adverbs of degree: *very* / *too***</td></tr>
</table>

That's	**very**	annoying.
It's	**too**	short.

Grammar Watch

- *very* = a lot
- *too* = more than you need or want

A IDENTIFY. **Cross out the incorrect words.**

1. This raincoat doesn't cost a lot. It's **very / ~~too~~** cheap.
2. She wears size 8. That dress is size 2. It's **~~very~~ / too** small for her.
3. The prices at the clearance sale are **very / ~~too~~** good. A lot of people are going to be there.
4. This sweater is **very / ~~too~~** pretty. I want to buy it.
5. These shoes aren't good for walking to work. They're **~~very~~ / too** tight.
6. This scarf is **very / ~~too~~** colorful. It looks great with my coat.

B COMPLETE. **Write *very* or *too*.**

1. **A:** The coffee shop on Oak Street is ___very___ good. I get breakfast there a lot.
   B: That place is ___too___ slow. I'm always late for work when I stop there.

2. **A:** I like that blouse. It's ___very___ beautiful.
   B: Thanks. But it's ___too___ big. I need to exchange it for a smaller size.

3. **A:** I don't like to shop online. For me, it's ___too___ slow. When I want something, I don't want to wait.
   B: Really? I shop online all the time. It's ___very___ easy to order what you need, and a few days later it's at your door.

4. **A:** That coat is ___very___ warm. It's perfect for cold winter days.
   B: I know. I want it, but it's ___too___ expensive. It's $90, and I only have $60.

I can use adverbs of degree *very* and *too* in a sentence. ■   I need more practice. ■

For more practice, go to MyEnglishLab.

Correlations

ELPS Level 2: 10
CASAS Reading: RDG 1.7
CASAS Competencies: 0.1.2
Complete standards language available on the Pearson English Portal.

Self-Directed Learning

State the **lesson objective**. Say: *In this lesson, we will learn to use adverbs of degree* very *and* too *in a sentence.*

Adverbs of degree: *very / too*

 ActiveTeach: Grammar Discovery

1. Warm up. Write:
   - *It's very expensive.*
   - *It's too expensive.*
2. Underline *very* and *too*.
3. Circle *expensive* in the examples and write the label *adjective*. Tell the class that *very* and *too* come in front of adjectives.
4. Read the **Grammar Watch** note.
5. Read the first sentence on the board. Say: *But it's possible for me to buy it.* Read the second sentence. Say: *It's impossible for me to buy it.*
6. Tell students to look at the grammar chart.
7. Read the first sentence in the chart. Stress the word *very*. Explain the meaning of *very annoying* with an example. Write: *My brother is usually late.* Say: *It is annoying, but it's not a big problem.*
8. Read the second sentence in the chart. Explain that *too* is negative. Give an example. Write: *These pants are too short.* Say: *They don't fit. I can't wear them.* Note: You can bring in a pair of pants or other piece of clothing that is too short for you to wear. Use it to illustrate the meaning of *too*.

 ActiveTeach: Grammar Coach

EXPANSION: Speaking practice for grammar presentation

1. Ask: *What is annoying to you?* As a class, come up with a list of annoying things (for example, a mosquito bite, clothes that are too small, waiting a long time for someone, burning dinner in the oven, forgetting a name, etc.). Encourage students to come up with light and humorous ideas.
2. Write the list as students volunteer ideas.

3. When the list is complete, begin to read the items in the list. Ask: *A mosquito bite?* Elicit a response from the entire class: *That's very annoying!* Make sure that the word *very* is stressed.
4. Continue for the entire list.

A IDENTIFY. **Cross out the incorrect words.**

1. Read the directions.
2. Read item 1. Ask: *Is it possible to buy the raincoat?* (yes) *Is the answer* very *or* too? (*very*)
3. Read item 2. Ask: *Is it possible for her to wear the dress?* (no) *Is the answer* very *or* too? (*too*)
4. Students compare answers with a partner. Tell them to take turns reading the sentences.
5. To check answers, call on students to read the sentences for the class.

B COMPLETE. **Write *very* or *too*.**

1. Read the directions.
2. Write item 1 and read it. Ask: *Can they go to the coffee shop? Is it possible?* (yes) *Is the answer* very *or* too? (very)
3. Students compare answers with a partner. Tell them to choose roles and read the conversations out loud.
4. To check answers, call on pairs to read the conversations for the class.

EXPANSION: Grammar and writing practice for B

1. Brainstorm adjectives and list them on the board.
2. Pair students and tell them to choose one adjective and write sentences with *very* and sentences with *too*. For example, for *cold: It's very cold today. I'm going to wear my wool coat. / I don't want to go to the beach today. It's too cold.*
3. Call on pairs to say their sentences for the class.

Self-Directed Learning

Point out the blue bar. Ask students if they can do the lesson learning objective or if they need more practice. Tell them to check one of the boxes. Assign Extra Practice as needed.

Extra Practice

  pp. 34–35

Lesson 10 | Writing

Correlations

ELPS Level 2: 3, 10
CCRS Level A: W.1.2, W.1.5, L.1.1
CASAS Reading: RDG 1.7, 1.8, 2.1
CASAS Listening: L2.1, 2.3
CASAS Competencies: 0.1.2, 0.1.5, 0.1.6
Complete standards language available on the Pearson English Portal.

Self-Directed Learning

1. State the **lesson objective**. Say: *In this lesson, we will learn to use a topic sentence.*
2. Say: *You will write about saving money.*

1 STUDY THE MODEL

1. Read the directions.
2. Point to the paragraph. Ask: *What is the title of the model?* (How I Save Money)
3. **Scaffold** the model. Write as a chart:

Ways to save money when shopping	
1	
2	
3	

4. Tell students to read the text and read the questions independently. Call on students to answer the questions. Ask: *What are the three ways the writer saves money?* (1. buys on sale, 2. uses cash, 3. checks receipt) Write the information in the chart on the board.
5. Ask students to think of some words and phrases that could be used to describe how they save money (for example, *buy things on sale, at a thrift store, at cheaper stores; pay with cash, pay with a check, pay with a debit card; use coupons, buy a lot at one time*). Make a list. Tell students they can use these ideas in their writing.

2 PLAN YOUR WRITING

1. Erase the information in the chart on the board.
2. Read the directions.
3. Model with a student. The student asks the teacher the questions. Make sure you say three ways you save money. They may be the same as the writer, or different.
4. Write the information into the chart.
5. Tell students to make their own chart on a piece of paper.
6. Have students work in pairs to ask and answer the questions. They should complete the chart with three ways they save money.

3 WRITE

1. Read the directions aloud.
2. Use your information in the chart from Exercise 2 to write sentences in a paragraph. Leave a blank for the topic sentence. Elicit the topic sentence.
3. Point to the **Writing Skill**. Read it aloud while students listen.
4. Ask: *Why is this a good topic sentence?* (It tells the main idea of the paragraph.) *Are there other good topic sentences for the paragraph?* (Possible answer: *I save money in different ways.*)
5. Tell students to write. Circulate to make sure students are writing in paragraph form and using topic sentences.

 ActiveTeach for 3: Writing Support

4 CHECK YOUR WRITING

1. Read the directions aloud. Point to the **Writing Checklist**. Call on students to read the checklist items aloud.
2. Pair students to review their writings together. Say: *Read your sentences with a partner. Use the Writing Checklist.* For additional help, remind students that a correct sentence:
   • *begins with a capital letter*
   • *has a subject*
   • *has a verb*
   • *has a period*
   • *is a complete idea*
3. Walk around and verify that students are using the checklist. Collect the papers for review or put them in the students' writing portfolios.

Teaching Tip: Digital skills

If you have a learning management system, tell students to post their paragraphs on a discussion board and provide feedback on other students' paragraphs. Model posting and replying for the class.

Self-Directed Learning

Point out the blue bar. Ask students if they can do the lesson learning objective or if they need more practice. Tell them to check one of the boxes. Assign Extra Practice as needed.

Extra Practice

 CCRS Plus   p. 36

Write about saving money

1 STUDY THE MODEL

READ. Answer the questions.

> Davit Babayan
>
> How I Save Money
>
> This is how I save money when
> I shop. I always buy things on sale.
> I pay with cash, not a credit card.
> I check the receipt to make sure the
> prices are correct.

1. What did Davit write about? Davit wrote about saving money.
2. Why does Davit buy things on sale? He buys things on sale to save money.
3. How does he pay? He pays with cash.
4. Why does he check the receipt? He checks the receipt to make sure the prices are correct.

2 PLAN YOUR WRITING

WORK TOGETHER. Ask and answer the questions.

1. How do you save money when you shop?
2. Do you buy things on sale?
3. How do you pay for things?
4. Do you look at your receipts? Why or why not?

3 WRITE

Now write about how you save money. Use the model, the Writing Skill, and your ideas from Exercise 2 to help you.

Writing Skill: Use a topic sentence

Start your paragraph with a topic sentence. A topic sentence tells the main idea of the paragraph. For example:

This is how I save money when I shop.

4 CHECK YOUR WRITING

WORK TOGETHER. Read the checklist. Read your writing aloud. Revise your writing.

WRITING CHECKLIST

☐ The paragraph answers the questions in Exercise 2.

☐ The paragraph starts with a topic sentence.

I can use a topic sentence. ■

I need more practice. ■

For more practice, go to MyEnglishLab.

Soft Skills at Work

Listen Actively

1 MEET RITA

Read about one of her workplace skills.

I'm a good listener. I listen actively. For example, I ask questions to make sure I understand the customer's needs.

2 RITA'S PROBLEM

READ. Circle *True* or *False*.

Rita is a salesperson at an electronics store. A customer shows her a laptop and says, "I want to return this laptop. I bought it here two months ago." Rita knows that customers can return items up to two weeks after they buy them. But when something is wrong with an item, they can return it up to two months after they buy it.

1. Rita sells computers in an electronics store.   (True)   False
2. A customer bought his laptop two weeks ago in that store.   True   (False)
3. Customers can return all items two months after they buy them.   True   (False)

3 RITA'S SOLUTION

A WORK TOGETHER. Rita listens actively to understand her customers' needs. What does she say? Explain your answer.

1. Rita says, "Sorry. There are no returns after two weeks."
2. Rita says, "OK. Is there something wrong with the laptop?"
3. Rita says, "OK. Did you buy the laptop here?"
4. Rita _____.

B ROLE-PLAY. Look at your answer to 3A. Role-play Rita's conversation.

Show what you know!

1. **THINK ABOUT IT.** Do you listen actively? How do you listen actively in class? At work? At home?

2. **WRITE ABOUT IT.** Write an example in your Skills Log.

   I listen actively in class. I repeat and ask questions.

3. **PRESENT IT.** Tell the class how you listen actively.

I can give an example of how I listen actively. ■

Unit Review: Go back to page 45. Which unit goals can you check off?

Correlations

ELPS Level 2: 2, 3, 7, 9
CASAS Reading: RDG 1.7, 1.8, 3.2
CASAS Listening: L2.1, 2.3, 4.1, 4.2
CASAS Competencies: 0.1.2, 0.1.4, 0.1.5, 0.1.6, 0.2.1, 4.8.3
Complete standards language available on the Pearson English Portal.

Self-Directed Learning

State the **lesson objective**. Say: *In this lesson, we will give an example of how we listen actively.*

1 MEET RITA

1. Ask: *What is the title of this lesson?* (Listen actively) *What does* actively *mean?* (making an effort)
2. Write *Workplace Skill*. Read the directions. Say: *Listen as I read* Meet Rita. Read the paragraph. Ask: *What is one of Rita's workplace skills?* (She listens actively.) Next to *Workplace Skill*, write: *Listen actively*.
3. Under *Workplace Skill*, write: *Examples*. Ask: *How does Rita listen actively?* (She asks questions. She tries to understand the customer's needs.) Write the examples. Elicit other ways to listen actively and write them under *Workplace Skill*.

2 RITA'S PROBLEM

1. Say: *Now we are going to read about Rita at work. Listen while I read.* Read the first sentence. Use the photo and the **Career Awareness** information to help students understand her job. Say: *Look at the photo. Where is Rita?* (electronics store) *She is smiling. Why?* (She is ready to help customers.)
2. Say: *Rita has a problem at work. Listen while I read.* Read the rest of the paragraph. Explain any unfamiliar vocabulary.
3. Read the directions. Call on students to answer. Ask them to **cite evidence**: *Where is that information?*
4. Ask: *What is Rita's problem?* (A customer wants to return a laptop two months after he bought it.)

Career Awareness: Salesperson

Salespeople work in stores and other businesses to sell products and help customers. No formal education is required.

3 RITA'S SOLUTION

A WORK TOGETHER. Rita listens actively...

1. Read the directions. Tell students to work together. Remind them that only one solution is correct.
2. Ask: *Is #1 a good way to listen actively?* (no) *Why not?* (She doesn't ask any questions.) *Is #2 a good way?* (yes) *Why?* (She asks a question for more information.) *Is #3 a good way?* (no) *Why not?* (She probably wasn't listening to the customer while he was talking.)
3. Elicit ideas from students for #4. Write them. Ask: *Are these good ways to listen actively?*

> **ActiveTeach for 3A: Academic Conversation Support**

B ROLE-PLAY. Look at your answer to 3A...

1. Group students in pairs. Explain one person will be Rita. The other person will be the customer. Model the activity with an above-level student.
2. Walk around and ask students to switch roles. If students aren't pronouncing their lines clearly, model correct pronunciation and ask them to repeat.

Show what you know!

1. THINK ABOUT IT. Do you listen actively?...

Read the directions. Students think about their answers and then share with a partner. Call on students to share.

2. WRITE ABOUT IT. Write an example in your...

Read the directions and the example. Have students write their examples in their **Skills Log** at the back of the book. Circulate and assist students as needed.

3. PRESENT IT. Tell the class how you listen...

Read the directions. Call on students to stand up in front of the class and read their sentences.

Self-Directed Learning

1. Point out the blue bar. Ask students if they can do the lesson learning objective or if they need more practice. Tell them to check one of the boxes. Assign Extra Practice as needed.
2. Ask students to turn to page 45. Go to the Unit Wrap-Up teaching notes on page T-45.

Extra Practice

 p. 37

Small Talk

4

Classroom Materials / Extra Practice

 ActiveTeach

 MyEnglishLab

 Workbook

 Life Skills Writing, MCA, Team Projects, Persistence Activities

Unit Overview

Goals
- See the list of goals on the facing page

Pronunciation
- Unpronounced syllables
- *Have to* and *has to*

Reading
- Read about different writing styles
- Predict the topic

Grammar
- Adverbs of frequency
- Questions with *How often* / frequency time expressions
- Simple present: *love / like / hate* + infinitive
- Modal: *Have to*

Writing
- Write about a free-time activity
- Use details in your writing

Document Literacy and Numeracy
- Complete a Venn Diagram
- Interpret calendars
- Interpret a bar graph
- Understand emojis

Workplace, Life, and Community Skills
- Understand a schedule of events
- Digital Skills: Find a digital calendar online. Add two events to a digital calendar. Invite a friend.

Life Skills Writing
- Complete a library card application

Soft Skills at Work
- Be professional

Preview

1. Set the context of the unit by asking questions about free-time activities (for example, *What do you do in your free time? How often do you do those activities?*).
2. Show the Unit Opener. Ask: *What is the unit title?* (Small Talk) Ask: *What are some examples of small talk?* (talking about the weather, plans for the weekend)
3. Say: *Look at the picture.* Ask the Preview questions. (Possible answers: a group of friends/family; outside, in a garden; talking about food)

Unit Goals

1. Point to the Unit Goals. Explain that this list shows what you will be studying in this unit.
2. Tell students to read the goals silently.
3. Say each goal. Explain unfamiliar vocabulary as needed.
4. Point to the ☐ next to the first goal. Say: *We will come back to this page again. You will write a checkmark next to the goals you learned in the unit.*

Oral Presentation

1. Tell students they will give a short presentation at the end of the unit.
2. Write the topics:
   Option 1: One of my free-time activities
   Option 2: Different writing styles
3. Assign the topics to two students.

Unit Wrap-Up

1. Review the Unit Goals with students.
2. Direct students to the Grammar Review.
3. If you assigned presentations, ask students to present.

 ActiveTeach for Wrap-Up: Team Project

 ActiveTeach for Wrap-Up: Persistence Activities

4 Small Talk

PREVIEW

Look at the picture. What do you see? Where are the people? What are they talking about?

UNIT GOALS

- [ ] Identify free-time activities
- [ ] Talk about free-time activities
- [ ] Read a community calendar
- [ ] Understand a schedule of events
- [ ] Communicate likes and dislikes

- [ ] Accept or decline an invitation
- [ ] **Academic skill:** Predict the topic
- [ ] **Writing skill:** Use details in your writing
- [ ] **Workplace soft skill:** Show how you are professional

A PREDICT. Look at the pictures. What are the people doing?

B ▶ LISTEN AND POINT. Then listen and repeat.

Correlations

ELPS Level 2: 2, 7, 8
CCRS Level A: SL.1.1, SL.K.6, L.1.5, L.1.6
CASAS Reading: RDG 1.7, 2.2, 2.3
CASAS Listening: L2.1, 2.3, 2.9, 4.1, 4.2
CASAS Competencies: 0.1.2, 0.1.5, 0.2.1, 0.2.4, 7.4.1
Complete standards language available on the Pearson English Portal.

Self-Directed Learning

State the **lesson objective**. Say: *In this lesson, we will learn to identify free-time activities.*

A PREDICT. Look at the pictures. What are the...

1. Read the directions. Tell students to cover the list on page 67.
2. Point to picture 1 and ask: *What free-time activity is this?* Say: *#1 is go swimming.*
3. Say: *Look at the other pictures. What free-time activities do you know?* Students call out answers. Help students pronounce the free-time activities if they have difficulty.
4. If a student calls out an incorrect free-time activity, ask a *yes/no* clarification question: *Is number 8 go fishing?* If nobody can identify the correct activity (*go to the beach*), tell students they will now listen to an audio and practice the names of the activities.

B LISTEN AND POINT. Then listen and repeat.

1. Read the directions. Play the audio. Students listen and point to the free-time activities.
2. While the audio is playing, walk around and check that students are pointing to the correct activities. Pause the audio after item 12.
3. Say each free-time activity in random order and ask students to point to the appropriate picture.
4. Tell students to look at page 67. Resume the audio. Students listen, read, and repeat.

ActiveTeach for B: Vocabulary Flashcards

■ EXPANSION: Writing practice for B

1. Tell the class to close their books. Say a free-time activity and tell students to write it. Repeat for several activities.
2. Students compare answers with a partner.
3. Walk around and spot-check answers. If many students have difficulty, tell them they will practice spelling later in the unit.

Culture Note

Most U.S. towns and cities have public areas for exercise and recreation. These range from parks and hiking paths to playgrounds, swimming pools, and ice-skating rinks. Most of these are usually free, although some may require a small fee. To find out more information, search online for your local parks and recreation department's website.

Vocabulary

C **ACT IT OUT. Student A, act out a free-time...**
1. Read the directions.
2. Model the game: Act out a free-time activity (for example, *go dancing*). Ask the class to guess the activity.
3. Form groups of 3. Students take turns playing the role of Student A.
4. Walk around and check that students who are guessing use question intonation. Model as needed (for example, *Go running?*).
5. To wrap up, call on a few individual students to act out a free-time activity while the class guesses.

D **CATEGORIZE. Look at the list of free-time...**
1. Read the directions.
2. Draw the chart on the board. Point to picture 1 and ask: *What activity is this?* (go swimming) *Is it an indoor activity, an outdoor activity, or can it be both indoor and outdoor?* (both) Write *go swimming* in the middle of the diagram.
3. Repeat with pictures 7 and 10. (*go to the gym, go to the park*)
4. Form groups of 3. Tell them to draw their own charts as a group, talk about where people do each activity, and write the activities in their charts.
5. To review, call on volunteers to add the rest of the vocabulary items to the chart on the board.
6. Ask the class if the activities are in the correct places in the chart. Point out that there may be different opinions about where to write the activities.

Study Tip: Write sentences
1. Point to the **Study Tip**. Read the directions and the examples.
2. Tell students to write sentences for five different activities that they like to do.
3. Walk around and spot-check for spelling. If misspellings occur, tell students to check the list on page 67.
4. Say: *You can remember new vocabulary when you apply it to your own life.* Remind students to use this strategy to remember other new vocabulary.

Show what you know!

1. THINK ABOUT IT. Write three activities...
1. Read the directions.
2. Model the activity. Write three activities from the list on page 67 that you do in your free time.

3. Tell students to write three activities from the list or their own activities.
4. Walk around and check spelling. As needed, help students to begin each activity with *go* or the base form of another verb.

2. TALK ABOUT IT. Ask your classmates about...
1. Read the directions. Write: *What do you do in your free time?* Say the question and ask the class to repeat.
2. Say: *Ask for more information. Ask:* Where do you go? How often do you go?
3. Model the activity with an above-level student. Point to the question on the board and direct the student to ask you the question. Answer with one of the activities you wrote on the board. Then the student asks for more information.
4. Form pairs. Students take turns asking and answering the questions.
5. Tell students to stand, mingle, and ask classmates: *What do you do in your free time?*

3. WRITE ABOUT IT. Now write about a...
1. Read the directions. Write an example.
2. Share the checklist below. Then write a checkmark next to each as you point back to the example sentence.
   - The sentence is about a free-time activity.
   - The sentence says where the student does this free-time activity.
   - The sentence says how often the student does this free-time activity.
3. Reform the pairs from Step 2. Partners write about each other, using the information that they exchanged already.
4. Give students time to write their sentences.
5. Tell students to show their sentences to their partner. Tell the students to use the checklist to review the sentences.
6. Walk around and verify that students are using the checklist. Collect the papers for review or put them in the students' writing portfolios.

Self-Directed Learning
Point out the blue bar. Ask students if they can do the lesson learning objective or if they need more practice. Tell them to check one of the boxes. Assign Extra Practice as needed.

Extra Practice
p. 38

Vocabulary

Free-time activities

1. go swimming	4. go dancing	7. go to the gym	10. go to the park
2. go shopping	5. go running	8. go to the beach	11. go for a walk
3. go fishing	6. go out to eat	9. go to the zoo	12. go for a bike ride

C **ACT IT OUT.** Student A, act out a free-time activity. Other students, guess the activity.

Student A acts out "go dancing."
B: Go running?
A: No.
C: Go dancing?
A: Yes!

D **CATEGORIZE.** Look at the list of free-time activities. Which are outdoor activities? Which are indoor activities? Which can be both? Complete the chart.
(Answers will vary.)

Indoor
go to the gym
go shopping
go dancing

Both
go swimming
go out to eat
go running
go to the zoo

Outdoor
go to the park
go fishing
go to the beach
go for a walk
go for a bike ride

Study Tip

Write Sentences

Look at the free-time activities. Which activities do you like to do? Write sentences.

I like to go swimming.
I don't like to go shopping.

Show what you know!

1. **THINK ABOUT IT.** Write three activities you do in your free time.

2. **TALK ABOUT IT.** Ask your classmates about their free-time activities.

   A: What do you do in your free time?
   B: I go to the beach.
   A: Where do you go?
   B: I go to Sunset Beach.
   A: Really? How often do you go?

3. **WRITE ABOUT IT.** Now write about a classmate's free-time activities.

   Wong goes to the beach in his free time. He likes Sunset Beach. He usually goes every weekend.

I can identify free-time activities. ■   I need more practice. ■

For more practice, go to MyEnglishLab.

Listening and Speaking

Talk about free-time activities

1 BEFORE YOU LISTEN

LABEL. Look at the pictures. Write the names of the classes.

a business class   an auto mechanics class   a guitar class

1. ___a guitar class___

2. ___a business class___

3. ___an auto mechanics class___

2 LISTEN

A ▶ **LISTEN FOR MAIN IDEA.** What are they talking about?

   a. weekend plans
   b. business
   c. going hiking

B ▶ **LISTEN FOR DETAILS.** Listen again. Answer the questions.

1. Who does Bi-Yun usually see on Sunday?
   a. her family   **b.** her friends   **c.** her classmates

Mario   Bi-Yun

2. What does Mario usually do on Saturday mornings?
   a.    **b.**    **c.**

C ▶ **EXPAND.** Listen to the whole conversation. Answer the question.

Which level class do you think Mario is in?
   a. beginning   **b.** intermediate   **c.** advanced

Correlations

ELPS Level 2: 2, 7
CASAS Reading: RDG 1.7, 2.2, 2.3
CASAS Listening: L1.4, 2.1, 2.3, 4.1, 4.2, 6.1, 6.2
CASAS Competencies: 0.1.2, 0.1.5, 0.2.1, 0.2.4
Complete standards language available on the Pearson English Portal.

Self-Directed Learning

State the **lesson objective**. Say: *In this lesson, we will learn to talk about free-time activities.*

1 BEFORE YOU LISTEN

LABEL. Look at the pictures. Write the names...

1. Say: *Sometimes people take classes in their free time. Look at the pictures of people taking classes.*
2. Read the directions. Say the words and phrases in the box.
3. Give students time to label the pictures.
4. Ask: *Which picture shows a business class?* Students call out the number of the picture.
5. Repeat for the remaining words in the box.

EXPANSION: Writing and speaking practice for 1

1. Pair students and have them list other popular classes people can take in your area.
2. Call on students to share their ideas and write them (for example: an English class, a Spanish class, a photography class, an exercise class, a swimming class). Say each one and have students repeat.
3. **Reinforce:** Call on students and ask: *Which class(es) do you want to take?* Remind them to use the correct pronunciation of *want to*.

Digital Skills for 1

1. Tell students to choose one class they would like to take in the future. As homework, tell them to research a place in the community that offers the class. Suggest that students search online.
2. Tell students to contact the place and find out when the class meets, how much it costs, and what students need to bring to class. Tell students to write the information and bring it to class.
3. At a later date, follow up by grouping students according to their interests and telling them to share the information they found.

2 LISTEN

A ▶ **LISTEN FOR MAIN IDEA. What are they...**

1. Tell students to look at the picture. Ask: *Who do you see?* (Mario and Bi-Yun) *What are they doing?* (talking and walking down the street)
2. Read the directions. Elicit the answer choices.
3. Play the audio. Students listen and circle the letter of the correct answer.
4. Elicit the correct answer from the class.
5. Ask about **register**: *What is the relationship between Mario and Bi-Yun?* (friends) *How do you know?* (They are talking about their weekends. They don't speak formally—for example, *yeah*.)

EXPANSION: Speaking practice for 2A

1. Have students work in pairs to describe the clothes and physical appearance of the people in the picture.
2. Have above-level students say what they are going to do next.

B ▶ **LISTEN FOR DETAILS. Listen again...**

1. Tell students to read the questions and answer choices silently. Ask the class to identify the activities in the photos (go to the beach, take a class, play the guitar / take a guitar class).
2. Play the audio again. Students circle the letter of the correct answer.
3. Students compare answers with a partner.
4. Call on volunteers to ask and answer the questions.

Teaching Tip: Use the script

Optional: If students need additional support, tell them to read the Audio Script on page 268 as they listen to the conversations.

C ▶ **EXPAND. Listen to the whole...**

1. Tell students to read the questions and answer choices silently.
2. Play the audio. Students answer the question.
3. Ask: *Do you need to listen one more time?* If yes, play the audio again.
4. Review the correct answer with the class. Ask: *How do you know?* (Mario says he doesn't know how to run a business.)

Listening and Speaking

3 PRONUNCIATION

A ▶ PRACTICE. Listen. Then listen again and...

1. Tell students to close their books. Write the words they will hear. Pronounce each word and elicit the number of syllables.
2. Tell students to open their books. Read the directions.
3. Read the **Pronunciation Note**. Ask: *Why are the syllables red?* (They are unpronounced.) Cross out the second *e* in *every* to show it is not pronounced.
4. Play the audio. Students listen. Pause the audio. Say: *Most people don't say* ev-e-ry *with three syllables. They say* ev-ry *with two syllables.* Repeat with *usually* and *interesting*.
5. Resume the audio. Students listen and repeat.

 ActiveTeach for 3A: Pronunciation Coach

B ▶ APPLY. Listen. Write the number of...

1. Read the directions. Write item 1. Pronounce *evening*. Ask: *How many syllables do you hear?* (two) *What syllable is unpronounced?* (-en) Cross out -en. Tell students to listen and cross out the vowel that's not pronounced (ev∅ning, fav∅rite, differ∅nt).
2. Play the audio. Tell students to listen and write the number of syllables they hear.
3. To review, tap on the desk to indicate each syllable as you pronounce *ev-ning, fa-vrite, dif-frent*.
4. Say each word. Ask students to repeat.

4 CONVERSATION

A ▶ LISTEN AND READ. Then listen and repeat.

1. Note: This conversation is the same one students heard in Exercise 2A on page 68.
2. Tell students to read the conversation and underline words with unpronounced syllables (*family, usually, business, every*).
3. Play the audio. Students read along silently. Then students listen and repeat.
4. Walk around and help with pronunciation as needed. Pay particular attention to the students' pronunciation of *family, usually, business,* and *every*.

B WORK TOGETHER. Practice the conversation.

1. Pair students and tell them to practice the conversation in Exercise 4A.
2. Tell students to take turns playing A and B.

C CREATE. Make new conversations. Use the...

1. Read the directions.
2. Tell students to look at the information in the boxes. Say each item and tell the class to repeat. Elicit the kind of information in each box (blue: activity, yellow: class, green: time/day).
3. Model a new conversation with an above-level student. Play B and say items from the blue, yellow, and green boxes.
4. Tell pairs to take turns playing A and B and to use the vocabulary words to fill in the blanks.
5. Walk around during the activity and check students' pronunciation of words with unpronounced syllables.
6. Tell students to stand, mingle, and practice the conversation with several new partners.
7. Call on pairs to perform for the class.

■■ **MULTILEVEL INSTRUCTION for 4C**
Pre-level scaffolding Ask pairs to fill in the blanks in their book before they practice.
Above-level expansion Tell pairs to practice without looking at the conversation and to use their own ideas.

D MAKE CONNECTIONS. Think about three...

1. Read the directions.
2. Write three things you are going to do in your free time this weekend. Then write:
   • *I'm going to _____.*
   • *I usually _____ on _____.*
   • *I _____ every _____.*
3. Model the conversation with an above-level student. Tell the student to use A's first two lines from Exercise 4C. Answer using the fill-in sentences and one of your plans from the board. Point to the information on the board as you say it. Then ask the student *What about you?* and prompt him or her to complete the sentences on the board with one of his or her plans.
4. Pair students and tell them to take turns starting the conversation.

Self-Directed Learning

Point out the blue bar. Ask students if they can do the lesson learning objective or if they need more practice. Tell them to check one of the boxes. Assign Extra Practice as needed.

Extra Practice

MyEnglishLab   Workbook pp. 39–40

Listening and Speaking

3 PRONUNCIATION

A ▶ **PRACTICE. Listen. Then listen again and repeat.**

every
(2 syllables)

usually
(3 syllables)

interesting
(3 syllables)

Some words have a syllable that is not pronounced. For example, the word *family* looks like it has three syllables (fam·i·ly), but we pronounce it as two syllables (fam·i·ly).

B ▶ **APPLY. Listen. Write the number of syllables you hear.**

1. __2__ evening   2. __2__ favorite   3. __2__ different

4 CONVERSATION

A ▶ **LISTEN AND READ. Then listen and repeat.**

A: What are you doing this weekend?
B: I'm going to go to the beach with my family.
A: Really? Sounds like fun.
B: Yeah. We usually go to the beach on Sunday in the summer. What about you?
A: Well, I have class on Saturday. I have a business class every Saturday morning.

B **WORK TOGETHER. Practice the conversation.**

C **CREATE. Make new conversations. Use the words in the boxes.**

A: What are you doing this weekend?
B: I'm going to _____ with my family.
A: Really? Sounds like fun.
B: Yeah. We usually _____ on Sunday. What about you?
A: Well, I have _____. I have _____ every _____.

go out to eat
go for a bike ride
go hiking

an auto mechanics class
a cooking class
a computer class

Friday evening
Saturday afternoon
Sunday morning

D **MAKE CONNECTIONS. Think about three things you are going to do in your free time. Talk about your free-time activities.**

I can talk about free-time activities. ■   I need more practice. ■

For more practice, go to MyEnglishLab.

Adverbs of frequency

Adverbs of frequency				
With action verbs			**With be**	

With action verbs

I		
We	always	
They	usually	go
	often	
He	sometimes	to the beach.
She	hardly ever	goes
	never	

With be

I	am	always	
We		usually	
They	are	often	
		sometimes	at the beach.
He	is	hardly ever	
She		never	

0%					100%
never	hardly ever	sometimes	often	usually	always

Grammar Watch

- Adverbs of frequency go *before* action verbs.
- Adverbs of frequency go *after* forms of *be*.

A IDENTIFY. Cross out the incorrect words.

1. She works on Saturday mornings. She **never / ~~often~~** sleeps late on Saturdays.

2. I can't go to the movies Thursday night. I **always / ~~hardly ever~~** take a computer class after work on Thursdays.

3. There are very few good restaurants near my office. I **hardly ever / ~~often~~** go out to eat for lunch.

4. Ty is an excellent worker. He **always / ~~sometimes~~** finishes his projects on time.

5. My friend Tanya takes the bus to work. She **~~often~~ / never** drives to her job.

6. He likes computer programming. He **sometimes / ~~never~~** spends hours on the computer.

B WRITE. Make sentences with the adverbs in parentheses.

1. (always) The kids are busy. (usually) They get homework help after school.
   The kids are always busy. They usually get homework help after school.

2. (never) Marc is on time. (sometimes) He gets to work thirty minutes late.
   Marc is never on time. He sometimes gets to work thirty minutes late.

3. (usually) They go dancing on weekends. (hardly ever) They stay home.
   They usually go dancing on weekends. They hardly ever stay home.

4. (never) They are home on Sundays. (always) They are at their cousin's house.
   They are never home on Sundays. They are always at their cousin's house.

Correlations

ELPS Level 2: 1, 2, 3, 4, 5, 6, 7, 8, 9, 10
CCRS Level A: L.1.1
CASAS Reading: RDG 1.7, 2.9, 4.9
CASAS Listening: L1.3, 2.1, 2.3, 3.1, 4.1, 4.2
CASAS Competencies: 0.1.2, 0.1.5, 0.2.1, 0.2.4, 7.1.4
Complete standards language available on the Pearson English Portal.

Self-Directed Learning

State the **lesson objective**. Say: *In this lesson, we will learn to use adverbs of frequency in sentences and questions.*

Adverbs of frequency

 ActiveTeach: Grammar Discovery

1. Warm up. Say: *The conversation on page 69 used this grammar.* Turn back to page 69. Point to the sentence in Exercise 4A and then write: *We usually go to the beach on Sunday.*
2. Say: *Let's look at some more examples.* Write:
   • *She often goes for a walk.*
   • *We are hardly ever at home.*
3. Copy the *never–always* continuum onto the board. Pronounce the adverbs of frequency and ask the class to repeat.
4. Point to *never* and *always* on the continuum and say: *If you never do something, you don't do it, not at any time. You do it 0% of the time. If you always do something, you do it all the time, or 100% of the time.*
5. Pair students. Say: *Never is 0% of the time. Always is 100% of the time. With your partner, write the percentages for the other adverbs of frequency on the continuum (hardly ever–20%; sometimes–40%; often–60%; usually–80%).*
6. Tell students to look at the grammar charts. Point to the left chart. Ask: *What is the verb?* (*go*) *Where are the adverbs of frequency?* (before the verb) Read the first point of the **Grammar Watch** note.
7. Point to the right grammar chart. Ask: *What is the verb?* (*be*) *Where are the adverbs of frequency?* (after *be* / after the verb) Read the second point of the **Grammar Watch** note.

8. Call on students to read examples from the left chart. Tell them to choose one word from each row (for example, *She always goes to the beach.*).
9. Call on students to read examples from the right chart. Tell them to choose one word from each row (for example, *We are hardly ever at the beach.*).

 ActiveTeach: Grammar Coach

■ **EXPANSION: Writing and grammar practice**
1. For each adverb on the continuum, tell students to write one activity that they do with that frequency.
2. To model the activity, write an activity you never do under *never* on the continuum (for example, *go fishing*). Write an activity you always do under *always* (for example, *eat breakfast*).

Ⓐ IDENTIFY. Cross out the incorrect words.
1. Read the directions.
2. Ask a student to read item 1. Ask: *What does she do on Saturday mornings?* (She works.) *Can she sleep late?* (no) *So, the answer is…?* (never)
3. Students compare answers with a partner.
4. Call on students to read the completed items.
5. Tell students to circle the verb in each sentence. Ask: *Are they action verbs or* be? (action verbs) *Are the frequency adverbs before or after the verbs?* (before)

Ⓑ WRITE. Make sentences with the adverbs in…
1. Read the directions.
2. Read item 1. Tell students to circle the verbs (*are, get*).
3. Ask: *Is* are *an action verb or a form of the verb* be? (*be*) *Does* always *go before or after* are? (after) Read the first sentence of the example.
4. Ask: *Is* get *an action verb or a form of the verb* be? (action verb) *Does* usually *go before or after* get? (before) Read the second sentence of the example.
5. Tell students to circle the verbs in items 2–4 before they write the sentences.
6. Walk around and check for correct placement of the adverbs of frequency.
7. Students compare answers with a partner.
8. Call on students to read their answers.

Grammar

Questions with *How often* / frequency time expressions

 ActiveTeach: Grammar Discovery

1. Show the grammar charts on the board.
2. Write: *exercise*. Say: *Ask me if I exercise*. Elicit and write: *Do you exercise?* Answer: *Yes, I do.*
3. Say: *Now you know that I exercise, but you don't know how often I exercise. Do I exercise every day or once a month?* To ask about frequency, use *How often*. Write *How often* in front of *Do you exercise?* and change *D* to *d*. Answer with a frequency time expression.
4. Post a calendar for a month. Use it to point out the meanings of the frequency time expressions in the right chart. Ask a student to read the **Grammar Watch**. Say: *For one time, we say "once." For two times, we say "twice." For numbers above two, we say, "three times, four times, five times, etc."*
5. Point to the question on the board and ask the class: *How often do you exercise?* Tell students to circle one of the time expressions in the right chart or write an answer next to the chart.
6. Call on several students and ask: *How often do you exercise?* Then call on different students and ask them to recall their classmates' answers: *How often does [Name] exercise?*

 ActiveTeach: Grammar Coach

C INTERPRET. **Look at the calendar. Ask and...**

1. Tell students to look at the calendar but to cover the example. Ask: *How often does Felipe eat dinner with his cousins?* Tell students to circle *eat dinner with cousins* each time it appears on the calendar. Elicit the answer: *Once a week.*
2. Pair students and tell them to take turns playing A and B and ask five questions each. Tell them to start each question with *How often does Felipe...* and complete it with an activity from the calendar.
3. To check answers, call on five students to ask a question. Tell them to call on a classmate to answer. Possible questions and answers: *How often does Felipe play soccer?* (twice a month) *How often does Felipe go to a computer class?* (every Monday) *How often does Felipe go jogging with Hong?* (twice a week) *How often does Felipe cook for his family?* (once a month)

Show what you know!

1. **THINK ABOUT IT. Write three questions...**

1. Read the directions and the example.
2. Tell students to begin their questions with *How often do you...* and end with a free-time activity. They can use the activities on page 67 or their own ideas.

2. **TALK ABOUT IT. Ask your questions. Answer...**

1. Read the directions. Ask three students to read one of their questions out loud. Write the questions.
2. Model surveying the class. Ask a student one of the questions. Write the student's name and answer under the question you asked. Repeat with different students and different questions.
3. Tell students to mingle and try to ask every classmate one of their questions. They should write down the answers.

3. **WRITE ABOUT IT. Now write about your...**

1. Read the directions.
2. Tell students to look at the example. Ask: *What's the verb?* (goes) *What does it end in?* (-s) Tell students to underline the -s. Ask: *What's the frequency time expression?* (rarely) *Where is it?* (before the action verb). Say: Rarely *means the same as* hardly ever.
3. Point to one name and answer on the board. Tell the class about this student's activity.
4. Tell students to write five sentences.
5. Pair students and ask them to check each other's sentences.
   • Sentences should use an adverb of frequency.
   • Adverbs should come before action verbs and after the verb *be*.
   • Sentences should use the correct form of the verb.
6. Have students volunteer to write their sentences so the class can see them.

Self-Directed Learning

Point out the blue bar. Ask students if they can do the lesson learning objective or if they need more practice. Tell them to check one of the boxes. Assign Extra Practice as needed.

Extra Practice

  pp. 39–40

Grammar

	Questions with *How often* / frequency time expressions				Grammar Watch

How often	do	you they	exercise?	Every day. Every Monday. Once a week. Twice a month.	once = one time twice = two times
	does	he she			

C **INTERPRET. Look at the calendar. Ask and answer five questions with *how often*.**

A: How often does Felipe eat dinner with his cousins?
B: Once a week.

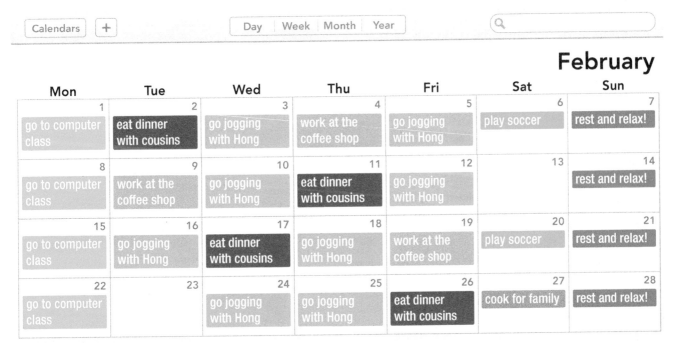

| Calendars | + | | | Day | Week | Month | Year | | 🔍 |

February

Mon	Tue	Wed	Thu	Fri	Sat	Sun
1 go to computer class	2 eat dinner with cousins	3 go jogging with Hong	4 work at the coffee shop	5 go jogging with Hong	6 play soccer	7 rest and relax!
8 go to computer class	9 work at the coffee shop	10 go jogging with Hong	11 eat dinner with cousins	12 go jogging with Hong	13	14 rest and relax!
15 go to computer class	16 go jogging with Hong	17 eat dinner with cousins	18 go jogging with Hong	19 work at the coffee shop	20 play soccer	21 rest and relax!
22 go to computer class	23	24 go jogging with Hong	25 go jogging with Hong	26 eat dinner with cousins	27 cook for family	28 rest and relax!

Show what you know!

1. **THINK ABOUT IT. Write three questions about your classmates' free-time activities. Use *how often*.**

   How often do you go to the movies?

2. **TALK ABOUT IT. Ask your questions. Answer your classmates' questions.**

3. **WRITE ABOUT IT. Now write about your classmates' free-time activities.**

   Safa rarely goes to the movies.

I can use adverbs of frequency in sentences and questions. ☐	I need more practice. ☐

For more practice, go to MyEnglishLab.

1 READ A COMMUNITY CALENDAR

A ▶ **EXAMINE. Read and listen to the recorded message. Write the times. Then listen and repeat.**

City Library Schedule of Events
March

Sun	Mon	Tue	Wed	Thu	Fri	Sat
				1 Beginning Computer Class 1:00–3:00 PM	**2** Writing a Resume Workshop 2:00–4:00 PM Teen Time 3–5:00 PM	**3** Citizenship Information Session 3:00 PM–5:00 PM
4	**5** ESL Classes for Adults from _6:00–8:00 PM_	**6** Beginning Computer Class 1:00–3:00 PM	**7** Story Time for Young Children 9:00 AM ESL Classes for Adults from 6:00 – 8:00 PM	**8** Beginning Computer Class 1:00–3:00 PM	**9** Writing a Resume Workshop 2:00–4:00 PM Teen Time 3–5:00 PM	**10** Special Lecture: Finding Your Perfect Job
11	**12** ESL Classes for Adults from 6:00 – 8:00 PM	**13** Beginning Computer Class 1:00–3:00 PM	**14** Story Time for Young Children 9:00 AM ESL Classes for Adults from 6:00 – 8:00 PM	**15** Beginning Computer Class 1:00–3:00 PM	**16** Writing a Resume Workshop 2:00–4:00 PM Teen Time 3–5:00 PM	**17**
18	**19** ESL Classes for Adults from 6:00 – 8:00 PM	**20** Beginning Computer Class 1:00–3:00 PM	**21** Story Time for Young Children 9:00 AM ESL Classes for Adults from 6:00 – 8:00 PM	**22** Beginning Computer Class 1:00–3:00 PM	**23** Writing a Resume Workshop 2:00–4:00 PM Teen Time 3–5:00 PM	**24** Job Fair 9:00 AM – 4:00 PM
25	**26**	**27**	**28**	**29**	**30**	**31**

B **INTERPRET. Circle *True* or *False*. Correct the false information.**

1. The Citizenship Information Session meets on the first Saturday of the month. ~~once~~   (True)   False
2. The Job Fair is ~~twice~~ a month.   True   (False)
3. The ESL Class for Adults meets every Monday and Wednesday.   (True)   False
4. The Beginning Computer Class meets twice a week.   (True)   False
5. The Beginning Computer Class meets from ~~9:00 to 1:00~~.1:00–3:00 p.m.   True   (False)
6. Story Time for Young Children meets every Wednesday ~~afternoon~~.morning   True   (False)
7. There is a special lecture once a ~~week~~. month   True   (False)

C **WORK TOGETHER. Ask and answer questions about the City Library Events Calendar.**

A: When does the ESL Class for Adults meet?
B: It meets every Monday and Wednesday from 6 to 8 p.m.

I can read a community calendar. ■   I need more practice. ■

For more practice, go to MyEnglishLab.

Correlations

ELPS Level 2: 1, 2, 3, 4, 5, 6, 7, 8, 9, 10
CCRS Level A: RI.1.7, W.1.7, W.1.8, SL.K.3
CASAS Reading: RDG 1.7, 1.8, 2.2, 2.3, 3.2, 4.9
CASAS Listening: L2.1, 2.3, 4.1, 4.2
CASAS Competencies: 0.1.2, 0.1.5, 2.8.3, 4.5.6, 7.4.4, 7.7.3
Complete standards language available on the Pearson English Portal.

Self-Directed Learning

State the **lesson objective**. Say: *In this lesson, we will learn to read a community calendar and understand a schedule of events.*

1 READ A COMMUNITY CALENDAR

A **EXAMINE. Read and listen to the…**

Document Literacy: Community calendar

Context: Community calendars are found anywhere that offers services and events for the public, such as community centers, schools, libraries, arts centers, etc.
Purpose: Community calendars give information about events that are open to the public.
Key Words: *schedule, events, days of the week, months*

1. Tell students to look at the community calendar. Orient them to the calendar. Ask: *What kind of document is this?* (a calendar) *What is listed for each day?* (events) Ask about **context**: *Where is this community calendar from?* (City Library). *What month is it for?* (March) Ask about **purpose**: *What are community calendars for?* (give information about events) Ask about **key words**: *What information is on a community calendar?* (events, dates, times, schedule)
2. Tell students to find and circle *Writing a Résumé Workshop* every time it appears on the calendar. Ask: *How many times does the résumé workshop meet in the month?* (four) Repeat with the Beginning Computer Class and ESL Classes for Adults.
3. Read the directions. Point out where students should write the times on the calendar.
4. Play the audio. Students listen and write the times. Pause after *the second Saturday of the month.*
5. Resume audio. Students listen and repeat.

Numeracy: Math skills

1. **Scaffold:** Say the ordinal numbers from 1 to 30 and ask the class to repeat. Then count from 1 to 30 in ordinal numbers as a class.
2. Say: *Point to Friday on the calendar. The second is the first Friday of the month. What is the date of the second Friday of the month?* (the 9th)
3. Write: *first, second, third, fourth.* Ask a few more questions with ordinal numbers— for example, *What's the date of the third Wednesday of the month?* (the 21st)

Classroom Communication

Tell students there are many places in their communities, such as public libraries, where they can go and do activities. Brainstorm, write, and discuss places. Have students research events online and share the information in class.

B **INTERPRET. Circle *True* or *False*. Correct…**

1. Read the directions. Read item 1. Tell students to point to the first Saturday of the month on the calendar. Ask: *What date are you pointing to?* (March 3rd) *Is the Citizenship Information Session on the calendar for this day?* (yes) Say: *So, the answer is true.*
2. Ask: *How often is the job fair?* (once a month) Point to item 2 in the book. Ask: *Is the answer true or false?* (false) Say: *We need to correct this false sentence. So we cross out* twice *and write* once *above it.*
3. Ask the class which other items are false. Call on students to read the corrected sentences.

C **WORK TOGETHER. Ask and answer…**

1. Read the directions.
2. Tell students to find *ESL Classes for Adults* on the calendar.
3. Ask two above-level students to read the example.
4. Pair students and tell them to take turns asking and answering questions about the other activities on the calendar.

Self-Directed Learning

Point out the blue bar. Ask students if they can do the lesson learning objective or if they need more practice. Tell them to check one of the boxes. Assign Extra Practice as needed.

Workplace, Life, and Community Skills

2 UNDERSTAND A SCHEDULE OF...

A ▶ **LISTEN. Check the events that will take...**

1. Tell students to look at the schedule of events. Remind students of the Events Calendar in Exercise 1A. Ask: *What kind of document is this?* (schedule of events) Ask about **context**: *Where is this schedule of events from?* (Atlas Community College Library). *What dates is it for?* (May 14 and May 15) Ask about **purpose**: *What are schedules of events for?* (to give information about events that are open to the public) Ask about **key words**: *What information is on a schedule of events?* (dates, events, times, locations)

2. Read the directions. Play the audio.

3. As needed, play the audio again and allow students to check their own answers before they compare with a partner.

B ▶ **IDENTIFY. Listen again and complete the...**

1. Read the directions. Play the audio, pausing briefly between the information for Monday and Tuesday to give students time to write in their answer.

2. Pair students and tell them not to show each other their calendars. Tell them to check their answers by asking and answering questions. Write an example: *A: When does the Resume Writing Workshop meet? B: It meets on Monday, May 14th, at 1:00.*

3. Direct students to circle any answers that are different from their partner's.

4. As needed, play the audio again. Tell students to listen again and correct their answers.

■ **MULTILEVEL INSTRUCTION for 2B**

Pre-level scaffolding Allow students to look at each other's calendars as they compare answers.

Above-level expansion Tell students to add two activities and times to the calendar and not show their calendar to their partner. Partners take turns telling each other what the activities are and when they meet. They write each other's activities on their calendars.

C **WORK TOGETHER. Invite a classmate to...**

1. Read the directions.

2. Pair students. Tell students to pick an event at the Atlas Community College Library and invite their partners.

3. Before accepting the invitation, partners should ask when the event is.

4. Switch partners and have the conversations again.

 ActiveTeach for 2C: Academic Conversation Support

■ **MULTILEVEL INSTRUCTION for 2C**

Pre-level scaffolding Write model sentences that students can use in the conversation. For example: *Do you want to go to _____ with me? When does it meet / When is it?*

Above-level expansion Tell students to invite their partners to activities that they added to the calendar in 2B. This activity will not be on their partner's calendar, so they need to tell their partner about it when they invite them.

D **GO ONLINE. Find the website of your local...**

1. Read the directions. Ask students what they would search in English if they wanted to visit the website of a local library. Brainstorm some local libraries. Write the names of the libraries.

2. Tell students to search for these libraries online. Have students find a schedule or list of events at the library.

3. Compare research as a class. Write a complete list of events that students discovered.

Digital Skills for 2D

Digital calendar apps are available on most mobile phones. There are also digital calendars that are offered through email services. Others can be found online by searching for "free online calendar," or similar keywords.

 ActiveTeach: Review

Self-Directed Learning

Point out the blue bar. Ask students if they can do the lesson learning objective or if they need more practice. Tell them to check one of the boxes. Assign Extra Practice as needed.

Extra Practice

  pp. 41–42   Life Skills Writing

Workplace, Life, and Community Skills

2 UNDERSTAND A SCHEDULE OF EVENTS

A ▶ **LISTEN.** Check the events that will take place at Atlas Community College Library.

☑ ESL Conversation Classes   ☐ Teen Time
☑ Computer Classes   ☑ Job Application Workshop
☑ Job Interview Workshop   ☐ Job Interviews
☐ Story Time for Children   ☑ Résumé Writing Workshop

B ▶ **IDENTIFY.** Listen again and complete the table.

🌐 Atlas Community College Library: Upcoming Events 🔍

Date	Event	Time	Location
Monday, May 14th	Open Computer Lab	1. 8:00 AM–8:00 PM	Computer Lab
	2. Résumé Writing Workshop	1:00 PM	Room 224
	ESL Conversation Class	3. 9:00–11:00 AM	Classroom A
	ESL Conversation Class	6:30–8:30 PM	Classroom B
	Job Interview Workshop Series	4:00–6:00 PM	Computer Lab
Tuesday, May 15th	4. Open Computer Lab	8:00 AM–1:00 PM	Computer Lab
	5. Computer Skills for Adults	1:00–3:00 PM	Classroom A
	Completing a Job Application	6. 5:00 PM	

C **WORK TOGETHER.** Invite a classmate to one of the college's library events.

D **GO ONLINE.** Find the website of your local library. Identify two events that interest you. Add those events to a digital calendar. Invite a friend to one of the events.

I can understand a schedule of events. ■   I need more practice. ■

For more practice, go to MyEnglishLab.

Lesson 5 — Listening and Speaking

Communicate likes and dislikes

1 BEFORE YOU LISTEN

MAKE CONNECTIONS. Look at the pictures. Which activities do you need to do at home or at work? What are some other activities that people need to do?

cook

vacuum

work outside

iron

2 LISTEN

A PREDICT. Look at the picture. What is the man's problem? What are some solutions?

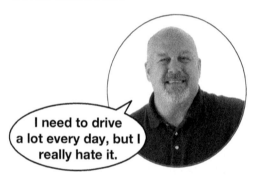

I need to drive a lot every day, but I really hate it.

B ▶ LISTEN FOR MAIN IDEA. What problem do the people discuss?

a. People often don't have a lot of free time.
b. People need to do things they don't enjoy.

C ▶ LISTEN FOR DETAILS. Listen to the whole podcast. Number the ideas in the order that you hear them.

a. __3__ After you do something you hate, do something you like.

b. __2__ Put a time limit on the activities you hate to do.

c. __1__ When you need to do something you hate, do something you like at the same time.

D ▶ EXPAND. Listen to the whole podcast. Match the solutions and examples.

When you do something you hate:

1. __b__ do something you like at the same time
2. __c__ put a time limit on it
3. __a__ do something you like after

a. work and then take a break
b. work and talk to a friend
c. work for two hours and then stop

Correlations

ELPS Level 2: 2, 3, 7, 9
CCRS Level A: SL.1.4
CASAS Reading: RDG 1.7, 2.2, 2.3
CASAS Listening: L2.1, 2.3, 4.1, 4.2, 5.8, 6.1, 6.2, 6.5
CASAS Competencies: 0.1.2, 0.1.5, 0.1.6
Complete standards language available on the Pearson English Portal.

Self-Directed Learning

State the **lesson objective**. Say: *In this lesson, we will learn to communicate likes and dislikes.*

1 BEFORE YOU LISTEN

MAKE CONNECTIONS. Look at the pictures…

1. Read the directions.
2. Tell students to look at the pictures. Say the activities and ask the class to repeat.
3. Ask: *What are some other activities that people have to do?* Elicit answers from the class and write them (for example, *clean the house, wash clothes, do dishes, do homework, work*).
4. **Reinforce:** Review the vocabulary for errands in Unit 3 as needed.

■■ **EXPANSION: Writing and speaking practice for 1**

1. Form groups of 4. Tell groups to assign one of the pictured activities to each member. Students form a question with *how often* for their activity (for example, *How often do you cook?*).
2. Explain that each group member should ask all group members his or her question and note their answers.
3. Remind students to answer with adverbs of frequency or frequency time expressions (for example, *I hardly ever cook. I cook twice a month.*).
4. Then tell students to write sentences about their group members' activities (for example, *[Name] hardly ever cooks.*). Remind students to use third-person singular *-s*.

2 LISTEN

Ⓐ PREDICT. Look at the picture. What is the…

1. Tell students to look at the picture. Read the directions.
2. Ask a student to read what the man says in the speech bubble.
3. Elicit answers to the questions. Write the solutions.

Ⓑ ▶ LISTEN FOR MAIN IDEA. What problem…

1. Read the question. Call on two students to read the answer choices.
2. Play the audio. Students listen and circle the letter of the correct answer.
3. Ask: *Was your guess in Exercise 2A correct?* Ask for a show of hands. Elicit the correct answer from the class.

Ⓒ ▶ LISTEN FOR DETAILS. Listen to the…

1. Read the directions. Ask three students to read the ideas.
2. Play the audio again. Students number the ideas in the order they hear them.
3. Students compare answers with a partner.
4. Call on students to read the items in the correct order.
5. *Optional:* Ask: *Do you think these are good ideas? Why or why not?*

Teaching Tip: Use the script

Optional: If students need additional support, tell them to read the Audio Script on pages 268–269 as they listen to the conversation.

Ⓓ ▶ EXPAND. Listen to the whole podcast…

1. Read the directions. Call on students to read the solutions and examples.
2. Play the audio. Students match solutions and examples.
3. Ask: *Do you need to listen one more time?* If yes, play the audio again.
4. Call on students to give the correct answers.
5. Ask about **register:** *Do the two speakers know each other well?* (probably not) *How can you tell?* (She calls him Dr. Goldberg. Using a title is more formal.)

■■ **EXPANSION: Speaking practice for 2D**

1. Pair students to give their own examples for each of the solutions for each activity they listed in Exercise 1 (for example, fold laundry and listen to music, clean the kitchen and then have a cup of tea, or work for 30 minutes and take a two-minute break).
2. Call on students to share their ideas. Write them on the board.

Listening and Speaking

Teaching Tip: Set the scene

For pre-level students or those with low first language literacy, use the pictures to help them anticipate the content of the conversation and preview vocabulary.

3 CONVERSATION

A ▶ LISTEN AND READ. Then listen and repeat.

1. Tell students to look at the picture. Ask: *Where are they?* (laundromat) *What are they doing?* (washing clothes)
2. Read the directions.
3. Play the audio. Students listen and read silently. Then students listen and repeat.

B WORK TOGETHER. Practice the…

1. Pair students and tell them to practice the conversation in Exercise 3A.
2. Tell students to take turns playing A and B.

Teaching Tip: Formative assessment

Model the conversation with multiple students to check comprehension. Formative assessment can inform instruction choices like multilevel pairings.

C CREATE. Make new conversations. Use the…

1. Read the directions.
2. Tell students to look at the information in the boxes. Say each item and have students repeat. Ask: *Which of these things do you really hate to do?*
3. Show the conversation with blanks. Elicit information from the boxes to complete the blanks.
4. Ask a pair of on-level students to practice the conversation on the board for the class.
5. Erase the words in the blanks and ask two above-level students to make up a new conversation.
6. Tell pairs to take turns playing A and B and to use the vocabulary words to fill in the blanks.
7. Tell students to stand, mingle, and practice the conversation with several new partners.
8. Call on pairs to perform for the class.

■ MULTILEVEL INSTRUCTION for 3C

Pre-level scaffolding Tell students to circle one thing they really hate in both boxes. They write the information in the blanks before they practice.
Above-level expansion Tell students to use a different reason in A's last line. Also, tell pairs to continue the conversation by giving each other tips on how they can make things they hate to do more enjoyable.

D PRESENT IT. Make a presentation about…

1. Read the directions.
2. Model the activity. Make a simple chart on the board with headings: *I hate to _____, Solutions, Helpful Ideas from Podcast.* Under each write an idea (for example, *clean my room, listen to happy music, doing something I like at the same time*). Present your ideas to the class.
3. Tell students to make a chart like yours with their own information.
4. Pair students to practice their presentations.
5. Call on students to give their presentation to the class.

■ EXPANSION: Writing practice for 3D

1. As students give their presentations, have the class take notes on helpful ideas and solutions.
2. Tell students to write sentences about the five best ideas.

Self-Directed Learning

Point out the blue bar. Ask students if they can do the lesson learning objective or if they need more practice. Tell them to check one of the boxes. Assign Extra Practice as needed.

Extra Practice

  pp. 43–44

Listening and Speaking

3 CONVERSATION

A ▶ **LISTEN AND READ. Then listen and repeat.**

A: You know, I really hate to do the laundry.
B: Me, too. And do you know what else I hate?
A: No. What?
B: I hate to iron.
A: Not me. I actually like it.
B: You're kidding.
A: No, really. I find it relaxing.

B **WORK TOGETHER. Practice the conversation in Exercise A.**

C **CREATE. Make new conversations. Use the words in the boxes.**

A: You know, I really hate to _____.
B: Me, too. And do you know what else I hate?
A: No. What?
B: I hate to _____.
A: Not me. I actually like it.
B: You're kidding.
A: No, really. I find it relaxing.

clean the office
do the dishes
get up early

cook
vacuum
work outside

D **PRESENT IT. Make a presentation about what you hate to do at work or at home. What are some solutions? Do the ideas in the podcast help? Which ideas are helpful? Explain you answer.**

I can communicate likes and dislikes. ■ 　　　　I need more practice. ■

For more practice, go to MyEnglishLab.

Grammar

Simple present: *love / like / hate* + infinitive

Simple present: *love / like / hate* + infinitive			
Affirmative		**Negative**	
I **love**		I **don't love**	
He **likes** to cook.		He **doesn't like** to vacuum.	
They **hate**		They **don't hate**	

Grammar Watch

love = 😊

like = 🙂

not like = 🙁

hate = 😣

A **COMPLETE. Use the verbs to complete the sentences.**

1. Zoya ___loves to go___ to work every day.
   (love / go)

2. She ___likes to help___ people.
   (like / help)

3. She ___loves to spend___ time with children.
   (love / spend)

4. She ___hates to see___ them sick or hurt.
   (hate / see)

5. Her supervisor is supportive. She

   ___doesn't like to have___ unhappy employees.
   (not like / have)

6. But Zoya and her co-workers

   ___don't like to work___ long hours overnight.
   (not like / work)

7. The worst shift is midnight to noon.

   They all ___hate to work___ that shift.
   (hate / work)

Correlations

ELPS Level 2: 1, 2, 3, 4, 5, 6, 7, 8, 9, 10
CCRS Level A: L.1.1
CASAS Reading: RDG 1.7, 2.9, 4.9
CASAS Listening: L2.1, 2.3, 3.1, 4.1, 4.2
CASAS Competencies: 0.1.2, 0.1.5, 0.1.6, 0.2.1, 0.2.4, 6.7.2
Complete standards language available on the Pearson English Portal.

Self-Directed Learning

State the **lesson objective**. Say: *In this lesson, we will learn to use the simple present with* love / like / hate + *infinitive.*

Simple present: *love / like / hate* + infinitive

 ActiveTeach: Grammar Discovery

1. Warm up. Say: *The conversation on page 75 used this grammar.* Turn back to page 75. Point to the sentences in Exercise 3A and then write:
   - *I really hate to do the laundry.*
   - *I hate to iron.*
2. Ask: *What follows the verb* hate? (an infinitive / to + base form of the verb) Underline *hate* and the infinitives.
3. Tell students to look at the faces in the **Grammar Watch**. Say the verbs and ask the class to repeat. Ask: *What are your likes and dislikes?* Tell students to write one activity next to each face.
4. Say: *To talk about activities you like and dislike, you use* love, like, not like, *or* hate + *an infinitive.* Ask a student: *What activity do you hate?* Write the student's response (for example, *vacuum*). Ask: *How do you make this an infinitive?* Add *to* to the example on the board.
5. Tell students to look at the left grammar chart. Ask: *How do you feel about cooking?* Tell students to circle the verb that expresses how they feel about cooking.
6. Ask a few students: *How do you feel about cooking?* Tell students to use words from the left or right charts (for example, *I don't like to cook.*).
7. Point to the right chart. Read the sentences and ask the class to repeat.
8. Write the names of the students who gave their opinions about cooking. Ask the class to recall their answers. As a class, write a sentence about each person (for example, *[Name] doesn't like to cook.*).
9. Tell the class to look at the sentences on the board. Ask: *Do any students have the same*

opinion about cooking? As a class, write a new sentence with *they* as the subject (for example, *[Name] and [Name] don't like to cook.*).

 ActiveTeach: Grammar Coach

Digital Skills for the Grammar Watch

Emojis are simple graphics of facial expressions that are used in casual digital exchanges to show emotions. Point out to students that emojis are not usually used in professional settings, but are frequently used with friends and family. Ask students to share an emoji that they like or have questions about and discuss it with the class. Teach new vocabulary as necessary (for example, *embarrassment*). Emoji meanings can also be researched online.

A COMPLETE. Use the verbs to complete the...

1. Read the directions. Remind students that an infinitive is *to* + base form of a verb.
2. Tell students to look at item 1. Ask: *What form of* love *goes with* Zoya? (loves) *What do you add to go* to make it an infinitive? (to) Ask a student to read the example.
3. Walk around and check that students are using the infinitive.
4. Call on students to read their answers.

■ EXPANSION: Writing practice for A

1. Point to the picture of Zoya. Tell students that Zoya is a doctor. Exercise A is about what she likes and doesn't like about her work. Say: *She likes to help people.*
2. Say: *Pick an activity that you do very often. It can be work or something else. What do you like about it? What don't you like about it?* Tell students to write at least five sentences about this activity using *to* + base form of the verb.
3. Call on students to read one of their sentences.

Career Awareness: Doctor

Doctors give medical care to sick and injured people. Doctors work in hospitals and private practices. There are many types of doctors, but all require many years of study and preparation.

■ EXPANSION: Career awareness for A

Ask students about the job in this lesson: *What does a doctor do? Where does a doctor work? Do you have to study to be a doctor? Do you like to look after sick people? Do you want to be a doctor?*

Grammar

B INTERPRET. Read the bar graph. Write three...

1. Read the directions.
2. Ask: *What is a survey?* Explain that in a survey, you ask a large number of people questions to find out what they think or do.
3. Tell students to read the information in the yellow box silently. Ask the class: *What question did the survey ask?* (What's your favorite activity?) *How many people answered the question?* (500)
4. Tell students to look at the bar graph to the right of the yellow box. Ask: *What is the title of the bar graph?* (Favorite things to do in the U.S.) Say: *The bar graph shows the results of the survey.* Ask: *What is the favorite activity in the U.S.?* (reading) *What percentage of people like to read?* (34%) *What activity is sixth most popular?* (using a computer) *What percentage of people like to use a computer?* (7%)
5. Tell students to point to the first bar in the bar graph. Ask a student to read the example. Tell students to choose three other activities in the bar graph and write sentences.
6. To review, elicit a sentence for each bar on the graph.

Numeracy: Interpret data

Ask students these additional questions:
1. *If we add the percentages for all the activities, what is the answer?* (100%)
2. *Does the graph show all activities that are popular the U.S.?* (No. It only shows what people said was their favorite activity, not all the activities they like to do.)
3. *What percentage of people in the U.S. have a favorite activity that involves reading or watching a screen?* (72%—read, watch TV, go to movies, use a computer)

■ EXPANSION: Speaking practice for B
Form pairs. Tell students to take turns reading their sentences. Say: *Listen for* to *in your partner's sentences.*

■ EXPANSION: Graphic organizer and speaking practice for B
1. Ask: *What do you think a bar graph of favorite things to do in your native country would look like?* Tell students to list favorite free-time activities in their country, rank them in order, guess a percentage for each activity, and then create a bar graph like the one in Exercise B.
2. Tell students to explain their bar graph to a partner by pointing to each bar and saying a sentence.

Show what you know!

1. THINK ABOUT IT. Write four sentences about...

1. Read the directions. Model the activity. Say four sentences about your likes and dislikes. Use *like, love,* and *hate.*
2. Encourage students to review the free-time activities on page 67.
3. Walk around and help with vocabulary. If students ask how to say or spell an activity that's not in the unit, write the activity. Explain the meanings of any activities on the board. Say the activities and ask the class to repeat.

2. TALK ABOUT IT. Talk about your likes and...

1. Read the directions. Ask two students to read the example.
2. Model the activity. Call on an above-level student to read one sentence from Step 1. Respond truthfully. Say: *Not me* or *Me, too.* Then say one of your sentences from Step 1. To prompt the student to respond to your like or dislike, you can say: *What about you?*
3. Pair students. Students take turns playing A and B.
4. Call on a few students to report one of their partner's likes or dislikes.

■ MULTILEVEL INSTRUCTION for 2
Cross-ability The pre-level student reads each sentence from Step 1, and the higher-level student responds. When partners switch roles, the pre-level student has had appropriate responses modeled.

3. WRITE ABOUT IT. Write four sentences about...

1. Read the directions.
2. Ask students to check each other's sentences.
   - Sentences should use the correct form of the verbs *love, like,* and *hate.*
   - Negative sentences should use the correct form of *do not.*
   - Sentences should use an infinitive.
3. Have students volunteer to write their sentences so the class can see them.

Self-Directed Learning

Point out the blue bar. Ask students if they can do the lesson learning objective or if they need more practice. Tell them to check one of the boxes. Assign Extra Practice as needed.

Extra Practice

  pp. 43–44

Grammar

B **INTERPRET.** Read the bar graph. Write three sentences about the information. Use *like to*, *love to*, and *hate to*.

We surveyed 500 people in the U.S. and asked, "What's your favorite activity?" Here are the results.

Favorite things to do in the U.S.

Read — 34%
Watch TV — 21%
Spend time with family — 20%
Go to movies — 10%
Go fishing — 8%
Use a computer — 7%

Thirty-four percent of the people like to read.

_____

_____

_____

Show what you know!

1. **THINK ABOUT IT.** Write four sentences about activities you like and dislike. Use *like, hate, love.*

_____

_____

_____

_____

2. **TALK ABOUT IT.** Talk about your likes and dislikes with your classmates.

   A: I love to . . .
   B: Not me. I love to . . .
   A: Well, I don't like to . . .

3. **WRITE ABOUT IT.** Write four sentences about your partner's likes and dislikes.

   Hu likes to go swimming. He doesn't like to go fishing.

I can use the simple present with *love / like / hate* + infinitive. ■   I need more practice. ■

For more practice, go to MyEnglishLab.

Read about different writing styles

1 BEFORE YOU READ

A **LABEL. Write the words under the pictures.**

abbreviations   emoji   mistake   punctuation

     `. , ' ?`   Great ~~Grate~~ job!   St. Ave. Rd.

1. an ____emoji____   **2.** ____punctuation____   **3.** a ____mistake____   **4.** ____abbreviations____

B **DISCUSS.**

What does the message say? What does the emoji tell you about the sender's feelings?

THX 😎
C U L8R

2 READ

▶ **LISTEN AND READ.**

Different Writing Styles

1 Technology is changing the way people write in English. Some of the changes are happening because of text messages.

It isn't easy to write on a phone, so people keep messages
5 short. They do this in several ways:
- They make changes in spelling (like *cuz* for *because* or *prolly* for *probably*).
- They leave out words (like *Will call* for *I will call you.*).
- They leave out punctuation.
10 - They use abbreviations (like *am* for *morning* or *LMK* for *Let me know*).
- They use emojis to show feelings (😂 for *That's funny!*).

People also leave out greetings, like "Dear Tom." They leave out closings, too, like "Best wishes." They usually don't sign
15 their name because the person getting the text knows them.

When you text a friend or family member, this style of writing is fine. Mistakes are usually okay, too. Text messages often have mistakes. That's because people write fast. They don't stop to check their message before they hit "Send."

20 But what about writing to other people? Do you ever write to a supervisor at work or a teacher at school? Some text messages or e-mails need a more formal writing style. It depends on your relationship with your reader. Sometimes you want to use a style that shows respect. Then you need
25 to take the time to write in a style that's clear and polite.

Dan Brown
RE: Meeting?

Hello Liz,

It was nice meeting you today and talking about the new project. I'd like to talk again soon. When are you free? Please text me at (202) 555-9876.

Best,

Dan

Hi Dan, Liz here. Happy to talk but this week not gd. Sorry. Mon @ 4 ok?

Clear and polite style	Friends and family style
Hello	Hey
Could you please	Cn u
I'm surprised!	WOW!!!
I'm sorry, but I'm afraid I'm going to be late.	Gonna be late.

Self-Directed Learning

1. State the **lesson objective**. Say: *In this lesson, we will learn to predict the topic.*
2. Say: *We will read about different writing styles.*

1 BEFORE YOU READ

A LABEL. Write the words under the pictures.

1. Read the directions. Say the words in the box.
2. Tell students to look at item 1. Ask: *What is this?* (an emoji) *What is an emoji?* (a small picture that shows a word or feeling.) Ask: *What are some of your favorite emojis?* Elicit ideas.
3. Tell students to label the other pictures.
4. Call on students to provide answers.

B DISCUSS.

1. **Scaffold:** Write common abbreviations and text shortcuts (for example, *c u l8r, np, thx, r u*) in a column. Then write the full form (*see you later, no problem, thanks, are you*) in random order in a second column. Tell students to match the abbreviation to the full form.
2. Read the directions and questions.
3. Have students compare their answers in pairs.
4. Elicit the full forms of the words in the message and write them on the board.
5. **Extend:** Write: *Text Messages.* Ask: *How are text messages different from your other writing?* Write students' ideas under the heading.

2 READ

▶ **LISTEN AND READ.**

1. Point to the **Academic Skill** and read it. Have students look at the article. Ask: *What is the title of this article?* (Different Writing Styles) Say: *Now let's look at the pictures to help us guess what the article is about.*

2. Introduce the visual. Ask: *What pictures or other visuals do you see?* (an email with a photo, a text message on a phone, a chart with "Clear and polite style" and "Friends and family style") *What do you think the topic is going to be?* Write students' predictions on the board.
3. Introduce the reading. Ask: *When do we use different writing styles?* (when we are writing to different people, with different technologies, in different situations) Ask: *How many paragraphs do you see?* (five) *What do you notice about the second paragraph?* (It has five bulleted items.)

 ActiveTeach for 2: Anticipation Guide – *Before* Reading exercise

4. Read the text.
   a. Say: *Now we are going to read and listen to the article* Different Writing Styles.
   b. **Scaffold:** Write questions about paragraphs 2–4: *2. How do people keep text messages short? 3. Why do text messages often have mistakes? 4. Why do some texts need a more formal style?* Tell students to underline the answers to these questions in the text as they read.
   c. Play the audio as students listen and read along silently.
   d. Have an above-level student read the first paragraph aloud or read it aloud yourself. Ask: *Why is the way we write changing?* (because of text messages)
   e. Ask the questions on the board about the other three paragraphs and elicit the answers (2. changes in spelling, leave out words, punctuation, use abbreviations and emojis 3. People write fast and don't check for mistakes. 4. Sometimes you need to show respect to the person you are writing to.)
   f. Ask: *Which of your predictions about the topic were correct?* Put a check next to the correct predictions.
   g. **Extend:** Tell students to look at their list of ideas about text messages from Exercise 1B. Ask: *Which of your ideas does the article mention?*

 ActiveTeach for 2: Anticipation Guide – *After* Reading exercise

3 CLOSE READING

A IDENTIFY. What is the main idea? Complete...

1. Say: *Now we are going to identify the main idea.*
2. Read the directions. Have students circle the answer.
3. Elicit the answer from the class.

B CITE EVIDENCE. Complete the sentences...

1. Say: *Now we are going to find information in the reading.*
2. Read the directions. Walk around as students work on the activity. If students are struggling, have them work in pairs or direct them to the text lines where they can find the information.
3. Call on students to read the sentence with the correct completion. Ask a different student to **cite evidence:** *Where is that information? What line number?*

4 SUMMARIZE

 ActiveTeach for 4: Vocabulary Practice

1. Read the directions. Ask students to read aloud the words in the box.
2. Tell students to complete the paragraph.
3. To check answers, call on students to read sentences in the summary with the blanks filled in. Ask other students to read the completed summary silently.
4. **Reinforce academic language:** Point to the word *Summarize.* Say: Summarize *means to give the most important information. We write a summary to explain what the reading is about. This is a summary of the article. The article is long. The summary is short.*

■ **EXPANSION: Speaking practice for 4**

1. Put students in pairs or small groups.
2. Tell them to discuss which things they do in text messages and when.

Culture Note

1. Say: *More and more people text in the U.S. every year. Young people often prefer to text than to use the telephone.*
2. Ask: *In your native country, do most people text? What about older people?*

Show what you know!

1. THINK ABOUT IT. In the chart, write the...

1. Read the directions.
2. Model the activity. Copy the chart. Write the names of people you email or text in the appropriate row.
3. Tell the class about your chart.
4. Tell students to complete the chart.

2. PRESENT IT. Tell the class about the people...

1. Read the directions.
2. Put students in small groups to explain their charts (who is included, what the right style of writing is, and why).
3. Walk around as students work on the activity and answer questions.
4. Call on students to present their charts to the class.

 ActiveTeach for 2: Academic Conversation Support

Self-Directed Learning

Point out the blue bar. Ask students if they can do the lesson learning objective or if they need more practice. Tell them to check one of the boxes. Assign Extra Practice as needed.

■ **EXPANSION: Self-directed learning**

Ask students to reflect: *What did you learn from this reading?* Call on students to share something they learned.

Extra Practice

 CCRS Plus   pp. 45–46

Reading

3 CLOSE READING

A IDENTIFY. What is the main idea? Complete the sentence.

There are different styles for writing messages in English.
The best style to use depends on _____.

(a.) who you are writing to   b. what you want to say   c. how you are feeling

B CITE EVIDENCE. Complete the sentences. Where is the information? Write the line numbers.

Lines

1. The way people write English is changing because of _____.
   a. new English words   (b.) writing on cell phones   c. changes in grammar   1–5

2. When people write text messages, they often don't use _____.
   a. emojis   b. abbreviations   (c.) punctuation   9

3. "Best wishes" is an example of _____.
   a. a mistake   b. a way to say hello   (c.) a way to end an e-mail   13–14

4. "Cn u wait 4 me" is an example of _____ in a message to someone like a teacher or a supervisor.
   a. leaving out words   (b.) the wrong style   c. showing respect   20–25

4 SUMMARIZE

Complete the summary with the words in the box.

leave out   mistakes   polite   style

Text messages are causing changes in the way people write English. When people write texts to friends, they often (1) ___leave out___ letters, words, and punctuation. They use "friends and family (2) ___style___." These messages are often full of (3) ___mistakes___. Sometimes writers need a more formal style that's more (4) ___polite___.

Show what you know!

1. **THINK ABOUT IT.** In the chart, write the names of people you e-mail or text. Which style is right for each person?

Friends and family style	
Clear and polite style	

2. **PRESENT IT.** Tell the class about the people in your chart. What is the right style for writing to each person? Why?

I can predict the topic. ☐   I need more practice. ☐

To read more, go to MyEnglishLab.

1 BEFORE YOU LISTEN

A **LABEL.** Look at the pictures. Write the reasons that people say no to invitations.

I have other plans.   I don't feel well.   I'm too busy.

1. <u>I don't feel well.</u>

2. <u>I'm too busy.</u>

3. <u>I have other plans.</u>

B **MAKE CONNECTIONS.** In the U.S., it is polite to give a reason when you decline an invitation. How about in your country?

2 LISTEN

A **PREDICT.** Look at the co-workers. Who looks like she is leaving? Who looks like she is staying?

B ▶ **LISTEN FOR MAIN IDEA.** Listen to the conversation. What does Meg ask?

a. "Do you want to get some lunch?"
b. "Do you have time to help me?"

C ▶ **LISTEN FOR DETAILS.** Listen again. Choose the correct answer.

1. _____ is very busy.
   a. Meg   **b.** Selda

2. Selda _____ go with Meg.
   a. can   **b.** can't

D ▶ **EXPAND.** Listen to the whole conversation. Answer the questions.

1. Who called Selda?
   a. her husband   **b.** her friend   **c.** her co-worker

2. What is Selda going to do?
   a. finish her work   **b.** go to lunch with Meg   **c.** go to lunch with Bob

Correlations

ELPS Level 2: 2, 7
CCRS Level A: SL.1.1, SL.K.6
CASAS Reading: RDG 1.7, 2.2, 2.3
CASAS Listening: L1.5, 2.1, 2.3, 4.1, 4.2, 6.1, 6.2, 6.5
CASAS Competencies: 0.1.2, 0.1.4, 0.1.5, 0.1.6, 0.2.3
Complete standards language available on the Pearson English Portal.

Self-Directed Learning

State the **lesson objective**. Say: *In this lesson, we will learn to accept or decline an invitation.*

1 BEFORE YOU LISTEN

A LABEL. Look at the pictures. Write the…

1. Say: *Look at some reasons people say no to invitations.* Call on students to read the sentences in the box.
2. Read the directions. Give students time to label the pictures.
3. Ask: *Which picture shows someone who doesn't feel well?* Students call out the number of the picture. Ask: *How do you know?* (He's in bed and looks sick.)
4. Repeat for the remaining sentences in the box.
5. *Optional:* Ask: *What other reasons can you think of?* Elicit students' ideas and write them (for example, *I'm too tired. I don't have any money. I don't like…*). Say each reason and ask the class to repeat.

▪▪ EXPANSION: Vocabulary and graphic organizer practice for 1A

1. Form small groups. Assign each group one of the reasons to decline, or say no to invitations. Tell groups to brainstorm related reasons and write them on small slips of paper (for example, for *I don't feel well: I have a headache. I have a cold. My stomach hurts.*).
2. Draw three web diagrams. Write one reason in each circle. Collect the slips of paper and put them in a box or bag. Ask students to draw a slip of paper, read the reason, and write it on the correct web diagram.

B MAKE CONNECTIONS. In the U.S., it is…

1. Read the directions. Tell students to underline the word *decline*. Ask: *If you decline an invitation, do you say yes or no to the invitation?* (no) Write *accept* and say: *When you say yes to an invitation, you accept the invitation.*

2. Ask: *What about in your native country? Is it polite to give a reason when you decline an invitation?*
3. If possible, pair students from different countries.
4. Write: *In your native country, do you need to give a reason when you decline an invitation?* Tell partners to talk about what is polite in their countries.
5. Call on students to tell the class about what is polite in their countries.

2 LISTEN

A PREDICT. Look at the co-workers. Who…

1. Tell students to look at the picture of Meg and Selda. Ask: *Where are they?* (at work/in an office) *What do you see?* Elicit a description of the office and the two co-workers.
2. Ask: *What time is it?* (12:05) *What is Meg carrying?* (a raincoat / a coat / a jacket) *What does she have over her shoulder?* (her purse)
3. Read the directions. Call on students to answer.

B ▶ LISTEN FOR MAIN IDEA. Listen to the…

1. Tell students to read the directions and the answer choices silently.
2. Play the audio. Students listen and circle the letter of the correct answer.
3. Ask: *Was your guess in Exercise 2A correct?* Ask for a show of hands. Elicit the question Meg asks.
4. Ask about **register**: *Do you think Meg and Selda are friends?* (yes) *How do you know?* (Meg asks Selda to lunch.)

C ▶ LISTEN FOR DETAILS. Listen again…

1. Tell students to read the questions and answer choices silently.
2. Play the audio again. Students circle the letter of the correct answers.
3. To check answers, call on students to read the sentences.

> **Teaching Tip: Use the script**
>
> *Optional:* If students need additional support, tell them to read the Audio Script on page 269 as they listen to the conversations.

D ▶ EXPAND. Listen to the whole…

1. Read the directions. Tell students to read the questions and answer choices silently.
2. Play the audio. Students listen and answer the questions.
3. Ask students to read the questions and call on classmates to answer. If an incorrect answer is given, play the audio again.

Listening and Speaking

3 PRONUNCIATION

A ▶ PRACTICE. Listen. Then listen again and...

1. Write *have to* and *has to*. Read the **Pronunciation Note**. Say: *We write* have to *and* has to, *but when people talk they usually say "hafta" and "hasta."*
2. Tell students to underline *have to* and *has to* in the examples.
3. Play the audio. Students listen. Then students listen and repeat.

 ActiveTeach for 3A: Pronunciation Coach

Language Note

Read the **Pronunciation Note** again and ask the class: *Why is this?* Tell them to refer back to the **Pronunciation Note** on page 49. Explain that *"wanna," "hafta,"* and *"hasta"* are called *reductions.* Ask: *What other reduction have we practiced?* (*"gonna"*) Pronounce all three reductions and ask the class to repeat.

B ▶ CHOOSE. Listen to the sentences. Circle...

1. Write: *a. I have a class tonight. b. I have to go.* Underline *have to* in b and ask: *Is this pronounced* "hafta" *or* "hasta"? (*"hafta"*) Write *"hafta"* in parentheses above *have to*. Read both sentences. Reduce *have to* to *"hafta"* in b. Ask the class to repeat. Remind students that we do not write *"hafta"* or *"hasta."* We only say them in conversation.
2. Read the directions.
3. Play the audio. Students listen and circle the words they hear.
4. To check answers, play the audio again and pause after each item. Elicit the answers from the class.

4 CONVERSATION

A ▶ LISTEN AND READ. Then listen and repeat.

1. Note: This conversation is the same one students heard in Exercise 2B on page 80.
2. Tell students to read the conversation and underline words with reductions (*want to, have to*). Tell students to write *"wanna"* in parentheses above *want to*, and *"hafta"* in parentheses above *have to*.
3. Play the audio. Students read along silently.
4. Resume the audio. Pause after each sentence for students to repeat.

5. Walk around and help with pronunciation as needed. Pay particular attention to the students' pronunciation of *want to* and *have to*.

B WORK TOGETHER. Practice the...

1. Pair students and tell them to practice the conversation in Exercise 4A.
2. Tell students to take turns playing A and B.

C CREATE. Make new conversations. Use the...

1. Read the directions.
2. Tell students to look at the information in the boxes. Say each item and have students repeat.
3. Show the conversation with blanks. Elicit information from the boxes to complete the blanks.
4. Tell pairs to take turns playing A and B and to use the vocabulary words to fill in the blanks.
5. Tell students to stand, mingle, and practice the conversation with several new partners.
6. Call on pairs to perform for the class.

D ROLE-PLAY. Make your own conversations...

1. Read the directions. Write the words *accept* and *decline*. To review, ask: *What does* accept *mean?* (say yes) *What does* decline *mean?* (say no)
2. Ask: *How do you accept an invitation?* Point to the yellow note. Say the phrases and ask the class to repeat. Write them on the board under *accept*.
3. Ask: *How do you decline an invitation?* Elicit the three ways in the conversations in Exercise 4A and 4C and write them under *decline*.
4. Model the role-play with an above-level student. Play B.
5. Pair students and tell them to take turns starting the conversation.
6. Tell students to stand, mingle, and role-play with several partners.

▬ MULTILEVEL INSTRUCTION for 4D

Pre-level scaffolding Ask pairs to write out their new conversations before performing the role-play.
Above-level expansion Tell pairs to ask follow-up questions after they accept an invitation (for example, *What time?* or *Where are you going?*).

Self-Directed Learning

Point out the blue bar. Ask students if they can do the lesson learning objective or if they need more practice. Tell them to check one of the boxes. Assign Extra Practice as needed.

Extra Practice

  p. 47

Listening and Speaking

3 PRONUNCIATION

A ▶ **PRACTICE. Listen. Then listen again and repeat.**

have to   I have to finish some work.
has to   She has to make some calls.

> **Have to and has to**
>
> In conversation, *have to* usually sounds like "hafta" and *has to* sounds like "hasta."

B ▶ **CHOOSE. Listen to the sentences. Circle the words you hear.**

1. **a.** have to
   (b.) have a

2. **(a.)** have to
   b. have a

3. **(a.)** has to
   b. has a

4. **a.** has to
   (b.) has a

4 CONVERSATION

A ▶ **LISTEN AND READ. Then listen and repeat.**

A: Do you want to get some lunch?
B: Sorry, I can't. I have to finish some work.
A: Oh. Are you sure?
B: Yes, I'm sorry. I'm really too busy.
A: Well, how about a little later?
B: Thanks, but I don't think so. Not today.

B **WORK TOGETHER. Practice the conversation in Exercise A.**

C **CREATE. Make new conversations. Use the words in the boxes.**

A: Do you want to _____ ?
B: Sorry, I can't. I have to _____ .
A: Oh. Are you sure?
B: Yes, I'm sorry. I really can't.
A: Well, how about a little later?
B: Thanks, but I don't think so. Not today.

> walk over to the deli
> take a walk
> get some coffee

> go to a meeting
> run some errands
> make some calls

D **ROLE-PLAY. Make your own conversations. Student A, invite your partner to do something. Student B, accept or decline the invitation.**

> To accept an invitation, you can say:
> • Sure. I'd love to.
> • That sounds like fun.
> • Sounds great.

I can accept or decline an invitation. ■   I need more practice. ■

For more practice, go to MyEnglishLab.

Lesson **9** Modal: *Have to*

Modal: *have to*				
Affirmative			**Negative**	
I You We They	**have to**	**finish** some work.	I You We They	**don't have to**
He She	**has to**		He She	**doesn't have to**

go to a meeting.

A DECIDE. Complete the sentences. Use the verbs in the box.

drive   get up   ~~go~~   study   stay   visit

1. We don't have _____*to go*_____ to the grocery store. We have a lot of food.
2. He has _____to study_____ tonight. There's a big test tomorrow.
3. Kara doesn't have _____to drive_____ to work. She takes the bus every day.
4. They start work at 6:00 in the morning. They have _____to get up_____ early.
5. Jon has _____to stay_____ home from work today. He's sick.
6. I have _____to visit_____ my co-worker. She's in the hospital.

Grammar Watch

- Use *have to / has to* + the base form of the verb.
- Use *have to / has to* when something is necessary.
- Use *don't / doesn't have to* when something is not necessary.

B APPLY. Complete the sentences. Use *have to* and the words in parentheses.

1. I'm coming home on time tonight. I ____*don't have to work late*____.
   (not work late)
2. Bik ____has to stay____ home with her son. He's sick.
   (stay)
3. I can help you finish. You ____don't have to do____ all the work.
   (not do)
4. Monica ____doesn't have to work____ this weekend. She can go to the zoo with us.
   (not work)
5. Omar ____has to take____ the bus to work. He doesn't have a car.
   (take)
6. The movie theater is always crowded. We ____have to buy____ tickets early.
   (buy)

C SELF-ASSESS. Compare your answers.

I can make sentences with the modal *have to.* ☐   I need more practice. ☐

For more practice, go to MyEnglishLab.

Correlations

CASAS Reading: RDG 1.7
CASAS Listening: L3.1
CASAS Competencies: 0.1.2
Complete standards language available on the Pearson English Portal.

Self-Directed Learning

State the **lesson objective.** Say: *In this lesson, we will learn to make sentences with the modal* have to.

Modal: *have to*

 ActiveTeach: Grammar Discovery

1. Warm up. Say: *The conversation on page 81 used this grammar.* Turn back to page 81. Point to the sentence in Exercise 4A and then write: *I have to finish some work.*
2. Say: *Let's look at another example.* Write: *You don't have to go to a meeting.*
3. Ask: *What words appear in each sentence?* (have to) *What follows* have to? (base form of verb)
4. Underline *have to finish* and *have to go* as students notice the pattern.
5. Point to the grammar charts.
6. Write: *I need to finish some work.* Read the sentence. Then cross out *need to* and write *have to.* Say: Have to *and* need to *have similar meanings.*
7. Rewrite the sentence: *I have to finish some work.* Read the sentence. Then cross out *I* and write *Selda.* Ask: *What else do I have to change?* Cross out *have* and write *has.* Rewrite and read the sentence: *Selda has to finish some work.*
8. Call on students to read examples from the grammar charts. Tell them to choose words from each column. For example: *They don't have to go to a meeting.* Ask students to say their sentences again with the "hafta" or "hasta" pronunciation of *have to* or *has to.*
9. Tell students to read the **Grammar Watch** note silently.

 ActiveTeach: Grammar Coach

A DECIDE. **Complete the sentences. Use the…**
1. Read the directions.
2. Say each verb in the box. Ask a student to read the example.
3. Walk around and check for *to.*

4. Call on students to read the completed sentences. Encourage them to use the "hafta" or "hasta" pronunciation of *have to* or *has to.*

B APPLY. **Complete the sentences. Use *have…***
1. Write item 1. Ask: *Is it affirmative or negative?* (negative) *What's the subject?* (I) Tell students to point to I on the chart on the right. Ask: *What's the correct negative form of* have to? (don't have to)
2. Complete item 1 on the board. Call on a student to read the example.
3. Walk around and check that students are forming the negative correctly. If students have difficulty, take them through the same steps used with the example.
4. Tell students to look at their answers and check that each one includes *to.*
5. Call on students to read the completed sentences. Encourage them to use the "hafta" or "hasta" pronunciation of *have to* or *has to.*

C SELF-ASSESS. **Compare your answers.**
1. Pair students and tell them to take turns reading the sentences. Tell them to practice the "hafta" and "hasta" pronunciation of *have to* and *has to.*
2. To check answers, call on a student to read item 2. Tell that student to call on another classmate to read item 3. Continue in the same way with the remaining items.

▬ **EXPANSION: Grammar and speaking practice for C**
1. Tell students to write a to-do list. Write your own to-do list as a model (for example, *go to the laundromat, clean the house, exercise, call my grandmother*).
2. Pair students. Say: *Tell your partner about your to-do list. Use* have to. *For example, you can say: I have to go to the laundromat. I have to clean the house…*
3. Tell students to exchange lists with their partner. Then form new pairs. Say: *Tell your new partner about your first partner's to-do list. Use* has to. Borrow a student's list and model the activity.

Self-Directed Learning

Point out the blue bar. Ask students if they can do the lesson learning objective or if they need more practice. Tell them to check one of the boxes. Assign Extra Practice as needed.

Extra Practice

MyEnglishLab   Workbook p. 47

Correlations

ELPS Level 2: 3, 10
CCRS Level A: W.1.2, W.1.5, L.1.1
CASAS Reading: RDG 1.7, 1.8, 2.1
CASAS Listening: L2.1, 2.3
CASAS Competencies: 0.1.2, 0.1.5, 0.1.6, 0.2.4
Complete standards language available on the Pearson English Portal.

Self-Directed Learning

1. State the **lesson objective**. Say: *In this lesson, we will learn to use details in our writing.*
2. Say: *You will write about a free-time activity.*

1 STUDY THE MODEL

1. Read the directions.
2. Point to the paragraph. Ask: *What is the title of the model?* (My Free Time)
3. **Scaffold** the model. Write as a graphic organizer:

1	Activity	
2	How often	
3	Who	
4	Where	

4. Tell students to read the text and read the questions independently. Call on students to answer the questions. Write the information in the graphic organizer on the board.
5. *Optional:* Ask students to think of some reasons they might like to do the activity (for example, *it's relaxing / fun / interesting / exciting*). Add a fifth row to the graphic organizer:

5	Reason	

2 PLAN YOUR WRITING

1. Erase the information in the right-hand column of the graphic organizer on the board.
2. Read the directions.
3. Model with a student. The student asks the teacher the questions.
4. Write the information into the graphic organizer.
5. Tell students to make their own graphic organizer on a piece of paper.
6. Have students work in pairs to ask and answer the questions and complete their own graphic organizers.

3 WRITE

1. Read the directions aloud.
2. Use your information in the graphic organizer from Exercise 2 to write sentences in a paragraph. Include indentation. Leave out some details, such as a person's name or the name of a place.
3. Point to the **Writing Skill**. Read it aloud while students listen.
4. Ask: *What details can we add?* For example, you can add the name of a person or place. Add the missing details to the sentences.
5. Tell students to write. Circulate to make sure students are writing in paragraph form.

 ActiveTeach for 3: Writing Support

4 CHECK YOUR WRITING

1. Read the directions aloud. Point to the **Writing Checklist**. Call on students to read the checklist items aloud.
2. Pair students to review their writings together. Say: *Read your sentences with a partner. Use the Writing Checklist.* For additional help, remind students that a correct sentence:
   - *begins with a capital letter*
   - *has a subject*
   - *has a verb*
   - *has a period*
   - *is a complete idea*
3. Walk around and verify that students are using the checklist. Collect the papers for review or put them in the students' writing portfolios.

Teaching Tip: Digital skills

Tell students to show photos from their phones to illustrate the ideas in their writing—what they do in their free time, with whom, and where.

Self-Directed Learning

Point out the blue bar. Ask students if they can do the lesson learning objective or if they need more practice. Tell them to check one of the boxes. Assign Extra Practice as needed.

Extra Practice

 CCRS Plus   p. 48

Writing

Write about a free-time activity

1 STUDY THE MODEL

READ. Answer the questions.

Nestor Cruz

My Free Time

In my free time, I like to go fishing.
I usually go on Sunday mornings. I go
fishing with my brother and my son.
We go to different places, like Spring
River and Silver Lake. I like to fish
because it is relaxing.

1. What does Nestor like to do in his free time? He likes to go fishing. He goes fishing on
2. How often does he do this activity? Sunday mornings.
3. Who does he go with? His brother and his son.
4. Where does he go? He goes to different places, like Spring River and Silver Lake.

2 PLAN YOUR WRITING

WORK TOGETHER. Ask and answer the questions.

1. What do you like to do in your free time?
2. How often do you do this activity?
3. Who do you go with?
4. Where do you go?

3 WRITE

Now write about your free time. Use the model, the Writing Skill, and your ideas from Exercise 2 to help you.

4 CHECK YOUR WRITING

WORK TOGETHER. Read the checklist. Read your writing aloud. Revise your writing.

Writing Skill: Use details in your writing

Put details in your writing. Write details about time, people, and places. For example:

No details: I go fishing.
With details: I go fishing with my brother and my son.

WRITING CHECKLIST

☐ The paragraph answers the questions in Exercise 2.

☐ The paragraph starts with a topic sentence.

☐ There are details about time, people, and places in the writing.

I can use details in my writing. ■ | I need more practice. ■

For more practice, go to MyEnglishLab.

Soft Skills at Work

Be professional

1 MEET ASAD

Read about one of his workplace skills.

> I am professional. For example, when I'm at work, I always take care of the customer. The customer's needs come first.

2 ASAD'S PROBLEM

READ. Circle *True* or *False*.

Asad works in a supermarket. There is a big sale today. Asad's supervisor told him to prepare items for the sale, and there isn't much time. Then a customer comes to Asad and says, "Excuse me. I can't find the coffee. Can you show me where it is?" But Asad still has a lot of work to do.

1. Asad has a very busy day today.   (True)   False
2. Asad's supervisor is helping him with the display.   True   (False)
3. The customer needs Asad's help.   (True)   False

3 ASAD'S SOLUTION

A **WORK TOGETHER.** Asad is professional. What does he say to the customer? Explain your answer.

(1.) Asad says, "Sure. Come with me."
2. Asad says, "I'm sorry, I'm busy. Can you ask someone else?"
3. Asad says, "I need to finish this. Then I can help you."
4. Asad _____.

B **ROLE-PLAY.** Look at your answer to 3A. Role-play Asad's conversation.

Show what you know!

1. **THINK ABOUT IT.** Are you professional? How are you professional at work? Give examples.

2. **WRITE ABOUT IT.** Write an example in your Skills Log.

   I am professional at work. For example, I stop talking to my co-workers when a customer needs help.

I can give an example of how I am professional. ☐

Unit Review: Go back to page 65. Which unit goals can you check off?

Correlations

CASAS Reading: RDG 1.7, 1.8, 3.2
CASAS Listening: L2.1, 2.3, 4.1, 4.2
CASAS Competencies: 0.1.2, 0.1.4, 0.1.5, 0.1.6, 0.2.1, 4.8.3, 4.8.4
Complete standards language available on the Pearson English Portal.

Self-Directed Learning

State the **lesson objective.** Say: *In this lesson, we will learn to give an example of how we are professional.*

1 MEET ASAD

1. Ask: *What is the title of this lesson?* (Be professional) Ask: *What does* professional *mean?* (doing your job well)
2. Read the directions. Read the paragraph. Ask: *What is one of Asad's workplace skills?* (He is professional.) Ask: *How is Asad professional?* (He takes care of customers. He puts the customer's needs first.)

2 ASAD'S PROBLEM

1. Say: *Now we are going to read about Asad at work.* Read the first sentence. Use the photo and the **Career Awareness** information to help students understand his job. Say: *Look at the photo. Where is Asad?* (supermarket) *What is he doing?* (putting items on the shelves)
2. Say: *Asad has a problem at work. Listen while I read.* Read the rest of the paragraph. Explain any unfamiliar vocabulary.
3. Read the directions. Call on students to answer. Ask them to **cite evidence:** *Where is that information?*
4. Ask: *What is Asad's problem?* (A customer needs help, but Asad has a lot of work to do.)

Career Awareness: Grocery clerk

Grocery clerks work in supermarkets and grocery stores. They use cash registers, put items on the shelves, and provide customer service. No formal education is required.

3 ASAD'S SOLUTION

A WORK TOGETHER. Asad is professional...

1. Read the directions. Ask students to work together. Walk around and check that students understand that only one solution is correct.
2. Ask: *Is #1 a good way to be professional?* (yes) *Why?* (He is taking care of the customer.) Ask: *Is #2 a good way to be professional?* (no) *Why not?* (He is not taking care of the customer.) Ask: *Is #3 a good way to be professional?* (no) *Why not?* (He is not putting the customer's needs first.)
3. Ask students if they have any other ideas. Write their responses. Ask: *Is this a good way to be professional? Why?*

 ActiveTeach for 3A: Academic Conversation Support

B ROLE-PLAY. Look at your answer to 3A...

1. Read the directions. Pair students. Tell pairs to choose a solution from Exercise 3A and decide who will be Asad and who will be the customer.
2. Model the conversation with an above-level student.
3. Walk around and assist students as needed.
4. Tell students to switch roles.

Show what you know!

1. THINK ABOUT IT. Are you professional?...

Read the directions. Have students think about their answers for a few minutes. Then ask them to share with a partner. Call on students to share with the class.

2. WRITE ABOUT IT. Write an example in your...

Read the directions and the example. Have students write their examples in their **Skills Log** at the back of the book. Circulate and assist students as necessary.

Self-Directed Learning

1. Point out the blue bar. Ask students if they can do the lesson learning objective or if they need more practice. Tell them to check one of the boxes. Assign Extra Practice as needed.
2. Ask students to turn to page 65. Go to the Unit Wrap-Up teaching notes on page T-65.

Extra Practice

 p. 49

5 At Home

Unit Overview

Goals
- See the list of goals on the facing page

Pronunciation
- Stress in two-word nouns
- Voiced and voiceless *th*

Reading
- Read about renters and homeowners
- Skimming

Grammar
- Present continuous
- *There is / There are*
- Imperatives

Writing
- Write about your home
- Structure paragraphs and use indents

Document Literacy and Numeracy
- Compare cost on rent and utilities
- Interpret a utility bill
- Interpret a bar graph
- Follow directions on a map
- Understand signs

Workplace, Life, and Community Skills
- Read apartment ads
- Read a utility bill
- Digital Skill: Search for an apartment in your town or city

Life Skills Writing
- Complete an application for an apartment

Soft Skills at Work
- Take initiative

Preview

1. Set the context of the unit by asking questions about homes (for example, *Do you live in an apartment or a house? What is your neighborhood like? Do you like where you live?*).
2. Show the Unit Opener. Ask: *What is the unit title?* (At Home)
3. Say: *Look at the picture.* Ask the Preview questions. (Possible answers: A woman is looking under a sink. She is looking at a problem with the sink.)

Unit Goals

1. Point to the Unit Goals. Explain that this list shows what you will be studying in this unit.
2. Tell students to read the goals silently.
3. Say each goal. Explain unfamiliar vocabulary as needed.
4. Point to the ☐ next to the first goal. Say: *We will come back to this page again. You will write a checkmark next to the goals you learned in the unit.*

Oral Presentation

1. Tell students they will give a short presentation at the end of the unit.
2. Write the topics:
   Option 1: My home
   Option 2: Is it better to rent or own a home?
3. Assign the topics to two students.

Unit Wrap-Up

1. Review the Unit Goals with students.
2. Direct students to the Grammar Review.
3. If you assigned presentations, ask students to present.

 ActiveTeach for Wrap-Up: Team Project

 ActiveTeach for Wrap-Up: Persistence Activities

5 At Home

PREVIEW

Look at the picture. What do you see? What is the woman doing? What is the problem?

UNIT GOALS

- [ ] Identify household problems
- [ ] Describe household problems
- [ ] Read apartment ads
- [ ] Read a utility bill
- [ ] Ask about an apartment

- [ ] Get directions
- [ ] **Academic skill:** Skimming
- [ ] **Writing skill:** Structure paragraphs and use indents
- [ ] **Workplace soft skill:** Show how you take initiative

Vocabulary

Household problems

A **PREDICT.** Look at the pictures. What do you see? What are the household problems?

B ▶ **LISTEN AND POINT.** Then listen and repeat.

Correlations

ELPS Level 2: 2, 7, 8
CCRS Level A: SL.1.1, SL.K.6, L.1.5, L1.6
CASAS Reading: RDG 1.7, 2.2, 2.3
CASAS Listening: L2.1, 2.3, 2.9, 4.2
CASAS Competencies: 0.1.2, 0.1.5, 7.4.1, 8.2.6
Complete standards language available on the Pearson English Portal.

Self-Directed Learning

State the **lesson objective.** Say: *In this lesson, we will learn to identify household problems.*

Ⓐ PREDICT. **Look at the pictures. What do you...**

1. Read the directions. Tell students to cover the list on page 87.
2. Write: *In number _____, the _____ is _____.*
3. Point to picture 1 and ask: *What household problem is this?* Say: *In #1, the ceiling is leaking.*
4. Say: *Look at the other numbers. What household problems do you know?* Students call out answers. Point to the model sentence and help students pronounce household problems if they have difficulty.
5. If a student calls out an incorrect event, ask a *yes/no* clarification question: *In #2, is the sink clogged?* If nobody can identify the correct problem, tell students they will now listen to audio and practice the names of the problems.

Ⓑ ▶ LISTEN AND POINT. **Then listen and repeat.**

1. Read the directions. Play the audio. Students listen and point to the household problems.
2. While the audio is playing, walk around and check that students are pointing to the correct problems. Pause the audio after item #12.
3. Say each household problem in random order and ask students to point to the appropriate picture.
4. Tell students to look at page 87. Resume the audio. Students listen, read, and repeat.

 ActiveTeach for B: Vocabulary Flashcards

▣ EXPANSION: Writing practice for B

1. Tell the class to close their books. Say a household problem and tell students to write it. Repeat for several household problems.
2. Students compare answers with a partner.
3. Walk around and spot-check students' answers. If students have difficulty with spelling, tell them to look at the vocabulary list on page 87.

▣ EXPANSION: Vocabulary practice for B

1. Pair students. Have them write the household words for numbers 1–10 on page 87 (for example, *ceiling, toilet, sink,* etc.) on individual small pieces of paper or index cards.
2. Next have students write all the problem words and phrases (for example, *leaking, clogged, isn't working*) on different individual small pieces of paper. They should write one problem word or phrase for each number on page 87, so some will be duplicated.
3. Tell pairs to place the papers with the household words at the top of their desks. Under each household word, students place the paper with the problem word or phrases that applies (for example, *Ceiling: leaking*).
4. Form groups of 5. For each group, scramble a set of the vocabulary scraps on a desk. Give the class 30 seconds to reassemble the problem words under the appropriate household words. The first group to do it successfully wins.

Vocabulary

C WORK TOGETHER. Look at the pictures...

1. Read each line in the example and ask the class to repeat. Model correct intonation.
2. Play A and model the example with an above-level student. Point to picture 2. Continue the conversation.
3. Play B. Prompt the student to point to another picture and ask: *What's the problem?*
4. Pair students and tell them to talk about at least three pictures each.
5. Walk around and check for correct pronunciation of the household problems.

▧ MULTILEVEL INSTRUCTION for C

Pre-level scaffolding Allow pairs to refer to the list of words at the top of page 87 as needed.

Above-level expansion Tell pairs to cover the list of words on page 87 when they practice.

D CATEGORIZE. Complete the chart. Use the...

1. Review the vocabulary in the box. Say: *Look at the pictures. Point to a ceiling. Point to a door.* Continue in the same way with the other words in the box.
2. Read the directions. Pair students. Students complete the chart on their own paper.
3. Tell students to switch partners and compare their chart with another classmate.
4. To check answers, copy the chart onto the board. Ask three students to write the words for a column in the chart.
5. Point to each word on the chart, say a sentence, and ask the class to repeat, for example: *The faucet is leaking. The door is stuck. The toilet is clogged.*

▧ EXPANSION: Vocabulary practice for D

1. Tell students to look at the list of household problems on page 87 and the chart in Exercise D. Ask: *Which household problems do you have today?* Tell students to write a checkmark next to any problems in their home.
2. Pair students. Say: *Tell your partner what problems you have.*
3. If necessary, model: *My ceiling is leaking. My lock is broken.*

Study Tip: Use the flashcards on MyEnglishLab

1. Point to the **Study Tip**. Read the directions.
2. Say: *You can remember new vocabulary when you test yourself with flashcards. You can also make your own flashcards.* Remind students to use this strategy to remember other new vocabulary.

Show what you know!

1. THINK ABOUT IT. Read the list of household...

1. Ask: *Which household problem do you <u>really</u> not want to have?* Tell students to circle this problem.
2. Ask students to tell you which is a really bad problem to have and why.
3. Read the directions. Say: *A <u>small</u> household problem is not dangerous. It is also easy to fix and not expensive.*
4. Tell students to identify two small household problems in the list.

2. TALK ABOUT IT. Talk about small household...

1. Read the directions and the example.
2. Model the activity with two above-level students. Play A and begin the conversation.
3. Form groups of 3. Students talk about the small household problems that they starred.
4. Reform the groups and repeat the activity.
5. To wrap up, say each household problem from the list and ask students: *Is this a small problem?*

3. WRITE ABOUT IT. Write a list of small...

1. Read the directions. Write an example: *The mailbox is broken.*
2. Remind students to capitalize the first word in the sentence. Remind them to end with a punctuation mark.
3. Share the checklist below. Then write a checkmark next to each as you point back to the example sentence.
   - The household problem is not dangerous.
   - The household problem is easy to fix.
   - The household problem is not expensive to fix.
4. Give students time to make their list.
5. Tell students to show their sentences to partner. Tell the students to use the checklist to review the sentences.
6. Walk around and verify that students are using the checklist. Collect the papers for review or put them in the students' writing portfolios.

Self-Directed Learning

Point out the blue bar. Ask students if they can do the lesson learning objective or if they need more practice. Tell them to check one of the boxes. Assign Extra Practice as needed.

Extra Practice

  p. 50

Vocabulary

Household Problems

1. The ceiling is leaking.
2. The faucet is leaking.
3. The toilet is clogged.
4. The sink is clogged.
5. The lock is broken.
6. The mailbox is broken.
7. The window is stuck.
8. The door is stuck.
9. The washing machine isn't working.
10. The stove isn't working.
11. There's no heat.
12. There's no hot water.

C **WORK TOGETHER.** Look at the pictures. Student A, point to a picture and ask, "What's the problem?" Student B, say the problem.

Student A points to Picture 2.
A: What's the problem?
B: The ceiling is leaking.
A: No, it isn't.
B: The faucet is leaking.
A: Right!

D **CATEGORIZE.** Complete the chart. Use the words in the box. Some words can be in more than one column.

Study Tip

Use the flashcards on MyEnglishLab

Click on each flashcard. Say the household problem. Play the audio to check your answer. To practice pronunciation, play the audio and repeat.

ceiling	~~faucet~~	sink	washing machine
door	lock	toilet	window

(Answers will vary.)

Things that leak	Things that get stuck	Things that get clogged
faucet toilet, ceiling	window, lock, door	sink, washing machine, toilet

Show what you know!

1. **THINK ABOUT IT.** Read the list of household problems again. Put a star (★) next to two small household problems.

2. **TALK ABOUT IT.** Talk about small household problems.

    A: The toilet is clogged. That's a small problem.
    B: I agree. The window is stuck. That's a small problem, too.
    C: I don't think so. It is dangerous.

3. **WRITE ABOUT IT.** Write a list of small household problems.

    Small Household Problems

    _____

    _____

I can identify household problems. ■   I need more practice. ■

For more practice, go to MyEnglishLab.

1 BEFORE YOU LISTEN

Ⓐ **LABEL. Write the words under the pictures.**

a locksmith   an electrician   a building manager   a plumber

1. _____an electrician_____   2. _____a plumber_____   3. _____a locksmith_____   4. _____a building manager_____

Ⓑ **MAKE CONNECTIONS. When there is a problem in your home, who fixes it?**

2 LISTEN

Ⓐ **PREDICT. Look at the picture. What is the man doing?**

Ⓑ ▶ **LISTEN FOR MAIN IDEA. Complete the sentence.**

Harry is talking to _____.
a. a plumber
b. the building manager
ⓒ his friend

Harry

Ⓒ ▶ **LISTEN FOR DETAILS. Listen again. What does Joe say?**

ⓐ Call the building manager.
b. Buy a new radiator.
c. Fix the radiator.

Ⓓ ▶ **EXPAND. Listen to the whole conversation. Why can't Harry follow Joe's advice?**

a. His phone doesn't work.
b. He doesn't have the manager's number.
ⓒ He is the building manager.

Correlations

ELPS Level 2: 2, 7
CASAS Reading: RDG 1.7, 2.2, 2.3
CASAS Listening: L2.1, 2.3, 4.1, 4.2, 6.1, 6.2, 6.5
CASAS Competencies: 0.1.2, 0.1.5, 4.1.8, 8.2.6
Complete standards language available on the Pearson English Portal.

Self-Directed Learning

State the **lesson objective**. Say: *In this lesson, we will learn to describe problems in our homes.*

1 BEFORE YOU LISTEN

A LABEL. Write the words under the pictures.

1. Read the directions.
2. Tell the class to look at the second picture. Ask: *What's the problem?* (The sink is clogged / leaking.) Tell the class to look at the third picture. Ask: *What's the problem?* (The lock is broken.)
3. Tell the class to look at the first picture. Ask: *What isn't working?* (the electricity) Tell the class to look at the fourth picture. Ask: *What isn't working?* (the light)
4. Say: *Different people fix different problems in your home.* Say each type of repairperson in the box and ask the class to repeat. Explain that if you own your own home, you call an electrician, a plumber, or a locksmith to fix problems. If you rent an apartment, you call the building manager to fix problems.
5. Give students time to label the pictures. Elicit the answers.
6. As a follow-up, ask: *When the toilet is clogged, who fixes it?* (a plumber) *If the ceiling in your rental apartment is leaking, who fixes it?* (a building manager) *If a light isn't working in a house you own, who fixes it?* (an electrician)

Career Awareness: Building manager

Building managers make sure a building is clean and safe. A building manager in a small building does repairs and takes care of the landscaping. In a large building, the manager oversees janitors, maintenance staff, and landscapers.

EXPANSION: Career awareness for 1A

Ask students about the job in this lesson: *What do building managers do? Where do they work? Do you want to be a building manager?*

B MAKE CONNECTIONS. When there is a...

1. Ask: *When there is a problem in your home, who fixes it?*
2. Pair students to discuss the question.
3. Call on students to answer the question. Write any new ideas (for example, *cable guy, carpenter, handyman*).

2 LISTEN

A PREDICT. Look at the picture. What is the...

1. Tell students to look at the picture of Harry. Ask: *Where is he?* (in a building) Tell students to point to Harry, the radiator, and the phone.
2. Ask: *What is the man doing?* (fixing the radiator, talking on the phone) *If the radiator is broken, what problem does Harry have?* (There's no heat.) *Do you have a radiator in your home?* Ask for a show of hands.

B ▶ LISTEN FOR MAIN IDEA. Complete the...

1. Read the directions and the answer choices.
2. Play the audio. Students listen and circle the letter of the correct answer. Ask: *Does Harry live in a house or an apartment?* (apartment)
3. Ask: *Is Harry talking to a plumber?* (No, he isn't.) *Is he talking to the building manager?* (No, he isn't.) *Is he talking to his friend?* (Yes, he is.) *What's his friend's name?* (Joe)
4. Ask: *Was your guess in Exercise 2A correct?*
5. Ask about **register**: *How do you know Harry and Joe are friends?* (They call each other by their first names, Joe knows Harry's voice.)

C ▶ LISTEN FOR DETAILS. Listen again. What...

1. Tell students to read the question and answer choices silently.
2. Play the audio. Students circle the letter of the correct answer.
3. Students compare answers with a partner.
4. Call on a volunteer to say the answer.

Teaching Tip: Use the script

Optional: If students need additional support, tell them to read the Audio Script on page 269 as they listen to the conversation.

D ▶ EXPAND. Listen to the whole...

1. Read the directions.
2. Play the audio. Students answer the question.
3. Ask: *Do you need to listen one more time?* If yes, play the audio again.
4. Review the correct answer with the class.

Listening and Speaking

3 CONVERSATION

Ⓐ ▶ LISTEN AND READ. Then listen and repeat.

1. Note: This is the same conversation students heard in Exercise 2B on page 88.
2. Read the directions.
3. Play the audio. Students listen and read silently. Then students listen and repeat.

Ⓑ WORK TOGETHER. Practice the...

1. Pair students and tell them to practice the conversation in Exercise 3A.
2. Tell students to take turns playing A and B.

> **Teaching Tip: Formative assessment**
>
> Model the conversation with multiple students to check comprehension. Formative assessment can inform instruction choices like multilevel pairings.

Ⓒ CREATE. Make new conversations. Use the...

1. Read the directions. Tell students to look at the information in the boxes. Remind them to use the information in the box that matches the color of the blank. Ask: *What do you see in the yellow boxes?* (people to call, repair people) *What do you see in the blue boxes?* (problems)
2. Show the conversation. Elicit information from the boxes to fill the blanks.
3. Ask two on-level students to practice the conversation.
4. Erase the words in the blanks and ask two above-level students to make up a new conversation.
5. Tell pairs to take turns playing A and B and to use the vocabulary words to fill in the blanks.
6. Tell students to stand, mingle, and practice the conversation with several new partners.
7. Call on pairs to perform for the class.

■ MULTILEVEL INSTRUCTION for 3C

Pre-level scaffolding A can show B the name for the correct type of repairperson to call.

Above-level expansion Tell A not to show B the name for the correct type of repairperson to call.

Ⓓ MAKE CONNECTIONS. Make your own...

1. Read the directions. Tell the class that they're going to practice the conversation in Exercise 3C again but with different household problems.
2. Point to each picture and elicit a possible problem (the window is stuck, there's no heat, there's no hot water)
3. **Scaffold:** Tell students to write the following in their notebooks:
   a. a different household problem (not one from the blue box in Exercise 3A)
   b. who they should call to fix this problem
4. Pair students. Tell B to use the household problem he or she wrote down. Tell A to respond with who to call to fix the problem. Say: *If you don't know the name for the correct type of repairperson, you can say* the building manager. Walk around and note any errors you hear.
5. To wrap up, write some of the errors you heard during the role-plays. Ask students to correct the mistakes. Go over the corrections by saying the words or sentences correctly and asking the class to repeat.

■ EXPANSION: Graphic organizer practice for 3D

1. On the board, draw a web diagram and write *plumber* in the circle. Draw four lines radiating out from the circle.
2. Ask students to look at the vocabulary on page 87. Tell them to copy the diagram and write on it the four problems that you should call a plumber to fix (vocabulary items 2, 3, 4, and 12).
3. Pair students and tell them to use the language from the Venn diagram to practice a new conversation like the one in Exercise 3C.

Self-Directed Learning

Point out the blue bar. Ask students if they can do the lesson learning objective or if they need more practice. Tell them to check one of the boxes. Assign Extra Practice as needed.

> **Extra Practice**
>
>   p. 51

Listening and Speaking

3 CONVERSATION

A ▶ **LISTEN AND READ.** Then listen and repeat.

A: Hello?
B: Hi, Harry. It's Joe.
A: Oh, hi, Joe. Can I call you back?
B: Sure. No problem.
A: Thanks. My radiator is broken and I'm trying to fix it.
B: You should call the building manager for your apartment.

B **WORK TOGETHER.** Practice the conversation in Exercise A.

C **CREATE.** Make new conversations. Use the words in the boxes.

A: Hello?
B: Hi, _____. It's

_____.

A: Oh, hi, _____. Can I
call you back?
B: Sure. No problem.
A: Thanks.

and I'm trying to fix it.
B: You should call

.

My lock is broken	a locksmith
My bathroom light isn't working	an electrician
My faucet is leaking	a plumber

D **MAKE CONNECTIONS.** Make your own conversations about a problem in your home.

I can describe problems in my home. ■   I need more practice. ■

For more practice, go to MyEnglishLab.

Present continuous

Present continuous		
Affirmative		**Negative**

I	**am**		I	**am**	
You			You		
We	**are**	**fixing** the radiator now.	We	**are**	**not calling** the building manager.
They			They		
He	**is**		He	**is**	
She			She		

A **COMPLETE. Use the present continuous and the verbs in parentheses to complete the sentences.**

1. The oven is broken. The electrician (look for) ____*is looking for*____ the problem.

2. The plumber (fix) ____is fixing____ the sink. It (not leak) ____isn't leaking____ now.

3. The dishwasher (not work) ____isn't working____. It (make) 's making / is making a loud noise.

4. That lock is broken. The locksmith (try) ____is trying____ to fix it.

5. Be careful! The paint is still wet, and you (sit) 're sitting / are sitting on it.

6. We (not wait for) 're not waiting / aren't waiting the building manager to fix the broken light. My husband and I (fix) ____are fixing____ it right now.

7. You (do) ____are doing____ all the work yourself. Do you want some help?

8. The painters (work) ____are working____, but they (not paint) 're not painting / aren't painting very quickly.

Grammar Watch

- Use the present continuous for events taking place at the present time.
- See page 258 for spelling rules with *-ing* verbs.
- See page 258 for contractions with forms of *be*.

B **EVALUATE. Correct the mistake in each sentence.**

1. The sink is ~~leak~~. *leaking*

2. We~~'re~~ are looking for a good plumber.

3. ~~I~~ not calling the building manager. *I'm / I am*

4. The stove in my apartment ~~not~~ working. *is not / isn't*

5. The building manager ~~are~~ fixing the problem. *is*

6. They're not ~~use~~ the broken sink. *using*

Correlations

ELPS Level 2: 2, 7, 10
CCRS Level A: L.1.1, L.1.2
CASAS Reading: RDG 1.7, 2.9, 4.9
CASAS Listening: L1.3, 2.1, 2.3, 3.9, 4.1, 4.2
CASAS Competencies: 0.1.2, 0.1.5, 8.2.6
Complete standards language available on the Pearson English Portal.

Self-Directed Learning

State the **lesson objective**. Say: *In this lesson, we will learn to use the present continuous in affirmative and negative sentences.*

Present continuous

 ActiveTeach: Grammar Discovery

1. Warm up. Say: *The conversation on page 89 used this grammar.* Turn back to page 89. Point to the sentences in Exercise 3C and then write:
   • *My bathroom light isn't working.*
   • *My faucet is leaking.*
   Underline *isn't working* and *is leaking*.
2. Point to the picture of Harry on page 88. Ask: *What is Harry doing?* Write: *Harry _____ fix _____ the radiator.*
3. Tell students to look at the grammar charts.
4. Point to the left chart. Ask: *What form of* be *goes with Harry?* Write *is* in the first blank in the sentence. Ask: *What do I add to* fix *to form the present continuous?* Write *ing* in the second blank. Read the completed sentence: *Harry is fixing the radiator.*
5. Change the subject of the sentence on the board by erasing *Harry* and writing *You.* Ask: *What else needs to change?* Elicit the answer. Erase *is* and write *are.*
6. Point to the picture of Harry on page 88 again. Write: *Harry is talking to a plumber.* Ask: *Is this sentence true or false?* (false) *How can I change it to make it true?* Point to the right chart. Add *not* between *is* and *talking.* Read the new sentence: *Harry is not talking to a plumber.*
7. Read the **Grammar Watch** note. Say: *Look around the classroom. What's taking place at the present time?* Elicit a few affirmative and negative sentences and write them. Elicit the contractions for the negative sentences (for example, *Ahmed isn't listening. Amaya and Yoko aren't talking.*).

 ActiveTeach: Grammar Coach

Ⓐ COMPLETE. Use the present continuous...
1. Read the directions.
2. Write item 1. Ask: *What's the subject?* (the electrician) *What's the correct form of* be? *(is)*
3. Point to the verb *look for.* Ask: *How do we form the present continuous?* (is looking for)
4. Write item 3. Point to the verb *make.* Ask: *What letter does* make *end in?* (-e) Say: *When a verb ends in* -e, *take off the* -e *before you add* -ing. Cross out the *-e* in *make* and add *-ing.* Then write *making.*
5. Tell students to complete the other items. Walk around and check for the correct form of *be* and the verb + *-ing.*
6. Students compare answers with a partner.
7. To check answers, call on students to read the sentences out loud. Elicit contractions as appropriate. Ask the student who reads item 3 how to spell *making.* Write it.

Career Awareness: Plumber

Plumbers fix or install household items through which water or gas runs, for example, pipes, faucets, toilets, sinks, and radiators. They usually work in homes. They don't need a high level of education, but do need special training.

■■ EXPANSION: Career awareness for A
Ask students about the job in this lesson: *What do plumbers do? Where do they work? Do you need to study to be a plumber? Do you want to be a plumber?*

Ⓑ EVALUATE. Correct the mistake in each...
1. Read the directions. Tell students to look for the verb to *be* in the correct form and the verb in the *-ing* form.
2. Write:
   • *the verb to* be
   • *-ing form of the verb*
3. Ask: *Is the mistake in item 1 in the form of* be *or in the verb +* -ing? (the verb + *-ing*)
4. Tell students to read each sentence and check for the two things on the board.
5. Walk around and check that students are using the present continuous correctly. If students have difficulty, tell them to underline the form of *be* and ask: *Is it correct?* Then tell them to underline the verb + *-ing* and ask: *Is it correct?*
6. Students compare answers with a partner.
7. Check answers by asking students to write the corrected sentences.

Grammar

C APPLY. Complete the text messages. Use...

1. Write the sentences for item 1: *I need help! The bathroom sink _____.* Read the sentence out loud. Ask: *What's the subject of the second sentence?* (*bathroom sink*) *What's the form of* be? (*is*)

2. Ask: *What's the verb in the example?* (*isn't working*) Say: *Point to the verb* not work *in the box. What was added in the example?* (*is* and *-ing*)

3. Read the first part of the text message. Stop after the sentence that contains item 2. Tell students to look at item 2. Ask: *What's the subject?* (*we*) *What's the correct form of* be? (*are*) *Which verb in the box goes with* we *and* the game? (*watch*) *What do you need to add to* watch? (*are* and *-ing*)

4. Tell students to complete the other items. Walk around and check for the correct form of *be*. If students have difficulty, tell them to underline the subjects.

5. Students compare answers with a partner.

6. Number from 2 to 8 on the board. Ask students to write answers on the board. If there are any incorrect answers, review the item with the class.

7. Tell students to read the text silently. Ask: *What are the problems?* (The bathroom sink is leaking. The landlord isn't calling back.)

■■■ EXPANSION: Speaking practice for C

Pair students. Tell them to read the text messages as a phone conversation. They take turns playing A (blue boxes) and B (yellow boxes).

■■■ EXPANSION: Writing and speaking practice for C

1. Say: *The landlord finally calls back. Write a new phone conversation between the landlord and the person who has the problem.*

2. Pairs write the conversation together. Walk around and help them with ideas about how to begin and end the conversation.

3. *Optional:* Write the beginning and end of a conversation:

   Landlord: Hello. What is the problem?...

   Landlord: I understand. I will call a plumber right away.

4. Pairs read their new conversation aloud and take turns being the landlord and A.

Show what you know!

1. THINK ABOUT IT. Look at the picture. List...

1. Tell students to review the household problems on pages 87–89.

2. Tell students to create a list of three problems in the picture (for example, *The window is stuck.*).

2. TALK ABOUT IT. Talk about the picture...

1. Read the directions. Ask two above-level students to read the example out loud.

2. Pair students. Tell pairs to decide who is Student A. Student A says a problem from the list they made in Step 1. Student B says what the people are doing to fix it. Say: *If nobody is fixing a problem, say:* Nobody is fixing it.

3. When Student A has said all the items on his or her list, partners switch roles.

4. Walk around and check that students are using the present continuous correctly.

5. To check answers, name a problem and call on students to respond with what the people are doing.

3. WRITE ABOUT IT. Now write three sentences...

1. Read the directions. Working individually, students write three sentences about the picture, using their list from Step 1.

2. Ask students to check each other's sentences:
   - Sentence should begin with a capital letter and end with a period.
   - Sentences should use the correct form of *be*.
   - Sentences should use a verb + *-ing*.

3. Have students volunteer to share sentences about the picture.

Self-Directed Learning

Point out the blue bar. Ask students if they can do the lesson learning objective or if they need more practice. Tell them to check one of the boxes. Assign Extra Practice as needed.

Extra Practice
MyEnglishLab   Workbook p. 51

Grammar

C **APPLY.** Complete the text messages. Use the present continuous and the words in the box.

come	not stop
leak	~~not work~~
make	try
not call	watch

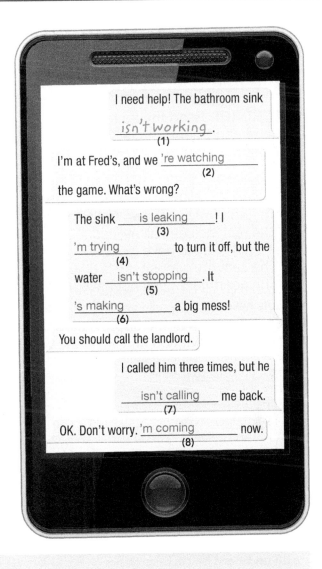

I need help! The bathroom sink _isn't working_.
(1)

I'm at Fred's, and we _'re watching_ the game. What's wrong?
(2)

The sink _is leaking_ ! I
(3)
'm trying to turn it off, but the
(4)
water _isn't stopping_ . It
(5)
's making a big mess!
(6)

You should call the landlord.

I called him three times, but he
isn't calling me back.
(7)

OK. Don't worry. _'m coming_ now.
(8)

Show what you know!

1. **THINK ABOUT IT.** Look at the picture. List three problems.

2. **TALK ABOUT IT.** Talk about the picture. Share your list of problems. What are the people doing?

   A: The window is stuck.
   B: A man is trying to close it.

3. **WRITE ABOUT IT.** Now write three sentences about what is happening in the picture.

I can use the present continuous in affirmative and negative sentences. ■   I need more practice. ■

For more practice, go to MyEnglishLab.

4

Workplace, Life, and Community Skills

Apartment ads and utility bills

1 READ APARTMENT ADS

A **INTERPRET. Read the ad for a rental apartment. Circle *True* or *False*.**

2 bedroom/2 bathroom apartment, living room, dining room, eat-in kitchen. 1200 square feet. Air-conditioning. Washer and dryer. Utilities included. Near transportation. Pets allowed. No fee. $1200 per month. One month's rent security deposit. CONTACT: Kim at kchan@yehee.com

1. The apartment has two bathrooms. (True) False
2. The rent includes all utilities. (True) False
3. It's not okay to have a pet. True (False)
4. The security deposit is $1200.00. (True) False
5. The apartment does not have a washer or dryer. True (False)

B **IDENTIFY. Look at the abbreviations. Then look at the ad above. Circle the words for each abbreviation and write the words on the line.**

1. A/C ___air conditioner___
2. apt. ___apartment___
3. DR ___dining room___
4. BA ___bathroom___
5. EIK ___eat-in kitchen___
6. BR ___bedroom___
7. LR ___living room___
8. W/D ___washer and dryer___
9. util. incl. ___utilities included___
10. trans. ___transportation___
11. sec.dep. ___security deposit___
12. sq. ft. ___square feet___

C **COMPARE. Read about the family. Read the ads. Which apartment is better for the family? Why?** *(Answers will vary.)* Apartment A is best for the Chens. It has two bedrooms. It is located where Mrs. Chen works. It's pet-friendly, and near transportation.

> **The Chens**
>
> The Chens are a family of three with a small dog (a mother and two children). Mrs. Chen works in the South End. She can spend $1450 a month on rent and utilities. She can pay $2000 for a security deposit. She doesn't have a car.

A.

South End. Large 2 BR, LR, EIK, 2 BA. 1200 square feet. W/D. Ht. + hw. not incl. Pets allowed. No fee. $1,200/mo. 1 mo. sec. dep. Near transportation. Available immediately. Call Rick 207-555-1212.

B.

North Square. Nice 2 BR, LR, DR. No pets. $1,200/mo. Util. incl. Near schools. Fee + 2 mo. sec. dep. Maven Realty Sam@mavenrealty.com

D GO ONLINE. **Search for an apartment in your town or city.**

Find an apartment that you like. How much is it? What is included? How much is the security deposit?

I can read apartment ads. ■   I need more practice. ■

For more practice, go to MyEnglishLab.

Correlations

ELPS Level 2: 1, 2, 3, 4, 5, 6, 7, 8, 9, 10
CCRS Level A: RI.1.9, W.1.7, W.1.8
CASAS Reading: RDG 1.7, 1.8, 2.2, 2.3, 3.2, 3.6, 3.16, 4.9
CASAS Listening: L2.1, 2.3, 4.2
CASAS Competencies: 0.1.2, 0.1.5, 1.4.2, 1.5.3, 4.5.6, 7.4.4, 7.7.3
Complete standards language available on the Pearson English Portal.

Self-Directed Learning

State the **lesson objective.** Say: *In this lesson, we will learn to read apartment ads and read a utility bill.*

1 READ APARTMENT ADS

Docment Literacy: Apartment ad

Context: *Where do you find apartment ads?* (online, newspapers, bulletin boards)
Purpose: *What are apartment ads for?* (to advertise apartments that are available for rent)
Key Words: *bedroom, bathroom, security deposit, utilities, washer, dryer, square feet, pets, fee*

A INTERPRET. Read the ad for a rental…

1. Tell students to look at the apartment ad. Orient them to the apartment ad. Ask: What kind of form is this? (apartment ad)
2. Tell the class to read the ad. Explain:
   • *Security deposit:* Money you give to the landlord before you rent. The landlord returns the money when you move out if you have not damaged the apartment.
   • *Fee:* Money you pay to the agent who showed you the apartment if you decide to rent it. (An agent helps people find apartments.)
3. Tell the class to look at the ad again. Ask: *How much is the rent?* ($1,200 a month) *How much is the security deposit?* (one month's rent = $1,200) *How much is the fee?* (no fee = $0)
4. Read the first sentence. Tell students to find and underline the number of bathrooms in the ad. Ask: *What did you underline?* (2 bathrooms) *Is the sentence true or false?* (true)
5. Tell students to read the sentences, underline information in the ad, and then circle *True* or *False*.

B IDENTIFY. Look at the abbreviations. Then…

1. Ask: *Why do classified ads use a lot of abbreviations?* (to save space) There are two reasons to save space in advertisements. In newspapers, people pay for advertisements per line, so longer ads are more expensive. Online, there is often a limit to the number of characters that can be used.
2. Tell students to look at the list. Say: *These are the short forms of words that are often in apartment ads. Look at item 1. Circle* air-conditioning *in the ad.* Ask: *Why is A/C the abbreviation for air-conditioning?* (because *air* starts with a and *conditioning* starts with c)
3. Read the directions.
4. Call on students to read the answers.

C COMPARE. Read about the family. Read the…

1. Read the directions.
2. Tell students to underline important information about the Chens and what they need in an apartment.
3. **Scaffold:** As a class, write a list of the Chens' housing requirements. Students volunteer information that they have underlined. For example: *Security deposit: $2,000 or less. Location: South End. Pets: Yes.* etc.
4. Students choose the ad for the apartment that is better for the Chens. Ask the class: *Who chose A? Who chose B?* Students raise their hands. If there is disagreement, compare the ads to each item in the list.

D GO ONLINE. Search for an apartment in your…

1. Read the directions. Ask students what they would search in English if they wanted to find an apartment in their town or city.
2. Write the search string: *apartments for rent in [town or city].* Have students search the internet and find information about apartments for rent.
3. Compare research as a class. Write a complete list of websites that advertise apartments for rent.

Digital Skills for 1D

Many websites list apartments for rent. Often, these sites give links to email for more information. Students can compose an email to a property manager, asking for more information.

Self-Directed Learning

Point out the blue bar. Ask students if they can do the lesson learning objective or if they need more practice. Tell them to check one of the boxes. Assign Extra Practice as needed.

2 READ A UTILITY BILL

A DISCUSS. What is a utility bill? What utility...

Document Literacy: Utility bill

Context: Utility bills are sent to customers by utility companies, which provide electricity, gas, water, sewage

Purpose: Utility bills tell you what you owe for utilities.

Key Words: *dates of service, account number, charges, balance, credits, due by, subtotal, total charges*

---

1. Tell students to look at the utility bill. Orient them to the bill. Ask: *What kind of form is this?* (Utility bill) Explain that a *utility* is an organization that provides basic services such as electricity, gas, water, and sewage. Ask about **context**: *Who sends utility bills?* (utility companies) *Who sent this utility bill?* (an electric company / Georgia Electric). Ask about **purpose**: *What are utility bills for?* (to tell you what you owe for utilities) Tell the class to read the utility bill. Ask about **key words**: *What information is on this type of form?* (account number, balance, due date, dates of service)

2. Ask: *What utility bills do most people need to pay?* (The most common utility bills are for electricity and gas, water and sewer, and trash and recycling.)

Language Note

Remind students that *utilities included / utilities not included* was in the apartment ads on page 92. Say: *If utilities are included in the rent, the landlord pays the utility bill. If utilities are not included, then the renter pays the utility bill.*

B MATCH. Read the descriptions. Then read...

1. Read the directions. Ask a student to read the example.
2. Tell students to circle the words in the utility bill.
3. Students match descriptions and words. Walk around and assist with new vocabulary and using context clues to find answers.
4. Students compare answers with a partner.
5. Call on students to read the answers.

■ EXPANSION: Learning strategy for 2B

1. Form groups of 3. Give each group 12 index cards.
2. Tell each group to write the descriptions and words on the index cards. Say: *Use one card for each description and one card for each word.*
3. Lay out the cards in two sets. On the left, arrange the description cards, face down. On the right, arrange the word cards, face down.
4. Model a matching activity: Groups take turns turning over a description card and then a word card, trying to find matches. If there is no match, the cards are put face-down again in the same place. When a match is made, those cards are removed by the student who makes the match.
5. Students read the cards out loud when they turn them over.

C INTERPRET. Review the utility bill. Answer...

1. Read the directions. Say: *The words in Exercise 2B will help you answer some of these questions.*
2. Students answer the questions.
3. Form pairs. Partners compare answers.
4. Call on pairs to read the answers.

 ActiveTeach: Review

Self-Directed Learning

Point out the blue bar. Ask students if they can do the lesson learning objective or if they need more practice. Tell them to check one of the boxes. Assign Extra Practice as needed.

Extra Practice

  pp. 52–53 Life Skills Writing

Workplace, Life, and Community Skills

2 READ A UTILITY BILL

A **DISCUSS.** What is a utility bill? What utility bills do most people need to pay?

B **MATCH.** Read the descriptions. Then read the utility bill. Match the descriptions with the words.

1. __c__ getting something brought to your house or apartment
2. __d__ a period of time
3. __b__ the number that identifies your service
4. __f__ the amount of money you need to pay
5. __a__ the amount of money you already paid
6. __e__ how much of something you get

a. credits
b. account number
c. ~~delivery~~
d. dates of service
e. supply
f. total charges

Georgia Electric

Dates of service:
June 2, 2019–July 1, 2019

Name: Lin Guo

Account number: 12 3456 7890

Charges:	
Delivery:	$26.72
Supply:	$36.43
Previous balance:	$74.22
Subtotal:	**$137.37**
Credits:	$74.22
Total charges:	**$63.15**

Due by July 22, 2019

C **INTERPRET.** Review the utility bill. Answer the questions.

1. What is the bill for? Electricity.
2. Who is the bill for? Lin Guo.
3. What time period does the bill cover? June 2, 2019–July 1, 2019.
4. What is the account number? 12 3456 7890.
5. How much money was paid? $74.22.
6. When should the bill be paid? Before July 22, 2019.
7. How much money needs to be paid? $63.15.

I can read a utility bill. ■

I need more practice. ■

For more practice, go to MyEnglishLab.

Ask about an apartment

1 BEFORE YOU LISTEN

MAKE CONNECTIONS. Read the questions. What other questions can you ask a rental agent about an apartment for rent?

10:15

How much is the rent?

How many bedrooms are there?

Is there a laundry room?

Are there two bathrooms?

2 LISTEN

Maria

Rental agen

Ⓐ PREDICT. Look at the picture. Who do you think is making the phone call?

Ⓑ ▶ LISTEN FOR MAIN IDEA. Why is the woman calling?

ⓐ. She wants information about an apartment.
b. She has a question about her rent.
c. She has a problem with her apartment.

Ⓒ ▶ LISTEN FOR DETAILS. Circle *True* or *False*.

1. There are two bedrooms.	(True)	False
2. There's a large living room.	(True)	False
3. There's a laundry room in the building.	True	(False)
4. There's a bus stop around the corner.	(True)	False

Ⓓ ▶ EXPAND. Listen to the whole conversation. How much is the rent?

ⓐ. $2,000 a month   **b.** $200 a month   **c.** $500 a month

Correlations

ELPS Level 2: 2, 7
CCRS Level A: SL.K.3
CASAS Reading: RDG 1.7, 2.2, 2.3
CASAS Listening: L2.1, 2.3, 4.2, 6.1, 6.2
CASAS Competencies: 0.1.2, 0.1.5, 0.1.6, 1.4.2
Complete standards language available on the Pearson English Portal.

Self-Directed Learning

State the **lesson objective**. Say: *In this lesson, we will learn to ask about an apartment.*

1 BEFORE YOU LISTEN

MAKE CONNECTIONS. Read the questions…

1. Read the directions. Call on students to read the questions.
2. Tell students to look at the ads on page 92 for ideas for other questions and write them on the board. (Some other possible questions: *Is there a fee? How many bathrooms are there? Is it near public transportation?*)

2 LISTEN

Ⓐ PREDICT. Look at the picture. Who do you…

1. Tell students to look at the picture. Ask: *Where is Maria?* (at home) *Where is the rental agent?* (in her office) *What is a rental agent?* Use the **Career Awareness** information to help students understand this job.
2. Ask: *Who do you think is making the phone call?* Say *Maria* and ask for a show of hands. Repeat with *the rental agent*.

Career Awareness: Rental agent

Rental agents often have offices in an apartment complex. They often meet possible renters and show them apartments. In addition to sales and marketing, they help with paperwork, including leases. Rental agents usually have an associate's degree or several years of training.

■ EXPANSION: Career awareness for 2B

Ask students about the job in this lesson: *What does a rental agent do? Where does a rental agent work? Do you need to study to be a rental agent? Do you want to be a rental agent?*

Ⓑ ▶ LISTEN FOR MAIN IDEA. Why is the…

1. Read the directions and the answer choices.
2. Play the audio. Students listen and circle the letter of the correct answer.
3. Ask: *Who is making the phone call?* (Maria) *Was your guess correct?* Ask for a show of hands.
4. Ask: *Why is the woman calling?* Elicit the correct answer from the class. Ask: *Who do you call if you have a problem with your apartment?* (the building manager)
5. Ask about **register**: *Do they introduce themselves?* (no) *Why not?* (Maria is only asking for information. They don't need to know each other's names yet.)

Ⓒ ▶ LISTEN FOR DETAILS. Circle *True* or *False*.

1. Read the directions. Tell students to read the statements silently.
2. Play the audio. Students circle the letter of the correct answer.
3. Students compare answers with a partner.
4. Call on students to read a sentence and say if it is true or false.
5. Ask a student to correct the false sentence (There's *no* laundry room…). Ask: *What is the apartment near?* (a laundromat and a park)

Teaching Tip: Use the script

Optional: If students need additional support, tell them to read the Audio Script on page 269 as they listen to the conversations.

Ⓓ ▶ EXPAND. Listen to the whole…

1. Read the directions.
2. Play the audio.
3. Ask: *Do you need to listen one more time?* If yes, play the audio again.
4. Ask: *According to the ad, how much is the rent?* Write: *$200/mo.* Ask: *Is the ad correct?* (no) How much is the rent really? Write: *$2,000/mo.* Ask: *What happened? What was the mistake?* (A zero was dropped from the price. / The rent is $2,000, but the ad says it is only $200.)
5. Elicit the correct answer.

Culture Note

1. Say: *In the U.S., many people own homes and many people rent. You will read more about this in Lesson 7.*
2. Ask: *In your native country, do more people rent or own their homes? Are some age groups more likely to rent than others?*

Listening and Speaking

3 PRONUNCIATION

A ▶ PRACTICE. Listen. Then listen and repeat.

1. Read the Pronunciation Note.
2. Tell students to look at the nouns in Exercise 3A. Say: *Nouns can be two words, like* bus stop *and* laundry room, *or one word, like* dishwasher. Ask: *Which is stressed,* bus *or* stop? (*bus*) laundry *or* room? (*laundry*) dish *or* washer? (*dish*)
3. Say: *Listen. Notice the stressed syllables.*
4. Play the audio. Students listen. Then students listen and repeat.

 ActiveTeach for 3A: Pronunciation Coach

Language Note

Two-word nouns are sometimes combined into one word, as in *dishwasher*, and sometimes remain as two separate words, as in *laundry room*. Tell students that there are no rules—they have to learn the form of each two-word noun.

B ▶ APPLY. Listen. Put a dot (•) above the...

1. Read the directions. Write item 1. Say: *washing machine.* Ask: *Which syllable is stressed?* (*wash-*) Put a dot over the syllable.
2. Say: *Listen.* Play the audio.
3. Say: *Listen again. Put a dot over the stressed syllable.* Play the audio again. Students listen and mark the stressed syllables.
4. Review the correct answers with students.
5. Say each noun. Tell students to repeat.

■ **EXPANSION: Pronunciation practice for 3B**

1. Put students in pairs to make sentences for each noun in Exercise 3A and 3B.
2. Call on students to say their sentences for the class. Correct pronunciation as needed.

4 CONVERSATION

A ▶ LISTEN AND READ. Then listen and repeat.

1. Note: This conversation is the same one students heard in Exercise 2B on page 94.
2. Tell students to read the conversation and underline nouns with two words. Elicit the nouns. (*bedrooms, living room, laundry room, bus stop*)
3. Play the audio. Students read along silently. Then students listen and repeat.
4. Walk around and help with pronunciation as needed. Pay particular attention to the students' pronunciation of *bedrooms, living room, laundry room,* and *bus stop.*

B WORK TOGETHER. Practice the conversation.

1. Read the directions. Pair students and tell them to take turns playing A and B.
2. Walk around and check that students are stressing the first word in a two-word noun.

C CREATE. Make new conversations. Use the...

1. Read the directions.
2. Tell students to find any two-word nouns in the colored boxes and underline the first word in each. Check that students circled and underlined as follows: *bathroom, dishwasher, parking lot, microwave, living room, subway stop, shopping center, supermarket.* Pronounce each two-word noun (with the stress on the first word) and ask the class to repeat.
3. Ask a pair of on-level students to practice the conversation for the class. Tell them to use the vocabulary in the colored boxes in the matching colored boxes in the conversation.
4. Pair students. Tell them to take turns playing A and B.
5. Tell students to stand, mingle, and practice the conversation with several new partners. Walk around and make sure students are using correct stress in two-word nouns.
6. Call on pairs to perform for the class.

■ **MULTILEVEL INSTRUCTION for 4C**
Pre-level scaffolding Tell pairs to fill in the blanks in their book before they practice.

D ROLE-PLAY. Make your own conversations...

1. Read the directions.
2. Model the conversation with an above-level student. Play A and answer B's questions.
3. Pair students and tell them to use their own information and make changes as needed. Tell students to take turns starting the conversation. Walk around and help as needed.
4. Tell students to practice the conversation with a new partner.
5. Call on pairs to perform for the class.

Self-Directed Learning

Point out the blue bar. Ask students if they can do the lesson learning objective or if they need more practice. Tell them to check one of the boxes. Assign Extra Practice as needed.

Extra Practice

  pp. 54–55

Listening and Speaking

3 PRONUNCIATION

A ▶ PRACTICE. Listen. Then listen and repeat.

Stress in two-word nouns

Sometimes we put two words together to make a noun. The first word is usually stressed.

•bus stop   •laundry room   •dishwasher   •living room

B ▶ APPLY. Listen. Put a dot (•) above the stressed syllable.

1. •washing machine   2. •mailbox   3. •locksmith   4. •rental agent   5. •microwave

4 CONVERSATION

A ▶ LISTEN AND READ. Then listen and repeat.

A: Hello?
B: Hi, I'm calling about the apartment for rent. Can you tell me about it?
A: Sure. There are two bedrooms and a large living room.
B: Is there a laundry room?
A: No, there isn't. But there's a laundromat down the street.
B: I see. Is there a bus stop nearby?
A: Yes, there is—just around the corner.

B WORK TOGETHER. Practice the conversation.

C CREATE. Make new conversations. Use the words in the boxes.

A: Hello?
B: Hi, I'm calling about the apartment for rent. Can you tell me about it?
A: Sure. There are two bedrooms and a _____ .
B: Is there a _____ ?
A: No, there isn't. But there's _____ .
B: I see. Is there a _____ nearby?
A: Yes, there is—just around the corner.

sunny kitchen	dishwasher	a microwave	subway stop
new bathroom	parking lot	free parking on the street	shopping center
big closet	balcony	a big window in the living room	supermarket

D ROLE-PLAY. Make your own conversations. Student A, you are going to rent your house or apartment. Student B, you want to rent a house or apartment. Ask and answer questions.

I can ask about an apartment. ■   I need more practice. ■

For more practice, go to MyEnglishLab.

Grammar

Lesson 6

There is / There are

There is / There are

Affirmative	Negative	
There is a bus stop nearby.	**There isn't a** **There's no**	park near here.
There are two bedrooms.	**There aren't any** **There are no**	restaurants in the neighborhood.

Questions		Short answers			
Is there	a laundry room?	Yes,	**there is.**	No,	**there isn't.**
Are there	a lot of windows?		**there are.**		**there aren't.**
How many bedrooms	**are there**?	Two. (**There are** two.)			
		One. (**There's** one.)			

A **IDENTIFY. Cross out the incorrect words.**

1. **There is /** ~~**There are**~~ a bus stop near the apartment.
2. **Are there /** ~~**Is there**~~ a lot of children in the neighborhood?
3. **Is there /** ~~**Are there**~~ a bathtub?
4. ~~**There is**~~ **/ There are** two windows in the kitchen.
5. **There's /** ~~**There isn't**~~ no elevator in the building.
6. ~~**There aren't**~~ **/ There isn't** a lot of traffic on this street.

B **COMPLETE. Use *there is / there are* to complete the conversation.**

A: So, tell me about your new apartment. How many bedrooms _____*are there*_____?

B: _____There are_____ two. And they're nice and big.

A: That's good. How are the neighbors?

B: Well, _____there is_____ an older woman next door. She seems very friendly.

A: And how's the neighborhood?

B: I like it a lot. _____There are_____ a lot of stores around the corner.

A: That's convenient. _____Are there_____ any supermarkets?

B: No, _____there aren't_____, but _____there's_____ a convenience store down the street.

Grammar Watch

We use *there is* and *there are* to say that something is in a place or to talk about how many things are in a place.

Self-Directed Learning

State the **lesson objective**. Say: *In this lesson, we will learn to make sentences and ask and answer questions with* there is / there are.

There is / There are

 ActiveTeach: Grammar Discovery

1. Warm up. Say: *The conversation on page 95 used this grammar.* Turn back to page 95. Point to the sentences in Exercise 4A and then write:
   - *There are two bedrooms and a large living room.*
   - *Is there a laundry room?*
   - *No, there isn't.*
2. Ask: *What is the verb?* (be; are, is) *What other word appears in all these sentences?* (there)
3. Underline the verbs as students notice the pattern.
4. Tell students to look at the grammar charts.
5. Read the **Grammar Watch** note.
6. On the board, draw a word box with *is* and *are*. Side-by-side write: *1. There _____ a dishwasher. 2. There _____ shops nearby.* Say: *Look at item 1. What comes after the blank?* (a dishwasher) *Look at item 2. What comes after the blank?* (shops) *Which do you think is the answer for item 1, is or are?* (is) *Why?* (because *dishwasher* is singular) *Which do you think is the answer for item 2, is or are?* (are) *Why?* (because *shops* is plural)
7. Point to item 1 on the board and ask: *How do I make this sentence negative?* Point to the grammar chart. Elicit and write under item 1: *There isn't a dishwasher. / There's no dishwasher.* Repeat with item 2 and write: *There aren't any shops. / There are no shops.*

8. Point to item 1 on the board and ask: *How do I make this sentence into a question?* Point to the grammar chart. Elicit and write under item 1: *Is there a dishwasher?* Repeat with item 2 and write: *Are there any shops?*
9. Elicit affirmative and negative short answers to each question and write them.
10. Tell students to point to the question with *How many* in the grammar chart. Read the question. Elicit other words to substitute for bedrooms when asking about an apartment (for example, *How many bathrooms / closets / windows are there?*).

 ActiveTeach: Grammar Coach

A **IDENTIFY. Cross out the incorrect words.**
1. Read the directions. Say: *Look at item 1. What comes after* There is / There are? (a bus stop) *Why is the answer* There is? (because *bus stop* is singular)
2. Say: *Look at item 2. With a lot of, look at what comes after. Is* children *singular or plural?* (plural) *When a subject is plural, does it take* is *or* are? (are). *What should you cross out?* (Is there)
3. Students complete the activity in pairs. Tell them to look first at what comes after *There is / There are.*
4 Call on students to read the sentences.

B **COMPLETE. Use *there is / there are* to...**
1. Read the directions and the example.
2. Point out that, for *there is*, students can also write *there's*.
3. Students complete the conversation by themselves. Then compare answers with a partner. Tell pairs to read the conversation to each other.
4. Call on pairs to perform the completed conversation for the class.

Grammar

C WRITE. Read the answers. Write questions…

1. Tell students to look at the *Questions* and *Short answers* boxes in the grammar charts on p. 96. Say one short answer from each line and elicit the corresponding question (for example, say: *Yes, there is.* Elicit: *Is there a laundry room?*).

2. Read the directions and the example. Walk around and remind students to read Speaker B's answer before they write Speaker A's question.

3. Say each item number and tell the class to call out their questions. Then tell students to check their questions and make sure they used question marks.

4. *Optional:* Pair students and tell them to read the completed questions and answers out loud. Students switch roles after item 3.

Show what you know!

1. THINK ABOUT IT. Imagine that you have an…

1. Draw the chart on the board. Read the directions.

2. Model the activity. Say: *My apartment has three bedrooms.* Write: **Three** in the *My Apartment* column.

3. Walk around and make sure that students are completing only the *My Apartment* column.

2. TALK ABOUT IT. Student A, ask questions…

1. Pair students. Tell pairs to decide who is Student A and Student B.

2. Read the directions. Play A and model the activity with an above-level student. Ask: *How many bedrooms are there [in your apartment]?* Fill in the answer in the *My Partner's Apartment* in the chart on the board.

3. Walk around and check that students are forming questions correctly. If they need help, tell them to look back at the grammar chart.

4. To follow-up, tell Student A to check the information in the chart by reading it back to Student B (for example, Student A: *There are two bedrooms, right?* or *Are there two bedrooms?*).

5. Still in pairs, students change roles. Tell Student B to note Student A's responses in the chart on page 97.

3. WRITE ABOUT IT. Write four sentences about…

1. Read the directions. Still in pairs, tell students to write four sentences about their partner's apartment.

2. Ask students to check each other's sentences.
   • Sentences should begin with a capital letter.
   • Sentences should use *There is / There are*.
   • Sentences should end with an end mark.

3. Have students volunteer to write their sentences on the board.

■ **EXPANSION: Speaking and grammar practice for 3**

Have students bring in apartment ads from the newspaper or online. Tell them to practice asking and answering questions about the ads.

■ **EXPANSION: Grammar and writing practice for 3**

1. Have students bring in apartment ads from the newspaper or online.

2. Say: *Imagine your friend is looking for an apartment. Write your friend an email about the apartment in one of the ads. Make up a neighborhood name for the apartment. Use There is / There are and has / have (for example, There's an apartment for rent in the River District. It has two bedrooms, and the rent is only $950! There's no fee.).*

Self-Directed Learning

Point out the blue bar. Ask students if they can do the lesson learning objective or if they need more practice. Tell them to check one of the boxes. Assign Extra Practice as needed.

Extra Practice
MyEnglishLab   Workbook pp. 54–55

Grammar

C **WRITE. Read the answers. Write questions with *Is there*, *Are there*, or *How many*.**

1. A: _Is there a bus stop near the apartment?_
  B: Yes, there is. The #2 bus stop is across the street.

2. A: Are there any families with children in the building?
  B: No. There are no families with children in the building.

3. A: Is there a supermarket nearby?
  B: Yes, there is. There's a supermarket 10 minutes from here.

4. A: Are there any furnished apartments available?
  B: Sorry. There aren't any furnished apartments available.

5. A: Is there a laundry room?
  B: Yes, there is. There's a laundry room in the basement.

6. A: How many closets are there?
  B: Four. There are four big closets in the apartment.

Show what you know!

1. THINK ABOUT IT. Imagine that you have an apartment for rent. Look at the chart. Complete the column under *My Apartment*.

	My Apartment	My Partner's Apartment
Number of bedrooms?		
Number of bathrooms?		
Laundry room? (yes or no)		
Parking? (street or lot)		

2. TALK ABOUT IT. Student A, ask questions about your partner's apartment. Write the answers in the last column. Student B, use your chart and answer the questions. Take turns.

3. WRITE ABOUT IT. Write four sentences about your partner's apartment.

There is one bathroom in Nico's apartment.

I can make sentences and ask and answer questions with *there is / there are.* ■   I need more practice. ■

For more practice, go to MyEnglishLab.

Read about renters and homeowners

1 BEFORE YOU READ

A DECIDE. Complete the sentences with the words in the box.

homeowners   investments   renter   value

1. The ___value___ of a house is how much it sells for.

2. They are new ___homeowners___.

3. A ___renter___ pays rent to live in a house or apartment.

4. People make ___investments___ so that their money will grow over time.

B MAKE CONNECTIONS.

In your native country, do most people live in houses? Are most adults homeowners or renters?

2 READ

▶ Listen and read.

Academic Skill: Skimming

Skimming means you do not read every word. Instead, you read quickly to get the general idea of the article.

Rent or Own?

1 In many countries, most people live in homes that they own. In China, for example, 90% of homes are owner-occupied. They belong to the people who live in them. In the United States, only about 63% of homes are owner-occupied. Renters
5 live in the other 37%.

Young adults often rent. Most American adults under age 35 are renters. After age 35, that changes. In the 35 to 44 age group, there are more homeowners than renters. People over 65 are the group most likely to own their homes.

10 Many renters don't like renting. Only 32% of renters say they rent because they want to. Most renters say they want to buy a home in the future (72%).

Which is better, renting a home or owning one? It depends. There are good reasons to buy a home, but there are good
15 reasons to rent, too.

Reasons to Buy a House

- A house can be a good investment. The value of a house usually goes up over time.
- If you stay in the house for three or more years, you'll
20 probably save money.
- You can make any changes you want to your home when you own it.
- Homeowners can save money on their taxes.

Reasons to Rent

25 • A house can be a bad investment. Sometimes the value of a house drops.
- It is easier to move (for another job or to a better home, for example).
- You don't have to spend time or money on home repairs.
30 • You don't have to pay property tax.

Who Rents in the U.S.?

Source: Pew Research Center

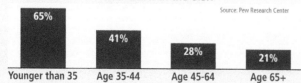

| 65% | 41% | 28% | 21% |
| Younger than 35 | Age 35-44 | Age 45-64 | Age 65+ |

Correlations

ELPS Level 2: 1, 2, 3, 4, 7, 9
CCRS Level A: RI/RL.1.1, RI.1.2, RI.1.4, RI.1.5, RI.1.7, SL.K.2, SL.1.4
CASAS Reading: RDG 1.7, 1.8, 2.3, 3.2, 3.4, 3.9, 3.11, 4.2, 4.9
CASAS Listening: L2.1, 2.3, 4.2, 5.8, 6.1, 6.2
CASAS Competencies: 0.1.2, 0.1.5, 1.5.2, 6.7.2, 7.2.3
Complete standards language available on the Pearson English Portal.

Self-Directed Learning

1. State the **lesson objective**. Say: *In this lesson, we will learn to skim an article.*
2. Say: *We will read about renters and homeowners.*

1 BEFORE YOU READ

A **DECIDE. Complete the sentences with the…**

1. Read the directions. Say the words in the box.
2. Point to each picture. Ask: *What do you see?* (a house with a dollar sign, a family standing in front of a house that was for sale, a couple moving in/getting keys to a new apartment, money)
3. Read the first sentence and elicit the correct completion. (value)
4. Tell students to complete the other sentences.
5. Call on students to read the completed sentences aloud.

B **MAKE CONNECTIONS.**

1. Read the questions.
2. Have students discuss the questions in pairs.
3. Call on students to tell the class about their native countries.
4. **Extend:** Ask: *Why do you think most adults are _____ (homeowners / renters)?*

Teaching Tip: Pairing strategies

Pairing or grouping students from different countries and language backgrounds allows for greater language practice as well as cross-cultural exchange. On the other hand, pairing or grouping students from the same country can help them develop their ideas more thoroughly and give them confidence. In some cases, you may want to put students first in same-country pairs and then in different-country pairs.

2 READ

▶ **Listen and read.**

1. Introduce the reading. Ask: *What is the title?* (Rent or Own) *What do you think the topic will be?* (comparing renting and owning a home)
2. Point to the **Academic Skill** and read it. Ask: *When you skim something, do you read it carefully or quickly?* (quickly) *Do you look for specific information or the general idea?* (the general idea) Say: *Important information about the general idea is often in certain places.* Tell students to read the first and last paragraph, and the first sentences of each paragraph when they skim. Tell students to skim the article. Ask: *What is the general idea?* Elicit ideas.
3. Introduce the graphic. Ask: *What graphic do you see?* (a bar graph) *What is the title of the bar graph?* (Who Rents in the U.S.?) *What word do you see many times in the graph?* (Age)

 ActiveTeach for 2: Anticipation Guide – *Before* Reading exercise

4. Read the text.
   a. Say: *Now we are going to read and listen to the article* Rent or Own?.
   b. Play the audio as students listen and read along silently.
   c. Have an above-level student read the first paragraph aloud or read it aloud yourself. Ask: *Do more people rent or own their homes?* (own)
   d. Ask: *How many paragraphs does the article have?* (four) Tell students to look at the second and third paragraphs. Ask: *Which sentence tells you what the paragraph is about?* (the first) Say: *The first sentence is often the topic sentence.* Tell students to underline the topic sentences.
   e. Ask: *What follows the fourth paragraph?* (bulleted lists of reasons to buy a house and to rent)
   f. **Extend:** Ask: *Which reason to buy do you think is the most important?* (Answers will vary.) *Which reason to rent do you think is the most important?* (Answers will vary.)

 ActiveTeach for 2: Anticipation Guide – *After* Reading exercise

Reading

3 CLOSE READING

A IDENTIFY. What is the main idea?

1. Say: *Now we are going to identify the main idea.*
   Reinforce: *Remember that skimming can help you find the main idea.*
2. Read the directions. Students circle the answer.
3. Elicit the answer from the class.

B CITE EVIDENCE. Complete the statements...

1. Say: *Now we are going to find information in the reading.*
2. Read the directions. Walk around as students work on the activity. If students are struggling, have them work in pairs or direct them to the text lines where they can find the information.
3. Call on students to read the sentence with the correct completion. Ask a different student: *Where is that information? What line number?*

C INTERPRET. Complete the sentences about...

1. Read the directions.
2. Students read the sentences and answer choices silently and complete.
3. Students compare answers with a partner.
4. Call on students to read the completed sentences.

Numeracy: Interpret data

Ask additional questions:

1. Say: *Look at the x-axis.* Ask: *What are the names of the bars?* (younger than 35, etc.) Ask: *What does each bar show?* (different age groups) Call on students and ask: *Which age group are you in?* Check their answers by asking how old they are.
2. Say: *Look at the y-axis. What is the unit of measure?* (percentage) *Look at the first bar. What does it show?* (65% of renters are younger than 35)

---

4 SUMMARIZE

 ActiveTeach for 4: Vocabulary Practice

1. Read the directions. Ask students to read aloud the words in the box.
2. Tell students to complete the paragraph. Tell them they can refer to their charts.
3. To check answers, call on students to read sentences in the summary with the blanks filled in. Ask other students to read the completed summary silently.

Show what you know!

1. THINK ABOUT IT. What are some good...

1. Read the directions.
2. Have students work in pairs to answer the questions. Encourage students to refer back to the reasons in the reading and to add ideas of their own.
3. Call on pairs to report their ideas.

2. WRITE ABOUT IT. Is it better to rent or...

1. Read the directions and the sentence frame. Encourage students to give at least two reasons.
2. Model the activity. Write the frame and ask an above-level student to complete the sentence.
3. Have students write their sentences on a sheet of paper. Walk around and answer any questions.
4. Say: *Share your sentences with at least two people. Check their sentences. If the sentences are not correct, help your partner correct them.*
5. Collect the papers for review or put them in the students' writing portfolios.

3. PRESENT IT. Give a short presentation on...

1. Read the directions. Ask: *Do you think it is better to rent or own?*
2. Form groups of 3 based on whether students think it is better to rent or own. In groups, students share their reasons.
3. Model the activity. Tell students whether you think it is better to rent or own and give reasons.
4. Call on students to present their ideas to a small group or the class.

 ActiveTeach for 3: Academic Conversation Support

Self-Directed Learning

Point out the blue bar. Ask students if they can do the lesson learning objective or if they need more practice. Tell them to check one of the boxes. Assign Extra Practice as needed.

■ **EXPANSION: Self-directed learning**

Ask students to reflect: *What did you learn from this reading?* Call on students to share something they learned.

Extra Practice

 CCRS Plus   pp. 56–57

Reading

3 CLOSE READING

A **IDENTIFY. What is the main idea?**

About 63% of U.S. homes are owner-occupied, _____.
a. so most Americans are renters
b. but it's usually better to rent
c. and most renters want to be homeowners *(circled)*

B **CITE EVIDENCE. Complete the statements. Where is the information? Write the line numbers.**

	Lines
1. About _____ of homes in the United States are owner-occupied. a. 10% b. 63% *(circled)* c. 90%	3–4
2. About _____ of U.S. renters are happy to be renters. a. 32% *(circled)* b. 37% c. 72%	10–11
3. Buying a house is a good investment when the value of the house _____. a. goes up *(circled)* b. goes down c. stays the same	17–18

C **INTERPRET. Complete the sentences about the bar graph.**

1. In the U.S., about _____ of people in the 35 to 44 age group are renters.
  a. 60%   b. 40% *(circled)*   c. 20%
2. Less than 30% of people aged _____ living in the U.S. rent houses.
  a. 45 to 64 *(circled)*   b. 35 to 44   c. 35 and younger

4 SUMMARIZE

Complete the summary with the words in the box.

investment   likely   owner-occupied   rented

About 63% of the homes in the United States are (1) _owner-occupied_. The rest (37%)
are (2) _rented_. Most adults under age 35 are renters. Older people are more (3)
likely to own their homes. It can be a good (4) _investment_ to own your home,
but sometimes it's better to rent.

Show what you know!

1. **THINK ABOUT IT.** What are some good reasons to buy a house? What are some
   good reasons to rent?

2. **WRITE ABOUT IT.** Is it better to rent or own a home? Explain your reasons.

   I think it's better to _____ because _____.

3. **PRESENT IT.** Give a short presentation on reasons to buy a home. Present reasons
   to rent. What is good and bad about each one?

I can skim an article. ■   I need more practice. ■

To read more, go to MyEnglishLab.

Lesson 8 — Listening and Speaking

Get directions

1 BEFORE YOU LISTEN

A **LABEL.** Look at the pictures. Write the words under the pictures.

Turn right.   Turn left.   ~~Go straight.~~   Go through one traffic light.

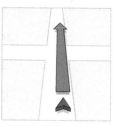
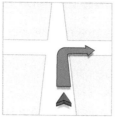

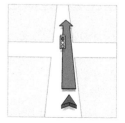

1. _Go straight._   2. ___Turn right.___   3. ___Turn left.___   4. Go through one traffic light.

B **MAKE CONNECTIONS.** How do you usually get directions? Do you use a map? Your phone? Other?

2 LISTEN

A **PREDICT.** Look at the map. What information do you see?

B ▶ **LISTEN FOR MAIN IDEA.** Listen to the directions. Number the directions in the order you hear them.

__1__ go straight

__4__ turn right

__2__ turn left

__3__ go straight

__5__ go through one traffic light

C ▶ **LISTEN FOR DETAILS.** Start at the red dot [•] on the map. Follow the directions. Draw the route on the map.

D ▶ **EXPAND.** Listen to the complete directions. Where are you going? Circle the building.

Correlations

ELPS Level 2: 2, 7

CASAS Reading: RDG 1.7, 2.2, 2.3, 3.4

CASAS Listening: L2.1, 2.3, 4.1, 4.2, 5.4, 5.5, 6.1, 6.2

CASAS Competencies: 0.1.2, 0.1.5, 0.1.6, 2.2.1, 2.2.5

Complete standards language available on the Pearson English Portal.

Self-Directed Learning

State the **lesson objective.** Say: *In this lesson, we will learn to get directions.*

1 BEFORE YOU LISTEN

Ⓐ LABEL. Look at the pictures. Write the…

1. Read the directions. Say the words in the box.
2. Stand with your back to the class. Say and use your hand to indicate *straight, right,* and *left.* Do it again and ask the class to repeat.
3. Students write the directions on the lines.
4. Point to each picture and elicit the direction from the class.
5. Point to each picture again, say the direction, and ask the class to repeat.

Ⓑ MAKE CONNECTIONS. How do you usually…

1. Read the first questions. Elicit and write different ways to get directions (for example, *use a phone app, look at a map, use a GPS in your car, call the place where you are going and ask*). *Optional:* Elicit some apps for getting directions.
2. For each way you listed, ask: *Do you usually use this way to get directions?* Ask for a show of hands. Keep a tally on the board.

2 LISTEN

Ⓐ PREDICT. Look at the map. What…

1. Tell students to look at the map. Ask: *What information do you see?* (street names, traffic lights, buildings, blocks, red dot)
2. Say: *Look at the red dot.* Ask: *What does this mean?* (you are here, your location)
3. **Extend:** Elicit the names of the streets. Ask: *How many traffic lights are there?* (six) *How many buildings are there?* (twelve) *Where is the red dot?* (on Warton Avenue)

Ⓑ ▶ LISTEN FOR MAIN IDEA. Listen to the…

1. Read the directions for the activity. Tell students to read the directions related to the map silently.
2. Play the audio. Students listen and number the directions in the order they hear them.
3. Elicit the correct answers from the class.

Ⓒ ▶ LISTEN FOR DETAILS. Start at the red…

1. Tell students to look at the map and find the red dot on the map. Ask: *What way will you go on Warton Avenue—east or west?* (east) Read the directions. Tell students to place their pencils or pens at the red dot. Remind students to listen for *traffic lights, blocks,* and direction words and phrases.
2. Play the audio. Students draw the route on the map.
3. Students compare routes with a partner.
4. Ask about **register:** *What kind of sentences do people use when they give directions?* (imperatives, sentences that start with the verb)

Teaching Tip: Use the script

Optional: If students need additional support, tell them to read the Audio Script on page 269 as they listen to the conversations.

Ⓓ ▶ EXPAND. Listen to the complete…

1. Read the directions.
2. Play the audio. Students circle the building.
3. Ask: *Do you need to listen one more time?* If yes, play the audio again.
4. Review the correct answer with the class. Ask a student to hold up the book and point to the circled building.
5. Pair students and tell them to practice giving directions from the red dot to one of the buildings on the map.
6. Tell students to circle another building on the map. Say: *Give your partner directions from the red dot to the building. Don't tell your partner which building it is. See if your partner can follow your directions and find the right building.*

Culture Note

1. Say: *In the U.S., more and more people are using their phones to get directions.*
2. Ask: *In your native country, do people use their phones for directions? Is there a difference between how young people and older people get directions?*

Listening and Speaking

3 PRONUNCIATION

A ▶ PRACTICE. Listen. Then listen and repeat.

1. Read the directions and the **Pronunciation Note**.
2. Tell students to practice the tongue position for the *th* sounds. Say: *Keep your tongue flat. Stick it out a little bit. Gently bite the tip of your tongue.*
3. Tell students to keep their tongues in this position. Tell them to put their hands on their throats. Say: *To make the* th *sound in* then, *use your voice. You should feel vibration in your throat.* Say the voiced *th* sound several times and ask the class to repeat.
4. Tell students to keep their tongues in position and their hands on their throats. Say: *To make the* th *sound in* thanks, *do not use your voice. You should not feel vibration in your throat.* Say the voiceless *th* sound several times and ask the class to repeat.
5. Tell students to look at the words in Exercise 3A and underline the ones with *th*.
6. Say: *Listen. Notice the* th *sounds.* Play the audio. Students listen. Then students listen and repeat.

 ActiveTeach for 3A: Pronunciation Coach

B ▶ CHOOSE. Listen. How does the *th* in...

1. Read the directions.
2. Tell students to listen carefully for the *th* sound. Play the audio. Students listen.
3. Play the audio again. Students check the column.
4. Call on students to say answers. Play each item after the student answers.

4 CONVERSATION

A ▶ LISTEN AND READ. Then listen and repeat.

1. Tell students to read the conversation and underline the words with *th* sounds. Ask: *Which word has a voiced* th? (the) *Which word has a voiceless* th? (Third)
2. Play the audio. Students listen and read along silently. Ask: *What street is the pharmacy on?* (Davis Street) *Are there any traffic lights or stop signs?* (Yes, there's a stop sign.)
3. Resume the audio. Students listen and repeat.
4. Walk around and help with pronunciation of *th*.

B WORK TOGETHER. Practice the conversation.

1. Pair students and tell them to practice the conversation in Exercise 4A.
2. Tell students to take turns playing A and B. Walk around and check pronunciation of *th*.

C CREATE. Make new conversations. Use the...

1. Read the directions.
2. Tell students to look at the maps. Say: *Speaker A asks for directions to a place on the maps and Speaker B gives directions using buildings, street signs, and traffic signals. Speaker A wants to make sure he remembers the directions and so repeats what Speaker B says.*
3. Model the conversation with an above-level student. Play A. Then switch roles with the student and play B.
4. Pair students and tell them to take turns playing A and B and to use the places on the maps.
5. Tell students to stand, mingle, and practice the conversation with several new partners. They use new places with each partner. Walk around and help as needed.
6. Call on pairs to perform for the class.

■ MULTILEVEL INSTRUCTION for 4C

Above-level expansion Tell pairs to add new buildings to the maps and continue practicing.
Cross-ability The pre-level student plays A first. When they switch roles, the above-level student says A's first line, and then helps B to write the directions before they practice the rest of the conversation.

D MAKE CONNECTIONS. Make your own...

1. Read the directions. If possible, post or distribute local maps for students to use.
2. Model a conversation with an above-level student. Play B. Tell the student to look at the conversation in Exercise 4C and complete A's first line with a place in your community. Give directions to the place. Pause after each direction for A to repeat.
3. Pair students and tell them to take turns starting the conversation.

Self-Directed Learning

Point out the blue bar. Ask students if they can do the lesson learning objective or if they need more practice. Tell them to check one of the boxes. Assign Extra Practice as needed.

Extra Practice

| MyEnglishLab | Workbook pp. 58–59 |

Listening and Speaking

3 PRONUNCIATION

A ▶ PRACTICE. Listen. Then listen and repeat.

Then turn right.   It's on the left.
It's on Third Street.   Thanks.

B ▶ CHOOSE. Listen. How does the *th* in these words sound? Check (✓) the column.

Voiced and voiceless *th*

There are two *th* sounds in English. To feel the difference, put your hand on your throat. When you say the *th* sound in *thanks,* you don't feel anything. (This is called a voiceless sound.) When you say the *th* sound in *then,* you feel a vibration in your throat. (This is a voiced sound.)

	voiced *th* (like *then*)	voiceless *th* (like *thanks*)		voiced *th* (like *then*)	voiceless *th* (like *thanks*)
1. there	✓		**4.** theater		✓
2. this	✓		**5.** the	✓	
3. things		✓	**6.** third		✓

4 CONVERSATION

A ▶ LISTEN AND READ. Then listen and repeat.

A: Can you give me directions to Save-Rite Pharmacy?
B: Sure. Go straight on Third Street.
A: OK. Go straight on Third Street.
B: Yep. At the stop sign, turn right onto Davis Road.
A: Turn right onto Davis Road.
B: Exactly. Save-Rite Pharmacy is on the left.

B WORK TOGETHER. Practice the conversation.

C CREATE. Make new conversations. Use the directions on the maps.

  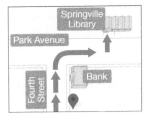 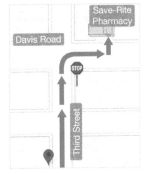

A: Can you give me directions to _____?
B: Sure. Go straight on _____.
A: OK. Go straight on _____.
B: Yep. At the _____, turn _____ onto _____.
A: At the _____, turn _____ onto _____.
B: Exactly. _____ is on the left.

D MAKE CONNECTIONS. Make your own conversations. Ask for and give directions from school to places in your community.

I can get directions. ■   I need more practice. ■

For more practice, go to MyEnglishLab.

Imperatives

Imperatives		Grammar Watch
Affirmative	**Negative**	• Use the imperative for instructions and directions.
Turn left at the stop sign.	**Don't turn** right.	• The imperative is the base form of the verb. • Use *don't* + the base verb for the negative.

A LABEL. Write the words under the pictures.

Don't park.   Don't text.   Don't walk.   Go straight.   Stop.

   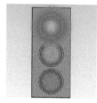         

1. _Don't park._   2. _____Stop._____   3. ___Don't walk.___   4. ___Don't text.___   5. ___Go straight___

B INTERPRET. Look at the pictures. Complete the instructions. Use the words in the box.

be   not go   not smoke   not use   ~~turn~~   watch for

1. ___Turn___ right.   2. ____Don't go____ straight.   3. ____Watch for____ people walking.

4. ___Don't smoke___.   5. ___Don't use___ your phone.   6. ___Be___ quiet.

I can use affirmative and negative imperatives. ☐	I need more practice. ☐

For more practice, go to MyEnglishLab.

Correlations

ELPS Level 2: 10
CASAS Reading: RDG 1.3, 1.7, 2.3, 3.6
CASAS Listening: L3.1, 3.4
CASAS Competencies: 0.1.2, 1.9.1
Complete standards language available on the Pearson English Portal.

Self-Directed Learning

State the **lesson objective**. Say: *In this lesson, we will learn to use affirmative and negative imperatives.*

Imperatives

 ActiveTeach: Grammar Discovery

1. Warm up. Say: *The conversation on page 101 used this grammar.* Turn back to page 101. Point to the sentences in Exercise 4A and then write:
   - *Go straight on Third Street.*
   - *Turn right onto Davis Road.*
2. Say: *These sentences are commands. Notice we don't say* you *with commands. Also, commands always use the base form of the verb. There is no -s at the end of the verb.*
3. Tell students to look at the grammar charts.
4. Point to the sentence on the left side of the chart. Read the affirmative sentence and have students repeat.
5. Point to the sentence on the right side of the chart. Read it and have students repeat. Say: *This is a negative command.*
6. Have a student read the **Grammar Watch** note.
7. Say: *Look at the sentences on the board.* Ask a student to come to the board and make them negative.
8. Have the class read the negative sentences.

▬ **EXPANSION: Grammar practice**

1. As a class, brainstorm action verbs (for example: *sit, stand, eat, jump,* etc.). Make sure that all students understand this vocabulary.
2. Write the verbs on the board.
3. Use the imperative form to give the class instructions using this vocabulary. Tell them to act out the commands.
4. Use the negative form occasionally and make sure that students do not do these actions.

A LABEL. **Write the words under the pictures.**

1. Read the directions.
2. Say each command in the box.
3. Tell students that a red circle with a bar across it means *Don't.* These are called *Don't* signs.
4. Students compare answers with a partner.
5. To check answers, call on students to read the instructions out loud.

Language Note

People also give driving directions using the word *take*—for example, *Take the third left.* This means the same thing as *Turn left at the third street.*

B INTERPRET. **Look at the pictures. Complete...**

1. Read the directions. Read the words in the box.
2. Students compare answers with a partner.
3. To check answers, call on students to read the instructions out loud.

▬ **EXPANSION: Grammar practice for B**

1. Say: *There are many types of* Don't *signs. Go online and find a* Don't *sign that is not in the book.* Students search online for "*Don't* signs." This can be done as homework if students cannot go online in the classroom. Some good examples of other *Don't* signs include signs for *Don't swim, Don't touch, Don't feed the wildlife,* and *Don't litter.*
2. Students print out or draw their signs and bring them to class.
3. Tell students to write a negative command for their sign. Help with vocabulary as needed.
4. Hang the *Don't* signs on the classroom wall.
5. Have half the class stand by their signs while the other half goes up to them and tries to guess what the negative command is for the sign.
6. Then have the other half of the class stand by their signs.

Self-Directed Learning

Point out the blue bar. Ask students if they can do the lesson learning objective or if they need more practice. Tell them to check one of the boxes. Assign Extra Practice as needed.

Extra Practice

  pp. 58–59

Correlations

ELPS Level 2: 3, 10
CCRS Level A: W.1.2, W.1.5, L.1.1
CASAS Reading: RDG 1.7, 1.8, 2.1
CASAS Listening: L2.1, 2.3
CASAS Competencies: 0.1.2, 0.1.5, 0.1.6, 0.2.4, 1.4.1
Complete standards language available on the Pearson English Portal.

Self-Directed Learning

State the **lesson objective**. Say: *In this lesson, we will learn to use the correct structure and indents in our writing. You will write about your home.*

1 STUDY THE MODEL

1. Read the directions.
2. Point to the paragraph. Ask: *What is the title of the model?* (My Home)
3. **Scaffold** the model. Write as a graphic organizer:

My Home		
	Things writer likes	Problems
1		
2		
3		

4. Tell students to read the text and read the questions independently. Call on students to answer the questions. Write the answers to questions 3 and 4 in the graphic organizer on the board. Point out that the first two sentences tell what the writer is writing about.
5. Point to the **Writing Skill**. Read it while students listen. Ask: *How many paragraphs does the model have?* (two) *What does the first paragraph talk about?* (things the writer likes) *What does the second paragraph talk about?* (problems with the home) *How many examples of each does the writer give?* (three)
6. Ask students to think of some other things they might like about a home (for example, *a lot of space, big closets, new appliances, close to school/work/shopping*). Write the ideas.
7. Brainstorm other problems a home might have (for example, *dirty neighborhood, not enough parking, traffic*). Write the ideas.

2 PLAN YOUR WRITING

1. Erase the information in the graphic organizer on the board.
2. Read the directions.

3. Model with a student. The student asks the teacher the questions.
4. Write your answers in the graphic organizer.
5. Tell students to make their own graphic organizer.
6. Have students work in pairs to ask and answer the questions and complete their own graphic organizers. Walk around and help students as necessary.

3 WRITE

1. Read the directions.
2. Use your information in the graphic organizer from Exercise 2 to write sentences in two paragraphs. Don't indent. Elicit where you should indent and add an arrow.
3. Tell students to write. Walk around and make sure students are writing in paragraph form and indenting.

 ActiveTeach for 3: Writing Support

4 CHECK YOUR WRITING

1. Read the directions aloud. Point to the **Writing Checklist**. Call on students to read the checklist items aloud.
2. Pair students to review their writings together. Say: *Read your sentences with a partner. Use the Writing Checklist.* For additional help, remind students that a correct sentence:
   • *begins with a capital letter*
   • *has a subject*
   • *has a verb*
   • *has a period*
   • *is a complete idea*
3. Walk around and verify that students are using the checklist. Collect the papers for review or put them in the students' writing portfolios.

Teaching Tip: Digital skills

Tell students that to indent your paragraph, you press the tab key on your keyboard. If possible, demonstrate.

Self-Directed Learning

Point out the blue bar. Ask students if they can do the lesson learning objective or if they need more practice. Tell them to check one of the boxes. Assign Extra Practice as needed.

Extra Practice

 CCRS Plus   p. 60

Write about your home

1 STUDY THE MODEL

READ. Answer the questions.

Anissa Bel

My Home

    I like my home. I live in an apartment.
It has a large kitchen and many windows.
There is a laundry room in the building.
There is a bus stop nearby.

    There are also some problems with
my apartment. Sometimes the elevators
don't work. The neighbors are noisy.
The school is far away.

1. What did Anissa write about?
2. Where does Anissa live?
3. What does she like about her home?
4. What are some problems with her home?

1. She wrote about her home.
2. She lives in an apartment.
3. She likes the large kitchen. It has many windows.
   There is a laundry room in the building. There is a
   bus stop nearby.
4. The elevators don't always work. The neighbors
   are noisy. The school is far away.

2 PLAN YOUR WRITING

WORK TOGETHER. Ask and answer
the questions.

1. What will you write about?
2. Where do you live?
3. What do you like about your home?
4. What are some problems with your
   home?

**Writing Skill: Structure paragraphs and use
indents**

The first line of a paragraph is indented. It
begins a little bit in from the left. For example:

  ◯ I like my home.

  ◯ There are also some problems with my
apartment.

3 WRITE

Now write about your home. Use the
model, the Writing Skill, and your ideas
from Exercise 2 to help you.

4 CHECK YOUR WRITING

WORK TOGETHER. Read the checklist.
Read your writing aloud. Revise your
writing.

WRITING CHECKLIST

☐ The paragraph answers the questions in
Exercise 2.

☐ The paragraph starts with a topic
sentence.

☐ The first line of each paragraph is
indented.

I can use the correct structure and indents in my writing. ■   I need more practice. ■

For more practice, go to MyEnglishLab.

Take initiative

1 MEET YUSEF

Read about one of his workplace skills.

I take initiative. For example, I try to fix problems at work. When I can't fix the problem myself, I find someone to help me fix it.

2 YUSEF'S PROBLEM

READ. Circle *True* or *False*.

Yusef has a new job. He is a cleaner in a grocery store. He works alone at night. Last night, his supervisor showed him all the cleaning equipment. Then the supervisor went home. Yusef vacuumed some of the floors in the building, but in the middle of the night the vacuum cleaner stopped working.

1. Yusef is a new employee in the building.	(True)	False
2. Yusef has many co-workers.	True	(False)
3. Yusef finished vacuuming all the floors.	True	(False)

3 YUSEF'S SOLUTION

WORK TOGETHER. Yusef takes initiative. What does he do? Explain your answer.

(1.) Yusef tries to fix the vacuum cleaner so he can finish cleaning the floors.
2. Yusuf calls his supervisor and leaves a voice message about the broken cleaner.
3. Yusef doesn't do anything about the vacuum cleaner.
4. Yusef _____.

Show what you know!

1. **THINK ABOUT IT.** Do you take initiative? How do you take initiative in class? At work? At home? Give examples.

2. **WRITE ABOUT IT.** Write an example in your Skills Log.

I take initiative in class. For example, when there aren't enough chairs in the classroom, I get some chairs from another classroom.

I can give an example of how I take initiative. ☐

Unit Review: Go back to page 85. Which unit goals can you check off?

Correlations

CASAS Reading: RDG 1.7, 1.8, 3.2
CASAS Listening: L2.1, 2.3, 4.1, 4.2
CASAS Competencies: 0.1.2, 0.1.4, 0.1.5, 0.1.6, 0.2.1, 4.8.3, 4.8.4
Complete standards language available on the Pearson English Portal.

Self-Directed Learning

State the **lesson objective**. Say: *In this lesson, we will give an example of how we take initiative.*

1 MEET YUSEF

1. Ask: *What is the title of this lesson?* (Take initiative) Explain *taking initiative.* (making decisions on your own; not asking for help)
2. Write: *Workplace Skill.* Read the directions. Say: *Listen as I read* Meet Yusef. Read the paragraph. Ask: *What is one of Yusef's workplace skills?* (He takes initiative.) Next to *Workplace Skill*, write: *Take initiative.*
3. Under *Workplace Skill*, write: *Examples.* Ask: *How does Yusef take initiative?* (He tries to fix problems himself.) Write the examples. Elicit other ways to take initiative and write them under *Workplace Skill.*

2 YUSEF'S PROBLEM

1. Say: *Now we are going to read about Yusef at work. Listen while I read.* Read the first sentence. Use the photo and the **Career Awareness** information to help students understand his job. Say: *Look at the photo. Where is Yusef?* (supermarket) *What is he doing?* (cleaning the floor)
2. Say: *Yusef has a problem at work. Listen while I read.* Read the rest of the paragraph. Explain any unfamiliar vocabulary.
3. Read the directions. Call on students to answer. Ask them to **cite evidence:** *Where is that information?*
4. Ask: *What is Yusef's problem?* (He is alone at work, and the vacuum cleaner stopped working.)

Career Awareness: Night cleaner

Night cleaners make sure that stores and offices are clean. They empty trash, clean bathrooms, and do other jobs to keep a building clean. No formal education is required.

3 YUSEF'S SOLUTION

1. Read the directions. Ask students to work together on the first three items. Walk around and check that students understand that only one solution is correct.
2. Ask: *Is #1 a good way to take initiative?* (yes) *Why?* (He is trying to fix the problem himself.) Ask: *Is #2 a good way to take initiative?* (no) *Why not?* (He is asking for help before he tries to fix the problem himself.) Ask: *Is #3 a good way to take initiative?* (no) *Why not?* (He is not fixing the problem.)
3. Ask students if they have any other ideas. Call on students to share item 4 with the class. Write their responses. Ask: *Is this a good way to take initiative? Why?*

 ActiveTeach for 3: Academic Conversation Support

Workplace Culture

Say: *Taking initiative also means asking questions when you do not understand how to do something. In U.S. workplaces, asking questions is encouraged.*

Show what you know!

1. THINK ABOUT IT. Do you take initiative? How...

Read the directions. Have students think about their answers for a few minutes. Then ask them to share with a partner. Call on students to share with the class.

2. WRITE ABOUT IT. Write an example in your...

Read the directions and the example. Have students write their examples in their **Skills Log** at the back of the book. Circulate and assist students as needed.

Self-Directed Learning

1. Point out the blue bar. Ask students if they can do the lesson learning objective or if they need more practice. Tell them to check one of the boxes. Assign Extra Practice as needed.
2. Ask students to turn to page 85. Go to the Unit Wrap-Up teaching notes on page T-85.

Extra Practice

 p. 61

6 In the Past

Unit Overview

Goals
• See the list of goals on the facing page

Pronunciation
• Extra syllable for -ed endings
• Statements as questions

Reading
• Read about President Barack Obama
• Scan for information

Grammar
• Simple past: Regular verbs
• Simple past: Irregular verbs
• Simple past: Information questions

Writing
• Write a biography
• Use commas with dates

Document Literacy and Numeracy
• Interpret a to-do list
• Identify holidays on a calendar
• Create a timeline

Workplace, Life, and Community Skills
• Recognize U.S. holidays
• Digital Skill: Search for U.S. holidays

Life Skills Writing
• Write a note to a teacher to explain an absence

Soft Skills at Work
• Be dependable

Preview
1. Set the context of the unit by asking questions about the past (for example, *What did you do in your native country? When did you move here?*).
2. Show the Unit Opener. Ask: *What is the unit title?* (In the Past)
3. Say: *Look at the picture.* Ask the Preview questions. (Possible answers: an old man and young boy / grandfather and grandson; looking at a postcard / a photo album; talking about the past)

Unit Goals
1. Point to the Unit Goals. Explain that this list shows what you will be studying in this unit.
2. Tell students to read the goals silently.
3. Say each goal. Explain unfamiliar vocabulary as needed.
4. Point to the ☐ next to the first goal. Say: *We will come back to this page again. You will write a checkmark next to the goals you learned in the unit.*

Oral Presentation
1. Tell students they will give a short presentation at the end of the unit.
2. Write the topics:
   Option 1: My favorite national holiday
   Option 2: The life of someone they know well
3. Assign the topics to two students.

Unit Wrap-Up
1. Review the Unit Goals with students.
2. Direct students to the Grammar Review.
3. If you assigned presentations, ask students to present.

 ActiveTeach for Wrap-Up: Team Project

 ActiveTeach for Wrap-Up: Persistence Activities

6 In the Past

PREVIEW

Look at the picture. What do you see? What are the people looking at? What are they talking about?

UNIT GOALS

- [ ] Identify events
- [ ] Talk about past activities
- [ ] Recognize U.S. holidays
- [ ] Talk about milestones
- [ ] Talk about something that happened

- [ ] **Academic skill:** Scan for information
- [ ] **Writing skill:** Use commas with dates
- [ ] **Workplace soft skill:** Show how you are dependable

A PREDICT. Look at the pictures. What do you see? What events are these?

B ▶ LISTEN AND POINT. Then listen and repeat.

Correlations

ELPS Level 2: 2, 7, 8
CCRS Level A: SL.1.1, SL.K.6, L.1.5, L.1.6
CASAS Reading: RDG 1.7, 2.3
CASAS Listening: L2.1, 2.3, 2.9, 4.2
CASAS Competencies: 0.1.2, 0.1.5, 0.2.4, 7.4.1
Complete standards language available on the Pearson English Portal.

Self-Directed Learning

State the **lesson objective**. Say: *In this lesson, we will learn to identify events.*

A **PREDICT. Look at the pictures. What do you...**

1. Read the directions. Tell students to cover the list on page 107.
2. Point to picture 1 and ask: *What event is this?* Say: *#1 is a birthday party.*
3. Say: *Look at the other pictures. Which events with family and friends do you know?* Students call out answers. Help students pronounce the events if they have difficulty.
4. If a student calls out an incorrect event, ask a *yes/no* clarification question: *Is #3 a birthday party?* If nobody can identify the correct event (anniversary party), tell students they will now listen and practice the names of the events.

B ▶ **LISTEN AND POINT. Then listen and repeat.**

1. Read the directions. Play the audio. Students listen and point to the events.
2. While the audio is playing, walk around and check that students are pointing to the correct events. Pause the audio after item 10.
3. Say each event in random order and ask students to point to the appropriate picture.
4. Tell students to look at page 107. Resume the audio. Students listen, read, and repeat.

 ActiveTeach for B: Vocabulary Flashcards

■■ **EXPANSION: Vocabulary practice for B**

Tell students to look at the pictures and vocabulary on page 107. Ask:

- *Which event celebrates the date on which a husband and wife got married?* (an anniversary party)
- *Which event celebrates the end of a person's career?* (a retirement party)
- *Which event marks the end of a person's life?* (a funeral)
- *Which event is a meeting of related people who haven't seen each other for a long time?* (a family reunion)
- *Which event is a ceremony in which a husband and wife get married?* (a wedding)

■■ **EXPANSION: Writing practice for B**

1. Tell the class to close their books. Say an event and tell students to write it. Repeat for several events.
2. Students compare answers with a partner.
3. Walk around and spot-check answers. If many students have difficulty, tell them they will practice spelling later in the unit.

Culture Note

Barbecues are outdoor events where grilled foods are served. Guests dress casually and often bring side dishes, such as salads or noodles. In the southern U.S., you will usually be served a specific dish made with grilled pork or beef, called *barbecue*. In other parts of the country, when you are invited to a barbecue, you might be served any grilled food (as shown in picture 7). Another word for this event is a *cookout*.

Vocabulary

C WORK TOGETHER. Look at the pictures…

1. Read the directions. Read each line in the example and ask the class to repeat. Model correct intonation.
2. Play Speaker A and model the example with an above-level student. Point to picture 3.
3. Continue the conversation. Then prompt Speaker B to point to a picture and ask: *What event is this?*
4. Pair students and tell them to ask about five pictures each.
5. Walk around and help students correct each other's mistakes.

D MAKE CONNECTIONS. Do you usually bring…

1. Read the directions. Tell students to complete the chart in their books.
2. Form groups of 3. Tell students to talk about similarities and differences in their answers.
3. Draw the chart from Exercise D on the board. As a class, complete the chart for events in the U.S.
4. Tell students to compare the chart on the board with their own charts. Ask: *Are there any differences?* Discuss as a class.
5. Tell the class to look at the pictures again. Ask: *Are there any events that don't happen in your native country? Do people have barbecues? Do they have family reunions?*

Study Tip: Self-test

1. Point to the **Study Tip**. Read the directions.
2. Tell students to write five different events.
3. Walk around and check spelling. If misspellings occur, tell students to check the list on page 107.
4. Say: *You can remember new vocabulary when you test yourself.* Remind students to use this strategy to remember other new vocabulary.

Show what you know!

1. THINK ABOUT IT. List two of your favorite…

1. Read the directions. Tell students to write their favorite two events.
2. Ask: *What are your favorite events?* Elicit answers. Tell students they will discuss their reasons in Step 2.

2. TALK ABOUT IT. Talk about your favorite…

■ **MULTILEVEL INSTRUCTION for 2**

Cross-ability Before students practice the conversation, group them according to the same favorite event. Tell groups to brainstorm reasons why they enjoy the event. Ask an above-level student to record the reasons on a sheet of paper. Tell group members to choose a few reasons and note them in their books. For the activity, group students with different favorite events and, to the extent possible, of different levels.

1. Ask two students to read the example out loud.
2. Tell students to note what they like about their two favorite events.
3. Model the activity. Prompt a student to ask you: *What are your favorite events?* Answer truthfully, in a manner similar to the example. Then ask an above-level student: *What are your favorite two events? Why?*
4. Form groups of 3. Walk around and listen to students' conversations. Help them explain their choices as needed.
5. Call on groups to perform for the class.

3. WRITE ABOUT IT. Write about your favorite…

1. Read the directions. Write an example.
2. Share the checklist below. Then write a checkmark next to each as you point back to the example sentence.
   • The event is clearly identified.
   • There are at least two reasons why the event is your favorite.
   • All sentences end with an end mark.
3. Give students time to write their sentences.
4. Tell students to show their sentences to a partner and to use the checklist to review the sentences.
5. Walk around and verify that students are using the checklist. Collect the papers for review or put them in the students' writing portfolios.

Self-Directed Learning

Point out the blue bar. Ask students if they can do the lesson learning objective or if they need more practice. Tell them to check one of the boxes. Assign Extra Practice as needed.

Extra Practice
MyEnglishLab   Workbook p. 62

Vocabulary

Events

1. a birthday party
2. a wedding
3. an anniversary party

4. a funeral
5. a family reunion
6. a graduation

7. a barbecue
8. a holiday party
9. a retirement party
10. a surprise party

C **WORK TOGETHER.** Look at the pictures. Student A, point to a picture. Student B, name the event.

Student A points to Picture 3.
A: What event is this?
B: It's an anniversary party.
A: Right!

D **MAKE CONNECTIONS.** Do you usually bring gifts to these events? Check (✓) your response. Talk about it with your classmates.

Event	Gifts	No Gifts
1. a birthday party		
2. a wedding		
3. an anniversary party		
4. a funeral		
5. a family reunion		
6. a graduation		
7. a holiday party		
8. a barbecue		
9. a retirement party		
10. a surprise party		

Study Tip

Self-test

Close your book. Write the name of events from the list. Open your book. Check your spelling.

Show what you know!

1. **THINK ABOUT IT.** List two of your favorite events.

2. **TALK ABOUT IT.** Talk about your favorite events. Why do you like them?

   I like weddings. I love dancing, and people are happy.

3. **WRITE ABOUT IT.** Write about your favorite kind of event. Explain why it is your favorite event.

I can identify events. ■

I need more practice. ■

For more practice, go to MyEnglishLab.

Talk about past activities

1 BEFORE YOU LISTEN

MAKE CONNECTIONS. Look at the pictures. Which of these activities do you do with your family or friends?

| listen to family stories | look at old photos | stay up late | dance all night |

2 LISTEN

A **PREDICT.** Look at the picture. The people are probably _____.

   a. married   **b.** family   **c.** co-workers

B ▶ **LISTEN FOR MAIN IDEA.** What are the people talking about?

   ⓐ the weekend   **b.** a meeting   **c.** a problem

Rose   Sam

C ▶ **LISTEN FOR DETAILS.** Listen again. Circle *True* or *False*.

1. Rose asks Sam about his weekend.   **True**   False
2. Sam was at a wedding last weekend.   True   **False**
3. Sam watched old movies last weekend.   True   **False**
4. Sam listened to family stories.   **True**   False

D ▶ **EXPAND.** Listen to the whole conversation. What did Rose do last weekend?

   a.

   b.

Correlations

ELPS Level 2: 2, 7
CASAS Reading: RDG 1.7, 2.2, 2.3
CASAS Listening: L2.1, 2.3, 4.1, 4.2, 6.1, 6.2, 6.5
CASAS Competencies: 0.1.2, 0.1.5, 0.2.4
Complete standards language available on the Pearson English Portal.

Self-Directed Learning

State the **lesson objective.** Say: *In this lesson, we will learn to talk about past activities.*

1 BEFORE YOU LISTEN

MAKE CONNECTIONS. Look at the pictures...

1. Read the directions. Point to each picture. Say each activity and have students repeat.
2. Ask: *Which of these activities do you do with your family or friends?* Tell students to put a checkmark next to the activities they do.
3. Say: *Raise your hand if you do any of these: When you get together with family or friends, do you listen to family stories?* Repeat with the other three activities.

2 LISTEN

A PREDICT. Look at the picture. The people...

1. Tell students to look at the picture. Ask: *Where are they?* (at work, in an office/break room) *What are they doing?* (talking and looking at a piece of paper)
2. Tell students to read the directions and the answer choices silently.
3. Students choose the answer.
4. Say each answer. Ask for a show of hands. Ask: *Why?* (because they are in an office, they are probably co-workers)

EXPANSION: Speaking practice for 2A

1. Have students work in pairs to describe the clothes and physical appearance of the people in the picture.
2. Have students guess what Rose and Sam are talking about.

B ▶ LISTEN FOR MAIN IDEA. What are the...

1. Call on a student to read the directions and the answer choices.
2. Play the audio. Students listen and circle the letter of the correct answer.
3. Elicit the correct answer from the class.

4. Ask: *Was your guess in Exercise 2A correct?* Ask for a show of hands.
5. Ask about **register:** *Are Rose and Sam friends?* (yes, probably) *How do you know?* (They are talking about their weekends and about family.)

C ▶ LISTEN FOR DETAILS. Listen again...

1. Read the directions. Tell students to read the statements silently.
2. Play the audio. Students circle *True* or *False.*
3. Students compare answers with a partner.
4. Call on students to read the sentences. Tell the class to call out *True* or *False.*
5. Write the false sentences on the board. As a class, change the false sentences to make them true. (2. *Sam was at a* <u>family reunion</u>. 3. *Sam* <u>looked at old pictures</u>.)
6. **Extend:** Ask the class: *Does your family have family reunions? What do you do at them?*

Teaching Tip: Use the script

Optional: If students need additional support, tell them to read the Audio Script on page 269–270 as they listen to the conversations.

D ▶ EXPAND. Listen to the whole...

1. Tell the class to look at the first picture. Ask: *What is the event?* (a birthday party) Tell the class to look at the second picture. Ask: *What are the people doing?* (talking, laughing, eating, drinking) *Is it a birthday party?* (no) *Is it a party?* (yes/maybe)
2. Play the audio. Students listen and answer the question.
3. Ask: *Do you need to listen one more time?* If yes, play the audio again.
4. **Extend:** Ask: *What did Rose do last weekend? Did she have a birthday party?* (no) *Did she have a party?* (yes) *Why was it a "surprise" party?* (because she didn't plan to have a party) *Who did she invite over?* (some friends) *Who else came?* (some other friends) *Which picture shows what Rose did?*

Culture Note

1. Say: *In the U.S., family reunions are very popular.*
2. Ask: *Are family reunions popular in your native country? What time of year do they usually happen? How big are they?*

Listening and Speaking

3 PRONUNCIATION

A ▶ PRACTICE. Listen. Then listen and repeat.

1. Say: *Look at the words. What do they all end in?* (-ed)
2. Write *invited* and *needed* on the board. Read the first sentence of the **Pronunciation Note**. Underline as follows: *invi<u>t</u>ed, nee<u>d</u>ed*. Pronounce *invited* and *needed*, emphasizing the /Id/ ending. Say: *The -ed ending does not add an extra syllable after other sounds.*
3. Write *looked* and *dropped*. Underline as follows: *loo<u>k</u>ed, dro<u>pp</u>ed*. Say: *After some sounds, the -ed ending sounds like /t/.* Pronounce *looked* and *dropped*, emphasizing the /t/ ending.
4. Write *called* and *showed*. Underline as follows: *cal<u>l</u>ed, sho<u>w</u>ed*. Say: *After some sounds, the -ed ending sounds like /d/.* Pronounce *called* and *showed*, emphasizing the /d/ ending.
5. Play the audio. Students listen and then listen and repeat.

 ActiveTeach for 3A: Pronunciation Coach

B ▶ IDENTIFY. Listen. Circle the words with...

1. Read the directions. Tell students to look at the words and underline the letter or sound that comes before the -ed ending. Ask: *After which sounds does the -ed ending add a syllable?* (/t/ and /d/)
2. Play the audio. Students listen.
3. Play the audio again. Students circle the words with an extra -ed syllable.
4. Call on students to say the answers. Play each item after the student answers.

4 CONVERSATION

A ▶ LISTEN AND READ. Then listen and repeat.

1. Note: This conversation is the same one students heard in Exercise 2D on page 108.
2. Tell students to read the conversation and underline words with -ed endings (*showed, looked, listened*).
3. Ask: *What words did you underline?* (showed, looked, listened) Say: *Does the -ed ending add a syllable for any of these verbs?* (no)
4. Play the audio. Students read along silently. Then students listen and repeat.
5. Walk around and help with pronunciation as needed. Pay particular attention to the students' pronunciation of *showed, looked,* and *listened*.

B WORK TOGETHER. Practice the...

1. Pair students and tell them to practice the conversation in Exercise 3A.
2. Tell students to take turns playing A and B.

C CREATE. Make new conversations. Use the...

1. Read the directions.
2. Tell students to look at the information in the boxes. Say each word or phrase and have students repeat. Have them pay attention to the pronunciation of any verbs with an -ed ending.
3. Model the conversation with an above-level student using information from the boxes.
4. Tell pairs to take turns playing A and B and to use the vocabulary words to fill in the blanks.
5. Tell students to stand, mingle, and practice the conversation with several new partners.
6. Walk around and make sure students are completing the conversation correctly. Correct the pronunciation of past tense verbs as needed.
7. Call on pairs to perform for the class.

D MAKE CONNECTIONS. Talk about a special...

1. Read the directions.
2. Model the activity. Ask an above-level student: *What special event did you go to recently? What did you do?*
3. Pair students. Say: *Before you practice, tell your partner what your special event is.* Students take turns asking and answering questions about the special event. Walk around and check that students form the past tense correctly.
4. Tell students to practice the conversation with a new partner.
5. Ask pairs to perform their conversations for the class.

■■ MULTILEVEL INSTRUCTION for 4D

Pre-level scaffolding Write two sentence frames on the board: *I went to a _____. We _____ and _____.* Students fill in the first blank with an event, and the other two blanks with verbs in the past tense plus nouns if needed.

Self-Directed Learning

Point out the blue bar. Ask students if they can do the lesson learning objective or if they need more practice. Tell them to check one of the boxes. Assign Extra Practice as needed.

Extra Practice	
MyEnglishLab	Workbook pp. 63–64

Listening and Speaking

3 PRONUNCIATION

A ▶ PRACTICE. Listen. Then listen and repeat.

Extra syllable	No extra syllable	
in·vit·ed	looked	danced
need·ed	dropped	showed

Extra syllable for -ed endings

The past tense -ed ending adds an extra syllable after the sound /t/ or /d/. It does not add an extra syllable after other sounds.

B ▶ IDENTIFY. Listen. Circle the words with an extra -ed syllable.

1. called   2. (visited)   3. watched   4. (wanted)   5. talked   6. stayed

4 CONVERSATION

A ▶ LISTEN AND READ. Then listen and repeat.

A: How was your weekend? How was the family reunion?
B: It was really nice, thanks. My whole family showed up.
A: Sounds great.
B: Yeah, it was fun. We looked at old pictures and listened to family stories.

B WORK TOGETHER. Practice the conversation in Exercise A.

C CREATE. Make new conversations. Use the information in the boxes.

A: How was your weekend? How was the _____?
B: It was really nice, thanks. My whole family showed up.
A: Sounds great.
B: Yeah, it was fun. We _____ and _____.

anniversary party	watched family movies	talked about old times
barbecue	cooked a lot of food	played games
wedding	stayed up late	danced all night

D MAKE CONNECTIONS. Talk about a special event. What did you do?

I can talk about past activities. ■   I need more practice. ■

For more practice, go to MyEnglishLab.

Grammar

Simple past: Regular verbs

Simple past: Regular verbs		Grammar Watch

Affirmative

I		
You		
He		
She	**invited** some co-workers over.	
We		
They		

Negative

I		
You		
He		
She	**didn't plan** a party.	
We		
They		

Grammar Watch

- For the simple past, regular verbs, add *-ed*.
- For example: want → want**ed**
- For verbs that end in *-e*, add *-d*.
- For example: invite → invite**d**

A COMPLETE. Use the simple past of the words in parentheses.

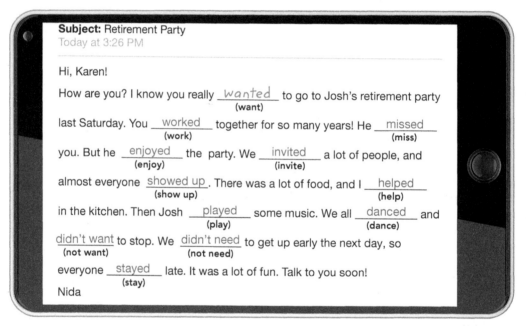

Subject: Retirement Party
Today at 3:26 PM

Hi, Karen!

How are you? I know you really __wanted__ to go to Josh's retirement party
(want)

last Saturday. You __worked__ together for so many years! He __missed__
(work) (miss)

you. But he __enjoyed__ the party. We __invited__ a lot of people, and
(enjoy) (invite)

almost everyone __showed up__. There was a lot of food, and I __helped__
(show up) (help)

in the kitchen. Then Josh __played__ some music. We all __danced__ and
(play) (dance)

__didn't want__ to stop. We __didn't need__ to get up early the next day, so
(not want) (not need)

everyone __stayed__ late. It was a lot of fun. Talk to you soon!
(stay)
Nida

B APPLY. Complete the conversation with the past tense form of the words in the box.

clean up	finish	not leave	visit	watch
decide	need	stay up	want	~~work~~

A: You look a little tired this morning.

B: Yeah, I __worked__ late last night. My supervisor __needed__ some help, so

I __decided__ to stay. We __finished__ the work, but the place was a mess!

So then we __cleaned up__. We __didn't leave__ until really late. You look a little

tired, too.

A: I am. I __visited__ my cousin last night. We __watched__ a soccer game on

TV. I __wanted__ to see the end so I __stayed up__ late.

Correlations

ELPS Level 2: 2, 7
CCRS Level A: L.1.1
CASAS Reading: RDG 1.7, 2.9, 4.9
CASAS Listening: L1.3, 2.1, 2.3, 3.9, 4.1, 4.2
CASAS Competencies: 0.1.2, 0.1.5, 0.2.4
Complete standards language available on the Pearson English Portal.

Self-Directed Learning

State the **lesson objective.** Say: *In this lesson, we will learn to use the simple past with regular verbs.*

Simple past: Regular verbs

 ActiveTeach: Grammar Discovery

1. Warm up. Say: *The conversation on page 109 used this grammar.* Turn back to page 109. Point to the sentences in Exercise 4A and then write:
   • *My whole family showed up.*
   • *We looked at old pictures and listened to family stories.*
2. Ask: *How do you make verbs in the past tense?* (Add *-ed.*)
3. Underline the verbs on the board as students notice the pattern.
4. Tell students to look at the grammar charts. Point to the left chart. Ask: *How do you form the simple past with regular verbs?* (add *-ed* to the base form of the verb) Say: *The form is the same with all subjects.* Read a sentence from the chart. Elicit a few other affirmative simple past statements with different subjects and write them.
5. Point to the right chart. Ask: *How do you form negative sentences in the simple past tense?* (*didn't* + base form of a verb) Say: *The form is the same with all subjects.* Read a sentence from the chart. Elicit a few other negative simple past statements with different subjects and write them.
6. Read the first two points of the **Grammar Watch** note. Write: *want.* Add *-ed* and write: *I wanted some water.*
7. Read the second two points of the **Grammar Watch** note. Write: *invite.* Add *-d* and write: *I invited a friend.*

 ActiveTeach: Grammar Coach

A COMPLETE. **Use the simple past of the...**

1. Read the second sentence of the email. Ask: *How do you form the simple past of* want? (add *-ed*) Write: *want → wanted.* Ask: *How would you form the simple past of* not want? (*didn't* + *want*) Write: *not want = didn't want.*
2. Say: *If a verb ends in* -e, *just add* -d *to form the simple past.* Write *dance* and ask the class how to form the past tense. Add *-d* to *dance.*
3. Read the directions. Students work individually.
4. Read the email as students check their answers.
5. Tell students to look at their answers. Ask: *For which verbs does* -ed *add a syllable?* (*wanted, invited*) Pronounce *invited* with the /Id/ ending and ask the class to repeat.
6. *Optional:* Tell students to take turns reading the letter to a partner.

B APPLY. **Complete the conversation with the...**

1. Read the directions. Tell students to use the words in the box only once.
2. Students compare answers with a partner. Tell them to read the conversation. Walk around and check students' pronunciation of the /Id/ ending in *visited* and *wanted.*
3. Call on two above-level students to read the conversation for the class.

Teaching Tip: Completion activities

Completion activities such as Exercises A and B are a great opportunity for students to demonstrate their reading comprehension. After Exercise A, ask: *What was the event?* (a retirement party) *What did people do?* (They played music and danced. They stayed up late.) After Exercise B, ask: *What did A do last night?* (watched a soccer game on TV with his or her cousin) *What did Speaker B do last night?* (worked late) *What did you do last night?* Write the questions. Tell students to ask and answer the questions with a partner or copy the questions into their notebooks and write answers in class or for homework.

■■ **EXPANSION: Grammar and writing practice for B**

Ask: *What did you do last weekend?* Tell students to write at least five sentences using verbs on this page and pages 108 and 109 (for example, *I watched a movie on Friday night. I stayed up late. On Saturday, I cleaned the house. On Saturday night, I talked to my best friend on the phone. On Sunday, I cooked dinner for my family.*).

C INTERPRET. Look at the pictures. Then...

1. Read the directions. Point to the first picture and ask: *What did Sofia do?* (She visited Mrs. Parker.) Say: *Find* visit Mrs. Parker *on Sofia's list and check it.* Tell students to do the same for the other three pictures.

2. Point to the second, third, and fourth pictures and ask: *What did Sofia do after work?* (She watched a movie. She walked the dog. She baked cookies.) Then read each item on Sofia's list and ask the class to call out *yes* or *no*.

D DISCUSS. Talk about what Sofia did and...

1. Read the directions.

2. Tell students to look at the first two items on Sofia's list. Ask: *Did she visit Mrs. Parker?* (yes) *Did she call her supervisor?* (no)

3. Ask two students to read the example out loud.

4. Tell students to look at the second item on Sofia's list. Write: *She didn't call supervisor.* Ask: *What's missing?* Add *her* before *supervisor.* Say: *You need to add words to some sentences.*

5. Pair students and tell them to take turns talking about the items on Sofia's list. Remind students to add *-ed* to the verb for the things she did and to use *didn't* + the verb for the things she didn't do.

E WRITE. Now write four sentences about...

1. Read the directions. Tell students to choose four items from Sofia's list, but not to choose the first and second items.

2. Tell students to use the sentences in Exercise B as a model. Remind students to start each sentence with a capital letter and end each sentence with a period.

3. Ask students to write a sentence on the board for each item, beginning with *watch a movie*. Read each sentence and correct as needed. Check that students added necessary words as follows: *She didn't respond to <u>her</u> work emails. She didn't look at <u>her</u> work schedule online.*

Show what you know!

1. THINK ABOUT IT. Complete the sentence...

1. Read the directions. Write the example on the board.

2. Model the activity. Think of one thing you did last week. Complete the example with an expression containing a regular simple past verb (for example, *I baked banana bread last week.*).

3. Tell students to think of one thing they did last week and to complete the sentence. Encourage them to use verbs from this unit.

4. Walk around and check that students are using a regular simple past verb and the *-ed* ending.

2. TALK ABOUT IT. Play the Memory Game...

1. Read the directions. Ask three students seated in a row to read the example out loud. Then ask the same three students to model the activity by substituting their own names and activities into the example.

2. Form groups of 5 and tell group members to count off. Say: *Student 1, read your sentence from Step 1. Student 2, say what Student 1 did and then read your own sentence. Student 3, say what Student 1 did, say what Student 2 did, and then read your own sentence, and so on.*

3. Call on the fifth student in each group to report what all the people in his or her group did.

■■ **MULTILEVEL INSTRUCTION for 2**
Cross-ability Instead of telling group members to count off, assign pre-level students number 1 or 2 and above-level students number 4 or 5.

3. WRITE ABOUT IT. Now write one sentence...

1. Read the directions.

2. Ask group members to check each other's sentences.
   - Sentences should begin with a capital letter.
   - Sentences should use the simple past.
   - Sentences should end with an end mark.

3. Call on students to share sentences about their group members' activities.

Self-Directed Learning

Point out the blue bar. Ask students if they can do the lesson learning objective or if they need more practice. Tell them to check one of the boxes. Assign Extra Practice as needed.

Extra Practice

  pp. 63–64

Grammar

C **INTERPRET.** Look at the pictures. Then read Sofia's to-do list and check the things she did.

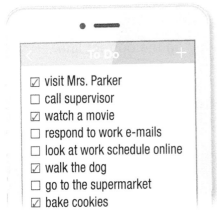

To Do

- ☑ visit Mrs. Parker
- ☐ call supervisor
- ☑ watch a movie
- ☐ respond to work e-mails
- ☐ look at work schedule online
- ☑ walk the dog
- ☐ go to the supermarket
- ☑ bake cookies

D **DISCUSS.** Talk about what Sofia did and did not do after work.

A: Sofia visited Mrs. Parker.
B: She didn't call her supervisor.

E **WRITE.** Now write four sentences about what Sofia did and did not do after work.

Show what you know!

1. **THINK ABOUT IT.** Complete the sentence about a past activity. Use the simple past.

   I _____ last week.

2. **TALK ABOUT IT.** Play the Memory Game. What did you do last weekend?

   Talib: I visited my sister.
   Alex: Talib visited his sister. I cooked dinner for my wife.
   Ying: Talib visited his sister. Alex cooked dinner for his wife. I worked Saturday and Sunday.

3. **WRITE ABOUT IT.** Now write one sentence about each person's weekend. Use the simple past.

   Talib visited his sister. Alex cooked dinner for his wife.

I can use the simple past with regular verbs. ■   I need more practice. ■

For more practice, go to MyEnglishLab.

1 RECOGNIZE U.S. HOLIDAYS

A **MATCH.** Look at the calendars. Write the name of each holiday on the correct line.

Christmas Day   Columbus Day   Independence Day   Labor Day
Martin Luther King, Jr. Day   Memorial Day   ~~New Year's Day~~   Presidents' Day
Thanksgiving Day   Veterans' Day

1. _New Year's Day_
2. _Martin Luther King Jr. Day_
3. _Presidents' Day_
4. _Memorial Day_
5. _Independence Day_
6. _Labor Day_
7. _Columbus Day_
8. _Veterans' Day_
9. _Thanksgiving Day_
10. _Christmas Day_

B ▶ **SELF-ASSESS.** Listen and check your answers. Then listen and repeat.

C ▶ **IDENTIFY.** Look at the calendars. Listen. Which U.S. holidays is she talking about? Write the name of each holiday.

1. _New Year's Day_
2. _Memorial Day_
3. _Independence Day_
4. _Labor Day_
5. _Thanksgiving Day_

Correlations

ELPS Level 2: 1, 2, 3, 4, 5, 6, 7, 8, 9, 10
CCRS Level A: RI/RL.1.1, RI.1.4, W.1.7, W.1.8
CASAS Reading: RDG 1.7, 1.8, 2.3, 3.2, 4.9
CASAS Listening: L2.1, 2.3, 4.2
CASAS Competencies: 0.1.2, 0.1.5, 2.7.1, 4.5.6, 7.7.3, 7.4.4
Complete standards language available on the Pearson English Portal.

Self-Directed Learning

State the **lesson objective**. Say: *In this lesson, we will learn to recognize U.S. holidays.*

1 RECOGNIZE U.S. HOLIDAYS

Ⓐ MATCH. Look at the calendars. Write the…

1. Read the directions. Tell students to look at the names of national holidays in the box. Say each holiday for the class to repeat.
2. Tell students to look at the pictures next to the calendars. Say: *Look at the first picture. What do you see?* (balloons and party things) *What month and date is it for?* (January 1st). *What day is this?* (Tuesday / New Year's Day / the first day of the year)
3. Explain other pictures. Say: *Look at the picture next to January 21st. Who is this man?* (Martin Luther King, Jr.) *Look at the picture next to February. Who are these men?* (George Washington, the 1st president of the U.S.; Abraham Lincoln, the 16th president of the U.S.) *Look at the picture next to July. What do you see?* (fireworks) *Look at the picture next to September. What event is this?* (a barbecue / cookout) *Look at the picture next to Thursday, November 27. What food is this?* (turkey) *Point to the pictures of soldiers. What months are they next to?* (May, November)
4. Pair students and tell them to look at the calendars and pictures. Say: *Write the names of the holidays you know first. Cross them off in the box. Then try to guess the other holidays.*

Culture Note

Say: *On national holidays, people don't have to go to work or school. What are some national holidays in your native country?* Write the countries represented in your class. For each country, elicit a couple of important national holidays and list them on the board.

Ⓑ ▶ SELF-ASSESS. Listen and check your…

1. Read the directions. Play the audio. Tell students to circle any incorrect answers. Pause the audio after item 10.
2. Say: *Correct the answers you circled.*
3. Resume the audio. Say: *Change any answers that are still not correct.*
4. Review the difference between written and spoken numbers. Write: *New Year's Day—January 1.* Say: *New Year's Day is on January 1st.* Ask: *When is Independence Day?* (on July 4th) Ask: *What do people usually call Independence Day?* (the Fourth of July) *When is your birthday?* Review ordinals as needed.
5. Play the audio again. Students listen and repeat.

Culture Note

Four national U.S. holidays are on the same date each year: New Year's Day, Independence Day, Veterans' Day, and Christmas Day. Six national holidays change day every year: Martin Luther King, Jr. Day, Presidents' Day, Memorial Day, Labor Day, Columbus Day, and Thanksgiving.

▬ EXPANSION: Vocabulary practice for 1B

1. Tell students to look at the dates of the holidays in Exercise 1A. Ask: *Which holidays are celebrated on the same date every year? Which holidays change dates every year?*
2. Draw a chart with the headings *Same date* and *Change dates*. Number 1–10 on the left side of the chart.
3. Call on students to complete the chart. Students put a check in the correct column for each holiday.

Ⓒ ▶ IDENTIFY. Look at the calendars. Listen…

1. Read the directions.
2. Play the audio. Pause after item 1. Ask: *What holiday begins the year?* (New Year's Day) Write: *new year's day.* Ask: *Is this correct?* (no) *What do I need to do?* (begin each word with a capital letter) Cross out *new year's day* and write *New Year's Day.*
3. Resume playing the audio. Students work individually, then compare their answers with a partner.
4. Play the audio again. Stop after each item and call on students for the answer.

Workplace, Life, and Community Skills

2 READ ABOUT HOLIDAYS

A **INTEPRET. Read the article. Then read the...**

1. Tell students to take out a piece of paper and number from 1 to 3. Tell students to cover the article with the piece of paper.
2. Say: *I'm going to ask you three questions about U.S. holidays. Write your guess.* Ask each question from the article.
3. Number from 1 to 3 on the board. Repeat each question, elicit answers from the class, and write them.
4. Read the directions, then have students read the article silently and check the answers on the board.
5. Read each question again. Point to each answer on the board and ask if it's correct. Correct as needed.
6. *Optional:* Read the article aloud. Pause after each question and answer section and ask: 1st question: *What are the "Big Six" holidays that many U.S. businesses observe?* (New Year's Day, Memorial Day, Independence Day, Labor Day, Thanksgiving Day, and Christmas Day) *Do you get these days off?* 2nd question: *What did Martin Luther King, Jr. do?* (He worked for the equality of all people.) 3rd question: *Who do we remember on Memorial Day?* (U.S. military personnel who died in wars)
7. Point to the *True / False* sentences below the article.
8. Ask: *What is the answer for number 1?* (True.) *How do you know it's true? Where in the article does it say that there are ten national holidays?* Elicit and tell students to underline in the article: *There are ten national holidays.*
9. For each answer, have students **cite evidence** by underlining the words in the article that gave them the answer.
10. Students compare answers with a partner.
11. Tell pairs to look at their false answers. Say: *For each false answer, look at the words you underlined in the article.* Tell pairs to correct the false information in the sentences.
12. Call on three students from different pairs to write corrected items 2 and 4 on the board (2. *Many businesses in the U.S. stay open* on national holidays. 4. President's Day celebrates *George Washington and Abraham Lincoln. / Martin Luther King, Jr. Day* celebrates the life of Martin Luther King, Jr.).

Classroom Communication

Bring in an actual calendar and use it for examples in this lesson. When the lesson is done, hang the calendar on the wall. Keep track of students' favorite holidays from their countries, class events, and birthdays. At the beginning of each week, spend a few moments in class looking at upcoming holidays and birthdays.

B GO ONLINE. **Search for other U.S. holidays...**

1. Read the directions. Ask students what they would search in English if they wanted a list of holidays in the U.S.
2. Write the search string: *holidays in the U.S.* Have students search the internet and write the names in the space provided.
3. Compare research as a class. Write a complete list of U.S. holidays that the class discovered.

Digital Skills for 2B

Information online is not always accurate. Students should always look for more than one source for the same information, such as lists of holidays. If the information matches from one website to another, it is more likely to be true.

Culture Note

Say: *In the U.S., the holiday season begins on Thanksgiving Day and ends on New Year's Day. During these five weeks, people say to each other, "Happy Holidays."* Ask: *Is there a special holiday season in your native country? When is it? What do people say to each other?*

 ActiveTeach: Review

Self-Directed Learning

Point out the blue bar. Ask students if they can do the lesson learning objective or if they need more practice. Tell them to check one of the boxes. Assign Extra Practice as needed.

Extra Practice

  pp. 65–66 (Find on English Portal) Life Skills Writing

Workplace, Life, and Community Skills

2 READ ABOUT HOLIDAYS

A INTERPRET. Read the article. Then read the sentences. Circle *True* or *False*. Correct the false information.

○ ○ ○

Q&A   HOME | TOPICS | FEEDS | BOOKMARKS   🔍 Holidays in the U.S.   **Add Question**

Q. How many national holidays are there in the United States?

A. There are ten national holidays, but most people don't know that because many businesses stay open on national holidays. Schools, banks, and government offices such as the post office are closed on all ten days. Many U.S. businesses observe only the "Big Six:" New Year's Day, Memorial Day, Independence Day, Labor Day, Thanksgiving Day, and Christmas Day.   More

Q. Which holidays celebrate specific people?

A. Presidents' Day, Martin Luther King, Jr. Day, and Columbus Day celebrate specific people. Presidents' Day celebrates George Washington, the first president of the United States, and Abraham Lincoln, the sixteenth president. Martin Luther King, Jr. Day celebrates Dr. King's work for the equality of all people. Columbus Day celebrates the day Columbus arrived in the Americas in 1492.   More

Q. What's the difference between Veterans' Day and Memorial Day?

A. Both holidays celebrate the U.S. military. On Veterans' Day, we celebrate all people in the U.S. military. On Memorial Day, we remember U.S. military personnel who died in wars.   More

---

1. There are ten national holidays.   (True)   False
   Many businesses stay open
2. ~~All businesses in the U.S. are closed~~ on national holidays.   True   (False)
3. Government offices are closed on national holidays.   (True)   False
   George Washington and Abraham Lincoln
4. Presidents' Day celebrates ~~the life of Martin Luther King, Jr.~~ True   (False)
   1492
5. Columbus Day celebrates the day Columbus arrived in ~~1942~~.   True   (False)
6. Veterans' Day celebrates all people in the U.S. military.   (True)   False

B GO ONLINE. Search for other U.S. holidays. Select a holiday you are not familiar with. What is the holiday? When is it celebrated? What does it celebrate?

I can recognize U.S. holidays. ■   I need more practice. ■

For more practice, go to MyEnglishLab.

Talk about milestones

1 BEFORE YOU LISTEN

LABEL. Write the words under the pictures.

getting a job   growing up
getting married   being born
having children   graduating from school

1. _____being born_____

2. _____growing up_____

3. _____graduating from school_____

4. _____getting a job_____

5. _____getting married_____

6. _____having children_____

2 LISTEN

Ⓐ PREDICT. Look at the picture. Where are the people? What are they doing?

Ⓑ ▶ LISTEN FOR MAIN IDEA. Look at the milestones in Exercise 1. Which milestones do the people talk about?
They talk about growing up and graduating from school.

Ⓒ ▶ LISTEN FOR DETAILS. Listen to the podcast again. Complete the sentences.

1. Daniel says his _____ isn't interesting.
   a. job   **ⓑ** life

2. Daniel was born in _____.
   ⓐ California   **b.** Colorado

3. Daniel went to _____.
   ⓐ college   **b.** acting classes

4. He wanted to be _____ when he was a child.
   a. an actor   **ⓑ** a plumber

Daniel

Amber

Ⓓ ▶ EXPAND. Listen to the whole podcast. Complete the sentences.

1. Daniel _____ last night.
   a. went to a party   **ⓑ** stayed home

2. Daniel says he is _____.
   a. a glamorous person   **ⓑ** a regular guy

Correlations

ELPS Level 2: 2, 3, 7, 9
CCRS Level A: SL.K.3, SL.1.4
CASAS Reading: RDG 1.7, 2.2, 2.3
CASAS Listening: L1.4, 2.1, 2.3, 4.2, 6.1, 6.2, 6.5
CASAS Competencies: 0.1.2, 0.1.5, 0.1.6, 0.2.1
Complete standards language available on the Pearson English Portal.

Self-Directed Learning

State the **lesson objective**. Say: *In this lesson, we will learn to talk about milestones.*

1 BEFORE YOU LISTEN

LABEL. Write the words under the pictures.

1. Read the lesson title. Ask: *What are milestones?* (important times in a person's life) Read the directions. Say the words in the box and ask the class to repeat.
2. Tell students to look at picture 1. Ask: *What do you see?* (mother, father, and baby, birth of a baby, hospital) Ask: *What milestone is this?* (being born)
3. Give students time to label the pictures.
4. Ask: *Which picture shows getting married?* Students call out the answer.
5. Repeat with the remaining pictures.
6. Tell students to check the milestones they have experienced.
7. Ask: *What are some other milestones?* Elicit students' ideas and list them (for example, *moving, buying a house, retiring, becoming a grandparent*).

Language Note

Write: *Being born is the first milestone.* Underline *being born* and ask if it's a noun or a verb. Point out that the *-ing* words at the beginning of the milestones act like nouns.

■ **EXPANSION: Graphic organizer and vocabulary practice for 1**

1. Draw a web diagram. Write *Milestones* in the circle and ask students to copy the diagram into their notebooks.
2. At the ends of the lines radiating from the circle, tell students to write the milestones they labeled in Exercise 1. Tell them to draw circles around the milestones and then more lines radiating from each circle. On these lines, students note some details about each milestone.
3. Model the activity with your own web diagram.

2 LISTEN

A PREDICT. Look at the picture. Where are...

1. Tell students to look at the picture. Ask: *What do you see?* (two people talking into microphones and wearing headphones, one with a laptop)
2. Ask: *Where are they?* (at a radio station/recording studio) *What are they doing?* (a radio interview, a podcast)

B ▶ LISTEN FOR MAIN IDEA. Look at the...

1. Read the directions.
2. Play the audio. Students listen and circle the milestones the people talk about.
3. Ask: *Was your guess in Exercise 2A correct?* Ask for a show of hands if they were correct.
4. Tell students to look at the picture again. Say: *Point to Amber Jenkins. Point to Daniel Campos. Which one is the host/interviewer?* (Amber Jenkins)
5. Call on students to say each milestone that they hear. Elicit all milestones.
6. Ask: *Who is Daniel Campos? / Why is Amber Jenkins interviewing him?* (He's a star / an actor / a celebrity.)

C ▶ LISTEN FOR DETAILS. Listen to the...

1. Read the directions.
2. Tell students to read the sentences and answer choices silently.
3. Play the audio. Students complete the sentences.
4. Students compare answers with a partner.
5. Call on students to read completed sentences.

Teaching Tip: Use the script

Optional: If students need additional support, tell them to read the Audio Script on pages 270 as they listen to the conversation.

D ▶ EXPAND. Listen to the whole podcast...

1. Read the directions. Have a student read the sentences and the answer choices.
2. Play the audio. Students complete the sentences.
3. Ask: *Do you need to listen one more time?* If yes, play the audio again.
4. Call on students to read the completed sentences aloud.

Listening and Speaking

3 PRONUNCIATION

A ▶ PRACTICE. Listen. Then listen and repeat.

1. Say: *Sometimes you can make a statement into a question without changing word order.* On the board, write: *You were born in California.* Say the statement for the class to repeat. Then change the period into a question mark. Say the question for the class to repeat.
2. Read the **Pronunciation Note.** Ask: *When can you say a statement as a question?* (to check understanding)
3. Write: *I was born in _____.* Call on several students to complete the statement. Model repeating the statement as a question to check understanding. For example, S: *I was born in Jakarta.* T: *You were born in Jakarta?* S: *Yes./Right.*
4. Play the audio. Students listen. Then students listen and repeat.

 ActiveTeach for 3A: Pronunciation Coach

B ▶ APPLY. Listen to the sentences. Add a...

1. Read the directions.
2. Play the audio. Students listen and add a period or a question mark.
3. Call on students to write the sentences with the correct punctuation on the board. Play the audio again. Ask the class to listen and check the sentences. Correct as needed.
4. Read the statements and then the questions for the class to repeat. Tell students to read the sentences with a partner.

4 CONVERSATION

A ▶ LISTEN AND READ. Then listen and repeat.

1. Tell students to look at the picture. Ask: *Where are they?* (in a break room at work) *What are they doing?* (eating, drinking coffee, talking) Tell students to read the conversation silently and underline the milestones in B's life. Ask: *What did you underline?* Elicit: *born in a small village, grew up in Beijing, came to the U.S. five years ago, got an apartment in Long Beach, moved to San Francisco.*
2. Tell students to read the conversation again and look for a clue to one more milestone in B's life. Tell students to circle the clue. Ask: *What did you circle?* (my wife) *What's the milestone?* (getting married)
3. Read the directions.
4. Play the audio. Students listen and read silently. Then students listen and repeat.

B WORK TOGETHER. Practice the...

1. Pair students and tell them to practice the conversation in Exercise 4A.
2. Tell students to take turns playing A and B.

■ **EXPANSION: Speaking and pronunciation practice for 4B**

1. Tell one partner in each pair to close his or her book. This student tries to remember the events in B's life by making statements with question intonation (for example, *He's from China?*).
2. The other partner looks at the conversation and answers *yes* or *no*. For *no* answers, he or she tells the first student to guess again.

C MAKE CONNECTIONS. Make new...

1. Read the directions.
2. Say: *When we answer questions, we often give more information.* Tell students to look at B's first sentence in Exercise 4A. Ask: *What additional information does the speaker give?* (where he was born, where he grew up)
3. Write a few things you know about a student's life on the board (for example, *came to U.S. in 2007, studied English in El Salvador, two children*). Start a conversation with the student by asking: *Where are you from?* Then say statements as questions to check your understanding of the events in the student's life (for example, *You came to the U.S. in 2007? You studied English in El Salvador? You have two children?*). Correct the information on the board as needed.
4. Tell pairs to ask each other: *Where are you from?* Say: *What do you already know about your partner? Use statements as questions to check information.*
5. Walk around and provide help as needed.

D PRESENT. Tell the class about your partner.

1. Read the directions.
2. Call on students to tell the class about their partners.

Self-Directed Learning

Point out the blue bar. Ask students if they can do the lesson learning objective or if they need more practice. Tell them to check one of the boxes. Assign Extra Practice as needed.

Extra Practice		
MyEnglishLab	Workbook	p. 67

Listening and Speaking

3 PRONUNCIATION

A ▶ PRACTICE. Listen. Then listen and repeat.

Sometimes we say a statement as a question. The voice goes up at the end.

You were born in California?

Sarah came to the U.S. last year?

Daniel always wanted to be an actor?

You got a job in a supermarket?

B ▶ APPLY. Listen to the sentences. Add a period (.) to statements. Add a question mark (?) to questions.

1. Maria grew up in Houston.
2. You came to the U.S. in 2015?
3. Ali graduated from college two years ago.
4. She got married last year?
5. Rob became a home caregiver in 2017.
6. You got your first job last month?

4 CONVERSATION

A ▶ LISTEN AND READ. Then listen and repeat.

A: So, tell me . . . Where are you from?
B: China. I was born in a small village, but I grew up in Beijing.
A: And you came to the U.S. five years ago?
B: Right. First, my wife and I got an apartment in Long Beach. Then we moved to San Francisco.
A: Your English is very good. Did you study English in China?
B: Yes, I did, but I didn't practice speaking a lot.

B WORK TOGETHER. Practice the conversation in Exercise A.

C MAKE CONNECTIONS. Make new conversations. Ask a classmate about milestones in his or her life. Take turns.

Angela: Where are you from?
Yu: China . . .

D PRESENT. Tell the class about your partner.

Yu is from China. He studied English in China.

I can talk about milestones. ■   I need more practice. ■

For more practice, go to MyEnglishLab.

Grammar

Simple past: Irregular verbs

Simple past: Irregular verbs			
Affirmative		**Negative**	
I		I	
You		You	
He	went to bed early.	He	didn't go to a party.
She		She	
We		We	
They		They	

Grammar Watch

Here are some examples of irregular past tense forms. See page 259 for more past tense forms.

Base form	Past-tense form
begin	**began**
come	**came**
do	**did**
go	**went**
get	**got**
grow	**grew**
have	**had**
leave	**left**
make	**made**
take	**took**

A IDENTIFY. Cross out the incorrect words.

1. I ~~don't grow~~ / **didn't grow** up in the U.S. I ~~grow~~ / **grew** up in India.

2. Rosa ~~meets~~ / **met** Carlos in 2016, and they ~~get~~ / **got** married in 2018.

3. My co-worker **took** / ~~takes~~ some college classes last year, but he didn't ~~graduated~~ / **graduate**.

4. Last year, they ~~leave~~ / **left** Colombia, and they **came** / ~~come~~ to the U.S.

5. Mike ~~goes~~ / **went** to Los Angeles, and he ~~finds~~ / **found** a good job there.

6. She ~~have~~ / **had** a good job, but she didn't **have** / ~~had~~ a nice supervisor.

B COMPLETE. Write the simple past of the words in parentheses.

I _____was born_____ in Venezuela in 1997. I _____grew_____ up
    1. (be born)   **2. (grow)**

in Caracas. My family _____had_____ a small store there. In
    3. (have)

2015, my family left Venezuela, and we _____came_____ to the
    4. (come)

U.S. I _____had to_____ find a job, but I ____didn't speak____ English
    5. (have to)   **6. (not speak)**

very well. So I _____took_____ classes. A supermarket near my
    7. (take)

house needed cashiers. I _____went_____ to the store, and I
    8. (go)

_____had_____ an interview that day. I _____got_____ the job.
    9. (have)   **10. (get)**

Today, I still work at the supermarket, but now I'm a manager.

Correlations

ELPS Level 2: 2, 7, 10
CCRS Level A: L.1.1
CASAS Reading: RDG 1.7, 2.9
CASAS Listening: L2.1, 2.3, 3.6, 3.9, 4.2
CASAS Competencies: 0.1.2, 0.1.5, 0.1.6, 0.2.1
Complete standards language available on the Pearson English Portal.

Self-Directed Learning

State the **lesson objective.** Say: *In this lesson, we will learn to use the simple past with irregular verbs.*

Simple past: Irregular verbs

 ActiveTeach: Grammar Discovery

1. Warm up. Say: *The conversation on page 115 used this grammar.* Turn back to page 115. Point to the sentences in Exercise 4A and then write:
   - *I grew up in Beijing.*
   - *You came to the U.S. five years ago?*
   - *My wife and I got an apartment in London.*
2. Ask: *How do you form the simple past with regular verbs?* (add -ed) Write *watch* and elicit the past tense. Write: *I watched some TV.*
3. Underline *grew up, came,* and *got.* Say: *Some verbs do not have -ed forms. They are irregular.*
4. Tell students to look at the grammar charts. Point to the left chart. Say: *Go is an irregular verb. What is the past form of go?* (went) Say a sentence from the left chart and ask the class to repeat. Say: *The form is the same with all subjects.*
5. Point to the right chart. Ask: *How do you form negative sentences with irregular verbs?* (didn't + base form of a verb) Say a sentence from the right chart and ask the class to repeat.
6. Tell students to look at the **Grammar Watch** note. Say: *These are some of the verbs that have irregular simple past forms.* Say each past-tense form and ask the class to repeat.
7. Say the base forms in random order and tell the class to call out the past-tense forms. Correct pronunciation as needed.
8. Tell students to turn to page 259 and read the list of other verbs that are irregular in the simple past.

 ActiveTeach: Grammar Coach

Classroom Communication

Encourage students to quiz each other. Tell students to study the irregular past-tense forms. Then tell them to quiz a partner. Say: *Student A, close your book. Student B, say the past-tense form and tell Student A to say the base form. Then say the base form and tell Student A to say the past-tense form.*

A **IDENTIFY. Cross out the incorrect words.**

1. Read the directions. Tell students that all the sentences are in the past tense. Remind students to look at the list on page 259 for past-tense forms of verbs that aren't in the **Grammar Watch.**
2. Students compare answers with a partner and take turns reading the sentences out loud.
3. Call on students to read the sentences for the class.

B **COMPLETE. Write the simple past of the...**

1. Read the directions. Ask: *What is the simple past of* be? (was, were) Tell students to look at the paragraph. Call on a student to read the first sentence.
2. Remind students to use *didn't* + the base form of the verb with negative sentences.
3. Walk around and spot-check students' spelling of irregular past forms.
4. Students compare answers with a partner. Tell them to each read half of the paragraph aloud.
5. Call on two above-level students to read the paragraph for the class. As they say the answers, write them. Tell students to check their spelling.

EXPANSION: Grammar and vocabulary practice for B

1. Tell students to read the paragraph in Exercise B again. Tell them to list five milestones in the person's life. Tell them to use the simple past tense.
2. Pair students. Write: *What was the first milestone?* Elicit the ordinal numbers *second* through *fifth* and list them under *first.* Say: *Take turns asking and answering the questions with a partner.*
3. Review as a class: *1st—born in Venezuela, 2nd—grew up in Caracas, 3rd—came to the U.S., 4th—found a job, 5th—got a promotion.*

Grammar

Simple past

 ActiveTeach: Grammar Discovery

1. Say: *Now we're going to study* yes/no *questions in the simple past tense.*
2. Tell students to look at the grammar charts on page 117. Point to the left chart. Ask: *How do you form* yes/no *questions in the simple past? What comes first? Next?* Elicit and write: Did + subject + base form of verb.
3. Point to the right chart. To elicit short answers, ask a few students: *Did you grow up in California?* (Yes, I did. / No, I didn't.) Then ask students about their classmates: *Did [Student] grow up in [State/Country]? Did [Student] and [Student] grow up in [State/Country]?*
4. Point to the **Grammar Watch**. Read it aloud.
5. Have students ask each other: *Were you born in [country]?* And have them answer: *Yes, I was.* or *No, I wasn't.*

 ActiveTeach: Grammar Coach

C WRITE. Make questions and answers. Use...
1. Read the directions.
2. Write item 1. Elicit the question step-by-step, writing each part: *What comes first? Next?* Then elicit the short answer and write it. Call on two students to read the question and answer.
3. Walk around and remind students to use the base form of the verb.
4. Students compare answers with a partner and take turns asking and answering the questions.
5. Call on pairs to read the questions and answers for the class.

▦ **EXPANSION: Speaking practice for C**
1. As a class, make a chart on the board. One column is headed **Name** and the other, **I grew up in...** Begin by putting your own name and the place where you grew up. Students take turns coming to the board and adding their information.
2. Ask *yes/no* questions about students. Call on other students to answer. For example, *Did Adam grow up in Angola?* Elicit the correct response, *Yes, he did.* Continue for several students. Include questions with negative responses.
3. Students take turns asking and answering. The student who answers asks the next question until everyone has had a turn.

Show what you know!

1. THINK ABOUT IT. Write four questions about...
1. Review the milestones on page 114. Point to each one and elicit the simple past form. (*got a job, had children, grew up,* etc.)
2. Say four milestone in your life. List your milestones in note form on the board (for example, *grew up, California; moved to Northeast, 10 yrs ago; married, 2001,* etc.)
3. Pair students. Say: *Tell each other about four of your milestones. Take notes about your partner.*
4. Read the directions and the example. Say: *Write* yes/no *questions in the simple past.*
5. Walk around and check that students form *yes/no* questions correctly.

▦ **MULTILEVEL INSTRUCTION for 1**
Pre-level scaffolding Tell pre-level students to write notes that they can use when speaking about their milestones. Partners still take notes about each other as well.

2. TALK ABOUT IT. Ask and answer the...
1. Read the directions. Ask two students to read the example.
2. Use the same pairs and students' notes from Step 1. Walk around and check that A forms *yes/no* questions correctly and B uses short answers.
3. Call on volunteers and ask several pairs to ask and answer their questions for the class.

3. WRITE ABOUT IT. Write four sentences about...
1. Read the directions. Students can use the notes that they made in Step 1.
2. Ask pairs to check each other's sentences.
   - Sentences should include a milestone.
   - Sentences should spell irregular past forms correctly.
   - Negative sentences should use *didn't* + base form of a verb.
3. Have students volunteer to write their sentences on the board.

Self-Directed Learning

Point out the blue bar. Ask students if they can do the lesson learning objective or if they need more practice. Tell them to check one of the boxes. Assign Extra Practice as needed.

Extra Practice

  p. 67

Grammar

Simple past		
Yes/No questions		**Short answers**

Did I / you / he / she / we / they **grow up in California?**

Yes, he / she / we / they **did.**
No, **didn't.**

Grammar Watch

Remember how to form past tense questions with *be.*

A: Were you born in Myanmar?

B: Yes, I **was.**

C **WRITE.** Make questions and answers. Use the simple past of the verbs.

1. **A:** _Did you grow up in a big city?_
(you / grow up / in a big city)
B: No, _I didn't_.

2. **A:** _Did Ana take English classes?_
(Ana / take / English classes)
B: Yes, _she did_.

3. **A:** _Did they move to San Diego?_
(they / move / to San Diego)
B: No, _they didn't_.

4. **A:** _Did Mr. Jung get a new job?_
(Mr. Jung / get / a new job)
B: Yes, _he did_.

Show what you know!

1. **THINK ABOUT IT.** Write four questions about milestones in your partner's life.

Did you grow up in Angola?

2. **TALK ABOUT IT.** Ask and answer the questions. Take turns.

A: Did you grow up in Angola?
B: No, I didn't. I grew up in the Democratic Republic of the Congo.

3. **WRITE ABOUT IT.** Write four sentences about your partner's life.

David grew up in the Democratic Republic of the Congo.

I can use the simple past with irregular verbs. ■   I need more practice. ■

For more practice, go to MyEnglishLab.

Read about President Barack Obama

1 BEFORE YOU READ

A DECIDE. Complete the words with the words in the box.

1. Washington, D.C., is the center of the U.S. _____government_____.
2. Before you can vote, you have to _____register_____.
3. All the people who live in the same town or area are a _____community_____.

community
government
register

B DISCUSS. Who is Barack Obama?

2 READ

▶ Listen and read.

Academic Skill: Scan for Information

Scanning an article means reading it quickly to find specific information, such as names and dates.

PRESIDENT BARACK OBAMA

1 "It doesn't matter who you are or where you come from or what you look like. . . . You can make it here in America if you're willing to try."   *President Barack Obama*

"America is a place where all things are possible!"
5 said Barack Obama. And he knows. Barack Obama was the first African-American president of the United States!

His Unusual Early Life
As a child, Obama learned about different races,
10 languages, and countries. He was born in Hawaii in 1961. His mother was a white woman from Kansas. His father was a black man from Kenya. They divorced, and his mother married a man from Indonesia. The family lived in Indonesia for four
15 years. At age 10, Obama returned to Hawaii and lived with his grandparents.

Helping People Build Better Lives
Obama went to college in New York. After he graduated in 1983, he became a community organizer
20 in Chicago. He helped poor people register to vote, get job training, and get into college.

In 1988, Obama went to law school. He became a lawyer and taught law in Chicago, Illinois. Finally, he

decided to go into politics. Working in government,
25 he could help more people. First, he worked for the people of Illinois. In 2009, he became president of the United States.

His Years in the White House
During his time in office, many changes happened.
30 Obama is famous for the Affordable Care Act. It's often called "Obamacare." This law helped millions of Americans get health insurance. The economy got better, too. Obama worked hard to improve U.S. relationships with other countries. He won the 2009
35 Nobel Peace Prize.

President Obama left the White House in 2017. He worked very hard while he was president.

Correlations

ELPS Level 2: 1, 2, 3, 4, 5, 6, 7, 8, 9, 10
CCRS Level A: RI/RL.1.1, RI.1.2, SL.K.2
CASAS Reading: RDG 1.7, 1.8, 2.3, 3.2, 3.10, 3.11, 4.2
CASAS Listening: L2.1, 2.3, 4.2, 5.8, 6.1, 6.2
CASAS Competencies: 0.1.2, 0.1.5, 5.2.1
Complete standards language available on the Pearson English Portal.

Self-Directed Learning

1. State the **lesson objective**. Say: *In this lesson, we will learn to scan for information.*
2. Say: *We will read about president Barack Obama.*

1 BEFORE YOU READ

Ⓐ DECIDE. Complete the sentences with the...

1. Read the directions. Say the words in the box.
2. Call on a student to read the first sentence and elicit the correct completion.
3. Tell students to complete the other sentences.
4. Call on students to provide answers.

Ⓑ DISCUSS. Who is Barack Obama?

1. Read the question.
2. Have students discuss the question in pairs.
3. Elicit and write what students know about Barack Obama.

2 READ

▶ Listen and read.

1. Introduce the reading. Ask: *What is the title?* (President Barack Obama) Tell students to skim the article. Ask: *What is the article about?* (Possible answer: the life of Obama)
2. Introduce the visual. Ask: *What does the photo show?* (Obama, his wife, and two daughters walking on the street, smiling and waving)

 ActiveTeach for 2: Anticipation Guide – *Before* **Reading exercise**

3. Read the text.
   a. Say: *Now we are going to read and listen to the article* President Barack Obama.
   b. Play the audio as students listen and read along silently.
   c. Explain that writers sometimes use quotations at the beginning of a text to introduce their writing. Ask: *Why do you think the writer chose this quote?* (Answers will vary. Possible answer: It is about both the U.S. in general and about Obama specifically.)
   d. Have an above-level student read the first paragraph aloud. Ask: *Why was Barack Obama special?* (He was the first African-American president of the United States.)

4. Point to the **Academic Skill** and read it.
   a. Ask: *When you scan something, do you read quickly or slowly?* (quickly) *Are you looking for general ideas or specific information?* (specific information) *What are examples of specific information that are easy to scan for?* (names and dates) Ask: *Why are names and dates easy to scan for?* (You can look for capital letters and numbers.) Tell students they can also use section headings to get a general idea of where the specific information can be found. Ask students to scan for these details: the year Obama was born, where he went to school, and when he became president (1961, New York, 2009).
   b. To help students practice scanning, write: *Affordable Care Act, Chicago, Hawaii, Indonesia, Kansas, Kenya, New York, Nobel Peace Prize, White House, 10, 1961, 1983, 1988, 2009, 2017.*
   c. Tell students to scan for each and underline them in the text.
   d. Pair students to compare what they underlined.

 ActiveTeach for 2: Anticipation Guide – *After* **Reading exercise**

Digital skills for 2

1. Tell students to go online and search for "famous quotes by Barack Obama."
2. Tell students to write down their favorite quote and bring it to the class to share.

Reading

3 CLOSE READING

Ⓐ IDENTIFY. What is the main idea?

1. Say: *Now we are going to identify the main idea.* **Reinforce:** Ask: *To identify the main idea, is it better to skim or scan?* (skim) *Where do you often find the main idea?* (in the first and last paragraphs, the headings, and the first sentences of paragraphs)
2. Read the directions. Students circle the correct answer.
3. Elicit the correct answer from the class.

Ⓑ CITE EVIDENCE. Complete the statements...

1. Say: *Now we are going to find information in the reading.* **Reinforce:** Ask: *To find the answers, is it better to skim or scan?* (scan) Tell students to read the statements so they know what to scan for. Tell students to underline the specific information when they find it.
2. Read the directions. Walk around as students work on the activity. If students are struggling, have them work in pairs or direct them to the text lines where they can find the information.
3. Call on students to read the sentence with the correct completion. Ask a different student: *Where is that information? What line number?*

▓▓ **EXPANSION: Speaking practice for 3B**

1. Tell students to write 3–5 questions about other details in the reading.
2. Pair students to take turns asking and answering their questions and citing evidence for their answers.
3. Call on students to ask a classmate a question.

4 SUMMARIZE

 ActiveTeach for 4: Vocabulary Practice

1. Read the directions. Ask students to read aloud the words in the box.
2. Tell students to complete the paragraph.
3. Call on students to read sentences in the summary aloud and provide the missing words. Ask the other students to read the completed summary silently.

Culture Note

1. Say: *U.S. presidents can serve no more than eight years.*
2. Ask: *In your native country, how long can the leader of the country serve?*

Show what you know!

1. **TALK ABOUT IT. Scan the article for...**

1. Read the directions.
2. Draw a timeline. Add the first event. Elicit the second event and add it.
3. Tell students to add five or more events to the timeline.

 ActiveTeach for 1: Academic Conversation Support

2. **WRITE ABOUT IT. Use your timeline to write...**

1. Read the directions and the sentence frame.
2. Model the activity. Ask a student to complete the sentence.
3. Tell students to write sentences about four more events.
4. Have students take turns sharing their sentences in pairs.
5. *Optional:* Collect the students' writing and put it in their portfolios.

Self-Directed Learning

Point out the blue bar. Ask students if they can do the lesson learning objective or if they need more practice. Tell them to check one of the boxes. Assign Extra Practice as needed.

▓▓ **EXPANSION: Self-directed learning**

Ask students to reflect: *What did you learn from this reading?* Call on students to share something they learned.

Extra Practice

 CCRS Plus   pp. 68–69

Reading

3 CLOSE READING

A IDENTIFY. What is the main idea?

Barack Obama, the first African-American president of the United States, _____.
a. came to the United States from Africa
b. cared about helping people have better lives
c. was a poor boy who became a rich man

B CITE EVIDENCE. Complete the statements. Where is the information? Write the line numbers.

Lines

1. President Obama's father was from _____.
   a. Hawaii   b. Kansas   c. Kenya   <u> 12 </u>

2. As a boy, Obama lived for four years in _____ with his mother and stepfather.
   a. Kenya   b. Indonesia   c. Illinois   <u>14–15</u>

3. From age 10 until college, Obama lived in Hawaii with his _____.
   a. mother   b. father   c. grandparents   <u>15–16</u>

4. Obama worked first as a community organizer and then as a lawyer in _____.
   a. Hawaii   b. Chicago   c. the White House   <u>18–23</u>

5. Obama decided to go into politics because it's a way to _____.
   a. help people   b. make money   c. become famous   <u>23–25</u>

4 SUMMARIZE

Complete the summary with the words in the box.

early   famous   health insurance   politics   president

Barack Obama was the first African-American (1) ___president___ of the United States. He learned a lot from his (2) ___early___ life in Hawaii and Indonesia. After college, he became a lawyer. He decided to work in (3) ___politics___ to help people. As president, he was (4) ___famous___ for helping millions of Americans get (5) ___health insurance___ with the Affordable Care Act.

Show what you know!

1. **TALK ABOUT IT.** Scan the article for important dates in President Obama's life. Mark five or more important events in his life on the timeline.

Born in Hawaii
●
1961

2. **WRITE ABOUT IT.** Use your timeline to write about events in President Obama's life.

1983 was an important year in President Obama's life because _____.

I can scan for information. ▢   I need more practice. ▢

To read more, go to MyEnglishLab.

Lesson 8

Talk about something that happened

1 BEFORE YOU LISTEN

A **LABEL.** Write the words under the pictures.

I got stuck in traffic.
I took the wrong train.

I forgot my lunch.
I overslept.

I lost my keys.
~~I had car trouble.~~

1. _I had car trouble._   2. _I overslept._   3. _I got stuck in traffic._

This train is going to Fremont?

4. _I forgot my lunch._   5. _I lost my keys._   6. _I took the wrong train._

B **MAKE CONNECTIONS.** What are some other things that can happen before work?

2 LISTEN

A **PREDICT.** Look at the picture. How does Adam feel?

a. sick   **b.** stressed out   **c.** nervous

B ▶ **LISTEN FOR MAIN IDEA.** What happened to Adam before work?

a. He had some free time.
b. He had a lot of problems.
c. He had a big breakfast.

Maria   Adam

Correlations

ELPS Level 2: 2, 7
CCRS Level A: SL.1.1, SL.K.6
CASAS Reading: RDG 1.7, 2.2, 2.3
CASAS Listening: L2.1, 2.3, 4.1, 4.2, 6.1, 6.2, 6.5
CASAS Competencies: 0.1.2, 0.1.5, 0.1.6, 0.1.8, 0.2.1
Complete standards language available on the Pearson English Portal.

Self-Directed Learning

State the **lesson objective.** Say: *In this lesson, we will learn to talk about something that happened. The conversation on page 121 used this grammar.*

1 BEFORE YOU LISTEN

▅ **EXPANSION: Grammar practice for 1A**

1. Before students look at page 120, write the words from the sentences in the box in scrambled order (for example, *car / had / I / trouble*).
2. Students write the words in the correct order to make sentences, then check by looking in their books.

A **LABEL. Write the words under the pictures.**

1. Read the directions. Say each sentence in the box and ask the class to repeat.
2. Tell the class to look at the first picture. Ask: *What happened?* (The person had car trouble.) *How do you know?* (Smoke is coming out, and the car is making noise.)
3. Give students time to label the pictures.
4. Tell students to compare answers in pairs.
5. To check answers, call on students to read the correct sentence for each picture and explain their answers.
6. Say: *Think about bad things that happened on your way to school or work. What happened? Look at the pictures. Did any of these things happen to you?* Ask for a show of hands about each bad thing (for example, *Who had car trouble? Who overslept?*).

▅ **EXPANSION: Vocabulary practice for 1A**

1. Act out one of the things that can happen on your way to school or work—for example, by pretending to grip a steering wheel and honk the horn. Ask the class to guess what happened. (You got stuck in traffic.)
2. Form groups of 3. Group members take turns acting out the things that can happen. Group members guess.

B **MAKE CONNECTIONS. What are some other...**

1. Ask: *What are some other things that can happen before work?*
2. Elicit student's ideas and write them (for example, *I missed the bus. There wasn't any hot water. I forgot my school / work bag.*). Ask: *How do you feel when things like this happen to you?*

▅ **EXPANSION: Grammar practice for 1B**

1. Students work in pairs to form a *yes/no* question from each statement in Exercise 1A and 1B (for example, *Did you have car trouble? Did you oversleep?*) and the other events that the class thought of. Call on students to write the questions on the board.
2. Tell students to copy the questions into their notebooks. Tell students to think about the last bad morning they had. Then tell students to stand, mingle, and, by asking the *yes/no* questions, try to find one classmate who had each problem. Tell them to write the classmate's name next to the question.
3. As a follow-up, ask: *Who had car trouble? Who overslept?* Call on students to say classmates' names.

2 LISTEN

A **PREDICT. Look at the picture. How does...**

1. Tell students to look at the picture. Ask: *Who do you see?* (Adam and Maria) *Where are they?* (at a coffee shop/diner/restaurant)
2. Call on a student to read the question and answer choices. Ask: *Are these good or bad feelings?* (bad) Check that students know what the words mean (for example, *nervous* means worried about something, like a test or a job interview).
3. Ask for a show of hands for each answer.

B ▶ **LISTEN FOR MAIN IDEA. What happened...**

1. Call on students to read the directions and the answer choices.
2. Play the audio. Students listen and circle the letter of the correct answer.
3. Ask: *Was your guess in Exercise 2A correct?* Ask for a show of hands for answer *b*.
4. Call on a student to read the correct main idea.
5. Ask about **register:** *Do Maria and Adam know each other well?* (yes) *How do you know?* (She asks him if everything is OK, and notices he looks stressed out.)

Listening and Speaking

C ▶ LISTEN FOR DETAILS. Listen again. Put...

1. Tell students to read the question and answer choices silently. Tell them to look at the pictures in Exercise 1A. Say: *Which two bad things happened to Adam? Circle them.* (Adam got stuck in traffic. Adam lost his keys.)
2. Play the audio again. Students circle the letter of the correct answer.
3. Students compare answers with a partner.
4. Call on a student to read the events in the correct order for the class.

> **Teaching Tip: Use the script**
>
> *Optional:* If students need additional support, tell them to read the Audio Script on page 270 as they listen to the conversations.

D ▶ EXPAND. Listen to the whole...

1. Read the directions. Tell students to read the questions and answer choices silently.
2. Play the audio. Students listen and answer the questions.
3. Students compare answers with a partner by taking turns reading the questions and answers.
4. Call on two pairs to read the questions and answers.

3 CONVERSATION

A ▶ LISTEN AND READ. Then listen and repeat.

1. Note: This is the same conversation students heard in Exercise 2A on page 120.
2. Read the directions.
3. Play the audio. Students listen and read silently. Then students listen and repeat.

B WORK TOGETHER. Practice the...

1. Pair students and tell them to practice the conversation in Exercise 3A.
2. Tell students to take turns playing A and B.

C CREATE. Make new conversations. Use the...

1. Read the directions.
2. Tell students to look at the information in the boxes. Say each word or expression and ask the class to repeat. Review unfamiliar vocabulary as needed. Ask: *What does* upset *mean?* (unhappy and worried because something bad has happened) *What does* exhausted *mean?* (very tired)
3. Show the conversation and add information from the boxes.

4. Ask a pair of on-level students to practice the conversation for the class.
5. Erase the words in the blanks and ask two above-level students to make up a new conversation.
6. Tell pairs to take turns playing A and B using the words in the boxes to fill in the blanks.
7. Tell students to stand, mingle, and practice the conversation with several new partners. Tell them to use a different problem each time they practice.
8. Circulate and make sure students are completing the conversation correctly. Correct the pronunciation as needed.
9. Call on pairs to perform for the class.

■ **MULTILEVEL INSTRUCTION for 3C**
Pre-level scaffolding Tell students to write the information in the blanks before they practice.

D ROLE-PLAY. Make your own conversations.

1. Read the directions.
2. Brainstorm a list of adjectives for negative feelings (*nervous, stressed out, sick, upset, unhappy, exhausted, tired, mad/angry*) and a list of problems and write them. Students can use any of the vocabulary from page 120 as well as the other problems they listed in Exercise 1.
3. Model the activity with two above-level students. Tell them to describe a bad morning they had. One student reads A's lines in Exercise 3C with a different adjective and the other reads B's lines with different problems.
4. Pair students and tell them to take turns playing A and B.
5. Tell students to practice the conversation with a new partner.

> **Teaching Tip: Formative assessment**
>
> Use the role-play to check students' use of grammar, including pronunciation of *-ed* endings and irregular verbs. Review/reteach as needed.

Self-Directed Learning

Point out the blue bar. Ask students if they can do the lesson learning objective or if they need more practice. Tell them to check one of the boxes. Assign Extra Practice as needed.

> **Extra Practice**
>
>   pp. 70–71

Listening and Speaking

C ▶ **LISTEN FOR DETAILS. Listen again. Put the events in the correct order.**

__2__ Adam got stuck in traffic.

__3__ Adam got to work late.

__1__ Adam lost his car keys.

D ▶ **EXPAND. Listen to the whole conversation. Circle the answers.**

1. What day is it?
    (a.) Tuesday.   **b.** Thursday.

2. What mistake did Adam make?
    (a.) He went to work on his day off.   **b.** He didn't go to work.

3 CONVERSATION

A ▶ **LISTEN AND READ. Then listen and repeat.**

A: Is everything OK? You look stressed out.
B: Well, I had a rough morning.
A: Why? What happened?
B: First, I lost my car keys.
A: Oh, no!
B: Then I got stuck in traffic.
A: When did you get to work?
B: At 10:00. I was really late.

B **WORK TOGETHER. Practice the conversation in Exercise A.**

C **CREATE. Make new conversations. Use the words in the boxes.**

A: Is everything OK? You look _____.

B: Well, I had a rough morning.

A: Why? What happened?

B: First, I _____.

A: Oh, no!

B: Then I _____.

A: When did you get to work?

B: At 10:00. I was really late.

upset
unhappy
exhausted

lost my wallet
overslept
forgot my lunch

had car trouble
missed the bus
took the wrong train

D **ROLE-PLAY. Make your own conversations.**

I can talk about something that happened. ■	I need more practice. ■

For more practice, go to MyEnglishLab.

Grammar

Simple past: Information questions

Simple past: Information questions		Grammar Watch

Simple past: Information questions

	I		
	you		
	he		
When **did**	she	**get** to work?	
	we		
	they		

Grammar Watch

Question words

What
What time
Why
When
Where

- Use a question word + *did* and the base form of the verb.
- Answer with a short answer (At 10:00.) or a full sentence (I got to work at 10:00.).

A **WRITE. Make questions about the past. Use the words in parentheses.**

1. (What time / you / get up yesterday) _____ *What time did you get up yesterday?*
2. (Where / you / go this morning) _____ Where did you go this morning?
3. (What / you / have for lunch yesterday) _____ What did you have for lunch yesterday?
4. (What time / you / get to work this morning) _____ What time did you get to work this morning?
5. (What / you / do last night) _____ What did you do last night?

B **WORK TOGETHER. Ask and answer the questions in Exercise A.**

A: What time did you get up yesterday?
B: I got up at 7:00.

C **WRITE. Read the answers. Then write questions about the underlined words.**

1. **A:** _What did Saul forget?_
   B: Saul forgot his wallet.
2. **A:** _What time did Jane finish work?_
   B: Jane finished work at 10:45.
3. **A:** _Why did Brad miss the bus?_
   B: Brad missed the bus because he overslept.
4. **A:** _Where did Lan find her keys?_
   B: Lan found her keys in the kitchen.

I can ask information questions with the simple past. ■   I need more practice. ■

For more practice, go to MyEnglishLab.

Correlations

ELPS Level 2: 2, 7, 10
CCRS Level A: L.1.1
CASAS Reading: RDG 1.7, 2.3, 2.6
CASAS Listening: L3.1, 3.9, 4.1, 4.2
CASAS Competencies: 0.1.2, 0.1.5, 0.1.6, 0.2.1
Complete standards language available on the Pearson English Portal.

Self-Directed Learning

State the **lesson objective**. Say: *In this lesson, we will learn to ask information questions with the simple past.*

Simple past: Information questions

 ActiveTeach: Grammar Discovery

1. Warm up. Say: *The conversation on page 121 used this grammar.* Turn back to page 121. Point to the sentence in Exercise 3A and then write: *When did you get to work?*
2. Say: *This is an information question in the simple past. Let's look at some more examples.* Write:
   - *What time did you get home?*
   - *Where did you grow up?*
3. Tell students to look at the grammar chart. Ask: *When did you get to work?* Call on students to make questions using other pronouns (for example, *When did she get to work?*). For each new question, erase and rewrite the subject pronoun in the sentence on the board.
4. Ask: *How does an information question in the simple past begin?* (with a question word) Point to the **Grammar Watch** note and read the list of question words.
5. Read the first point of the **Grammar Watch** note. Point to the questions on the board. Ask: *What comes after the question word?* (did + base form of the verb). On the board, underline *did / get* and *did / grow up*.
6. Read the second point of the **Grammar Watch** note. Ask: *When you did you get to class?* Elicit an answer from an above-level student. The student may answer: *At six o'clock* or *I got to class at six o'clock.* Ask this question to a few other students and elicit answers—some short and some long.

 ActiveTeach: Grammar Coach

A WRITE. Make questions about the past. Use...

1. Read the directions.
2. Write item 1. Ask: *What do you need to add to form a question about the past?* (did) *Where do you need to add it?* (between *What time* and *you* / between the question word and the subject) Insert *did* into the words on the board. Read the example: *What time did you get up yesterday?*
3. Walk around and remind students to begin their questions with a capital letter and end with a question mark.

B WORK TOGETHER. Ask and answer the...

1. Tell students to look at Exercise A and to circle the verb in each item. Then say each verb and ask the class to call out the past tense for statements (1. *get up–got up*, 2. *go–went*, 3. *have–had*, 4. *get–got*, 5. *do–did*).
2. Ask two above-level students to read the example out loud. Prompt Student A to ask B the next question: *Where did you go this morning?*
3. Pair students and tell them to take turns answering and asking the questions in Exercise A.
4. Walk around and check that Student B is using the correct simple past forms of the irregular verbs.
5. Call on a pair to ask and answer each question for the class.

C WRITE. Read the answers. Then write...

1. Read the directions.
2. Write item 1. Point to *his wallet* and ask: *What, Where, Why,* or *When?* Write *What* on the line. Elicit the rest of the question and write it on the line. Ask: *What form of the verb do we use with did?* (the base form)
3. Walk around and spot-check for word order and the base form of the verbs.
4. Students compare answers with a partner by reading the conversations.
5. Call on pairs to read the conversations for the class.

Self-Directed Learning

Point out the blue bar. Ask students if they can do the lesson learning objective or if they need more practice. Tell them to check one of the boxes. Assign Extra Practice as needed.

Extra Practice

  pp. 70–71

Correlations

ELPS Level 2: 3, 10
CCRS Level A: W.1.2, W.1.5, L.1.1
CASAS Reading: RDG 1.7, 1.8, 2.1
CASAS Listening: L2.1, 2.3
CASAS Competencies: 0.1.2, 0.1.5, 0.1.6
Complete standards language available on the Pearson English Portal.

Self-Directed Learning

1. State the **lesson objective.** Say: *In this lesson, we will learn to use commas with dates.*
2. Say: *You will write a biography.*

1 STUDY THE MODEL

1. Read the directions.
2. Point to the paragraph. Ask: *What is the title of the model?* (My Mother)
3. **Scaffold** the model. Write as a graphic organizer:

1	Person	
2	Where / Year born	
3	Move(s)	
4	Married	
5	Children	
6	Job	

4. Tell students to read the text and read the questions independently. Call on students to answer the questions. Write the information in the graphic organizer on the board.

2 PLAN YOUR WRITING

1. Erase the information in the right-hand column of the graphic organizer on the board.
2. Read the directions. Say: *You can talk about more than one move. You can also talk about a past job if the person doesn't work now.*
3. Model with a student. The student asks the teacher the questions.
4. Write the information into the graphic organizer. Add an extra row to the bottom of the organizer. Tell the class another detail about the person (for example, *After he retired, he went back to school.*) and add it to the chart.
5. Tell students to make their own graphic organizer on a piece of paper.
6. Have students work in pairs to ask and answer the questions and complete their own graphic organizers. Encourage students to add more details.

3 WRITE

1. Read the directions aloud.
2. Point to the **Writing Skill.** Read it aloud while students listen.
3. Use your information in the graphic organizer from Exercise 2 to write sentences in a paragraph. Include indentation. Begin some sentences with a date but leave out the commas.
4. Ask: *Where does it need commas?* Elicit and add commas to dates at the beginning of a sentence.
5. Tell students to write. Circulate to make sure students are writing in paragraph form and using commas if needed.

 ActiveTeach for 3: Writing Support

4 CHECK YOUR WRITING

1. Read the directions aloud. Point to the **Writing Checklist.** Call on students to read the checklist items aloud.
2. Pair students to review their writings together. Say: *Read your sentences with a partner. Use the Writing Checklist.* For additional help, remind students that a correct sentence:
   - *begins with a capital letter*
   - *has a subject*
   - *has a verb*
   - *has a period*
   - *is a complete idea*
3. Walk around and verify that students are using the checklist. Collect the papers for review or put them in the students' writing portfolios.

Teaching Tip: Digital skills

If students use a word-processing application to write their paragraphs, make sure students know how to save their documents using *Save* on the drop-down menu.

Self-Directed Learning

Point out the blue bar. Ask students if they can do the lesson learning objective or if they need more practice. Tell them to check one of the boxes. Assign Extra Practice as needed.

Extra Practice

 CCRS Plus   p. 72

Lesson 10

Write a biography

1 STUDY THE MODEL

READ. Answer the questions.

> Pablo Rivera
>
> ### My Mother
>
> My mother's name is Frida. She was born in 1955, in a small town in Mexico. In 1975, she moved to Mexico City and met my father. They got married in 1978. Then I was born in 1979. In 1985, my parents opened a store. They worked in the store for 30 years. In 2015, my father died, and my mother moved back to her small town in Mexico.

1. Who did Pablo write about?
2. Where was she born? In what year?
3. Where did she move? In what year?
4. When did she get married?
5. When did she have children?
6. Where did she work?

1. He wrote about his mother, Frida.
2. She was born in Mexico in 1955.
3. She moved to Mexico City in 1975.
4. She got married in 1978.
5. She had children in 1979.
6. She worked in a store.

2 PLAN YOUR WRITING

WORK TOGETHER. Ask and answer the questions.

1. Who will you write about?
2. Where was the person born? In what year?
3. Did the person move? When and where?
4. Did the person get married? When?
5. Did the person have children? When?
6. Does the person work? Where?

Add more details about the person.

Writing Skill: Use commas with dates

When you begin a sentence with a date, add a comma. For example:

In 1985, my parents opened a store.

When you end a sentence with a date, do not add a comma. For example:

I was born in 1979.

3 WRITE

Now write about a person you know well. Use the model, the Writing Skill, and your ideas from Exercise 2 to help you.

4 CHECK YOUR WRITING

WORK TOGETHER. Read the checklist. Read your writing aloud. Revise your writing.

WRITING CHECKLIST

☐ The paragraph answers the questions in Exercise 2.

☐ There is a comma after a date at the beginning of a sentence.

☐ There is no comma next to a date at the end of a sentence.

I can use commas with dates. ■   I need more practice. ■

For more practice, go to MyEnglishLab.

Be dependable

1 MEET CHUNHUA

Read about one of her workplace skills.

> I am dependable. People can count on me. For example, when I am going to be late, I always let people know.

2 CHUNHUA'S PROBLEM

READ. Circle *True* or *False*.

Chunhua takes the bus to work every morning. This morning, her alarm did not go off, and she overslept. She hurried, but she couldn't get to the bus stop in time. She missed the bus, and she is going to be late for work.

1. Chunhua always takes the bus to work.	(True)	False
2. Chunhua didn't set her alarm.	True	(False)
3. Chunhua can get to work on time today.	True	(False)

3 CHUNHUA'S SOLUTION

WORK TOGETHER. Chunhua is dependable. What does she do? Explain your answer.

1. Chunhua takes the next bus. She hopes no one will see that she is late.
2. Chunhua calls her supervisor and says she is going to be late for work.
3. Chunhua calls her supervisor and says she can't come to work today.
4. Chunhua _____.

Show what you know!

1. **THINK ABOUT IT.** Are you dependable? How are you dependable in class? At work? At home? Give examples.

2. **WRITE ABOUT IT.** Write an example in your Skills Log.

I am dependable. When I am going to meet a friend and I'm running late, I always call to let my friend know.

I can give an example of how I am dependable. ■

Unit Review: Go back to page 105. Which unit goals can you check off?

Correlations

CASAS Reading: RDG 1.7, 1.8, 3.2
CASAS Listening: L2.1, 2.3, 4.1, 4.2
CASAS Competencies: 0.1.2, 0.1.4, 0.1.5, 0.1.6, 0.2.1, 7.3.2
Complete standards language available on the Pearson English Portal.

Self-Directed Learning

State the **lesson objective**. Say: *In this lesson, we will give an example of how we are dependable.*

1 MEET CHUNHUA

1. Ask: *What is the title of this lesson?* (Be dependable) Ask: *What does* dependable *mean?* (doing what you say you will do and doing it well)
2. Write: *Workplace Skill*. Read the directions. Say: *Listen as I read* Meet Chunhua. Read the paragraph. Ask: *What is one of Chunhua's workplace skills?* (She is dependable.) Next to *Workplace Skill*, write: *Be dependable.*
3. Under *Workplace Skill*, write: *Examples*. Ask: *How is Chunhua dependable?* (She does what she says she will do. She says when she is going to be late.) Write the examples. Elicit other ways to be dependable and write them under *Workplace Skill*.

2 CHUNHUA'S PROBLEM

1. Say: *Now we are going to read about Chunhua going to work. Listen while I read.* Read the first sentence. Say: *Look at the photo. How does Chunhua go to work?* (takes the bus). Ask: *Do we know her job?* (no)
2. Say: *Chunhua has a problem. Listen while I read.* Read the rest of the paragraph. Explain any unfamiliar vocabulary. For example, say: Oversleep *means to sleep too long.*
3. Read the directions. Call on students to answer. Ask them to **cite evidence**: *Where is that information?*
4. Ask: *What is Chunhua's problem?* (She is going to be late for work.)

3 CHUNHUA'S SOLUTION

1. Read the directions. Ask students to work together on the first three items. Walk around and check that students understand that only one solution is correct.
2. Ask: *Is #1 dependable?* (no) *Why not?* (She does not let people know she is going to be late.) Ask: *Is #2 dependable?* (yes) *Why?* (She tells her supervisor she will be late.) Ask: *Is #3 dependable?* (no) *Why not?* (She does not even go to work.)
3. Ask students if they have any other ideas. Call on students to share item 4 with the class. Write their responses. Ask: *Is this dependable? Why?*

 ActiveTeach for 3: Academic Conversation Support

Workplace Culture

Say: *It is always important to tell your supervisors and co-workers when you will be late to work. This is being dependable. It is also being professional. Make sure that you have a list of phone numbers that you can use when you need to call your work.*

Show what you know!

1. THINK ABOUT IT. Are you dependable? How...

Read the directions. Have students think about their answers for a few minutes. Then ask them to share with a partner. Call on students to share with the class.

2. WRITE ABOUT IT. Write an example in your...

Read the directions and the example. Have students write their examples in their **Skills Log** at the back of the book. Circulate and assist students as needed.

Self-Directed Learning

1. Point out the blue bar. Ask students if they can do the lesson learning objective or if they need more practice. Tell them to check one of the boxes. Assign Extra Practice as needed.
2. Ask students to turn to page 105. Go to the Unit Wrap-Up teaching notes on page T-105.

Extra Practice

 p. 73

7 Health Watch

Classroom Materials / Extra Practice

 ActiveTeach

 MyEnglishLab

Workbook

 English Portal

Life Skills Writing, MCA, Team Projects, Persistence Activities

Unit Overview

Goals
- See the list of goals on the facing page

Pronunciation
- Linking sounds
- *t* between two vowel sounds
- Using pauses

Reading
- Read about stress
- Use formatting cues

Grammar
- Prepositions of time
- Simple past: More irregular verbs
- Ways to express reasons: *because* and *for*

Writing
- Write about treating a health problem
- Give a reason

Document Literacy and Numeracy
- Interpret appointment cards
- Identify dosage on medicine labels

Workplace, Life, and Community Skills
- Read medicine lablels
- Digital Skills: Search for an online pharmacy. Find information on a medicine.

Life Skills Writing
- Complete a medical history form

Soft Skills at Work
- Respect others

Preview
1. Set the context of the unit by asking questions about health (for example, *Are you healthy? What health problems did you have in the past?*).
2. Show the Unit Opener. Ask: *What is the unit title?* (Health Watch)
3. Say: *Look at the picture.* Ask the Preview questions. (Possible answers: a young woman; in a robe; eating soup; she doesn't feel well)
4. Write the answers.

Unit Goals
1. Point to the Unit Goals. Explain that this list shows what you will be studying in this unit.
2. Tell students to read the goals silently.
3. Say each goal. Explain unfamiliar vocabulary as needed.
4. Point to the ☐ next to the first goal. Say: *We will come back to this page again. You will write a checkmark next to the goals you learned in the unit.*

Oral Presentation
1. Tell students they will give a short presentation at the end of the unit.
2. Write the topics:
   Option 1: Information on a medicine label
   Option 2: How to manage stress
3. Assign the topics to two students.

Unit Wrap-Up
1. Review the Unit Goals with students.
2. Direct students to the Grammar Review.
3. If you assigned presentations, ask students to present.

 ActiveTeach for Wrap-Up: Team Project

 ActiveTeach for Wrap-Up: Persistence Activities

7 Health Watch

PREVIEW

Look at the picture. What do you see?
What is the problem?

UNIT GOALS

- ☐ Describe health problems
- ☐ Identify health problems
- ☐ Make a doctor's appointment
- ☐ Read medicine labels
- ☐ Talk about an injury

- ☐ Call about missing work
- ☐ **Academic skill:** Use formatting cues
- ☐ **Writing skill:** Give a reason
- ☐ **Workplace soft skill:** Show how you respect others

125

A **PREDICT.** Look at the pictures. What do you see? What are the health problems?

B ▶ **LISTEN AND POINT.** Then listen and repeat.

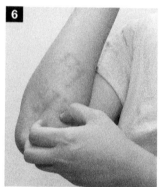

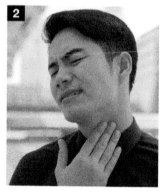

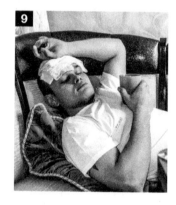

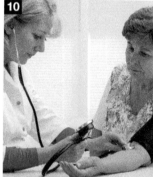

Health problems

1. a headache
2. a sore throat
3. a cough
4. a cold

5. a fever
6. a rash
7. an earache
8. an upset stomach

9. the flu
10. high blood pressure
11. heartburn
12. chest pains

Correlations

ELPS Level 2: 2, 7, 8
CCRS Level A: SL.1.1, SL.K.6, L.1.5, L.1.6
CASAS Reading: RDG 1.7, 2.3
CASAS Listening: L2.1, 2.3, 2.9, 4.2
CASAS Competencies: 0.1.2, 0.1.5, 3.6.3, 7.4.1
Complete standards language available on the Pearson English Portal.

Self-Directed Learning

State the **lesson objective**. Say: *In this lesson, we will learn to describe health problems.*

A PREDICT. **Look at the pictures. What do you...**

1. Read the directions. Tell students to cover the list on page 126.
2. Point to picture 1. Ask: *What health problem is this?* Say: *#1 is a headache.*
3. Say: *Look at the other pictures. What health problems do you know?* Students call out answers. Help students pronounce the health problems if they have difficulty.
4. If a student calls out an incorrect health problem, ask a *yes/no* clarification question: *Is #11 a sore throat?* If nobody can identify the correct health problem, tell students they will now listen to the audio and practice the vocabulary for health problems.

B ▶ LISTEN AND POINT. **Then listen and...**

1. Read the directions. Play the audio. Students listen and point to the health problems.
2. While the audio is playing, walk around and check that students are pointing to the correct health problems. Pause the audio after item 12.
3. When the audio finishes, say each health problem in random order and ask students to point to the appropriate picture.
4. Tell students look at page 126. Resume the audio. Students listen, read, and repeat.

 ActiveTeach for B: Vocabulary Flashcards

■ EXPANSION: Writing practice for B

1. Tell the class to close their books. Say a health problem and tell students to write it. Repeat for several health problems.
2. Students compare answers with a partner.
3. Walk around and spot-check students' answers. If many students have difficulty, tell them they will practice spelling later in the unit.

Culture Note

Some health problems are annoying—such as a headache or a cold—but other health problems can be very dangerous and need immediate attention. In the U.S., you can call 911 for medical emergencies. For example, if someone you know has sudden chest pains, it might be a heart attack. Call 911 right away.

Teaching Tip: Assign homework

Many students have busy schedules, but homework has a role in helping students focus on English learning outside of class. Assign activities that are real world, concrete, and relevant to students' lives. For example, to extend the lesson about health problems, tell them to visit the American Heart Association online (www.heart.org) to learn more about the warning signs of a heart attack. Ask them to write at least one warning sign. In the next class, be sure to use the homework as an opportunity for vocabulary building as well as health education.

Vocabulary

C ▶ ANALYZE. Listen to the sentences...

1. Tell students to look at the list of words on page 126. Elicit one health problem with *a* before it and one with *an*. Write them on the board. Ask: *Why does* earache *have an* before it instead of *a?* (because *earache* begins with a vowel sound)
2. Elicit one health problem with *the* before it and one with no word before it. Write them on the board.
3. Use the four health problems on the board in sentences with *I have _____.* As you say each sentence, act out the meaning (for example, hold your throat and say: *I have a sore throat.*).
4. Read the directions. Play the audio.
5. Call on students for answers.

■■ **EXPANSION: Vocabulary practice for C**

Pair students. One partner acts out the health problems on page 126. The other guesses by saying complete sentences.

D WORK TOGETHER. Look at the pictures...

1. Read the directions.
2. Play B and model the example with an above-level student. Prompt the student to point to picture 1 and ask: *What's the matter?* You answer. Then point to picture 12 and ask the question.
3. Pair students and tell them to take turns pointing to a picture and asking *What's the matter?* Walk around and check that students are using *a, an, the,* or no word appropriately before each health problem.
4. To check answers, point to each picture and ask: *What's the matter?* The class calls out sentences with *He / She has...*

■■ **MULTILEVEL INSTRUCTION for D**

Cross-ability Ask above-level students to cover the list of words on page 126 as they practice. Lower-level students can consult the list as needed and also use it to check their partner's use of *a, an,* and *the.*

Classroom Communication

Model the activity and how students should correct each other's mistakes. Ask an above-level student to play Speaker B and make a mistake. Say: *No, try again.* After the correct answer, say: *Yes. Good!*

Study Tip: Translate

1. Provide each student with five index cards or tell students to cut up notebook paper into five pieces.
2. Point to the **Study Tip.** Read the directions.
3. Say: *You can use your native language to help you remember new words.* Remind students to use this strategy to remember other new vocabulary.

Teaching Tip: Be an active language learner

As you visit with students, show them you are an active language learner yourself by trying to pronounce health problems in their native languages.

Classroom Communication

Ask several students to present their cards to the class and teach the class to say health problems in their native languages.

Show what you know!

1. **THINK ABOUT IT. For some health problems...**

Read the directions. Students complete the chart with all of the health problems from page 126.

2. **TALK ABOUT IT. Use your chart. Talk about...**

1. Read the directions. Pair students.
2. Read the example with an above-level student.
3. Tell students that Student B should say: *I agree* or *I don't agree* and give reasons.

3. **WRITE ABOUT IT. Now write three sentences...**

1. Copy the chart onto the board. Call on students to write in answers. Discuss any differences of opinion.
2. Read the directions and the examples.
3. Give students time to write their sentences.
4. Collect the papers for review or put them in the students' writing portfolios.

Self-Directed Learning

Point out the blue bar. Ask students if they can do the lesson learning objective or if they need more practice. Tell them to check one of the boxes. Assign Extra Practice as needed.

Extra Practice

  pp. 74–75

Vocabulary

C ▶ **ANALYZE.** Listen to the sentences. Write the words you hear. Circle the words *a*, *an*, *the*. Find and circle those words in the "Health Problems" list.

1. I have _____ (a) cold _____.

2. I have _____ (an) earache _____.

3. I have _____ (the) flu _____.

4. I have _____ heartburn _____.

D **WORK TOGETHER.** Look at the pictures. Student A, point to a picture and ask, "What's the matter?" Student B, say the problem. Take turns.

Student A points to Picture 1.
A: What's the matter?
B: She has a headache.
Student B points to Picture 12.
B: What's the matter?
A: He has chest pains.

Study Tip

Translate
Look at the list of health problems. Make cards for five new words. Write the word in English on one side of the card. Write the word in your native language on the other side.

Show what you know!

1. **THINK ABOUT IT.** For some health problems you need to go to an emergency room immediately. For some health problems you can wait to see a doctor. Other health problems get better with rest. Look at the health problems again. Complete the chart.

Go to the Emergency Room	Call for an appointment	Wait a couple of days
		headache

2. **TALK ABOUT IT.** Use your chart. Talk about health problems.

A: Wait a couple of days when you have a headache.
B: I don't agree. A headache can be very serious. Some people have to go to the emergency room.

3. **WRITE ABOUT IT.** Now write three sentences about health problems.

Wait a couple of days when you have _____.

Call your doctor for an appointment when you have _____.

Go to the emergency room when you have _____.

I can describe health problems. ■   I need more practice. ■

For more practice, go to MyEnglishLab.

Unit 7, Lesson 1 **127**

Lesson 2
Make a doctor's appointment

1 BEFORE YOU LISTEN

LABEL. Write the words under the pictures.

It's itchy.   It's swollen.   He's nauseous.   She's dizzy.

1. ___She's dizzy.___   2. ___He's nauseous.___   3. ___It's itchy.___   4. ___It's swollen.___

2 LISTEN

Ⓐ PREDICT. Look at the pictures. Where is the woman? Where is the man?

Ⓑ ▶ LISTEN FOR MAIN IDEA. What does the woman say?

a. What are your symptoms?
ⓑ. What's the matter?

Ⓒ ▶ LISTEN FOR DETAILS. Check (✓) the man's symptoms.

☑ He has a fever.   ☑ He's nauseous.
☐ He has heartburn.   ☐ He's dizzy.

Ⓓ ▶ EXPAND. Listen to the whole conversation. Write the day and time of the appointment.

Receptionist   Roberto

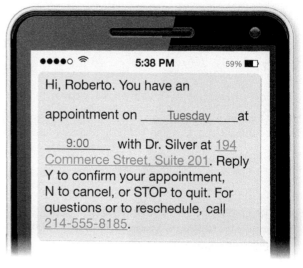

5:38 PM   59%

Hi, Roberto. You have an

appointment on ___Tuesday___ at

___9:00___ with Dr. Silver at 194 Commerce Street, Suite 201. Reply Y to confirm your appointment, N to cancel, or STOP to quit. For questions or to reschedule, call 214-555-8185.

Correlations

ELPS Level 2: 2, 7
CCRS Level A: SL.K.3
CASAS Reading: RDG 1.7, 2.2, 2.3
CASAS Listening: L1.2, 2.1, 2.3, 4.2, 6.1, 6.2, 6.5
CASAS Competencies: 0.1.2, 0.1.5, 3.1.2
Complete standards language available on the Pearson English Portal.

Self-Directed Learning

State the **lesson objective**. Say: *In this lesson, we will learn to make a doctor's appointment.*

1 BEFORE YOU LISTEN

LABEL. Write the words under the pictures.

1. Say: *Look at the pictures of health problems.* Read each sentence in the box and have the class repeat.
2. Explain any unfamiliar vocabulary through modeling, if possible. For example, to demonstrate *dizzy,* spin around a couple of times, act unsteady, and say: *I'm dizzy.*
3. Give students time to label the pictures.
4. Point to picture 1. Ask: *What does it show?* (She's dizzy.) Repeat with remaining pictures.
5. **Extend:** Say: *These words are also called symptoms.* Write the symptoms on the board. Ask: *When do people have these symptoms?* Tell students to review the vocabulary on page 126 for ideas. List students' responses under each symptom (for example, for dizzy: *when they have a headache, when they have an earache*).

Language Note

Point out that the symptoms in Exercise 1 are adjectives, while the health problems on page 126 are nouns.

2 LISTEN

A PREDICT. Look at the pictures. Where is...

1. Read the directions.
2. Call on students to answer. Write their guesses (for example, *The woman is in an office / in a doctor's office. The man is at home / in bed.*).

B ▶ LISTEN FOR MAIN IDEA. What does the...

1. Read the directions and the answer choices.
2. Play the audio. Students listen and circle the letter of the correct answer.

3. Elicit the correct answer from the class.
4. Ask: *Where is the woman?* Read the guesses you wrote in Exercise 2A. Elicit and circle the best answer. Repeat with *Where is the man?*

C ▶ LISTEN FOR DETAILS. Check (✓) the...

1. Tell students to read the questions and answer choices silently.
2. Call on students to read a sentence and act it out.
3. Play the audio. Students listen and check the man's symptoms.
4. Students compare answers with a partner. Elicit the answers from the class.

Career Awareness: Receptionist

Receptionists perform many tasks in offices like answering phones and greeting visitors. A high school diploma is usually required.

■■ EXPANSION: Career awareness for 2C

Ask students about the job in this lesson: *What does a receptionist do? Where does a receptionist work? Do you need to study to be a receptionist? Do you want to be a receptionist?*

Teaching Tip: Use the script

Optional: If students need additional support, tell them to read the Audio Script on page 271 as they listen to the conversations.

D ▶ EXPAND. Listen to the whole...

1. Read the directions. Tell students to read the text message silently.
2. Ask: *Who is the message from?* (the clinic) *What is it about?* (an appointment) *Who is the doctor?* (Dr. Silver)
3. Play the audio. Students listen and write the day and time.
4. Ask: *Do you need to listen one more time?* If yes, play the audio again.
5. Ask: *When is the appointment?*

Culture Note

1. Say: *In the U.S., some doctor's offices charge you for missed appointments. To avoid charges, call at least 24 hours ahead of time to cancel an appointment you can't keep.*
2. Ask: *In your native country, do doctor's offices charge for missed appointments?*

Listening and Speaking

3 PRONUNCIATION

A ▶ PRACTICE. Listen. Then listen and repeat.

1. Write: *I have a fever.* Point to and pronounce distinctly each word in the sentence.
2. Read the **Pronunciation Note**. Mark the linking in the sentence on the board as you say: *I ha-va fever.* Ask students to repeat.
3. Read the directions. Point to the linking symbol in the sentence you wrote. Ask: *What's the consonant sound?* Write *v* under the linking symbol. Ask: *What's the vowel sound?* Write *a* under the linking symbol. Point to *va* and say: *We say the v from* have *together with the next word,* a.
4. Tell students to read the sentences. Say: *The curved lines show linking between words.*
5. Play the audio. Students listen. Then students listen and repeat.

 ActiveTeach for 3A: Pronunciation Coach

B ▶ APPLY. Listen. Draw lines to connect...

1. Read the directions. Tell students to read the sentences and underline words they predict will have linking.
2. Play the audio. Students listen and draw lines to connect linked sounds. If necessary, play the audio again and have students listen twice before answering.
3. Ask: *What words are linked?*
4. Review the correct answers with students.
5. Say the linked words. Ask students to repeat them.

4 CONVERSATION

A ▶ LISTEN AND READ. Then listen and repeat.

1. Note: This conversation is from the one students heard in Exercise 2B on page 128.
2. Tell students to read the conversation silently and look for sentences that they practiced in Exercise 3A and 3B. Tell them to draw a line to connect linked sounds in these sentences.
3. Play the audio. Students listen. Then students listen and repeat.
4. Walk around and help with pronunciation as needed. Pay particular attention to the students' use of linking.

B WORK TOGETHER. Practice the...

1. Pair students and tell them to practice the conversation in Exercise 4A.
2. Tell students to take turns playing A and B.
3. Walk around and check that students are using linking correctly.

C CREATE. Make new conversations. Use...

1. Read the directions.
2. Call on students to say each item in the boxes.
3. Model each pair of symptoms (in random order) and ask the class to identify them. For example, scratch your leg and elicit: *rash / my leg is itchy.*
4. Tell students to look at the words in blue and write *a, an, the,* or no word before them (*a cough, a headache, a rash*).
5. Show the conversation with blanks and fill it in with information from the boxes.
6. Ask a pair of on-level students to practice the conversation for the class.
7. Erase the words in the blanks and ask two above-level students to make up a new conversation. Tell B to choose a pair of symptoms. Tell A to choose a day and time from one of the rows in the boxes.
8. Tell pairs to take turns playing A and B and to use the vocabulary words to fill in the blanks.
9. Walk around during the activity and check that students are using *a* before the health problems in blue.
10. Call on pairs to perform for the class.

D ROLE-PLAY. Make your own conversations.

1. Read the directions.
2. Tell students to note a pair of symptoms and a day and time. Tell them to use the vocabulary on page 126 and at the top of page 128.
3. Pair students and tell them to practice the conversation.
4. Walk around and check the symptoms and days that students have noted. Make corrections as necessary.
5. Call on pairs to perform for the class.

Self-Directed Learning

Point out the blue bar. Ask students if they can do the lesson learning objective or if they need more practice. Tell them to check one of the boxes. Assign Extra Practice as needed.

Extra Practice
p. 76

Listening and Speaking

3 PRONUNCIATION

A ▶ PRACTICE. Listen. Then listen and repeat.

I have a fever.

I need to make an appointment.

Please come at eight.

We close at noon on Friday.

Linking sounds

We often link sounds in words together without a break when we speak.

B ▶ APPLY. Listen. Draw lines to connect sounds that are linked in speech.

1. He has a fever.

2. I have an upset stomach.

3. My hand is itchy.

4. She's a medical assistant.

4 CONVERSATION

A ▶ LISTEN AND READ. Then listen and repeat.

A: Hello. Westview Clinic.
B: Hi. This is Roberto Cruz. I'm sick, and I need to make an appointment, please.
A: All right. What's the matter?
B: I have a fever and I'm nauseous.
A: OK. How about Tuesday morning? At 9:00?
B: Yes, that's fine.

B WORK TOGETHER. Practice the conversation.

C CREATE. Make new conversations. Use the words in the boxes.

A: Hello. Westview Clinic.
B: Hi. This is _____. I'm sick, and I need to make an appointment, please.
A: All right. What's the matter?
B: I have a _____ and _____.
A: OK. How about _____?
   At _____?
B: Yes, that's fine.

cough	my throat is swollen	on Thursday	noon
headache	I'm dizzy	this afternoon	3:00
rash	my leg is itchy	first thing tomorrow	8:30

D ROLE-PLAY. Make your own conversations.

I can make a doctor's appointment. ☐   I need more practice. ☐

For more practice, go to MyEnglishLab.

3 Grammar

Lesson **3**

Prepositions of time

Prepositions of time: *on / at / by / in / from . . . to*		
Are you available	**on**	Tuesday morning?
The appointment is	**at**	9:00 A.M.
Please get here	**by**	5:00 today.
I'm going to see the doctor	**in**	an hour.
The pharmacy is open	**from**	8:00 A.M. **to** 9:00 P.M.

Grammar Watch

- Use *on* with a day or date.
- Use *at* with a specific time on the clock.
- Use *by* with a specific time in the future. It means *at that time or earlier*.
- Use *in* with an amount of time in the future.
- Use *from . . . to* with a starting time and an ending time.

A **IDENTIFY. Cross out the incorrect words.**

1. The appointment is ~~on~~ / at 9:15 A.M. on April 1.
2. You need to get here **by** / ~~in~~ 5:00.
3. The clinic is open from 8:00 A.M. ~~at~~ / **to** 5:00 P.M.
4. The office is closed **on** / ~~in~~ Saturday and Sunday.
5. The doctor can see you ~~from~~ / in an hour.
6. Dr. Evans has openings ~~at~~ / **from** 3:40 P.M. to 5:00 P.M.
7. My appointment is **at** / ~~in~~ 2:30 this afternoon.

B **DECIDE. Complete the sentences with *on*, *at*, *by*, *in*, or *from . . . to*.**

1. The dentist has appointments available ___on___ June 6 and 7.
2. The doctor can call you back ___in___ a few minutes.
3. The appointment is ___at___ 4:30 today.
4. The clinic has openings ___from___ 3:30 ___to___ 5:00 tomorrow afternoon.
5. The doctor's office closes ___at___ noon for lunch.
6. Please come ___on___ Monday.
7. The doctor wants to see you again ___in___ a week.
8. The drugstore is open ___from___ 9:00 A.M. ___to___ 7:00 P.M.
9. You need to call ___by___ 5:00 P.M. because the office closes then.
10. Is the office open ___on___ Saturdays?

Correlations

ELPS Level 2: 1, 2, 3, 4, 5, 6, 7, 8, 9, 10
CCRS Level A: L.1.1
CASAS Reading: RDG 1.7, 2.9, 4.9
CASAS Listening: L1.3, 2.1, 2.3, 4.1, 4.2
CASAS Competencies: 0.1.2, 0.1.5, 0.2.1, 3.1.2
Complete standards language available on the Pearson English Portal.

Self-Directed Learning

State the **lesson objective**. Say: *In this lesson, we will learn to use prepositions of time.*

Prepositions of time: *on / at / by / in / from…to*

 ActiveTeach: Grammar Discovery

1. Warm up. Say: *The pronunciation on page 129 used this grammar.* Turn back to page 129. Point to the sentences in Exercise 3A and then write:
   • *Please come at eight.*
   • *We close at noon on Friday.*
2. Underline the prepositions *at, at,* and *on*. Point to them and ask: *What are these words?* (prepositions)
3. Tell students to look at the grammar chart. Call on students to read each of the sentences.
4. Explain expressions as needed. Say: Please get here by 5:00 today *means arrive here before 5:00. 5:00 is the latest you can arrive. After 5:00 is too late.*
5. Say: I'm going to see the doctor in an hour *means I'm going at [say the time one hour from now].*
6. Say: The pharmacy is open from 8:00 a.m. to 9:00 p.m. *means the pharmacy opens at 8:00 a.m. and closes at 9:00 p.m.*
7. Read the **Grammar Watch** note and ask the class to read along silently.

8. Say: *Let's use prepositions of time to talk about when our English class is.* Draw a web diagram and write *English class* in the circle. Write the prepositions of time (*on, at, by, in, from…to*) at the ends of the lines out from the circle.
9. Point to *on* in the web diagram and ask: *When is our English class?* Elicit and write the day(s) your class meets (for example, *on Tuesdays and Thursdays*). Repeat with the other prepositions. For *by*, ask about the due date for a homework assignment. For *in*, ask when today's class is over.

 ActiveTeach: Grammar Coach

A IDENTIFY. **Cross out the incorrect words.**

1. Read the directions and the example. Ask: *Why is the answer* at? (because 9:15 is a specific time on the clock)
2. Students compare answers with a partner.
3. Call on students to read the sentences. Correct as needed.

■ **EXPANSION: Grammar practice for A**

1. Write item 1. Cross out *at* and the rest of the sentence. Circle *on*. Say: *Rewrite the sentence with* on. Elicit and write an alternative ending to the sentence with *on* (for example, *on Wednesday*). Read the new sentence: *The appointment is on Wednesday.*
2. Tell students to rewrite items 2–7 using the other preposition. For item 3, tell students to cross out *from* and the rest of the sentence.
3. Students compare answers with a partner.
4. Call on students to read the sentences. Correct as needed.

B DECIDE. **Complete the sentences with…**

1. Read the directions and the example. Ask: *Why is the answer* on? (because June 6 and 7 are dates)
2. Students compare answers with a partner.
3. Call on students to read the sentences. Correct as needed.

Grammar

C INTERPRET. Look at the text message...

1. Tell students to look at the appointment reminder on the mobile phone. Ask: *Who is the patient?* (Liz) *What is her doctor's name?* (Dr. Meed)
2. Say: *Point to the day of Liz's appointment. Point to the time. Point to the hours the office is open.*
3. Ask a student to read the last sentence of the reminder. Ask: *Does Liz need to arrive on time for her appointment, or does she need to arrive early?* (early) *How early?* (10 minutes) *What time is that?* (10:05 a.m.)
4. Read the directions and the example. Ask: *Why do we use* on? (because *Wednesday* is a day)
5. Pair students and tell them to take turns reading the questions and answers. Tell them to talk about any answers that are different and make corrections as necessary.
6. Read each question and call on students to read the answers.

▬ EXPANSION: Speaking practice for C

1. Write the day, date, and time of an appointment that you have. Use *on* and *at* to talk about when your appointment is. Use *in* to talk about how soon your appointment is.
2. Tell students to note the day, date, and time of an appointment or plan they have. Tell students they can make up the information.
3. Form small groups and tell students to talk about when and how soon their appointments are (for example, *My appointment is on... at... It's in...*).

Digital Skills for C

Most medical practices give information about making appointments on their websites. Tell students to visit their doctor's website or choose a local medical practice. Look for information on the website about making an appointment. Can appointments be made online? Can they be made by phone? Does the medical practice offer walk-in or after-hours care?

Show what you know!

1. THINK ABOUT IT. On the first appointment...

1. Pair students.
2. Read the first three sentences of the directions (about the first appointment card) and model. Show the appointment cards on the board. Write an appointment for an above-level student. Use *Friday, January 15,* and *3:30 p.m.*

3. Read the last sentence of the directions (about the second appointment card) and model.

2. TALK ABOUT IT. Ask questions with *When*...

1. Read the directions. Play B and read the example with the above-level student you chose in Step 1. Prompt the student to ask: *When is the appointment?* Answer with the date and prompt the student to ask: *What time is the appointment?* Answer with the time.
2. Write: *When is the appointment? What time is the appointment?*
3. Students complete the activity in the same pairs as Step 1. They should write the time and date for their appointment on card 2.
4. To check their work, tell pairs to read their appointments out loud. Their partners listen and check the information.

3. WRITE ABOUT IT. Write two sentences about...

1. Read the directions and the example.
2. Pair students and ask them to check each other's sentences.
   - One sentence should answer the question: *What day is the appointment?*
   - One sentence should answer the question: *What time is the appointment?*
3. To check answers, ask each student: *What time is your appointment?*

▬ EXPANSION: Grammar and speaking practice for 3

When you check answers, after each student's response, ask another student: *When is his* [or *her*] *appointment?* They answer: *His* [or *her*] *appointment is on...* Then ask that student: *What time is your appointment?*

Self-Directed Learning

Point out the blue bar. Ask students if they can do the lesson learning objective or if they need more practice. Tell them to check one of the boxes. Assign Extra Practice as needed.

Extra Practice

  p. 76

Grammar

C INTERPRET. Look at the text message. Answer the questions. Use *on*, *at*, *by*, *in*, or *from . . . to.*

●●●○○ 📶   3:57 PM   33% 🔋

Hi, Liz. This is a reminder that you have an appointment with Dr. Meed on Wednesday, October 6 at 10:15 A.M. at 114 Main St., Springfield, IL 62702. Reply 1 to confirm your appointment. Please arrive at least 10 minutes before the time of your appointment.

Call 909-555-1234 if you need to reschedule. Office hours: M–F 8:00–5:00

1. What day is Liz's appointment?

   It is ___on Wednesday___.

2. What time is her appointment?

   It is ___at 10:15 A.M.___.

3. When is the doctor's office open?

   It is open ___from 8:00 to 5:00___.

4. It is now 8:15 A.M. on October 6. How soon is Liz going to see the doctor?

   She is going to see him ___in two hours___.

5. What time does Liz need to arrive at the doctor's office?

   She should be there ___by 10:05 A.M.___.

Show what you know!

1. **THINK ABOUT IT.** On the first appointment card, write your partner's name. Choose a time and date for your partner's appointment. Write them on the card. Write your name on the second card.

2. **TALK ABOUT IT.** Ask questions with *When* and *What time*. Write the information on the second card. Take turns.

   A: When is the appointment?
   B: It's on Friday, January 15.

3. **WRITE ABOUT IT.** Write two sentences about the day and time of your appointment.

   My appointment is on Friday, January 15. It's at 3:30 P.M.

1

Appointment for _____

Date: _____

Time: _____

2

Appointment for _____

Date: _____

Time: _____

I can use prepositions of time. ■   I need more practice. ■

For more practice, go to MyEnglishLab.

Medicine labels

1 READ OTC MEDICINE LABELS

A IDENTIFY. Over-the-counter (OTC) medicine is medicine you can buy from any drugstore. For other medicine, you need to get a prescription from a doctor. Circle the OTC medicine you buy or have at home.

a
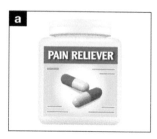
PAIN RELIEVER

b
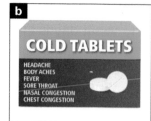
COLD TABLETS
HEADACHE
BODY ACHES
FEVER
SORE THROAT
NASAL CONGESTION
CHEST CONGESTION

B MATCH. Which medicine from Exercise A should you take?

1. _d_ You have a sore throat.
2. _a_ You have a headache.
3. _f_ Your skin itches.
4. _b_ You have a cold.
5. _c_ You have a cough.
6. _e_ You have red eyes.

c
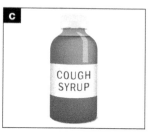
COUGH SYRUP

d

Throat Lozenges
16 Lozenges

e

EYE DROPS

f

OINTMENT

C MATCH. Read the medicine label. Match the questions and answers.

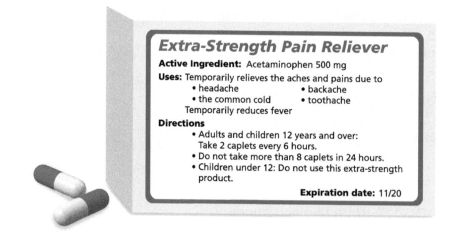

Extra-Strength Pain Reliever

Active Ingredient: Acetaminophen 500 mg
Uses: Temporarily relieves the aches and pains due to
• headache   • backache
• the common cold • toothache
Temporarily reduces fever
Directions
• Adults and children 12 years and over:
  Take 2 caplets every 6 hours.
• Do not take more than 8 caplets in 24 hours.
• Children under 12: Do not use this extra-strength product.
Expiration date: 11/20

1. _b_ What is this medicine for?
2. _d_ Who can take this medicine?
3. _c_ What is the dosage?
4. _e_ Who cannot use this product?
5. _a_ What is the expiration date?

a. November, 2020
b. Aches and pains, and fever
c. Two caplets every six hours
d. Adults and children over 12
e. Children under 12

Lesson 4 | Workplace, Life, and Community Skills

Correlations

ELPS Level 2: 1, 2, 3, 4, 5, 6, 7, 8, 9, 10
CCRS Level A: W.1.7, W.1.8
CASAS Reading: RDG 1.7, 1.8, 2.3, 3.2, 3.6, 4.9
CASAS Listening: L2.1, 2.3, 4.2, 5.4, 5.5
CASAS Competencies: 0.1.2, 0.1.5, 3.3.2, 3.4.1,
4.5.6, 7.7.3, 7.4.4
Complete standards language available on the Pearson English Portal.

Self-Directed Learning

State the **lesson objective**. Say: *In this lesson, we will learn to read medicine labels.*

1 READ OTC MEDICINE LABELS

A IDENTIFY. Over-the-counter (OTC) medicine...

1. Ask: *Do you take medicine? When?* Write: *I take medicine when I _____.* Complete the sentence yourself (for example, say: *I take medicine when I have a headache.*). Tell students to copy and complete the sentence in their notebooks.
2. Form small groups. Say: *Talk to your classmates. When do you take medicine?*
3. Ask: *What's a prescription?* (a piece of paper on which a doctor writes what medicine you need) *Do you need a prescription for over-the-counter medicine?* (no) *Where can you buy OTC medicine?* (at any drugstore and most grocery stores)
4. *Optional:* Bring in containers for prescription and OTC medicine. Hold up the containers and ask: *Which one is an over-the-counter medicine? Which one can I buy at any drugstore?*
5. Read the directions. Write: *pain reliever.* Ask: *Who has pain relievers at home?* Students respond by raising their hands. Repeat for *cold tablets, cough syrup, throat lozenges, eye drops,* and *ointment.*
6. Ask: *What other OTC medicine do you buy?* Write the names of medicines that students say on the board.

Culture Note

Ask: *Are there any medicines that you can buy over-the-counter in your native country but need a prescription for in the United States?* Write students' responses.

B MATCH. Which medicine from Exercise A...

1. Read the directions. Tell students to look at the example. Ask: *What do you take when you have a sore throat?* Elicit the name of the medicine (*throat lozenges*).

2. Students match the OTC medicine from Exercise 1A and the sentences. Walk around and assist with vocabulary.
3. Students compare answers with a partner.
4. Check answers by asking questions. For example: *What do you take when you have a headache?* Note that pain reliever and cold tablets can be the answer for more than one health problem.

C MATCH. Read the medicine label. Match...

Document Literacy: Over-the-counter (OTC) medicine labels

Context: OTC medicine labels are found on OTC medicine, available at drugstores and grocery stores.
Purpose: OTC medicine labels give directions and warnings for using OTC medicine.
Key Words: *active ingredient, uses, directions, expiration date, temporarily relieves*

1. Tell students to look at the medicine label. Ask about **context**: *What kind of medicine is this label for?* (pain reliever) Ask about **purpose**: *What are OTC labels for?* (to give directions and warnings for using OTC medicine) Ask about **key words**: *What information is on an OTC medicine label?* (active ingredient, uses, directions, expiration date)
2. Read the directions. Tell students to read the medicine label silently.
3. Tell students to find *temporarily* on the label and underline it. Say: Temporarily *means for a short time. Now find a word that means* make better. (relieves)
4. Tell students to find the items on the right (a–e) on the label and underline them. Tell students to use this information to answer the questions.
5. Students compare answers with a partner. Tell them to take turns asking and answering the questions.
6. Read the questions and call on students to say answers. After each question and answer, check comprehension by asking an additional question (for example, *What kinds of aches does this medicine relieve?*)

EXPANSION: Speaking practice for 1C

Ask students to bring in labels from OTC medicines. Pair students. Tell them to ask each other the questions in Exercise 1C. Students answer using information from their label.

Workplace, Life, and Community Skills

2 READ PRESCRIPTION MEDICINE...

A INTERPRET. Look at the prescription and...

> **Document Literacy: Prescriptions and prescription medicine labels**
>
> **Context:** Prescription medicine is available at pharmacies. It is not available over the counter. To get prescription medicine, you need a prescription written by a doctor. Prescription medicine labels are found on prescription medicine.
>
> **Purpose:** Prescriptions are for getting prescription medicine. Prescription medicine labels give information about refills as well as dosage and warnings for using the medicine.
>
> **Key Words:** *refills, Rx, warning, dosage, patient, doctor*

1. Tell students to look at the medicine label and prescription. Ask: *Who gives you a prescription?* (a doctor) *Can you buy this medicine at any drugstore?* (no) Ask about **context**: *Where can you buy prescription medicine?* (at pharmacies; you need a prescription) Ask about **purpose**: *What are prescriptions for?* (to get prescription medicine) *What are prescription medicine labels for?* (to give information about refills, dosage, and warnings for using prescription medicine) Ask about **key words**: *What types of information are on prescription medicine labels?* Elicit a few words (for example, *warning, doctor, patient*).
2. Ask the class what *dosage* means and write a definition (*how much medicine you take*).
3. Read the directions.
4. Read the questions and elicit answers from the class.
5. Tell students to cover the medicine label. Say the specific pieces of information from the label in random order. Point to the board and tell students to call out the type of information (for example, T: *Do not take with aspirin.* Class: *Warning*).

B MATCH. Read the medicine label in Exercise...

1. Read the directions.
2. Ask the class what *refills* means and write a definition (*times that you can get more medicine with the same prescription*).
3. Tell students to find the items on the right (a–e) on the prescription and label and underline them. Tell students to use this information to answer the questions.

C ▶ SELF-ASSESS. Listen and check your...

1. Play the audio. Students listen and check their answers. Pause after item 5.

2. Say: *Now listen and repeat. Practice the questions because you're going to ask them in Exercise D.*
3. Resume the audio. Tell students to repeat.

D ACT IT OUT. With a partner, take turns being...

1. Read the directions. Tell students to look at Exercise 2B. Point to the questions and ask: *Who asks the questions?* (the customer) *Who answers the questions?* (the pharmacist)
2. Tell students to look at the medicine labels. Write: *an eyedropper, a tube of ointment.* Ask: *What's the picture next to the first label?* (an eyedropper) Ask: *What's the picture next to the second label?* (a tube of ointment)
3. Pair students. Say: *Talk to your partner. Decide who's going to be the pharmacist for the eyedrops and who's going to be the pharmacist for the ointment.*
4. Tell students to look at the questions in Exercise 2B and find answers to the questions on their label.
5. Say: *Take turns being the customer and the pharmacist. The customer asks the questions in Exercise 2B. The pharmacist answers the questions using the underlined information on his or her label.*
6. Call on pairs to perform for the class.

E GO ONLINE. Search for an online pharmacy...

1. Read the directions. Ask students what they would search in English if they wanted to find online pharmacies.
2. Write the search strings: *online pharmacy.* Have students search the internet and write the name of a medicine and instructions for taking it.
3. Compare research as a class. Write down different examples of instructions.

> **Digital Skills for 2E**
>
> Warn students that there are illegal online pharmacies. To find a legal online pharmacy, consumers need to look for a website name that ends *.pharmacy*.

 ActiveTeach: Review

Self-Directed Learning

Point out the blue bar. Ask students if they can do the lesson learning objective or if they need more practice. Tell them to check one of the boxes. Assign Extra Practice as needed.

> **Extra Practice**
>
> Workbook pp. 77–78 Life Skills Writing

Workplace, Life, and Community Skills

2 READ PRESCRIPTION MEDICINE LABELS

A **INTERPRET.** Look at the prescription and the medicine label. Answer the questions.

```
Washington Medical Group
Leora Fishman, M.D.
1123 W. Main Street, Washington Heights, New York
914-222-2222 (Fax) 914-222-1111

Name:    Kate Reed              Date: 11/11/2019
Address: 123 Main Street        DOB:  7/4/1996
City:    Washington Heights, NY Rx:   Milacam, 15 MG

                         Two refills

Signature: 1054996076V
```

1. Who wrote the prescription? Dr. Leora Fishman.
2. Who is it for? Kate Reed.
3. What is the dosage? 2 TBs once a day.
4. Where can you get this medicine? Bio-Med Pharmacy
5. What information is on the label?
   The doctor, the patient, the dosage, any warnings,
   the name and amount of medicine, the number of refills, and the expiration date.

B **MATCH.** Read the medicine label in Exercise A again. Match the questions and answers.

Bio-Med Pharmacy
Doctor: Leora Fishman
Patient: Kate Reed
Dosage: Take 2 tablespoons by mouth once a day. Take with food.
Warning: Do not take with aspirin.

Milacam 15 MG
2 Refills   Exp: 11/20/21

1. __e__ What is the name of the medicine?   **a.** Two
2. __d__ How often do I take it?   **b.** Two tablespoons
3. __b__ What is the dosage?   **c.** November 20, 2021
4. __c__ What is the expiration date?   **d.** Once a day
5. __a__ How many refills can I get?   **e.** Milacam

C ▶ **SELF-ASSESS.** Listen and check your answers. Then listen and repeat.

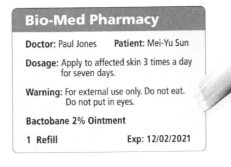

D **ACT IT OUT.** With a partner, take turns being the customer and the pharmacist. Ask and answer the questions in Exercise B about these prescriptions.

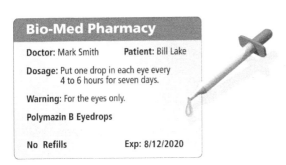

Bio-Med Pharmacy

Doctor: Mark Smith   Patient: Bill Lake

Dosage: Put one drop in each eye every 4 to 6 hours for seven days.

Warning: For the eyes only.

Polymazin B Eyedrops

No Refills   Exp: 8/12/2020

Bio-Med Pharmacy

Doctor: Paul Jones   Patient: Mei-Yu Sun

Dosage: Apply to affected skin 3 times a day for seven days.

Warning: For external use only. Do not eat. Do not put in eyes.

Bactobane 2% Ointment

1 Refill   Exp: 12/02/2021

E GO ONLINE. Search for an online pharmacy. On the website, find information on a medicine you saw in an advertisement. Check the instructions on how to take the medicine.

I can read medicine labels. ■   I need more practice. ■

For more practice, go to MyEnglishLab.

Talk about an injury

1 BEFORE YOU LISTEN

LABEL. Write the sentences under the pictures.

I broke my arm.   I cut my finger.   I hurt my head.
I burned my hand.   I fell.   I sprained my ankle.

1. _I fell._

2. _I broke my arm._

3. _I cut my finger._

4. _I sprained my ankle._

5. _I hurt my head._

6. _I burned my hand._

2 LISTEN

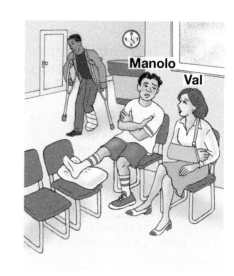

Manolo
Val

A **PREDICT.** Look at the picture. Where are the people?

B ▶ **LISTEN FOR MAIN IDEA.** Read the sentences. Circle *True* or *False*.

1. Val had an accident.   (True)   False
2. Manolo was at a soccer game.   (True)   False

C ▶ **LISTEN FOR DETAILS.** Listen again. Circle *True* or *False*.

1. Val sprained her arm.   True   (False)
2. Manolo thinks he broke his ankle. True   (False)

D ▶ **EXPAND.** Listen to the whole conversation. What happened to Manolo? Circle the letter.

a.

b.

Correlations

ELPS Level 2: 2, 7
CCRS Level A: SL.K.3
CASAS Reading: RDG 1.7, 2.3
CASAS Listening: L1.5, 2.1, 2.3, 4.2, 6.1, 6.2, 6.5
CASAS Competencies: 0.1.2, 0.1.5, 0.1.6, 0.2.1, 3.6.2
Complete standards language available on the Pearson English Portal.

Self-Directed Learning

State the **lesson objective**. Say: *In this lesson, we will learn to talk about an injury.*

1 BEFORE YOU LISTEN

LABEL. Write the sentences under the…

1. Say: *Look at the pictures. What's an* injury? (when a person gets hurt / has an accident) Ask: *Does anyone have an injury?* Elicit examples. Help students describe their injuries.
2. Read the directions and the example.
3. Read the sentences in the box. Ask the class to repeat.
4. Tell students to underline the parts of the body in the sentences. Say: *If you know the parts of the body, you can match the pictures with the sentences.*
5. Tell students to write the answers under the correct picture.
6. Walk around and spot-check students' written answers.
7. Call on students to read the sentence that matches each picture. Explain or elicit unfamiliar words (for example, *sprains* are injuries to joints, or parts of your body that can bend). Write: *I sprained my _____.* Demonstrate bending each joint. Elicit and list on the board the parts of the body that a person can sprain (*ankle, knee, elbow, wrist, fingers*).

2 LISTEN

A PREDICT. Look at the picture. Where are…

1. Read the directions. Ask: *How many people are in the picture?* (three) *What do they all have?* (an injury)
2. Ask: *What are Manolo and Val doing?* (sitting, waiting, talking) *Where are they?* (in the waiting room at a doctor's office or hospital)

B ▶ LISTEN FOR MAIN IDEA. Read the…

1. Read the directions. Tell students to read the sentences silently.
2. Play the audio. Students circle *True* or *False*.
3. Ask: *Was your guess in Exercise 2A correct?* Ask for a show of hands if their guess was correct.
4. Call on students to read the sentences and say if they are true or false.

Teaching Tip: Use the script

Remember that if students need additional support, tell them to read the Audio Script on page 271 as they listen to the conversation.

C ▶ LISTEN FOR DETAILS. Listen again…

1. Direct students to look at the picture again. Ask: *What part of his body did Manolo hurt?* (his ankle or foot) *What part of her body did Val hurt?* (her arm)
2. Read the directions. Tell students to read the sentences silently.
3. Play the audio. Students circle *True* or *False*.
4. Call on students to read the sentences and say if they are true or false.
5. Tell students to rewrite the sentences to make them true.

D ▶ EXPAND. Listen to the whole…

1. Read the directions.
2. Direct students to look at the pictures. Ask: *What do you think happened to Manolo?*
3. Play the audio. Students listen and circle the letter of the correct answer.
4. Students compare answers with a partner.
5. Ask: *What happened to Manolo?* Ask students to say what happens to Manolo in each picture. (a. He sprained/hurt his ankle at a soccer game. b. He fell down the bleachers). Write their responses. Ask: *Which is true?* Elicit and circle a. Ask: *Was your guess correct?*

■ **EXPANSION: Graphic organizer practice for 2D**

1. Say: *Think about an accident you had or an accident a friend or family member had when you were with them.*
2. Draw a *Wh-* question chart on the board (with *What, Where, When,* and *How* as headings) and complete it with information about an accident you or your friend/family member had. In the *What?* box, write a sentence similar to the ones in the box in Exercise 1A. Write short answers in the other boxes.
3. Tell students to draw a complete *Wh-* question chart about their accident.

Listening and Speaking

3 PRONUNCIATION

A ▶ PRACTICE. Listen. Then listen and repeat.

1. Write the first sentence. Point to each word and pronounce it distinctly. Ask: *Is this how people speak?* (no)
2. Say the sentence again, running *What* and *are* together as you would in normal speech. Point to the underlined *t* in the sentence, say the sentence and ask: *What sound do you hear?* (/d/)
3. Read the **Pronunciation Note**. Point to the underlined *t* and ask: *Is it between two vowel sounds?* (yes) *What does it sound like?* (/d/)
4. Write the second sentence on the board. Ask: *Is the underlined* t *between two vowel sounds?* (yes) Say the sentence and ask: *Does the* t *sound like a quick /d/?* (yes) Repeat with the third sentence.
5. Play the audio. Students listen. Then students listen and repeat.

 ActiveTeach for 3A: Pronunciation Coach

B ▶ CHOOSE. Listen. Which *t*'s have the...

1. Read the directions.
2. Write item 1. Underline the *t* in *What*. Ask: *Is the underlined* t *between two vowel sounds?* (yes) Say the sentence and ask: *Does the* t *sound like a quick /d/?* (yes) Circle the item number.
3. Play the audio. Students listen and circle the words with the sound /d/. If necessary, play the audio again and have students listen twice before answering.
4. Write items 2–4. Underline the *t* in each sentence. Say each sentence and ask: *Is the underlined* t *between two vowel sounds? Does the* t *sound like a quick /d/?*
5. Have pairs practice saying items 1 and 4.

4 CONVERSATION

A ▶ LISTEN AND READ. Then listen and repeat.

1. Note: This conversation is the same one students heard in Exercise 2B on page 134.
2. Tell students to read the conversation silently and underline words and phrases that they practiced in Exercise 3A and 3B.
3. Play the audio. Students listen. Then students listen and repeat.

B WORK TOGETHER. Practice the conversation.

1. Pair students and tell them to practice the conversation in Exercise 4A.
2. Tell students to take turns playing A and B.

C CREATE. Make new conversations. Use the...

1. Tell students to look at the information in the boxes. Call on students to say each item. Then they act out the blue items and point to the green items.
2. Show the conversation with blanks. Ask: *What goes in the first two blanks?* (their names)
3. Ask a pair of students to model a new conversation.
4. Tell pairs to take turns playing A and B and to use the vocabulary lists to fill in the blanks.
5. Walk around and check students' pronunciation of *what are* and *what about*.
6. Tell students to stand, mingle, and practice the conversation with several new partners.

D ROLE-PLAY. Make your own conversations.

1. Brainstorm and write body parts people can hurt. Say the words and ask the class to point to the part of the body and repeat.
2. Choose a body part from the list and elicit the class's help to make sentences about injuries. Tell students to look at the sentences in the box in Exercise 1A on page 134.
3. Ask two above-level students to model a new conversation.
4. Pair students and tell them to use information you wrote or their own information in the conversation in Exercise 4C. Walk around during the activity and help as needed.

Self-Directed Learning

Point out the blue bar. Ask students if they can do the lesson learning objective or if they need more practice. Tell them to check one of the boxes. Assign Extra Practice as needed.

Extra Practice		
MyEnglishLab	Workbook	p. 79

Listening and Speaking

3 PRONUNCIATION

A ▶ **PRACTICE. Listen. Then listen and repeat.**

What are you doing here?

I was at a soccer game.

What's the matter?

> **t between two vowel sounds**
>
> When the letter *t* is between two vowel sounds, it often sounds like a quick /d/.

B ▶ **CHOOSE. Listen. Which *t*'s have the sound /d/? Circle the words.**

1. (What) about you?
2. I hurt my ankle.
3. That's too bad.
4. See you (later).

4 CONVERSATION

A ▶ **LISTEN AND READ. Then listen and repeat.**

A: Hi, Val. What are you doing here?
B: Oh, hi, Manolo. I had an accident. I broke my arm.
A: Oh, no! I'm sorry to hear that.
B: Thanks. What about you?
A: I hurt my ankle at a soccer game. I think I sprained it.

B **WORK TOGETHER. Practice the conversation.**

C **CREATE. Make new conversations. Use the words in the boxes.**

A: Hi, _____. What are you doing here?
B: Oh, hi, _____. I had an accident.

A: Oh, no! I'm sorry to hear that.
B: Thanks. What about you?
A: I hurt my _____ at a soccer game.
   I think I sprained it.
B: That's too bad.

I cut my hand.	foot
I burned my finger.	wrist
I fell.	back

D **ROLE-PLAY. Make your own conversations.**

I can talk about an injury. ■	I need more practice. ☐

For more practice, go to MyEnglishLab.

Simple past: More irregular verbs

Simple past: More irregular verbs		
She	**had**	an accident.
	broke	her arm.
	got	hurt.
	hurt	her ankle.

Grammar Watch

Common irregular verbs

Base form	Past-tense form
break	**broke**
cut	**cut**
fall	**fell**
get	**got**
have	**had**
hurt	**hurt**

- See page 259 for more past tense forms.

A COMPLETE. Write the past-tense forms of the words in parentheses.

1. I (get) _____got_____ hurt on my way to work last week. I was in a hurry, and I (fall) _____fell_____ down the stairs. My foot (hurt) _____hurt_____ for a few days after that, but I (not go) _____didn't go_____ to the doctor.

2. The floor in the bathroom at work was wet. Nishi slipped, and she (fall) _____fell_____. She (hurt) _____hurt_____ her hand pretty bad, but she (not break) _____didn't break_____ it.

3. Luis (have) _____had_____ an accident at his job in the restaurant. He (cut) _____cut_____ his finger. It was serious, and he (go) _____went_____ to the hospital.

4. Ling was out of the office yesterday. She (have) _____had_____ a sore throat, and her head (hurt) _____hurt_____. She (not have) _____didn't have_____ any medicine at home, so I (get) _____got_____ some for her at the pharmacy.

B APPLY. Make sentences about the past. Use the words in the box.

~~break~~   cut   fall   get   have   hurt

1. Oscar / his ankle _Oscar broke his ankle._
2. The kitchen manager / her finger with a knife _The kitchen manager cut her finger with a knife._
3. You / a fever last night _You had a fever last night._
4. My co-worker and I / sick on the same day _My co-worker and I got sick on the same day._
5. The patient / in the bathroom _The patient fell in the bathroom._
6. Lan / her arm _Lan hurt her arm._

Correlations

ELPS Level 2: 2, 7, 10
CCRS Level A: L.1.1
CASAS Reading: RDG 1.7, 2.9
CASAS Listening: L2.1, 2.3, 3.9, 4.2
CASAS Competencies: 0.1.2, 0.1.5, 0.1.6, 0.2.1
Complete standards language available on the Pearson English Portal.

Self-Directed Learning

State the **lesson objective**. Say: *In this lesson, we will learn to talk about an injury.*

Simple past: More irregular verbs

 ActiveTeach: Grammar Discovery

1. Warm up. Say: *The conversation on page 135 used this grammar.* Turn back to page 135. Point to the sentences in Exercise 4A and then write:
   • *I had an accident.*
   • *I broke my arm.*
2. Write *burn* and *sprain*. Ask: *How do we usually form the past tense?* Elicit the answer and add *-ed* to the words on the board. Say *burned* and *sprained* and ask the class to repeat.
3. Say: *Some verbs do not have -ed forms. They have irregular past-tense forms.* Tell students to look at the sentences on the board. Ask: *What is the past-tense form of* have? (*had*) Repeat with *break*. Say: *Have and break have irregular past-tense forms.*
4. Tell students to look at the grammar chart. Read sentences from the chart and have students repeat.
5. Point to the **Grammar Watch** note. Ask: *What other verbs have irregular past-tense forms?* Say the irregular past-tense forms in the **Grammar Watch** note and ask the class to repeat.
6. Point to the picture of Manolo and Val on page 134. Ask: *What happened to Manolo? What happened to Val?* Elicit and write the sentences (*He hurt his ankle. She broke her arm.*). Read them and ask the class to repeat.

EXPANSION: Grammar practice

1. Tell students to look at the Grammar Reference on page 259. Say the past-tense forms and ask the class to repeat.
2. Give students time to study the irregular past-tense forms on page 136 and in the Grammar Reference on page 259.
3. Tell students to close their books. Say base forms in random order and ask the class to call out the past tense forms.
4. Pair students and tell them to quiz each other. Tell students to mark the verbs their partner doesn't know.
5. Provide students with index cards or tell them to cut up notebook paper. Tell them to make flashcards for the verbs they need to practice more.

 ActiveTeach: Grammar Coach

A **COMPLETE. Write the past-tense forms of…**

1. Read the directions. Write: *I (get) _____ hurt.* Ask: *What is the past tense of* get? (*got*) Write *got* on the line.
2. Erase the sentence and write: *I (not get) _____ hurt.* Ask: *How do you make a negative sentence in the past tense?* (*didn't* + base form) Write *didn't get* on the line.
3. Remind students that they can also use the Grammar Reference on page 259.
4. Students compare answers with a partner. Walk around and spot-check students' spelling of the past-tense forms.
5. Call on students to read the completed items.

B **APPLY. Make sentences about the past. Use…**

1. Read the directions. Write item 1 and point to the answer. Ask: *Which verb from the box is used?* (*break*) *What is the past-tense form of break?* (*broke*) Read the sentence.
2. Say each verb in the box and ask the class to call out the past-tense form.
3. Say: *First, choose the correct verb. Then write a past tense sentence.*
4. Students compare answers with a partner. Walk around and spot-check students' spelling of the past-tense forms.
5. Call on students to read the completed sentences.

Grammar

C DESCRIBE. Look at the pictures. What...

1. Read the directions. Tell students to underline *last weekend*. Ask: *Are you going to use the present or the past tense?* (past tense)
2. Say: *Look at item 1. What happened to Jessica last weekend?* Write the example. Ask the class to complete the second sentence. Write: *cut her hand.*
3. Pair students. Say: *Look at the other pictures. What happened to David, Theo, and Mandy last weekend? Talk to your partner. Try to think of two things to say about each picture. To get ideas, look at the exercises on page 136.*
4. For items 2–4, ask: *What happened to [David]?* Call on pairs to give their answers. For each item, ask if there are any different answers.

D WRITE. Make two sentences about what...

1. Read the directions and the sentences about Jessica on the board. Say: *Use the sentences as an example.*
2. Remind students to start each sentence with a capital letter and end with a period. Tell students to check their spelling of irregular past-tense verbs by looking at the grammar chart and the Grammar Reference on page 259.
3. For items 2–4 in Exercise C, ask students to write their sentences on the board. Correct as needed.
4. Call on different students to read the sentences.

■■ EXPANSION: Speaking practice for D

1. Tell students to read the conversation between Manolo and Val in Exercise 4A on page 135 again.
2. Choose two pictures from Exercise C. With the class, create a phone conversation between the two people. Write it. For example:
   Jessica: *Hi, Mandy. How was your weekend?*
   Mandy: *Terrible. I got sick. I had a fever.*
   Jessica: *That's too bad.*
   Mandy: *What about you? How was your weekend?...*
3. Form like-ability pairs. Pre-level pairs practice the conversation on the board. Above-level pairs create a conversation between the other two people in Exercise C.

Show what you know!

1. THINK ABOUT IT. Complete the questions.

1. Read the directions. Ask: *Did you ever cut your finger? Did you ever sprain your ankle?* For each question, ask for a show of hands. Ask a student whose hand is raised: *When?*
2. Advise students to review the vocabulary on page 126 for help with completing the last question.
3. Elicit a variety of endings for each question. Write three complete questions of your choice (for example, *Did you ever <u>hurt your leg</u>? Did you ever <u>break your toe</u>? Did you ever <u>have the flu</u>?*).

2. TALK ABOUT IT. Ask your questions. Take...

1. Form groups of 5. Read the directions and example.
2. Model the activity. Next to your questions on the board, write the names of four above-level students as column headings of a chart. Point to the names and say: *This is my group.*
3. Demonstrate asking each group member a question and taking notes on the chart.
4. Tell students to create charts for their group and to continue asking questions until they complete their charts.

3. WRITE ABOUT IT. Write two sentences about...

1. Read the directions.
2. Tell students to look at their charts and circle the most interesting answer from each partner.
3. Point to the verbs in the questions on the board. Elicit the past-tense forms (*hurt, broke, had*).
4. Ask group members to check each other's sentences.
   • Sentences should use the past tense.
   • Past-tense forms should be spelled correctly.
5. Call on students to share sentences about their group members' activities.

Self-Directed Learning

Point out the blue bar. Ask students if they can do the lesson learning objective or if they need more practice. Tell them to check one of the boxes. Assign Extra Practice as needed.

Extra Practice

MyEnglishLab	Workbook p. 79

Grammar

C **DESCRIBE.** Look at the pictures. What happened last weekend?

Jessica had an accident in the kitchen. She . . .

Jessica

1. _____

_____

David

2. _____

_____

EMERGENCY

Theo

3. _____

_____

Mandy

4. _____

_____

D **WRITE.** Make two sentences about what happened in each picture in Exercise C.

Show what you know!

1. THINK ABOUT IT. Complete the questions.

Did you ever hurt _____?
Did you ever break _____?
Did you ever have _____?

2. TALK ABOUT IT. Ask your questions. Take notes.

A: Did you ever break your toe?
B: No, but I broke my finger at work last year.

3. WRITE ABOUT IT. Write two sentences about your classmates' injuries.

_____

_____

I can talk about an injury. ■   I need more practice. ■

For more practice, go to MyEnglishLab.

Read about stress

1 BEFORE YOU READ

A **DECIDE. Complete the sentences with the words in the box.**

attitude   avoid   situation   sources   stress

1. When you feel _____stress_____, you worry and you can't relax.
2. Things that cause stress are called _____sources_____ of stress.
3. Anna's co-workers always try to do their best work. They have a good _____attitude_____.
4. Tom's car won't start and he's late for an important meeting. He's in a bad _____situation_____.
5. Doctors say to _____avoid_____ eating junk food.

B **MAKE CONNECTIONS.**

What's happening in the photo? Are you ever in the same situation? When do you feel stressed?

2 READ

▶ Listen and read.

> **Academic Skill: Use formatting cues**
>
> Authors sometimes use formatting such as **boldface** type, bullets (•), and color to help readers find the main point.

STRESS

1 Everyone feels stress sometimes. That *can* be a good thing. For example, stress about important things, like a job interview or a test, can make you work hard
5 to prepare for it. But some people feel so much stress that they become sick.

What causes stress?

Change The biggest source of
10 stress is change. It may be a bad change, like losing a job or getting divorced. But even a good change, like going on vacation, causes stress.

15 **Loss of Control** You also feel stress in situations that you can't control. Maybe you are stuck in traffic or your kids are sick. When you can't change bad things in your life, then you feel stress.

Negative Attitudes The way you think can cause stress.
20 For example, you worry a lot or you think about only the bad things in your life. These kinds of negative attitudes cause stress.

Unhealthy Habits The way you live can cause stress. Do you eat too
25 much junk food? Do you work too many hours? Unhealthy habits like these add stress to your life.

How can you manage stress?

Pay attention to the times you feel
30 stressed. Look for what causes stress in your life.

Think about ways to change the things that cause you stress.

Accept the things you can't change. Some-
35 times you can't avoid a stressful situation.

Get regular exercise. It will help you relax. You'll also sleep better.

Talk about your stress with a family member, friend, counselor, or doctor.

Correlations

ELPS Level 2: 1, 2, 3, 7, 9
CCRS Level A: RI/RL.1.1, RI.1.2, RI.1.4, RI.1.5, SL.K.2, SL.L.3, SL.1.4
CASAS Reading: RDG 1.7, 1.8, 2.3, 3.2, 3.10, 3.11, 4.2, 4.9
CASAS Listening: L2.1, 2.3, 4.2, 5.8, 6.1, 6.2
CASAS Competencies: 0.1.2, 0.1.5, 0.2.1, 7.5.4
Complete standards language available on the Pearson English Portal.

Self-Directed Learning

1. State the **lesson objective**. Say: *In this lesson, we will learn to use formatting cues.*
2. Say: *We will read about stress.*

1 BEFORE YOU READ

A DECIDE. Complete the sentences with the...

1. Write: *STRESS*. Ask: *What is stress?* Use the word STRESS as the center of a web diagram and note student's ideas (for example, *worry, no time, too much work, can't relax, tired*). If students need help, tell them to look at the picture in the article.
2. Read the directions. Say the words in the box and have students repeat.
3. Read the first sentence. Ask: *What word is like worrying?* (stress) Tell students to write *stress* to complete the sentence.
4. Tell students to complete the sentences.
5. Call on students to read the completed sentences aloud.

B MAKE CONNECTIONS. What's happening...

1. **Scaffold:** With the class, brainstorm a list of words they can use to describe the photo (for example, *bus, rush, hurry, miss*).
2. Ask: *What's happening in the picture?* (A man is running to catch a bus.)
3. Pair students to answer the second and third questions.
4. Call on students to share their ideas.

2 READ

▶ Listen and read.

1. Point to the **Academic Skill** and read it. Say: *Formatting is a way to change text. It makes the text look different.* Ask: *What is boldface?* (The print is thicker and darker than usual, as in the word *boldface* in the note.) Have students look at the article. Ask: *What kinds of formatting do you see?* (the colors purple and red, the headings

and subheads are larger and bold) Ask: *What do you think each color means?* (the purple text introduces the main ideas of the article, the red text introduces support for the first main idea)

2. Introduce the reading. Ask: *What is the title?* (Stress) *What does stress feel like?* (worry, anxiety) *How does the formatting of the title connect to the topic?* (The lettering is big, red, and uneven. Stress feels big, angry, and messy.)
3. Introduce the visual. Elicit descriptions of the picture. Ask: *Why does it have that shape?* (to show that she is upset, stressed)
4. Have an above-level student read the first paragraph or read it yourself. Ask: *Do you think this article will be about good or bad things that stress causes?*

 ActiveTeach for 2: Anticipation Guide – *Before* **Reading exercise**

5. Read the text.
   a. Say: *Now we are going to read and listen to the article* Stress.
   b. Play the audio as students listen and read along silently.
   c. Say: *I am going to ask you questions about details in the text. For each question, underline the place in the text where you find the answer.*
   d. Ask: *What are the two main topics the writer talks about in the article?* (what causes stress and how you can manage stress)
   e. Ask: *How many causes does the writer talk about?* (four) *What are they?* (change, loss of control, negative attitudes, unhealthy habits) Elicit examples of each.
   f. Ask: *How many ways to manage stress does the writer mention?* (five) Tell students to number them and underline the key words. (1 - *look for what causes stress*; 2 - *ways to change*; 3 - *accept*; 4 - *exercise*; 5 - *talk about your stress*)
   g. Pair students. Tell them to list the five ways to manage stress.

Teaching Tip: Multiple reads

Tell students to read articles several times. On the first read, they focus on the general idea, or gist. They should not stop to look up words they don't know. On a later read, they can focus on details. If they have detail questions to answer, they should read the questions first, and scan for information.

 ActiveTeach for 2: Anticipation Guide – *After* **Reading exercise**

Reading

3 CLOSE READING

A IDENTIFY. What is the main idea?

1. Say: *Now we are going to identify the main idea.* **Reinforce the Academic Skill.** Say: *Look at the formatting to help you find the main points the writer wants to make.*
2. Read the directions. Have students circle the answer.
3. Elicit the answer from the class. Ask: *What word in special formatting helped you choose the correct answer?* (manage)

B CITE EVIDENCE. Complete the sentences…

1. Say: *Now we are going to find information in the reading and cite evidence.*
2. Read the directions. Walk around as students work on the activity. If students are struggling, have them work in pairs or direct them to the text lines where they can find the information.
3. Call on students to read the sentence with the correct completion. Ask a different student: *Where is that information? What line number?*

Career Awareness: Counselor

Counselors usually work with people to improve their mental health and solve problems. People talk about their feelings and problems with counselors. Some counselors give advice about jobs and colleges. They work in schools, mental health organizations, and workplaces. In most states, you need at least a bachelor's degree in counseling. You may also need a master's degree and/or two years of supervised experience.

■■ **EXPANSION: Career awareness for 3B**

Ask students about the job in this lesson: *What does a counselor do? Where does a counselor work? Do you need to study to be a counselor? Do you want to be a counselor?*

4 SUMMARIZE

 ActiveTeach for 4: Vocabulary Practice

1. Read the directions. Ask students to read the words in the box.
2. Tell students to complete the paragraph.
3. To check answers, call on students to read sentences in the summary with the blanks filled in. Other students read along silently.

Show what you know!

1. THINK ABOUT IT. What causes you stress?…

1. Read the directions.
2. Tell students to take notes on their ideas.

2. WRITE ABOUT IT. Write about your sources…

1. Read the directions. Point to the sentence frames.
2. Model the activity. Say and write sentences about when you feel stress and how you manage it.
3. Have students write their sentences on a sheet of paper. Walk around and answer any questions.
4. Say: *Share your sentences with at least two people. Check their sentences. If the sentences are not correct, help your partner correct them.*
5. Collect the papers for review or put them in the students' writing portfolios.

3. PRESENT IT. Make a presentation about…

1. Write the different ways to manage stress: *pay attention, change things, accept, get exercise, talk about it.*
2. Read the directions.
3. Put students in groups of 3. Explain what it means to *rank-order* ideas. Tell students to rank-order the five ways to manage stress from most helpful to least helpful. Tell them to give reasons and to add any other ideas they have. One student takes notes.
4. Groups take turns presenting their rank orders to the class.
5. Elicit any other ways to manage stress that the class can think of.

 ActiveTeach for 3: Academic Conversation Support

Self-Directed Learning

Point out the blue bar. Ask students if they can do the lesson learning objective or if they need more practice. Tell them to check one of the boxes. Assign Extra Practice as needed.

■■ **EXPANSION: Self-directed learning**

Ask students to reflect: *What did you learn from this reading?* Call on students to share something they learned.

Extra Practice

 CCRS Plus   pp. 80–81

Reading

3 CLOSE READING

A IDENTIFY. What is the main idea?

Everybody feels stress but _____.
a. not all stress is bad
(b.) you can learn to manage it
c. you just have to accept it

B CITE EVIDENCE. Complete the sentences. Where is the information? Write the line numbers.

Lines

1. The thing that causes the most stress is _____.
   a. a person's job   (b.) change   c. a negative attitude   <u>9–10</u>

2. Being in a car stuck in traffic is an example of _____.
   a. something you can change   b. avoiding a stressful situation   (c.) a situation that you cannot control   <u>15–17</u>

3. Eating junk food is an example of _____.
   (a.) an unhealthy habit   b. a good way to relax   c. a thing you have to accept   <u>23–25</u>

4. Start managing the stress in your life by _____.
   (a.) understanding the sources of your stress   b. avoiding all changes   c. thinking about happy things only   <u>29–31</u>

5. Try talking about your stress with a friend, family member, doctor, or _____.
   a. employer   b. pharmacist   (c.) counselor   <u>38–39</u>

4 SUMMARIZE

Complete the summary with the words in the box.

accept   attitudes   control   manage   sources

Too much stress is bad for you. Big (1) <u>sources</u> of stress are change, loss of
(2) <u>control</u>, negative (3) <u>attitudes</u>, and unhealthy habits. There are things
you can do to (4) <u>manage</u> the stress in your life, but sometimes you have to
(5) <u>accept</u> things you can't change.

Show what you know!

1. **THINK ABOUT IT.** What causes you stress? How do you manage stress?

2. **WRITE ABOUT IT.** Write about your sources of stress and how you can manage stress.

   I feel stress when _____. To manage my stress, I _____.
   I can also _____.

3. **PRESENT IT.** Make a presentation about the five ways to manage stress in the article. Which ones are the most helpful? What are other ways to manage stress?

I can use formatting cues. ■   I need more practice. ■

To read more, go to MyEnglishLab.

Call in when you have to miss work

1 BEFORE YOU LISTEN

A **LABEL.** Write the sentences under the pictures.

I have a checkup.
I have to go to the dentist.

I'm getting my flu shot.
My child is sick.

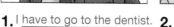

1. I have to go to the dentist.   **2.** _____ My child is sick. _____   **3.** _____ I have a checkup _____   **4.** _____ I'm getting my flu shot _____

B **MAKE CONNECTIONS.** What are some other reasons that people miss work? Did you ever have to miss work or school?

2 LISTEN

A **PREDICT.** Look at the picture. Who is Sung calling?

B ▶ **LISTEN FOR MAIN IDEA.** Why is Sung calling?

a. She's going to be late.
(b.) She's not going to work today.
c. She has an emergency.

C ▶ **LISTEN FOR DETAILS.** Answer the questions.

1. Where is Sung going?
  a. to the hospital (b.) to the doctor's office c. to the dentist's office

2. What is the problem?
  (a.) Sung doesn't feel well. b. Sung's son is sick. c. Sung forgot her appointment.

3. What does the supervisor say?
  a. Take your medicine. b. See you tomorrow. (c.) Take care of yourself.

D ▶ **EXPAND.** Listen to the whole conversation. Answer the questions.

1. What does the supervisor ask?
  a. When is your appointment? b. Do you feel better? (c.) Do you think you'll be in tomorrow?

2. What will Sung do later?
  (a.) call her supervisor again b. go to work c. call the doctor

Correlations

ELPS Level 2: 2, 7
CCRS Level A: SL.1.1, SL.K.6
CASAS Reading: RDG 1.7, 2.3
CASAS Listening: L1.4, 2.1, 2.3, 4.1, 4.2, 6.1, 6.2, 6.5
CASAS Competencies: 0.1.2, 0.1.4, 0.1.5, 0.1.6, 0.1.8, 0.2.1, 4.6.5
Complete standards language available on the Pearson English Portal.

Self-Directed Learning

State the **lesson objective**. Say: *In this lesson, we will learn to call in when we have to miss work.*

1 BEFORE YOU LISTEN

A LABEL. Write the sentences under the…

1. Say: *Look at the pictures.* Ask: *What is happening?* (The man has a toothache, the child is sick in bed, the woman is getting weighed, the woman is getting a shot.)
2. Say: *Look at the sentences about reasons people miss work.* Call on students to read the sentences in the box.
3. Tell students to look at picture 1. Ask: *What does he have to do?* (go to the dentist)
4. Give students time to label the pictures.
5. Call on students to read the sentence that matches each picture. Explain or elicit unfamiliar words. For example, *a checkup* is a regular visit to the doctor. You don't have to be sick or have an injury.

B MAKE CONNECTIONS. What are some other…

1. Ask: *What are some other reasons that people miss work?* Elicit examples and write them.
2. Ask: *Did you ever have to miss work or school? What was the problem? Did you call anyone? Who?* Add any new reasons to the list.

Culture Note

1. Say: *When you miss work because of sickness or injury, some employers require a doctor's note. If you're not sure if you need one, ask the doctor or dentist for a note just in case.*
2. Ask: *Do employers in your native country require a doctor's note when you miss work?*
3. Say: *Some doctors ask, "Do you need a note for your employer?" If your doctor doesn't ask, what can you say?* Write students' ideas on the board (for example, *Can you please write a note for my manager?* or *I need a note for my employer.*).

2 LISTEN

A PREDICT. Look at the picture. Who is Sung…

1. Tell students to look at the picture. Say: *Point to Sung. Point to Eva. How does Sung look?* (sick / like she has a headache / like she doesn't feel well)
2. Ask: *Who is Sung calling? Who is Eva?* Elicit answers and write them. (her work supervisor, a friend, her coworker)

B ▶ LISTEN FOR MAIN IDEA. Why is Sung…

1. Read the directions. Call on students to read the answer choices.
2. Play the audio. Students listen and circle the letter of the correct answer.
3. Elicit the correct answer from the class.
4. Ask: *Was your guess in Exercise 2A correct?* Ask for a show of hands.

C ▶ LISTEN FOR DETAILS. Answer the…

1. Tell students to read the questions and answer choices silently.
2. Play the audio. Students circle the letter of the correct answers.
3. Students compare answers with a partner.
4. Ask about **register**: *How does Eva show that she understands that Sung is not well and feels sorry for her?* (She says, *I'm sorry to hear that* and *Take care of yourself.*) Write these two expressions on the board and have students repeat them after you.

Teaching Tip: Use the script

Optional: If students need additional support, tell them to read the Audio Script on page 271 as they listen to the conversations.

D ▶ EXPAND. Listen to the whole…

1. Read the directions. Tell students to read the questions and answer choices silently.
2. Play the audio. Students listen and answer the questions.
3. Ask: *Do you need to listen one more time?* If yes, play the audio again.
4. Call on students to ask and answer the questions.

Listening and Speaking

3 PRONUNCIATION

A ▶ PRACTICE. Listen to the sentences...

1. Read the Pronunciation Note.
2. Write the first sentence. Ask: *Where is the pause?* (between *sorry* and *to*) *What are the two thought groups?* (*I'm sorry* and *to hear that*) Read the sentence, pausing between the two thought groups, and ask the class to repeat.
3. Read the directions. Play the audio. Students listen. Then students listen and repeat.

 ActiveTeach for 3A: Pronunciation Coach

B ▶ APPLY. Listen. Draw lines to separate...

1. Read the directions. Show the sentences on the board.
2. Play the audio. Students listen and draw lines to separate the thought groups.
3. Ask: *Do you need to hear it again?* Play the audio again as needed.
4. Call on students to draw lines to separate thought groups in the sentences you wrote.
5. Say the first sentence. Emphasize the pauses. Ask students to repeat the sentence.
6. Repeat for the other sentences.

4 CONVERSATION

A ▶ LISTEN AND READ. Then listen and repeat.

1. Note: This conversation is the same one students heard in Exercise 2B on page 140.
2. Tell students to read the conversation. Tell them to find sentences similar to the examples and mark the pauses (*I can't come in / today; I have to / go to the doctor; Sorry / to hear that*).
3. While students are marking pauses, write the conversation. Ask students who have marked the pauses correctly to mark them on the board.
4. Say: *I'm going to read the conversation. Listen for one more pause to mark.* Point out that periods and commas also represent pauses, but that it's not necessary to mark them. Read the conversation, pausing between *today* and *because*. Ask the class where the pause was and mark it on the board.
5. Play the audio. Students listen and read silently. Pause the audio after *Thanks.* Tell students to practice pausing between thought groups. Resume the audio. Students listen and repeat. As needed, say the lines and ask students to repeat.

B ▶ WORK TOGETHER. Practice the...

1. Read the directions.
2. Model the conversation with two above-level students. Emphasize the pauses for sentences practiced in Exercise 4A.
3. Pair students. Walk around and check that students are using the correct pausing.

C CREATE. Make new conversations. Use the...

1. Tell students to look at the information in the boxes. Say each phrase or sentence and ask the class to repeat.
2. Point to the second blue phrase and ask: *Take who to the clinic?* (my son) *What pronoun goes with* my *son?* (he) Tell students to underline *my son, he,* and *he* in the second row in the boxes. Repeat with *my mother, she,* and *she* in the third row.
3. Ask two above-level students to practice a conversation in front of the class. Tell them to use their own names and information from the same row in the boxes to fill in the blanks. Walk around and make sure they are using the correct pronouns.
4. Call on pairs to perform for the class.

D ROLE-PLAY. Make your own conversations.

1. Brainstorm other situations and explanations with the class and write them.
2. Read the directions.
3. Play B and make up a conversation with an above-level student. Use the information you brainstormed. Prompt the student playing A to choose a yellow phrase from Exercise 4C and change the pronoun as needed.
4. Walk around and check that A uses a pronoun that matches B's information.
5. Call on pairs to role-play for the class.

Self-Directed Learning

Point out the blue bar. Ask students if they can do the lesson learning objective or if they need more practice. Tell them to check one of the boxes. Assign Extra Practice as needed.

Extra Practice

MyEnglishLab   Workbook **pp. 82–83**

Listening and Speaking

3 PRONUNCIATION

Using pauses

We use pauses to break sentences into smaller thought groups. These pauses make sentences easier to say and understand.

A ▶ PRACTICE. Listen to the sentences. Then listen and repeat.

I'm sorry / to hear that.
Do you think / you'll be in / tomorrow?
I have to / take my son / to the clinic.

B ▶ APPLY. Listen. Draw lines to separate the thought groups.

1. I can't come in today. I can't / come in / today.
2. She has an appointment. She has / an appointment.
3. Thanks for calling. Thanks / for calling.
4. Take care of yourself. Take care of / yourself.

4 CONVERSATION

A ▶ LISTEN AND READ. Then listen and repeat.

A: Hello. Eva Pérez speaking.
B: Hi, Eva. This is Sung. I can't come in today because I have to go to the doctor. I don't feel well.
A: Sorry to hear that. Thanks for calling, and take care of yourself.
B: Thanks.

B WORK TOGETHER. Practice the conversation in Exercise A.

C CREATE. Make new conversations. Use the words in the boxes.

A: Hello. _____ speaking.
B: Hi, _____. This is _____. I can't come in today because I have to _____. _____.
A: Sorry to hear that. Thanks for calling, and _____.
B: Thanks.

go to the dentist
take my son to the clinic
take care of my mother

I broke my tooth
He has a fever
She's sick

good luck
I hope he feels better
I hope she gets well soon

D ROLE-PLAY. Make your own conversations.

I can call in when I have to miss work. ■   I need more practice. ■

For more practice, go to MyEnglishLab.

Ways to express reasons		
Sung missed work yesterday	**because**	she didn't feel well.
She went to the doctor	**for**	a prescription.

Grammar Watch

- Use *because* + a subject and a verb.
- Use *for* + a noun.

A COMPLETE. Write *because* or *for*.

1. I can't go to work ___because___ I have a cold.
2. We have to go to the pharmacy ___for___ some medicine.
3. My co-worker is going to the doctor ___for___ a blood test.
4. Carlo went to the clinic ___because___ he hurt his back.
5. You went to the store ___for___ cold medicine.
6. Our supervisor wasn't at work yesterday ___because___ she had a fever.

B WRITE. Where do they have to go? Write one sentence with *because* and one with *for*. Use the words in parentheses.

1. (Jack / the pharmacy / some medicine)
   Jack has to go to the pharmacy because he needs some medicine.
   Jack has to go to the pharmacy for some medicine.

2. (Ping / the doctor / a flu shot)
   Ping has to go the doctor because she needs a flu shot.
   Ping has to go to the doctor for a flu shot.

3. (Grace / the dentist / a checkup)
   Grace has to go to the dentist because she needs a checkup.
   Grace has to go to the dentist for a checkup.

I can express reasons with *because* and *for*. ■   I need more practice. ■

For more practice, go to MyEnglishLab.

Correlations

ELPS Level 2: 10
CCRS Level A: L.1.1
CASAS Reading: RDG 1.7, 2.3
CASAS Listening: L4.1, 4.2
CASAS Competencies: 0.1.2
Complete standards language available on the Pearson English Portal.

Self-Directed Learning

State the **lesson objective.** Say: *In this lesson, we will learn to express reasons with* because *and* for.

Ways to express reasons

 ActiveTeach: Grammar Discovery

1. Warm up. Say: *The conversation on page 141 used this grammar.* Turn back to page 141. Point to the sentence in Exercise 4A and then write: *I can't come in today because I have to go to the doctor.*
2. Underline *because.*
3. Tell students to look at the grammar chart.
4. Show the grammar chart. Read the sentences. Ask: *Why did Sung miss work yesterday?* (because she didn't feel well) *Why did she go to the doctor?* (for a prescription) Explain: *Both sentences give reasons.*
5. Underline and read *she didn't feel well* and *a prescription.* Ask: *Which is a noun?* (a prescription) *Which is a subject and a verb?* (she didn't feel well)
6. Read the **Grammar Watch** note.
7. *Optional:* Review parts of speech. Read the first sentence in the grammar chart. Point to the underlined portion and ask: *What is the subject?* (she) *What is the verb?* (didn't feel) Read the second sentence. Point to the underlined portion. Circle *a* and say: *Nouns often have* a, an, *or* some *before them.*
8. Write: *He went to the doctor* because... and *He went to the doctor* for... Elicit several endings to each sentence and write them (for example, *because... he had chest pains / he sprained his ankle / he needed a prescription; for... a physical / eye drops / an X-ray*).

 ActiveTeach: Grammar Coach

 COMPLETE. Write *because* **or** *for.*

1. Read the directions and the example. Tell students to underline *I have a cold.* Ask: *Why is the answer* because? (because there's a subject and a verb in *I have a cold*)

2. Tell students to look at what comes after the blank in each sentence and decide whether it's a subject and a verb or a noun.
3. Students compare answers with a partner.
4. Call on students to say answers.
5. *Optional:* Tell students to read the sentences again and find the two items that match the picture. (items 1 and 5)

 WRITE. Where do they have to go? Write...

1. Read the directions.
2. Tell students to look at the items. To review the modal *have to,* ask where each person has to go. Elicit complete sentences (for example, T: *Where does Jack have to go?* S: *He has to go to the pharmacy.*).
3. Ask: *Are you going to write sentences in the simple past or the simple present?* (simple present)
4. Read the **Grammar Watch** note again. Write: *because* + *a subject and a verb.* Tell students to look at item 1. Read the example. Say: *Look at the part of the sentence after* because. *What's the subject?* (he) *Why* he? (he is the pronoun for *Jack*) *What's the verb?* (needs) *Why* need**s**? (with *he,* the simple present verb ends in *-s*)
5. Write: *for* + *a noun.* Ask the class to help write the second sentence for item 1. Write the answer.
6. Walk around and check that students add a subject and verb after *because* and use correct subject pronouns and subject–verb agreement.
7. Call on students to write answers on the board.

■ **EXPANSION: Grammar practice for B**

1. Write three new exercise items like the ones in Exercise B. Each item should include:
   - A person's name or a pronoun
   - Where the person has to go
   - What the person needs there
   For example: *Roberto / store / a swimsuit.*
2. Form groups of 3 and tell them to make sentences with *because* and *for.*
3. *Optional:* Above-level students create their own prompts, using the list above. Students exchange prompts and write sentences.

Self-Directed Learning

Point out the blue bar. Ask students if they can do the lesson learning objective or if they need more practice. Tell them to check one of the boxes. Assign Extra Practice as needed.

Extra Practice

MyEnglishLab	Workbook pp. 82–83

Self-Directed Learning

1. State the **lesson objective**. Say: *In this lesson, we will learn to give reasons in our writing.*
2. Say: *You will write about treating a health problem.*

1 STUDY THE MODEL

1. Read the directions.
2. Point to the paragraph. Ask: *What is the title of the model?* (Treating a Cough) Ask: *What does treat a cough mean?* Tell students to read the first sentence. Explain: *Treat means what you do to get better when you are sick.*
3. Tell students to read the text and the questions independently.
4. **Scaffold** the model. Write as a graphic organizer:

1	Health problem:	
	What he does	Why it helps
2	→	
3	→	
4	→	

5. Call on students to answer the questions. When students answer item 1, write: *A cough* next to *Health problem*.
6. As students answer items 2–4, write the answer to the first part of each item under the heading *What he does*. Write the answer to the second part of each item under the heading *Why it helps*.
7. Point out that the answers in the right column are the *reasons* that the writer does the things in the left column. Stress the word *reasons*.
8. Point to the **Writing Skill**. Call on a student to read it. Point out that sometimes what we do and the reason we do it are in different sentences as in the example in the **Writing Skill** box. Tell students to look at the second things Hasti does (wear a scarf). Ask: *Is the reason in the same sentence?* (yes) Point out that we can use *because* to add a reason to a sentence. Repeat for the third thing. (take medicine)

2 PLAN YOUR WRITING

1. Erase the information in the graphic organizer.
2. Read the directions.
3. Model with a student. The student asks the teacher the questions.
4. Write the information into the graphic organizer.
5. Tell students to make their own graphic organizer on a piece of paper.
6. Have students work in pairs to ask and answer questions to complete their graphic organizers.

3 WRITE

1. Read the directions aloud.
2. Tell students to use their information in the graphic organizer from Exercise 2 to write sentences.
3. As students write, circulate to make sure they are writing in paragraph form and using reasons.

 ActiveTeach for 3: Writing Support

4 CHECK YOUR WRITING

1. Read the directions. Point to the **Writing Checklist**. Call on students to read the checklist aloud.
2. Pair students to review their writings together. Say: *Read your sentences with a partner. Use the Writing Checklist.* For additional help, remind students that a correct sentence:
   - *begins with a capital letter*
   - *has a subject*
   - *has a verb*
   - *has a period*
   - *is a complete idea*
3. Walk around and verify that students are using the checklist. Collect the papers for review or put them in the students' writing portfolios.

Teaching Tip: Digital skills

Tell students that they can find a lot of information about health conditions and how to treat them online. Suggest students use their phones to research the health problem they are writing about.

Self-Directed Learning

Point out the blue bar. Ask students if they can do the lesson learning objective or if they need more practice. Tell them to check one of the boxes. Assign Extra Practice as needed.

Extra Practice

 CCRS Plus   p. 84

Write about treating a health problem

1 STUDY THE MODEL

READ. Answer the questions.

Hasti Kumar

Treating a Cough

There are three things I do when I have a cough. I drink a lot of hot tea. The tea relaxes my chest. Also, I wear a scarf because it keeps my chest warm. I take cough medicine at night. It helps me sleep. I usually feel better in a couple of days.

1. What is Hasti's health problem?
2. What does Hasti drink? Why?
3. What does Hasti wear? Why?
4. What medicine does Hasti take? Why?

1. He has a cough.
2. He drinks hot tea because it relaxes his chest.
3. He wears a scarf because it keeps his chest warm.
4. He takes cough medicine because it helps him sleep.

2 PLAN YOUR WRITING

WORK TOGETHER. Ask and answer the questions.

1. Think of a health problem. What is it?
2. What's one thing you do to get better? Why?
3. What's another thing you do to get better? Why?
4. What's one more thing you do to get better? Why?

3 WRITE

Write about how you treat a health problem. Use the model, the Writing Skill, and your ideas from Exercise 2 to help you.

4 CHECK YOUR WRITING

WORK TOGETHER. Read the checklist. Read your writing aloud. Revise your writing.

Writing Skill: Give a reason

Give a reason why you do something. For example:

I drink a lot of hot tea. (The tea relaxes my chest.)

WRITING CHECKLIST

☐ The paragraph answers the questions in Exercise 2.

☐ There is a topic sentence.

☐ There is a reason for each thing the writer does.

I can give reasons in my writing. ■   I need more practice. ■

For more practice, go to MyEnglishLab.

Lesson 11 Respect others

1 MEET BELVIE

Read about one of her
workplace skills.

> I show respect for others. For example,
> I respect my co-workers' needs, and I
> try not to cause problems for them.

2 BELVIE'S PROBLEM

READ. Circle *True* or *False*.

Belvie works at a factory. She is ready to start work,
but she suddenly feels very sick. Belvie thinks she
has the flu. She can work today, but then she will
probably give the flu to her co-workers. She can go
home, but then she will lose a day's pay.

1. Belvie is late for work.   True   (False)
2. Belvie probably has the flu.   (True)   False
3. Belvie might make her co-workers sick. (True)   False

3 BELVIE'S SOLUTION

**WORK TOGETHER. Belvie shows respect for others. What does she do?
Explain your answers.**

1. Belvie starts to work. She doesn't say that she is sick.
2. Belvie tells her supervisor that she's sick. Then she goes home.
3. Belvie starts to work. She tells everyone she's sick.
4. Belvie _____.

Show what you know!

1. **THINK ABOUT IT.** Do you respect others? How do you show respect for others
   in class? At work? At home? Give examples.

2. **WRITE ABOUT IT.** Write an example in your Skills Log.

   *I show respect for others in class. For example, I turn off my phone during class.
   I don't want someone to call me and interrupt the class.*

I can give an example of how I show respect for others. ■

Unit Review: Go back to page 125. Which unit goals can you check off?

Correlations

CASAS Reading: RDG 1.7, 1.8, 3.2
CASAS Listening: L2.1, 2.3, 4.1, 4.2
CASAS Competencies: 0.1.2, 0.1.4, 0.1.5, 0.1.6, 0.2.1, 4.8.5, 7.3.2
Complete standards language available on the Pearson English Portal.

Self-Directed Learning

State the **lesson objective**. Say: *In this lesson, we will give an example of how we show respect for others.*

1 MEET BELVIE

1. Ask: *What is the title of this lesson?* (Respect others) Ask: *What does* respect others *mean?* (treat people well, be polite and listen to them)
2. Write: *Workplace Skill*. Read the directions. Say: *Listen as I read* Meet Belvie. Read the paragraph. Ask: *What is one of Belvie's workplace skills?* (She respects others.) Next to *Workplace Skill*, write: *Respect others*.
3. Under *Workplace Skill*, write: *Examples*. Ask: *How does Belvie respect others?* (She respects co-workers' needs. She tries not to cause problems for them.) Write the examples. Elicit other ways to respect others and write them under *Workplace Skill*.

2 BELVIE'S PROBLEM

1. Say: *Now we are going to read about Belvie at work. Listen while I read.* Read the first sentence. Use the photo and the **Career Awareness** information to help students understand her job. Say: *Look at the photo. Where is Belvie?* (factory) *What is she doing?* (She is sewing / making a product / operating equipment.)
2. Say: *Belvie has a problem at work. Listen while I read.* Read the rest of the paragraph. Explain any unfamiliar vocabulary as needed.
3. Students complete the questions after the reading. Call on students to answer. Ask them to **cite evidence**: *Where is that information?*
4. Ask: *What is Belvie's problem?* (Belvie could make her co-workers sick.)

Career Awareness: Factory worker

Factory workers help to make products in a factory. Specific duties include working on an assembly line and operating machinery. No formal education is required.

3 BELVIE'S SOLUTION

1. Read the directions. Ask students to work together. Walk around and check that students understand that only one solution is correct.
2. Ask: *Is #1 a good way to respect others?* (no) *Why not?* (She could make her co-workers sick.) Ask: *Is #2 a good way to respect others?* (yes) *Why?* (She goes home after talking to her supervisor.) Ask: *Is #3 a good way to respect others?* (no) *Why not?* (She could make her co-workers sick.)
3. Ask students if they have any other ideas. Write their responses. Ask: *Is this a good way to respect others? Why?*

 ActiveTeach for 3: Academic Conversation Support

Workplace Culture

1. Say: *In the U.S., some employers—not all—give their workers sick leave. Workers get paid when they are too sick to come to work.*
2. Ask: *In your native country, do most employers give sick leave?*

Show what you know!

1. THINK ABOUT IT. Do you respect others?...

Read the directions. Have students think about their answers for a few minutes. Then ask them to share with a partner. Call on students to share with the class.

2. WRITE ABOUT IT. Write an example in your...

Read the directions and the example. Have students write their examples in their **Skills Log** at the back of the book. Circulate and assist students as needed.

Self-Directed Learning

1. Point out the blue bar. Ask students if they can do the lesson learning objective or if they need more practice. Tell them to check one of the boxes. Assign Extra Practice as needed.
2. Ask students to turn to page 125. Go to the Unit Wrap-Up teaching notes on page T-125.

Extra Practice

 p. 85

8 Job Hunting

Unit Overview

Goals
- See the list of goals on the facing page

Pronunciation
- Pronunciation of *can* and *can't*
- Intonation of questions with *or*

Reading
- Read about jobs in the U.S.
- Predict the topic

Grammar
- *Can* to express ability
- Time expressions with *ago, last, in,* and *later*
- Ways to express alternatives: *or, and*

Writing
- Write about your job history
- Use the correct tense

Document Literacy and Numeracy
- Interpret a timeline
- Interpret a bar graph

Workplace, Life, and Community Skills
- Read help wanted ads
- Identify job requirements
- Digital Skills: Search for a job posting website

Life Skills Writing
- Complete a job application

Soft Skills at Work
- Be honest

Preview

1. Set the context of the unit by asking questions about jobs (for example, *Do you have a job? What jobs did you have in the past?*).
2. Show the Unit Opener. Ask: *What is the unit title?* (Job Hunting)
3. Say: *Look at the picture.* Ask the Preview questions. (Possible answers: men talking in an office; a job interview)
4. Write the answers.

Unit Goals

1. Point to the Unit Goals. Explain that this list shows what you will be studying in this unit.
2. Tell students to read the goals silently.
3. Say each goal. Explain unfamiliar vocabulary as needed.
4. Point to the ☐ next to the first goal. Say: *We will come back to this page again. You will write a checkmark next to the goals you learned in the unit.*

Oral Presentation

1. Tell students they will give a short presentation at the end of the unit.
2. Write the topics:
   Option 1: How to find a job
   Option 2: A job you want in the future
3. Assign the topics to two students.

Unit Wrap-Up

1. Review the Unit Goals with students.
2. Direct students to the Grammar Review.
3. If you assigned presentations, ask students to present.

 ActiveTeach for Wrap-Up: Team Project

 ActiveTeach for Wrap-Up: Persistence Activities

8 Job Hunting

PREVIEW

Look at the picture. What do you see?
What's happening?

UNIT GOALS

- [ ] Identify job titles and duties
- [ ] Talk about your job skills
- [ ] Read help-wanted ads
- [ ] Identify job requirements
- [ ] Answer questions about work history
- [ ] Answer questions about availability
- [ ] **Academic skill:** Predict the topic
- [ ] **Writing skill:** Use the correct tense
- [ ] **Workplace soft skill:** Show how you are honest

145

Vocabulary

Job titles and duties

Ⓐ **PREDICT.** Look at the pictures. What do you see? What are the jobs? What do the people do in each job?

Ⓑ ▶ **LISTEN AND POINT.** Then listen and repeat.

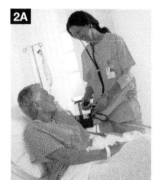

Correlations

ELPS Level 2: 2, 3, 7, 8, 9

CCRS Level A: SL.1.1, SL.K.6, L.1.5, L.1.6

CASAS Reading: RDG 1.7, 2.3

CASAS Listening: L2.1, 2.3, 2.9, 4.2, 5.8

CASAS Competencies: 0.1.2, 0.1.5, 4.4.4, 7.1.1, 7.4.1

Complete standards language available on the Pearson English Portal.

Self-Directed Learning

State the **lesson objective**. Say: *In this lesson, we will learn to identify job titles and duties.*

A **PREDICT. Look at the pictures. What do...**

1. Tell students to cover the list on page 147. Read the first three questions in the directions: *Look at the pictures. What do you see? What are the jobs?*

2. Point to each set of pictures. Ask: *What are your ideas?* The photos do not always provide enough information to answer with certainty, but encourage students to take guesses (for example, for picture 1, elicit: *someone who works with computers*). You can also ask about where the people are working (for example, for picture 2, *someone who works in a hospital*).

3. Number from 1 to 7 on the board. Say each job title on page 147 in random order. Tell students to match the job titles with the pairs of pictures.

4. As students call out answers, write them: *1. computer system administrator; 2. nursing assistant; 3. warehouse worker; 4. stock clerk; 5. receptionist; 6. food service worker; 7. manager.* Help students pronounce the jobs if they have difficulty.

5. If students call out an incorrect job, ask a *yes/no* clarification question: *Is number 5 is a manager?*

6. Point to each pair of pictures, say the job, and ask the class to repeat again.

7. Ask: *What do the people do in each job? What are their duties?*

8. Brainstorm duties and write them next to the jobs on the board. (Phrase the duties in the same way as the job duties listed on page 147, beginning with the base form of a verb.) Try to brainstorm at least one duty for each job. For example, for picture 6, elicit: *wash dishes, make food*.

B ▶ **LISTEN AND POINT. Then listen and...**

1. Read the directions. Play the audio. Students listen and point to the jobs.

2. While the audio is playing, walk around and check that students are pointing to the correct jobs. Pause the audio after item 7B.

3. Say each job in random order and ask students to point to the appropriate picture.

4. Tell students to look at page 147. Resume the audio. Students listen, read, and repeat.

 ActiveTeach for B: Vocabulary Flashcards

Teaching Tip: Check comprehension

To make sure students are connecting the new words with their meanings, tell them to point to the pictures as they listen / listen and repeat.

Vocabulary

C IDENTIFY. Student A, say a job title. Student…

1. Read the directions. Ask two on-level students to read the example.
2. Ask an above-level student to stand up and play Speaker A. Tell the class that they are Speaker B. The above-level student says a few jobs and the class calls out the corresponding duties.
3. Pair students. Tell them to take turns playing Speakers A and B.
4. To wrap up, say each pair of job duties and ask the class to call out the job.

D EXTEND. Think of jobs. Write the job duties.

1. Read the directions. Say: *A duty of many jobs is to assist people. Who do you assist at a job?* Ask a student to read the first example.
2. Say: *A duty of many jobs is to clean things. What do you clean at a job?* Ask a student to read the second example.
3. Write the verbs on the board. Check answers by saying: *A duty of many jobs is to [greet] people. Who do you [greet] at a job?* Write students' answers next to the verbs.

Study Tip: Make connections

1. Provide each student with seven index cards or tell students to cut up notebook paper into seven pieces.
2. Point to the **Study Tip**. Draw two rectangles on the board representing the two sides of a card. Write a job duty in one and the corresponding job in the other.
3. Walk around as students work. If misspellings occur, tell them to check the list on page 147.
4. Say: *You can learn new words by pairing them with related words.* Remind students to use this strategy to remember other new vocabulary.

Show what you know!

1. THINK ABOUT IT. What job do you want in…

1. Tell students to look at the list of job duties in Exercise D and underline the duties they would like in a job.
2. Read the directions.
3. As a model, write the job title you would like to have in five years' time and three duties on the board and read them.
4. Tell students to choose a job from the list on page 147 or a different job. Say: *To get an idea of what job you would enjoy, look at the duties you underlined or we listed on the board.*
5. Walk around and help students who choose a different job.

2. WRITE ABOUT IT. Now write about the job…

1. Read the directions and the example. Tell students to write three sentences about their job.
2. Share the checklist below. Then write a checkmark next to each as you point back to the example sentence.
   - Each sentence starts with a capital letter.
   - Each sentence describes a different job duty.
   - Each sentence ends with a period.
3. Give students time to write their sentences.
4. Tell students to show their sentences to a partner. Tell the students to use the checklist to review the sentences.
5. Walk around and verify that students are using the checklist. Collect the papers for review or put them in the students' writing portfolios.

3. PRESENT IT. Tell your classmates about the…

1. Read the directions.
2. Model the activity. Tell the class about the job you want to have in five years' time. Point to the job title and duties that you wrote on the board in Step 1. Say: *The job I would like to have in five years' time is… The duties are…*
3. Call on students to tell the class about the jobs they want to have.

Self-Directed Learning

Point out the blue bar. Ask students if they can do the lesson learning objective or if they need more practice. Tell them to check one of the boxes. Assign Extra Practice as needed.

Extra Practice

  pp. 86–87

Vocabulary

Job titles and duties

1. computer system administrator
   A install computer systems
   B problem solve

2. nursing assistant
   A take care of patients
   B record patient information

3. warehouse worker
   A receive shipments
   B unload materials

4. stock clerk
   A assist customers
   B stock shelves

5. receptionist
   A greet visitors
   B handle phone calls

6. food service worker
   A prepare food
   B clean kitchen equipment

7. manager
   A supervise employees
   B plan work schedules

C IDENTIFY. Student A, say a job title. Student B, say the job duties for that job.

A: Manager.
B: Plan work schedules. Supervise employees.

D EXTEND. Think of jobs. Write the job duties.

assist: _visitors, patients_
clean: _the dishes, the floor_
greet: _____
handle: _____
install: _____

prepare: _____
record: _____
stock: _____
supervise: _____
unload: _____

Study Tip

Make connections
Make cards for job duties. Write a job title on the front of the card. Write two job duties of that job on the back.

Show what you know!

1. **THINK ABOUT IT.** What job do you want in five years? What are the job duties?

   Job title: _____

   Job duties: _____   _____   _____

2. **WRITE ABOUT IT.** Now write about the job you want.

   A medical assistant takes care of patients.

3. **PRESENT IT.** Tell your classmates about the job you want.

   I want to be a medical assistant. A medical assistant takes care of patients.

I can identify job titles and duties. ■   I need more practice. ■

1 BEFORE YOU LISTEN

A LABEL. Write the words under the pictures.

operate a forklift   speak Spanish   use a computer
order supplies   use a cash register   work as a team

1. _operate a forklift_

2. _use a computer_

3. _use a cash register_

4. _order supplies_

5. _work as a team_

6. _speak Spanish_

2 LISTEN

A PREDICT. Look at the picture. Who is the supervisor?
a. Albert   **b.** Manny

B ▶ **LISTEN FOR MAIN IDEA.** Complete the sentence.

Manny is at the store _____.
a. to buy something   **b.** for a job interview

C ▶ **LISTEN FOR DETAILS.** Complete the sentences.

1. Albert is a _____.
   a. salesperson   **b.** store manager

2. Albert asks about Manny's _____.
   a. job duties   **b.** customer experience

3. Manny assists customers and _____ at his job.
   a. stocks shelves   **b.** orders supplies

D ▶ **EXPAND.** Listen to the whole conversation. Complete the sentence.

Manny _____ use a cash register.
a. can   **b.** can't

Correlations

ELPS Level 2: 2, 7
CCRS Level A: SL.K.3
CASAS Reading: RDG 1.7, 2.3
CASAS Listening: L1.4, 2.1, 2.3, 4.2, 6.1, 6.2, 6.5
CASAS Competencies: 0.1.2, 0.1.5, 4.1.5
Complete standards language available on the Pearson English Portal.

Self-Directed Learning

State the **lesson objective**. Say: *In this lesson, we will learn to talk about our skills at a job interview.*

1 BEFORE YOU LISTEN

LABEL. Write the words under the pictures.

1. Say: *Let's talk about skills you can use in different jobs.* Say the words and phrases in the box and ask the class to repeat.
2. Act out each skill in random order. As you act, talk about what you're doing. For example, sit down at your computer and say: *I'm writing a letter.* Tell the class to call out the skill (*use a computer*).
3. Read the directions. Give students time to label the pictures.
4. Ask: *Which picture shows a man driving a forklift truck?* Students call out the number of the picture.
5. Repeat for the remaining words in the box.
6. Talk about your skills. Say: *I can... I can't...*
7. Tell students to circle the skills they have. Pair students to compare their skills.
8. For each skill, ask the class: *Who can (operate a forklift)?* Ask for a show of hands.

▪▪ **EXPANSION: Vocabulary and writing for 1**

1. Ask students to look at the job titles and duties on page 147 and circle the skills they have.
2. Tell student to write a list of their skills, using the vocabulary from pages 147 and 148.
3. Say: *Exchange lists with a partner. Read your partner's list and suggest a job for him or her. You can say:* I think _____ is a good job for you.

2 LISTEN

A PREDICT. **Look at the picture. Who is the...**

1. Tell students to look at the picture. Ask: *Where are they?* (at work, in an office). *What are they doing?* (smiling, talking, shaking hands)
2. Ask: *Who do you think is the supervisor?*

B ▶ LISTEN FOR MAIN IDEA. **Complete the...**

1. Read the directions. Have students read the sentence and answer choices silently.
2. Play the audio. Students listen and complete the sentence.
3. Elicit the correct answer from the class.
4. Ask: *Who is the supervisor?* (Albert) *Was your guess in Exercise 2A correct?* Ask for a show of hands.
5. Ask about **register**: *Do they know each other?* (no) *How do you know?* (Albert introduces himself.)

C ▶ LISTEN FOR DETAILS. **Complete the...**

1. Read the directions. Tell students to read the sentences and answer choices silently.
2. Play the audio. Students circle the letter of the correct answer.
3. Students compare answers with a partner.
4. Call on students to read their completed sentences.
5. **Extend:** Ask: *What does Albert have in his hand?* (Manny's application) To review, ask: *What are Manny's duties in the job he has now?* (assist customers, stock shelves) Tell students to look at the list of job duties on page 147. Ask: *What is Manny's current job?* (sales associate / stock clerk)

Teaching Tip: Use the script

Optional: If students need additional support, tell them to read the Audio Script on page 271 as they listen to the conversations.

D ▶ EXPAND. **Listen to the whole...**

1. Read the directions and play the audio.
2. Ask: *Do you need to listen one more time?* If yes, play the audio again.
3. Review the correct answer with the class.

Workplace Culture

1. Tell students to look at the picture of Albert and Manny and to describe it.
2. Say: *The following are useful tips for a job interview in the U.S.*
   - *Wear formal clothes. Look neat and clean. It is important to dress professionally.*
   - *Make good eye contact. In the U.S., making good eye contact shows confidence.*
   - *Shake hands firmly at the beginning and end of the interview.*
3. Ask: *Are there any special tips for a job interview in your native country?*

Listening and Speaking

3 PRONUNCIATION

A ▶ PRACTICE. Listen. Then listen and repeat.

1. Read the first bullet of the **Pronunciation Note**.
2. Tell students to look at the sentences and underline *can*. Write the three sentences with *can*. Point to *can* in each sentence and ask: *Does another word come after it? I can learn* and *Can you speak Chinese?* Label *can* in these sentences: *weak*.
3. Read the second bullet of the **Pronunciation Note**. Point to *Yes, I can* on the board. Ask: *Does* can *have a weak or a strong pronunciation?* Label *can* in this sentence: *strong*.
4. Read the last bullet of the **Pronunciation Note**. Write *I can't use a cash register*. Underline *can't*. Ask: *Does it have a weak or a strong pronunciation?* Label *can't*: *strong*.
5. Play the audio. Students listen. Then students listen and repeat.

> **ActiveTeach for 3A: Pronunciation Coach**

B ▶ CHOOSE. Listen. Circle *can* when it has...

1. Read the directions. Tell students to read the sentences. Elicit where they predict *can* will have a strong pronunciation.
2. Play the audio. Students circle *can* when it has a strong pronunciation.
3. Review the correct answers with students. Ask: *Were your guesses correct?*

4 CONVERSATION

A ▶ LISTEN AND READ. Then listen and repeat.

1. Note: This conversation is the same one students heard in Exercise 2D on page 148.
2. Tell students to read the conversation and underline *can* and *can't*. Tell students to read the **Pronunciation Note** again and label each *can* or *can't* they underlined *weak* or *strong*.
3. Play the audio. Students read along silently. Then students listen and repeat.
4. Walk around and help with pronunciation as needed. Pay particular attention to the students' pronunciation of *can* and *can't*.

B WORK TOGETHER. Practice the...

1. Pair students and tell them to practice the conversation in Exercise 4A.
2. Tell students to take turns playing A and B. Walk around and check that students are using the correct pronunciation of *can* and *can't*.

C CREATE. Make new conversations. Use the...

1. Read the directions.
2. Tell students to look at the information in the boxes. Say the duties/skills in each row and ask the class to repeat. At the end of each row, ask: *What job are these duties/skills for?* (row 1: warehouse worker; row 2: receptionist; row 3: food service worker)
3. Ask two above-level students to make up a new conversation using information from the boxes.
4. Tell pairs to take turns playing A and B and to use information from the same row in the boxes to fill in the blanks.
5. Tell students to stand, mingle, and practice the conversation with several new partners.
6. Walk around and check that students correctly substitute names and information into the conversation. Listen for correct pronunciation of *can* and *can't* in the last two lines of the conversation.

D ROLE-PLAY. Make your own conversations.

1. Model the activity. Write a job from the list on page 147. Ask: *What are three duties/skills for this job?* Write the duties/skills.
2. Label the first two duties/skills on the board: *B*. Label the last duty/skill: *A*.
3. Model a conversation with an above-level student.
4. Tell students to choose a job they would like from the list on page 147 or a different job. Tell them to note three duties/skills for the job. Direct them to label the first two duties/skills: *B* and the last duty/skill: *A*.
5. Pair students and tell them to practice the conversation.
6. Walk around and check that students correctly substitute names and information into the conversation. Listen for correct pronunciation of *can* and *can't* in the last two lines of the conversation.
7. Call on pairs to perform for the class. Ask the class to listen and guess the job that B is applying for.

Self-Directed Learning

Point out the blue bar. Ask students if they can do the lesson learning objective or if they need more practice. Tell them to check one of the boxes. Assign Extra Practice as needed.

> **Extra Practice**
>
>   pp. 88–89

Listening and Speaking

3 PRONUNCIATION

A ▶ PRACTICE. Listen. Then listen and repeat.

I can't use a cash register.   I can learn.
Can you speak Chinese?   Yes, I can.

B ▶ CHOOSE. Listen. Circle *can* when it has a strong pronunciation.

1. I can't plan work schedules.
2. Can you handle phone calls?
3. Yes, I can.
4. My manager can supervise employees.

4 CONVERSATION

A ▶ LISTEN AND READ. Then listen and repeat.

A: Manny? Hi, I'm Albert Taylor, the store manager. Please have a seat.
B: Thank you. It's nice to meet you.
A: I have your application here. I see that you're working now. What are your job duties?
B: Well, I assist customers and stock shelves.
A: OK. Tell me about your skills. Can you use a cash register?
B: No, I can't, but I can learn.

B WORK TOGETHER. Practice the conversation in Exercise A.

C CREATE. Make new conversations. Use the words in the boxes.

A: _____? Hi, I'm _____, the
store manager. Please have a seat.
B: Thank you. It's nice to meet you.
A: I have your application here. I see that
you're working now. What are your job
duties?
B: Well, I _____ and _____.
A: OK. Tell me more about your skills. Can
you _____?
B: No, I can't, but I can learn.

receive shipments	unload materials	operate a forklift
greet visitors	handle phone calls	use a computer
prepare food	clean equipment	order supplies

D ROLE-PLAY. Make your own conversations.

> **Pronunciation of *can* and *can't***
>
> - *Can* often has a weak pronunciation when another word comes after it. It sounds like "c'n" because "a" becomes short and quiet.
> - *Can* has a strong pronunciation at the end of a sentence.
> - *Can't* always has a strong pronunciation.

I can talk about my skills at a job interview. ■   I need more practice. ■

For more practice, go to MyEnglishLab.

Grammar

Can to express ability

Can to express ability					
Affirmative			**Negative**		
I			I		
She	**can**	stock shelves.	She	**cannot**	speak Chinese.
They			They	**can't**	

Yes/No questions				**Short answers**	
Can	you	**use**	a cash register?	**Yes**, I can.	**No**, I can't.

Grammar Watch

- Use *can* + the base form of the verb.
- *Can't = cannot*. We use *can't* more often.

A **WRITE. Look at the pictures. Write one question for each picture. Use *can*.** *(Answers will vary.)*

1. <u>*Can Pat lift heavy boxes?*</u>
2. <u>Can Pat use a computer?</u>

3. <u>Can Mike operate a forklift?</u>
4. <u>Can Mike fix the sink?</u>

5. <u>Can Paco and Lisa fix the computer?</u>
6. <u>Can Paco and Lisa fix the cash register?</u>

B **WORK TOGETHER. Ask and answer the questions in Exercise A.**

A: Can Pat lift heavy boxes?
B: No, she can't.

Correlations

ELPS Level 2: 2, 7
CASAS Reading: RDG 1.7, L3.1
CASAS Listening: L1.3, 2.1, 2.3, 4.1, 4.2
CASAS Competencies: 0.1.2, 0.1.5, 0.2.1, 3.1.2
Complete standards language available on the Pearson English Portal.

Language Note

Ask: *What is the negative of* can? Elicit and write *can't* and *cannot.* Say: *Use* can't *in informal conversation:* I can't go to the party. *In more formal speech and writing, don't use abbreviations.* Write: *The president cannot / can not attend the event.* Point to *cannot* and say: *Both spellings are correct, but* cannot *as one word is more usual.*

Self-Directed Learning

State the **lesson objective**. Say: *In this lesson, we will learn to use* can *to express ability.*

Can to express ability

 ActiveTeach: Grammar Discovery

1. Warm up. Say: *The conversation on page 149 used this grammar.* Turn back to page 149. Point to the sentences in Exercise 4A and then write:
   - *Can you use a cash register?*
   - *No, I can't, but I can learn.*
2. Underline the words *can, can't,* and *can.*
3. Tell students to look at the grammar charts. Point to the top grammar chart. Read the sentences and ask the class to repeat.
4. Read the first point of the **Grammar Watch** note aloud and ask the class to read along silently.
5. Write: *I can speak English.* Underline *can* and *speak* and say: *Use* can + *the base form of a verb.*
6. Read the second point of the **Grammar Watch** note aloud. Point to the sentence *I can speak English* on the board and elicit two ways to make it negative. Write: *I can't speak English. / I cannot speak English.* Ask: *Which do we use more often?* (*I can't speak English.*)
7. Point to the bottom grammar chart. Read the question and answers. Tell the class to repeat.
8. Point to the sentence *I can speak English* and ask the class to make a *yes/no* question.
9. Write: *Can you speak English?* Ask a few students the question and elicit the short answer: *Yes, I can.* Ask a few students: *Can your mother / father / grandparents speak English?* to elicit the short answer: *No, she / he / they can't.*

 ActiveTeach: Grammar Coach

A WRITE. **Look at the pictures. Write one…**
1. Read the directions and the example.
2. Elicit another question for item 2: *Can Pat type / use a computer?*
3. Remind students to use the base form of the verb and to begin each question with a capital *C* and end with a question mark.
4. Walk around and help with vocabulary and spelling as needed. Check that students form *yes/no* questions correctly.

EXPANSION: Grammar and speaking practice for A
1. Tell students to change the subject of the questions in Exercise A to *you.*
2. Direct pairs to ask each other the questions in Exercise A (for example, A: *Can you lift heavy boxes?* B: *Yes, I can.*).

B WORK TOGETHER. **Ask and answer the…**
1. Read the directions.
2. Play Speaker A and model the example with an above-level student. Model continuing the activity by asking another question: *Can Pat type?* Elicit the short answer: *Yes, she can.*
3. Pair students. Walk around and check Student B's use of pronouns.
4. Call on three pairs to ask and answer the questions for the class. Make corrections as necessary.

MULTILEVEL INSTRUCTION FOR B
Cross-ability Direct the pre-level student to play the role of Speaker A first so that he or she has the short answers modeled before having to produce them.

C INTEPRET. **Look at Amy's job application...**

1. Read the directions.
2. Tell students to look at the job application. Say the skills and ask the class to repeat. Explain unfamiliar vocabulary. Say: Sort materials *means organize them. For example, a warehouse worker puts boxes that are going to New York, Philadelphia, and Washington, D.C., in different areas of the warehouse.* To illustrate, draw boxes labeled *NYC, Phila.,* and *D.C.* in three separate areas on the board.
3. Tell students to look at the example. Read A's question. Tell students to point to *use a computer* on the application. Ask: *Did Amy check* use a computer? (yes) *Can she help with computer problems?* (no)
4. Pair students. Say: *One partner asks questions about Amy's office skills. The other partner asks questions about Amy's warehouse skills.*
5. Call on one pair to ask and answer questions about Amy's office skills. Call on another pair to ask and answer questions about Amy's warehouse skills.

D WRITE. **Make sentences about Amy's skills...**

1. Read the directions. Tell students to write one sentence for each skill on the application.
2. Remind students to use the base form of the verbs. Remind them to begin each sentence with a capital letter and end with a period.
3. Walk around and spot-check students' grammar and punctuation.

■ EXPANSION: Pronunciation practice for D

1. Pair students and direct them to take turns reading the sentences in Exercise D out loud. Tell them to practice the weak pronunciation of *can* and the strong pronunciation of *can't.*
2. Walk around and monitor students' pronunciation. Model as needed.

E MAKE CONNECTIONS. **Describe your skills...**

1. Read the directions.
2. Tell students to look at the application and check the skills they have. Direct them to make their checkmarks to the right of each skill.
3. Model the activity by writing one sentence about your skills on the board (for example, *I can use a computer.*).
4. Check answers by surveying the class. Ask about each of the skills (for example, *Who can help with computer problems?*). Students raise their hands and say *I can.*

Show what you know!

1. **THINK ABOUT IT. Complete the questions.**

1. Read the directions.
2. Tell students to choose three skills and complete the questions in the chart. Tell them to look at the vocabulary on pages 147 and 148 and Amy's application for ideas.
3. Show the chart on the board. Ask for ideas for completing the questions. Write three of them in the chart.

2. **TALK ABOUT IT. Interview each member of...**

1. Read the directions.
2. Use the chart on the board to model the activity. Ask three students the questions on the chart (one question each). Record the students' names and answers.
3. Form groups of 4. Direct students to ask each partner one question. Remind students to use short answers: *Yes, I can* or *No, I can't.*

3. **WRITE ABOUT IT. Now write one sentence...**

1. Read the directions.
2. Use the chart on the board to model the activity. Point to each row of the chart and write a sentence with *can* or *can't* about the student's skills.
3. Ask students to check each other's sentences.
   • There should be a sentence about all members of the group.
   • Sentences should use *can* or *can't.*
   • Sentences should use the base form of the verb.
4. Call on students to talk about their group's job skills.

Self-Directed Learning

Point out the blue bar. Ask students if they can do the lesson learning objective or if they need more practice. Tell them to check one of the boxes. Assign Extra Practice as needed.

Extra Practice
MyEnglishLab   Workbook pp. 88–89

Grammar

C **INTERPRET. Look at Amy's job application. Ask and answer questions about her skills. Use *can*.**

A: Can Amy help with computer problems?
B: No, she can't.

○○○

Amy Ruiz

Please check the skills you have.

Office skills
○ help with computer problems
● use a computer
● record information

Warehouse skills
○ operate a forklift
● sort materials
○ lift up to 50 lbs.

D **WRITE. Make sentences about Amy's skills. Use *can* and *can't*.**

1. Amy can't help with computer problems.
2. Amy can use a computer.
3. Amy can record information.
4. Amy can't operate a forklift.
5. Amy can sort materials.
6. Amy can't lift up to 50 lbs.

E **MAKE CONNECTIONS. Describe your skills. Use *can* and *can't*.**

1. _____
2. _____
3. _____
4. _____

Show what you know!

1. THINK ABOUT IT. Complete the questions.

Question	Name	Answer
Can you use a computer?	Paola	Yes
1. Can you _____?		
2. Can you _____?		
3. Can you _____?		

2. TALK ABOUT IT. Interview each member of your group. Ask questions and complete the chart.

3. WRITE ABOUT IT. Now write one sentence about each person's skills.

Paola can use a computer.

I can use *can* to express ability. ■
I need more practice. ■

For more practice, go to MyEnglishLab.

1 READ HELP WANTED ADS

A **IDENTIFY.** Read the help wanted ads. Where can you find these ads? Where else can people find out about jobs?

Job-ads.com

Home Job Listings Post Resume Career Advice Help

CAR SERVICE DRIVERS NEEDED

Job description: Drivers for evening and weekend airport car service. Experience: 1 year of driving service. Part-time. Pay: $12/hr. For more information, and to apply, please send a letter of interest to Jonna Kern at jkern@carservice.org

Career.com

Home | Post My Resume | Job Listings | Resource Center | Help

Office Assistant

Responsibilities: handle phone calls, greet visitors, and organize customer files. Preferred experience: 1 year of working in a busy office environment and formal training in computer application software. Class and hours: Full-time, M-F, 8 am-5 pm. Health benefits. Required materials: Cover letter, résumé, and list of references. Send to: erinhubs@hroffice.com. For full consideration, apply by 1/31.

B **MATCH.** Connect the sentence parts.

1. _g_ A full-time employee works
2. _d_ Responsibilities are
3. _b_ A résumé includes
4. _e_ A cover letter is
5. _f_ Experience is
6. _a_ References are
7. _c_ Health benefits are

a. people who can describe you and your work.
b. a list of your job experiences and skills.
c. when your company pays some of your health insurance.
d. the activities and things you will do at a job.
e. a way to introduce yourself to your future employer.
f. your past work activities.
g. 40 hours a week.

C **INTERPRET.** Read the ads again. Answer the questions.

1. Which job is full-time? Office assistant.
2. What should someone do to apply for the car service driver position? They should send an email or a letter of interest.
3. Which job requires evening and weekend work? Car service driver.
4. What is the pay for Car Service Drivers? $12/hr.
5. What are the responsibilities of an office assistant? The office assistant handles phone calls, greets visitors, and organizes customer files.
6. What kind of experience is preferred for the Office Assistant position? One year of working in a busy office and computer software training.
7. When does the Office Assistant need to be able to work? Mondays–Fridays, 8 A.M.–5 P.M.

I can read help wanted ads. ■	I need more practice. ■

Correlations

ELPS Level 2: 1, 2, 3, 4, 5, 6, 7, 8, 9, 10
CCRS Level A: W.1.7, W.1.8
CASAS Reading: RDG 1.7, 1.8, 2.2, 2.3, 3.2
CASAS Listening: L2.1, 2.3, 4.2, 5.4, 5.5
CASAS Competencies: 0.1.2, 0.1.5, 4.1.3, 4.1.5, 4.5.6, 7.4.4, 7.7.3
Complete standards language available on the Pearson English Portal.

Self-Directed Learning

State the **lesson objective**. Say: *In this lesson, we will learn to read help wanted ads and identify job requirements.*

1 READ HELP WANTED ADS

A IDENTIFY. **Read the help wanted ads. Where...**

Document Literacy: Help wanted ad

Context: Help wanted ads are found online, in newspapers, and on bulletin boards.
Purpose: Help wanted ads advertise job opportunities.
Key Words: *job description, responsibilities, experience, cover letter, résumé, references*

1. Tell students to look at the help wanted ads. Ask about **context**: *Where were these ads found?* (online) Direct students to circle the names of the websites (job-ads.com, career.com) *Where else can people find out about jobs?* (newspapers, bulletin boards, job fairs, friends and family) Ask about **purpose**: *What are these ads for?* (advertise job opportunities) *Do you work? Where did you find out about your job?* Ask about **key words**. Elicit a few words (for example, *job description, experience, responsibilities*).
2. Read the ads aloud. After you read each ad, ask: *What is the job?* (car service driver; office assistant) *What skills do you need for the job?* (drive; organizational, telephone, and people skills)

EXPANSION: Speaking practice for 1A

1. Ask students to raise their hand if they had a job in their native country. Ask those students: *How did you find it?*
2. Ask the whole class: *How do people usually find out about jobs in your country?*
3. List students' responses on the board.

B MATCH. **Connect the sentence parts.**

1. Read the directions.
2. Direct students to look at item 1. Tell them to find and underline the word *full-time* in the ads. Ask: *What comes after the word* full-time*?* (M–F, 8 am–5 pm). *What do you think* M–F *is an abbreviation for?* (Monday–Friday). *How many hours per week does a full-time employee work?* Ask students for the answer to item 1. If necessary, explain that *8 am–5 pm* usually includes an unpaid lunch hour, which means there are 8 work hours in a day.
3. Direct students to look at the rest of the items. Tell them to find and underline the key words in the ads (*responsibilities, résumé, cover letter, experience, references, health benefits*). Say: *Use the words you underlined to connect the sentence parts.*
4. Students check answers with partners.
5. Call on students to read the full sentences.

C INTERPRET. **Read the ads again. Answer the...**

1. Read the directions.
2. To model the activity, write the first item. Ask: *Which job is full-time?* Remind students that they underlined *full-time* in Exercise 1B. Elicit the correct answer and write it on the line: *Office assistant*.
3. Students compare answers with a partner.
4. Check answers by asking students the questions.

Self-Directed Learning

Point out the blue bar. Ask students if they can do the lesson learning objective or if they need more practice. Tell them to check one of the boxes. Assign Extra Practice as needed.

2 IDENTIFY JOB REQUIREMENTS

A WORK TOGETHER. Look at the résumés...

1. Read the directions.
2. Tell students to read the four résumés silently. Say: *As you read, underline words that match the car service driver job and circle words that match the office assistant job.*
3. Pair students. Say: *Compare the words you underlined and circled. Decide which job each candidate should apply for. Write your answers on the lines.*
4. Give pairs time to work. Ask: *What are the names of the candidates?* (Jin Mong, Ann Lopez, Kim Kiska, Bin Fang) List them on the board as students identify them.
5. Check answers by asking pairs what job they picked for each candidate. Write the job title next to each name.

B COMPARE. Look at the résumés. Answer...

1. Read the directions. Then draw the chart below on the board.

	Driving Experience	Office Experience	Computer Skills
Jin Mong			
Ann Lopez			
Kim Kiska			
Bin Fang			

Ask: *What are the requirements for the Car Service Driver job?* Elicit: *1 Year Driving Experience.*
Ask: *What are the requirements for the Office Assistant?* Elicit: *Preferred 1 Year Office Experience* and *Formal Computer Training.*

2. Tell pairs to look at each résumé and put checkmarks in the rows of the chart for each candidate if they meet the requirements. Model by filling out the chart for Jin Mong as a class.
3. Read the first question. Say: *Jin Mong and Bin Fang both have driving experience. But who is best qualified?* Tell pairs to discuss and choose a candidate. Ask each pair which candidate they picked and why. Tally the results on the board next to the names.
4. Read the second question. Say: *Ann Lopez and Kim Kiska both have office experience. But which is best qualified for the Office Assistant job?* Pairs discuss and choose a candidate. Ask each pair which candidate they picked and why. Tally the results on the board next to the names.

C ROLE-PLAY. Act out a job interview. Choose...

1. Read the directions.
2. Ask: *What is an interview about?* (the candidate, the job). *What questions does an interviewer ask?* Write ideas on the board (for example: *How much experience do you have? Can you work weekends and evenings? Did you like working in a busy office environment?*).
3. Ask: *What questions does a candidate ask?* (for example, *What are the responsibilities? What are the benefits? Is it full-time?*)
4. Pair students. Explain that one person will be the candidate. The other person will be the interviewer. Tell pairs to use one of the job ads in Exercise 1A and the ideas on the board.
5. Model the activity with an above-level student. Have students practice the conversation with different partners.
6. Walk around and assist. Have students switch roles and act out the interview again.
7. Ask a few pairs to act out the interview in front of the class.

 ActiveTeach for 2C: Role-Play Support

D GO ONLINE. Search for a job posting...

1. Read the directions. Ask students what they would search in English if they wanted to find a job posting website.
2. Write the search string: *jobs in [City].* Have students search the internet and find a job they are interested in and answer the questions.
3. Compare research as a class. Write jobs students are interested in. Discuss the jobs as a class.

Digital Skills for 2D

Remember that while you can search online for a job, an employer can also search for you online. Make sure that what you post online, in social media for example, does not make you look bad to an employer.

 ActiveTeach: Review

Self-Directed Learning

Point out the blue bar. Ask students if they can do the lesson learning objective or if they need more practice. Tell them to check one of the boxes. Assign Extra Practice as needed.

Extra Practice

  p. 90 Life Skills Writing

Workplace, Life, and Community Skills

2 IDENTIFY JOB REQUIREMENTS

A **WORK TOGETHER.** Look at the résumés. Which job from 1A is each candidate applying for? Write your answers on the lines. How do you know?

B **COMPARE.** Look at the résumés. Answer the questions.

Which candidate is best qualified for the Car Service Driver job? Why? Bin Fang is best qualified for the Car Service Driver job.

Which candidate is best qualified for the Office Assistant job? Why? Kim Kiska is best qualified for the Office Assistant job.

C **ROLE-PLAY.** Act out a job interview. Choose a job from 1A. Student A, you are the interviewer. Student B, you are the applicant. Take turns.

D GO ONLINE. Search for a job posting website. Find a job you are interested in.

What are the job responsibilities? What experience do you need? How can you apply for the job?

Jin Mong
1234 New Moon Road, New Jersey 11112

Education: Jones Community College
Major: Hospitality
Work experience: OMBER Driver, June 2018-present, Moon Gas, gas station attendant, June 2017-June 2018
Languages: English and Chinese
Skills: can operate a cash register

Car Service Driver

Ann Lopez
42 North Shore Road, Boynton Beach, FL
alopez@qmail.com

Education: Palm Beach High School, currently enrolled in Palm Beach State College, Office Technology
Work Experience: Starland Coffee Shop, server January 2018-present.
Relevant Experience: Work with customers, handle customer problems, train new staff
Languages: Spanish and English
Skills: Can type, order supplies, use a cash register

Office Assistant

Kim Kiska
22 West Lane Street, #3A
Stockton, CA
kimkas@yippe.com

Education: Stockton High School, A.A in Office Systems and Technology.
Work Experience: Office Assistant, Gem Restaurant Supply, March 2017-present
Responsibilities: Handle phone calls, organize file room, work with customers; Office Clerk, Bel Blue Office Systems, October 2015-March 2017.
Responsibilities: Greet customers, enter new data in database
Languages: Polish, Russian, and English
Skills: Fluent in all Office Software Systems

Office Assistant

Bin Fang
807 Kates Place, #21. Chicago, IL binfang@macro.com

Education: Jones Driving School, C-License
Work Experience: John's Taxi Service, September 2018-present; Roberto's Car Service, December 2015-present
Skills: Can type, use a computer, operate a commercial vehicle

Car Service Driver

I can identify job requirements. ■   I need more practice. ■

For more practice, go to MyEnglishLab.

Listening and Speaking

Answer questions about work history

1 BEFORE YOU LISTEN

A **READ.** What are the reasons people change jobs?

B **MAKE CONNECTIONS.** Have you ever changed jobs? What was the reason?

1 I'd like to make more money.

2 I'd like a different schedule.

3 I'd like a job closer to home.

4 I'd like to do something different.

2 LISTEN

A **PREDICT.** Look at the picture. What are they talking about?

a. things Manny wants to buy
b. Manny's work experience

B ▶ **LISTEN FOR MAIN IDEA.** Put Manny's experiences in the correct order. Write numbers on the lines.

1. __3__ got a job as a stock clerk
2. __1__ came to the U.S.
3. __2__ got a job as a gardener

Manny

Albert

C ▶ **LISTEN FOR DETAILS.** Why does Manny want to change jobs?

a. He wants to be a stock clerk.
b. He wants to do something different.

D ▶ **EXPAND.** Listen to the whole conversation. Answer the questions.

1. When was Manny unemployed?
   a. two months ago   b. two years ago

2. Why was Manny unemployed?
   a. His mother was sick.   b. He was sick.

3. How long was Manny unemployed?
   a. for two years   b. for two months

Correlations

ELPS Level 2: 2, 7
CASAS Reading: RDG 1.7, 2.3
CASAS Listening: L2.1, 2.3, 4.2, 6.1, 6.2, 6.5
CASAS Competencies: 0.1.2, 0.1.5, 0.1.6, 0.2.1, 4.1.5
Complete standards language available on the Pearson English Portal.

Self-Directed Learning

State the **lesson objective.** Say: *In this lesson, we will learn to answer questions about our work history.*

1 BEFORE YOU LISTEN

A READ. What are the reasons people change...

1. Say: *Look at the people. Read the reasons they changed jobs.* Call on students to read the reasons.
2. Ask: *What are some other reasons people change jobs?* Brainstorm reasons and write them on the board. Begin each reason with *I'd like...* (for example, *I'd like to learn new skills / a job with benefits / a promotion / to move to a new city.*).

B MAKE CONNECTIONS. Have you ever...

1. Read the questions.
2. Ask an above-level student to ask you each question (for example, S: *Have you ever changed jobs?* T: *Yes. First I was a business manager. Then I got a job as a teacher.* S: *What was the reason?* T: *I wanted to do something different.*).
3. Write: *old job: _____ / new job: _____ / reason for change: _____.* Tell students to write their answers in their notebooks.
4. Pair students and tell them to ask each other the questions in the directions.
5. Call on a few students to answer the questions for the class.

MULTILEVEL INSTRUCTION for 1B
Pre-level scaffolding Students can answer the first question *yes* or *no.*
Above-level expansion Students can explain their reason (for example, *I wanted a job closer to home because I wanted to spend more time with my family.*).

2 LISTEN

A PREDICT. Look at the picture. What are...

1. Tell students to look at the picture. Ask: *Who do you see?* (Albert and Manny). Ask: *What do you remember about them from Lesson 2? What is Albert's job?* (store manager) *What is Manny doing?* (interviewing for a new job) *Does Manny have a job now?* (yes)
2. Read the directions. Students circle their prediction.

B ► LISTEN FOR MAIN IDEA. Put Manny's...

1. Tell students to read the directions and the answer choices silently.
2. Play the audio. Tell students to write *1* on the space next to the event that happened first, *2* for the next event, and *3* for the last.
3. Ask: *What are they talking about?* (Manny's work experience) *Was your guess in Exercise 2A correct?* Ask for a show of hands. Use the **Career Awareness** information to help students understand Manny's first job.
4. Call on a student to read the events in order.
5. Say: *When we speak in more formal situations, we often use longer sentences. In informal situations we use shorter sentences.* Ask about **register:** *Does Manny use longer or shorter sentences?* (longer)

Career Awareness: Gardener

Gardeners work outside and take care of plants, trees, and shrubs. They can work in parks, plant stores, private homes, or business properties. They don't need a particular level of education, but they need to be physically fit and strong.

C ► LISTEN FOR DETAILS. Why does Manny...

1. Ask: *What is Manny's job now?* (stock clerk)
2. Review the reasons to change jobs. Say them and ask the class to repeat.
3. Read the directions. Tell students to listen for one of the reasons.
4. Play the audio. Ask: *Why does Manny want to change jobs?* (He'd like to do something different.) If the class can't answer, play the audio again. Elicit the answer.

D ► EXPAND. Listen to the whole...

1. Read the directions. Tell students to read the questions and answers silently.
2. Write *unemployed.* Tell students to listen for Albert to say *unemployed* and then listen to Manny's explanation.
3. Play the audio. Students answer the questions.
4. Ask: *What do you think* unemployed *means?* (He didn't have a job.) If the class can't answer, play the audio again.
5. Say *unemployed* and ask the class to repeat.
6. Pair students to ask and answer the questions.
7. Call on pairs to ask and answer the questions.

3 CONVERSATION

A ▶ LISTEN AND READ. Then listen and repeat.

1. Note: This conversation is the same one students heard in Exercise 2B on page 154.
2. Play the audio. Students read along silently. Then students listen and repeat.
3. Walk around and help with pronunciation as needed.

B WORK TOGETHER. Practice the...

1. Pair students and tell them to practice the conversation in Exercise 3A.
2. Tell students to take turns playing A and B. Walk around and help as needed.

C CREATE. Make new conversations. Use the...

1. Read the directions.
2. Tell students to look at the information in the boxes. Say each word or phrase and ask the class to repeat.
3. Make sure that students understand the six jobs in the orange and green boxes. Elicit what these workers do in their jobs.
4. Show the conversation with blanks on the board. Elicit information from the boxes to fill in the blanks.
5. Ask a pair of on-level students to practice the conversation for the class.
6. Erase the words in the blanks and ask two above-level students to make up a new conversation.
7. Tell pairs to take turns playing A and B and to use the vocabulary words to fill in the blanks.
8. Tell students to stand, mingle, and practice the conversation with several new partners.
9. Walk around and make sure students are completing the conversation correctly. Model stress in two-word nouns as needed.
10. Call on pairs to perform for the class.

■ EXPANSION: Speaking practice for 3C

1. Tell students to look again at the six jobs listed in the green and orange boxes.
2. Form groups of 3. Tell students to discuss which job they would most like to have and why.
3. Call on students to say which jobs the people in their groups most wanted to have.

D ROLE-PLAY. Make your own conversations.

1. Read the directions.
2. Provide pens or highlighters in blue, green, orange, and yellow, or tell students to write the color name next to each piece of information as follows.

   - Ask: *When did you come to the U.S.?* Write: _____ *ago.* Tell students to note their answer in blue.
   - Ask: *What was your first job in the U.S.?* Tell students to note their answer in green. (Direct students who don't work or haven't changed jobs to make up the work history information.)
   - Ask: *What job do you have now?* Tell students to note their answer in orange.
   - Ask: *What was the reason for your job change?* Tell students to note their answer in yellow.

3. Pair students and tell them to substitute their own information into the conversation in Exercise 3C.
4. Walk around and remind students to switch roles.
5. Call on pairs to perform for the class.

■ MULTILEVEL INSTRUCTION for 3D

Cross-ability Pair a pre-level student with an above-level student. The above-level student helps the pre-level student write notes about his/her work experience.

Self-Directed Learning

Point out the blue bar. Ask students if they can do the lesson learning objective or if they need more practice. Tell them to check one of the boxes. Assign Extra Practice as needed.

Extra Practice
p. 91

Listening and Speaking

3 CONVERSATION

A ► LISTEN AND READ. Then listen and repeat.

A: So, tell me more about your work experience.
B: Well, I came to the U.S. three years ago. First, I got a job as a gardener.
Then last year I got a job as a stock clerk.
A: OK. So now you're a stock clerk. Why are you looking for another job?
B: Things in my life have changed, and now I'd like to do something different.

B WORK TOGETHER. Practice the conversation in Exercise A.

C CREATE. Make new conversations. Use the words in the boxes.

A: So, tell me more about your work experience.
B: Well, I came to the U.S.   ago. First, I got a job as a   .
Then last year I got a job as a   .
A: OK. So now you're a   . Why are you looking for another job?
B: Things in my life have changed, and now I'd like   .

a year	warehouse worker	truck driver	to make more money
a few years	nurse assistant	receptionist	a different schedule
ten months	food service worker	cook	a job closer to home

D ROLE-PLAY. Make your own conversations.

I can answer questions about my work history. ■   I need more practice. ■

For more practice, go to MyEnglishLab.

6 Grammar

Time expressions with *ago*, *last*, *in*, and *later*

	Time expressions with *ago*, *last*, *in*, and *later*			
I got a job	three years 10 months	ago.	One month	
	last	year. week.	Two days	later, I got a better job.
	in	July. the fall.	A week	

A DECIDE. Use the words in the boxes to complete the sentences.

1.
ago
in
last

Luz came to the U.S. two years ___ago___. She studied English ___last___ year. She got a job ___in___ December.

2.
ago
last
later

Six months ___later___, Meng came to the U.S. She started working in a factory one month ___ago___. She left that job ___last___ week because she got a better job.

3.
in
last
later

___In___ 2004, Omar came to the U.S. One year ___later___, he got a job in a supermarket. He got a new job in a warehouse ___last___ month.

B APPLY. Write each sentence a different way. Use *ago* or *in*.
(Answers will vary depending on the current year.)

1. Tina got a new job last month. _Tina got a new job a month ago._
2. She learned to take care of patients in 2015. _She learned to take care of patients 4 years ago._
3. Frank got his job a year ago. _Frank got his job in 2018._
4. He left his job in January. _He left his job 10 months ago_
5. They started school six months ago. _They started school in 2018._
6. Yan changed jobs last week. _Yan changed jobs a week ago._

Lesson

Correlations

ELPS Level 2: 1, 2, 3, 4, 5, 6, 7, 8, 9, 10
CASAS Reading: RDG 1.7, 2.9
CASAS Listening: L2.1, 2.3, 3.11, 4.2
CASAS Competencies: 0.1.2, 0.1.5, 0.1.6, 0.2.1
Complete standards language available on the Pearson English Portal.

Self-Directed Learning

State the **lesson objective**. Say: *In this lesson, we will learn to use time expressions with* ago, last, in, *and* later.

Time expressions with *ago, last, in,* and *later*

 ActiveTeach: Grammar Discovery

1. Warm up. Say: *The conversation on page 155 used this grammar.* Turn back to page 155. Point to the sentences in Exercise 3A and then write:
   - *I came to the U.S. three years ago.*
   - *Then last year I got a job as a stock clerk.*
2. Underline *three years ago* and *last year*.
3. Tell students to look at the grammar chart. Read sentences and ask the class to repeat.
4. Write:
   - *time* + ago
   - *time* + later
   - last + *time*
   - in + *time*

   Say: Ago *and* later *go after a time expression.* Last *and* in *go before a time expression.*
5. Ask: *When did this class meet for the first time?* Write a date (for example, *September 2018*). Use the date to compose sentences with *ago, last,* and *in* about when the class started (for example, *The class started four months ago. The class started last fall. The class started in September.*). Write the sentences.
6. Think of an event that has happened since the start of school (for example, the arrival of a new student), and write the event and date. Compose a sentence with *later* (for example, *Two months later, Juan joined the class.*).
7. Read the sentences on the board and ask the class to repeat.

 ActiveTeach: Grammar Coach

■ EXPANSION: Grammar practice

1. As a class make a list of milestones on the board. For example, *got a job, changed jobs, had children, got married, graduated, came to the U.S.,* etc. (If necessary, review milestones in Unit 6, Lessons 5 and 6.)
2. Tell students to use the list of milestones to write four sentences using *ago, later, last,* and *in.* Tell students to use the grammar chart as a model, substituting their own information. Say: *The sentences can be about you or members of your family.*
3. Model the activity with your own information. For example, write:
   1. *I got married _____ ago. _____ later, we had a daughter.*
   2. *Last _____, my daughter had a baby.*
   3. *I got a new job in _____.*
4. Ask students what words or dates could fill in the blanks. Then write the missing information.
5. Students write their own sentences. Walk around and assist.
6. Pair students and tell them to read their sentences to their partner.

A DECIDE. **Use the words in the boxes to…**

1. Read the directions. Write the example and point to the answer. Ask: *Why is the answer* ago? (because *in* and *last* go before a time)
2. Students compare answers with a partner.
3. Call on students to read the completed items.

B APPLY. **Write each sentence a different way…**

1. Read the directions. Write the example. Underline *last month* and *a month ago.* Say: *The meaning is the same.* Ask: *What month was last month?* Elicit the answer and say: *Another possible answer is:* Tina got a new job in [last month]. Write this sentence.
2. Write the current date. Tell students to use today's date to figure out how long ago or in what month or year the events happened.
3. Students compare answers with a partner.
4. Call on students to read the completed sentences.

Grammar

C WRITE. Look at Aram's timeline. Write...

1. Say: *Here is a timeline about Aram's life in the U.S. You're going to write sentences about it.*
2. Tell students to read the directions and the events on the timeline silently.
3. Write the example. Explain: *There's another way to write about this.* Write: *Aram came to the U.S. _____ years _____.* Write the current year and 2015 and elicit the class's help to rewrite the sentence with *ago*.
4. Tell students to look at the first and second events on the timeline. Elicit a sentence about the second event with *later*. This sentence can begin just with *Later...*, as in the example, or challenge students to rewrite it with a time expression (for example, *One / A month later, he started English classes.*).
5. Tell students to write one sentence about each event. Using *in, ago,* and *later* at least once each. For sentences with *ago*, tell students to compare the event date with today's date. For sentences with *later*, tell students to compare an event date with the event date right before it.
6. Check answers by calling on students to read sentences for each event in the timeline.

EXPANSION: Grammar and speaking practice for C

1. Pair students and tell them to exchange books and read each other's sentences.
2. Tell partners to point out differences in their sentences and help each other make corrections.
3. Call on a few students to read all five sentences about Aram together, without the numbers, as if they were reading a paragraph.

Show what you know!

1. THINK ABOUT IT. Answer the question about...

1. Read the directions.
2. Ask an above-level student the question: *When did you start learning English?* Write the student's answer. If the student doesn't use *in, ago,* or *later* (or uses them incorrectly), prompt the class to help rephrase the student's response using one of the time expressions.
3. Point out that students can't use *later* to answer the question.

2. TALK ABOUT IT. Take turns asking *When did...*

1. Ask five students: *When did you start learning English?* Note their names and the month or year on the board. If a student uses *ago* to answer, ask the class to figure out the arrival month or year.

2. Elicit the class's help to put the dates on the board in order. Ask: *Who started learning English first?... Second?* etc.
3. Draw a timeline like the one in the example with the students' names and start dates.
4. Form groups of 5. Tell group members to count off from 1 to 5. Say: *Number 1, you are the recorder. Take notes. Write down each group member's name and date when they started learning English.*
5. Read the directions and the example. Say: *Each group member asks the person to the right: When did you start learning English? Go around the circle until everyone has asked and answered the question.*
6. Say: *Now use the recorder's notes to create a timeline showing when each person in your group started learning English. Number 2, draw the timeline.*

3. WRITE ABOUT IT. Now write a sentence...

1. Read the directions.
2. Use the timeline on the board to model the activity. Say a sentence about each person in order from left to right. Use *in, ago,* and *later* at least once each.
3. Ask pairs to check each other's sentences.
   - Sentences should include time expressions with *in, ago,* or *later*.
   - *Ago* and *later* should be after the time expression.
   - *In* should be before the time expression.
4. Have students volunteer to write their sentences on the board.

EXPANSION: Speaking practice for 3

1. Say: *Practice talking about your timeline in your group.* Tell students to read to each other the sentences they wrote in Step 3.
2. Say: *Number 3, draw the group's timeline on the board.*
3. Call on students 4 and 5 from each group to come to the board and explain the timeline to the class.

Self-Directed Learning

Point out the blue bar. Ask students if they can do the lesson learning objective or if they need more practice. Tell them to check one of the boxes. Assign Extra Practice as needed.

Extra Practice

MyEnglishLab   Workbook p. 91

Grammar

C WRITE. Look at Aram's timeline. Write sentences. Use *in*, *ago*, and *later*. *(Answers will vary.)*

| May 2015 came to the U.S. | June 2015 started English classes | January 2016 got his first job | July 2017 got a better job | December 2018 became a supervisor |

1. *Aram came to the U.S. in May 2015.*
2. *Later he* started English classes.
3. In January 2016, he got his first job.
4. A year and a half later, he got a better job.
5. A few months ago, he became a supervisor.

Show what you know!

1. **THINK ABOUT IT. Answer the question about yourself. When did you start learning English? Use *in* or *ago*.**

2. **TALK ABOUT IT. Take turns asking *When did you start learning English?* Draw a time line to show each person's answer.**

Victor   Dani

July 2017   September   today

Victor: I started learning English in July, 2017.
Dani: I started learning English four months ago.

3. **WRITE ABOUT IT. Now write a sentence about when each person started learning English.**

_____

_____

_____

I can use time expressions with *ago*, *last*, *in*, and *later*. ☐   I need more practice. ☐

For more practice, go to MyEnglishLab.

Read about jobs in the U.S.

1 BEFORE YOU READ

A **LABEL.** Label the pictures with the words in the box.

agriculture   health care   manufacturing   technology

1. ___health care___   2. ___agriculture___   3. ___technology___   4. ___manufacturing___

B **MAKE CONNECTIONS.** Think about the fields of employment in A. Which fields have the most jobs these days? What kinds of jobs are they?

2 READ

▶ **LISTEN AND READ.**

Today's Hot Jobs

1 The U.S. job market is changing fast. At one time, most workers in the U.S. had jobs on farms. Now, less than 2 percent of workers have agricultural jobs. In 1960, 25 percent of workers had jobs in manufacturing.
5 Now, only 10 percent of workers are making things in factories. So where are the jobs today?

Health Care
Many of the fastest-growing jobs
10 are in health care. The U.S. population is getting older. These older Americans need
15 medical care and help with daily living. The greatest need is for personal care aides. There may be more than 750 thousand new jobs of this kind by 2026. Personal care aides take care of people in their homes or in
20 day programs. They sometimes work with people with disabilities or long-term illnesses. On average, they make about $22,000 a year. There are other fast-growing jobs in health care, too. For example, by 2026, there may be a need for 437 thousand
25 more registered nurses. On average, they make about $69,000 a year.

Computer and Information Technology
There are also many fast-growing jobs in computer and information technology. By 2026, there may be
30 more than 546 thousand new jobs in this field. Almost 300 thousand of those jobs will be for software developers. Some software developers create programs for computers and cell phones. Others design computer networks (where many
35 computers work together). On average, they make more than $100,000 a year.

Many of today's fastest-growing jobs are in these two fields. Where will tomorrow's jobs be?

Source: U.S. Department of Labor

Percentage of Growth in Jobs

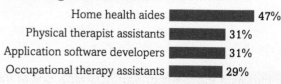

Home health aides — 47%
Physical therapist assistants — 31%
Application software developers — 31%
Occupational therapy assistants — 29%

Correlations

ELPS Level 2: 1, 2, 7
CCRS Level A: RI/RL.1.1, RI.1.2, RI.1.4, SL.K.2
CASAS Reading: RDG 1.7, 1.8, 2.3, 3.2, 3.8, 3.11, 4.2
CASAS Listening: L2.1, 2.3, 4.2, 5.8, 6.1, 6.2
CASAS Competencies: 0.1.2, 0.1.5, 0.2.1, 7.1.1
Complete standards language available on the Pearson English Portal.

Self-Directed Learning

1. State the **lesson objective**. Say: *In this lesson, we will learn to predict the topic.*
2. Say: *We will read about jobs in the U.S.*

1 BEFORE YOU READ

A LABEL. **Label the pictures with the words…**

1. Write: *job market.* Say: *When people talk about the job market, they're talking about whether it's easy or difficult to find jobs.*
2. Read the directions.
3. Say the words in the box. Students repeat them.
4. Ask: *Which picture shows agriculture?* (2)
5. Tell students to complete the other sentences.
6. Call on students to provide answers.

B MAKE CONNECTIONS. **Think about the…**

1. Read the directions and questions.
2. Have students discuss the questions in pairs.
3. Call on students to share their ideas. Ask: *Where are the jobs in [your area]? What fields are they in?* Tell students to circle the field in Exercise 1A that is easiest to find jobs in. Write the fields on the board. Ask: *What field did you circle?* Say each field and ask for a show of hands. Keep a tally on the board.

2 READ

▶ **LISTEN AND READ.**

1. Point to the **Academic Skill** and read it. Ask: *What should you look at to help you predict the topic?* (the title and any visuals or graphs) Say: *When you predict the topic of a reading, you begin to think about it and start asking yourself questions. This helps you pay attention to what you read, as you see if your predictions are correct and your questions answered.*
2. Introduce the reading. Say: *Now let's look at the title and the pictures to predict the topic.* Ask: *What is the title of this article?* (Today's Hot Jobs)

What do you think "hot jobs" means? (popular jobs) Write: *Today's Hot Jobs.* Underline *hot* and say: *If something is* hot, *it's popular.* Ask: *What jobs are hot at the moment?*

3. Introduce the visual/graphic. Ask: *What pictures or other visuals do you see?* Elicit descriptions of the visuals and the graphic. Ask: *What does the photo show?* (a healthcare worker serving food to an older person) *What is the title of the bar graph?* (Percentage of Growth in Jobs) *What jobs are in the graph?* (home health aides, physical therapist assistants, application software developers, occupational therapy assistants) *What fields are these?* (health care and technology)

4. Say: *So, the title of the article is* Today's Hot Jobs, *and the picture and graph show jobs in health care and technology. What do you think the topic of the article is?* Elicit and write: *Popular job fields right now: health care and technology.*

 ActiveTeach for 2: Anticipation Guide – *Before* Reading exercise

5. Read the text.
   a. Say: *Now we are going to read and listen to the article* Today's Hot Jobs.
   b. Play the audio as students listen and read along silently.
   c. Have an above-level student read the first paragraph or read it yourself. Ask: *What are differences between jobs today and jobs in the past?* (In the past, people worked on farms and in factories. Fewer people work in those places now.)
   d. **Reinforce the Academic Skill** from Unit 7. Ask: *What are the two headings in purple?* (Healthcare and Computer and Information Technology)
   e. *What job or jobs does the writer talk about under the first heading?* (personal care aides) *What job does the writer talk about under the second heading?* (software developers) Tell students to circle the two jobs and underline the job descriptions. Circle the annual salaries.
   f. Read students' ideas from Exercise 1B on the board and ask: *Were your ideas the same as those in the article?*
   g. Ask: *Which field are you more interested in? Health care or technology?* Ask for a show of hands.

 ActiveTeach for 2: Anticipation Guide – *After* Reading exercise

3 CLOSE READING

A IDENTIFY. What is the main idea?

1. Say: *Now we are going to identify the main idea.* **Reinforce Academic Skills.** Say: *Remember to use the headings or formatting to help when identifying the main idea.*
2. Read the directions. Have students circle the answer.
3. Elicit the answer from the class.

B CITE EVIDENCE. Complete the statements.

1. Say: *Now we are going to find information in the reading.*
2. Read the directions. Walk around as students work on the activity. If students are struggling, have them work in pairs or direct them to the text lines where they can find the information.
3. Call on students to read the sentence with the correct completion. Ask a different student: *Where is that information? What line number?*

C INTERPRET. Complete the sentences about…

1. Say: *Now we are going to interpret the bar graph. A bar graph is a way to show numerical information or numbers in a visual, easy-to-understand way.*
2. Tell students to look at the bar graph. Ask: *What does each bar or column show?* (jobs) *How are they groups arranged?* (largest number on top, smallest on bottom)
3. Students read the sentences and answer choices silently and complete.
4. Students compare answers with a partner.
5. Call on students to read the completed sentences to the class.

Numeracy: Math skills

A percentage is a number or ratio as a fraction of 100. We can express percentages as a number followed by % (25%), or we can present them as decimals (.25). We can also say the same thing as a fraction. For example, 25% = 25/100 = 1/4, or one quarter.

---

4 SUMMARIZE

 ActiveTeach for 4: Vocabulary Practice

1. Read the directions. Ask students to read aloud the words in the box.
2. Tell students to complete the paragraph.
3. To check answers, call on students to read sentences in the summary with the blanks filled in. Ask other students to read the completed summary silently.

Show what you know!

1. **THINK ABOUT IT. What job do you want to…**
   1. Read the directions.
   2. Students take notes in answer to the questions.

2. **TALK ABOUT IT. Talk about the jobs you…**
   1. Read the directions. Call on a student to read the example.
   2. Model the activity. Ask an above-level student to talk about a job he or she wants.
   3. Pair students to take turns talking about jobs they want and how to get them.

 ActiveTeach for 2: Academic Conversation Support

3. **WRITE ABOUT IT. Now write about the job…**
   1. Read the directions.
   2. Give students time to write about a job they want.
   3. Pair students to read their writing.
   4. Collect students' writing to put in their portfolios.

Self-Directed Learning

Point out the blue bar. Ask students if they can do the lesson learning objective or if they need more practice. Tell them to check one of the boxes. Assign Extra Practice as needed.

■ **EXPANSION: Self-directed learning**

Ask students to reflect: *What did you learn from this reading?* Call on students to share something they learned.

Extra Practice

 CCRS Plus   pp. 92–93

---

3 CLOSE READING

A IDENTIFY. What is the main idea?

The fastest-growing jobs in the United States _____.
a. are in health care and in computer and information technology
b. are some of the highest-paid jobs in the United States
c. are jobs creating programs for computers and cell phones

B CITE EVIDENCE. Answer the questions. Where is the information? Write the line numbers.

Lines

1. The number of jobs in manufacturing today is _____ it was in the past.
   a. higher than   b. lower than   c. the same as   3–6

2. Personal care aides make about _____ on average.
   a. $2026 a month   b. $22,000 a year   c. $69,000 a year   21–22

3. By 2026, there will probably be _____ new jobs for software developers.
   a. about 100,000   b. more than 546,000   c. almost 300,000   29–32

C INTERPRET. Complete the sentences about the bar graph.

1. The bar graph shows _____.
   a. growing jobs in numbers   b. growing jobs in percentage   c. dying jobs in percentage   _____

2. The growth in jobs for application software developers _____.
   a. is higher than for home health aides   b. is lower than for occupational therapy assistants   c. is the same as for physical therapist assistants   _____

4 SUMMARIZE

Complete the summary with the words in the box.

| employment | health care | job market | software | technology |

The (1) ___job market___ in the U.S. is changing. Two fields of (2) ___employment___ are growing fast. There will be many new jobs in (3) ___health care___, especially jobs for personal care aides. There will also be many new jobs in computer and information (4) ___technology___, especially for (5) ___software___ developers.

Show what you know!

1. **THINK ABOUT IT.** What job do you want to have in five years? Why? What do you need to do to get that job?

2. **TALK ABOUT IT.** Talk about the jobs you want. Talk about how to get those jobs.

   In five years, I want to be a software developer. I need to learn about technology.

3. **WRITE ABOUT IT.** Now write about the job you want in five years.

I can predict the topic. ■   I need more practice. ■

To read more, go to MyEnglishLab.

Answer questions about availability

1 BEFORE YOU LISTEN

MATCH. Read the information about job interviews. Then match the words with the definitions.

At a job interview, the interviewer asks you about your **availability**. For example,"Which shift can you work, day or night? and "Can you work on weekends?" The interviewer may ask if your hours are **flexible**. For example, "Can you work different hours if the schedule changes?" The interviewer also asks when you can start. If you are working, you should give your boss one or two weeks' **notice** that you are leaving your job. This will help your boss find a new employee to fill your position when you leave.

1. __c__ easy to change
2. __a__ when you can work
3. __d__ information or warning that something will happen
4. __b__ a scheduled period of work time

a. availability
b. shift
c. flexible
d. notice

2 LISTEN

A **PREDICT.** Look at the picture. What do you think is happening?

B ▶ **LISTEN FOR MAIN IDEA.** What does Albert ask? Check the questions.

☑ Do you prefer mornings or afternoons?
☐ Are you flexible?
☑ Can you work on weekends?
☑ When could you start?

Albert   Manny

C ▶ **LISTEN FOR DETAILS.** Circle *True* or *False*.

1. Manny prefers to work in the morning.   (True)   False
2. Manny can work on weekends.   (True)   False
3. Manny can start working today.   True   (False)

D ▶ **EXPAND.** Listen to the whole conversation. Does Manny know if he got the job? No, he doesn

Correlations

ELPS Level 2: 2, 7
CCRS Level A: RI.1.5, SL.1.1, SL.K.3, SL.1.4, SL.K.6
CASAS Reading: RDG 1.7, 2.3, 3.8
CASAS Listening: L1.4, 2.1, 2.3, 4.1, 4.2, 6.1, 6.2, 6.5
CASAS Competencies: 0.1.2, 0.1.4, 0.1.5, 0.1.6, 0.1.8, 0.2.1, 4.1.5, 4.6.5
Complete standards language available on the Pearson English Portal.

Self-Directed Learning

State the **lesson objective**. Say: *In this lesson, we will learn to answer questions about availability.*

1 BEFORE YOU LISTEN

MATCH. Read the information about job...

1. Read the directions.
2. Tell students to look at the paragraph. Ask: *What are the words in boldface?* Write: *availability, flexible,* and *notice.* Say each word in boldface and ask the class to repeat.
3. Tell students to read the paragraph silently.
4. Read the first two sentences out loud, stressing *For example.* Ask the class: *What do you think* availability *means?* Elicit a definition and write it on the board (for example, *when you can work*).
5. Pair students and tell them to read the first two sentences again and write a definition for *shift.* Call on pairs to read their definition. Write a definition on the board (for example, *the time of day when you work*).
6. Tell pairs to read the next two sentences (starting with *The interviewer may ask...*) and write a definition for *flexible.* Call on pairs to read their definition. Write a definition on the board (for example, *you can change your hours if necessary*).
7. Tell pairs to read the last three sentences (starting with *The interviewer also asks...*) and write a definition for *notice.* Call on pairs to read their definition. Write a definition on the board (for example, *telling your manager that you are leaving your job*).

Teaching Tip: Guess meaning from context

In Exercise 1, students are using context to guess the meaning of unfamiliar words. Explain that guessing meaning from context is a good strategy to learn new vocabulary. Elicit the specific cues that show the meanings of the words.

2 LISTEN

A PREDICT. Look at the picture. What do you...

1. Tell students to look at the picture. Ask: *What do you remember about Albert and Manny?* (Albert is a manager. He is interviewing Manny for a job. Manny is a stock clerk now but he wants to do something different.)
2. Ask: *What do you think is happening?* (end of interview, job offer) Write the ideas.

B ▶ LISTEN FOR MAIN IDEA. What does...

1. Read the directions. Call on students to read the questions. Ask: *What do these questions ask about?* (availability)
2. Play the audio. Students listen and check the questions.
3. Elicit the correct answers from the class.
4. Say: *Sometimes we use polite phrases to introduce questions.* Ask about **register**: *What is a phrase that Albert uses to introduce questions?* (Let me ask you a few questions about...)

C ▶ LISTEN FOR DETAILS. Circle *True* or *False*.

1. Read the directions. Tell students to read the statements silently.
2. Play the audio. Students circle *True* or *False*.
3. Students compare answers with a partner.
4. Call on students to read a completed sentence.
5. **Extend:** Elicit a correction for the false statement.

D ▶ EXPAND. Listen to the whole...

1. Read the directions.
2. Play the audio. Students answer the question.
3. Review the correct answer with the class. Ask: *When will he learn about the job?* (next week)

Workplace Culture

1. Ask: *What does Manny ask in his interview?* (When can I expect to hear from you?)
2. Say: *In the U.S. it's OK to ask questions in an interview. In fact, it's a good idea to prepare a few questions to ask about the job and the company before an interview. But don't ask about salary and benefits; wait until the interviewer brings them up.*
3. Have students brainstorm questions to ask in an interview and write them on the board (for example, *Can you describe a typical day for someone in this job? What are the job duties? What skills are most important for this job? What new skills can I learn on the job?*).

Listening and Speaking

3 PRONUNCIATION

A ▶ PRACTICE. Listen. Then listen and repeat.

1. Read the **Pronunciation Note**. Ask: *In which choice does the voice go down?* (the last)
2. Read the directions. Tell students to look at the questions and circle *or*.
3. Play the audio. Students listen. Then students listen and repeat.

 ActiveTeach for 3A: Pronunciation Coach

B ▶ APPLY. Listen and draw arrows where...

1. Read the directions. Tell students to read the sentences and circle *or*. Elicit where they predict the voice will go up.
2. Play the audio. Students listen and draw arrows where the voice goes up and down.
3. Review the correct answers with students. Ask: *Were your guesses correct?*

4 CONVERSATION

A ▶ LISTEN AND READ. Then listen and repeat.

1. Note: This conversation is the same one students heard in Exercise 2B on page 160.
2. Tell students to read the conversation and underline the question with a choice. Tell them to circle *or* and mark the voice going up on the first choice and down on the last choice.
3. Say: *Do you prefer mornings or afternoons?* Ask the class to repeat. Model again and ask individual students to repeat.
4. Read the directions.
5. Play the audio. Students read along silently. Then students listen and repeat.

B WORK TOGETHER. Practice the...

1. Pair students and tell them to practice the conversation in Exercise 4A.
2. Tell students to take turns playing A and B. Walk around and check that students are using the correct intonation for the question with *or*.

C CREATE. Make new conversations. Use the...

1. Read the directions.
2. Tell students to look at the information in the blue box. Tell them to circle *or* and mark the voice going up on the first choice and down on the last choice. Say: *Do you prefer first or second shift?* and *Do you prefer days or nights?* Ask the class to repeat.

3. Explain that *first shift* is usually morning to afternoon and *second shift* is afternoon to evening.
4. Show the conversation with blanks. Read through the conversation. When you come to a blank, fill it in with information from the first row in the boxes. As you fill in each blank, say the color of the answer space and point to the same-color word or phrase you choose from the boxes.
5. Ask two on-level students to read the conversation in front of the class.
6. Tell pairs to take turns playing each role and to use information from the same row in the boxes to fill in the blanks. Walk around and check that students are using correction intonation.

D ROLE-PLAY. Make your own conversations.

1. Tell students to look at the conversation in Exercise 4A. Ask: *Who is Speaker A?* (the manager) Read A's first line. Write: *Do you prefer _____?* Tell students to look at the information in the blue box. Ask: *What other choices related to availability can the manager ask about?* Brainstorm ideas and write them (for example, *mornings or afternoons, part-time or full-time*). Draw a box around this information and label it *blue*. Ask students to come to the board and mark the pronunciation/intonation.
2. Tell students to look at the conversation in Exercise 4A. Read A's second line. Write: *Can you work on _____?* Tell students to look at the information in the yellow box. Brainstorm and write the other days the manager can ask about (for example, *weekends, Friday nights, holidays*). Draw a box around this information and label it *yellow*.
3. Read the directions. Play A and make up a conversation with an above-level student. Use the information on the board.
4. Pair students and tell them to take turns playing A and B.
5. Call on pairs to role-play for the class.

Self-Directed Learning

Point out the blue bar. Ask students if they can do the lesson learning objective or if they need more practice. Tell them to check one of the boxes. Assign Extra Practice as needed.

Extra Practice
MyEnglishLab   Workbook pp. 94–95

Listening and Speaking

3 PRONUNCIATION

Intonation of questions with *or*

Some questions with *or* ask the listener to make a choice. In these questions, the voice goes up on the first choice and down on the last choice.

A ▶ PRACTICE. Listen. Then listen and repeat.

Do you prefer mornings or afternoons?

Can you work first shift or second shift?

Do you work days or nights?

B ▶ APPLY. Listen and draw arrows where the voice goes up and down.

1. Do you work the morning shift or the night shift?

2. Are you a sales associate or a stock clerk?

3. Do you prefer to work Saturday or Sunday?

4 CONVERSATION

A ▶ LISTEN AND READ. Then listen and repeat.

A: Let me ask you a few questions about your availability.
Do you prefer mornings or afternoons?
B: Well, I prefer mornings, but I'm flexible.
A: All right. Can you work on weekends?
B: Yes, I can.
A: Great. And when could you start?
B: In two weeks. I need to give two weeks' notice at my job.

B WORK TOGETHER. Practice the conversation in Exercise A.

C CREATE. Make new conversations. Use the words in the boxes.

A: Let me ask you a few questions about your availability.
Do you prefer _____?
B: Well, I prefer _____, but I'm flexible.
A: All right. Can you work on _____?
B: Yes, I can.
A: Great. And when could you start?
B: In two weeks. I need to give two weeks' notice at my job.

first or second shift
days or nights

first shift
days

Saturdays
Sundays

D ROLE-PLAY. Make your own conversations.

I can answer questions about availability. ■

I need more practice. ■

For more practice, go to MyEnglishLab.

Ways to express alternatives: *or, and*				Grammar Watch
He can		**or**		Use *or* (not *and*) in negative statements.
They can	work Saturdays	**and**	Sundays.	
I can't		**or**		

A COMPLETE. Write *and* or *or*.

1. **A:** Which shift do you prefer?

   B: I'm flexible. I can work first shift _____or_____ second shift.

2. **A:** Can you work weekends?

   B: Sure! I can work both Saturday _____and_____ Sunday. I want a lot of hours.

3. **A:** Can you work both Saturday and Sunday?

   B: I'll be happy to work Saturday _____or_____ Sunday, but I can't work both days.

4. **A:** Can you take classes in the morning _____or_____ in the evening?

   B: In the morning. I can't take classes in the evening because I work second shift.

B INTERPRET. Look at the job applications. Write two sentences about each person's availability. Use *or* with *can* and *can't*.

1. *Carlos can work second shift or third shift.*
2. Carlos can't work first shift or weekends.

○○○

Carlos Hernández

When can you work? Check the boxes.

○ first shift ● second shift ● third shift ○ weekends

3. Mila can work first shift or second shift.
4. Mila can't work third shift or weekends.

○○○

Mila Pérez

When can you work? Check the boxes.

● first shift ● second shift ○ third shift ○ weekends

C WRITE. Now write two sentences about your work availability. Use *or* with *can* and *can't*.

I can express alternatives with *or* and *and*. ■   I need more practice. ■

For more practice, go to MyEnglishLab.

Correlations

ELPS Level 2: 10
CCRS Level A: L.1.1
CASAS Reading: RDG 1.7, 2.3
CASAS Listening: L3.5, 4.1, 4.2
CASAS Competencies: 0.1.2
Complete standards language available on the Pearson English Portal.

Self-Directed Learning

State the **lesson objective**. Say: *In this lesson, we will learn to express alternatives with or and and.*

Ways to express alternatives: *or, and*

 ActiveTeach: Grammar Discovery

1. Warm up. Say: *The conversation on page 161 used this grammar.* Turn back to page 161. Point to the sentence in Exercise 4A and then write: *Do you prefer mornings or afternoons?* Underline *or*.
2. Tell students to look at the grammar chart. Read the sentences and tell the class to repeat.
3. Read a sentence from the chart: *He can work Saturdays or Sundays.* Ask: *Can he work on both days?* (no) *Can he work on Saturdays?* (yes) *Can he work on Sundays?* (yes) Say: *But he can't work both days because we used or not and.*
4. Read another sentence from the chart: *They can work Saturdays and Sundays.* Ask: *Can they work both Saturdays and Sundays?* (yes)
5. Read the **Grammar Watch** note aloud.
6. Read the negative sentence from the chart: *I can't work Saturdays or Sundays.* Ask: *Can I work Saturdays?* (no) *Can I work Sundays?* (no) Say: *So, both days are not OK for me. Why or, not and?* (because the sentence is negative)

 ActiveTeach: Grammar Coach

A COMPLETE. Write *and* or *or*.

1. Read the directions and the example. Ask: *Why is the answer or?* (because this person can work first shift, or this person can work second shift—but not both)
2. Students compare answers with a partner by reading the conversations.
3. Call on pairs to read the conversations.

B INTERPRET. Look at the job applications...

1. Read the directions.
2. Tell students to look at Carlos's job application. Read the example. Say: *Now write a sentence with can't.* Allow time for students to complete item 2.
3. Elicit the sentence and write it on the board. Ask: *Can Carlos work first shift?* (no) *Can he work weekends?* (no) Say: *So, both times are not OK for Carlos. Why or, not and?* (because the sentence is negative)
4. Students check answers with a partner.
5. Call on students to write answers on the board.

C WRITE. Now write two sentences about your...

1. Remind students that *first shift* is from morning to afternoon and *second shift* is from afternoon to evening. Ask: *When do you think third shift is?* (usually from evening to early morning) Explain: *In workplaces that are open 24 hours, usually:*
   - *First shift—8:00 a.m. to 4:00 p.m.*
   - *Second shift—4:00 p.m. to 12:00 a.m.*
   - *Third shift—12:00 a.m. to 8:00 a.m.*
2. Tell students to look at Exercise B on page 162 and copy the job application form in their notebooks. Have them answer the question by checking the two work shifts they can work.
3. Read the directions. Tell students to write one sentence with *can* and one sentence with *can't* using the sentence in Exercise B as a model.
4. Ask one student to write a sentence with *can* on the board and one student to write a sentence with *can't*.

Self-Directed Learning

Point out the blue bar. Ask students if they can do the lesson learning objective or if they need more practice. Tell them to check one of the boxes. Assign Extra Practice as needed.

Extra Practice

  pp. 94–95

Correlations

ELPS Level 2: 3, 10
CCRS Level A: W.1.2, W.1.5, L.1.1
CASAS Reading: RDG 1.7, 1.8
CASAS Listening: L2.1, 2.3, 3.9
CASAS Competencies: 0.1.2, 0.1.5, 0.1.6
Complete standards language available on the Pearson English Portal.

Self-Directed Learning

1. State the **lesson objective**. Say: *In this lesson, we will learn to use the correct tense to describe our job history.*
2. Say: *You will write about your job history.*

1 STUDY THE MODEL

1. Read the directions.
2. Point to the paragraph. Ask: *What is the title of the model?* (My Job History)
3. **Scaffold** the model. Write as a graphic organizer:

First job (when and title)	Duties
Second job (when and title)	Duties
Job now (title)	Duties

4. Tell students to read the text and read the questions independently. Ask the first two questions. Elicit the two jobs Ana had and write them in the chart along with the duties. Tell students to mark the text. Ask questions 3 and 4. Write the information in the graphic organizer on the board.
5. Point to the **Writing Skill**. Read it aloud while students listen. Ask: *What tense do you use for your current job?* (present) *What tense do you use for your previous jobs?* (simple past) Ask: *What past tense verbs do you see in the model?* (was, stocked, became, helped, used) Tell students to underline them. Ask: *What verbs are in the present tense?* (have, live, am, supervise, plan) Tell students to mark the text.

2 PLAN YOUR WRITING

1. Erase the information in the graphic organizer on the board.
2. Read the directions.
3. Model with a student. The student asks the teacher the questions.
4. Write the information into the graphic organizer.

5. Explain: *Some people don't have a long job history. Your topic sentence can be different from the model.* Elicit and write other topic sentences (for example, *My job history is not very long, I have a short job history.*).
6. Tell students to make their own graphic organizer on a piece of paper.
7. Have students work in pairs to ask and answer the questions and complete their own graphic organizers.

3 WRITE

1. Read the directions aloud.
2. Use your information in the chart from Exercise 2 to write sentences in a paragraph. Include indentation. Use present tense for previous jobs and simple past for your current job.
3. As students write, circulate to make sure they are using correct tenses.

 ActiveTeach for 3: Writing Support

4 CHECK YOUR WRITING

1. Read the directions. Point to the **Writing Checklist**. Call on students to read the checklist aloud.
2. Pair students to review their writings together. Say: *Read your sentences with a partner. Use the Writing Checklist.* For additional help, remind students that a correct sentence:
   • *begins with a capital letter*
   • *has a subject*
   • *has a verb*
   • *has a period*
   • *is a complete idea*
3. Walk around and verify that students are using the checklist. Collect the papers for review or put them in the students' writing portfolios.

Teaching Tip: Digital skills

Tell students to use their phones to check the spelling of job titles or duties they talk about in their writing.

Self-Directed Learning

Point out the blue bar. Ask students if they can do the lesson learning objective or if they need more practice. Tell them to check one of the boxes. Assign Extra Practice as needed.

Extra Practice

 CCRS Plus   p. 96

Lesson 10

Write about your job history

1 STUDY THE MODEL

READ. Answer the questions.

Ana Pino

My Job History

I have a long job history. From 2012 to 2014, I was a stock clerk at Nexo in Mexico City. I stocked the shelves in the store. Three years later, I became a sales associate there. I helped customers and used the cash register. Now, I live in Houston, Texas. I am a store manager at World Mart. I supervise employees and plan work schedules.

1. Where did Ana work?
2. What did she do?
3. Where does Ana work now?
4. What does she do?

1. Ana worked in a store in Mexico.
2. She stocked shelves, helped customers, and used the cash register.
3. She now works at World Mart.
4. She supervises employees and plans work schedules.

2 PLAN YOUR WRITING

WORK TOGETHER. Ask and answer the questions.

1. Where did you work in the past?
2. What did you do?
3. Where do you work now?
4. What do you do?

3 WRITE

Now write about your job history. Use the model, the Writing Skill, and your ideas from Exercise 2 to help you.

Writing Skill: Use the correct tense

Use the simple past to explain your previous jobs. Use the present tense to explain your current job. For example:

Past: I was a stock clerk at Nexo in Mexico City.
Present: Now, I am a store manager at World Mart.

4 CHECK YOUR WRITING

WORK TOGETHER. Read the checklist. Read your writing aloud. Revise your writing.

WRITING CHECKLIST

☐ The paragraph answers all the questions in Exercise 2.

☐ The paragraph is indented.

☐ The verbs tenses are correct.

I can use the correct tense to describe my job history. ■   I need more practice. ■

For more practice, go to MyEnglishLab.

11 Lesson

Be honest

1 MEET RODRIGO

Read about one of his workplace skills.

> I am honest. I always tell the truth. I admit when I am wrong, and I try to learn from my mistakes.

2 RODRIGO'S PROBLEM

READ. Circle *True* or *False*.

Rodrigo wants to work at a company. He is in a job interview at the company. At his last job, he had a problem. He made a mistake, and his boss fired him. Rodrigo was upset, but he knows he made the mistake.

The interviewer asks, "Why did you leave your last job?" Rodrigo is not sure what to say.

1. Rodrigo is working at a company now.   True   (False)
2. Rodrigo's boss told him to leave his last job.   (True)   False
3. Rodrigo did something wrong at his last job.   (True)   False

3 RODRIGO'S SOLUTION

A **WORK TOGETHER.** Rodrigo is honest. He knows it is important to tell the truth. What does he say?

1. Rodrigo says, "My last job was awful, so I decided to leave."
2. Rodrigo says, "I was fired," and then he explains why his boss made a mistake.
3. Rodrigo says, "I was fired," and then he explains what he learned from the experience.
4. Rodrigo says, _____.

B **ROLE-PLAY.** Look at your answer to 3A. Role-play Rodrigo's conversation.

Show what you know!

1. **THINK ABOUT IT.** How are you honest in class? At work? At home? Give examples.

2. **WRITE ABOUT IT.** Write an example in your Skills Log.

   I am honest in class. When I don't know the answers in a test, I don't copy the answers from a classmate. I get the answers wrong and then learn from my mistakes.

I can give an example of how I am honest. ☐

Unit Review: Go back to page 145. Which unit goals can you check off?

Correlations

CASAS Reading: RDG 1.7, 1.8, 3.2
CASAS Listening: L2.1, 2.3, 4.1, 4.2
CASAS Competencies: 0.1.2, 0.1.4, 0.1.5, 0.1.6, 0.2.1, 4.8.1, 4.8.5
Complete standards language available on the Pearson English Portal.

Self-Directed Learning

State the **lesson objective**. Say: *In this lesson, we will give an example of how we are honest.*

1 MEET RODRIGO

1. Ask: *What is the title of this lesson?* (Be honest) Ask: *What does* honest *mean?* (telling the truth, being truthful)
2. Write: *Workplace Skill*. Read the directions. Say: *Listen as I read* Meet Rodrigo. Read the paragraph. Ask: *What is one of Rodrigo's workplace skills?* (He is honest.) Next to *Workplace Skill*, write: *Be honest*.
3. Under *Workplace Skill*, write: *Examples*. Ask: *How is Rodrigo honest?* (He always tells the truth. He admits when he is wrong. He learns from his mistakes.) Write the examples. Elicit other ways to be honest and write them under *Workplace Skill*.

2 RODRIGO'S PROBLEM

1. Say: *Now we are going to read about Rodrigo. Listen while I read.* Read the first two sentences. Say: *Look at the photo. Where is Rodrigo?* (a job interview) *Do we know what kind of job Rodrigo wants?* (no)
2. Say: *Rodrigo has a problem in his job interview. Listen while I read.* Read the rest of the paragraph. Explain any unfamiliar vocabulary as needed.
3. Students complete the questions after the reading. Call on students to answer. Ask them to **cite evidence**: *Where is that information?*
4. Ask: *What is Rodrigo's problem?* (He was fired from his last job. He is not sure what to say about it.)

3 RODRIGO'S SOLUTION

Ⓐ WORK TOGETHER. Rodrigo is honest. He…

1. Read the directions. Ask students to work together. Walk around and check that students understand that only one solution is correct.

2. Ask: *Is #1 being honest?* (no) *Why not?* (He does not tell the truth about being fired.) Ask: *Is #2 being honest?* (no) *Why not?* (He says he was fired, but he doesn't tell the truth about why.) Ask: *Is #3 being honest?* (yes) *Why?* (He tells the truth about being fired and learning from his mistakes.)
3. Ask students if they have any other ideas. Write their responses. Ask: *Is this being honest? Why?*

 ActiveTeach for 3A: Academic Conversation Support

Ⓑ ROLE-PLAY. Look at your answer to 3A…

1. Group students in pairs. Explain one person will be Rodrigo. The other person will be the interviewer. Model the activity with an above-level student. Have students practice the conversation with different partners.
2. Walk around and ask students to switch roles and continue practicing. If students aren't pronouncing their lines clearly, model correct pronunciation and ask them to repeat.
3. Invite one or two pairs of students to role-play the interaction for the whole class.

Show what you know!

1. THINK ABOUT IT. How are you honest in…

Read the directions. Have students think about their answers for a few minutes. Then ask them to share with a partner. Call on students to share with the class.

2. WRITE ABOUT IT. Write an example in your…

Read the directions and the example. Have students write their examples in their **Skills Log** at the back of the book. Circulate and assist students as needed.

Self-Directed Learning

1. Point out the blue bar. Ask students if they can do the lesson learning objective or if they need more practice. Tell them to check one of the boxes. Assign Extra Practice as needed.
2. Ask students to turn to page 145. Go to the Unit Wrap-Up teaching notes on page T-145.

Extra Practice

 p. 97

Classroom Materials / Extra Practice

ActiveTeach

MyEnglishLab

Workbook

Life Skills Writing, MCA, Team Projects, Persistence Activities

Unit Overview

Goals
- See the list of goals on the facing page

Pronunciation
- Pronunciation of *will*
- Extra syllables with *'s*

Reading
- Read about going to college
- Use information in graphs and tables

Grammar
- Future with *will*
- Adverbs of manner
- Object pronouns
- Possessive nouns

Writing
- Write about school
- Use commas between words in a list

Document Literacy and Numeracy
- Interpret a bar graph
- Compare cost of tuition

Workplace, Life, and Community Skills
- Leave a phone message
- Leave a voice message
- Digital Skills: Search how to set up a personal voicemail greeting message on your mobile phone

Life Skills Writing
- Complete an enrollment form

Soft Skills at Work
- Plan well

Preview

1. Set the context of the unit by asking questions about parents and children (for example, *Do you have children? How old are they? What are the most important jobs of a parent? What is difficult about being a parent?*).
2. Show the Unit Opener. Ask: *What is the unit title?* (Parents and Children)
3. Say: *Look at the picture.* Ask the Preview questions. (Possible answers: a mother and son; writing/doing homework; the mother helping the son)
4. Write the answers.

Unit Goals

1. Point to the Unit Goals. Explain that this list shows what you will be studying in this unit.
2. Tell students to read the goals silently.
3. Say each goal. Ask the class to repeat. Explain unfamiliar vocabulary as needed.
4. Point to the ☐ next to the first goal. Say: We will come back to this page again. *You will write a checkmark next to the goals you learned in the unit.*

Oral Presentation

1. Tell students they will give a short presentation at the end of the unit.
2. Write the topics:
   Option 1: Your school
   Option 2: Your educational goals
3. Assign the topics to two students.

Unit Wrap-Up

1. Review the Unit Goals with students.
2. Direct students to the Grammar Review.
3. If you assigned presentations, ask students to present.

 ActiveTeach for Wrap-Up: Team Project

 ActiveTeach for Wrap-Up: Persistence Activities

9 Parents and Children

PREVIEW

Look at the picture. What do you see?
Who are the people? What are they doing?

UNIT GOALS

- [ ] Identify school subjects
- [ ] Make plans for school events
- [ ] Leave a phone message
- [ ] Talk about school progress
- [ ] Discuss your child's behavior in school

- [ ] **Academic skill:** Use information in graphs and tables
- [ ] **Writing skill:** Use commas between words in a list
- [ ] **Workplace soft skill:** Show how you plan well

School subjects

A **PREDICT.** Look at the pictures. What school subjects are the students learning in each picture?

B ▶ **LISTEN AND POINT.** Then listen and repeat.

Self-Directed Learning

State the **lesson objective**. Say: *In this lesson, we will learn to identify school subjects.*

Ⓐ PREDICT. Look at the pictures. What school…

1. Read the directions. Tell students to cover the list on page 167.
2. Point to picture 1 and ask: *What school subject is this?* Say: *#1 is math.*
3. Say: *Look at the other numbers. What school subjects do you know?* Students call out answers. Help students pronounce the subjects if they have difficulty.
4. If students call out an incorrect subject, ask a *yes/no* clarification question: *Is #9 English?* (no) If nobody can identify the correct activity (world languages), tell students they will now listen to audio and practice the vocabulary for school subjects.

Ⓑ ▶ LISTEN AND POINT. Then listen and repeat.

1. Read the directions. Play the audio. Students listen and point to the school subjects.
2. While the audio is playing, walk around and check that students are pointing to the correct subjects. Pause the audio after item 10.
3. Say each subject in random order and ask students to point to the appropriate picture.
4. Tell students look at page 167. Resume the audio. Students, listen, read, and repeat.

 ActiveTeach for B: Vocabulary Flashcards

■ **EXPANSION: Vocabulary practice for B**
Tell students to look at the pictures and vocabulary on pages 166–167. Ask the class comprehension questions to reinforce vocabulary. Call on students to answer. For example:
• *Which subject teaches about songs?* (music)
• *Which subject teaches about numbers?* (math)
• *Which subject teaches about Spanish?* (world languages)
• *Which subject teaches about painting?* (art)

• *Which subject teaches about computers?* (technology)

Culture Note

1. Explain: *In the U.S., children have to attend school until they are 16 years old. This is the law. Public schools provide a free education. Local property taxes pay for public schools.*
2. Write the levels of education in the U.S. as headings on the board: *preschool, elementary school, middle school,* and *high school.*
3. Elicit or provide the grades/ages for each level of education. Note the grades and ages next to each heading on the board (preschool: usually 3–5 year olds; elementary school: K–5th grade / ages 5–11; middle school: 6th–8th grade / ages 11–14; high school: 9th–12th grade / ages 14–18). Ask: *About how old are preschoolers?* (4 years old) *Kindergartners?* (5 years old) *6th graders?* (11) *9th graders?* (14)
4. Explain: *Public education usually begins in kindergarten, but some districts have preschool.*
5. *Optional:* Explain: *Private schools require tuition.* Write: *tuition.* Say: *Tuition is the money you pay to go to a school. Private schools are not free.*
6. Ask: *Do children have to go to school in your native country? What are the laws? Are there schools that children can attend for free?*

Culture Note

One of the subjects on page 167 is "community service." More than half of all public schools in the U.S. organize community service activities for students. This is especially true in high school. These activities are not usually done as a separate class, but may be included in teaching other subjects. Some examples of community service are planting trees or a garden, collecting food for a food bank, making cards for the elderly, and collecting toys for children who may not have them.

Digital Skills for B

1. Ask: *What schools are in our community?* Say: *Go online and find out. Make a list. Find out information about that school.*
2. Tell students they can search online for *schools in [place].* They can also search for *[place] public schools* and *[place] private schools.*
3. After students complete their research, ask volunteers to come to the board and list schools in each category.

C WORK TOGETHER. Choose a school subject...

1. Read the directions. Write the example on the board. Ask: *What's the subject?* (science) *What do students learn about in science?* (the earth, the sun, health, electricity)
2. Tell the class to look at the list of words on page 167. Choose another school subject—not science. Elicit students' ideas for what students learn in that subject and write them on the board.
3. Pair students. Tell them to choose another school subject—not the ones on the board. Walk around and offer ideas as needed.
4. Each pair presents their list to the class. One partner reads the words and the other writes them on the board. They do not include the name of the subject, but only present the list of things learned in that subject.
5. The rest of the class guesses the subject after all the words are presented.

Study Tip: Test with a partner

1. Point to the **Study Tip**. Read the directions.
2. Pair students. Tell pairs to decide who is Student A. When pairs have finished, tell them to switch partners and repeat.
3. Say: *You can learn new words by using clues and testing with a partner.* Remind students to use this strategy to remember other new vocabulary.

Teaching Tip: Be an active language learner
As you visit with students, show them you are an active language learner yourself by trying to say school subjects in their native languages.

Show what you know!

1. THINK ABOUT IT. What are three very...

1. Read the directions.
2. Write a subject you think is very important and explain why (for example, *I think math is very important because you need to be able to manage your money.*).
3. Tell students to write a subject they think is very important and note why they think it's important.
4. Form groups of 3. Say: *Tell your group what subject you think is very important and why.*
5. Say: *Do you agree with your partners? Write the other two subjects you think are very important. Use your partners' ideas or your own ideas.*

2. WRITE ABOUT IT. Write two sentences about...

1. Read the directions. Show the example on the board.
2. Remind students to capitalize the first word in the sentence. Remind them to end with a period.
3. Share the checklist below. Then write a checkmark next to each as you point back to the example sentence.
   - The sentence names the subject.
   - The sentence starts with a capital letter.
   - The sentence ends with a period.
4. Give students time to write their sentences.
5. Tell students to show their sentences to a partner. Tell the students to use the checklist to review the sentences.
6. Walk around and verify that students are using the checklist. Collect the papers for review or put them in the students' writing portfolios.

■ EXPANSION: Vocabulary and speaking practice for 2

1. Ask: *What was your favorite school subject when you were a child? Why?* Tell students to write their answer in their notebooks.
2. Form groups of 3. Say: *Tell your group what your favorite school subject was when you were a child and why.*
3. Call on a few students to say what a partner's favorite subject was as a child and why.

3. PRESENT IT. Make a presentation to your...

1. Read the directions and the example.
2. Ask: *What are three important subjects for students to learn? Why?*
3. Form groups of 3. Tell students to take turns making a presentation to their group.
4. Call on volunteers to present to the whole class.

Self-Directed Learning

Point out the blue bar. Ask students if they can do the lesson learning objective or if they need more practice. Tell them to check one of the boxes. Assign Extra Practice as needed.

Extra Practice
pp. 98–99

Vocabulary

School subjects

1. math
2. English language arts
3. P.E. (physical education)
4. social studies/history

5. art
6. music
7. technology
8. community service

9. world languages
10. science

C WORK TOGETHER. Choose a school subject. What do students learn in that subject? Make a list. Talk about your list with the class.

science
the earth
the sun
health
electricity

Study Tip

Test with a Partner

Student A, close your book. Say all the school subjects you can remember. Student B, listen and check the list on this page. Help your partner remember all the school subjects.

Show what you know!

1. **THINK ABOUT IT.** What are three very important subjects for all students to learn? Why?

   _____   _____   _____

2. **WRITE ABOUT IT.** Write two sentences about an important subject.

   I think _____ is an important school subject.

3. **PRESENT IT.** Make a presentation to your classmates about three important subjects to learn and why they are important.

   I think science is important. There are a lot of jobs in science. You can work with computers. You can be a nursing assistant.

I can identify school subjects. ■   I need more practice. ■

For more practice, go to MyEnglishLab.

Make plans for school events

1 BEFORE YOU LISTEN

MATCH. Write the words next to the definitions.

notice   parent-teacher conference   PTO

1. _____parent-teacher conference_____ meeting with a student's teacher and his or her parents
2. _____PTO_____ Parent-Teacher Organization; group of teachers and parents of students in a school
3. _____notice_____ information that something will happen

2 LISTEN

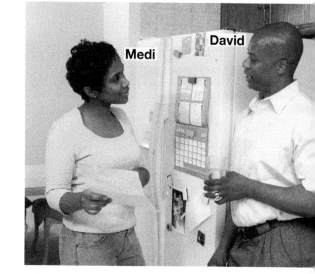
Medi   David

A PREDICT. Look at the picture. What are they talking about?

a. dinner plans
b. a problem with the refrigerator
c. a notice from school

B ▶ LISTEN FOR MAIN IDEA. What happens in two weeks?

a. There is a PTO meeting.
b. There is a parent-teacher conference.
c. They will get a notice.

C ▶ LISTEN FOR DETAILS. Listen again. Answer the questions.

1. When is the parent-teacher conference?
   a. Tuesday the 19th at 6:00
   b. Thursday the 19th at 6:00
   c. Thursday the 19th at 9:00

2. What does David have to do on the day of the conference?
   a. go to work
   b. go to class
   c. watch the kids

D ▶ EXPAND. Listen to the whole conversation. What is David going to do on Monday the 23rd?

a. go to work   b. go to a parent-teacher conference   c. go to a band concert

Correlations

ELPS Level 2: 2, 7
CCRS Level A: SL.K.3
CASAS Reading: RDG 1.7, 2.3
CASAS Listening: L1.4, 2.1, 2.3, 4.2, 6.1, 6.2, 6.5
CASAS Competencies: 0.1.2, 0.1.5
Complete standards language available on the Pearson English Portal.

Self-Directed Learning

State the **lesson objective**. Say: *In this lesson, we will learn to make plans for school events.*

1 BEFORE YOU LISTEN

MATCH. Write the words next to the definitions.

1. Say: *Most schools have regular events. Parents go to the school and meet with the teachers.*
2. Read the directions. Say the words and phrases in the box.
3. Ask students to read the definitions silently.
4. Form groups of 3. Together, students match the words and definitions.
5. Read each definition and call on a student to answer.
6. *Optional:* Give students a couple of minutes to study the words and definitions. While students are studying, write the words. Pronounce each word and ask the class to repeat. Tell them to close their books. Read the definitions in random order and ask the class to call out the words.
7. **Extend:** Write *parent-teacher conference* and *PTO meeting* on the board. Brainstorm things people talk about in each setting. List students' ideas on the board (for example, *parent-teacher conference: grades, attendance, behavior, homework*; *PTO meeting: school events, fundraisers*).

2 LISTEN

A PREDICT. **Look at the picture. What are...**

1. Tell students to look at the picture. Ask: *Where are they?* (in a kitchen). *What are they doing?* (talking, holding a paper)
2. Ask: *What do you think they are talking about?*
3. Ask students to raise their hands if they circled *a*. Repeat with *b* and *c*.

B ▶ LISTEN FOR MAIN IDEA. **What happens...**

1. Read the directions. Have students read answer choices silently.
2. Play the audio. Students listen and choose the correct answer.
3. Ask: *Was your guess in Exercise 2A correct?*
4. Ask students to raise their hands if they circled *a*. Repeat with *b* and *c*.
5. Ask about **register:** *What is Medi's and David's relationship?* (They are married/parents.) *How do you know?* (They are talking about a parent-teacher conference at school for their son.)

C ▶ LISTEN FOR DETAILS. **Listen again...**

1. Read the directions. Tell students to read the sentences and answer choices silently.
2. Play the audio. Students circle the letter of the correct answer.
3. Students compare answers with a partner.
4. Call on students to answer the questions.

Teaching Tip: Use the script

Optional: If students need additional support, tell them to read the Audio Script on page 272 as they listen to the conversations.

D ▶ EXPAND. **Listen to the whole...**

1. Read the directions. Tell students to read the answer choices silently.
2. Play the audio. Students choose the correct answer.
3. Ask: *Do you need to listen one more time?* If yes, play the audio again.
4. Review the correct answer with the class.

Culture Note

1. Say: *In the U.S., parent-teacher conferences are usually held twice a year—in the fall and in the spring. Teachers tell parents how their children are doing in school, and parents ask questions.*
2. Ask: *In your native country, do parents and teachers have conferences? If so, how often are they? What do they talk about?*

Listening and Speaking

3 PRONUNCIATION

A ▶ **PRACTICE. Listen. Then listen and repeat.**

1. Read the **Pronunciation Note**. Tell students to underline *'ll / will* in the sentence.
2. Read the directions.
3. Play the audio. Students listen. Then students listen and repeat.
4. Say each of the pronouns contracted with *will* in the first four sentences. Ask the class to repeat. Ask: *What other pronouns are there?* Write the contractions of the board (*you'll, it'll, they'll*). Pronounce them and ask the class to repeat.
5. Ask: *Why is* will *not contracted after* mother? (because it comes after *mother*, which is not a pronoun)

 ActiveTeach for 3A: Pronunciation Coach

B ▶ **CHOOSE. Listen and circle the words you...**

1. Read the directions. Tell students to read the sentences.
2. Play the audio. Students circle the words they hear.
3. Call on students to read the sentences with the correct words.

4 CONVERSATION

A ▶ **LISTEN AND READ. Then listen and repeat.**

1. Note: This conversation is the same one students heard in Exercise 2B on page 168.
2. Tell students to read the conversation and underline *will* and *'ll*.
3. Play the audio. Students read along silently. Then students listen and repeat.
4. Walk around and help with pronunciation as needed. Pay particular attention to the students' pronunciation of *will*.

B **WORK TOGETHER. Practice the...**

1. Pair students and tell them to practice the conversation in Exercise 4A.
2. Tell students to take turns playing A and B. Walk around and check that students are using the correct pronunciation of *will* and *'ll*.

C **CREATE. Make new conversations. Use the...**

1. Read the directions.
2. Tell students to look at the school events in the blue box. To check comprehension, describe the events in random order and ask the class to

call out the event: *parents and teachers talking about how to improve the school* (PTO meeting), *students acting on stage with parents and friends watching in the audience* (school play), *students showing their projects on things like health, technology, the environment, and space* (science fair). *Optional:* Call on above-level students to describe each event in random order and ask the class to call out the event.
3. Show the conversation on the board with blanks. Read it and when you come to a blank, fill it in with information from the boxes.
4. Ask two on-level students to practice the conversation on the board for the class.
5. Erase the words in the blanks and ask two above-level students to make up a new conversation in front of the class.
6. Tell pairs to take turns playing A and B and to use the information in the boxes.
7. Walk around and check students' pronunciation of *will* and *I'll*. As needed, pronounce the words and ask students to repeat.
8. Tell students to stand, mingle, and practice the conversation with several new partners.
9. Call on pairs to practice for the class.

D **ROLE-PLAY. Make your own conversations.**

1. Point to the blue box and ask: *What other school events can you think of?* (a parent-teacher conference, a band concert, an art show, a baseball game, a college fair)
2. Point to the yellow box and ask: *What else can you do to leave work early?* (change my shift, take personal/vacation time, talk to my boss)
3. Pair students and tell them to practice the conversation.
4. Walk around and check students' pronunciation of *will* and *I'll*.
5. Call on pairs to perform for the class.

■■■ **MULTILEVEL INSTRUCTION for 4C**
Above-level expansion Direct students to change other information in the conversation, such as dates, times, names, and who will watch the kids.

Self-Directed Learning
Point out the blue bar. Ask students if they can do the lesson learning objective or if they need more practice. Tell them to check one of the boxes. Assign Extra Practice as needed.

Extra Practice

  p. 100

Listening and Speaking

3 PRONUNCIATION

A ▶ PRACTICE. Listen. Then listen and repeat.

I'll try.　　　　　She'll meet him there.
We'll both go.　　My mother will watch the kids.
He'll be at work.

B ▶ CHOOSE. Listen and circle the words you hear.

1. **She will / (She'll)** send a notice.
2. **(I'll) / I will** be there after work.
3. **(We'll) / We will** go to the meeting.
4. **They will / (They'll)** meet next Tuesday.

4 CONVERSATION

A ▶ LISTEN AND READ. Then listen and repeat.

A: Carlo brought a notice home from school today. There's a parent-teacher conference in two weeks.
B: Oh yeah? What day?
A: Thursday the 19th at 6:00. My mother will watch the kids. That way we can both go.
B: Oh, I have to work that day until 9:00, but I'll try to change my shift.

B WORK TOGETHER. Practice the conversation in Exercise A.

C CREATE. Make new conversations. Use the words in the boxes.

A: Carlo brought a notice home from school today.
There's a _____ in two weeks.
B: Oh, yeah? What day?
A: Thursday the 19th at 6:00. My mother will watch the kids. That way we can both go.
B: Oh, I have to be at work that day until 9:00, but I'll _____ .

school play
PTO meeting
science fair

switch hours with someone
ask if I can leave early
change my schedule

D ROLE-PLAY. Make your own conversations.

I can make plans for school events. ☐　　　　I need more practice. ☐

For more practice, go to MyEnglishLab.

Future with *will*

Future with *will*			Grammar Watch
Affirmative		**Negative**	

Affirmative

I	will 'll	**try** to change my shift.

Negative

I	will not won't	**be** late.

Grammar Watch

- Use *will* + the base form of a verb.
- *won't* = *will not.*
- Use contractions *'ll* and *won't* for speaking and informal writing.

A COMPLETE. Use *will* and the words in parentheses to talk about the future.

1. Abe ____will work____ the evening shift this week.
   (work)

2. Her manager ____will call____ the supplier about the problem.
   (call)

3. They ____will have____ a meeting tomorrow.
   (have)

4. Rico ____won't be____ at work this morning. He has an appointment.
   (not / be)

5. The office ____won't open____ on Monday because it is a holiday.
   (not / open)

6. Drew ____will be____ late for dinner.
   (be)

7. Kids ____won't have____ school on Friday, so a lot of people ____will take____
   (not / have)   (take)
   that day off work.

B APPLY. Complete the sentences with the words in the box and *will* to talk about the future.

> meet   go   send   not be   ~~see~~   check   talk about

A: I _____'ll see_____ you at the PTO meeting on Thursday night, right?

B: I'm sorry, I _____won't be_____ there. I have to work.

A: That's too bad. We _____'ll talk about_____ some important things.

B: Well, you _____'ll meet_____ again next month, right?

A: I think so. I _____'ll check_____ the date of the next meeting, and I _____'ll send_____ you a text.

B: Yes, please. I _____'ll go_____ to the next meeting. I promise.

Correlations

ELPS Level 2: 2, 7, 10
CCRS Level A: L.1.1
CASAS Reading: RDG 1.7, L3.1
CASAS Listening: L1.3, 2.1, 2.3, 3.3, 4.1, 4.2
CASAS Competencies: 0.1.2, 0.1.5, 0.2.1, 3.1.2
Complete standards language available on the Pearson English Portal.

Self-Directed Learning

State the **lesson objective**. Say: *In this lesson, we will learn to use the future with* will.

Future with *will*

 ActiveTeach: Grammar Discovery

1. Warm up. Say: *The conversation on page 169 used this grammar.* Turn back to page 169. Point to the sentences in Exercise 4A and then write:
   - *My mother will watch the kids.*
   - *I'll try to change my shift.*
2. Read the sentences and underline *will* and *I'll*. Ask: *What is* I'll *a contraction of?* (I will)
3. Tell students to look at the grammar charts. Read the sentences and ask the class to repeat.
4. Read the first point of the **Grammar Watch** note. Point to the left chart and read the first sentence (*I will try to change my shift.*). Ask: *What is the base form of the verb?* (try)
5. Read the second point of the **Grammar Watch** note. Point to the right chart and read both sentences (*I will not / won't be late.*).
6. Point to the sentence on the board. Ask: *How do you make this sentence negative?* (add *not* after *will*) Erase *will* and write *will not*: *My mother will not watch the kids.*
7. Read the third point of the **Grammar Watch** note. Point to the left chart and read the second sentence (*I'll try to change my shift.*).
8. Write: *He will change his schedule.* Ask the class to change the sentence to what people say (*He'll change his schedule.*). Then ask the class to change the sentence to make it negative (*He won't change his schedule.*).

 ActiveTeach: Grammar Coach

A COMPLETE. **Use** *will* **and the words in…**

1. Read the directions and the example.
2. Students compare answers with a partner. Tell them to take turns reading the sentences.
3. Call on students to read the sentences. Correct as needed.

■ **EXPANSION: Grammar and writing practice for A**

Tell students to rewrite the sentences in Exercise A using pronouns and contractions. For example, *He'll work the evening shift this week. / She'll call the supplier about the problem. / It won't open on Monday because it is a holiday.*

■ **EXPANSION: Grammar and writing practice for A**

Tell students to rewrite the sentences in Exercise A switching negative to affirmative and affirmative to negative. To make the sentences work, they may need to change other information. For example, *Rico will be at work this morning. His appointment was cancelled. / The office will open on Monday after all. / Kids have school on Friday. It's a normal day. Most people won't take that day off.*

B APPLY. **Complete the sentences with the…**

1. Read the directions. Say the verbs in the box. Say: *These are the base forms of verbs.*
2. Read the example. Tell students that it is OK to use contractions.
3. Students compare answers with a partner by reading the conversation. After they correct their answers, tell them to read the conversation again.
4. Call on pairs to perform the conversation for the class. Correct as needed.

Culture Note

Point to the picture in the book and ask: *Who do you think these people are?* (a student, his family, and his teacher). Exercise B mentions a PTO meeting. *PTO* stands for "Parent Teacher Organization." A similar organization is the PTA, which stands for "Parent Teacher Association." Both PTOs and PTAs are groups at schools in which teachers and parents work together to improve the school and help students. PTOs and PTAs conduct fundraising activities for the school and discuss issues that the school faces. They meet regularly—usually once a month.

Grammar

C COMPLETE. Use *will* and the words in...

1. Read the directions. Ask: *Is an email to a friend formal or informal writing?* (informal) *Is it OK to use contractions?* (yes)
2. Students compare answers with a partner.
3. Call on an above-level student to read the email out loud.
4. Ask comprehension questions: *What is the event?* (Sue's school play) *Will Anita's husband, Jack, go?* (no) *Who will go?* (Anita and her kids) *What time does Anita have to work until?* (6:30) *What time is the play?* (at 8:00) *When will Anita call Jane?* (on Sunday)

Show what you know!

1. THINK ABOUT IT. Look at the chart. Choose...

1. Tell students to look at the picture of a school bake sale. Ask: *What is for sale?* (cookies, cupcakes, bread) Explain that at a school bake sale the members of a club or school group, such as the PTO or PTA, make desserts like cookies and cupcakes and sell them to make money for the club or school.
2. Read the directions.
3. Show the chart on the board. Say each event task and ask the class to repeat. Ask: *What's a flyer?* (a piece of paper advertising something) If possible, show the class flyers for events at your school or in your community.
4. Model the activity. Say: *I will design a flyer and clean up after the event.* Write your name on the chart for these tasks. Say: *Choose two tasks that you can do.* Students write their names next to the tasks in their books.

■ EXPANSION: Vocabulary practice for 1

1. Explain that a *bake sale* is a type of *fundraiser*—an event to make money for a specific cause or group.
2. Ask: *Can you think of any other types of school fundraisers?* (a car wash, a candy sale, a school fair / carnival)

2. TALK ABOUT IT. Work in a group. Decide...

1. Read the directions and the example.
2. Model the activity. Ask four above-level students to stand up. Say: *We are a group.* For each task on the chart, ask: *Who wants to...?* and write the name of a group member.

3. Form groups of 5. Tell group members to take turns asking *Who wants to...?* Direct each group member to volunteer to do one task.
4. Groups take turns presenting their plans to the class. Model the presentation. Tell the class to look at the chart on the board. Point to each row and say who will do each task. Use *will* (for example, *Phuong will get permission from the school. Arturo will design a flyer.*).
5. One student from each group tells the class about the group's plans.

■ EXPANSION: Writing and speaking practice for 2

1. Brainstorm what information to include on an event flyer for the bake sale. Make a list on the board (for example, *when the event is, where the event is, the cost of the event, what is going to be sold,* etc.).
2. Direct each group to create a flyer for their event. If possible, provide students with poster paper and markers. Tell students to first plan on a sheet of notebook paper.
3. Ask one student from each group to show the flyer to the class and talk about when and where the bake sale will take place.

3. WRITE ABOUT IT. Now write a sentence...

1. Read the directions and the example. Tell students to include a sentence about themselves: *I'll...*
2. Ask groups to check each other's sentences.
   - There should be five sentences.
   - Sentences should use *will* + the base form of the verb.
   - Sentences should use contractions.
3. Ask for volunteers to write a few sentences on the board.

Self-Directed Learning

Point out the blue bar. Ask students if they can do the lesson learning objective or if they need more practice. Tell them to check one of the boxes. Assign Extra Practice as needed.

Extra Practice
MyEnglishLab Workbook p. 100

Grammar

C **COMPLETE. Use *will* and the words in parentheses.**

To: jane@abc.com
Subject: Invitation

Hi Jane,

Thank you for inviting us to Sue's school play next Friday night. Unfortunately, Jack has a class, so he _won't be_
                                                                                                    1. (not / be)

there. But the kids and I _will come_. I usually get out of work at around 6:30, but I _will leave_ early if I can. The
                           2. (come)   **3. (leave)**

kids and I _will eat_ a quick dinner, and we _will get_ to the school around 8:00. Don't worry—we
              4. (eat)   **5. (get)**

won't be late! I'm going out now, so I _won't call_ you tonight. I _will call_ you on Sunday, and we
6. (not / be)   **7. (not / call)**   **8. (call)**

will talk some more then.
9. (talk)

Anita

Show what you know!

1. **THINK ABOUT IT. Look at the chart. Choose two tasks that you can do for a bake sale at school.**

a school bake sale

Event: School Bake Sale	
Event task	**Group member**
get permission from the school	
design a flyer	
decide who will bring what	
set up before the event	
clean up after the event	

2. **TALK ABOUT IT. Work in a group. Decide who will do each task in the chart. Complete the chart.**

   A: Who wants to get permission from the school?
   B: I'll call the principal tomorrow.

3. **WRITE ABOUT IT. Now write a sentence about what each person will do.**

   Marta will call the principal tomorrow.

I can use the future with *will.* ■	I need more practice. ■

For more practice, go to MyEnglishLab.

Voicemail messages

1 LEAVE A PHONE MESSAGE

Winter Hill Elementary School.

A **PREDICT.** Look at the picture. Why is the woman calling the school?

B ▶ **LISTEN.** Was your guess in Exercise A correct?

C ▶ **IDENTIFY.** Read the phone messages. Listen to the conversation again. Circle the number of the correct message.

1.

Date _3/9_ Time _1:15_

To _Mr. Taylor_

> **While You Were Out**

From _Elsa Vega (Maria's teacher)_

Phone _(718) 555-4343_

Message: _Will call back._

_____

②

Date _3/9_ Time _1:15_

To _Mr. Taylor_

> **While You Were Out**

From _Elsa Vega (Maria's mom)_

Phone _(718) 555-4343_

Message: _Please call back._

_____

2 LEAVE A VOICEMAIL MESSAGE

A ▶ **LISTEN.** The teacher leaves Ms. Vega a message on her mobile phone. Complete the missing information.

●●●○○ 🔊 **3:57 PM** 33% 🔋

‹ **Voicemail** +

John Taylor
May 23 at 2:15 PM

▶ ●━━━

Transcript
"Ms. Vega, this is Mr. Taylor. I'm returning your call. Since Maria was home sick today, she _won't_ need to complete next week's unit, but she _will_ need to complete this week's unit. _She'll_ take the quiz on Tuesday. Please _call_ me or _email_ me at jtaylor@winterhill.edu. if you have questions."

I can leave a phone message. ■   I need more practice. ■

For more practice, go to MyEnglishLab.

Workplace, Life, and Community Skills

Correlations

ELPS Level 2: 1, 2, 3, 4, 5, 6, 7, 8, 9, 10
CCRS Level A: W.1.7, W.1.8
CASAS Reading: RDG 1.7, 1.8, 2.3, 3.2
CASAS Listening: L2.1, 2.3, 4.2, 6.5
CASAS Competencies: 0.1.2, 0.1.5, 2.1.7, 4.5.6, 7.4.4, 7.7.3
Complete standards language available on the Pearson English Portal.

Self-Directed Learning

State the **lesson objective**. Say: *In this lesson, we will learn to leave a phone message and leave a voicemail message.*

1 LEAVE A PHONE MESSAGE

A PREDICT. **Look at the picture. Why is the...**

1. Ask: *Do you take phone messages at home? Where do you write them?*
2. Ask the class: *Do you answer the phone at work? What do you do if someone's not available to take a call?*
3. Read the directions. Pair students.
4. Give pairs time to come up with an answer to the question. Then point to the woman in the right half of the picture and ask: *Why is the woman calling the school?* (to talk to her child's teacher)
5. Elicit students' guesses and list them on the board.

B ► LISTEN. **Was your guess in Exercise A...**

1. Read the directions. Play the audio.
2. Ask: *Why is the woman calling the school?* Read the guesses on the board. Elicit and circle the best answer.
3. Ask: *What does the woman have a question about?* (her daughter's math homework)

C ► IDENTIFY. **Read the phone messages...**

1. Read the directions. Tell students to read the messages silently. Tell them to circle what is different in each message (1. *Will* call back. / Elsa Vega (Maria's *teacher*), 2. *Please* call back. / Elsa Vega (Maria's *mom*))
2. Say: *Now listen again.* Point to the woman in the right half of the picture and ask: *Is she Maria's teacher or Maria's mom? Who will call back, Ms. Vega or Mr. Taylor?*
3. Play the audio.

4. Repeat the questions above and elicit answers. (*Elsa Vega is Maria's mom; Mr. Taylor will call back.*) Then ask the class to call out the number of the correct message (#2).
5. *Optional:* To review prepositions of time, ask: *When did Elsa Vega call?* (on March 9th at 1:15)

Self-Directed Learning

Point out the blue bar at the bottom of page 172. Ask students if they can do the lesson learning objective or if they need more practice. Tell them to check one of the boxes. Assign Extra Practice as needed.

2 LEAVE A VOICEMAIL MESSAGE

A ► LISTEN. **The teacher leaves Ms. Vega a...**

Document Literacy: Voicemail message

Context: You leave voicemail messages on home phones and mobile phones when someone doesn't answer.
Purpose: A voicemail message explains why you called and gives information about calling you back.
Key Words: *voicemail, transcript*

1. Tell students to look at the voicemail message. Orient them to the message. *Who left this voicemail message?* (John Taylor) *When did he leave it?* (May 23 at 2:15 PM) Ask about **context**: *Where is this voicemail messages?* (on a mobile phone) *Whose phone is it?* (Ms. Vega's) Ask about **purpose**: *What are voicemail messages for?* (to explain why you called and give information about calling you back) Tell students to circle John Taylor's email address in the message. Elicit the **key words** (*voicemail, transcript*). Say: *A transcript is a written copy of something that is said.*
2. Read the directions. Tell students to read the message silently.
3. Play the audio. Tell students to write the missing information.
4. Students compare answers with a partner.
5. Play the audio again for students to check answers.

Culture Note

1. Say: *Parents in the U.S. generally keep their children home when they are sick, especially if they have a fever.*
2. Ask: *In your native country, when do parents keep their children home from school?*

Workplace, Life, and Community Skills

B INTEPRET. **Read the voicemail messages...**

1. Read the directions.
2. Tell students to read the two voicemail messages silently. Ask: *Who are the messages from?* (Laura Jeffrey and Sasha Burton) *Who received the messages?* (Elsa Vega)
3. Read item 1. Ask: *Who is the first message for?* (Ms. Vega) Say: *So, the answer is true.*
4. Tell students to find information in the voicemails and answer the questions. If necessary, for item 3, clarify that this is the meeting that Laura Jeffrey invites Lisa Vega to.
5. Ask the class which items are false. Call on students to read the corrected sentences.
6. **Extend:** Ask: *Who do you think Sasha Burton is?* Give student's a hint if necessary. Have them look back at Exercise 1C on page 172 to remember that Elsa Vega is a mom. (Sasha Burton is therefore probably another mom, who can't make the meeting.)

C APPLY. **Take turns leaving messages or...**

1. Read the directions.
2. Pair students. Students use the chart to pretend to leave voicemails on each other's phones.
3. Circulate to help students as needed.
4. Call on pairs to perform for the class.

 Active Teach for 2C: Academic Conversation Support

■■ EXPANSION: Writing practice for 2C

Instead of leaving a voicemail, have students send a text with the same information. If you do not want students to send actual texts, tell them to write their message on a piece of paper and exchange it. Their partner can then write a short reply (for example, *No problem. I'll tell you about the meeting later.*) and give the paper back.

Culture Note

Voicemails and text messages should be as brief as possible. State who you are, what you need, a brief reason why, and how to contact you. Say your phone number or email slowly twice to make it easier to write them down.

■■ MULTILEVEL INSTRUCTION for 2C

Pre-level scaffolding Students write out their voicemail first before they say it out loud.

Above-level expansion Challenge above-level students to use information for a voicemail that is not in the book.

D GO ONLINE. **Search how to set up a...**

1. Read the directions. Ask students what they would search in English if they wanted to find information about recording a voicemail greeting.
2. Write the search string: *setting up my voicemail greeting.* Have students search the internet. As a class, brainstorm what a greeting should say. Write ideas on the board. Say: *You want a greeting that is short and says who you are.*
3. Ask students to help each other set up voicemail greetings. Challenge them to record bilingual greetings.

Digital Skills for 2D

When you receive a phone call from a number that you don't recognize, it is a good idea to let it go to voicemail. It may be a call from someone you don't want to talk to, for example, someone trying to cheat you or sell you something.

 ActiveTeach: Review

Self-Directed Learning

Point out the blue bar. Ask students if they can do the lesson learning objective or if they need more practice. Tell them to check one of the boxes. Assign Extra Practice as needed.

Extra Practice

| MyEnglishLab | Workbook p. 101 | English Portal Life Skills Writing |

Workplace, Life, and Community Skills

B **INTERPRET.** Read the voicemail messages below. Circle *True* or *False*.

1.

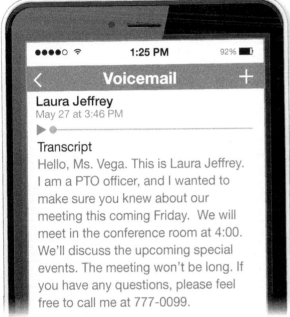

●●●●○ 📶	1:25 PM	92% 🔋

‹ Voicemail +

Laura Jeffrey
May 27 at 3:46 PM

▶ ●───────────

Transcript
Hello, Ms. Vega. This is Laura Jeffrey. I am a PTO officer, and I wanted to make sure you knew about our meeting this coming Friday. We will meet in the conference room at 4:00. We'll discuss the upcoming special events. The meeting won't be long. If you have any questions, please feel free to call me at 777-0099.

2.

●●○○○ 📶	3:18 PM	52% 🔋

‹ Voicemail +

Sasha Burton
June 16 at 9:15 PM

▶ ●───────────

Transcript
Hi, Elsa. It's Sasha. Will you be at the meeting on Friday? I won't be there. I have to work. Can you get an extra copy of the special events calendar for me? I'll get it from you when I see you on Sunday. Thanks!

1. The first message is for Ms. Vega.   (True)   False
2. The PTO officer invites Elsa to a meeting.   (True)   False
3. The meeting will be long.   True   (False)
4. Sasha will be at the meeting on Friday.   True   (False)
5. Sasha asks her friend for help.   (True)   False
6. The friends will see each other on Sunday.   (True)   False

C **APPLY.** Take turns leaving messages or voicemails. Use the information in the chart below.

What you need	You need a ride home from work	The homework assignment for tomorrow
Who you need to call	Mario	Lin
The reason you need something	Your car is broken	You missed class
How to contact you	Call back at 555-1122	E-mail happyday@gletter.com

D GO ONLINE. Search how to set up a personal voicemail greeting message on your mobile phone. If you don't have a greeting message, set one up.

I can leave a voicemail message. ⬜   I need more practice. ⬜

For more practice, go to MyEnglishLab.

Lesson 5

Talk about progress in school

1 BEFORE YOU LISTEN

A **READ.** How can students get extra help in school?

> Sometimes students have trouble in their classes. Students can get help from their parents and older brothers and sisters. Sometimes they can get extra help from teachers or older students before or after school. Most local libraries also have programs to help students with their schoolwork.

2 LISTEN

A **PREDICT.** Look at the picture. Where are they? Who is Mr. Thompson?

Mr. Thompson

Medi

B ▶ **LISTEN FOR MAIN IDEA.** Answer the questions.

1. What does Medi say?
   a. How are you doing?   **b.** How's Carlo doing?

2. What are they talking about?
   a. Carlo's progress   **b.** the parent-teacher conference

C ▶ **LISTEN FOR DETAILS.** Listen again. Answer the questions.

1. What subject is Carlo doing well in?
   Math.

2. What subject *isn't* Carlo doing well in?
   Social studies.

D ▶ **EXPAND.** Listen to the whole conversation. What does Carlo's teacher suggest?

a. help from older students
b. extra homework
c. help from his parents

Correlations

ELPS Level 2: 2, 7
CCRS Level A: SL.K.3
CASAS Reading: RDG 1.7, 2.3
CASAS Listening: L2.1, 2.3, 4.2, 6.1, 6.2, 6.5
CASAS Competencies: 0.1.2, 0.1.4, 0.1.5, 0.1.6, 2.8.6
Complete standards language available on the Pearson English Portal.

Self-Directed Learning

State the **lesson objective**. Say: *In this lesson, we will learn to talk about progress in school.*

1 BEFORE YOU LISTEN

READ. How can students get extra help in...

1. Tell students to read the paragraph silently.
2. Ask: *What are some ways students can get extra help in school?* Tell students to read again and underline the people and place students can go to for extra help.
3. Ask again: *What are some ways students can get extra help with school?* Elicit and list on the board: *parents, older brothers and sisters, teachers (before or after school), older students (before or after school), local libraries.*

2 LISTEN

A PREDICT. Look at the picture. Where are...

1. Tell students to look at the picture. Ask: *Who do you see?* (Mr. Thompson and Medi, a man and a woman) *Where are they?* (at school, in a classroom). *Who do you think Mr. Thompson is?* (a teacher, her child's teacher)
2. Elicit ideas and write them.

B ▶ LISTEN FOR MAIN IDEA. Answer the...

1. Read the directions. Have students read the questions and answer choices silently.
2. Play the audio. Students listen and choose the correct answers.
3. Call on students to answer the questions.
4. Ask: *Was your guess in Exercise 2A correct?* Ask for a show of hands.
5. Ask about **register**: *Have Mr. Thompson and Medi met before?* (no) *How do you know?* (He says *Nice to meet you*, and she says *Nice to meet you, too.*)

Career Awareness: Elementary school teacher

Elementary school teachers work in schools where the children are usually between the ages of six and eleven. They often have to be able to teach all subjects. They need to be patient and caring. They must have a bachelor's degree and some special training in the field of education.

■ EXPANSION: Career awareness for 2B

Ask students about the job in this lesson: *What does an elementary school teacher do? Where does an elementary teacher work? Do you need to study to be an elementary school teacher? Do you want to be an elementary school teacher?*

C ▶ LISTEN FOR DETAILS. Listen again...

1. Read the directions. Tell students to read the questions silently.
2. Play the audio. Students answer the questions.
3. Students compare answers with a partner by asking and answering one question each.
4. Call on students to answer the questions.

Teaching Tip: Use the script

Optional: If students need additional support, tell them to read the Audio Script on page 272 as they listen to the conversations.

D ▶ EXPAND. Listen to the whole...

1. Read the directions. Tell students to read the answer choices silently.
2. Play the audio. Students choose the correct answer.
3. Ask students to raise their hands for each answer choice.
4. To review, ask: *What does Carlo's teacher suggest?* (homework help after school / help from older students)
5. **Extend:** Ask: *Is the homework help program before or after school?* (after school) *How much does it cost?* (It's free.) *Do schools here have homework help?*

Culture Note

1. Say: *In the U.S., students usually have homework every night. Students in elementary school often have about 30 minutes of homework a night. In high school, students usually have between 2–3 hours of homework a night.*
2. Ask: *In your native country, do kids have homework every day? If so, how much homework do they have?*

Listening and Speaking

3 CONVERSATION

A ▶ LISTEN AND READ. Then listen and repeat.

1. Note: This conversation is the same one students heard in Exercise 2B on page 174.
2. Play the audio. Students read along silently. Then students listen and repeat.

B WORK TOGETHER. Practice the…

1. Pair students and tell them to practice the conversation in Exercise 3A.
2. Tell students to take turns playing A and B.

C CREATE. Make new conversations. Use the…

1. Read the directions.
2. Tell students to look at the information in the boxes. Ask: *What do you see in the blue and orange boxes?* (school subjects) *What is in the green box?* (things someone does well in school) *What is in the yellow box?* (suggestions, advice) Say each word or phrase and have students repeat.
3. Show the conversation on the board with blanks. Fill in the blanks with information from the boxes.
4. Ask two on-level students to practice the conversation on the board for the class. Tell A to use his/her own name. Tell B to use *mother* if female, and *father* if male.
5. Erase the words in the blanks and ask two above-level students to make up a new conversation in front of the class.
6. Tell pairs to take turns playing A and B and to use information from the boxes to fill in the blanks.
7. Tell students to stand, mingle, and practice the conversation with several new partners.
8. Walk around and assist students as necessary.
9. Call on pairs to perform for the class.

D ROLE-PLAY. Make your own conversations.

1. Point to the blue and orange boxes and ask: *What other subjects can you think of?* Encourage students to add subjects from their own classes (*English, grammar, listening, speaking, citizenship,* etc.) List students' ideas on the board.
2. Point to the green box and ask: *What are other things students do well?* (reads quickly, asks good questions, takes notes, practices new vocabulary, pays attention, etc.) List students' ideas on the board.
3. Point to the yellow box and ask: *What are some other suggestions to help students improve?* (take more notes, practice more, get homework help, etc.) List students' ideas on the board.
4. Model the conversation with an above-level student.
5. Pair students and tell them to practice the conversation.
6. Walk around and remind students to switch roles.
7. Call on pairs to perform for the class.

■■■ MULTILEVEL INSTRUCTION for 3D

Above-level expansion Tell students to role-play conversations in which they get feedback from the teacher about their own performance in class.

Self-Directed Learning

Point out the blue bar. Ask students if they can do the lesson learning objective or if they need more practice. Tell them to check one of the boxes. Assign Extra Practice as needed.

Extra Practice
pp. 102–103

Listening and Speaking

3 CONVERSATION

A ▶ **LISTEN AND READ. Then listen and repeat.**

A: Hi, I'm Harold Thompson, Carlo's teacher. Nice to meet you.
B: I'm Carlo's mother. Nice to meet you, too. So, how's Carlo doing?
A: Carlo's a good student. I enjoy having him in class.
B: That's good to hear.
A: He does very well in math. He works carefully.
B: He likes math a lot. What about social studies?
A: Well, he's having a little trouble in that class. He needs to do his homework.
B: OK. I'll talk to him.

B **WORK TOGETHER. Practice the conversation in Exercise A.**

C **CREATE. Make new conversations. Use the words in the boxes.**

A: Hi, I'm _____, Carlo's teacher. Nice to meet you.
B: I'm Carlo's _____. Nice to meet you, too.
   So, how's Carlo doing?
A: Carlo's a good student. I enjoy having him in class.
B: That's good to hear.
A: He does very well in _____. He _____.
B: He likes _____ a lot. What about _____?
A: Well, he's having a little trouble in that class.
   He needs to _____.
B: OK. I'll talk to him.

science	learns quickly	language arts	ask more questions
social studies	studies hard	science	spend extra time on it
language arts	writes well	math	study a little more

D **ROLE-PLAY. Make your own conversations.**

I can talk about progress in school. ■   I need more practice. ■

For more practice, go to MyEnglishLab.

Lesson 6 Adverbs of manner

Adverbs of manner				
Adjective			**Adverb**	
	careful			carefully.
Carlo is a	quick	worker.	Carlo works	quickly.
	good			well.

Grammar Watch

- To create most adverbs of manner, add -*ly* to the adjective. See page 259 for more spelling rules.
- A few adverbs of manner are irregular:
  good → **well**
  hard → **hard**
  fast → **fast**

A **COMPLETE. Change the underlined adjectives to adverbs of manner. Then complete the sentences.**

1. Sonia is a <u>careless</u> worker. She works _____*carelessly*_____.
2. Kevin's pronunciation is <u>clear</u>. He speaks _____clearly_____.
3. Amad is a <u>fast</u> learner. He learns _____fast_____.
4. Your children are <u>good</u> students. They do _____well_____ in school.
5. My team leader is a <u>hard</u> worker. He works _____hard_____.
6. Chi is very <u>quiet</u>. She does her work _____quietly_____.
7. Luke's handwriting is <u>neat</u>. He writes _____neatly_____.

B **APPLY. Change the adjectives to adverbs of manner. Then complete the sentences.**

careful   creative   good   hard   quick   ~~slow~~

1. Chen isn't fast. He works _____*slowly*_____.
2. Mona gets good grades. She does _____well_____ in school.
3. We don't have much time. Please work _____quickly_____.
4. Nan is very careful with her schoolwork. She does her work _____carefully_____.
5. Nelson has great ideas to solve problems at work. He always thinks _____creatively_____.
6. John has a test tomorrow. He needs to study _____hard_____.

I can use adverbs of manner. ■   I need more practice. ■

For more practice, go to MyEnglishLab.

176 Unit 9, Lesson 6

Correlations

ELPS Level 2: 2, 7, 10
CCRS Level A: L.1.1, L.1.2
CASAS Reading: RDG 1.7, 2.9
CASAS Listening: L2.1, 2.3, 3.2, 4.2
CASAS Competencies: 0.1.2, 0.1.5, 0.1.6
Complete standards language available on the Pearson English Portal.

Self-Directed Learning

State the **lesson objective**. Say: *In this lesson, we will learn to use adverbs of manner and object pronouns.*

Adverbs of manner

 ActiveTeach: Grammar Discovery

1. Warm up. Say: *The conversation on page 175 used this grammar.* Turn back to page 175. Point to the sentences in Exercise 3A and then write:
   - *He does very well in math.*
   - *He works carefully.*
2. Underline *well* and *carefully*.
3. Tell students to look at the grammar charts.
4. Point to the left chart and read the sentences. Say: Careful, quick, *and* good *are adjectives. What word do they describe?* (worker) *What part of speech is* worker? (a noun) Write *noun* above *worker* on the chart and say: *An adjective describes a noun.*
5. Point to the right chart and read the sentences. Say: Carefully, quickly, *and* well *are adverbs. What word do they describe?* (works) *What part of speech is* works? (a verb) Write *verb* above *works* on the chart and say: *An adverb describes the action of a verb. These adverbs tell you how Carlo works.*
6. Read the first point of the **Grammar Watch** note. Write: *careful + -ly = carefully, quick + -ly = quickly.* Say the first two sentences from the right chart and ask the class to repeat.
7. Read the second point of the **Grammar Watch** note. Say the last sentence from the right chart and ask the class to repeat.

 ActiveTeach: Grammar Coach

A **COMPLETE. Change the underlined...**

1. Read the directions and the example. Ask: *Why is the answer* carelessly? Write: *careless + -ly = carelessly.*
2. Remind students that a few adverbs of manner are irregular (for example, *good, hard,* and *fast*). Ask the class to call out the adverbs (*well, hard,* and *fast*).
3. Students compare answers with a partner. Tell them to take turns reading the sentences.
4. Call on students to read the completed sentences.

▨ **EXPANSION: Grammar and speaking practice for A**

1. Demonstrate different adjectives using your voice. For example, make your voice a whisper and say: *My voice is quiet.* Adjectives you can use include *quiet, loud, slow,* and *fast.*
2. After you use each adjective in a sentence, say the adjective in a normal voice and write it. The adjectives should be in list form on the board.
3. Point to the first word in the list. Whisper: *I am talking quietly.* Next to the adjective (*quiet*), write: + *-ly = quietly.*
4. Call on students to choose one of the adjectives on the board and use them as adverbs of manner, changing their own voices to match the word.
5. As students use the adverbs, write them next to the adjectives: *loud + -ly = loudly / slow + -ly = slowly / fast = fast.*

B **APPLY. Change the adjectives to adverbs...**

1. Read the first sentence of the directions. Tell students to add *-ly* to the adjectives in the box or write the irregular form.
2. Say the adjectives in the box and ask the class to call out the adverbs of manner.
3. Read the second sentence of the directions and the example.
4. Students compare answers with a partner. Tell them to take turns reading the sentences.
5. Call on students to read the completed sentences.

Extra Practice

MyEnglishLab   Workbook pp. 102–103

Grammar

Object pronouns

 ActiveTeach: Grammar Discovery

1. Warm up. Say: *The conversation on page 175 used this grammar.* Turn back to page 175. Point to the sentences and then write:
   • *Nice to meet you.*
   • *I enjoy having him in class.*
2. Underline *you* and *him*. Say: *These are object pronouns.*
3. Tell students to look at the grammar charts on page 177. Read the sentences and tell the class to repeat.
4. Read the **Grammar Watch** note while the class reads along silently.
5. Write: *Carlo needs to do his homework. His mother will talk to _____.* Ask: *What noun are we going to replace?* Underline *Carlo.* Ask: *What object pronoun takes the place of* Carlo? (him) Write *him* in the blank.
6. Circle *to* in the sentence *His mother will talk to him.* Ask: *In this sentence, does the object pronoun come after a verb or a preposition?* (a preposition)

 ActiveTeach: Grammar Coach

C DECIDE. Look at the underlined noun. Write...

1. Read the directions. Show the answer to item 1 on the board. Ask: *Why is the answer* her? *What noun does* **her** *take the place of?* Underline *Ms. Carson.*
2. Tell students to underline the noun in the first sentence before they write the object pronoun in the second sentence.
3. Students compare answers with a partner. Tell them to take turns reading the sentences.
4. Call on students to read the completed sentences.

Show what you know!

1. THINK ABOUT IT. Look at the skills in the...

1. Read the directions.
2. Tell students to look at the second column and write the adverbs of manner.
3. Show the chart on the board. Call on students to read the adverbs. Write their answers in the chart on the board.

2. TALK ABOUT IT. Which classmates or...

1. Read the directions. Model the activity. In the chart on the board, write names. Use the name *Mimi* for row 1 and the names of people you know for the other rows (for example, nieces, nephews, and neighbors—not students in your class).
2. Point to the first name and say: *Mimi speaks English well.* Point to the second name and say: *[Name] studies hard.* Do the same for the other three names.
3. Say: *Write the names of your classmates or co-workers in the third column.*

3. WRITE ABOUT IT. Now write one sentence...

1. Read the directions.
2. Point to row 1 in the chart. Write the example (*Mimi speaks English well.*)
3. Pair students and ask them to check each other's sentences.
   • Adverbs of manner with *-ly* are spelled correctly.
   • Irregular adverbs use the correct form.
4. Have students volunteer to write their sentences on the board.

Self-Directed Learning

Point out the blue bar. Ask students if they can do the lesson learning objective or if they need more practice. Tell them to check one of the boxes. Assign Extra Practice as needed.

Extra Practice
pp. 102–103

Grammar

Object pronouns

Object pronouns			
Singular		**Plural**	
Can you help	**me**?	Come with	**us**.
	you.		
I need to see	**him**.		
	her.	I am proud of all of	**you**.
You can do	**it**.		**them**.

Grammar Watch

- An object pronoun takes the place of a noun.
- Use an object pronoun after a verb or a preposition.

C **DECIDE.** Look at the underlined noun. Write the correct object pronoun.

1. <u>Ms. Carson</u> was at the parent-teacher conference. I met _____ *her* _____.
2. There is <u>a PTO meeting</u> on Friday. We can't attend _____ *it* _____.
3. <u>Emily and Mary</u> are doing very well in school. We're proud of _____ *them* _____.
4. <u>My daughter</u> is not doing well in science. I am worried about _____ *her* _____.
5. <u>My son</u> needs help in math class. Can you help _____ *him* _____?
6. Are <u>you</u> busy? I need to talk to _____ *you* _____.
7. When <u>we</u> don't understand something, our teacher helps _____ *us* _____.
8. <u>Art class</u> is hard for me. I don't like _____ *it* _____.
9. <u>My son</u> does his homework every day. I never have to remind _____ *him* _____.

Show what you know!

1. **THINK ABOUT IT.** Look at the skills in the first column of the chart. Look at the adjectives in the second column. Write adverbs of manner.

2. **TALK ABOUT IT.** Which classmates or co-workers have these skills? Write their names in the third column.

3. **WRITE ABOUT IT.** Now write one sentence about a person with each skill.

   Mimi speaks English well.

Skill	Adjective / Adverb	Name
speaks English	good / *well*	
studies	hard / *hard*	
learns	quick / *quickly*	
writes	neat / *neatly*	
listens	careful / *carefully*	

I can use adverbs of manner and object pronouns. ■   I need more practice. ■

For more practice, go to MyEnglishLab.

Lesson 7

Read about going to college

1 BEFORE YOU READ

A **MATCH. Write the words in the box next to the correct definitions.**

college degree   non-profit   private   profit

1. _____private_____ = owned by a person or group (not by the government, not public)

2. _____profit_____ = the money you get by doing business (after your costs have been paid)

3. _____non-profit_____ = making money to help people (instead of making money to keep)

4. _____college degree_____ = what a student gets after completing a course of study at a university, college, or community college

B **MAKE CONNECTIONS. What kinds of colleges are there in your community?**

	Community College	College	University
Degrees offered	Certificate (Up to 1 year) Associate's Degree (2 years)	Bachelor's Degree (4 years)	Bachelor's Degree (4 years) Master's Degree (1-2 more years) Ph.D.* (3-8 more years)

*Doctor of Philosophy

2 READ

▶ **Listen and read.**

Academic Skill: Use Information in Graphs and Tables

Authors sometimes use graphs and tables to present information. This information supports the author's main ideas.

GOING TO COLLEGE

1 Are you thinking of going to college*? Here are some things you should know.

Rising Numbers of Students Going to College
In 1990, 59 percent of U.S. high school graduates
5 went to college. In 2007, over 66 percent went to college. In 2016, almost 70 percent went to college. Every year, more and more Americans decide that going to college is their way to a better future.

The Cost of College
10 But going to college costs a lot. Today, the average cost of tuition is between $4,800 and $34,000 a year. This does not include the cost of books, housing, food, or transportation. These can cost $12,000 to $20,000 more a year.

Type of school	Average cost of tuition (1 year)
Public community college	About $3,520
Public college or university	About $10,000
Private non-profit college or university	About $33,000
For-profit college or university	About $16,000

Percentages of full-time college students receiving financial aid

[Bar graph: At 2-year colleges: 79%; At 4-year colleges: 86%. Vertical axis labeled 0 to 100.]

Source: National Center for Education Statistics

15 **Paying for College**
How do people pay for college? Most students get financial aid—scholarships, grants, and loans.

Scholarships and grants are the best kind of financial aid. You don't have to pay them back.
20 Some students get scholarships because their grades are good. Some students get grants because their income is low. About half of all college students receive some form of scholarship or grant. Students usually get them from their college, a state
25 program, or a community group.

Most students get loans. You have to pay back loans after you graduate.

Most students use a combination of scholarships, grants, and government loans to pay the high cost
30 of college.

*College is a general word for community colleges, colleges, and universities.
Sources: The College Board, the U.S. Census Bureau

Correlations

ELPS Level 2: 1, 2, 3, 4, 5, 6, 7, 8, 9, 10
CCRS Level A: RI/RL.1.1, RI.1.2, RI.1.4, RI.1.7, SL.K.2
CASAS Reading: RDG 1.7, 1.8, 2.3, 3.2, 3.4, 3.8, 3.11, 4.2
CASAS Listening: L2.1, 2.3, 4.2, 5.8, 6.1, 6.2
CASAS Competencies: 0.1.2, 0.1.5, 0.2.1, 6.7.2, 7.1.1
Complete standards language available on the Pearson English Portal.

Self-Directed Learning

1. State the **lesson objective**. Say: *In this lesson, we will learn to use information in graphs and tables.*
2. Say: *We will read about going to college.*

1 BEFORE YOU READ

A MATCH. Write the words in the box next to…

1. Read the directions. Say the words in the box and ask the class to repeat.
2. Call on students to read the definitions.
3. Give students time to match the words to the definitions.
4. Call on students to give the correct answers.

B MAKE CONNECTIONS. What kinds of…

1. Write: *community college, college,* and *university.*
2. Tell students to look at the chart. Ask: *What degree does a college offer?* (bachelor's) *Where can you get a master's degree?* (at a university) *How long does it take to get an associate's degree?* (two years) *Where can you get a certificate?* (a community college)
3. Read the question in the directions. Ask: *Are there community colleges in our community?* Write the names of local community colleges on the board. Repeat with colleges and universities.

2 READ

▶ Listen and read.

1. Introduce the reading. Ask: *What is the title?* (*Going to College*) *What are the things to think about when you want to go to college?* (cost, location, degree) Ask: *What are the headings?* (Rising Numbers of Students Going to College, The Cost of College, Paying for College) *What do you think the main idea will be?* Elicit and write students' ideas.

2. Point to the **Academic Skill** and read it or ask a student to read it. Ask: *Why do authors use graphs and tables?* (to present information, to support the author's main ideas) *Do you like graphs and tables? Why or why not?*
3. Introduce the visuals. Ask: *What visuals do you see?* (a column/bar graph and a table) Point to the bar graph and ask: *What does the bar graph show?* (the percentage of full-time college students receiving financial aid) Point to the table and ask: *What does this table show?* (the average cost per year of different types of colleges or universities)

 ActiveTeach for 2: Anticipation Guide – *Before* Reading exercise

4. Read the text.
   a. Say: *Now we are going to read and listen to the article* Going to College.
   b. Play the audio as students listen and read along silently.
   c. Ask if there are words they do not understand and explain them (for example, *tuition:* what you pay to go to college; *housing:* what you pay to live at college).
   d. Play the audio again. Pause the audio after the following sections and ask the following questions. Tell students to underline the places in the reading where they found the answers.

   Rising Numbers of Students Going to College: *Is the number of Americans going to college going up or down?* (up)

   The Cost of College: *Tuition is a big cost of college. What other costs are there?* (books, housing, food, transportation)

   Paying for College: Ask the class: *What types of financial aid can students get to help them pay for college?* (scholarships, grants, and loans) Check that students understand the differences between these types of funding.

   e. **Reinforce the Academic Skill** from Unit 6. Ask: *What is scanning?* (reading quickly to find specific information) *What are some things we can scan for easily?* (numbers and names)
   f. Write: *70%, $10,000, $12,000 to $20,000, 59%, 66%.* Tell students to scan the article and find the numbers and what they refer to.
   g. Pair students to take turns asking and answering questions about the numbers.

 ActiveTeach for 2: Anticipation Guide – *After* Reading exercise

Reading

3 CLOSE READING

A IDENTIFY. What is the main idea?

1. Say: *Now we are going to identify the main idea.*
2. Read the directions. Have students circle the answer.
3. Elicit the answer from the class. Ask: *Were your predictions correct?*

B CITE EVIDENCE. Complete the statements...

1. Say: *Now we are going to find information in the reading.*
2. Read the directions. Walk around as students work on the activity. If students are struggling, have them work in pairs or direct them to the text lines where they can find the information.
3. Call on students to read the sentence with the correct completion. Ask a different student: *Where is that information? What line number?*

Numeracy: Interpret data

1. Say: *Now we are going to interpret the bar graph. A bar graph is a way to show numerical information or numbers in a visual, easy-to-understand way.*
2. Tell students to look at the bar graph. Ask: *What does each bar show?* (students on financial aid at different types of colleges) *How are the groups arranged?* (2-year colleges on left, 4-year on right) *What kind of numbers does it show?* (percentages) *Which group has the largest number of students on financial aid?* (4-year colleges)

4 SUMMARIZE

 ActiveTeach for 4: Vocabulary Practice

1. Read the directions. Ask students to read aloud the words in the box.
2. Tell students to complete the paragraph. Tell them they can refer to their charts.
3. To check answers, call on students to read sentences in the summary with the blanks filled in. Ask other students to read the completed summary silently.

Show what you know!

1. THINK ABOUT IT. Is going to college one...

1. Read the directions and questions.
2. Model the activity with an above-level student. Ask the questions and take notes on the student's answers.
3. Students take notes on their answers to the questions.

2. TALK ABOUT IT. Explain your educational...

1. Read the directions.
2. Model the activity. Ask two above-level students to take turns asking and answering the questions about goals.
3. Pair students to take turns talking about their educational goals.

 ActiveTeach for 2: Academic Conversation Support

3. WRITE ABOUT IT. Write about your...

1. Read the directions.
2. Write the sentence frames. Call on an above-level student to fill it in.
3. Give students time to complete the sentence frames.
4. Call on students to read their sentences.

Self-Directed Learning

Point out the blue bar. Ask students if they can do the lesson learning objective or if they need more practice. Tell them to check one of the boxes. Assign Extra Practice as needed.

■ **EXPANSION: Self-directed learning**

Ask students to reflect: *What did you learn from this reading?* Call on students to share something they learned.

Extra Practice

 CCRS Plus   pp. 104–105

Reading

3 CLOSE READING

A IDENTIFY. What is the main idea?

More and more Americans are going to college, and most of them _____.
a. say college is their way to a better future
b. probably think the cost of college is too high
c. get some form of financial aid to help pay for it *(c is circled)*

B CITE EVIDENCE. Complete the statements. Where is the information? Write the line numbers.

Lines

1. The average _____ is between $4,800 and $34,000.   10–11
   a. cost of a college education
   b. college tuition for one year *(b is circled)*
   c. amount of financial aid

2. _____ can get scholarships.   20–21
   a. Some students with good grades *(a is circled)*
   b. Students who work part-time
   c. About half of all students

3. Some students can get grants because they're _____.   21–22
   a. lucky
   b. full-time
   c. low-income *(c is circled)*

4. Community groups sometimes give college students _____.   22–25
   a. good advice
   b. scholarships or grants *(b is circled)*
   c. low-cost loans

5. Students who get _____ have to pay it back.   26–27
   a. any financial aid
   b. a scholarship or grant
   c. a loan *(c is circled)*

4 SUMMARIZE

Complete the summary with the words in the box.

costs   degree   loans   scholarship   tuition

Many Americans believe a college (1) ___degree___ is the way to a better future.
But college is expensive. College (2) ___tuition___ is thousands of dollars a year,
and there are other (3) ___costs___, too, like books and transportation. About half
of all college students get some form of (4) ___scholarship___ or grant. Most students
get (5) ___loans___.

Show what you know!

1. **THINK ABOUT IT.** Is going to college one of your goals? Why or why not? If yes, what type of college would be best for you to reach your goals?

2. **TALK ABOUT IT.** Explain your educational goals. Tell how you plan to reach your goals.

3. **WRITE ABOUT IT.** Write about your educational goals.

   I want to _____ because _____. I plan to _____.

I can use information in graphs and tables. ☐   I need more practice. ☐

To read more, go to MyEnglishLab.

Lesson 8

Discuss your child's behavior in school

1 BEFORE YOU LISTEN

LABEL. Write the words under the pictures.

be disrespectful   fool around in class   bully other kids
skip class   not pay attention   not get along with others

☐ _____bully other kids_____

☑ _____not pay attention_____

☐ _____not get along with others_____

☐ _____fool around in class_____

☐ _____be disrespectful_____

☑ _____skip class_____

2 LISTEN

Ana   Tito

A **PREDICT.** Look at the picture. What do you think happened? Complete the sentence.

Ana and Tito's son Luis _____.
a. got a good report card   **b.** is in trouble at school   **c.** finished his homework early

B ▶ **LISTEN FOR MAIN IDEA.** What trouble is Luis having? Check the boxes in Before You Listen.

C ▶ **LISTEN FOR DETAILS.** Listen again. Complete the sentence.

Luis's parents are going to _____.
(**a.**) talk to him   **b.** call the principal   **c.** go to a parent-teacher conference

D ▶ **EXPAND.** Listen to the whole conversation. Complete the sentence.

Luis usually _____ at school.
(**a.**) does well   **b.** has problems   **c.** talks a lot

Correlations

ELPS Level 2: 2, 7
CCRS Level A: SL.1.1, SL.K.3, SL.K.6, L.1.1
CASAS Reading: RDG 1.7, 2.3
CASAS Listening: L1.2, 2.1, 2.3, 4.1, 4.2, 6.1, 6.2, 6.5
CASAS Competencies: 0.1.2, 0.1.4, 0.1.5, 0.1.6, 2.8.6
Complete standards language available on the Pearson English Portal.

Self-Directed Learning

State the **lesson objective**. Say: *In this lesson, we will learn to discuss a child's behavior in school.*

1 BEFORE YOU LISTEN

LABEL. Write the words under the pictures.

1. Note: The checkboxes are for Exercise 2B.
2. Tell students to look at the pictures. Say: *These students are behaving badly.*
3. Read the directions. Say the words and phrases in the box and ask the class to repeat.
4. Give students time to label the pictures and then compare answers with a partner.
5. To check understanding, describe the pictures in random order and ask the class to call out the behaviors. Say: *Steve's not in class today, but he's not sick.* (skip class) *The girl is not listening to her math teacher.* (not pay attention) *The girl is arguing with another student.* (not get along with others) *The student is making fun of the teacher.* (be disrespectful) *The boy is frightening a smaller and weaker student.* (bully other kids) *The boy is playing in class.* (fool around in class)
6. Explain unfamiliar vocabulary (for example, *disrespectful* means you aren't showing respect, you are rude; *fool around* means to spend time doing silly things; *bully* means to harm someone else, or force them to do something).

Culture Note

1. Tell students to look at the behaviors in Exercise 1 again.
2. Say: *In the U.S., there are many forms of punishment in schools for children who behave in these ways. For example, a teacher may make a student move to another seat, make a student stay behind after school and do extra work, or suspend a student (not allow the student to attend school for a certain period of time).*

3. Ask: *In your native country, what happens to students who behave in these ways?* Write students' responses on the board.

2 LISTEN

A PREDICT. Look at the picture. What do you…

1. Tell students to look at the picture. Ask: *Where are they?* (at home, in a living room). *What do you think their relationship is?* (husband and wife) *Why?* (They are at home. They are sitting casually.)
2. Tell students to read the sentence and answer choices silently. Tell students to complete the sentence.
3. Ask students to raise their hands if they completed the sentence with *a, b,* or *c.*

B ▶ LISTEN FOR MAIN IDEA. What trouble is…

1. Read the directions. Tell students to underline the question in the directions: *What trouble is Luis having?* Tell students to listen and check the boxes in Exercise 1.
2. Play the audio. Students listen and check the behaviors.
3. Elicit the behaviors they heard and checked.
4. Write: *What's up?* Ask about **register**: *What does Ana mean when she asks this question?* (What has happened? What's the problem?) *Is this formal language or informal?* (informal—the sort of language used between husband and wife)

C ▶ LISTEN FOR DETAILS. Listen again…

1. Read the directions. Tell students to read the sentence and answer choices silently.
2. Play the audio. Students circle the letter of the correct answer.
3. Students compare answers with a partner.
4. Call on a student to read the completed sentence.

D ▶ EXPAND. Listen to the whole…

1. Read the directions. Tell students to read the answer choices silently.
2. Play the audio. Students choose the correct answer.
3. Ask: *Do you need to listen one more time?* If yes, play the audio again.
4. Review the correct answer with the class.
5. **Extend:** Ask the class: *Why do you think Luis is having problems in school now? What are some reasons students behave badly?*

Listening and Speaking

3 PRONUNCIATION

Ⓐ ▶ PRACTICE. Listen. Then listen and repeat.

1. Read the **Pronunciation Note**. Write a few possessive nouns that don't add a syllable on the board (for example, *Justin's band, Brianna's job, the baby's seat*). Say them and ask the class to repeat.

2. Write the names from the **Pronunciation Note**. Point to and pronounce the underlined sound in each name. Say: *After these sounds, the 's ending adds an extra syllable.*

3. Add an 's ending to each name and a noun (for example, *Luis's parents, Liz's homework, Josh's teacher, Mitch's class, George's grades, Felix's book*). Say each phrase and ask the class to repeat.

4. Tell students to look at the examples and underline 's. Ask: *Which words do you think will have an extra syllable?* Write their guesses.

5. Play the audio. Students listen. Ask: *Were your guesses correct?* (boss's, Alex's, George's)

6. Resume the audio. Students listen and repeat.

 ActiveTeach for 3A: Pronunciation Coach

Ⓑ ▶ CHOOSE. Listen. Circle the possessive...

1. Read the directions. Tell students to read the items. Elicit where they predict 's will add an extra syllable.

2. Play the audio. Students circle the possessive nouns that add a syllable.

3. Review the correct answers with students. Say each item and ask the class to repeat. Ask: *Were your guesses correct?*

4 CONVERSATION

Ⓐ ▶ LISTEN AND READ. Then listen and repeat.

1. Note: This is from the conversation students heard in Exercise 2B on page 180.

2. Read the directions. Tell students to read the conversation silently and to underline the possessive nouns. Ask: *What did you underline?* (friend's) *Does the 's ending in* friend's *add an extra syllable?* (no) Say *friend's* and ask the class to repeat.

3. Play the audio. Students read along silently. Then students listen and repeat.

4. Walk around and help with the pronunciation of possessives as needed.

Ⓑ WORK TOGETHER. Practice the...

1. Pair students and tell them to practice the conversation in Exercise 4A.

2. Tell students to take turns playing A and B. Walk around and check that students are using the correct pronunciation of possessives.

Ⓒ CREATE. Make new conversations. Use the...

1. Read the directions.

2. Tell students to look at the information in the boxes. Say each phrase and ask the class to repeat.

3. Show the conversation on the board with blanks. Read through it and fill it in with information from the top row in the boxes.

4. Ask two on-level students to read the conversation in front of the class.

5. Tell pairs to take turns playing each role and to use information from the same row in the boxes to fill in the blanks.

6. Tell students to stand, mingle, and practice the conversation with several new partners.

7. Call on pairs to perform for the class.

Ⓓ DISCUSS. What should Luis's parents do?...

1. Read the directions.

2. Review by asking: *What trouble is Luis having in school?* (not paying attention and skipping class) *What are Luis's parents going to do?* (talk to Luis)

3. Say: *When Luis's parents talk to him, what should they say? What can they do to change his behavior?* Tell students to write a couple of ideas in their notebooks (for example, *They need to ask why he's not paying attention and skipping class. They can get him help with his schoolwork. They can punish him.*).

4. Form groups of 3. Tell group members to take turns saying their ideas and talking about them.

5. Ask: *What's your group's best idea?* Ask each group to write one idea on the board. Read and talk about the ideas on the board.

Self-Directed Learning

Point out the blue bar. Ask students if they can do the lesson learning objective or if they need more practice. Tell them to check one of the boxes. Assign Extra Practice as needed.

Extra Practice
MyEnglishLab　　Workbook pp. 106–107

Listening and Speaking

3 PRONUNCIATION

A ► **PRACTICE. Listen. Then listen and repeat.**

my boss**'s** name   his friend**'s** house
Alex**'s** friend   Sue**'s** homework
George**'s** class   her aunt**'s** car

B ► **CHOOSE. Listen. Circle the possessive nouns that add a syllable.**

1. (Lucas's) computer
2. the department's meetings
3. the (class's) assignment
4. our supervisor's office
5. the employee's tasks
6. (Aziz's) schedule
7. the (language's) sounds

4 CONVERSATION

A ► **LISTEN AND READ. Then listen and repeat.**

A: Where's Luis?
B: He's at a friend's house. Why? What's up?
A: Well, his teacher called. He's having some trouble at school.
B: Uh-oh. What kind of trouble?
A: She said he's not paying attention and skipping class.
B: What? Well, we need to talk to him right away.
A: Definitely. Let's all talk tonight after dinner.

B **WORK TOGETHER. Practice the conversation in Exercise A.**

C **CREATE. Make new conversations. Use the words in the boxes.**

A: Where's Luis?

B: He's at a friend's house. Why? What's up?

A: Well, his teacher called. He's having some trouble at school.

B: Uh-oh. What kind of trouble?

A: She said he's _____ and _____ .

B: What? Well, we _____ right away.

A: Definitely. Let's all talk tonight after dinner.

> not getting along with others
> getting to school late
> being disrespectful to his teachers

> bullying some other kids
> not doing his homework
> fooling around in class

> have to find out what's going on
> need to have a talk with him
> need to have a family meeting

D **DISCUSS. What should Luis's parents do? What would you do in their situation?**

I can discuss a child's behavior in school. ☐   I need more practice. ☐

For more practice, go to MyEnglishLab.

Grammar

Possessive nouns

Possessive nouns		
Singular		**Plural**

Their son**'s**
        name is Luis.
The child**'s**

Their sons**'**
        names are Luis and Lucas.
The children**'s**

Grammar Watch

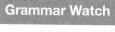

To form a possessive noun:

- Add *'s* to most singular nouns.
- Add only an apostrophe to plural nouns that end in -*s*.
- Add *'s* to plural nouns that do not end in -*s*.
- See page 260 for more spelling rules.

A **IDENTIFY.** Cross out the incorrect words.

1. Who is your ~~daughters~~ / daughter's teacher?
2. My **sons** / ~~son's~~ are in the first and second grades.
3. The ~~teachers~~ / **teacher's** first name is Alex.
4. Sometimes a teacher calls a ~~students~~ / **student's** parents.
5. I know the names of all my **classmates** / ~~classmates'~~.
6. My ~~daughter's~~ / **daughters'** names are Alicia and Rita.
7. The guidance **counselor's** / ~~counselors'~~ name is Ms. White.

B **EVALUATE.** Find and correct the error in each sentence.

1. My ~~sons~~ *son's* grades are poor, so I need to talk to his teacher.
2. The new ~~teacher's~~ *teachers'* names are Ms. Gómez and Ms. Bates.
3. Where is the school ~~nurse'~~ *nurse's* office?
4. My ~~daughters~~ *daughter's* report card was good, but my son is having a hard time.
5. The principal will try to answer all the ~~parents's~~ *parents'* questions.
6. Teachers like to meet their ~~students~~ *students'* parents.

I can use possessive nouns. ☐   I need more practice. ☐

For more practice, go to MyEnglishLab.

Correlations

CCRS Level A: L.1.1, L.1.2
CASAS Reading: RDG 1.7
CASAS Listening: L4.1, 4.2, 3.8
CASAS Competencies: 0.1.2
Complete standards language available on the Pearson English Portal.

Self-Directed Learning

State the **lesson objective**. Say: *In this lesson, we will learn to use possessive nouns.*

Possessive nouns

 ActiveTeach: Grammar Discovery

1. Warm up. Say: *The conversation on page 181 used this grammar.* Turn back to page 181. Point to the sentence in Exercise 4A and then write: *He's at a friend's house.* Underline *friend's*.
2. Tell students to look at the grammar charts. Point to the left chart and read the first sentence. Have students repeat.
3. Write: *Their son's name is Luis.* Above it, write: *They have a son.* Read the two sentences. Underline *son* and *son's*. Ask: *Which noun is possessive?* (son's) Say: *Possessive nouns are followed by another noun. They show that one thing or person belongs to or is related to another thing or person.* Point to the bottom sentence and ask: *What belongs to their son?* (his name) Write: *son name*, with space between the two words. Ask: *What do you add to a singular noun to make it possessive?* Add *'s* to *son*.
4. Point to the right chart and read the first sentence. Have students repeat.
5. Write: *Their sons names are Luis and Lucas*, with space between *sons* and *names*. Ask: *What do you add to a plural noun that ends in* -s *to make it possessive?* Add an apostrophe to *sons*.
6. Read the second sentence in the right chart. Have students repeat.
7. Write: *The children names are Luis and Lucas*, with space between *children* and *names*. Ask: *What do you add to a plural noun that doesn't end in* -s *to make it possessive?* Use a different color to add *'s* to *children*.
8. Tell students to read the **Grammar Watch** note silently. Then tell them to turn to page 260 and read the spelling rules for possessive nouns.

 ActiveTeach: Grammar Coach

A IDENTIFY. **Cross out the incorrect words.**
1. Read the directions.
2. Show the example on the board. Point to the answer and ask: *Why is the answer* daughter's? (because it's followed by another noun / because it's possessive)
3. Note: In items 1–5, students determine whether the nouns are possessive or not. In items 6–7, students choose the correct possessive form.
4. Students compare answers with a partner.
5. Call on students to write the answers on the board.

B EVALUATE. **Find and correct the error in...**
1. Read the directions.
2. Show the example on the board. Point to the answer and ask: *Why is* sons *incorrect?* (because it's followed by another noun and should be possessive) Read the sentence. Underline *his* and ask: *Is it one son or more than one son?* (one son) Write *son* on the board and ask: *What do you add to a singular noun to make it possessive?* Use a different color to add *'s* to *son*.
3. Tell students that every sentence has one error. Direct them to cross out the noun that has an error and write the correct form above. Tell them to look at the rest of the sentence for clues to whether the noun is singular or plural.
4. Call on students to write answers on the board.
5. Tell students to check their own answers and then ask a partner to double-check them.

■ **EXPANSION: Grammar practice for B**
1. Tell students to write sentences telling the names of people in their family.
2. Model the activity by writing your own sentences on the board (for example, *My parents' names are Robert and Karen. My husband's name is William. My sons' names are Lucas and Shawn. My daughter's name is Samantha.*).
3. Tell students to ask a partner to check their possessive forms and correct any errors.

Self-Directed Learning

Point out the blue bar. Ask students if they can do the lesson learning objective or if they need more practice. Tell them to check one of the boxes. Assign Extra Practice as needed.

Extra Practice

  pp. 106–107

Correlations

ELPS Level 2: 3, 10
CCRS Level A: W.1.2, W.1.5, L.1.1, L.1.2
CASAS Reading: RDG 1.7, 1.8, 2.1
CASAS Listening: L2.1, 2.3, 3.9
CASAS Competencies: 0.1.2, 0.1.5, 0.1.6
Complete standards language available on the Pearson English Portal.

Self-Directed Learning

1. State the **lesson objective**. Say: *In this lesson, we will learn to use commas between words in a list.*
2. Say: *You will write about your school.*

1 STUDY THE MODEL

1. Read the directions.
2. Point to the paragraph. Ask: *What is the title of the model?* (My School)
3. **Scaffold** the model. Write as a graphic organizer:

1	Name of school	
2	Classes/subjects	
3	Times/days	
4	Cost	
5	Goal	

4. Tell students to read the text and read the questions independently. Tell students to underline the answers to the questions. Call on students to answer the questions. Write the information in the graphic organizer on the board.

2 PLAN YOUR WRITING

1. Erase the information in the graphic organizer on the board.
2. Read the directions.
3. Model with an above-level students. The student asks the teacher the questions.
4. Write the information into the graphic organizer.
5. Tell students to make their own graphic organizer on a piece of paper.
6. Have students work in pairs to ask and answer the questions and complete their own graphic organizers.

3 WRITE

1. Read the directions.
2. Point to the **Writing Skill**. Read it aloud while students listen. Tell students to look at the model. Ask: *What lists do you see?* (classes, times for classes)
3. Use the information in the chart from Exercise 2 to write sentences in a paragraph. Leave out commas between items in a list.
4. Ask: *Does this paragraph need commas? Where?* Add commas between items in a list.
5. Tell students to write. Walk around to make sure students are writing in paragraph form.

 ActiveTeach for 3: Writing Support

4 CHECK YOUR WRITING

1. Read the directions. Point to the **Writing Checklist**. Call on students to read the checklist aloud.
2. Pair students to review their writings together. Say: *Read your sentences with a partner. Use the Writing Checklist.* For additional help, remind students that a correct sentence:
   • *begins with a capital letter*
   • *has a subject*
   • *has a verb*
   • *has a period*
   • *is a complete idea*
3. For additional help, remind students that a correct paragraph:
   • *is indented*
   • *begins with a topic sentence*
4. Walk around and verify that students are using the checklist. Collect the papers for review or put them in the students' writing portfolios.

Teaching Tip: Digital skills

Tell students that if their school has a website, they can go online to find more information about the school.

Self-Directed Learning

Point out the blue bar. Ask students if they can do the lesson learning objective or if they need more practice. Tell them to check one of the boxes. Assign Extra Practice as needed.

Extra Practice

 CCRS Plus   p. 108

Write about school

1 STUDY THE MODEL

READ. Answer the questions.

Tam Dang

My School

New Neighbors is a school for adult students in Boston, Massachusetts. It has classes in English, citizenship, and computer skills. Classes are in the mornings, in the evenings, and on Saturdays. The classes are free. I am taking English and computer skills classes there so I can get a job as a software developer.

1. What's the name of Tam's school?
2. What classes does it have?
3. When are the classes?
4. How much does it cost?
5. What is Tam's goal?

1. New Neighbors.
2. It has English, citizenship, and computer skills classes.
3. They are in the mornings, in the evenings, and on Saturdays.
4. They're free.
5. To get a job as a software developer.

2 PLAN YOUR WRITING

WORK TOGETHER. Ask and answer the questions.

1. What's the name of the school?
2. What classes does it have?
3. When are the classes?
4. How much do they cost?
5. Are you taking classes there?
6. What is your goal?

Writing Skill: Use commas between words in a list

Put commas between words in a list. For example:

It has classes in English, citizenship, and computer skills.

3 WRITE

Now write about a school. Use the model, the Writing Skill, and your ideas from Exercise 2 to help you.

4 CHECK YOUR WRITING

WORK TOGETHER. Read the checklist. Read your writing aloud. Revise your writing.

WRITING CHECKLIST

☐ The paragraph answers the questions in Exercise 2.

☐ There is a topic sentence.

☐ There are commas between words in lists.

I can use commas between words in a list. ■   I need more practice. ■

For more practice, go to MyEnglishLab.

Plan well

1 MEET RASHA

Read about one of her
workplace skills.

I plan well. For example, I plan my schedule
so that I can both complete all my work and
also be available for important family events.

2 RASHA'S PROBLEM

READ. Circle *True* or *False*.

Rasha is at work. Her son Omar plays soccer on his
school team. He calls her and says, "Mom, we won
the game! Our team is going to be in the final!" Rasha
says, "That's great! When's the final?" Omar says,
"It's on Friday afternoon at 4 p.m." Rasha wants to go to the final game because she
knows it is important to Omar, but she always works on Friday at 4 p.m.

1. Rasha and Omar are at work.   True   (False)
2. Omar will play soccer on Friday. (True)   False
3. Rasha has to work on Friday.   (True)   False

3 RASHA'S SOLUTION

A WORK TOGETHER. Rasha plans well. What does she say to her son? Explain your answer.

(1.) Rasha says, "OK. I'll ask a co-worker to change shifts with me on Friday."
2. Rasha says, "I can't come to the game. I have to work on Friday."
3. Rasha says, "OK. I'll plan to tell my supervisor I'm sick on Friday."
4. Rasha should _____.

B ROLE-PLAY. Look at your answer to 3A. Role-play Rasha's conversation.

Show what you know!

1. **THINK ABOUT IT.** Do you plan well? How do you plan well in class? At work?
   At home? Give examples.

2. **WRITE ABOUT IT.** Write an example in your Skills Log.

   *I plan well in class. When I have class and my son is home, I ask my neighbor to
   watch him. Then I can go to class.*

I can give an example of how I plan well. ☐

Unit Review: Go back to page 165. Which unit goals can you check off?

Correlations

CASAS Reading: RDG 1.7, 1.8, 3.2
CASAS Listening: L2.1, 2.3, 4.1, 4.2
CASAS Competencies: 0.1.2, 0.1.4, 0.1.5, 0.1.6, 0.2.1, 7.1.2
Complete standards language available on the Pearson English Portal.

Self-Directed Learning

State the **lesson objective**. Say: *In this lesson, we will give an example of how we plan well.*

1 MEET RASHA

1. Ask: *What is the title of this lesson?* (Plan well) Ask: *What does* plan *mean?* (deciding what to do and when to do it)
2. Write: *Workplace Skill*. Read the directions. Say: *Listen as I read* Meet Rasha. Read the paragraph. Ask: *What is one of Rasha's workplace skills?* (She plans well.) Next to *Workplace Skill*, write: *Plan well*.
3. Under *Workplace Skill*, write: *Examples*. Ask: *How does Rasha plan well?* (She plans her schedule so that she can complete all her work and also be available for her family.) Write the example. Elicit other ways to plan well and write them under *Workplace Skill*.

2 RASHA'S PROBLEM

1. Say: *Now we are going to read about Rasha at work. Listen while I read.* Read the first three sentences. Ask: *Where is Rasha when her son calls?* (at work) Say: *Look at the photo. What sport does her son play at school?* (soccer)
2. Say: *Rasha has a problem at work. Listen while I read.* Read the rest of the paragraph. Explain any unfamiliar vocabulary as needed.
3. Students complete the questions after the reading. Call on students to answer. Ask them to **cite evidence**: *Where is that information?*
4. Ask: *What is Rasha's problem?* (Her son has a big soccer game, but she has to work.)

3 RASHA'S SOLUTION

A WORK TOGETHER. **Rasha plans well. What...**
1. Read the directions. Ask students to work together. Walk around and check that students understand that only one solution is correct.

2. Ask: *Is #1 a good way to plan well?* (yes) *Why?* (She is changing her schedule ahead of time.) Ask: *Is #2 a good way to plan well?* (no) *Why not?* (She is not trying to plan ahead.) Ask: *Is #3 a good way to plan well?* (no) *Why not?* (She is not telling the truth. She is planning, but not doing it in a good way.)
3. Ask students if they have any other ideas. Write their responses. Ask: *Is this a good way to plan well? Why?*

 ActiveTeach for 3A: Academic Conversation Support

B ROLE-PLAY. **Look at your answer to 3A...**
1. Group students in pairs. Explain one person will be Rasha. The other person will be Omar. Model the activity with an above-level student. Have students practice the conversation with different partners.
2. Walk around and ask students to switch roles and continue practicing. If students aren't pronouncing their lines clearly, model correct pronunciation and ask them to repeat.
3. Invite one or two pairs of students to role-play the interaction for the whole class.

Show what you know!

1. THINK ABOUT IT. Do you plan well? How do...

Read the directions. Have students think about their answers for a few minutes. Then ask them to share with a partner. Call on students to share with the class.

2. WRITE ABOUT IT. Write an example in your...

Read the directions and the example. Have students write their examples in their **Skills Log** at the back of the book. Circulate and assist students as needed.

Self-Directed Learning

1. Point out the blue bar. Ask students if they can do the lesson learning objective or if they need more practice. Tell them to check one of the boxes. Assign Extra Practice as needed.
2. Ask students to turn to page 165. Go to the Unit Wrap-Up teaching notes on page T-165.

Extra Practice

 p. 109

10 Let's Eat!

Unit Overview

Goals
- See the list of goals on the facing page

Pronunciation
- Pronunciation of *to, the, a,* and *of*

Reading
- Read about the effects of coffee
- Get meaning from context

Grammar
- Count nouns/Non-count nouns and *How much / How many*
- Comparative adjectives with *than*
- Quantifiers with plural and non-count nouns

Writing
- Write about nutrients in a dish
- Use *like* and *such as* to introduce examples

Document Literacy and Numeracy
- Identify food containers and quantities
- Understand nutritional information on food labels
- Compare food price in ads
- Interpret a bar graph
- Read a menu

Workplace, Life, and Community Skills
- Read food labels
- Digital Skills: Search for ingredients in a food you like

Life Skills Writing
- Complete a healthy eating log

Soft Skills at Work
- Ask for help

Preview

1. Set the context of the unit by asking questions about shopping and food (for example, *Do you like to cook? What do you like to eat? Do you go grocery-shopping a lot?*).
2. Show the Unit Opener. Ask: *What is the unit title?* (Let's Eat)
3. Say: *Look at the picture.* Ask the Preview questions. (Possible answers: a man shopping for groceries in a supermarket; looking at a can)
4. Write the answers.

Unit Goals

1. Point to the Unit Goals. Explain that this list shows what you will be studying in this unit.
2. Tell students to read the goals silently.
3. Say each goal. Explain unfamiliar vocabulary as needed.
4. Point to the ☐ next to the first goal. Say: *We will come back to this page again. You will write a checkmark next to the goals you learned in the unit.*

Oral Presentation

1. Tell students they will give a short presentation at the end of the unit.
2. Write the topics:
   Option 1: A favorite dish
   Option 2: Information on a food label
3. Assign the topics to two students.

Unit Wrap-Up

1. Review the Unit Goals with students.
2. Direct students to the Grammar Review.
3. If you assigned presentations, ask students to present.

 ActiveTeach for Wrap-Up: Team Project

 ActiveTeach for Wrap-Up: Persistence Activities

10 Let's Eat!

PREVIEW

Look at the picture. What do you see?
Where is this person? What is he doing?

UNIT GOALS

- [ ] Identify food containers and quantities
- [ ] Ask for quantities of food
- [ ] Read food labels
- [ ] Compare information in food ads
- [ ] Order food in a restaurant

- [ ] **Academic skill:** Get meaning from context
- [ ] **Writing skill:** Use *like* and *such as* to introduce examples
- [ ] **Workplace soft skill:** Show how you ask for help

A **PREDICT.** Look at the pictures. What do you see?

There's a bag of potato chips.
There's a box of cereal.

B ▶ **LISTEN AND POINT.** Then listen and repeat.

C ▶ **IDENTIFY.** Listen. Check (✓) the foods you hear.

1 ✓ ☐ ☐

2  ✓ ☐

3  ☐ ✓

4  ☐ ☐ ✓

5  ✓ ☐ ☐

6  ✓ ☐ ☐

7  ☐ ☐ ✓

8 ☐ ✓ ☐

9 ☐ ☐ ✓

10  ✓ ☐ ☐

11  ✓ ☐ ☐

12  ☐ ☐ ✓

13  ☐ ☐ ✓

6 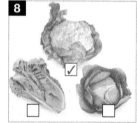

14  ✓ ☐ ☐

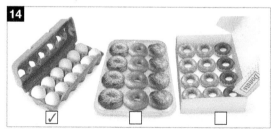

Correlations

ELPS Level 2: 1, 2, 3, 4, 5, 6, 7, 8, 9, 10
CCRS Level A: SL.1.1, SL.K.6, L.1.5, L.1.6
CASAS Reading: RDG 1.7, 2.3
CASAS Listening: L2.1, 2.3, 2.9, 4.2
CASAS Competencies: 0.1.2, 0.1.5, 1.2.8, 7.4.1
Complete standards language available on the Pearson English Portal.

Self-Directed Learning

State the **lesson objective**. Say: *In this lesson, we will learn to identify food containers and quantities.*

A PREDICT. Look at the pictures. What do you...

1. Read the directions. Tell students to cover the list on page 187.
2. Point to picture 1 and ask: *What foods are these?* Say: *#1 has potato chips. What else?* Elicit *potatoes* and *rice.*
3. Say: *Look at the other pictures. What foods do you know?* Students call out answers. Help students pronounce foods if they have difficulty.
4. Say: *Look at the pictures again. Which food containers and quantities do you know?* Elicit a container or quantity and write it (for example, *#1 is* bag.).
5. Students call out additional answers. Help students pronounce containers and quantities if they have difficulty.
6. If students call out an incorrect container or quantity, ask a *yes/no* clarification question: *Is #8 jar?* (no) If nobody can identify the correct container or quantity, tell students they will now listen to the audio and practice the vocabulary for food containers and quantities.

B ▶ LISTEN AND POINT. Then listen and repeat.

1. Read the directions. Play the audio. Students listen and point to the containers and quantities.
2. While the audio is playing, walk around and check that students are pointing to the correct activities. Pause the audio after item 14.
3. Say each container or quantity in random order and ask students to point to the appropriate picture.
4. Tell students to look at page 187. Resume the audio. Students listen, read, and repeat.

 ActiveTeach for B: Vocabulary Flashcards

Teaching Tip: Pointing and repeating

To make sure students are connecting the new words with their meanings, tell them to point to the pictures as they listen / listen and repeat.

C ▶ IDENTIFY. Listen. Check (✓) the foods...

1. Read the directions. Say: *For example, when you hear* a bag of potato chips, *write a checkmark in the box under the potato chips.*
2. Tell students to look at the pictures and read the labels on the food containers.
3. Play the audio. Students listen and write a checkmark under the correct items.
4. Pair students and tell them to compare checkmarks.
5. Play the audio again so that students can check their answers.
6. *Optional:* Tell pairs to look at the pictures they didn't check and identify the container or quantity and the food.

▬ EXPANSION: Writing practice for C

1. Tell the class to close their books. Say a food, with container or quantity, and tell students to write it. Do this for several foods.
2. Students compare answers with a partner.
3. Repeat the foods and ask students to write each answer on the board.
4. For foods that students have difficulty spelling, give them an index card and tell them to write the food on the card. Say: *Go home and stick it to the refrigerator.*

Classroom Communication

This unit provides opportunities to have a class event in which students bring in food to share. This can be an occasion for students to share foods from their native countries—or it can be just an occasion for students to eat together and talk. It can even be as simple as bringing in snacks for the first few minutes of class. Look for opportunities to reinforce vocabulary (for example, by making labels to go in front of the dishes).

Vocabulary

D **CATEGORIZE. Which foods come in these...**

1. Read the directions.
2. Copy the chart on the board and write the example.
3. Ask: *Which picture shows bag?* (picture 1) *What foods are in picture 1?* List: *potato chips, rice, potatoes.* Ask: *What other foods come in a bag?* Use students' responses to add to the list on the board (for example, *pasta, flour, pretzels, frozen vegetables*).
4. Form groups of 3. Walk around and check spelling. If you see a misspelled food, write the word correctly on the board.
5. Ask an above-level student to be the recorder for each column. Call on students to say what foods come in each container, and the recorder writes the answers on the board.

Study Tip: Draw pictures

1. Provide each student with four index cards or tell students to cut up notebook paper into four pieces.
2. Point to the **Study Tip**. Read the directions. Pair students with mixed abilities.
3. Walk around as students work. If misspellings occur, tell them to check the list on page 187.
4. Say: *You can make cards with pictures to remember new words.* Remind students to use this strategy to remember other new vocabulary.

Show what you know!

1. THINK ABOUT IT. What foods do you have at...

1. Read the directions.
2. Write examples on the board (for example, *a gallon of milk, cans of tomatoes, a head of lettuce*). Underline *of* in each item. Add *a dozen eggs* to the list. Point out that we use *of* after all the containers and quantities except *dozen*.
3. Model the activity. Write your own list (for example, *a box of cereal, a bag of pretzels, a bottle of apple juice, a half-gallon of milk, a dozen bagels*). Underline *a* and *of* in each item.
4. Tell each student to make a list on their own paper.
5. Walk around and spot-check students' spelling. Remind students to use *a* and *of* (except with *dozen*).

2. TALK ABOUT IT. Work with a partner. Talk...

1. Read the directions and example.
2. Model the activity. Ask an above-level student to read you the first item on his or her list and continue the conversation. Circle foods that are on both lists.
3. Pair students. Students write lists, compare them, and discuss.

■■ **EXPANSION: Speaking practice for 2**

Pairs take turns reading their circled items. As each pair reads, tell other pairs to check the circled items that are also on their lists. Ask the class: *Are there any foods that everyone in class has at home?* Write these.

3. WRITE ABOUT IT. Now write about the food...

1. Read the directions. Show the example on the board.
2. Share the checklist below. Then write a checkmark next to each as you point back to the example sentence.
   - The sentence starts with a capital letter and ends with a period.
   - There is a container or quantity for each food item.
   - The word *of* is used with the container or quantity, except for *dozen*.
3. Give students time to write their sentences.
4. Tell students to show their sentences to a partner. Tell the students to use the checklist to review the sentences.
5. Walk around and verify that students are using the checklist. Collect the papers for review or put them in the students' writing portfolios.

Self-Directed Learning

Point out the blue bar. Ask students if they can do the lesson learning objective or if they need more practice. Tell them to check one of the boxes. Assign Extra Practice as needed.

Extra Practice		
MyEnglishLab	Workbook	p. 110

Vocabulary

Food containers and quantities

1. bag	**3.** can	**5.** jar	**7.** bunch	**9.** pound	**11.** quart	**13.** gallon
2. box	**4.** bottle	**6.** container	**8.** head	**10.** pint	**12.** half-gallon	**14.** dozen

D **CATEGORIZE. Which foods come in these containers?**

Study Tip

Draw pictures
Make cards for food containers. On one side, write the word. On the other side, draw a picture of the container.

a bag of	a box of	a can of	a jar of
oranges			

Show what you know!

1. **THINK ABOUT IT. What foods do you have at home now? Make a list.**

2. **TALK ABOUT IT. Work with a partner. Talk about the food you have at home. Take notes. Circle the foods you both have at home.**

   A: I have a gallon of milk and boxes of cereal.
   B: Me too! I have cans of tomatoes and tuna.
   A: I don't. What else do you have?

3. **WRITE ABOUT IT. Now write about the food both you and your partner have at home.**

   We both have _____.

I can identify food containers and quantities. ■   I need more practice. ■

For more practice, go to MyEnglishLab.

Ask for quantities of food

1 BEFORE YOU LISTEN

A **LABEL.** Write the words under the pictures.

a convenience store   an outdoor market   a supermarket

1. _____a supermarket_____   **2.** _____a convenience store_____   **3.** _____an outdoor market_____

B **MAKE CONNECTIONS.** Where do you go food shopping? Why do you shop there?

2 LISTEN

A **PREDICT.** Look at the picture. Where are they?

B ▶ **LISTEN FOR MAIN IDEA.** What are they talking about?

a. a problem with the refrigerator   **b.** food they need to buy

C ▶ **LISTEN FOR DETAILS.** Check (✓) the things that Agnes will buy.

- ☑ milk
- ☐ butter
- ☐ two tomatoes
- ☑ a can of tomatoes
- ☑ two onions
- ☐ a dozen eggs

Agnes

Yuka

D ▶ **EXPAND.** Listen to the whole conversation. What does Agnes need to do?

a. take more money   **b.** get a bigger refrigerator   **c.** write the things down

Correlations

ELPS Level 2: 1, 2, 3, 4, 5, 6, 7, 8, 9, 10
CCRS Level A: SL.K.3
CASAS Reading: RDG 1.7, 2.3
CASAS Listening: L1.4, 2.1, 2.3, 4.2, 6.1, 6.2, 6.5
CASAS Competencies: 0.1.2, 0.1.5, 1.2.8
Complete standards language available on the Pearson English Portal.

Self-Directed Learning

State the **lesson objective**. Say: *In this lesson, we will learn to ask for quantities of food.*

1 BEFORE YOU LISTEN

A LABEL. Write the words under the pictures.

1. Read the directions. Call on a student to say the words and phrases in the box. Correct pronunciation if needed.
2. Give students time to label the pictures and then compare answers with a partner. Call on students to say the correct answers.
3. To check understanding, ask questions: *Which is bigger, a supermarket or a convenience store? Which one usually has better prices? Where can you find the freshest fruits and vegetables?*

B MAKE CONNECTIONS. Where do you go...

1. Ask: *Where do you go food shopping?* Tell students to write down the name of the store where they usually shop for food. Ask: *What kind of store is it?* Tell students to circle the kind of store in Exercise 1A.
2. Tell students to stand, mingle, and ask each other: *Where do you go food shopping?* Say: *When you find a classmate who shops at the same kind of food store, stay together. Look for other classmates who shop at the same kind of food store. When you've formed a small group, sit down and talk about why you shop there.*
3. Write the three types of stores as headings. Ask a member from each group to write a couple of the group's reasons under the appropriate heading.
4. Read the reasons why students shop at each kind of store. Ask the class: *Which type of store is most popular? Why?*

Culture Note

1. Say: *Most people in the U.S. shop for food at supermarkets. A few people prefer to go to outdoor markets.*
2. Ask: *In your native country, where do most people go food-shopping? Why?*

2 LISTEN

A PREDICT. Look at the picture. Where are they?

1. Tell students to look at the picture. Ask: *Who do you see?* (two women, Agnes and Yuka). *Where are they?* (in a kitchen, in front of the refrigerator)
2. Ask: *What do you think their relationship is?* Elicit ideas and write them (for example, *roommates, friends, coworkers*)

B ▶ LISTEN FOR MAIN IDEA. What are they...

1. Tell students to read the directions and answer choices silently. Ask: *Which one do you think is correct?* Say *a* and ask for a show of hands. Repeat with *b*.
2. Play the audio. Students listen and choose the correct answer.
3. Ask students to raise their hands if they circled *a*. Repeat with *b*. Ask: *Was your guess correct?* Ask for a show of hands.
4. Ask about **register:** *Now what do you think their relationship is?* (roommates) *How do you know?* (They are talking about what they need at the grocery store.)

C ▶ LISTEN FOR DETAILS. Check (✓) the...

1. Tell students to look at the picture again. Say: *Point to Agnes. Point to Yuka.* Ask: *Which roommate is going to the grocery store?* (Agnes)
2. Read the directions. Tell students to read the items silently.
3. Play the audio. Students check the things Agnes will buy.
4. Students compare answers with a partner.
5. Ask: *What does Agnes need from the grocery store?* (milk) *What does Yuka need?* (a can of tomatoes and two onions)

Teaching Tip: Use the script

Optional: If students need additional support, tell them to read the Audio Script on page 273 as they listen to the conversations.

D ▶ EXPAND. Listen to the whole...

1. Read the directions. Tell students to read the answer choices silently.
2. Play the audio. Students choose the correct answer.
3. Ask: *Do you need to listen one more time?* If yes, play the audio again.
4. Call on a student to read the answer.

Listening and Speaking

3 CONVERSATION

A ▶ **LISTEN AND READ. Then listen and repeat.**

1. Note: This conversation is the same one students heard in Exercise 2B on page 188.
2. Tell students to read the conversation and underline the food items.
3. Play the audio. Students read along silently. Then students listen and repeat.

B **WORK TOGETHER. Practice the...**

1. Pair students and tell them to practice the conversation in Exercise 3A.
2. Tell students to take turns playing A and B. Walk around and help with pronunciation as needed.

C **CREATE. Make new conversations. Use the...**

1. Read the directions.
2. Tell students to look at the pictures. Ask the class to call out the food items. Say each food and ask the class to repeat. Use the plurals *cucumbers, apples,* and *oranges.*
3. Show the conversation on the board with blanks. Read it and when you come to a blank, elicit information from the boxes.
4. Ask two on-level students to practice the conversation for the class.
5. Erase the words in the blanks and ask two above-level students to make up a new conversation in front of the class.
6. Tell pairs to take turns playing A and B and to use information from the boxes to fill in the blanks.
7. Tell students to stand, mingle, and practice the conversation with several new partners.
8. Walk around and check that students use the plurals *cucumbers, apples,* and *oranges* when appropriate.
9. Call on pairs to perform for the class.

Teaching Tip: Use realia

The topic of food is effectively reinforced with realia. Bring in food items in various containers, or bring in grocery store circulars with photos of items. Pre-level students can use the realia to prompt their conversations in Exercise 3C and 3D.

D **ROLE-PLAY. Make your own conversations.**

1. Read the directions.
2. Tell students to look at the headings and write their own food items in each category. Walk around and check that the food items students choose work with the containers in the headings.
3. Model the role-play with an above-level student. Play A.
4. Pair students and tell them to role-play the conversation. Walk around and make sure they take turns playing each role.
5. Call on pairs to perform for the class.

■■■ **MULTILEVEL INSTRUCTION for 3D**

Cross-ability Direct the above-level student to play A first and model by repeating B's food items in A's second and third lines.

Self-Directed Learning

Point out the blue bar. Ask students if they can do the lesson learning objective or if they need more practice. Tell them to check one of the boxes. Assign Extra Practice as needed.

Extra Practice

  pp. 111–112

Listening and Speaking

3 CONVERSATION

A ▶ **LISTEN AND READ. Then listen and repeat.**

A: Hi, Yuka. I'm going to the grocery store for some milk.
Do you need anything?
B: Uh, let me see. Could you get a can of tomatoes?
A: A can of tomatoes? Sure, no problem.
B: Oh, and I need some onions.
A: How many onions?
B: Two.
A: All right. A can of tomatoes and two onions.
I'll be back in a little while.

B **WORK TOGETHER. Practice the conversation in Exercise A.**

C **CREATE. Make new conversations. Use the pictures of food in the boxes.**

A: I'm going to the grocery store for some
_____. Do you need anything?
B: Uh, let me see. Could you get a can
of _____?
A: A can of _____? Sure, no problem.
B: Oh, and I need some _____.
A: How many _____?
B: Two.
A: All right. A can of _____ and
two _____. I'll be back in a
little while.

D **ROLE-PLAY. Make your own conversations.**

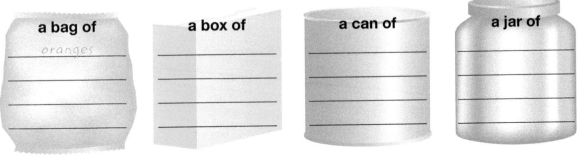

a bag of	a box of	a can of	a jar of
oranges			

I can ask for quantities of food. ■   I need more practice. ■

For more practice, go to MyEnglishLab.

Lesson 3

Count nouns / Non-count nouns and *How much / How many*

Count nouns/Non-count nouns		
Singular count nouns	**Plural count nouns**	**Non-count nouns**
an onion a sandwich	two onions some sandwiches	bread milk fish rice

Yes/No questions	Affirmative answers	Negative answers
Are there **any** onions? **Is** milk?	**Yes**, there **is** / **are** some.	**No**, there **isn't** / **aren't** any.

A **COMPLETE. Use the correct forms of** *there is / there are* **to make questions and answers.**

1. **A:** _____*Is there any*_____ bread?

   B: Yes, _____*there's*_____ some on the counter.

2. **A:** _____Are there any_____ tomatoes?

   B: No, _____there aren't_____ any.

3. **A:** _____Is there any_____ coffee?

   B: Yes, _____there's_____ some in the breakroom.

4. **A:** _____Are there any_____ carrots?

   B: Yes, _____there are_____ some in the refrigerator.

5. **A:** _____Is there any_____ butter?

   B: No, _____there isn't_____, but we have jelly.

6. **A:** _____Are there any_____ bananas in the cafeteria today?

   B: No, _____there aren't_____. I bought the last one.

Grammar Watch

- *There is* = *There's*
- See page 260 for spelling rules for plurals.
- See page 261 for more examples of non-count nouns.

B **WORK TOGETHER. Practice the conversations in Exercise A.**

Correlations

ELPS Level 2: 1, 2, 3, 4, 5, 6, 7, 8, 9, 10
CCRS Level A: L.1.1, L.1.2
CASAS Reading: RDG 1.7, 2.6
CASAS Listening: L1.3, 2.1, 2.3, 3.3, 4.1, 4.2
CASAS Competencies: 0.1.2, 0.1.5, 1.2.8, 2.6.3
Complete standards language available on the Pearson English Portal.

Self-Directed Learning

State the **lesson objective**. Say: *In this lesson, we will learn to use count and non-count nouns and how much / how many.*

Count nouns / Non-count nouns

 ActiveTeach: Grammar Discovery

1. Warm up. Say: *The conversation on page 189 used this grammar.* Turn back to page 189. Point to the sentences in Exercise 3A and then write:
   • *I'm going to the store for some milk.*
   • *A can of tomatoes and two onions.*
2. Underline *some milk* and *two onions*.
3. Tell students to look at the grammar charts. Show the top charts on the board (Singular count nouns, Plural count nouns, Non-count nouns).
4. Point to the first chart on the board. Ask: *What are the singular count nouns?* Underline <u>an</u> and <u>a</u> in *an onion* and *a sandwich*.
5. Point to the second chart on the board. Ask: *What are the plural forms of the count nouns?* Underline the plural endings in *onion<u>s</u>* and *sandwiche<u>s</u>*.
6. Point to the third chart on the board. Ask: *What are the non-count nouns?* (bread, fish, milk, rice) Next to the heading *Non-count nouns*, write and then cross out *a, an* and *-s*. Say: *Do not use* a *or* an *with non-count nouns. Non-count nouns do not have plural forms.*
7. Tell students to look at the bottom charts on page 190. Point to the first chart on the bottom. Tell students to circle the plural count noun (*onions*). Read the sentences for the plural count noun across the charts (*Are there any onions? Yes, there are some. / No there aren't any.*) and ask the class to repeat. Say: *Use* there are *with plural count nouns.*
8. Read the sentences for the non-count nouns across the bottom charts (*Is there any milk? Yes, there is some. / No there isn't any.*) and ask the class to repeat. Say: *Use* there is *with non-count and count nouns.*

9. Read the *yes/no* questions and the negative answers again and ask the class to repeat. Say: *Use* any *in questions and negative sentences.*
10. Read the affirmative answers and ask the class to repeat. Say: *Use* some *in affirmative sentences.*
11. Tell students to read the **Grammar Watch** note silently. Tell them to turn to pages 260–261 and read more about nouns.

 ActiveTeach: Grammar Coach

A COMPLETE. Use the correct forms of *there...*

1. Read the directions. Show the first line of the example. Ask: *Why is the answer* Is there any? (because *bread* is non-count)
2. Show the second line of the example. Ask: *Why is the answer* there's? (because *bread* is non-count and the answer is affirmative)
3. Tell students to look at the noun in each item. Remind students that nouns with plural endings are count nouns.
4. Walk around as students complete the exercise and spot-check students' answers. If you see an incorrect answer, ask the student to circle the noun in the item and then ask: *Is the answer* Is there any *or* Are there any? *or* Is the answer *There's* or *There are?* If the error is with affirmative/negative, tell the student to circle *Yes* or *No* in the second line.

B WORK TOGETHER. Practice the...

1. Pair students and tell them to compare answers by asking and answering the questions.
2. Call on pairs to ask and answer the questions for the class. Correct as needed.

■ **EXPANSION: Speaking practice for B**

1. Tell students to look at the foods on page 186 and make a list of five count and five non-count nouns. Model by writing the headings *count* and *non-count* and numbering from 1 to 5. Elicit and list on the board a couple of count nouns (for example, *oranges, eggs*) and a couple of non-count nouns (for example, *rice, olive oil*).
2. Pair students. Say: *Ask your partner about the food in his or her fridge or cupboard at home. Use* Are there any *or* Is there any *and the foods on your lists.* Model by pointing to a count noun on the board and asking an above-level student: *Are there any [eggs] in your fridge?* Then point to a non-count noun and ask the same student: *Is there any [rice] in your cupboard?*

How much / How many

 ActiveTeach: Grammar Discovery

1. Say: *Now we're going to study questions with* How much *and* How many.
2. Show the grammar chart from page 191 on the board.
3. Read the sentences and ask the class to repeat.
4. Ask: *Do we use* How many *or* How much *with plural count nouns like* eggs *or* oranges? (*How many*) *What do we use with non-count nouns like* chicken *or* sugar? (*How much*)
5. Point out that containers and quantities can be used to make non-count nouns countable. *Optional:* For practice with this, write on the board: *rice—2, soda—5, yogurt—8, milk—3, meat—1.* Tell students to use containers or quantities to write the amounts (*2 bags of rice, 5 bottles of soda, 8 containers of yogurt, 3 gallons of milk, a pound of meat*)
6. Write: *How _____ rice? How _____ bags of rice?* Ask the class to complete the questions. (*much, many*)

 ActiveTeach: Grammar Coach

C **IDENTIFY. Cross out the incorrect words.**

1. Read the directions and the example. Ask: *Why is the answer* many? (because *potatoes* is a plural count noun)
2. Remind students to refer to page 261 for more examples of non-count nouns.
3. Students compare answers by reading the conversation with a partner.
4. Call on two above-level students to read the conversation for the class.

D **WRITE. Read the conversation in Exercise C...**

1. Read the directions. Read the first two lines of the conversation in Exercise C. Then point to the shopping list and read: *5 lbs. of potatoes.*
2. Write: *lbs. = pounds, lb. = pound.*
3. Check answers by asking students: *How much cheese are they going to get? How many oranges... How much milk... How much sugar...*
4. As students answer, tell them to write the items from the shopping list on the board.

Show what you know!

1. THINK ABOUT IT. Plan a company picnic...

1. Read the directions. To model, elicit a couple of ideas and write them on the board. Ask: *What do you like to eat at a picnic? What do you like to drink?*
2. Tell students to come up with at least five items. Walk around and check for the correct use of count and non-count nouns (no -s).
3. Ask several students to write three items each on the board. Ask the class to check that the count nouns end in -s and the non-count nouns don't.

2. TALK ABOUT IT. Decide how much food you...

1. Pair students. Read the directions.
2. Play A and model the example with an above-level student. Student B finishes his or her sentence (for example, *I think we need five chicken sandwiches*). Write the item and then introduce the next item (*OK, let's also take some...*). Prompt Student B to ask: *How much / How many do we need?* After each item is decided, write it. Keep the conversation going until there are five items on the list.
3. Say: *Take turns suggesting a food item to take. You can say:* Let's also take some... *Then the other person asks:* How much / How many do we need?
4. Walk around and make sure pairs are taking turns and asking *How much / How many do we need?*

3. WRITE ABOUT IT. Now write five sentences...

1. Read the directions and the example.
2. Pair students and ask them to check each other's sentences.
   - Sentences should use *a* and *an* with singular count nouns.
   - Sentences should use the correct plural form for count nouns
   - Sentences should not use *a* and *an* or plural forms for non-count nouns.
3. Have students volunteer to write their sentences on the board.

Self-Directed Learning

Point out the blue bar. Ask students if they can do the lesson learning objective or if they need more practice. Tell them to check one of the boxes. Assign Extra Practice as needed.

Extra Practice

  pp. 111–112

Grammar

How much / How many

		bread	
How	**much**	milk	do we need?
		onions	
	many	cans of soup	

C **IDENTIFY. Cross out the incorrect words.**

A: How ~~much~~ / **many** potatoes do we have? Do we need more?

B: Yes. I'll get a five-pound bag at the store.

A: OK. Are you going to get **cheese** / ~~cheeses~~?

B: Yeah. But how **much** / ~~many~~ cheese do we need?

A: Oh, a pound is fine. We need some **fruit** / ~~fruits~~, too.

B: OK. I'll get a dozen ~~orange~~ / **oranges**. I love them!

A: How **much** / ~~many~~ milk do we have?

B: None. I'll get a half-gallon.

A: Could you get some **sugar** / ~~sugars~~, too?

B: Sure. How **much** / ~~many~~ sugar do you want?

A: One pound is enough.

Shopping List

5 lbs. of potatoes

1 lb. of cheese

1 dozen oranges

0.5 gallon of milk

1 lb. of sugar

_____

D **WRITE. Read the conversation in Exercise C again. Complete the shopping list.**

Show what you know!

1. **THINK ABOUT IT. Plan a company picnic. Decide what food and drinks you want to bring. Write the list of food.**

2. **TALK ABOUT IT. Decide how much food you need. Write how much you need.**

   A: Let's bring some chicken sandwiches.
   B: Good idea. How many do we need?
      I think . . .

3. **WRITE ABOUT IT. Now write five sentences about your picnic. Write where you will go and what you will bring.**

   The company will have a picnic in Central Park. We will bring ten chicken sandwiches and three gallons of orange juice. We'll also take . . .

I can use count and non-count nouns and *how much / how many.* ☐

I need more practice. ☐

For more practice, go to MyEnglishLab.

Workplace, Life, and Community Skills

Nutrition information

READ FOOD LABELS

A **DISCUSS.** Work with a small group. Do you eat a healthy diet? How do you know the foods you eat are healthy?

B **IDENTIFY.** Read the article. Complete the information below.

What's in My Food?

Carbohydrates, cholesterol, fiber, protein, sodium, and sugar are some of the nutrients in food. All of these nutrients are good for you, but only in the right amounts.

Carbohydrates give you energy for several hours. Foods such as pasta, bread, and potatoes have a lot of carbohydrates.

Cholesterol is only in animal fat. Foods such as butter, mayonnaise, red meat, and eggs have a lot of cholesterol. Too much cholesterol is not good for you.

Fiber is from plants. Foods such as vegetables, fruits, and grains all have lots of fiber. Fiber is good for you. It helps your stomach digest food.

Protein makes your body strong. Foods such as chicken, fish, and beans have a lot of protein.

Sodium is another word for salt. Foods such as potato chips, canned soups, and olives have a lot of sodium. Too much sodium is not good for you.

Sugar gives you quick energy. Candy, cookies, and soda have a lot of sugar. Too much sugar is not good for you. Watch out! Sometimes sugar has a different name, such as high-maltose corn syrup or high-fructose corn syrup.

How do you find out what's in your food?

Read the ingredient and nutrition labels on your food packages. An ingredient label lists all the ingredients in the food. The ingredients are listed in the order of amount. The first ingredient on the list is the main (or largest) ingredient. The last ingredient is the smallest one. A nutrient label lists the amount of each nutrient in one serving of the food. To eat a healthy diet, you need to ask, "What's in my food?" and make sure you eat the right amount of each nutrient.

1. **carbohydrates:** bread, potatoes, _____*pasta*_____
2. **cholesterol:** butter, mayonnaise, red meat, _____eggs_____
3. **fiber:** vegetables, grains, _____fruits_____
4. **protein:** chicken, beans, _____fish_____
5. **sodium:** potato chips, olives, _____canned soups_____
6. **sugar:** candy, soda, _____cookies_____

C **INTERPRET.** Read the sentences. Circle *True* or *False*. Correct the false statements.

1. To find out what is in your food, you need to read the ~~nutrition~~ label. *ingredient*	True	(False)
2. The ingredients are listed in ~~alphabetical order.~~ the order of amount	True	(False)
3. The main ingredient of the food is listed first. *serving*	(True)	False
4. The label lists the amount of nutrients in one ~~container.~~	True	(False)

Correlations

ELPS Level 2: 1, 2, 3, 4, 5, 6, 7, 8, 9, 10
CCRS Level A: W.1.7, W.1.8
CASAS Reading: RDG 1.7, 1.8, 2.3, 3.2
CASAS Listening: L2.1, 2.3, 4.2
CASAS Competencies: 0.1.2, 0.1.5, 1.2.8, 1.6.1, 3.5.1, 3.5.2, 4.5.6, 7.4.4, 7.7.3
Complete standards language available on the Pearson English Portal.

Self-Directed Learning

State the **lesson objective**. Say: *In this lesson, we will learn to read food labels.*

A DISCUSS. Work with a small group. Do you…

1. Read the directions.
2. Form groups of 3. Write the following questions:
   1. *Do you eat a healthy diet?*
   2. *What foods do you eat?*
   3. *How do you know the foods you eat are healthy?*
3. Tell the groups to discuss these questions.
4. Call on students to answer. Elicit brief answers for questions 2 and 3 and write them.

B IDENTIFY. Read the article. Complete the…

1. Introduce the reading. Ask: *Does this reading have a title?* (yes) *What is it?* (What's in My Food?) *Does the reading have headings?* (yes) *What color are they?* (orange) *What do you notice about them?* (Most of them are single words. Most of them are nutrients.)
2. Direct students to read the article silently.
3. Read the directions and the example. Tell students to find the part of the article that talks about carbohydrates and underline the foods that have a lot of carbohydrates.
4. Students compare answers with a partner.
5. Say each nutrient category and ask the class to repeat.
6. Tell students to close their books. Say the groups of food items in random order and ask the class to call out the nutrient categories.

■ **EXPANSION: Vocabulary practice for B**

1. Say: *Scanning an article means reading it quickly to find specific information. Look quickly at the article to find the word* nutrient. Tell students that it appears five times.
2. Ask: *What is a nutrient?* (Possible answers: *the things in food that are good for you; things like carbohydrates, cholesterol, fiber*) Write students' responses.

■ **EXPANSION: Speaking and vocabulary practice for B**

1. Tell students to look at the food items in Exercise B and underline the ones they eat.
2. Write: *All of these* _____ *are good for you, but only in the right* _____. *To eat a healthy* _____, *you need to ask,* _____, *and make sure you eat the right* _____ *of each* _____. Tell students to read the article again and complete the sentences (*nutrients, amounts, diet, "What's in my food?" amount, nutrient*).
3. Ask students for the answers and write them in the blanks.

■ **EXPANSION: Graphic organizer for C**

1. Draw a chart on the board with the column headings: *Nutrient, Foods with a lot, What it does,* and *Eat a lot or a little?* Use the nutrient categories as row headings.
2. Tell students to read the article again and complete the chart. Say: *Some information will be missing from the chart.*
3. To model, read the *Carbohydrates* section of the article and fill in the first row of the chart: *pasta, bread, potatoes; gives you energy.* Explain to students that for *carbohydrates*, they can leave the last column blank, since the article does not provide information about how many carbohydrates to eat.

C INTERPRET. Read the sentences. Circle…

1. Read the directions.
2. Read item 1. Tell students to scan the article for *nutrition label.* Ask them to **cite evidence:** *Where is that information?* (*How do you find out what's in your food?*) Ask an above-level student to read the sentence with *nutrition label* in it (*Read the ingredient and nutrition labels on your food packages.*) Ask: *Is the answer true?* (yes)
3. Ask the class which items are false (2, 4). Say: *Now we need to correct the false information.*
4. Read item 2. Say: *What order are the ingredients lists in?* (in the order of amount) Tell students to underline this sentence in the article. Say: *Correct the false statement in item 2.*
5. Read item 4. Say: *What is the amount that the label uses?* (servings) Tell students to underline this sentence in the article. Ask: *What is a serving?* Explain that a *serving* is the amount of the food that one person would normally eat. Say: *Correct the false statement in item 4.*

Workplace, Life, and Community Skills

D COMPARE. Read the nutrition labels. Circle...

Document Literacy: Nutrition labels
Context: Nutrition labels are found on food packages.
Purpose: They give information about how healthy a food is.
Key Words: *nutrition facts, serving size, calories, fat, carbohydrate, sugar, protein*

1. Say: *Read the nutrition labels for a gallon of whole milk and a gallon of non-fat milk.* Ask about **context**: *Where do you find nutrition labels?* (On food packages) *What foods are these labels for?* (whole milk, non-fat milk) *What is the main difference between the two foods?* (fat) Ask about **purpose**: *What are nutrition labels for?* (Show how healthy a food is) Ask about **key words**: *What information is on nutrition labels?* Elicit a few words (for example, *nutrition facts, sugar, servings per container*).

2. Tell students to find *servings per container* on each label. Ask: *How much milk is in one serving?* (one cup) Say: *The nutrition information on each label is for one cup of milk.*

3. Explain *cup* as a unit of measure. Say: *One cup is equal to 340 grams.* Write: *1 cup = 340 g.* Bring in a cup measure to show the class.

4. Ask: *What nutrient does milk have that makes your body strong?* (protein) *How many grams of protein are in whole milk and non-fat milk?* (8 grams in both) *How many grams of fat does one serving of whole milk have?* (8 grams) *How many grams of fat does one serving of non-fat milk have?* (0 grams)

5. Tell students to find *calories* on the labels. Explain: *Calories measure how much energy a food can produce. People need calories every day to stay healthy. We burn calories through activities. People gain weight when they eat a lot of calories and don't burn them.* Write: *If you aren't trying to gain weight, eat foods that are <u>high / low</u> in calories.* Tell the class to call out the answer. Circle *low.*

6. Read the directions.

7. Students compare answers with a partner.

8. Tell pairs to correct the false sentences (3. <u>per serving</u>, 7. <u>0 grams</u>, 8. <u>8 grams</u>).

E COMPARE. Look at the two nutrition labels...

1. Form groups of 3.

2. Say: *Look at the two nutrition labels again. Circle the numbers that are different for each.*

3. Ask groups: *Which milk do you think is better for your health? Why?* Say: *Take turns completing the*

example with one reason. Each group member should try to give a different reason.

4. Discuss as a class. Ask: *Which milk do you think is better for your health? Why?* Ask students to **cite evidence**.

F EXAMINE. Read the labels. Circle the main...

1. Read the directions.

2. Tell students to silently re-read the last section of the article on page 192. Students circle the main ingredient on each label.

3. Tell students to silently re-read the *Sugar* section of the article. Students underline the other names for sugar on each label (*high-maltose corn syrup, high-fructose corn syrup*).

4. Students compare answers with a partner.

5. Ask questions to check answers. For example: *What's the main ingredient in the peanut energy bar?* (peanuts) *What are the sugar ingredients in the orange drink?* (high-fructose corn syrup, sugar)

G GO ONLINE. Search for the ingredients in a...

1. Read the directions. Ask students what they would search in English if they wanted to find information about food ingredients.

2. Write the search string: *ingredients for [Product].* Have students search the internet and decide if the ingredients in their favorite foods are healthy or not.

3. Compare research as a class. Discuss what makes these foods healthy and why students like them.

Digital Skills for G
1. Tell students to search online for a nutrition calculator. Say: *A nutrition calculator gives you the calories, fat, carbohydrates, protein, and other nutrients for many foods.* Write the search strings: *food calculator* and *nutrition calculator.*
2. Write the websites that students find.
3. Tell students to calculate the nutrition information for their favorites foods.

 ActiveTeach: Review

Self-Directed Learning

Point out the blue bar. Ask students if they can do the lesson learning objective or if they need more practice. Tell them to check one of the boxes. Assign Extra Practice as needed.

Extra Practice
Workbook pp. 113–114   Life Skills Writing

Workplace, Life, and Community Skills

D **COMPARE. Read the nutrition labels.**
Circle *True* or *False*. Note that *g* = grams
and *mg* = milligrams.

WHOLE MILK, 1 gallon

Nutrition Facts	
16 servings per container	
Serving size	**1 cup**
Amount per serving	
Calories	**160**
Total Fat 8g	
Cholesterol 35mg	
Sodium 125mg	
Total Carbohydrate 13g	
Dietary Fiber 0g	
Sugar 12g	
Added sugars 0g	
Protein 8g	

1. There are 16 servings in a gallon of milk. (True) False

2. The whole milk has 160 calories per serving. (True) False

3. The whole milk has 8 grams of total fat per gallon. True (False)

4. The non-fat milk has 5 milligrams of cholesterol per serving. (True) False

5. The whole milk has 125 milligrams of sodium per serving. (True) False

6. Both kinds of milk have 12 grams of sugar per serving. (True) False

7. The non-fat milk has 12 grams of added sugars per serving. True (False)

8. The non-fat milk has zero grams of protein per serving. True (False)

NON-FAT MILK, 1 gallon

Nutrition Facts	
16 servings per container	
Serving size	**1 cup**
Amount per serving	
Calories	**90**
Total Fat 0g	
Cholesterol 5mg	
Sodium 130mg	
Total Carbohydrate 13g	
Dietary Fiber 0g	
Sugar 12g	
Added sugars 0g	
Protein 8g	

E **COMPARE. Look at the two nutrition labels in Exercise D.**
Which milk do you think is better for your health? Why?

I think whole milk is better because . . .

F **EXAMINE. Read the labels.**
Circle the main ingredient.
Underline the sugar ingredients.
Do you think these foods are
good for your health? Why?

G GO ONLINE. Search for the
ingredients in a food you like.
Are the ingredients good for
you? Report your findings.

Ingredients: peanuts, high-maltose corn syrup, sugar, rolled oats, high-fructose corn syrup.

SUNSHINE ORANGE DRINK

Ingredients: water, high-fructose corn syrup, sugar, 2% or less of each of the following juices — orange, apple, lime, grapefruit.

I can read food labels. ☐   I need more practice. ☐

For more practice, go to MyEnglishLab.

Make decisions when shopping for food

1 BEFORE YOU LISTEN

A **READ. Look at some things that are important to people when they buy food.**

1.

Convenience is important to me. I buy food that's easy to prepare.

2.

I buy food that **tastes good**. That's all I care about.

3.

I think about **price**. I get store brands and things on sale.

4.

I buy **healthy** food like low-fat milk and whole wheat bread.

5.

I like **fresh** fruits and vegetables. I don't buy frozen or canned food.

B **MAKE CONNECTIONS. What's important to *you* when you buy food?**

2 LISTEN

A ▶ **LISTEN FOR MAIN IDEA. What is the commercial for? Circle the answer.**

a.

b.

c.

B ▶ **LISTEN FOR DETAILS. Check (✓) the words you hear.**

☑ better taste   ☐ lower price   ☑ fresher
☑ healthier meals   ☑ better for you   ☐ easier to prepare

Correlations

ELPS Level 2: 2, 7
CCRS Level A: SL.K.3
CASAS Reading: RDG 1.7, 2.3
CASAS Listening: L2.1, 2.3, 4.2, 6.1, 6.2, 6.5
CASAS Competencies: 0.1.2, 0.1.4, 0.1.5, 0.1.6, 1.2.8
Complete standards language available on the Pearson English Portal.

Self-Directed Learning

State the **lesson objective**. Say: *In this lesson, we will learn to make decisions when shopping for food.*

1 BEFORE YOU LISTEN

A READ. Look at some things that are…

1. Read the directions. Tell students to read the reasons silently.
2. Say each boldfaced word or phrase and have students repeat.
3. Write the boldfaced words, and tell students to close their books. Say the following and ask the class to call out a word or phrase from the board:
   It doesn't cost a lot. (price)
   It's not frozen or canned. (fresh)
   It's easy to prepare. (convenience)
   It's good for you. (healthy)
   I like to eat it. (tastes good)
4. Tell students to open their books. Call on students to read each reason.

B MAKE CONNECTIONS. What's important to…

1. Ask: *What's important to you when you buy food? Draw a star next to the reason that's most important to you.*
2. Say each reason and ask for a show of hands. Tally the responses on the board and circle the most popular answer.

2 LISTEN

A ▶ LISTEN FOR MAIN IDEA. What is the…

1. Point to each picture and ask the class to call out the food item (pasta, soup, bread).
2. Read the directions. Play the audio. Students listen and circle the answer.
3. Ask: *What is the commercial for?* Ask the class to call out the answer.
4. Ask about **register**: *What kind of customer do you think the commercial is talking to, a college student or a parent?* (parent) *Why do you think so?* (It says, *Your family is important to you. You want to take care of them.*)

B ▶ LISTEN FOR DETAILS. Check (✓) the…

1. Read the directions. Tell students to read the words silently.
2. Play the audio. Students listen and check.
3. Ask the class: *How many boxes did you check?* Ask for a show of hands: *One box? Two boxes?* etc. Play the audio again as needed.
4. Call on students to say the answers.

Teaching Tip: Use the script

Optional: If students need additional support, tell them to read the Audio Script on page 273 as they listen to the conversations.

Culture Note

1. Say: *The majority of food shoppers in the U.S. shop where they can get the best prices. Secondly, they choose a store that is convenient or close by. Another reason they may choose a particular store is if it is clean and has fast service. Other important reasons are convenience and availability of products. Customers also like a clean store and fast service.*
2. Ask: *In your native country, what do you think are the most important reasons for where people shop for food?*

Listening and Speaking

3 CONVERSATION

A PREDICT. Look at the picture. What are...

1. Read the directions. Ask: *Who do you see?* (two women, shoppers) *Where are they?* (in a supermarket/grocery store)
2. Ask: *What are they shopping for?* Elicit guesses and write them. Ask: *What is the woman holding in her hand?* (coffee)

B ▶ LISTEN. What are they talking about?

1. Read the directions. Tell students to read the answer choices silently.
2. Play the audio. Students listen and choose the answer.
3. Call on a student to say the correct answer.

C ▶ LISTEN AND READ. Then listen and repeat.

1. Note: This conversation is the same one students heard in Exercise 3B.
2. Play the audio. Students read along silently. Pause the audio. Ask: *What brand of coffee does the shopper buy?* (Franklin) *Why?* (It tastes great and it's not expensive.)
3. Resume the audio. Students listen and repeat.

D WORK TOGETHER. Practice the...

1. Pair students and tell them to practice the conversation in Exercise 3C.
2. Tell students to take turns playing A and B.

E CREATE. Make new conversations. Use the...

1. Read the directions.
2. Tell students to look at the information in the boxes. Call on a student to say each item.
3. Show the conversation on the board with blanks. Fill in the blanks with information from the boxes.
4. Ask two on-level students to practice the conversation on the board for the class.
5. Erase the words in the blanks and ask two above-level students to make up a new conversation in front of the class.
6. Tell pairs to take turns playing A and B and to use information from the boxes to fill in the blanks.
7. Tell students to stand, mingle, and practice the conversation with several new partners.
8. Walk around and assist students as needed.
9. Call on pairs to perform for the class.

F MAKE CONNECTIONS. Talk about a product...

1. Read the directions. Tell students to think about a product they like. Tell them to draw a simple picture of the product that shows the brand name. Do the same on the board.
2. Model a conversation with an above-level student. Ask an above-level student to read A's lines from Exercise 4C, substituting your brand and product in the first line. Respond with B's lines from Exercise 4C. For B's last line, give your own two reasons.
3. Pair students and tell them to practice the conversation. Tell A to ask about the product in B's drawing. Tell B to give two reasons for liking the product.
4. Walk around and remind students to switch roles and practice both parts.
5. Call on pairs to perform for the class.

▦ MULTILEVEL INSTRUCTION for 3F

Pre-level scaffolding Direct students to write down two reasons why they like their product.

Above-level expansion Tell pairs to talk about a few products.

▦ EXPANSION: Listening and graphic organizer practice for 3F

- Draw a six-column chart on the board with the headings: *Brand and product, Convenient, Tastes good, Low price, Healthy,* and *Fresh.*
- As students listen to classmates' conversations, tell them to write the brand and product in the first column of the chart, then check the reasons they hear.

Self-Directed Learning

Point out the blue bar. Ask students if they can do the lesson learning objective or if they need more practice. Tell them to check one of the boxes. Assign Extra Practice as needed.

Extra Practice
MyEnglishLab Workbook p. 115

Listening and Speaking

3 CONVERSATION

A PREDICT. Look at the picture. What are they shopping for?

B ▶ LISTEN. What are they talking about?

a. a brand of coffee
b. who is going to pay for the coffee
c. how much coffee they need

C ▶ LISTEN AND READ. Then listen and repeat.

A: Oh, you buy Franklin brand coffee. Is it good?
B: Yes, it's excellent. I think it's better than all the other brands.
A: Really? Why?
B: It tastes great and it's not expensive.

D WORK TOGETHER. Practice the conversation in Exercise C.

E CREATE. Make new conversations. Use the words in the boxes.

A: Oh, you buy _____ brand _____. Is it good?
B: Yes, it's excellent. I think it's better than all the other brands.
A: Really? Why?
B: _____ and it's not expensive.

Sunshine	orange juice	It tastes good
Captain Cook	fish	It's always fresh
Dairy Glenn	ice cream	It's low-fat

F MAKE CONNECTIONS. Talk about a product you like. Explain why you like it.

I can make decisions when shopping for food. ■   I need more practice. ■

For more practice, go to MyEnglishLab.

6 Grammar

Comparative adjectives with *than*

Comparative adjectives with *than*

This coffee is	fresh.	It's	**fresher**	than the other brands.
	tasty.		**tastier**	
	expensive.		**more expensive**	

To form comparative forms of:

one-syllable adjectives ⟶ Add *-er*

two-syllable adjectives ending in *y* ⟶ change *y* to *i* and add *-er*

adjectives with two or more syllables ⟶ use *more* + an adjective

Grammar Watch

- Some comparative adjectives are irregular. For example: *good* ⟶ *better.*
- See page 261 for more spelling rules.

A APPLY. Make comparative forms with *-er* or *more*.

1. fresh   _fresher_
2. fast   faster
3. good   better
4. delicious   more delicious
5. sweet   sweeter
6. expensive   more expensive
7. healthy   healthier
8. fattening   more fattening
9. salty   saltier

B COMPLETE. Write the comparative form of the adjective. Add *than*.

1. Bananas are (sweet) _sweeter than_ apples.
2. Jelly is (cheap) _cheaper than_ butter.
3. Fresh orange juice tastes (good) _better than_ frozen orange juice.
4. Homemade meals are (tasty) _tastier than_ fast food.
5. Fresh fruit is (nutritious) _more nutritious than_ canned fruit.
6. Canned soup is (convenient) _more convenient than_ homemade soup.
7. Vegetables are (good for you) _better for you than_ cookies.
8. Sandwiches are (easy to make) _easier to make than_ hamburgers.

Lesson **6** | Grammar

Correlations

ELPS Level 2: 1, 2, 3, 4, 5, 6, 7, 8, 9, 10
CCRS Level A: SL.1.4, L.1.1, L.1.2
CASAS Reading: RDG 1.7, 2.2, 2.6, 2.9
CASAS Listening: L2.1, 2.3, 3.10, 4.2, 5.8
CASAS Competencies: 0.1.2, 0.1.5, 0.1.6, 1.2.1
Complete standards language available on the Pearson English Portal.

Self-Directed Learning

State the **lesson objective**. Say: *In this lesson, we will learn to use comparative adjectives with* than.

Comparative adjectives with *than*

 ActiveTeach: Grammar Discovery

1. Warm up. Say: *The conversation on page 195 used this grammar.* Turn back to page 195. Point to the sentences in Exercise 3C and then write:
   - *Is it good?*
   - *Yes, it's excellent. I think it's better than all the other brands.*
2. Underline *better than.*
3. Tell students to look at the grammar charts. Point to the top chart. Read sentences and tell the class to repeat.
4. Write: *fresh, tasty,* and *expensive.*
5. Tell students to read the bottom grammar chart silently.
6. Read the first row, about one-syllable adjectives. Point to and say: *fresh.* Ask: *How many syllables does* fresh *have?* (one) *How do we form the comparative?* Add *-er* to *fresh* on the board. Say *fresher* and ask the class to repeat.
7. Read the second row, about two-syllable adjectives. Point to and say: *tasty.* Ask: *How many syllables does* tasty *have?* (two) Draw a line between *ta* and *sty. Does it end in* -y? (yes) *How do we form the comparative?* Change the *y* in *tasty* to *i* and add *-er.* Say *tastier* and ask the class to repeat.
8. Read the third row, about adjectives with two or more syllables. Point to and say: *expensive.* Ask: *How many syllables does* expensive *have?* (three) Draw lines between *ex* and *pen* and *pen* and *sive. How do we form the comparative?* Write *more* in front of *expensive* on the board. Say *more expensive* and ask the class to repeat.
9. Tell students to read the first point of the **Grammar Watch** note silently. Say: *There are no rules for forming irregular comparatives. You have to study and practice them.* Write: *good → better,*

bad → worse, far → farther. Write: This coffee is better than other brands. *This coffee is worse than other brands. Ten kilometers is farther than six miles.* Read these sentences and underline *better than, worse than,* and *farther than.*

10. Tell students to read the second point of the **Grammar Watch** note silently. Tell them to turn to page 261 and read more about adjectives.

 ActiveTeach: Grammar Coach

A APPLY. Make comparative forms with -er...

1. Read the directions and the example. Ask: *Why is the answer* fresher? (because it is a one-syllable adjective)
2. Tell students to say the adjectives and count the syllables. Walk around and pronounce adjectives for students as needed.
3. Students compare answers with a partner.
4. Call on students to write answers on the board and correct as needed. Say the comparative adjectives and ask the class to repeat.
5. *Optional:* Draw a four-column chart on the board with the headings:
   - *1 syllable (-er)*
   - *2 syllables ending in -y (y → i + -er)*
   - *2+ syllables: (more _____)*
   - *irregular*
   Ask students who come to the board to write answers in the appropriate column. Say the comparative adjectives in each column and ask the class to repeat.

B COMPLETE. Write the comparative form of...

1. Read the directions and the example.
2. Tell students to look at their answers and check that they all include *than.*
3. Students compare answers with a partner. Tell them to take turns reading the sentences.
4. Call on students to read the completed sentences. Ask students who read items 4 and 8 to spell *tastier* and *easier.*

■ **EXPANSION: Grammar practice for B**

1. Tell students to use the answers from Exercise B in new sentences.
2. Model by writing your own sentence with *sweeter than* on the board (for example, *Ice cream is sweeter than yogurt.*).
3. Pair students. Say: *Student A, read your sentences to your partner. Student B, say whether you agree or disagree with each statement.* Write: *I agree. I disagree.*

Grammar

C APPLY. Compare the food in the…

1. Read the directions. Say the adjectives in the box and ask the class to call out the comparatives.
2. *Optional:* Direct students to write the comparative forms next to the adjectives in the box.
3. Read the example. Tell students to look at the supermarket ad. Ask: *How much is a small salad?* ($2.99) *How much is a large salad?* ($4.99) Elicit another comparison from the class (for example, *The potato chips are saltier than the pretzels.*). If necessary, explain that *sodium* means *salt*.
4. Pair students. Walk around and check that students are using the correct comparative forms and *than*.

Numeracy: Math skills

1. Tell students to imagine that they are shopping at this store and give the checkout clerk a ten-dollar bill.
2. Ask: *How much change will you get from the ten-dollar bill if you buy:*
   • *a pizza and a small salad?* ($1.02)
   • *two bags of potato chips and a box of pretzels?* ($6.33)
3. Ask: *How much more money will you need if you buy one of each item in the ad?* (an extra $1.76)
4. Tell students to use a calculator from their phone or computer to do the math. Have them compare answers in pairs.

D WRITE. Now write six sentences comparing…

1. Read the directions. Tell students to write on notebook paper and use the example in Exercise C as a model.
2. To provide an additional model, call on a pair to say a comparison. Write the sentence on the board. Correct as needed.
3. Tell partners to exchange papers and check each other's sentences. Tell students to check that the sentences are true, that the comparative forms are correct and correctly spelled, and that the sentences contain *than*.
4. Call on students to write sentences on the board with each of the adjectives from the box. Read them and correct as needed.

Show what you know!

1. THINK ABOUT IT. Think of a food or drink…

1. Read the directions.
2. Ask: *What do you like to eat or drink?* Tell students that they can answer with a type of food or drink

or a specific brand. Model by saying what you like (for example, *I like homemade pizza.*) Write this on the board.
3. Say: *Think of three reasons why you like your product.* Point out that students can use adjectives from the box in Exercise C or other adjectives they have learned. Model by writing reasons of your own on the board (for example, *Homemade pizza is delicious. It's easy to make. It's cheap.*).

2. WRITE ABOUT IT. Now write three sentences…

1. Read the directions.
2. Tell students to make comparisons using the adjectives they wrote in Step 1. Give an example: *Homemade pizza is more delicious than pasta and other Italian food.*
3. Ask pairs to check each other's sentences.
   • Sentences should use the correct forms of comparative adjectives.
   • Comparative adjectives should be spelled correctly.
   • Sentences should contain *than*.
4. Have students volunteer to write their sentences on the board.

3. PRESENT IT. Make a presentation about your…

1. Read the directions and the example.
2. Model the activity. Point to your favorite product on the board. Say: *I like homemade pizza. It is more delicious than… Homemade pizza is also easy to make. It's easier to make than…* etc.
3. Tell students that they should not just read the sentences that they wrote in Step 2, but use them to talk about their products.
4. Call on students to volunteer.

■■ MULTILEVEL INSTRUCTION for 3
Pre-level scaffolding Students can read their sentences from Step 2.
Above-level expansion Challenge students to make their presentation without notes.

Self-Directed Learning
Point out the blue bar. Ask students if they can do the lesson learning objective or if they need more practice. Tell them to check one of the boxes. Assign Extra Practice as needed.

Extra Practice

  p. 115

Grammar

C APPLY. Compare the food in the supermarket ad. Use adjectives from the box or other adjectives.

A small salad is cheaper than a large salad.

cheap
delicious
expensive
fattening
fresh
good
nutritious
salty

Super prices this week!

14" Ready-to-bake pizza $5.99 each 2 for $10.99

Try our salads! $2.99 small large $4.99

Super Salty potato chips 89¢ 12-oz. bag

Hart's fat-free, low-sodium pretzels $1.89 12-oz. box

D WRITE. Now write six sentences comparing the food in the ad.

Show what you know!

1. **THINK ABOUT IT.** Think of a food or drink you like. Complete the information below.

   My product: _____

   Three things I like about this product:

   1. _____
   2. _____
   3. _____

2. **WRITE ABOUT IT.** Now write three sentences comparing it to other brands or products.

   1. _____
   2. _____
   3. _____

3. **PRESENT IT.** Make a presentation about your product. Explain how or why it is better than other brands.

   Happy Cows yogurt is more delicious than other brands. It is . . .

I can use comparative adjectives with *than.* ☐   I need more practice. ☐

For more practice, go to MyEnglishLab.

1 BEFORE YOU READ

A **MATCH.** Write the letter of the word next to the correct definition.

_a_	**1.** = the substance in coffee that makes people feel more awake	**a.** caffeine
_d_	**2.** = a change caused by an event or action	**b.** consume
_e_	**3.** = something that is made or grown, usually to be sold	**c.** contain
_c_	**4.** = have something inside	**d.** effect
_b_	**5.** = eat or drink something	**e.** product

B **IDENTIFY.** Which products contain caffeine? Which one has the most caffeine?
(Answers will vary.)

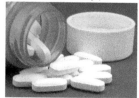

A pain reliever for headaches

An energy drink

Cola

Lemon/lime soda

Among the four products, only lemon/lime soda doesn't contain caffeine. Energy drinks contain the most caffeine.

2 READ

▶ Listen and read.

Academic Skill: Get Meaning from Context

You can sometimes guess the meaning of a word from its context (the words and sentences around it).

Caffeinated Nation

1 You have a cup of coffee for breakfast. Later, you have a cola with lunch. After work, you take some pain reliever for a headache. You may not know it, but each of these products contains caffeine. About 90 percent of the
5 people in the United States consume caffeine every day. Most of them get it from coffee. Some get it from energy drinks, tea, chocolate, or medicines.

What are the effects of caffeine?

Fifteen minutes after caffeine enters your body, you
10 start to feel changes. Your heart beats faster. You have more energy and feel more awake. You feel happier. These effects can last for several hours. When they go away, you may feel a little tired and sad.

Is caffeine bad for you?

15 For most adults, up to 400 milligrams of caffeine a day is not harmful.* That is the amount in one to four cups of coffee. Small amounts of caffeine may even be good for you. But caffeine affects people in different ways, so it's hard to say how much is the right amount.

20 Too much caffeine can be bad for your health. It can make you feel nervous and irritable. It can give you a headache or an upset stomach. If you consume caffeine too late in the day, you may find it hard to sleep at night.

25 It's a good idea to read the labels on medicines, foods, and beverages. Find out if they contain caffeine and how much.

*Source: The U.S. Food and Drug Administration

Amount of caffeine per cup

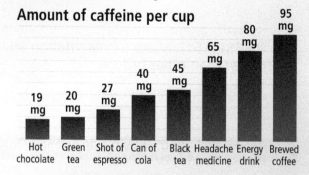

Hot chocolate	Green tea	Shot of espresso	Can of cola	Black tea	Headache medicine	Energy drink	Brewed coffee
19 mg	20 mg	27 mg	40 mg	45 mg	65 mg	80 mg	95 mg

Correlations

ELPS Level 2: 1, 2, 7, 8
CCRS Level A: RI/RL.1.1, RI.1.2, RI.1.4, SL.K.2, L.1. 4
CASAS Reading: RDG 1.7, 1.8, 2.3, 3.2, 3.11, 4.2, 4.9
CASAS Listening: L2.1, 2.3, 3.5.1, 4.2, 5.8, 6.1, 6.2
CASAS Competencies: 0.1.2, 0.1.5, 0.2.1
Complete standards language available on the Pearson English Portal.

Self-Directed Learning

1. State the **lesson objective**. Say: *In this lesson, we will learn to get meaning from context.*
2. Say: *We will read about the effects of caffeine.*

1 BEFORE YOU READ

Ⓐ MATCH. Write the letter of the word next to…

1. Read the directions and the words on the right.
2. Call on students to read the definitions on the left.
3. Ask: *What is the substance in coffee that makes people feel more awake?* Elicit *a. caffeine.*
4. Give students time to match the words to the definitions.
5. Call on students to give the correct answers.

Ⓑ IDENTIFY. Which products contain caffeine?…

1. Tell students to look at the products. Call on students to identify each product.
2. Ask: *Which products do you think have caffeine? Write a checkmark under them.*
3. Ask the class: *Which product do you think has the most caffeine? Circle it.* Ask for a show of hands for each product. Write the most popular guess on the board.

2 READ

▶ Listen and read.

1. Introduce the reading. Ask: *What is the title? What are the headings in the article?* Call on students to answer. Ask: *What do you think the article will be about?* (health effects of caffeine)
2. Introduce the graphic. Ask: *What is the title of the bar graph?* Say: *Look at the x-axis. What are these things?* (drinks that contain caffeine)

ActiveTeach for 2: Anticipation Guide – *Before* Reading exercise

3. Read the text.
   a. Say: *Now we are going to read and listen to the article* Caffeinated Nation.
   b. Play the audio as students listen and read silently.
   c. Play the audio again. Pause the audio after the first paragraph. Ask: *What is the caffeinated nation in the title?* (the United States) *What percentage of Americans consumes caffeine every day?* (90 percent) Tell students to underline this information.
   d. Resume playing the audio. Pause after the *What are the effects of caffeine?* section and ask: *How does caffeine make people feel?* (Your heart beats faster. You have more energy. You feel more awake. You feel happier.) *How do they feel several hours later?* (a little tired and sad) Tell students to number the effects.
   e. Finish playing the audio. Ask: *What is the main idea of the third paragraph?* (some caffeine can be good for you / some caffeine isn't bad for you) Underline *not harmful* in line 16. Point to *harmful.* Say: *We will come back to this word later.*
   f. Ask: *What is the main idea of the fourth paragraph?* (Too much caffeine can be bad for you.) Underline the first sentence of the paragraph. Ask: *What examples does the article give?* Tell students to number the effects.
   g. Tell students to look at the last paragraph. Ask: *How can you find out how much caffeine is in something?* (read the label) Tell students to underline this information.
4. Point to the **Academic Skill** and read it. Ask: *What is context?* (the words and sentences around a word)
5. Point to *consume* in line 5. Call on a student to read the sentence. Ask: *Do you remember what* consume *means?* Remind students of the definition in Exercise 1A. Ask: *What words or sentences here help us know that?* Elicit *get it from coffee* in line 6. Write: *consume = get it from coffee = drink.*
6. Point to *harmful* in line 16. Ask: *Can you guess what this word means?* (bad, dangerous) *How do you know?* (the next lines explain that a small amount can be good for you so we know *not harmful* means *not bad*)
7. **Reinforce:** Help students use context to guess the meaning of other words they don't know.

ActiveTeach for 2: Anticipation Guide – *After* Reading exercise

Reading

3 CLOSE READING

A IDENTIFY. What is the main idea?

1. Say: *Now we are going to identify the main idea.*
2. Read the directions. Have students circle the answer.
3. Elicit the answer from the class.

B CITE EVIDENCE. Complete the sentences...

1. Say: *Now we are going to find information in the reading.*
2. Read the directions. Walk around as students work on the activity. If students are struggling, have them work in pairs or direct them to the text lines where they can find the information.
3. Call on students to read the sentence with the correct completion. Ask a different student: *Where is that information? What line number?*

C INTERPRET. Complete the sentences about...

1. Tell students to look at the bar graph. Ask: *Where is the x-axis?* (the bottom) *What does the x-axis show?* (different products that contain caffeine) Ask: *What does each bar show?* (the amount of caffeine in the product) *How are the bars organized?* (from smallest / least amount of caffeine to largest / most amount of caffeine) *How do you know?* (the length of the bar, the number above the bar) *What is the unit of measure?* (mg) *What does mg mean?* (milligrams) *Is this heavy or light?* Elicit light by asking about a can of cola: *Is a can of cola heavy?* (no) *Do you think a milligram is heavy?* (no)
2. Students read the sentences and answer choices silently and complete.
3. Students compare answers with a partner.
4. Call on students to read the completed sentences to the class.

> **Numeracy: Interpret a bar graph**
>
> A bar graph has three parts: the x-axis (bottom), the y-axis (left), and the bars. The x-axis tells you the groups (who or what the chart is about). The y-axis tells you how much. It can use different units of measure. Each bar tells you the data or amount for a specific group.

4 SUMMARIZE

 ActiveTeach for 4: Vocabulary Practice

1. Read the directions. Ask students to read aloud the words in the box.

2. Tell students to complete the paragraph.
3. To check answers, call on students to read sentences in the summary with the blanks filled in. Ask other students to read the completed summary silently.

Show what you know!

1. **THINK ABOUT IT. List the products you...**

1. Read the directions.
2. Model the activity. List the products you consume with caffeine and amounts of each. Note that drinks can be in cups, ounces, or milliliters. If you include headache medication, list the dose (for example, *four pills*).
3. Students make a list of products.

2. **TALK ABOUT IT. Which products with...**

1. Read the directions and questions.
2. Model the activity. Ask an above-level student the questions. Use examples from the reading to guide the student. For example, ask: *Do you have more energy?*
3. Pair students to take turns talking about the caffeine they consume.

 ActiveTeach for 2: Academic Conversation Support

3. **WRITE ABOUT IT. Write about the caffeine...**

1. Read the directions.
2. Show the sentence frames. Call on an above-level student to fill them in.
3. Give students time to complete the sentence frames.
4. Call on students to read their sentences.

Self-Directed Learning

Point out the blue bar. Ask students if they can do the lesson learning objective or if they need more practice. Tell them to check one of the boxes. Assign Extra Practice as needed.

■ **EXPANSION: Self-directed learning**

Ask students to reflect: *What did you learn from this reading?* Call on students to share something they learned.

> **Extra Practice**
>
> CCRS Plus   pp. 116–117

Reading

3 CLOSE READING

A IDENTIFY. What is the main idea?

Most people in the U.S. consume caffeine every day _____.
a. in many different products
b. and it can have both good and bad effects
c. but they don't know how much they're consuming

B CITE EVIDENCE. Complete the sentences. Where is the information? Write the line numbers.

Lines

1. Caffeine starts to have effects on the body after _____ minutes.
   a. 5   **b.** 15   c. 25   ___9–10___

2. When the effects of caffeine go away, people _____.
   a. sometimes feel a   b. need to consume   c. often get headaches   ___12–13___
   little sad and have   more caffeine
   less energy

3. Up to _____ milligrams of caffeine a day is safe for most adults.
   a. 40   b. 100   **c.** 400   ___15–16___

C INTERPRET. Complete the sentences about the bar graph.

1. Which drink has the highest level of caffeine per cup?
   a. energy drink   b. tea   c. espresso

2. Headache medicine contains _____.
   a. 6.5 mg of caffeine   **b.** 65 mg of caffeine   c. 85 mg of caffeine
   per cup   per cup   per cup

4 SUMMARIZE

amounts   effects   products
consume   health

Complete the summary with the words in the box.

Most people in the U.S. (1) ___consume___ caffeine every day. They get it from coffee and
(2) ___products___ such as tea, cola, chocolate, and some medicines. Caffeine has several
(3) ___effects___ on the body. It affects people in different ways. Small (4) ___amounts___
are probably safe and may be good for your (5) ___health___. Too much caffeine is bad for you.

Show what you know!

1. **THINK ABOUT IT.** List the products you consume that have caffeine. Write how
   much you consume in a day.

2. **TALK ABOUT IT.** Which products with caffeine do you consume?
   How does caffeine affect you? Is it ever a problem for you?

3. **WRITE ABOUT IT.** Write about the caffeine you consume and how it affects you.

   I get caffeine from _____. Caffeine makes me feel _____.
   Caffeine (is sometimes / isn't) a problem for me because _____.

I can get meaning from context. ■   I need more practice. ■

To read more, go to MyEnglishLab.

Lesson 8 Order food in a restaurant

1 BEFORE YOU LISTEN

DISCUSS. Look at the menu. Which dishes and drinks do you know? Which look good?

Mom's Café

Main Dishes
Main dishes are served with a house salad and your choice of one side.

All Main Dishes **$9.95**

meatloaf   roast chicken   pork chops

Asian noodles   hamburger   fish sandwich   macaroni and cheese

Sides

coleslaw   French fries

mixed vegetables   onion rings

mashed potatoes

Drinks

soda   bottled water
apple juice   iced tea

2 LISTEN

A **PREDICT. Look at the picture. Where are they? What is happening?**

B ▶ **LISTEN FOR MAIN IDEA. Which of these sentences do you hear?**

- ☑ Are you ready to order?
- ☐ What do you want to eat?
- ☑ And what would you like with that?
- ☐ Would you like something else?

Sally

Edgar   Lina

C ▶ **LISTEN FOR DETAILS. What do they order?**
They order meatloaf with mixed vegetables and a hamburger with onion rings.

D ▶ **EXPAND. Listen to the whole conversation. Why is the server surprised?**

- a. The woman wants to change her order.
- b. The man ordered a lot of food.
- c. The people decide to leave the restaurant.

Self-Directed Learning

State the **lesson objective**. Say: *In this lesson, we will learn to order food in a restaurant.*

1 BEFORE YOU LISTEN

DISCUSS. Look at the menu. Which dishes and…

1. Tell students to look at the menu. Ask: *What's the name of the restaurant?* (Mom's Café) *How much are the main dishes?* ($9.95) *What do the main dishes come with?* (a house salad and one side) Say: *Point to the sides. Do you have to pay extra for the salad or the sides?* (no)
2. Say each main dish, side, and drink and ask the class to repeat.
3. Ask: *Which foods do you know?* Tell students to write a checkmark next to the foods they know.
4. Ask: *Which foods do you not know?* Call on students to name foods they don't know. Describe these foods or elicit descriptions from other students (for example, S: *I don't know macaroni and cheese.* Classmate: *It's pasta with cheese sauce. My kids love it!*).
5. Ask: *Which foods look good?* Call on a few students to answer. Then ask questions with comparatives: *Which looks better, the hamburger or the fish sandwich? Which looks tastier, the French fries or the mashed potatoes?*

■ **EXPANSION: Speaking practice for 1**

1. Form groups of 3. Ask groups: *If you're trying to eat a healthy diet, what can you order at Mom's Café?* Tell groups to talk about the main dishes, sides, and drinks and choose the healthiest one in each group. Ask: *Which foods and drinks are not healthy? Why? Why is the food or drink you chose healthier than the others?*
2. Say: *Talk about one choice and explain your choice to your group.* Provide an example: *Mixed vegetables are healthy. Vegetables have fiber. French fries and onion rings have more sodium (also more calories, fat, and cholesterol) than mixed vegetables.*

2 LISTEN

A **PREDICT. Look at the picture. Where are…**

Tell students to look at the picture. Ask: *Where are they?* (in a restaurant). *What is happening?* (Edgar and Lina are looking at menus. They are ordering. Sally is taking their orders.)

B ▶ **LISTEN FOR MAIN IDEA. Which of these…**

1. Read the directions. Call on students to read the questions.
2. Play the audio. Students listen and check the questions they hear.
3. Elicit the sentences they heard and checked.
4. Ask about **register**: *Do you think Sally knows Edgar and Lina?* (no) *Why or why not?* (They don't call each other by name.)

C ▶ **LISTEN FOR DETAILS. What do they order?**

1. Read the directions. Tell students to listen and circle the items in Exercise 1.
2. Play the audio. Students listen and circle the items.
3. Students compare answers with a partner.
4. Call on students to say the main dishes and sides.

Teaching Tip: Use the script

Optional: If students need additional support, tell them to read the Audio Script on page 273 as they listen to the conversations.

D ▶ **EXPAND. Listen to the whole…**

1. Read the directions. Tell students to read the answer choices silently.
2. Play the audio. Students choose the correct answer.
3. Review the correct answer with the class.

■ **EXPANSION: Numeracy practice for 2D**

1. Tell students to make a guest check for Edgar and Lina. Tell them to fill in the prices on the guest check. Assign a price for the drinks, such as $1.50 each. Write the sales tax for your state on the board. Tell pairs to calculate the tax and total.
2. Elicit the total and write it on the board. Ask pairs to calculate a 15% tip and a 20% tip for Edgar and Lina's waitress.
3. **Extend:** Ask: *Do servers usually receive tips in your native country? Is the tip/service included in the bill? How much do customers generally tip?*

Listening and Speaking

3 PRONUNCIATION

A ▶ PRACTICE. Listen. Then listen and repeat.

1. Read the Pronunciation Note.
2. Read the Directions.
3. Play the audio. Students listen. Then students listen and repeat.

 ActiveTeach for 3A: Pronunciation Coach

B ▶ APPLY. Listen and complete each...

1. Read the directions. Tell students to read the items silently. Say: *Think about what word you will hear.*
2. Play the audio. Students complete the sentences. Ask: *Were your guesses correct?*
3. Show the items with blanks on the board. Call on students to write in the words.
4. Read the sentences with the weak pronunciation of *a, to, the,* and *of*. Ask the class to repeat.
5. Tell students to take turns reading the sentences to a partner. Tell them to practice the weak pronunciation of *a, to, the,* and *of*. Walk around and listen. Model as needed.

4 CONVERSATION

A ▶ LISTEN AND READ. Then listen and repeat.

1. Note: This is the conversation students heard in Exercise 2B on page 200.
2. Read the directions. Tell students to read the conversation silently and to underline the words *to, the, a,* and *of*.
3. Play the audio. Students read along silently. Then students listen and repeat.
4. Walk around and check that students are using the weak pronunciation of *to, the, a,* and *of*.

B WORK TOGETHER. Practice the...

1. Pair students and tell them to practice the conversation in Exercise 4A.
2. Tell students to take turns playing A and B. Tell them to practice the weak pronunciation of *a, to, the,* and *of*. Walk around and listen. Model as needed.

Workplace Culture

1. Say: *In the U.S., food servers usually take orders in the same way. They take drink orders first, and then come back for food orders. In many places, they are encouraged to "upsell" or to get customers to buy or order more. They say things like* Would you like anything else with that? *Or* Would you like to add a(n) _____?
2. Ask: *In your native country, do food servers try to get you to order more?*

C ROLE-PLAY. Make your own conversations...

1. Read the directions.
2. Model a conversation with two above-level students. Play the server. To prompt the customer, write: *I'd like the _____.* Ask: *Are you ready to order? And what would you like with that?* Repeat the student's orders back to them. End the conversation by saying: *I'll be right back with your salads.*
3. Tell students to look at the conversation in Exercise 4A and underline language they can use when they're the server (*Are you ready to order? And what would you like with that?*).
4. Tell students to look at the menu on page 200 and circle the main dish and the side they will order.
5. Pair students to take turns playing A and B. Walk around and check that the server takes the customer's orders. Listen for the weak pronunciation of *to, the, a,* and *of*.
6. Call on pairs to role-play for the class.
7. *Optional:* As pairs role-play, tell students to listen and write down their orders.

▬ MULTILEVEL INSTRUCTION for 4C

Pre-level scaffolding Direct students to cross out the food in Edgar's lines in Exercise 4A and write in new foods.

Above-level expansion Direct students to also take their customers' drink orders. Provide language as necessary: *What would you like to drink? Can I get you (started with) some drinks?*

Self-Directed Learning

Point out the blue bar. Ask students if they can do the lesson learning objective or if they need more practice. Tell them to check one of the boxes. Assign Extra Practice as needed.

Extra Practice

  pp. 118–119

Listening and Speaking

3 PRONUNCIATION

A ▶ PRACTICE. Listen. Then listen and repeat.

Are you ready **to** order?
I'd like **the** meatloaf.
A side **of** mixed vegetables.

to, the, a, of

The words *to*, *the*, *a*, and *of* usually have a weak pronunciation. The vowel sound is short and quiet.

B ▶ APPLY. Listen and complete each sentence with *to*, *the*, *a*, or *of*.

1. I'd like ____a____ soda.
2. I'm ready ____to____ order now.
3. I'll have ____the____ roast chicken.
4. Could I have a side ____of____ coleslaw?

4 CONVERSATION

A ▶ LISTEN AND READ. Then listen and repeat.

A: Here are your iced teas. Are you ready to order?
B: Yes. I'd like the meatloaf.
A: And what would you like with that?
B: A side of mixed vegetables.
A: OK. Meatloaf with mixed vegetables.
B: And a hamburger with a side of onion rings.
A: A hamburger with onion rings.

B WORK TOGETHER. Practice the conversation in Exercise A.

C ROLE-PLAY. Make your own conversations. Use the menu on page 200 and the suggestions in the boxes. Take turns being a server and a customer.

Server:

Are you ready to order?
What would you like with that?
I'll be right back with your _____.

Customer:

I'd like _____
I'll have _____.
Could I have _____?

I can order food in a restaurant. ■   I need more practice. ■

For more practice, go to MyEnglishLab.

Quantifiers with plural and non-count nouns

Quantifiers with plural nouns					
Affirmative			**Negative**		
We have	**a lot of** **many** **some** **a few**	apples.	We don't have	**a lot of** **many** **any**	apples.

Quantifiers with non-count nouns					
Affirmative			**Negative**		
We have	**a lot of** **some** **a little**	sugar.	We don't have	**a lot of** **much** **any**	sugar.

Grammar Watch

Don't use *much* + a non-count noun in affirmative statements.

Example: *We eat a lot of rice.*

(**Not:** *We eat much rice.*)

A IDENTIFY. Cross out the incorrect words.

1. Apple juice has ~~many~~ / **a lot of** sugar.
2. You should eat **some** / ~~a few~~ fruit every day.
3. Vegetables have **a lot of** / ~~many~~ fiber.
4. Athletes eat ~~much~~ / **a lot of** carbohydrates to get energy.
5. There aren't ~~a few~~ / **many** nutrients in a bag of candy.
6. There is usually **a lot of** / ~~much~~ salt and fat in cheese.

B COMPLETE. Use a correct quantifier from the box. Use each word only once.

a few   any   a little   ~~a lot of~~   many

1. **A:** Do you eat _____ a lot of _____ eggs? You know, they have a lot of cholesterol.
   B: No, not really. I only eat _____ a few _____ eggs a week.
2. **A:** I really like fish. Do you eat a lot of fish?
   B: No, I don't eat _____ any _____ fish. I don't like it.
3. **A:** I think we have milk.
   B: We have _____ a little _____ milk, but it's not enough.
4. **A:** I want to make banana bread. Do we have bananas?
   B: I'm afraid we don't have _____ many _____ bananas, only one or two.

I can use quantifiers with plural and non-count nouns. ☐   I need more practice. ☐

For more practice, go to MyEnglishLab.

<table>
<tr><th colspan="2">Correlations</th></tr>
</table>

Correlations

ELPS Level 2: 10
CCRS Level A: L.1.1
CASAS Reading: RDG 1.7
CASAS Competencies: 0.1.2
Complete standards language available on the Pearson English Portal.

Self-Directed Learning

State the **lesson objective.** Say: *In this lesson, we will learn to use quantifiers with plural and non-count nouns.*

Quantifiers with plural and non-count nouns

 ActiveTeach: Grammar Discovery

1. Warm up. Write:
   • *I'll have a few apples.*
   • *I'll have some sugar.*
   Underline *a few* and *some.*
2. Tell students to look at the grammar charts. Point to the top chart.
3. Read each affirmative sentence and then its corresponding negative sentence (*We have many apples. We don't have many apples.* etc.). Students repeat.
4. Ask: *Which quantifiers for plural nouns can you use in both the affirmative and the negative?* (*many, a lot of*). Tell students to draw a circle around these words in the top chart.
5. *Which quantifiers can only be used in the affirmative?* (*some, a few*) *What do* some *and a* few *change to in the negative?* (*any*) Tell students to underline these words in the top chart.
6. Point to the bottom chart.
7. Read each affirmative sentence and then its corresponding negative sentence (*We have a lot of sugar. We don't a lot of sugar.* etc.). Students repeat.
8. Ask: *Which quantifier for non-count nouns can be used in the affirmative and the negative?* (*a lot of*) Tell students to draw a circle around these words in the bottom chart.
9. Ask: *Which quantifiers can only be used in the affirmative?* (*some, a little*) *What does* some *change to in the negative?* (*any*) Tell students to underline these words in the bottom chart. *What does* a little *change to in the negative?* (*much*)
10. Read the **Grammar Watch** to the students.

 ActiveTeach: Grammar Coach

■ **EXPANSION: Grammar practice**

1. Read all of the affirmative sentences with both plural nouns and with non-count nouns. Ask: *Which quantifiers can you use with plural nouns and non-count nouns?* (a lot of, some) Say: *a lot of apples, a lot of sugar, some apples, some sugar.*
2. Ask: *Which quantifiers can only be used with plural nouns?* (many, a few) Say: *many apples, a few apples.*
3. Ask: *Which quantifier can only be used with non-count nouns?* (a little) Say: *a little sugar.*

Ⓐ **IDENTIFY. Cross out the incorrect words.**

1. Read the directions and the example. Ask: *Why is the answer* a lot of? (because the sentence is affirmative and *sugar* is non-count)
2. Students compare answers with a partner. Tell them to take turns reading the sentences out loud.
3. Call on students to read the sentences.

Ⓑ **COMPLETE. Use a correct quantifier from...**

1. Read the directions.
2. Show item 1 on the board. Read the conversation. Point to: *I only eat _____ eggs a week.* Ask: *Is the sentence affirmative or negative?* (affirmative) *Is* eggs *a plural noun or a non-count noun?* (a plural noun) Point to the top left grammar chart. Ask: *What are the possible answers?* (a lot of, many, some, a few) Ask: *What is the best answer?* (a few)
3. Walk around and spot-check students' answers. If you see an incorrect answer, ask questions: *Is the sentence negative or affirmative? Is the noun after the blank a plural noun or a non-count noun?*
4. Students compare answers with a partner by reading the conversations.
5. Call on pairs to read the conversations.

Self-Directed Learning

Point out the blue bar. Ask students if they can do the lesson learning objective or if they need more practice. Tell them to check one of the boxes. Assign Extra Practice as needed.

Extra Practice
[MyEnglishLab] [Workbook] pp. 118–119

Correlations

ELPS Level 2: 3, 10
CCRS Level A: W.1.2, W.1.5, L.1.1, L.1.2
CASAS Reading: RDG 1.7, 1.8, 2.1
CASAS Listening: L2.1, 2.3, 3.11
CASAS Competencies: 0.1.2, 0.1.5, 0.1.6
Complete standards language available on the Pearson English Portal.

Self-Directed Learning

1. State the **lesson objective**. Say: *In this lesson, we will learn to use* like *and* such as *to introduce examples.*
2. Say: *You will write about your favorite dish.*

1 STUDY THE MODEL

1. Read the directions.
2. Point to the paragraph. Ask: *What is the title of the model?* (My Favorite Dish)
3. **Scaffold** the model. Write as a graphic organizer:

1	Name of dish	
2	Ingredients	
3	Healthy nutrients	
4	Unhealthy nutrients	

4. Tell students to read the text and read the questions independently. Call on students to answer the questions. Write the information in the graphic organizer on the board.
5. Point to the **Writing Skill**. Read it or call on an above-level student to read it while students listen. Tell students to look at the model and find and underline the examples using *such as* and *like*. Elicit what they are examples of (ingredients, healthy nutrients, unhealthy nutrients).

2 PLAN YOUR WRITING

1. Erase the information in the right-hand column of the graphic organizer on the board.
2. Read the directions.
3. Model with an above-level student. The student asks you the questions.
4. Write the information into the graphic organizer.
5. Write: *Healthy* and *Unhealthy*. Brainstorm examples of each (for example, Healthy: protein, fiber, vitamins, complex carbohydrates, minerals, olive oil, etc.; Unhealthy: cholesterol, sodium, sugar, artificial ingredients, a lot of caffeine, etc.).
6. Tell students to make their own graphic organizer on a piece of paper.

7. Have students work in pairs to ask and answer the questions and complete their own graphic organizers.

3 WRITE

1. Read the directions.
2. Use the information in the chart from Exercise 2 to write sentences in a paragraph. Leave out examples of healthy nutrients.
3. Ask: *Does this paragraph need examples? Where?* Add examples of healthy nutrients from your chart.
4. Tell students to write. Walk around to make sure students are writing in paragraph form and using examples.

 ActiveTeach for 3: Writing Support

4 CHECK YOUR WRITING

1. Read the directions. Point to the **Writing Checklist**. Call on students to read the checklist aloud.
2. Pair students to review their writings together. Say: *Read your sentences with a partner. Use the Writing Checklist.* For additional help, remind students that a correct sentence:
   - *begins with a capital letter*
   - *has a subject*
   - *has a verb*
   - *has a period*
   - *is a complete idea*
3. Walk around and verify that students are using the checklist. Collect the papers for review or put them in the students' writing portfolios.

Teaching Tip: Digital skills

Tell students to use their phones or a computer to go to a website to find the ingredients and the nutrients in their favorite dishes.

Self-Directed Learning

Point out the blue bar. Ask students if they can do the lesson learning objective or if they need more practice. Tell them to check one of the boxes. Assign Extra Practice as needed.

Extra Practice

 CCRS Plus   p. 120

Lesson 10

Write about nutrients in a dish

1 STUDY THE MODEL

READ. Answer the questions.

> Badrul Dewan
>
> My Favorite Dish
>
> Rice and beans is a tasty and healthy dish. It has many ingredients like rice, beans, and vegetables. It has healthy nutrients such as protein and fiber. It does not have unhealthy nutrients like cholesterol and sugar.

1. What is Badrul's favorite dish? It's rice and beans.
2. What ingredients are in the dish? Rice, beans, and vegetables.
3. What healthy nutrients does the dish have? It has protein and fiber.
4. What unhealthy nutrients does the dish have? It has no unhealthy nutrients.

2 PLAN YOUR WRITING

WORK TOGETHER. Ask and answer the questions.

1. What is a dish you like?
2. What ingredients are in the dish?
3. What healthy nutrients does the dish have?
4. What unhealthy nutrients does the dish have?

3 WRITE

Now write about the nutrients in a dish you like. Use the model, the Writing Skill, and your ideas from Exercise 2 to help you.

4 CHECK YOUR WRITING

WORK TOGETHER. Read the checklist. Read your writing aloud. Revise your writing.

Writing Skill: Use *like* and *such as* to introduce examples

Give examples in your writing. Use *like* and *such as* to introduce examples. For example:

It has healthy nutrients such as protein and fiber.

It does not have unhealthy nutrients like cholesterol and sugar.

WRITING CHECKLIST

☐ The paragraph answers the questions in Exercise 2.

☐ There are commas between words in lists.

☐ There are examples of ingredients and nutrients.

I can use *like* and *such as* to introduce examples. ■   I need more practice. ■

For more practice, go to MyEnglishLab.

Ask for help

1 MEET ANH

Read about one of her workplace skills.

I know when to ask for help. For example, when a customer asks a question and I don't know the answer, I ask my co-workers.

2 ANH'S PROBLEM

READ. Circle *True* or *False*.

Anh works in a bakery. She sells baked goods to customers. A customer points at a pie. She says, "That pie looks delicious, but I can't eat eggs. Does it have eggs in it?" Anh doesn't know the answer to the question.

1. Anh bakes food at a bakery.   True   **(False)**
2. Maybe the customer will buy the pie. **(True)**   False
3. Anh knows the ingredients in the pie. True   **(False)**

3 ANH'S SOLUTION

A WORK TOGETHER. Anh knows when to ask for help. What does she say? Explain your answer.

1. Anh says, "Don't worry. There aren't any eggs in it."
2. Anh says, "I don't know, but let me ask. I'll be right back."
3. Anh says, "I'm not sure. it probably doesn't have eggs."
4. Anh says _____.

B ROLE-PLAY. Look at your answer to 3A. Role-play Anh's conversation.

Show what you know!

1. **TALK ABOUT IT.** Do you know when to ask for help? How do you ask for help in class? At work? At home? Give examples.

2. **WRITE ABOUT IT.** Write an example in your Skills Log.

   I can ask for help in class. When I don't know the meaning of an English word, I ask the teacher.

I can give an example of how I ask for help. ☐

Unit Review: Go back to page 185. Which unit goals can you check off?

Correlations

CASAS Reading: RDG 1.7, 1.8, 3.2
CASAS Listening: L2.1, 2.3, 4.1, 4.2
CASAS Competencies: 0.1.2, 0.1.4, 0.1.5, 0.1.6,
0.2.1, 4.6.5, 4.8.3
Complete standards language available on the
Pearson English Portal.

Self-Directed Learning

State the **lesson objective**. Say: *In this lesson, we
will learn to give an example of how we ask for help.*

1 MEET ANH

1. Ask: *What is the title of this lesson?* (Ask for help)
2. Write: *Workplace Skill*. Read the directions. Say:
   Listen as I read Meet Anh. Read the paragraph.
   Ask: *What is one of Anh's workplace skills?* (She
   knows when to ask for help.) Next to *Workplace
   Skill*, write: *Ask for help.*
3. Under *Workplace Skill*, write: *Examples.* Ask: *When
   does Anh ask for help?* (She asks for help when
   she doesn't know the answer.) Write the example.
   Elicit other times when it is good to ask for help
   and write them under *Workplace Skill*.

2 ANH'S PROBLEM

1. Say: *Now we are going to read about Anh at work.
   Listen while I read.* Read the first sentence. Ask:
   Where does Anh work? (a bakery) Say: *Look at the
   photo. What does a bakery sell?* (baked goods,
   like bread, pastry, and muffins).
2. Say: *Anh has a problem at work. Listen while I
   read.* Read the rest of the paragraph. Explain any
   unfamiliar vocabulary as needed.
3. Students complete the questions after the reading.
   Call on students to answer. Ask them to **cite
   evidence**: *Where is that information?*
4. Ask: *What is Anh's problem?* (She doesn't know
   the answer to the customer's question.)

3 ANH'S SOLUTION

A WORK TOGETHER. Anh knows when to ask...

1. Read the directions. Ask students to work together
   on the first three items. Walk around and check
   that students understand that only one solution
   is correct.
2. Ask: *Is #1 asking for help?* (no) *Why not?* (She is
   making up the answer when she doesn't know.)
   Ask: *Is #2 asking for help?* (yes) *Why?* (She is going
   to ask someone who knows the answer.) Ask: *Is #3

asking for help? (no) *Why not?* (She is not asking
for help, but only guessing the answer.)
3. Ask students if they have any other ideas. Call on
   students to share item 4 with the class. Write their
   responses. Ask: *Is this asking for help? Why?*

 **ActiveTeach for 3A: Academic
Conversation Support**

B ROLE-PLAY. Look at your answer to 3A...

1. Group students in pairs. Explain that one person
   will be Anh. The other person will be the customer.
   Model the activity with an above-level student.
   Have students practice the conversation with
   different partners.
2. Walk around and ask students to switch roles and
   continue practicing. If students aren't pronouncing
   their lines clearly, model correct pronunciation and
   ask them to repeat.

■ MULTILEVEL INSTRUCTION for 3B

Cross-ability Form groups of 3. Have a pre-level
student be the customer with the question, have an
above-level student be Anh, and have an on-level
student be a co-worker who knows the answer
to the customer's question. The customer asks
the question; Anh says she'll ask a co-worker; the
co-worker makes up an answer; Anh reports the
answer to the customer.

Show what you know!

1. TALK ABOUT IT. Do you know when to ask...

Read the directions. Have students think about
their answers for a few minutes. Then ask them to
share with a partner. Call on students to share with
the class.

2. WRITE ABOUT IT. Write an example in your...

Read the directions and the example. Have students
write their examples in their **Skills Log** at the back of
the book. Circulate and assist students as needed.

Self-Directed Learning

1. Point out the blue bar. Ask students if they can do
   the lesson learning objective or if they need more
   practice. Tell them to check one of the boxes.
   Assign Extra Practice as needed.
2. Ask students to turn to page 185. Go to the Unit
   Wrap-Up teaching notes on page T-185.

Extra Practice

 p. 121

11 Call 911!

Unit Overview

Goals
• See the list of goals on the facing page

Pronunciation
• Stressed syllables
• *H* sound

Reading
• Read about being safe at work
• Identify supporting details

Grammar
• Present continuous: Statements and questions
• *There was / There were*
• Compound imperatives

Writing
• Write about an emergency
• Answer *wh-* questions to give information

Document Literacy and Numeracy
• Interpret a fire escape plan
• Interpret a bar graph

Workplace, Life, and Community Skills
• Identify fire hazards
• Understand fire safety procedures
• Digital Skills: Search for workplace fire-escape plans or your own workplace's fire-escape plan

Life Skills Writing
• Complete an employee accident form

Soft Skills at Work
• Follow safety procedures

Preview
1. Set the context of the unit by asking questions about safety (for example, *Did you have an accident in the past? What happened?*).
2. Show the Unit Opener. Ask: *What is the unit title?* (Call 911)
3. Say: *Look at the picture.* Ask the Preview questions. (Possible answers: an ambulance, two paramedics helping someone; a person hurt or injured)
4. Write the answers.

Unit Goals
1. Point to the Unit Goals. Explain that this list shows what you will be studying in this unit.
2. Tell students to read the goals silently.
3. Say each goal. Explain unfamiliar vocabulary as needed.
4. Point to the ☐ next to the first goal. Say: *We will come back to this page again. You will write a checkmark next to the goals you learned in the unit.*

Oral Presentation
1. Tell students they will give a short presentation at the end of the unit.
2. Write the topics:
   Option 1: What to do in case of fire
   Option 2: What to do if you are in a car accident
3. Assign the topics to two students.

Unit Wrap-Up
1. Review the Unit Goals with students.
2. Direct students to the Grammar Review.
3. If you assigned presentations, ask students to present.

 ActiveTeach for Wrap-Up: Team Project

 ActiveTeach for Wrap-Up: Persistence Activities

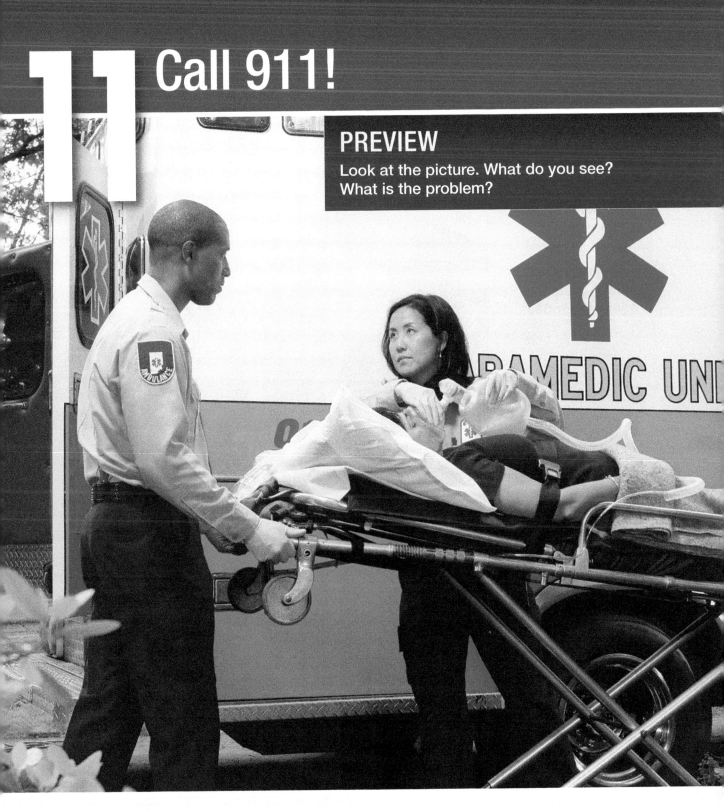

11 Call 911!

PREVIEW

Look at the picture. What do you see?
What is the problem?

UNIT GOALS

- ☐ Describe medical emergencies
- ☐ Call 911
- ☐ Identify fire hazards
- ☐ Understand fire safety procedures
- ☐ Describe an emergency
- ☐ Respond to police instructions

- ☐ **Academic skill:** Identify supporting details
- ☐ **Writing skill:** Answer *wh-* questions to give information
- ☐ **Workplace soft skill:** Show how you follow safety procedures

205

Vocabulary

Medical emergencies

A PREDICT. Look at the pictures. What do you see? Which medical emergencies do you know?

B ▶ LISTEN AND POINT. Listen again and repeat.

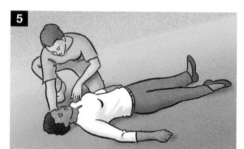

Correlations

ELPS Level 2: 2, 7, 8
CCRS Level A: SL.1.1, SL.K.6, L.1.5, L.1.6
CASAS Reading: RDG 1.7, 2.3
CASAS Listening: L2.1, 2.3, 2.9, 4.2
CASAS Competencies: 0.1.2, 0.1.5, 2.1.2, 7.4.1
Complete standards language available on the Pearson English Portal.

Self-Directed Learning

State the **lesson objective**. Say: *In this lesson, we will learn to describe medical emergencies.*

A PREDICT. **Look at the pictures. What do...**

1. Tell students to cover the list on page 207.
2. Say: *Look at the pictures. Which medical emergencies do you know?* Elicit a medical emergency (for example, *In number 9, he fell.*).
3. Students call out answers. Help students pronounce the medical emergencies if they have difficulty. As needed, restate students' responses to match the vocabulary on page 207.
4. If a student calls out an incorrect medical emergency, ask a *yes/no* clarification question: *In #4, is he choking?* If nobody can identify the correct medical emergency, tell students they will now listen to audio and practice the vocabulary for medical emergencies.

B ▶ LISTEN AND POINT. **Listen again and...**

1. Read the directions. Play the audio. Students listen and point to the medical emergencies.
2. While the audio is playing, walk around and check that students are pointing to the correct emergencies. Pause the audio after item 9.
3. Say each medical emergency in random order and ask students to point to the appropriate picture.
4. Tell students to look at page 207. Resume the audio. Students listen, read, and repeat.

 ActiveTeach for B: Vocabulary Flashcards

▬ **EXPANSION: Vocabulary practice for B**

1. Act out some of the medical emergencies on page 206 (for example, for *choking*, pretend to take a bite of food, then grab your throat and try to speak without any sound coming out). Ask students to guess the emergency by putting sentences in the second person (for example, *You are choking.*)
2. *Optional:* Ask for volunteers to stand up in front of the class and act out other emergencies. The other students guess.

Teaching Tip: Act out new vocabulary

Acting out new vocabulary is especially helpful for kinesthetic learners. The exercises in this vocabulary lesson allow opportunities for teachers to call on volunteers to act out medical emergencies for the class to guess. This method is also useful in teaching action verbs and vocabulary.

Digital Skills for B

1. For some emergencies the best thing is to take steps to prevent them in the first place. An example of this is accidental poisoning.
2. Tell students to go online and research tips to prevent accidental poisoning. Tell them to find one tip and share it with the class. Write the search string: *preventing accidental poisoning.*
3. Write the tips. Possible tips that students may find:
   • Store all medicine out of reach of children.
   • Never tell a child that medicine tastes like candy.
   • Always keep pills in their original containers.
   • Never take or give medicine in the dark.

Culture Note

1. For serious emergencies, you should call 911. In the U.S., the 911 emergency number began in the 1960s. Every year, about 240 million calls are made to 911 in the U.S. You can use 911 to save a life, report a crime, and report a fire. If you call 911, it is important to know your location and to let the 911 dispatcher know it as soon as you are asked.
2. Many other countries also have emergency numbers—for example, 112 is used in many parts of Europe. Ask: *Is there an emergency number in your native country. Is it 911 or a different number? Can you use the same emergency number for ambulance, police, and fire?*

Vocabulary

C IDENTIFY. Student A, point to a picture and...

1. Read the directions. Read each line in the example and ask the class to repeat.
2. Play A and model the example with an above-level student. Point to picture 5 and ask: *What's the emergency?* (she's unconscious) Point to another picture and ask: *What's the emergency?*
3. Model changing roles. Tell the student to point to a picture and ask you: *What's the emergency?*
4. Pair students and tell them to take turns playing A and B.

D ANALYZE. Look at the list of medical...

1. Read the directions. Say: *You're going to look at the list of medical emergencies and decide which ones are happening now and which ones happened in the past. How can you tell?* Elicit students' ideas.
2. Point to *happened in the past* and ask: *What is the ending for regular past-tense verbs?* (-ed) Remind students that some verbs are irregular in the past tense.
3. Point to *happening right now* and ask: *What is an emergency that's happening now?* Elicit an answer (for example, *She's bleeding.*). Underline the *'s* and *-ing*.
4. Pair students and tell them to look at each medical emergency and decide where to write it in the chart.
5. Call on students to write the medical emergencies in the chart on the board. Correct as needed.

Language Note

Point to the left side of the chart and ask: *Which emergency isn't present continuous?* Write *She's unconscious* on the board. Underline *unconscious* and ask: *What part of speech is* unconscious? (adjective) Point to the right side of the chart and ask: *Which emergency had an irregular past-tense verb?* (*He fell.*) *What's the base form of* fell? (*fall*)

Study Tip: Self-test your pronunciation

1. Point to the **Study Tip** and read the directions.
2. Tell students to use the voice recorder on their phones.
3. Walk around as students work. Model correct pronunciations if necessary.
4. Say: *You can record yourself to improve your pronunciation.* Remind students to use this strategy to practice pronunciation.

Show what you know!

1. THINK ABOUT IT. Look at the medical...

1. Read the directions.
2. Tell students to use the list of medical emergencies at the top of page 207.

2. TALK ABOUT IT. 911 is a special phone...

1. Read the directions. Ask students to read the examples silently.
2. Form groups of 3. Tell students to take turns saying an emergency they checked in Step 1.
3. Ask the class if you should call 911 for each emergency (for example, *Do you call 911 when someone is bleeding?*). Students raise their hands if they would call 911.

3. WRITE ABOUT IT. Write a list of medical...

1. Read the directions. Show the examples on the board.
2. Share the checklist below. Then write a checkmark next to each as you point back to the example sentence.
   • The sentence starts with a capital letter.
   • The present continuous and past tenses are formed correctly.
   • The sentence ends with a period.
3. Give students time to write their sentences.
4. Tell students to show their sentences to a partner. Tell the students to use the checklist to review the sentences.
5. Walk around and verify that students are using the checklist. Collect the papers for review or put them in the students' writing portfolios.

Self-Directed Learning

Point out the blue bar. Ask students if they can do the lesson learning objective or if they need more practice. Tell them to check one of the boxes. Assign Extra Practice as needed.

Extra Practice

MyEnglishLab   Workbook pp. 122–123

Vocabulary

Medical emergencies

1. She's bleeding.
2. He's choking.
3. She's having trouble breathing.
4. He's having a heart attack.
5. She's unconscious.
6. He's having an allergic reaction.
7. He swallowed poison.
8. She burned herself.
9. He fell.

C **IDENTIFY.** Student A, point to a picture and ask about the emergency. Student B, say the emergency.

Student A points to picture 5.
A: What's the emergency?
B: She's unconscious.

Study Tip

Self-Test Your Pronunciation
Record yourself. Read each sentence aloud. Listen. If you don't like your pronunciation, record the sentence again.

D **ANALYZE.** Look at the list of medical emergencies in Exercise B. Underline the verbs. Then write the sentences in the correct column below.

happened in the past	happening right now
He <u>swallowed</u> poison.	She<u>'s bleeding</u>.
She <u>burned</u> herself.	He<u>'s chocking</u>.
He <u>fell</u>.	She<u>'s having</u> trouble breathing.
	He<u>'s having</u> a heart attack.
	She<u>'s</u> unconscious.
	He<u>'s having</u> an allergic reaction.

Show what you know!

1. **THINK ABOUT IT.** Look at the medical emergencies. Check (✓) the most serious emergencies.

2. **TALK ABOUT IT.** 911 is a special phone number for medical emergencies. Compare your serious emergencies. Do you call 911 in these emergencies?

   A: Call 911 when a person is choking.
   B: Call 911 when a person is having a heart attack.

3. **WRITE ABOUT IT.** Write a list of medical emergencies for 911.

   Call 911
   The person is choking.
   The person is having a heart attack.

I can describe medical emergencies. ■   I need more practice. ■

For more practice, go to MyEnglishLab.

Unit 11, Lesson 1 **207**

Call 911 to report a medical emergency

1 BEFORE YOU LISTEN

A **MATCH.** Write the words under the pictures.

heart attack   hurt knee   poison   sinus infection

1. _____hurt knee_____   **2.** _____heart attack_____   **3.** _____poison_____   **4.** _____sinus infection_____

B **IDENTIFY.** Call 911 for free from any phone when there is an emergency. Circle the pictures that show an emergency.

2 LISTEN

A **PREDICT.** Look at the picture. Who is the woman calling?

B ▶ **LISTEN.** What is the woman doing?

   a. reporting an emergency
   b. checking in to a hospital
   c. ordering a taxi

C ▶ **LISTEN FOR DETAILS.** What does the 911 operator ask? Check the questions.

   ☑ What's your emergency?
   ☐ Where are you?
   ☑ What's the location of the emergency?
   ☑ What are the cross streets?
   ☐ What are you doing?
   ☑ What's your name?

D ▶ **EXPAND.** Listen to the whole conversation. What will happen next?

   a. An ambulance will come for the man.   **b.** The woman will drive to the hospital.

Correlations

ELPS Level 2: 1, 2, 3, 4, 5, 6, 7, 8, 9, 10
CCRS Level A: SL.K.3,
CASAS Reading: RDG 1.7, 2.3
CASAS Listening: L1.4, 2.1, 2.3, 4.2, 6.1, 6.2, 6.5
CASAS Competencies: 0.1.2, 0.1.5, 2.1.2
Complete standards language available on the Pearson English Portal.

Self-Directed Learning

State the **lesson objective**. Say: *In this lesson, we will learn to call 911 to report a medical emergency.*

1 BEFORE YOU LISTEN

A MATCH. Write the words under the pictures.

1. Read the directions. Read the words and phrases in the box and have students repeat them.
2. Give students time to label the pictures and then compare answers with a partner.
3. Direct students to look at the first picture. Ask the class: *What is the situation?* (She has a hurt knee.) Repeat with the other pictures (2. He's having a heart attack. 3. She swallowed poison. 4. He has a sinus infection.)

B IDENTIFY. Call 911 for free from any phone…

1. Read the directions. Ask: *What makes something an emergency?* (It is a situation that can kill someone or cause very serious damage quickly.)
2. Tell students to look at picture 1 in Exercise 1A. Ask: *Is it an emergency? Do you need to call 911?* (no/no)
3. Repeat with the other pictures (2. yes/yes; 3. yes/yes; 4. no/no). Tell students to give reasons for their answers. (Possible answers: A heart attack and poison can kill someone. A hurt knee and a sinus infection are not as serious.)

2 LISTEN

A PREDICT. Look at the picture. Who is the…

1. Tell students to look at the picture. Ask: *Who do you see?* (a woman and a man) *Where are they?* (in a store) *What are they doing?* (the woman is on the phone, the man is sitting and holding his chest)
2. Ask: *Who is the woman calling?* Write students' guesses.

B ► LISTEN. What is the woman doing?

1. Read the directions. Have students read answer choices silently. Ask: *Which do you think is correct?* Ask students to raise their hands if they guess *a*. Repeat with *b* and *c*.
2. Play the audio. Students listen and choose the correct answer.
3. Elicit the correct answer.
4. Write: *9-1-1. What's your emergency?* Ask about **register**: *Do you think an emergency call operator will always answer with these words?* (yes) *Do emergency operators in your native language always use the same words when they answer an emergency call? What do they say?*

C ► LISTEN FOR DETAILS. What does the 911…

1. Read the directions. Tell students to read the questions silently or call on students to read each question aloud.
2. Play the audio. Students check the questions they hear.
3. Students compare answers with a partner.
4. Ask the class: *How many questions did you check?* (Students should have checked four questions.) Play the audio again as needed.
5. Call on students to read the questions they checked.

Career Awareness: 911 operator

911 operators respond to emergency calls and send people, such as firefighters and police officers, out to locations. They can work at police stations, fire stations, call centers, and hospitals. They usually need a high school diploma and special training or certification.

■ **EXPANSION: Career awareness for 2C**

Ask students about the job in this lesson: *What does a 911 operator do? Where does one work? Do you need to study to be a 911 operator? Do you want to be a 911 operator?*

D ► EXPAND. Listen to the whole…

1. Read the directions. Tell students to read the answer choices silently.
2. Play the audio. Students choose the correct answer.
3. Ask: *Do you need to listen one more time?* If yes, play the audio again.
4. Ask the class: *What will happen next?*

Listening and Speaking

3 PRONUNCIATION

A ▶ PRACTICE. Listen to the words. Then...

1. Read the directions. Then read the **Pronunciation Note**.
2. Write *allergic* on the board and pronounce it slowly. Ask: *How many syllables does* allergic *have?* (three) Pronounce *allergic* again, exaggerating the stress on the second syllable. Ask: *Which syllable is longer and louder?* Mark the stress on the second syllable. Pronounce *allergic* again and ask the class to repeat.
3. Play the audio. Students listen. Then students listen and repeat.

■ **EXPANSION: Pronunciation practice for 3A**

1. Write these questions:
   - *Are you allergic to anything?*
   - *Have you ever been in an ambulance?*
   - *Have you ever had an emergency?*
2. Pair students to take turns asking and answering the questions. Walk around and make sure students are stressing the correct syllables.

 ActiveTeach for 3A: Pronunciation Coach

B ▶ APPLY. Listen. Mark (•) the stressed...

1. Read the directions. Tell students to read the items silently.
2. Play the audio. Students mark the stressed syllables.
3. Write the words on the board. Call on students to mark the stress. Make corrections as needed.
4. Pronounce the words and ask the class to repeat.

4 CONVERSATION

A ▶ LISTEN AND READ. Then listen and repeat.

1. Note: This conversation is the same one students heard in Exercise 2B on page 208.
2. Tell students to read the conversation and underline words from Exercise 3A (*emergency, location*) and mark the stressed syllables.
3. Play the audio. Students read along silently. Then students listen and repeat.

B WORK TOGETHER. Practice the...

1. Pair students and tell them to practice the conversation in Exercise 3A.
2. Tell students to take turns playing A and B. Walk around and help with the pronunciation of multi-syllable words.

C CREATE. Make new conversations. Use...

1. Read the directions.
2. Tell students to look at the boxes. Call on students to read each item. Ask: *What information is in blue boxes?* (emergency) *In green boxes?* (location) *In yellow boxes?* (cross streets)
3. Show the conversation on the board with blanks. Read it and when you come to a blank, elicit information from a box with the same color.
4. Ask two on-level students to practice the conversation for the class.
5. Erase the words in the blanks and ask two above-level students to make up a new conversation in front of the class.
6. Tell pairs to take turns playing A and B and to use information from the boxes to fill in the blanks.
7. Tell students to stand, mingle, and practice the conversation with several new partners.
8. Walk around and check that students use correct syllable stress.

D ROLE-PLAY. Make your own conversations.

1. Model the activity. Write three headings: *Emergency, Location, Cross streets*.
2. Fill in the information you will use in your conversation.
3. Ask an on-level student to play A and read the questions. Play B, or ask an above-level student to play B, and answer the questions using the information you wrote.
4. Tell students to fill in the blanks (in pencil) with an emergency, a location, and cross streets to use when they play B. Remind students to refer back to the list of medical emergencies on page 207.
5. Pair students and tell them to take turns playing A and B.
6. Walk around and check A's pronunciation of *emergency* and *location*. Check that B correctly provides information about an emergency.
7. Call on pairs to perform for the class.

■ **MULTILEVEL INSTRUCTION for 4D**
Cross-ability Direct pre-level students to play A first.

Self-Directed Learning

Point out the blue bar. Ask students if they can do the lesson learning objective or if they need more practice. Tell them to check one of the boxes. Assign Extra Practice as needed.

Extra Practice

  pp. 124–125

Listening and Speaking

3 PRONUNCIATION

A ▶ PRACTICE. Listen to the words. Then listen and repeat.

al·ler·gic   lo·ca·tion   sit·u·a·tion   am·bu·lance   e·mer·gen·cy

B ▶ APPLY. Listen. Mark (•) the stressed syllable.

1. e·lec·tric

2. re·ac·tion

3. con·ver·sa·tion

4. un·con·scious

4 CONVERSATION

A ▶ LISTEN AND READ. Then listen and repeat.

A: 9-1-1. What's your emergency?
B: I think a man is having a heart attack.
A: OK. What's the location of the emergency?
B: Dave's Sports Shop at 103 Elm Street.
A: What are the cross streets?
B: 17th and 18th Avenues.
A: All right. What's your name?
B: Olivia Ramos.

B WORK TOGETHER. Practice the conversation in Exercise A.

C CREATE. Make new conversations. Use different emergencies and locations.

A: 9-1-1. What's your emergency?
B:
A: OK. What is the location of the emergency?
B:
A: What are the cross streets?
B:
A: All right. What's your name?
B: _____.

A woman is having trouble breathing.	Fresh Supermarket on Coral Way.	42nd and 43rd Avenues.
A man is unconscious.	S & S Pharmacy on Route 1.	36th and 37th Streets.
Someone is hurt and is bleeding a lot.	All-Day Café on Palm Street.	Oak and Maple Avenues.

D ROLE-PLAY. Make your own conversations.

I can call 911 to report a medical emergency. ■   I need more practice. ■

For more practice, go to MyEnglishLab.

Grammar

Present continuous: Statements and questions

- You can use contractions in the present continuous.
- See page 258 for spelling rules for *-ing* verbs.

Present continuous: Statements and questions

Statements

| The man | **is** | **having** | a heart attack. |
| | **is not** | | |

Yes / No questions			**Short answers**		
Is	he	**bleeding?**	Yes,	he	**is.**
			No,		**isn't.**

Information questions				**Answers**		
What	**are**	they	**doing?**	They	**'re**	**talking** to the police.
	is		**happening?**	The driver	**is**	
Where	**are**	you	**going?**	I	**'m**	**going** to the hospital.
	is	he		He	**'s**	
Who	**is**	**calling** 911?		The driver	**is**	**calling.**

A **COMPLETE. Use the present continuous and the verbs in parentheses.**

1. Help! My co-worker _____*is choking*_____!
   (choke)

2. A man just fell down in the parking lot. He _____is not breathing_____.
   (not breathe)

3. _____Are_____ you _____talking_____ to the 911 operator now?
   (talk)

4. A woman _____is lying_____ on the ground. She's unconscious.
   (lie)

5. They are taking Frank to the hospital. Who _____is going_____
   (go)
   with him?

6. The police _____are leaving_____. Where _____are_____
   (leave)
   they _____going_____?
   (go)

7. What _____is happening_____? There are a lot of fire trucks.
   (happen)

8. I cut my finger. It hurts, but it _____is not bleeding_____ a lot.
   (not bleed)

9. Mike _____is having_____ an allergic reaction. I _____am taking_____ him
   (have)   (take)
   to the emergency room.

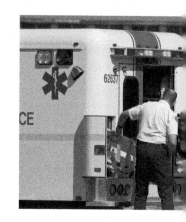

Correlations

ELPS Level 2: 2, 7, 10
CCRS Level A: L.1.1, L.1.2
CASAS Reading: RDG 1.7, 2.6
CASAS Listening: L1.3, 2.1, 2.3, 3.3, 3.9, 4.1, 4.2
CASAS Competencies: 0.1.2, 0.1.5
Complete standards language available on the Pearson English Portal.

Self-Directed Learning

State the **lesson objective**. Say: *In this lesson, we will learn to use present continuous in statements and questions.*

Present continuous: Statements and questions

 ActiveTeach: Grammar Discovery

1. Warm up. Say: *The conversation on page 209 used this grammar.* Turn back to page 209. Point to the sentence in Exercise 4A and then write: *I think a man is having a heart attack.*
2. Underline *is having.*
3. Remind students: *Use the present continuous for events happening at the present time.* Ask: *What's happening in our classroom right now?* Elicit a few present continuous sentences and write them on the board (for example, *You are talking. We are listening. Wen is looking at the clock.*). Underline *am, is,* or *are* in the sentences and *-ing.*
4. Tell students to look at the grammar charts. Point to the top three charts (for statements, *yes/no* questions, and short answers). Read sentences and ask the class to repeat.
5. Tell students to turn to Exercise D on page 207 and choose one medical emergency from the *happening right now* side of their charts. Write:
   Affirmative:
   Negative:
   Yes/no question:
   Short answer:
6. Tell students to write the affirmative statement, make it negative, use it to form a *yes/no* question, and write short answers. Do one example on the board with students: *He is choking. He is not choking. Is he choking? Yes, he is. No, he's not.* Direct students to choose another emergency and write the four types of sentences in their notebooks.
7. Tell students to read their sentences to a partner. Walk around and check that students are forming the present continuous correctly.

8. Read the first point of the **Grammar Watch** note and ask the class to read along silently. Tell students to rewrite their affirmative and negative statements using contractions (for example, *He's choking. He's not choking. He isn't choking.*). Ask: *When do we use contractions?* (in conversation and informal writing)
9. Point to the bottom charts. Read each information question and its answers and ask the class to repeat.
10. Tell students to look at the picture in Exercise 2A on page 208 and write a couple of information questions. Call on students to write questions on the board (for example, *What is happening? What is the woman / Olivia doing? Who is calling 911?*). Make corrections as needed. Read the questions and call on students to answer using the present continuous.
11. Tell students to read the second point of the **Grammar Watch** note silently. Tell them to turn to page 258 and read more about spelling rules for *-ing* verbs.

 ActiveTeach: Grammar Coach

Ⓐ COMPLETE. Use the present continuous...

1. Read the directions and the example. Write: *choke.* Cross out the *e* and write *-ing.* Review the spelling rules for *-ing* verbs on page 258 as needed.
2. Walk around and encourage students to use contractions.
3. Students compare answers with a partner, taking turns reading the sentences.
4. Call on students to read the sentences. Write the answers on the board. Write all possible answers (for example, for item 2: *is not breathing, isn't breathing, 's not breathing*). Tell students to check their spelling.

Career Awareness: Emergency medical technician

Emergency medical technicians (EMTs) respond to 911 calls, such as car accidents, childbirth, and heart attacks. They are usually the first medical workers to arrive. A high school diploma and special emergency training are required.

▬ **EXPANSION: Career awareness for A**

Ask students about the job in this lesson: *What does an EMT worker do? Where does an EMT worker work? Do you need to study to be an EMT worker? Do you want to be an EMT worker?*

Grammar

B COMPLETE. Use the present continuous...

1. Read the directions.
2. Ask two students to read the first two lines of the conversation. Show the example on the board. Circle *'s* and say: *Remember, we use contractions in the present continuous in conversation.*
3. Walk around and check that students use *is* or *'s* and the verb + *-ing.*
4. Students compare answers by reading the conversation with a partner.
5. Ask a pair to read the conversation for the class. Write the answers on the board. Tell students to check their spelling.
6. *Optional:* Call on pairs to perform for the class.

Show what you know!

1. THINK ABOUT IT. Look at the picture. What...

1. Ask the class: *Where are the people?* (in the emergency room of a hospital / in an ER).
2. Read the directions. Tell students to look at the people and write a verb + *-ing* next to their pictures (for example, *bleeding, hurting, walking, talking,* etc.). Tell the students that they can look at the parents together, not separately.
3. Walk around and assist with vocabulary.

2. TALK ABOUT IT. Ask and answer questions...

1. Read the directions and model the example with an above-level student.
2. Pair students. Say: *Decide who is A first. Have the conversation about half the people. Then switch roles.*
3. Check answers as a class. Ask: *What are the parents doing?* Elicit multiple answers. Write *parents* and list the answers underneath (for example, *worrying, helping the baby, calming the baby*).

■ **MULTILEVEL INSTRUCTION for 2**

Cross-ability Pair or group pre-level and above-level students. Have the above-level student play B for all the people, and then switch roles.

■ **EXPANSION: Grammar and speaking practice for 2**

In pairs, students take turns guessing the people in the picture. The first student says three sentences about the person, using a pronoun. They can describe personal appearance as well as use the present continuous. For example, *He is wearing blue shoes. He is sitting. He is bald.* The second student guesses the identity of the person.

3. WRITE ABOUT IT. Now write five sentences...

1. Read the directions. Say: *Study the picture. What are the people doing?*
2. Tell students to write five sentences about the people in their notebooks, using the present continuous.
3. Ask pairs to check each other's sentences.
   - Sentences should use the present continuous.
   - Sentences should spell *-ing* words correctly.
4. Call on students to read sentences about the picture.

■ **EXPANSION: Grammar practice for 1–3**

1. Find another picture that contains many people doing different things.
2. Bring copies of the picture to class. Possibilities for pictures range from fine art, to a *Where's Waldo* book, to photos that you find online. An alternative is to create a collage of pictures from different sources, illustrating action verbs (people swimming, walking, skating, eating a picnic, etc.). These could be pictures that you find or that you ask students to bring to class. This is also a good way to introduce vocabulary.
3. Repeat all or some of the activities in Steps 1–3.

Self-Directed Learning

Point out the blue bar. Ask students if they can do the lesson learning objective or if they need more practice. Tell them to check one of the boxes. Assign Extra Practice as needed.

Extra Practice
pp. 124–125

Grammar

B COMPLETE. Use the present continuous and the verbs in parentheses.

A: You won't believe this. There is an accident in front of my house!

B: Oh, no! What's _____*happening*_____ ?
   1. (happen)

A: Well, one man _____is calling_____ 911. Wait . . . Now I see an ambulance. It
   2. (call)

   _____is coming_____ down the street. And a fire truck.
   3. (come)

B: Is anyone hurt?

A: I'm not sure. A man _____is helping_____ a woman. He _____is talking_____ to
   4. (help)   **5. (talk)**

   her and she _____is holding_____ her head. I think she _____is bleeding_____ .
   6. (hold)   **7. (bleed)**

Show what you know!

1. **THINK ABOUT IT.** Look at the picture. What are the people doing?

2. **TALK ABOUT IT.** Ask and answer questions about what each person is doing. Take turns.

   A: What is the baby doing?
   B: The baby is crying.

3. **WRITE ABOUT IT.** Now write five sentences about what people are doing.

   The woman is _____ .

   _____

   _____

   _____

   _____

I can use present continuous in statements and questions. ☐   I need more practice. ☐

For more practice, go to MyEnglishLab.

Workplace, Life, and Community Skills

Fire hazards and safety procedures

1 IDENTIFY FIRE HAZARDS

A **DESCRIBE.** Look at the picture. Match the fire hazards to their descriptions.

1. __E__ a heater close to paper files
2. __D__ no window exit
3. __C__ an electrical cord under a rug
4. __A__ cloth on a lamp
5. __B__ too many plugs in an electrical outlet

B **WORK TOGETHER.** What are other fire hazards? What can people do to make their workplaces safe?

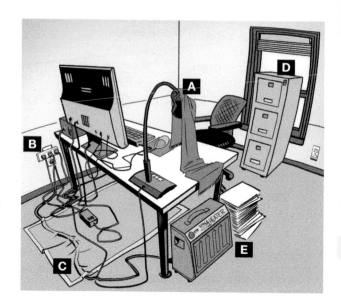

2 UNDERSTAND FIRE SAFETY PROCEDURES

A **LABEL.** Match each picture with a word or phrase from the box.

an escape plan   exit   a fire escape   ~~a fire extinguisher~~   a smoke alarm

a fire extinguisher

a smoke alarm

a fire escape

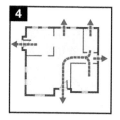

an escape plan

exit

B ▶ **SELF-ASSESS.** Listen and check your answers. Then listen and repeat.

I can identify fire hazards. ■   I need more practice. ■

For more practice, go to MyEnglishLab.

Correlations

ELPS Level 2: 2, 5, 7
CCRS Level A: W.1.7, W.1.8
CASAS Reading: RDG 1.7, 1.8, 2.3, 3.2, 3.4, 3.6
CASAS Listening: L2.1, 2.3, 4.2
CASAS Competencies: 0.1.2, 0.1.5, 1.4.8, 3.4.1, 3.4.2, 4.3.1, 4.5.6, 7.4.4, 7.7.3
Complete standards language available on the Pearson English Portal.

Self-Directed Learning

State the **lesson objective**. Say: *In this lesson, we will learn to identify fire hazards and understand fire safety procedures.*

1 IDENTIFY FIRE HAZARDS

A DESCRIBE. Look at the picture. Match the...

1. List the following words from Exercise 1A on the board: *lamp, electrical cord, rug, window, heater, filing cabinet, paper files, electrical outlet.*
2. Say the words and ask the class to repeat.
3. Ask: *Do we have any of these objects in our classroom?* Call on students to point out the objects.
4. *Optional:* Ask volunteers to write the words on cards and label the objects in your classroom.
5. Write *hazards* on the board. Explain: Hazards *are things that may be dangerous or cause accidents.* Fire hazards *are things that may cause a fire.*
6. Read the directions. Tell students to look for words from the board in the descriptions.
7. Read each description and ask the class to call out the letter of the fire hazard.

B WORK TOGETHER. What are other fire...

1. Read the directions.
2. Form groups of 3. Tell groups to discuss the first question. Say: *Think of fire hazards at home as well as at work.* (Possible answers: *unattended cooking, bad electrical wiring, no smoke alarms, no fire extinguishers, curtains near heaters*)
3. Have each group report back a couple of their answers.
4. Tell groups to discuss the second question. Say: *There are many types of workplaces, and the answers may be different for each place.* If some students work, tell them to describe the safety procedures at their workplace.

5. Have each group report back a couple of their answers.
6. Tell students this activity was just a brainstorm— there will be other opportunities to discuss fire safety in this lesson.

Digital Skills for 1B

1. Tell students to research fire safety online and to write down one safety fact that they did not know.
2. At the next class, discuss what students learned and write safety facts and URLs on the board. Good starting points are the American Red Cross, the National Fire Protection Association (NFPA), and FireFacts.org.

2 UNDERSTAND FIRE SAFETY...

A LABEL. Match each picture with a word or...

1. Read the directions and the words from the box.
2. Tell students to match as many fire safety words and pictures as they can.

B ▶ SELF-ASSESS. Listen and check your...

1. Read the directions.
2. Play the audio. As needed, pause to allow students time to fill in missing answers and make corrections.
3. Play the audio again. Tell students to point to the pictures in Exercise 2A as they listen and repeat.
4. Call on students for the answers in Exercise 2A.
5. Say: *Look at the fire safety pictures and words again. Which things does your home have?*

■ EXPANSION: Speaking and writing practice for 2B

1. Write these headings: *Home fire hazards* and *Ways to make your home safer.*
2. As a class, brainstorm home fire hazards. Say: *Think of the hazards we discussed in Exercise 1.* Write answers.
3. Brainstorm safety ideas. Say: *Look at the fire safety words in Exercise 2A. What can people do to make their homes safer?* (for example, have a fire extinguisher on each floor of the house, install smoke alarms). Write answers.
4. Ask students to read the ideas under each heading.
5. Tell students each to write down one thing they will do to make their home safer.

Workplace, Life, and Community Skills

C ▶ **LISTEN. Then listen again and complete...**

1. Ask: *Do you know what to do in case of a fire?* List students' ideas on the board.
2. Tell students to read the fire safety tips silently.
3. Play the audio. Students listen. Pause after item 7.
4. Resume the audio. Students listen and complete the tips.
5. Students compare answers with a partner.
6. Call on students to read the sentences. Write the answers. Tell students to check their spelling.
7. Ask comprehension questions. For example: *When should you call 911?* (after you leave your home) *What should you take with you?* (nothing) *Should you open a hot door?* (no)

■ **EXPANSION: Digital skills and listening practice for 2C**

1. Tell students that short public service announcements (PSAs) are available online about fire safety from the U.S. Fire Administration.
2. Have students search for *FEMA fire safety PSAs* and listen to the audio clips, which are each fifteen to thirty seconds long.
3. If possible, play some clips in class. Have students listen, check their comprehension, and discuss.

D **DETERMINE. Read about Carmen. Which of...**

1. Tell students to read the paragraph silently.
2. Read the directions.
3. Pair students. Tell pairs to read the paragraph again and highlight the fire safety tips Carmen followed in one color and the mistakes she made in another color.
4. Ask the class: *Which of the fire safety tips did Carmen follow?* Call on students to read the sentences they highlighted (*She touched the door to office, but it was not hot. She opened the door. She didn't take the elevator. She waited across the street from the building.*).
5. Ask the class: *What mistakes did Carmen make?* Call on students to read the sentences they highlighted. For each mistake, ask the class to identify the tip she didn't follow and then read the tip (for example, S: *First, she called 911.* T: *Which tip did she not follow?* Class: *Number 2.* T: *Don't stop to call 911...*).

E **INTERPRET. Look at the fire escape plan for...**

1. Say: *Look at the fire escape plan for Carmen's workplace. It shows how workers should exit the building quickly and safely if there is a fire.*
2. Pair students and tell them to answer the questions about the fire escape plan.

3. Call on pairs to ask and answer each question. Help as needed (for example, for item 1, count on your fingers as you say the offices: (1) Office *401*, (2) *402*, (3) *403*, etc.).
4. Say: *Fire escape plans should clearly indicate exits and exit routes. They should have a meeting place away from the home. Does your work have a fire escape plan?*
5. Explain that fire escape plans are important for workers' safety and also make it easier for fire fighters to make sure no one is left in the building.

■ **EXPANSION: Speaking and listening practice for 2E**

As a class, look at the fire escape plan for your school building. Discuss how you would leave the building in the event of a fire.

F <u>GO ONLINE.</u> **Search for workplace...**

1. Read the directions. Ask students what they would search in English if they wanted fire escape plans.
2. Write the search string: *fire escape plans.* Have students search the internet and find an image of a fire-escape plan.
3. Pair students and tell them to take turns describing the escape procedures. Hang the fire-escape plans on the walls for everyone to see.

Digital Skills for 2F

1. Tell students that short fire safety quizzes are available online.
2. Have students search for *fire safety quiz.* Tell students to complete the quiz online if that is possible.
3. If they are able to, have students print a quiz and bring it to class to share, complete, and discuss.

 ActiveTeach: Review

Self-Directed Learning

Point out the blue bar. Ask students if they can do the lesson learning objective or if they need more practice. Tell them to check one of the boxes. Assign Extra Practice as needed.

Extra Practice

 MyEnglishLab   Workbook **pp. 126–127**   English Portal **Life Skills Writing**

C ▶ **LISTEN. Then listen again and complete the tips below.**

Fire Safety Tips for the Workplace

GET OUT STAY OUT CALL 911

1. Leave your _____work area_____ immediately. Do not take anything with you, but alert your co-workers.
2. Don't stop to call _____911_____. Call from a safe location outside of the building.
3. Don't use an _____elevator_____ to exit the building. Use the stairs.
4. Close any open doors. This will _____prevent_____ the fire from spreading quickly.
5. Feel every closed _____door_____ before opening it. Don't open a door that is hot. Try to find another exit.
6. If you smell _____smoke_____, stay close to the floor. Cover your mouth and nose with a wet cloth.
7. When you get outside, do not go back to your workplace for any reason. Tell _____firefighters_____ about anyone still inside the building.

D **DETERMINE. Read about Carmen. Which of the fire safety tips from Exercise C did she follow? Did she make any mistakes?**

Yesterday afternoon, there was a fire at Carmen's workplace. First, she called 911. Then, she got her wallet and keys from her desk. She touched the door to her office, but it was not hot. She opened the door. She saw a few other open doors. She took the stairs to the first floor. There was a lot of smoke on the first floor. She continued to walk towards the exit. She waited across the street with a few of her co-workers.

E **INTERPRET. Look at the fire escape plan for Carmen's workplace. Answer the questions.**

1. How many offices are there? Eight.
2. How many exits are there? Two.
3. If you are in office 403, where should you exit? Exit 1.
4. If you are in office 406, where should you exit? Exit 2.
5. If you are in the Meeting Room, where should you exit? Exit 1.
6. Where should you wait for help in case of emergency? In the parking lot across the street.

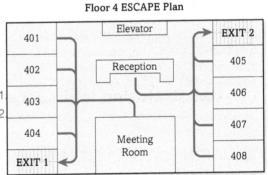

Floor 4 ESCAPE Plan

401, 402, 403, 404 | Elevator | Reception | Meeting Room | EXIT 1 | EXIT 2 | 405, 406, 407, 408

MEETING PLACE: parking lot across the street

F GO ONLINE. Search for workplace fire-escape plans or your own workplace's fire-escape plan. Select one image. Describe the escape procedure to a classmate.

I can understand fire safety procedures. ■   I need more practice. ■

For more practice, go to MyEnglishLab.

5 Listening and Speaking

Describe an emergency

1 BEFORE YOU LISTEN

MATCH. Write the words under the pictures.

a car accident   a construction accident   an explosion   a robbery

1. _a construction accident_   2. _a car accident_   3. _a robbery_   4. _an explosion_

2 LISTEN

Ⓐ PREDICT. Look at the picture. What are they talking about?

a. bad traffic   **b.** bad news   **c.** bad weather

Ⓑ ▶ LISTEN. Which story are they talking about?

a.
City Herald   HEADLINES | WEATHER
Fire Destroys Hotel, No Injuries Reported

b.
Greenville Times   🔍
Route 52 Car Accident Leaves Two Hospitalized

c.
Village News   LOCAL | SPORTS
Gas Explosion Injures Two

d.
Journal News
First Federal Bank Robbed, No One Hurt

Ⓒ ▶ LISTEN FOR DETAILS. Listen again. What happened to two people?

a. They called 911.   **ⓑ.** They went to the hospital.   **c.** They had a car accident.

Ⓓ ▶ EXPAND. Listen to the whole conversation. What happened after the emergency situation?

ⓐ. Some streets were closed.   **b.** The hospital was full.   **c.** There was a car accident.

Correlations

ELPS Level 2: 2, 7
CCRS Level A: SL.K.3
CASAS Reading: RDG 1.7, 2.3
CASAS Listening: L1.1, 2.1, 2.3, 4.2, 6.1, 6.2, 6.5
CASAS Competencies: 0.1.2, 0.1.4, 0.1.5, 0.1.6
Complete standards language available on the Pearson English Portal.

Self-Directed Learning

State the **lesson objective**. Say: *In this lesson, we will learn to describe an emergency.*

1 BEFORE YOU LISTEN

MATCH. Write the words under the pictures.

1. Tell students to look at the pictures. Ask: *What do you see?* Elicit descriptions (Possible answers: 1. A building, scaffolding/platform and paint can are falling; 2. An accident/crash, two cars hit each other, a man and woman on a city street; 3. Two men are running out of a building/bank carrying money; 4. A building is on fire, a lot of smoke).
2. Read the directions. Say: *Look at the dangerous situations.* Say each dangerous situation in the box and ask the class to repeat.
3. Give students time to label the pictures and then compare answers with a partner.
4. Direct students to look at the first picture. Ask the class: *What is the situation?* (a construction accident) Repeat with the other pictures.
5. Ask: *What are some other dangerous situations?* Write students' ideas (for example, *a fire, a natural disaster [a hurricane, an earthquake, a tornado], a fall, a wild animal*).

2 LISTEN

A PREDICT. Look at the picture. What are...

1. Tell students to look at the picture. Ask: *Who do you see?* (a woman and a man). *Where are they?* (In an office) *What are they doing?* (looking at a screen)
2. Tell students to read the answer choices silently.
3. Ask: *What are they talking about?* Ask for a show of hands for each answer.

B ▶ LISTEN. Which story are they talking...

1. Read the directions.
2. Tell students to read the newspaper headlines silently and underline the dangerous situations.

3. Say each newspaper name and ask the class to call out the dangerous situation (a. *fire*, b. *car accident*, c. *gas explosion*, d. *bank robbery*).
4. Play the audio. Ask: *Which answer in Exercise 2A is correct?*
5. Play the audio again. Students listen and circle the letter of the story they hear.
6. Write: *That's terrible.* Ask about **register**: *When do people use this expression?* (when they hear some bad or sad news)

C ▶ LISTEN FOR DETAILS. Listen again. What...

1. Read the directions. Tell students to read the answer choices silently or call on students to read each choice aloud.
2. Play the audio again. Students choose the correct answer.
3. Students compare answers with a partner.
4. Elicit the correct answer.

Teaching Tip: Use the script

Optional: If students need additional support, tell them to read the Audio Script on page 274 as they listen to the conversations.

D ▶ EXPAND. Listen to the whole...

1. Read the directions. Tell students to read the answer choices silently.
2. Play the audio. Students choose the correct answer.
3. Elicit the correct answer.

■ EXPANSION: Graphic organizer practice for 2D

1. Draw a *Wh-* question chart on the board. In the *What?* box, write *gas explosion*. Play the audio again. Tell students to listen for the *Who? Where? When?* and *Why?* of the story.
2. Elicit the class's help to complete the chart on the board (*Who?* two people hurt; *Where?* downtown; *When?* yesterday; *Why?* They don't know yet.)
3. Ask: *What is the name of our local newspaper? What were the headlines today?*
4. Bring in newspapers or tell students to look at the local paper online for homework. Tell students to choose a story about a dangerous situation and complete a *Wh-* question chart with information from the story.

Listening and Speaking

3 PRONUNCIATION

A ▶ PRACTICE. Listen to the words. Notice...

1. Read the directions. Then read the **Pronunciation Note**.
2. Model pronouncing the /h/ sound. Say: *First, open your mouth. Then use your throat to breathe out.* Say the /h/ sound and ask the class to repeat.
3. Play the audio. Students listen. Then students listen and repeat.

 ActiveTeach for 3A: Pronunciation Coach

B ▶ APPLY. Listen to each pair of words...

1. Read the directions.
2. Play the audio. Students listen and write *S* or *D*.
3. Play the audio again if students have difficulty.
4. Say each pair of words and ask the class to call out *same* or *different*.

4 CONVERSATION

A ▶ LISTEN AND READ. Then listen and repeat.

1. Note: This conversation is the same one students heard in Exercise 2B on page 214.
2. Tell students to read the conversation and underline words that begin with *h* (*hear, happened, hurt, hospital*).
3. Play the audio. Students read along silently. Then students listen and repeat.

B WORK TOGETHER. Practice the...

1. Pair students and tell them to practice the conversation in Exercise 4A.
2. Tell students to take turns playing A and B. Walk around and help with pronunciation as needed.

C CREATE. Make new conversations. Use the...

1. Read the directions.
2. Tell students to look at the boxes. Call on students to read each item.
3. Show the conversation on the board with blanks. Read it and when you come to a blank, elicit information from a box with the same color.
4. Ask two on-level students to practice the conversation for the class.
5. Erase the words in the blanks and ask two above-level students to make up a new conversation in front of the class.
6. Tell pairs to take turns playing A and B and to use information from the boxes to fill in the blanks.

7. Tell students to stand, mingle, and practice the conversation with several new partners.
8. Walk around and check students' pronunciation of words beginning with *h*.

D ROLE-PLAY. Make your own conversations.

1. Write information about an emergency situation in the news. Include *what, where, when,* and *who*.
2. Model the activity with an on-level student. Play A and use the information you wrote. The student reads B's lines.
3. Ask the class: *Do you read the newspaper? Where do you get your news?*
4. Pair students. Say: *Think about an emergency situation you have heard about. In your notebooks, write down the type of situation and the number of injuries and/or deaths.*
5. *Optional:* Bring in newspapers or have students search for a local news website. Tell students to look for stories about dangerous emergency situations. Tell them to write down the type of situation and the number of injuries. Tell partners to choose different stories.
6. Say: *Student A, talk about the information you wrote down. Begin the conversation by saying:* Did you hear what happened yesterday?
7. Call on pairs to perform for the class.

■■ MULTILEVEL INSTRUCTION for 4D

Pre-level scaffolding Tell students to write new words for the blue and yellow boxes. Direct pairs to use this new information in the conversation in Exercise 4C.

Above-level expansion Tell above-level pairs to talk about the information they wrote in their notebooks without looking at the conversation in Exercise 4C.

Teaching Tip: Formative assessment

Listen to multiple pairs perform their role-plays. Pay attention to pronunciation, use of vocabulary, and comprehension of the news article. Reteach as necessary.

Self-Directed Learning

Point out the blue bar. Ask students if they can do the lesson learning objective or if they need more practice. Tell them to check one of the boxes. Assign Extra Practice as needed.

Extra Practice

 MyEnglishLab   Workbook p. 128

Listening and Speaking

3 PRONUNCIATION

A ▶ PRACTICE. Listen to the words. Notice the sound /h/ at the beginning of the second word in each pair. Then listen and repeat.

1. ear   hear   **3.** art   heart

2. I   high   **4.** ow   how

B ▶ APPLY. Listen to each pair of words. Are the two words the same (S) or different (D)? Write S or D.

1. _S_   **2.** _D_   **3.** _D_   **4.** _S_   **5.** _D_   **6.** _S_

4 CONVERSATION

A ▶ LISTEN AND READ. Then listen and repeat.

A: Did you hear what happened yesterday?
B: No. What happened?
A: There was a gas explosion downtown.
B: Oh my gosh. That's terrible. Was anybody hurt?
A: Yes. Two people went to the hospital.

B WORK TOGETHER. Practice the conversation in Exercise A.

C CREATE. Make new conversations. Use the words in the boxes.

A: Did you hear what happened yesterday?
B: No. What happened?
A: There was a _____ downtown.
B: Oh my gosh. That's terrible. Was anybody hurt?
A: _____

robbery	No one was hurt.
car accident	There were no injuries.
construction accident	Four people were hurt.

D ROLE-PLAY. Make your own conversations.

I can describe an emergency. ■   I need more practice. ■

For more practice, go to MyEnglishLab.

Grammar

There was / There were

There was / There were				
Affirmative			**Negative**	
There	**was** a gas explosion	yesterday.	**There**	**wasn't a** / **was no** fire.
	were two car accidents			**weren't any** / **were no** injuries.

Yes / No questions		**Short answers**	
Was	a fire?	Yes,	**was.**
there		**there**	**were.**
Were	any injuries? No,		**wasn't.**
			weren't.

A **COMPLETE. Use** *there was*, *there were*, *was there*, or *were there*.

1. **A:** What happened downtown last night?
   B: _____*There was*_____ a robbery at the jewelry store.
   A: _____Were there_____ any customers there?
   B: Yes, _____there were_____. But no one was hurt.

2. **A:** _____There was_____ a problem at the high school last night.
   B: I know. _____There was_____ a fight after the basketball game.
   A: Wow! Did the police come?
   B: Yes, _____there were_____ five police cars in the parking lot.

3. **A:** _____There was_____ an explosion at the factory yesterday.
   B: Was anybody hurt?
   A: No, luckily _____there were_____ no injuries.

4. **A:** _____Was there_____ an accident on Main Street this morning?
   B: Yes, _____there was_____. I heard about it on the radio.
   A: I thought so. _____There was_____ a lot of traffic, and I was late to work.

Correlations

ELPS Level 2: 2, 3, 7, 9
CCRS Level A: SL.1.4
CASAS Reading: RDG 1.7, 2.9
CASAS Listening: L2.1, 2.3, 3.5, 4.2, 5.8
CASAS Competencies: 0.1.2, 0.1.5, 0.1.6, L5.8
Complete standards language available on the Pearson English Portal.

Self-Directed Learning

State the **lesson objective**. Say: *In this lesson, we will learn to use* there was / there were.

There was / There were

 ActiveTeach: Grammar Discovery

1. Warm up. Say: *The conversation on page 215 used this grammar.* Turn back to page 215. Point to the sentence in Exercise 4A and then write: *There was a gas explosion downtown.*
2. Show these two sentences from the grammar chart on the board. Use blanks for *was* and *were*:
   • *There _____ a gas explosion yesterday.*
   • *There _____ two car accidents yesterday.*
3. Say: *Look at the first sentence.* Ask: *What comes after the blank?* (a gas explosion) *Should* was *or* were *go in the blank?* (was) *Why?* (because *explosion* is singular)
4. Say: *Look at the second sentence.* Ask: *What comes after the blank?* (two car accidents) *Should* was *or* were *go in the blank?* (were) *Why?* (because *accidents* is plural)
5. Underline *yesterday* in the sentences on the board. Say: *Use* there was / there were *to talk about the past.*
6. Tell students to look at the grammar charts. Point to the top charts. Read the sentences and ask the class to repeat.
7. Point to sentence 1 on the board and ask: *How do I make this sentence negative?* Tell students to look at the top left grammar chart. Elicit and write under sentence 1: *There wasn't a gas explosion yesterday. There was no gas explosion yesterday.* Repeat with sentence 2 and write: *There weren't any car accidents yesterday. There were no car accidents yesterday.*
8. Point to the bottom charts. Read the sentences and ask the class to repeat.
9. Point to sentence 1 on the board and ask: *How do I make this sentence into a question?* Tell students to look at the grammar chart. Elicit

and write under sentence 1: *Was there a gas explosion yesterday?* Repeat with sentence 2 and write: *Were there any car accidents yesterday?*
10. Elicit affirmative and negative short answers to each question and write them.

 ActiveTeach: Grammar Coach

A COMPLETE. Use *there was, there were,…*

1. Read the directions. Write the example and point to the answer. Ask: *Why is the answer* There was? (because *robbery* is singular)
2. Students compare answers with a partner by reading the conversations.
3. *Optional:* Pair students and ask them to practice the completed conversations. Call on pairs to perform the completed conversations for the class.

Digital Skills for A

1. Ask: *Where do you find news about what is happening in [City or Town]?* Elicit a range of answers (television news, radio, online news, word of mouth, community groups, etc.) and write them. Circle all the answers that relate to online media.
2. Tell students to go online and find sites that give local news and information. Suggest the search strings: *[City or Town] news* and *local news*. Tell students to choose an online site and find one headline for what is happening locally.
3. Students write the headlines on the board and the URL.

Culture Note

1. Tell students that when emergencies in the U.S. affect many people, there are alerts on television, radio, online, and even mobile phones that provide you with emergency notification. These include the national Emergency Alert System (www.fema.gov), the National Weather Service (www.weather.gov), and Wireless Emergency Alerts (www.ready.gov).
2. Say: *For example, in the event of a tornado, the National Weather Service will issue a tornado warning that is broadcast on television, radio, and online, telling people to take action and seek safety.*
3. Ask: *How do you find out about emergencies in your native country?*

Grammar

B WRITE. Use *there was* or *there were* and...

1. Read the directions.
2. Say the words from the box and ask the class to repeat.
3. Say the words from the box again and ask the class to call out *singular* or *plural*. Tell students to look at the first item. Explain: A crowd of people *is singular because* crowd *is non-count. You use* There was *with* a lot of *and* There were *with* lots of.
4. Tell students to look at picture 1. Ask the class for the answer. Write: *There was a lot of smoke.*
5. Say: *For each picture, use your own idea to write the first sentence and words from the box to write the second sentence. There is more than one correct answer.*
6. Tell students to take turns reading their sentences for each picture.
7. Ask the class: *Were there many differences between your sentences and your partner's sentences? What situation did you say there was in picture 4? What situation did your partner say there was?*
8. Call on a couple of students to read their sentences for each picture.

C WORK TOGETHER. Ask and answer...

1. Read the directions. Model the example with an above-level student.
2. Tell pairs to take turns having the conversation about each picture. For pictures 2 and 4, they can use an emergency from Lesson 5.
3. Have volunteer pairs perform a conversation for each picture.

Show what you know!

1. THINK ABOUT IT. Think about an emergency...

1. Read the directions.
2. Ask for a show of hands: *Did you watch the news on TV last night? Did you read the newspaper this morning? Did you listen to the news on the radio today or yesterday? Did you read the news online today or yesterday?*
3. Tell students to think of an emergency situation they have heard about. Tell them to write down notes about what they remember: the situation, where it happened, when it happened, the number of injuries.
4. Ask a few students to name their emergency situations. Write them on the board. As a class, brainstorm questions that can be asked and write them on the board.

5. Ask questions to elicit details: Ask: *What time of day was it? Was anybody hurt? How did it happen? Did the police come?* etc. List the details on the board.

2. WRITE ABOUT IT. Write three sentences...

1. Read the directions. Ask an on-level student to read the example.
2. Tell students to use their notes or the notes on the board from Step 1 to write their sentences.
3. Students compare sentences with a partner.
   - Sentences should use *there was* or *there were*.
   - Plural count nouns should use *there were*.
   - Singular count nouns and non-count nouns should use *there was*.
4. Tell partners to take turns reading the sentences to each other.

■ **EXPANSION: Listening and writing practice for 2**

For homework, tell students to watch the local news on TV in English. Tell students to write two sentences with *There was / There were* about three different emergency situations. Call on students to tell the class about one emergency situation.

3. PRESENT IT. Give a short presentation...

1. Read the directions. Ask an on-level student to read the example.
2. Model the activity. Tell the class about one of the emergency situations discussed in 1 (for example, *I read the newspaper this morning. There was a robbery...*). Include the details listed on the board.
3. Tell students to practice telling a partner about their emergency situation.
4. Call on students to tell the class about their emergency situation. Check that students use *There was / There were* correctly.

Self-Directed Learning

Point out the blue bar. Ask students if they can do the lesson learning objective or if they need more practice. Tell them to check one of the boxes. Assign Extra Practice as needed.

Extra Practice
MyEnglishLab   Workbook p. 128

Grammar

B **WRITE.** Use *there was* or *there were* and words from the box. Write two sentences to describe each emergency situation.

a crowd of people

a lot of smoke

lots of police

a traffic jam

1. _____

   _____

2. _____

   _____

3. _____

   _____

4. _____

   _____

C **WORK TOGETHER.** Ask and answer questions about the situations in Exercise B.

A: What happened last night?
B: There was a fire. There was a lot of smoke.

Show what you know!

1. **THINK ABOUT IT.** Think about an emergency situation you have heard about.

2. **WRITE ABOUT IT.** Write three sentences about one of the emergency situations.

   There was a fire last night. There was a lot of smoke.
   There was a fire on Center Street yesterday. Some people went to the hospital.

3. **PRESENT IT.** Give a short presentation about an emergency situation you had or you heard about.

   I watched the news on TV last night. There was a fire on Center Street. Some people went to the hospital.

I can use *there was / there were.* ☐   I need more practice. ☐

For more practice, go to MyEnglishLab.

Read about being safe at work

1 BEFORE YOU READ

A MATCH. Complete the sentences with words from the box.

safety gear   a safety hazard   toxic chemicals

1. Toxic chemicals are dangerous.

2. Some workers need to wear _____safety gear_____.

3. A wet floor is _____a safety hazard_____.

B BRAINSTORM. Accidents sometimes happen at work. What are some ways that workers can get hurt?

2 READ

▶ Listen and read.

> **Academic Skill: Identify Supporting Details**
>
> Authors use supporting details to help explain the main ideas. Supporting details can be reasons, examples, or steps.

1 **What is OSHA?**
OSHA is the Occupational Safety and Health Administration. It's part of the U.S. government. Its job is to help workers avoid getting hurt or
5 sick at work.

What does OSHA do?
OSHA tries to make sure workers stay safe and healthy. It sets safety and health standards for workplaces. Employers must obey these rules.
10 OSHA also provides information and training. OSHA inspectors often visit workplaces. They look for health and safety hazards.

Do workers in the U.S. have the right to a safe workplace?
15 Yes, they do.

What are some other rights that workers have?
Workers have the right to:
• get job training in a language they understand
20 • receive the safety gear they need
• be protected from toxic chemicals
• report a work-related injury or illness
• see records of injuries in the workplace

Tests are sometimes done to find hazards in the
25 workplace. Workers have the right to see test results.

What can workers do if they are afraid for their health or safety?
They can talk about health or safety hazards with
30 their employer. They have the right to ask questions without fear. They have the right to ask for an OSHA inspection. If they want, they can speak to the inspector.

How can workers contact OSHA?
35 They can call OSHA. They can also visit an OSHA office. Every state has OSHA offices. Workers can also e-mail OSHA from the OSHA website.

Source: https://www.osha.gov/workers/index.html

Occupational Injuries

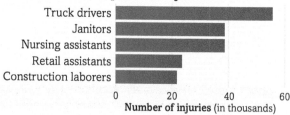

Number of injuries (in thousands)

Correlations

ELPS Level 2: 1, 2, 7
CCRS Level A: RI/RL.1.1, RI.1.2, RI.1.4, SL.K.2
CASAS Reading: RDG 1.7, 1.8, 2.3, 3.2, 3.11, 4.2, 4.9
CASAS Listening: L2.1, 2.3, 4.2, 5.8, 6.1, 6.2
CASAS Competencies: 0.1.2, 0.1.5, 4.2.6, 4.3.1
Complete standards language available on the Pearson English Portal.

Self-Directed Learning

1. State the **lesson objective**. Say: *In this lesson, we will learn to identify supporting details.*
2. Say: *We will read about being safe at work.*

1 BEFORE YOU READ

A MATCH. **Complete the sentences with words...**

1. Read the directions. Say the words in the box and ask the class to repeat.
2. Call on students to describe each picture. (Possible answers: 1. A yellow and black sign, with a skull and crossbones; 2. A worker on the side of the building with ropes, a mask, a helmet; 3. A sign, a wet floor, someone slipped)
3. Ask: *What is the man wearing in picture 2?* (a helmet, ropes) *What kind of equipment is that?* (safety equipment)
4. Give students time to complete the sentences.
5. Call on students to give the correct answers. Point out that *toxic chemicals* is correct for item 1 because it is plural. *A safety hazard* is also dangerous, but it is singular.

B BRAINSTORM. **Accidents sometimes...**

1. Read the directions. Ask: *What are some common jobs? Are some jobs more dangerous than others? Think about how workers in different jobs can get hurt.*
2. Form groups of 3. Students discuss ways workers can get hurt.
3. Elicit and write students' ideas.

2 READ

▶ **Listen and read.**

1. Introduce the reading. Ask: *Does this reading have a title?* (no) *Does it have headings?* (yes) *What color are the headings?* (red) *What do you notice about them?* (They are all questions.) *Where does this information come from?* (www.osha.gov) Say:

Many websites, including government websites, have a section called Frequently Asked Questions, *or FAQs. This reading has a similar format.* Ask: *What do you think this will be about?* (OSHA, safety at work)

2. Introduce the graphic. Ask: *What graphic do you see?* (a bar graph) Point to the graph and ask: *What does the graph show?* (the number of injuries for different kinds of jobs)

ActiveTeach for 2: Anticipation Guide – *Before* **Reading exercise**

3. Read the text.
   a. Say: *Now we are going to read and listen to the information.*
   b. Play the audio as students listen and read along silently.
4. Point to the **Academic Skill** and read it or ask a student to read it. Ask: *What are different kinds of supporting details?* (reasons, examples or steps) *What do they help explain?* (the main idea)
5. Ask: *What are the main ideas in this article?* (how OSHA protects U.S. workers; what rights U.S. workers have; steps workers can take if they are afraid for their safety; ways to contact OSHA)
6. Tell students to underline any reasons, examples, or steps that support the main ideas in the reading.
7. Write a graphic organizer:

Main ideas	Supporting details
How OSHA protects	
Workers rights	
Steps if afraid	
Ways to contact OSHA	

8. Tell students to write two supporting details for each main idea in the graphic organizer.
9. Go over what students put in their graphic organizers. (*How OSHA protects:* sets standards, provides information and training, looks for hazards; *Workers rights:* See bulleted list in article; *Steps if afraid:* talk with employer, have an OSHA inspection, speak to an inspector; *Ways to contact OSHA:* call, go to their office, email)

ActiveTeach for 2: Anticipation Guide – *After* **Reading exercise**

Reading

3 CLOSE READING

A IDENTIFY. What is the main idea?

1. Say: *Now we are going to identify the main idea.*
2. Read the directions. Have students circle the answer.
3. Elicit the answer from the class. Ask: *Where is the sentence that tells you the main idea?* (the end of the first section) Tell students to mark the text.

B CITE EVIDENCE. Complete the sentences…

1. Say: *Now we are going to find information in the reading.*
2. Read the directions. Walk around as students work on the activity. If students are struggling, have them work in pairs or direct them to the text lines where they can find the information.
3. Call on students to read the sentence with the correct completion. Ask a different student: *Where is that information? What line number?*

C INTERPRET. Complete the sentences about…

1. Tell students to look at the bar graph. Say: *This kind of bar graph is sometimes called a horizontal bar graph. The numbers are along the x-axis and the types of jobs are on the y-axis.* Ask: *What jobs do you see?* (truck drivers, janitors, nursing assistants, retail assistants, construction laborers) *How is the information organized?* (the job with the most injuries is on top)
2. Students read the sentences and answer choices silently and complete.
3. Students compare answers with a partner.
4. Call on students to read the completed sentences to the class.

Numeracy: Interpret data

Ask additional questions:
1. *Which job has about the same number of injuries as janitors?* (nursing assistants)
2. *Which job has the fewest injuries?* (construction laborers)
3. *Approximately how many injuries take place among retail assistants?* (22,000)

4 SUMMARIZE

 ActiveTeach for 4: Vocabulary Practice

1. Read the directions. Tell students to read the words in the box silently.
2. Tell students to complete the paragraph.

3. To check answers, call on students to read aloud sentences in the summary with the blanks filled in.

Show what you know!

1. TALK ABOUT IT. What rights do you have in…

1. Read the directions. Ask: *What are some dangers workers face in the workplace?* Elicit and write students' ideas. (Possible answers: chemicals, falling, dangerous equipment like knives, lifting heavy things, repeated movements)
2. Tell students to reread the rights workers have on page 218. Pair students to take turns talking about the rights they have in the workplace.
3. Call on students to share their ideas.

 ActiveTeach for 1: Academic Conversation Support

2. WRITE ABOUT IT. Write about your rights in…

1. Read the directions.
2. Show the sentence frame on the board. Model the activity. Say: *At work I have a right to see records of injuries in the workplace. For example, I can ask where teachers get hurt at the school.* Then, call on an above-level student to say one right and give an example from their discussion in Step 1.
3. Give students time to complete the sentence frame with as many rights as they can. **Reinforce the Writing Skill** from Unit 9. Remind them to use commas between items in a list. Encourage students to give at least one example of a situation when the right is important.
4. Call on students to read their sentences.

Self-Directed Learning

Point out the blue bar. Ask students if they can do the lesson learning objective or if they need more practice. Tell them to check one of the boxes. Assign Extra Practice as needed.

■ **EXPANSION: Self-directed learning**

Ask students to reflect: *What did you learn from this reading?* Call on students to share something they learned.

Extra Practice

 CCRS Plus   pp. 129–130

Reading

3 CLOSE READING

A IDENTIFY. What is the main idea?

OSHA is a part of the U.S. government that _____.
a. helps people who lose their job
b. takes care of people with injuries or illnesses
c. protects people from health and safety hazards at work

B CITE EVIDENCE. Complete the sentences. Where is the information? Write the line numbers.

Lines

1. OSHA is responsible for helping workers avoid _____.
   a. working   **b.** getting hurt or   c. inspections in   4–5
                        sick at work   their workplace

2. Employers have to give their workers _____ when the workers need it.
   a. a hazard   b. a rule   **c.** safety gear   20

3. Employers have to protect workers from _____.
   a. toxic chemicals   b. records of   c. OSHA inspectors   21
                                    workplace injuries

C INTERPRET. Complete the sentences about the bar graph.

1. Almost _____ injuries take place among janitors.
   a. 50,000   b. 30,000   **c.** 40,000

2. The most hazardous occupation is _____.
   a. a retail assistant   b. a construction laborer   **c.** a truck driver

4 SUMMARIZE

Complete the summary with the words in the box.

contact   employers   hazards   inspectors   right

OSHA is a part of the U.S. government. It makes rules about health and safety in the
workplace. (1) __Employers__ have to follow these rules. Workers have the (2) __right__
to a safe workplace. OSHA (3) __inspectors__ sometimes check for (4) __hazards__ in the
workplace. Workers can (5) __contact__ OSHA to learn more.

Show what you know!

1. **TALK ABOUT IT.** What rights do you have in the workplace to help you stay safe
   and healthy? Talk with your class.

2. **WRITE ABOUT IT.** Write about your rights in the workplace.

   At work, I have the right to _____.

I can identify supporting details. ■   I need more practice. ■

To read more, go to MyEnglishLab.

Respond to a police officer's instructions

1 BEFORE YOU LISTEN

A **MATCH.** Write the words under the pictures. Do you know any other traffic violations?

distracted driving   not wearing a seat belt   running a red light   speeding   tailgating

1. running a red light   2. ___tailgating___   3. not wearing a seat belt   4. ___speeding___   5. distracted driving

B **DISCUSS.** Do you know what to do if you are pulled over by the police?

C **CHOOSE.** Take the quiz. Check *True* or *False*.

Do you know what to do if you get pulled over?

1. Always pull over to the ~~left~~.   *right*   ☐ True   ☑ False

2. After you pull over, ~~get out of your car~~.   *roll down your window*   ☐ True   ☑ False

3. Keep your hands on the steering wheel.   ☑ True   ☐ False

4. Give the officer your driver's license, registration, and proof of insurance.   ☑ True   ☐ False

5. Don't argue with the police officer.   ☑ True   ☐ False

6. If a police officer gives you a ticket, you ~~need to~~ pay immediately.   *should not*   ☐ True   ☑ False

Correlations

ELPS Level 2: 2, 7
CCRS Level A: SL.1.1, SL.K.3, SL.K.6
CASAS Reading: RDG 1.7, 2.3
CASAS Listening: L1.4, 2.1, 2.3, 4.1, 4.2, 6.1, 6.2
CASAS Competencies: 0.1.2, 0.1.5, 0.1.6, 5.5.6
Complete standards language available on the Pearson English Portal.

Self-Directed Learning

State the **lesson objective**. Say: *In this lesson, we will learn to respond to a police officer's instructions.*

1 BEFORE YOU LISTEN

A MATCH. Write the words under the pictures...

1. Read the directions.
2. Say: *Look at the traffic violations.* Ask: *What does* violation *mean?* (doing something wrong, breaking a rule) Say the words in the box and have students repeat.
3. Give students time to label the pictures and then compare answers with a partner.
4. To check understanding, ask questions: *What are things that can distract you when you're driving?* (kids, phone, radio) *Why is tailgating unsafe?* (It's hard to stop quickly. You might run into the back of the car in front of you.) *Which one means driving too fast?* (speeding) *Which one means not stopping?* (running a red light)
5. Ask the class: *What are some other violations you know of?* List students' ideas on the board (for example, *running a stop sign, making an illegal turn, not using car seats for young children, passing a school bus, driving too slowly, talking on a cell phone [in some states]*).

B DISCUSS. Do you know what to do if you are...

1. Read the question.
2. Tell students to look at the picture. Ask: *What does it mean to get* pulled over *by the police?* (A police car signals—usually with its lights and its siren—that you should drive to the side of the road and stop.)
3. Repeat the question. Elicit students' ideas and write them.

C CHOOSE. Take the quiz. Check *True* or *False*.

1. Read the directions.
2. Tell students to look at the quiz. Explain unfamiliar vocabulary. Point out that when you *get pulled over*, the police are signaling you to stop. When you *pull over*, you are driving to the side of the road. Tell students to look at #4. If possible, bring in your car registration and proof-of-insurance card to show the class.
3. Read the quiz title. Read each quiz item and ask students to raise their hands for *True* or *False*.

Culture Note

1. Explain that laws about car registration and car insurance vary from state to state in the U.S.
2. Say: *In most states, you go to the Department of Motor Vehicles (DMV) to register a car. You show your owner's certificate, pay a fee, and receive a registration card, license plate(s), and a sticker for your car window that shows your registration is valid for one year.*
3. Say: *Most states require car insurance—to cover the cost of damage, medical expenses, etc. if you are in an accident. Many states require drivers to carry proof of insurance, a card from the insurance company that has your policy number and the dates your insurance is valid.*
4. Ask: *What are the laws about car registration and car insurance in your native country? Are they similar to the laws in the U.S.?*

Listening and Speaking

2 LISTEN

A ▶ SELF-ASSESS. Listen. Check your...

1. Read the directions.
2. Play the audio. Students listen and check their answers on the quiz. To aid comprehension, pause the audio after each section and/or play the audio as many times as needed.
3. Ask the class: *Did you change any of your answers? Which ones?* Tell students to circle the item number of any answers they changed.
4. Play the audio again. Pause after each answer in the recording, read the quiz item, and elicit the correct answer.

> **Teaching Tip: Note-taking**
>
> When students listen to a talk, such as the one by the police officer, suggest they take notes. Remind them to write down only the important words.

B ▶ LISTEN FOR DETAILS. Listen again...

1. Read the directions. Tell students to read the items silently.
2. Play the audio. Tell students to listen and correct the false items in the quiz (1, 2, and 6).
3. Students compare answers with a partner.
4. Call on students to read the corrected items: 1. ...*pull over to the* <u>right</u>. 2. ...*you should* <u>stay in</u> *your car.* 6. *If a police officer gives you a ticket,* <u>don't</u> *pay the police officer.*

> **Teaching Tip: Use the script**
>
> *Optional:* If students need additional support, tell them to read the Audio Script on page 274 as they listen to the conversations.

C ▶ EXPAND. Listen to the whole...

1. Read the directions. Tell students to read the answer choices silently. Ask: *Which do you think is correct?* Say each answer and ask for a show of hands.
2. Play the audio. Students choose the correct answer.
3. Review the correct answer with the class. Ask: *Was your guess correct?* Ask for a show of hands.

3 CONVERSATION

A ▶ LISTEN AND READ. Then listen and repeat.

1. Read the directions.
2. Play the audio. Students listen. Pause the audio.

3. Ask: *What did the police officer ask for?* (license, registration, and proof of insurance) *Did the driver wait for the police officer to ask for his documents before he got them out?* (yes) *Why did the officer pull him over?* (for speeding) *Did he argue with the officer?* (no)
4. As needed, explain *glove compartment*. Ask: *Where is the* glove compartment *in a car?* (in front of the passenger's seat) *What did the driver from the conversation have in his glove compartment?* (registration and proof of insurance) *What do you have in your glove compartment?*
5. Resume the audio. Students listen and repeat.
6. *Optional:* Play the audio again to aid comprehension and give students more practice saying the new vocabulary.

B WORK TOGETHER. Practice the...

1. Pair students and tell them to practice the conversation in Exercise 3A.
2. Tell students to take turns playing A and B. Walk around and help with pronunciation as needed.

C ROLE-PLAY. Make new conversations. Use...

1. Read the directions.
2. Tell pairs to underline the information in the conversation in Exercise 3A that they will need to change. Ask the class: *What did you underline?* (speeding) Point out that students may also want to change *pocket* to *purse, pocketbook, backpack,* etc.
3. Pair students to take turns playing A and B. Tell A to substitute traffic violations from the top of the page or the board for *speeding* in the conversation in Exercise 3A. Tell B to substitute for *pocket.*
4. Tell students to stand, mingle, and practice the conversation with several new partners.
5. Call on pairs to perform for the class. Encourage students to act out the traffic stop by having B sit in a chair.

■■ **MULTILEVEL INSTRUCTION for 3C**
Cross-ability Direct the above-level student to play A first.

Self-Directed Learning

Point out the blue bar. Ask students if they can do the lesson learning objective or if they need more practice. Tell them to check one of the boxes. Assign Extra Practice as needed.

> **Extra Practice**
>
>   p. 131

Listening and Speaking

2 LISTEN

A ▶ SELF-ASSESS. Listen. Check your answers on the quiz.

B ▶ LISTEN FOR DETAILS. Listen again. Correct the false sentences in the quiz.

C ▶ EXPAND. Listen to the whole conversation. When is it OK to leave?

a. after the officer gives you a ticket
b. after the officer gives you permission to go
c. after the officer leaves

3 CONVERSATION

A ▶ LISTEN AND READ. Then listen and repeat.

A: I need to see your license, registration, and proof of insurance.
B: OK. My license is in my pocket. The other things are in the glove compartment.
A: That's fine. You can get them.
B: Here you go.
A: I'll be back in a moment. Please turn off your engine and stay in your car.

[a few minutes later]

A: Do you know why I pulled you over?
B: I'm not sure.
A: I pulled you over for speeding.
B: I see.

B WORK TOGETHER. Practice the conversation in Exercise A.

C ROLE-PLAY. Make new conversations. Use different traffic violations.

I can respond to a police officer's instructions. ■   I need more practice. ■

For more practice, go to MyEnglishLab.

Grammar

Compound imperatives

Compound imperatives				
Affirmative				
Turn off	your engine	**and**	**stay**	in your car.
Negative				
Don't get out	of your car	**or**	**take off**	your seat belt.

Grammar Watch

- Connect two affirmative imperatives with *and*.
- Connect two negative imperatives with *or*.

A APPLY. Write *and* or *or*.

1. Drive carefully ___and___ follow all traffic laws.
2. Wear your seat belt ___and___ use car seats for children.
3. Don't text ___or___ use your phone while driving.
4. Drive more slowly ___and___ leave extra room between cars in bad weather.
5. Don't tailgate ___or___ change lanes without signaling.

B WRITE. Rewrite each pair of sentences as two imperatives with *and*.

What to do during a traffic stop:

1. You should use your turn signal. You should pull over to a safe spot.
   Use your turn signal and pull over to a safe spot.

2. You should wait for the police officer. You should roll down your window.
   Wait for the police officer and roll down your window.

3. You should be polite. You should follow the officer's instructions.
   Be polite and follow the officer's instructions.

4. You should not argue with the officer. You should not offer money to the officer.
   Don't argue with the officer and don't offer money to the officer.

5. You should not start your car. You should not leave until the officer gives you permission to go.
   Don't start your car and don't leave until the officer gives you permission to go.

I can use compound imperatives. ■

I need more practice. ■

For more practice, go to MyEnglishLab.

Correlations

ELPS Level 2: 10
CCRS Level A: L.1.1
CASAS Reading: RDG 1.7, 2.9
CASAS Listening: L3.4
CASAS Competencies: 0.1.2
Complete standards language available on the Pearson English Portal.

Self-Directed Learning

State the **lesson objective**. Say: *In this lesson, we will learn to use compound imperatives.*

Compound imperatives

 ActiveTeach: Grammar Discovery

1. Warm up. Say: *The conversation on page 221 used this grammar.* Turn back to page 221. Point to the sentence in Exercise 3A and then write: *Please turn off your engine and stay in your car.*
2. Underline *turn off* and *stay*.
3. To review, say: *Imperatives are the form of the verb you use when you give someone a command, directions, or advice. To form imperatives, use the base form of a verb or* don't + *the base form of a verb.* Write: *Call 911. Don't call 911.*
4. Say: *Compound imperatives are two imperatives joined together in the same sentence.*
5. Tell students to look at the grammar chart.
6. Write: *Turn off your engine. Stay in your car.*
7. Read the first point of the **Grammar Watch** note. Write *and* between the two affirmative imperatives on the board. Read the first sentence in the chart and ask the class to repeat.
8. Write: *Don't get out of your car. Don't take off your seat belt.*
9. Read the second point of the **Grammar Watch** note. Write *or* between the two negative imperatives on the board and cross out *Don't* in the second one. Read the second sentence in the chart and ask the class to repeat.

 ActiveTeach: Grammar Coach

A APPLY. Write *and* or *or*.

1. Read the directions and the example. Ask: *Why is the answer* and? (because *drive carefully* and *follow all traffic laws* are affirmative)
2. *Optional:* Tell students to circle *Don't* in the sentences. Say: *If* Don't *is at the beginning of a sentence, use* or.
3. Students compare answers with a partner. Tell pairs to take turns reading the sentences.
4. Call on students to read the completed sentences.

B WRITE. **Rewrite each pair of sentences as...**

1. Read the directions.
2. Show item 1. Cross out *You should* in both sentences. Write *and* between the two sentences. Read the example.
3. Walk around and check students' work. If you see mistakes in items 4 and 5, write item 4 on the board; cross out *You should not* in both sentences and write *or* between the sentences.
4. Students compare answers with a partner. Tell pairs to take turns reading the sentences.
5. Call on students to read the sentences.

■ EXPANSION: Grammar practice for B

1. Tell students to read the fire safety tips on page 213 again. *Optional:* Play the audio about fire safety tips.
2. Write: *If there's a fire...*
3. Pair students. Tell them to choose two affirmative imperatives and combine them with *and*. Tell them to choose two negative imperatives and combine them with *or*.
4. Call on pairs to read their sentences (for example, *Leave your house immediately and call 911 from a neighbor's house. Don't take anything with you or stop to call 911.*).

Self-Directed Learning

Point out the blue bar. Ask students if they can do the lesson learning objective or if they need more practice. Tell them to check one of the boxes. Assign Extra Practice as needed.

Extra Practice

  p. 131

Correlations

ELPS Level 2: 3, 10
CCRS Level A: W.1.2, W.1.5, L.1.1
CASAS Reading: RDG 1.7, 1.8, 2.1
CASAS Listening: L2.1, 2.3, 3.6
CASAS Competencies: 0.1.2, 0.1.5, 0.1.6
Complete standards language available on the Pearson English Portal.

Self-Directed Learning

1. State the **lesson objective**. Say: *In this lesson, we will learn to answer* wh- *questions to give information.*
2. Say: *You will write about an emergency.*

1 STUDY THE MODEL

1. Read the directions.
2. Point to the paragraph. Ask: *What is the title of the model?* (My Neighbor's Emergency)
3. Point to the **Writing Skill**. Read it or call on an above-level student to read it while students listen.
4. **Scaffold** the model. Write as a graphic organizer:

1	Who?	
2	When?	
3	Where?	
4	Why?	
5	What happened?	
6	How person is now	

Point out that the rows in the graphic organizer will help students answer the questions in Exercise 1 and understand the organization of the paragraph.

5. Tell students to read the text and read the questions independently. Tell students to write the number of the question next to the sentence where they find the answer. Call on students to answer the questions. Write the information in the graphic organizer on the board.

2 PLAN YOUR WRITING

1. Erase the information in the right-hand column of the graphic organizer on the board.
2. Read the directions.
3. Model with an above-level student. The student asks the teacher the questions.
4. Write the information into the graphic organizer.
5. Brainstorm and write other types of emergencies.

6. Tell students to make their own graphic organizer on a piece of paper.
7. Have students work in pairs to ask and answer the questions and complete their own graphic organizers.

3 WRITE

1. Read the directions.
2. Use the information in the chart from Exercise 2 to write sentences in a paragraph. Then ask *wh-* questions about the paragraph (for example, Who had the emergency? When did it happen?).
3. Tell students to write. Walk around to make sure students are writing in paragraph form and answering *wh-* questions to add information.

 ActiveTeach for 3: Writing Support

4 CHECK YOUR WRITING

1. Read the directions. Point to the **Writing Checklist**. Call on students to read the checklist aloud.
2. Pair students to review their writings together. Say: *Read your sentences with a partner. Use the Writing Checklist.* For additional help, remind students that a correct sentence:
   - *begins with a capital letter*
   - *has a subject*
   - *has a verb*
   - *has a period*
   - *is a complete idea*
3. Walk around and verify that students are using the checklist. Collect the papers for review or put them in the students' writing portfolios.

Teaching Tip: Digital skills

For students using a computer to write their paragraphs, tell them that many instructors want students to use a standard font, such as Times New Roman, for their assignments using 12-point font. Explain or show how to change font and size.

Self-Directed Learning

Point out the blue bar. Ask students if they can do the lesson learning objective or if they need more practice. Tell them to check one of the boxes. Assign Extra Practice as needed.

Extra Practice

 CCRS Plus   p. 132

Lesson 10

Write about an emergency

1 STUDY THE MODEL

READ. Answer the questions.

> Ivan Popov
>
> My Neighbor's Emergency
>
> My neighbor had an emergency last week. She had a car accident on Main Street. She had a heart attack and hit a parked car. There was a big crowd of people and everyone was worried. My neighbor went to the hospital, but now she's feeling much better.

1. Who had the emergency? Ivan's neighbor.
2. When did it happen? Last week.
3. Where did it happen? On Main Street.
4. Why did it happen? She had a heart attack.
5. What happened? She went to the hospital.
6. How is the person now? She's better now.

2 PLAN YOUR WRITING

WORK TOGETHER. Ask and answer the questions.

1. Think of an emergency. Who had the emergency?
2. When did it happen?
3. Where did it happen?
4. Why did it happen?
5. What happened?
6. How is the person now?

3 WRITE

Write about an emergency. Use the model, the Writing Skill, and your ideas from Exercise 2 to help you.

4 CHECK YOUR WRITING

WORK TOGETHER. Read your writing with a partner.

Writing Skill: Answer *wh-* questions to give information

Wh- questions begin with words like *who, what, when, where, why,* and *how.*

Answer *wh-* questions to give information about an event. For example:

(Who) had the emergency?

WRITING CHECKLIST

☐ The paragraph answers the questions in Exercise 2.

☐ The paragraph answers *wh-* questions.

☐ The paragraph includes details about time, people, and places.

I can answer *wh-* questions to give information. ■   I need more practice. ■

For more practice, go to MyEnglishLab.

11 Soft Skills at Work

Follow safety procedures

1 MEET LUIS

Read about one of his workplace skills.

I follow safety procedures. For example, when I have an accident at work, I report it. That way, I can stop more accidents from happening and make the workplace safer for everyone.

2 LUIS'S PROBLEM

READ. Circle *True* or *False*.

Luis just had an accident at work. He had to get a box from a high shelf. He climbed to the top of a ladder, but the shelf was too high. He couldn't reach the box. He fell off the ladder and hurt his leg. Workers are supposed to report accidents, but that takes time. Luis is busy today. He's not sure what to do.

1. Luis reached for a box and it fell on him.   True   (False)
2. Luis hurt his hand when he reached for a box.   True   (False)
3. Luis has to complete a report about his accident.   (True)   False

3 LUIS'S SOLUTION

WORK TOGETHER. Luis follows safety procedures. What does he do? Explain your answer.

1. Luis keeps working. He doesn't report the accident.
2. Luis tells his supervisor about the accident.
3. Luis tells his co-workers about the accident.
4. Luis should _____.

Show what you know!

1. **TALK ABOUT IT.** Do you follow safety procedures? How do you follow safety procedures in class? At work? At home? Give examples.

2. **WRITE ABOUT IT.** Write an example in your Skills Log.

   I follow safety procedures in class. When the fire alarm rings, I always follow the rules. I go outside until the fire alarm stops.

I can give an example of how I follow safety procedures. ☐

Unit Review: Go back to page 205. Which unit goals can you check off?

Correlations

CASAS Reading: RDG 1.7, 1.8, 3.2
CASAS Listening: L2.1, 2.3, 4.1, 4.2
CASAS Competencies: 0.1.2, 0.1.5, 0.1.6, 0.2.1, 4.3.4
Complete standards language available on the Pearson English Portal.

Self-Directed Learning

State the **lesson objective**. Say: *In this lesson, we will give an example of how we follow safety procedures.*

1 MEET LUIS

1. Ask: *What is the title of this lesson?* (Follow safety procedures) Ask: *What does* procedures *mean?* (the way to do something, a specific plan, a series of steps)
2. Write: *Workplace Skill*. Read the directions. Say: *Listen as I read* Meet Luis. Read the paragraph. Ask: *What is one of Luis's workplace skills?* (He follows safety procedures.) Next to *Workplace Skill*, write: *Follow safety procedures*.
3. Under *Workplace Skill*, write: *Examples*. Ask: *How does Luis follow safety procedures?* (He reports accidents at work. He helps stop more accidents from happening. He makes the workplace safer.) Write the examples. Elicit other ways to follow safety procedures and write them under *Workplace Skill*.

2 LUIS'S PROBLEM

1. Say: *Now we are going to read about Luis at work. Listen while I read.* Read the first sentence. Ask: *Where is Luis?* (at work) Say: *Look at the photo. What happens to Luis at work?* (He has an accident.)
2. Say: *Luis has a problem at work. Listen while I read.* Read the rest of the paragraph. Explain any unfamiliar vocabulary as needed.
3. Students complete the questions after the reading. Call on students to answer. Ask them to **cite evidence:** *Where is that information?*
4. Ask: *What is Luis's problem?* (He hurt his leg, but he doesn't want to report it because he's busy.)

3 LUIS'S SOLUTION

1. Read the directions. Ask students to work together. Walk around and check that students understand that only one solution is correct.
2. Ask: *Is #1 following safety procedures?* (no) *Why not?* (He does not report the accident.) Ask:

Is #2 following safety procedures? (yes) *Why?* (He reports the accident.) Ask: *Is #3 following safety procedures?* (no) *Why not?* (He tells his co-workers, but that is not reporting an accident.)
3. Ask students if they have any other ideas. Write their responses. Ask: *Is this following safety procedures? Why?*

 ActiveTeach for 3: Academic Conversation Support

■ **EXPANSION: Writing practice for 3**

1. Find a generic accident report form online. Search for *workplace accident report form*. Print copies for students. Or write your own form and have students copy it in their notebooks. Key fields include time and date of accident, name, address, phone number, date of birth, type of injury, details of incident, and signature.
2. Tell students to fill out the form, making up the details.

Workplace Culture

In the U.S., all employers must provide a workers' compensation program. This program allows workers to receive money (compensation) if they suffer an on-the-job illness or injury.

Show what you know!

1. TALK ABOUT IT. Do you follow safety...

Read the directions. Have students think about their answers for a few minutes. Then ask them to share with a partner. Call on students to share with the class.

2. WRITE ABOUT IT. Write an example in your...

Read the directions and the example. Have students write their examples in their **Skills Log** at the back of the book. Circulate and assist students as needed.

Self-Directed Learning

1. Point out the blue bar. Ask students if they can do the lesson learning objective or if they need more practice. Tell them to check one of the boxes. Assign Extra Practice as needed.
2. Ask students to turn to page 205. Go to the Unit Wrap-Up teaching notes on page T-205.

Extra Practice

 p. 133

12 The World of Work

Classroom Materials/Extra Practice

 ActiveTeach

 MyEnglishLab

 Workbook

 English Portal — Life Skills Writing, MCA, Team Projects, Persistence Activities

Unit Overview

Goals
• See the list of goals on the facing page

Pronunciation
• Intonation in *yes/no* questions
• Intonation in information questions and statements

Reading
• Read about the Social Security program
• Think about what you know

Grammar
• Expressions of necessity and prohibition
• Information questions with *Who / What / Which / When / Where*
• *Can / Could* to ask permission

Writing
• Write about job responsibilities
• Give details to support an idea

Document Literacy and Numeracy
• Calculate earnings from a pay stub
• Understand types of deduction
• Calculate overtime pay
• Interpret a work schedule

Workplace, Life, and Community Skills
• Read a paystub
• Understand payroll deductions and overtime hours
• Digital Skills: Search for other common deductions that can appear on a paystub

Life Skills Writing
• Complete a vacation request form

Soft Skills at Work
• Be a team player

Preview
1. Set the context of the unit by asking questions about work (for example, *What rules do you have to follow in your job? Would you like a different job?*).
2. Show the Unit Opener. Ask: *What is the unit title?* (The World of Work)
3. Say: *Look at the picture.* Ask the Preview questions. (Possible answers: workers working in a big hole in the street; a truck and equipment for digging; workers wearing hardhats and safety vests)
4. Write the answers.

Unit Goals
1. Point to the Unit Goals. Explain that this list shows what you will be studying in this unit.
2. Tell students to read the goals silently.
3. Say each goal. Explain unfamiliar vocabulary as needed.
4. Point to the ☐ next to the first goal. Say: *We will come back to this page again. You will write a checkmark next to the goals you learned in the unit.*

Oral Presentation
1. Tell students they will give a short presentation at the end of the unit.
2. Write the topics:
   Option 1: The responsibilities of a job you know
   Option 2: Social Security
3. Assign the topics to two students.

Unit Wrap-Up
1. Review the Unit Goals with students.
2. Direct students to the Grammar Review.
3. If you assigned presentations, ask students to present.

ActiveTeach for Wrap-Up: Team Project

ActiveTeach for Wrap-Up: Persistence Activities

12 The World of Work

PREVIEW
Look at the picture.
What do you see?

UNIT GOALS

- [ ] Identify job responsibilities
- [ ] Ask about policies at work
- [ ] Read a pay stub
- [ ] Understand payroll deductions and overtime
- [ ] Ask a co-worker to cover hours
- [ ] Request a schedule change
- [ ] **Academic skill:** Think about what you know
- [ ] **Writing skill:** Give details to support an idea
- [ ] **Workplace soft skill:** Show how you are a team player

Job Responsibilities

A PREDICT. Look at the pictures. What do you see? Which job responsibilities do you know?

B ▶ LISTEN AND POINT. Listen again and repeat.

Correlations

ELPS Level 2: 2, 7, 8
CCRS Level A: SL.1.1, SL.K.6, L.1.5, L.1.6
CASAS Reading: RDG 1.7, 2.3
CASAS Listening: L2.1, 2.3, 2.9, 4.2
CASAS Competencies: 0.1.2, 0.1.5, 4.4.4, 7.4.1
Complete standards language available on the Pearson English Portal.

Self-Directed Learning

State the **lesson objective**. Say: *In this lesson, we will learn to identify job responsibilities.*

A PREDICT. **Look at the pictures. What do…**

1. Read the directions. Tell students to cover the list on page 227.
2. Say: *Look at the pictures. What are the people doing? Which job responsibilities do you know?* Elicit a job responsibility (for example, *#9 is wash hands.*).
3. Students call out answers. Help students pronounce the job responsibilities if they have difficulty.
4. If students call out an incorrect job responsibility, ask a *yes/no* clarification question: *#9 is wear a uniform?* If nobody can identify the correct job responsibility, tell students they will now listen to the audio and practice the vocabulary for job responsibilities.

B ▶ LISTEN AND POINT. **Listen again and…**

1. Read the directions. Play the audio. Students listen and point to the job responsibilities.
2. While the audio is playing, walk around and check that students are pointing to the correct job responsibilities. Pause the audio after item 12.
3. Tell students to look at picture 6. Explain: Work as a team *means work together to do a job.*
4. Tell students to look at pictures 11 and 12. Explain: Maintain the equipment *means take care of the equipment.* Store the equipment *means put the equipment away properly.*
5. Say each job responsibility in random order and ask students to point to the appropriate picture.
6. Tell students to look at page 227. Resume the audio. Students listen, read, and repeat.

 ActiveTeach for B: Vocabulary Flashcards

Digital Skills for B

1. Job responsibilities are often listed in job advertisements. As a class, brainstorm some jobs that students have learned about in previous lessons (for example, night cleaner in Unit 5).
2. Tell students to pick one of these jobs and search online for job advertisements that list responsibilities.
3. Have students report back to the class what they found.

Vocabulary

C DISCUSS. Look at the job titles. What are...

1. Read the directions.
2. Say the jobs from the box and ask the class to repeat.
3. Ask: *Do you remember these jobs from Unit 8: a computer system administrator, a nursing assistant, a warehouse worker?*
4. Ask: *What are other responsibilities of these jobs?* Ask two students to read the example.
5. Pair students. Write: *What are the responsibilities of a _____?* Say: *Student A, ask about the responsibilities of a job from the box on page 147. Student B, say at least two job responsibilities from the list on page 227. Then switch roles.*
6. Write each job from the box as a heading on the board. Ask the class: *What are the responsibilities of a computer system administrator?* List students' ideas on the board. Repeat with the other jobs from the box.

D GIVE EXAMPLES. Complete the chart with...

1. Read the directions.
2. Say: *Look at the example.* Wear a uniform *is a job responsibility in the category* dress appropriately. *What's another job responsibility in this category?*
3. Form groups of 3. Tell groups to talk about job responsibilities for each category and to choose one to write in the chart.
4. List the categories on the board. Ask one student from each group to write the group's answers to the right of each category on the board. Tell the students to write only answers that are not already on the board.
5. Read the categories and job responsibilities on the board. Talk about how the job responsibilities fit into the categories.

Study Tip: Study words that go together

1. Provide each student with six index cards or tell students to cut up notebook paper into six pieces.
2. Point to the **Study Tip**. Read the directions.
3. Walk around as students work. If misspellings occur, tell them to check the list on page 227.
4. Say: *You can remember new vocabulary when you write words that go together.* Remind students to use this strategy to remember other new vocabulary.

Show what you know!

1. THINK ABOUT IT. Think of a job you have or...

1. Read the directions. Tell students to look at the example silently.
2. Model the activity. List the responsibilities for your job on the board.
3. Tell students to look at the list of job responsibilities and circle the responsibilities for their job.
4. Tell them to write the job title and list the responsibilities.

2. TALK ABOUT IT. Tell your classmates about...

1. Read the directions. Tell students to read the example silently.
2. Model the activity. Tell the class about your job. Point to the job title and responsibilities on the board. Say: *I am a teacher. Teachers have to follow directions, ask questions, and work as a team.*
3. Pair students. Tell them to take turns describing their job's responsibilities.
4. To wrap up, ask a few students to tell the class about the job his or her partner has or wants.

3. WRITE ABOUT IT. Write three sentences...

1. Read the directions. Write an example.
2. Share the checklist below. Then write a checkmark next to each as you point back to the example sentence.
   - One sentence names the job.
   - There are at least three job responsibilities named.
3. Give students time to write their sentences.
4. Tell students to show their sentences to partner. Tell the students to use the checklist to review the sentences.
5. Walk around and verify that students are using the checklist. Collect the papers for review or put them in the students' writing portfolios.

Self-Directed Learning

Point out the blue bar. Ask students if they can do the lesson learning objective or if they need more practice. Tell them to check one of the boxes. Assign Extra Practice as needed.

Extra Practice

  pp. 134–135

Vocabulary

Job responsibilities

1. clock in/out
2. call in late
3. follow directions
4. ask questions
5. report problems with the equipment
6. work as a team
7. wear a uniform
8. wear safety gear
9. wash hands
10. wear gloves
11. maintain the equipment
12. store the equipment

C **DISCUSS.** Look at the job titles. What are the responsibilities for each job?

nursing assistant

computer system administrator

sales associate

warehouse worker

A: What are the responsibilities of a nursing assistant?
B: A nursing assistant has to wash hands, wear gloves . . .

Study Tip

Study words that go together

Choose six job responsibilities. Make cards. Write the verb on the front of the card and the other words on the back.

wear / a uniform
wash / hands

D **GIVE EXAMPLES.** Complete the chart with examples. There may be more than one correct answer.

An employee has to . . .	EXAMPLE
dress appropriately	wear a uniform
follow health and safety rules	
be on time	
communicate well with others	
treat equipment correctly	

Show what you know!

1. **THINK ABOUT IT.** Think of a job you have or want to have. List the responsibilities for that job.

   warehouse worker — clock in and clock out

2. **TALK ABOUT IT.** Tell your classmates about the job and the responsibilities.

   A: I am a warehouse worker. I have to clock in every day.
   B: I want to be a computer systems administrator. A computer systems administrator has to maintain the computer equipment.

3. **WRITE ABOUT IT.** Write three sentences about a job and its responsibilities.

I can identify job responsibilities. ■   I need more practice. ■

For more practice, go to MyEnglishLab.

Lesson 2
Ask about policies at work

1 BEFORE YOU LISTEN

A **INTERPRET.** Look at the picture of a hotel guest and an employee of the hotel. What is the employee doing wrong?

A **DISCUSS.** What other things are employees often not allowed to do at work?

2 LISTEN

A **PREDICT.** Look at the picture. Who is Michelle? Who are the other people?

B ▶ **LISTEN FOR MAIN IDEA.** Check (✓) the topics that Michelle talks about.

- ☑ wearing the right clothing
- ☐ wearing safety gear
- ☑ being on time
- ☐ working as a team

New employee orientation

MICHELLE

Greenvi -Hotel

C ▶ **LISTEN FOR DETAILS.** Listen again. Complete the sentences.

1. You must wear your _____ during your work shift.
   a. name tag   **b.** employee ID badge   c. safety gear

2. Employees in housekeeping and food service must wear _____.
   a. a uniform   b. latex gloves   c. boots

3. During your 6-hour shift you must _____.
   a. not take a break   b. take a 15-minute break   **c.** take a 30-minute break

4. You must not _____ for another employee.
   a. clock in or clock out   b. call in late   c. ask questions

D ▶ **EXPAND.** Listen to the whole conversation. Next, Michelle will talk about the company's _____.
   a. vacation-time policy   **b.** sick-day policy   c. policy for calling in late

Correlations

ELPS Level 2: 2, 7
CCRS Level A: SL.K.3
CASAS Reading: RDG 1.7, 2.3
CASAS Listening: L1.4, 2.1, 2.3, 4.2, 6.1, 6.2, 6.5
CASAS Competencies: 0.1.2, 0.1.4, 0.1.5, 4.2.4
Complete standards language available on the Pearson English Portal.

Self-Directed Learning

State the **lesson objective**. Say: *In this lesson, we will learn to ask about policies at work.*

1 BEFORE YOU LISTEN

A INTERPRET. Look at the picture of a hotel...

1. Read the directions. Say: *Point to the guest. Point to the employee.* Ask: *Where are they?* (in a hotel)
2. Ask: *What is the employee doing wrong?* Elicit students' ideas and write them on the board. (Possible answers: *He's eating. He's drinking. He's talking on the phone. He isn't wearing the right clothing. He isn't helping the guest.*)

B DISCUSS. What other things are employees...

1. Say: *The employee in Exercise 1A is doing many things wrong.* Ask: *What other things are employees usually not allowed to do at work?*
2. Elicit students' ideas and list them (for example, *chew gum, smoke, text, arrive late, use alcohol or drugs*).

2 LISTEN

A PREDICT. Look at the picture. Who is...

1. Tell students to look at the picture and point to Michelle. Ask: *Where are they?* (Greenville Hotel, meeting room) *What does the sign say?* (New employee orientation)
2. Ask: *Who is Michelle?* Elicit ideas and list them (a supervisor, a manager, a hotel employee, a trainer) *Who are the other people?* (new employees) *What is an orientation?* (a meeting for new employees) Say: *At an orientation, new employees learn about company policies, or what they are expected to do and what they are not allowed to do.*

B ▶ LISTEN FOR MAIN IDEA. Check (✓) the...

1. Tell students to read the directions and answer choices silently.
2. Play the audio. Students listen and check the boxes of topics they hear.

3. Students compare the topics they checked with a partner.
4. Ask: *What does Michelle talk about?* Call on students to say the answers.
5. Write *dress code* on the board. Ask: *Which of the four answers has the same meaning as dress code?* (wearing the right clothing) Tell students to write *dress code* next to *wearing the right clothing*.

Career Awareness: Human resources worker

Human resources (HR) workers work in the HR department of a company or a business. They are involved in hiring new employees, creating job descriptions, listening to employee and employer complaints; and keeping records of employee performance, pay, and benefits. A bachelor's degree is usually required.

■■■ **EXPANSION: Career awareness for 2B**

Ask students about the job in this lesson: *What does an HR worker do? Where does an HR worker work? Do you need to study to be an HR worker? Do you want to be an HR worker?*

C ▶ LISTEN FOR DETAILS. Listen again...

1. Read the directions. Tell students to read the sentences silently.
2. Play the audio. Students listen and write the answers.
3. Play the audio again to aid comprehension.
4. Students compare answers with a partner. Tell them to take turns reading the completed sentences.
5. Call on students to read the sentences. Correct if necessary.
6. Ask: *What's an ID badge?* Tell students to point to Michelle's ID badge in the picture. Tell students to look at the picture in Exercise 1A. Ask: *Is the employee wearing his ID badge?* (no) *Do you wear an ID badge at your job?*

D ▶ EXPAND. Listen to the whole...

1. Read the directions. Tell students to read the answer choices silently.
2. Play the audio. Students choose the correct answer.
3. Ask: *What is Michelle going to talk about next?*
4. Say: *Michelle is giving a presentation.* Ask about **register**: *How does she ask for questions?* (Are there any questions?)

Listening and Speaking

3 PRONUNCIATION

A ▶ PRACTICE. Listen. Then listen and repeat.

1. Read the directions. Then read the **Pronunciation Note**.
2. Tell students to look at the questions. Ask (with rising intonation): *Are they all yes/no questions?* (yes) Say: *Listen for the voice to go up at the end of each question. Then practice making your voice go up at the end of each question.*
3. Play the audio. Students listen. Then students listen and repeat.

 ActiveTeach for 3A: Pronunciation Coach

B ▶ APPLY. Listen. Use an arrow to mark...

1. Read the directions. Tell students to read the sentences. Ask: *Are they all yes/no questions?* (yes)
2. Play the audio. Students listen and mark the intonation with an arrow.
3. Show the sentences on the board. Call on students to use an arrow to mark where the voice goes up.

4 CONVERSATION

A ▶ LISTEN AND READ. Then listen and repeat.

1. Tell students to read the conversation silently and underline the *yes/no* questions.
2. Ask: *Which questions did you underline?* Write *Can I ask you a question?* and *Am I allowed to wear sneakers?* on the board and mark the intonation with an arrow as in Exercise 3A and 3B. Tell students to mark the sentences in their books. Say the questions and ask the class to repeat.
3. *Optional:* Point out that *What do you want to know?* is an information question and has different intonation/pronunciation.
4. Play the audio. Students listen and read. Then students listen and repeat.
5. Ask: *Are employees at the Greenville Hotel allowed to wear sneakers?* (no) *What do they have to wear?* (boots) Say: *Look at the picture in Exercise 1A on page 228 again. Is the employee wearing black shoes?* (no) *What is he wearing?* (sneakers)

B WORK TOGETHER. Practice the...

1. Pair students and tell them to practice the conversation in Exercise 4A.
2. Tell students to take turns playing A and B. Walk around and pay particular attention to intonation in *yes/no* questions.

C CREATE. Make new conversations. Use the...

1. Read the directions.
2. Tell students to look at the boxes. Say each item and ask the class to repeat.
3. Show the conversation on the board with blanks. Read it and when you come to a blank, fill in a student's name or information from the same row in the boxes.
4. Ask the student whose name you used and another on-level student to practice the conversation.
5. Tell pairs to take turns playing each role and to use information from the same row in the boxes to fill in the blanks.
6. Walk around and check that A uses rising intonation in the *yes/no* questions.
7. Tell students to stand, mingle, and practice the conversation with several new partners.

▬ MULTILEVEL INSTRUCTION for 4C
Cross-ability Pre-level students play A first and write in the information. Above-level students play B with books closed.

D ROLE-PLAY. Make your own conversations.

1. Read the directions. Write: *Am I allowed to _____?* and *No, you aren't. You have to _____.* as headings on the board. As a class, brainstorm pairs of phrases to complete the sentences and write them on the board (for example, *wear shorts / wear pants, drink in the warehouse / drink in the break room, leave early / talk to a manager*).
2. Pair students and tell them to practice the conversation in Exercise 4A with the information on the board or their own information.
3. Walk around and check that pairs substitute information correctly and that A uses rising intonation in the *yes/no* questions.
4. Call on pairs to perform for the class.

Self-Directed Learning

Point out the blue bar. Ask students if they can do the lesson learning objective or if they need more practice. Tell them to check one of the boxes. Assign Extra Practice as needed.

Extra Practice	
MyEnglishLab	Workbook p. 136

Listening and Speaking

3 PRONUNCIATION

A ▶ PRACTICE. Listen. Then listen and repeat.

In *yes/no* questions, the voice usually goes up at the end.

Can I ask you a few questions?

Do we have to clock out?

Are we allowed to wear sneakers?

B ▶ APPLY. Listen. Use an arrow to mark where the voice goes up.

1. Do we need to wear gloves?

2. Did you clock in?

3. Can I report a problem?

4 CONVERSATION

A ▶ LISTEN AND READ. Then listen and repeat.

Employee: Hi, Michelle. Can I ask you a question?
Trainer: Sure. What do you want to know?
Employee: Am I allowed to wear sneakers?
Trainer: No, you aren't. You have to wear boots.
Employee: OK. Thanks. I'm glad I asked.

B WORK TOGETHER. Practice the conversation in Exercise A.

C CREATE. Make new conversations. Use the words in the boxes.

A: Hi, _____. Can I ask you a question?
B: Sure. What do you want to know?
A: Am I allowed to [   ]?
B: No, you aren't. You have to [   ].
A: OK. Thanks. I'm glad I asked.

eat in front of customers	eat in the break room
park anywhere	park in the back
trade shifts	talk to a manager

D ROLE-PLAY. Make your own conversations.

I can ask about policies at work. ■   I need more practice. ■

For more practice, go to MyEnglishLab.

Expressions of necessity and prohibition

Expressions of necessity: *must / have to*			
You	**have to**		
	must		
		wear	boots.
He	**has to**		
	must		

Grammar Watch

Use *have to* for questions (not *must*).
Do you have to wear a uniform?
Where do we have to clock in?

Expressions of prohibition: *must not / can't*			
You	**must not**		
		wear	sneakers.
	can't		

Ⓐ **COMPLETE. Use *must*, *must not*, *have to*, or *can't* and the verbs in parentheses. There may be more than one correct answer.**

1. **A:** ___Do I have to go___ (I / go) to the orientation meeting today?

   B: Yes. All new employees ___must go / have to go___ (go) to the meeting.

2. **A:** Can we smoke in the break room?

   B: No, you ___can't smoke / must not smoke___ (smoke) anywhere in the building. You ___have to go / must go___ (go) outside to the designated smoking area.

3. **A:** What's the uniform for supervisors?

   B: Supervisors ___have to wear / must wear___ (wear) dark suits and black shoes.

4. **A:** I need to take a sick day. Who do I have to tell?

   B: You ___have to call / must call___ (call) your manager at least 30 minutes before the start of your shift.

5. **A:** I'm going to eat lunch at my desk.

   B: Sorry, it's not allowed. You ___can't eat / must not eat___ (eat) at your desk. You ___have to eat / must eat___ (eat) in the break room.

Correlations

ELPS Level 2: 2, 7
CASAS Reading: RDG 1.7, 1.8, 2.3, 3.2
CASAS Listening: L1.3, 2.1, 2.3, 3.9, 4.1, 4.2
CASAS Competencies: 0.1.2, 0.1.5, 4.4.4
Complete standards language available on the Pearson English Portal.

Self-Directed Learning

State the **lesson objective**. Say: *In this lesson, we will learn to use expressions of necessity and prohibition.*

Expressions of necessity: *must / have to*

 ActiveTeach: Grammar Discovery

1. Warm up. Say: *The conversation on page 229 used this grammar.* Turn back to page 229. Point to the sentence in Exercise 4A and then write: *You have to wear boots.*
2. Write below that sentence: *You must clock in at the start of your shift.* Underline *have to wear* and *must clock in*.
3. Tell students to look at the grammar charts. Point to the top chart. Say: Necessity *means that you are required to do something. You must do it.*
4. Read the first two sentences in the top chart. Write: *have to wear = must wear.* Say: *These two sentences have the same meaning: You need to wear boots.*
5. Read the first and third sentences in the top chart. Write: have / has to + *base form of a verb.*
6. Read the second and fourth sentences in the top chart. Write: must + *base form of a verb.* Explain: Must *does not change, and we don't use* to *after* must.
7. Read all of the sentences in the top chart and ask the class to repeat. Write: *He has to wear boots.* Ask the class to make it into a question. Elicit and write: *Does he have to wear boots?*

 ActiveTeach: Grammar Coach

Expressions of prohibition: *must not / can't*

1. Tell students to look at the grammar charts again. Point to the bottom chart. Say: Prohibition *means that you are not allowed to do something. You must not do it.*

2. Read the two sentences in the bottom chart and tell the class to repeat. Say: *These two sentences have the same meaning: Don't wear sneakers.*
3. Write: must not / can't + *base form of a verb.*

 ActiveTeach: Grammar Coach

A COMPLETE. Use *must, must not, have to,* or…

1. Read the directions and the example. Elicit an answer for B's line (for example, *have to go*). Ask: *What is another possible answer?* (*must go*)
2. Students compare answers with a partner by reading the conversations. Remind students that there is more than one correct answer. For *must not* and *can't*, tell them to look for words in the sentences that make the meaning negative.
3. There are two possible answers for each item. Elicit both answers by calling on two pairs to read each conversation. For each item, write both possible answers.
4. *Optional:* Call on pairs to perform the completed conversations for the class.

■ **EXPANSION: Digital skills and grammar practice for A**

1. Tell students to go online and visit a hotel website. Say: *Find a list of rules that guests must follow in the hotel.* Students might need to search for keywords like *check-in hours, check-out hours, pet policy,* or *smoking policy.*
2. Make a list of common hotel rules on the board. Help with unfamiliar vocabulary.
3. Ask students to take three of the rules and make sentences with *must, have to, must not,* and *can't.*
4. *Optional:* Identify a local hotel's website beforehand and ask students to all use the same one. Write the URL.

Culture Note

1. Say: *In the U.S. there are laws that ban smoking in many places. In public places and some businesses, there are "designated smoking areas" for smokers that are set apart from the rest of the building. Outside of these areas, you must not smoke a cigarette.*
2. Ask: *In your native country, are there places that you cannot smoke? Are there special areas for smokers?*

Grammar

B READ. The email is about responsibilities...

1. Read the directions. Ask students to read the email silently and circle who it was sent to.
2. Read the email out loud as a class. Call on a different student to read each bullet.
3. Ask: *Who was the email sent to?* (new employees) *Whose responsibilities are listed?* (all employees)

C COMPLETE. Read the email again. Use the...

1. Tell students to look at the email again. Ask: *What are an employee's responsibilities?* Read the directions.
2. Show the example. Point out that *have to* changes to *has to* because *The employee* is the subject. Ask: *How do we know to use the verb* be? Tell students to circle *Be* in the first reminder in the list. Ask: *What is another possible answer?* (*must be*)
3. Remind students to use verbs from the list in the email. Say: *There is more than one correct answer.*
4. Pair students. Students compare answers by taking turns reading the sentences.
5. Say: *If you both have the same answer, talk about the other possible answer. Write the other possible answer to the right of each sentence.*
6. Call on students to read the sentences. Elicit both possible answers for each item.

Show what you know!

1. THINK ABOUT IT. Think about one role you...

1. Read the directions.
2. Ask for a show of hands as you ask the questions from the directions: *Are you an employee? A student? A parent?*
3. Give time for students to complete the activity.
4. Designate an area of the classroom for employees, parents, and students to meet. If groups are very disproportionate, switch students who are members of more than one group to the smaller groups.
5. Tell groups to share their ideas for other responsibilities.

2. TALK ABOUT IT. Tell your partner what your...

1. Read the directions. Play A and model the example with an on-level student.
2. Pair students from different groups in Step 1 (for example, pair employees with students or parents). Partners take turns telling each other about their roles and responsibilities.
3. Students switch partners and repeat.

3. WRITE ABOUT IT. Now write six sentences...

1. Read the directions.
2. Tell students to use ideas from Steps 1 and 2 to write six sentences on a sheet of notebook paper.
3. Put the students back in the same groups as Step 1. Students exchange papers with a partner within the group and compare sentences.
   - Sentences should use the correct form of *have to*.
   - Sentences should use the base form of the verb after *have to* and *must*.
   - Sentences should not use *to* after *must*.
4. Tell partners to take turns reading their sentences to each other.

▣ EXPANSION: Grammar practice for 3

1. Ask: *How many different responsibilities do you have as a group?*
2. Provide highlighters. For each responsibility that they identified, tell groups to highlight one sentence on someone's paper.
3. Write the headings: *Your Duties as an Employee, Your Duties as a Student,* and *Your Duties as a Parent.*
4. Ask each group to write the sentences that they highlighted under their heading on the board.
5. Ask the class: *Which group has the most responsibilities: employees, students, or parents?* Discuss as a class.

Self-Directed Learning

Point out the blue bar. Ask students if they can do the lesson learning objective or if they need more practice. Tell them to check one of the boxes. Assign Extra Practice as needed.

Extra Practice		
MyEnglishLab	Workbook	p. 136

Grammar

B READ. The e-mail is about responsibilities. Who is the information for?
The information is for all new employees.

C COMPLETE. Read the e-mail again. Use the correct form of *have to*, *must*, *must not*, or *can't* to complete the statements. There may be more than one correct answer.

1. The employee __*has to be*__ on time for work.

2. He _____ if he's going to be late.
   has to call (his supervisor)

3. He _____ his breaks on time.
   has to begin and end

4. He _____ in and out.
   has to clock / can't forget to clock / must not forget to clock

5. He _____ in and out for other employees.
   must not clock / can't clock

6. He _____ personal calls at work.
   must not make / can't make

○○○

To: All new employees
From: HR department
Subject: Your Duties as an Employee

Hello, and welcome again to B.T. Corporation.

To make your work more successful, here is a list of reminders:
* Be on time. This is very important.
* Call your supervisor if you are going to be late.
* Begin and end your breaks at the scheduled times.
* Don't forget to clock in and out.
* Don't clock in or out for other employees.
* Don't make personal calls at work.

Show what you know!

1. **THINK ABOUT IT.** Think about one role you have (for example, an employee, a parent, or a student). Write it on the line. Check the responsibilities you have in that role. Add other responsibilities that you have.

2. **TALK ABOUT IT.** Tell your partner what your role is. Tell about your responsibilities in that role. Take turns.

   A: *I'm a parent. I have to work a lot of hours.*
   B: *I'm a student. I have to work a lot of hours, too!*

   Responsibilities of a/an _____
   ☐ work a lot of hours
   ☐ not be late
   ☐ supervise people
   ☐ communicate in English
   ☐ _____
   ☐ _____

3. **WRITE ABOUT IT.** Now write six sentences about your responsibilities.

   I'm a _____. *I have to* _____.

   _____

I can use expressions of necessity and prohibition. ☐   I need more practice. ☐

For more practice, go to MyEnglishLab.

Lesson 4 — Pay stubs, payroll deductions, and overtime hours

1 READ A PAY STUB

A **INTERPRET.** Look at Kim's pay stub. How much money did she earn? She earned $490.00. How much money did she get? She got $359.50.

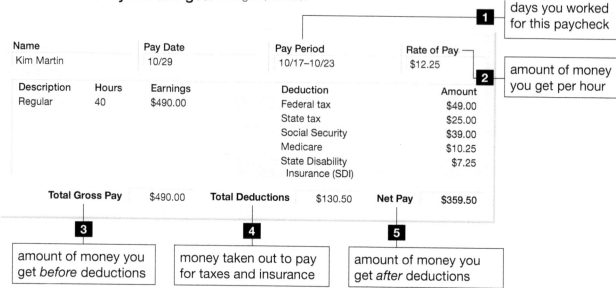

Name	Pay Date	Pay Period	Rate of Pay
Kim Martin	10/29	10/17–10/23	$12.25

1 days you worked for this paycheck

2 amount of money you get per hour

Description	Hours	Earnings		Deduction	Amount
Regular	40	$490.00		Federal tax	$49.00
				State tax	$25.00
				Social Security	$39.00
				Medicare	$10.25
				State Disability Insurance (SDI)	$7.25

Total Gross Pay	$490.00	**Total Deductions**	$130.50	**Net Pay**	$359.50

3 amount of money you get *before* deductions

4 money taken out to pay for taxes and insurance

5 amount of money you get *after* deductions

B **DETERMINE.** Look at the pay stub again. Correct the incorrect statements.

1. The pay stub is for ~~two weeks~~ one week of work.
2. The pay stub ~~includes~~ doesn't include Kim's job title.
3. The company paid her on ~~10/23~~ 10/29 for this pay period.
4. She gets paid ~~$40~~ $12.25 per hour.
5. Kim gets paid for ~~50~~ 40 hours of work.
6. Kim's ~~gross~~ net pay is $359.50.

I can read a pay stub. ■   I need more practice. ■

Correlations

ELPS Level 2: 1, 2, 3, 4, 5, 6, 7, 8, 9, 10
CCRS Level A: W.1.7, W.1.8
CASAS Reading: RDG 1.7, 1.8, 2.3, 3.2, 3.4
CASAS Listening: L2.1, 2.3, 4.2
CASAS Competencies: 0.1.2, 0.1.5, 4.2.1, 4.5.6, 7.4.4, 7.7.3
Complete standards language available on the Pearson English Portal.

Self-Directed Learning

State the **lesson objective.** Say: *In this lesson, we will learn to read a pay stub and understand payroll deductions and overtime hours.*

1 READ A PAY STUB

A INTEPRET. **Look at Kim's pay stub. How...**

Document Literacy: Pay stub

Context: A pay stub is the piece of paper that's attached to your paycheck from work.
Purpose: Pay stubs tell you how much money you earned and how much was taken out for taxes, insurance, etc.
Key Words: *pay date, pay period, rate, deduction, federal tax, state tax, Social Security, earnings, gross pay, net pay*

1. Tell students to look at the pay stub. Ask about **context**: *Where do you get pay stubs?* (at work) Explain as needed: *The pay stub is the piece of paper that's attached to your paycheck.* Ask about **purpose**: *What are pay stubs for?* (to tell how much money you earned and how much was taken out for taxes, insurance, etc.) Ask about **key words**: *What information is on your pay stub?* Elicit a few words (for example, *name, pay, tax*).
2. Write *deductions*. Tell students to look at the pay stub and find the definition for *deductions*. Ask: *What are deductions?* (money taken out of your paycheck to pay for taxes and insurance) *How much money was taken out of Kim's paycheck for deductions?* ($130.50) Say: *We'll look more closely at deductions later in the lesson.*
3. Write *rate of pay*. Tell students to look at the pay stub and find the definition for *rate of pay*. Ask: *How much did Kim earn per hour?* ($12.25)
4. Write *pay period*. Tell students to look at the pay stub and find the definiton for *pay period*. Ask: *How many days is the pay period?* (7 days)
5. Read the directions.

6. Pair students. Tell them to read the pay stub and circle the answers to the two questions.
7. Ask: *How much money did Kim earn?* ($490) Say: *$490 is her gross pay, the amount of money she earns before deductions.*
8. Ask: *How much money did Kim get?* ($359.50) Say: *$359.50 is her net pay, the amount of money she gets after deductions.* Net pay *is also called* take-home pay.
9. Use the numeracy box to show students how to calculate gross pay and net pay.

Numeracy: Math Skills

In this lesson, students need to calculate the gross and net pay. Gross pay is how much someone earns before deductions. Net pay is how much someone earns after deductions. Write the following:

Gross Pay
hours x rate of pay = gross pay
40 hours x $12.25/hour = $490

Net Pay
gross pay – deductions = net pay
$490 – $130.50 = $359.50

B DETERMINE. **Look at the pay stub again...**

1. Read the directions. Write the example. Ask: *Why is the answer* one week*?* (because the pay period is 10/17–10/23: seven days).
2. Write item 2. Ask: *Is Kim's job title on the pay stub?* (no) *Is the sentence true or false?* (false) Ask: *How can we correct this sentence?* (make it negative; substitute another word for *job title*, such as *last name* or *rate of pay*)
3. Students compare answers with a partner.
4. Call on students to read the corrected sentences.

Culture Note

1. Ask: *What is Social Security?* (money from the government for older people not working now) *What is Medicare?* (money from the government for health care for people who are 65 years old and over)
2. Ask: *Do older people receive money and health care from the government in your native country?*

Self-Directed Learning

Point out the blue bar. Ask students if they can do the lesson learning objective or if they need more practice. Tell them to check one of the boxes. Assign Extra Practice as needed.

Workplace, Life, and Community Skills

2 UNDERSTAND PAYROLL...

Ⓐ MATCH. Look at the pay stub again. Match...

1. Read the directions.
2. Students compare answers with a partner.
3. Call on students for answers. Ask them to **cite evidence:** *Where is that information?*

Ⓑ INTERPRET. Read the except from the...

1. Read the directions and note.
2. Point to item 1. Ask: *When do you get overtime pay?* (when you work more than 40 hours a week) *Do you get paid more or less for overtime?* (more)
3. Tell students to write answers to the questions on a piece of paper.
4. Read the questions and call on students to say the answers.

Ⓒ DETERMINE. Read Alex's pay stub. Answer...

1. Read the directions.
2. Students compare answers with a partner. Tell them to take turns asking and answering the questions.
3. Read the questions and call on students to say the answers.
4. Ask: *How many deductions were taken out of Alex's paycheck?* (four) *What were they?* (federal tax, state tax, Social Security, and Medicare)
5. Explain: *Social Security and Medicare taxes are employment taxes collected by the U.S. government. FICA, or Federal Insurance Contributions Act, is the law that requires employees and employers to pay Social Security and Medicare taxes.*

Ⓓ IDENTIFY. Look at Alex's pay stub. How...

1. Read the note about overtime pay again. Write: *overtime = 1.5 x regular hourly rate of pay.*
2. Use the Numeracy box to show students how to calculate overtime hourly rate.
3. Remind students how to calculate earnings, or gross pay. Say: *We learned how to calculate gross pay in Exercise 1A.* Write: *hours x rate = earnings.* Ask: *How can we calculate the rate of pay? What equation can we use?* Elicit or write: *earnings / hours = rate.*
4. Explain: *We can do the same to find overtime pay.* Use the Numeracy box. Write:
   overtime pay / overtime hours = overtime rate
   _____ / _____ = _____
5. Point to the first blank, then the second blank. Ask: *What is Alex's overtime pay? How many overtime hours did he work?* Write the values in the blanks. Pair students and tell students to calculate Alex's overtime rate.

6. Ask two students to show how to calculate Alex's overtime pay rate on the board: *$180 ÷ 10 = $18/hour.*

Numeracy: Math skills

For students to calculate overtime hourly rate, write the following:

Total overtime pay	÷	Number of hours	=	Overtime hourly rate
$63	÷	3	=	$21/hour

■ **EXPANSION: Numeracy practice for 2D**
Change the number of hours that Alex worked. Ask students to calculate the new earnings and then the total gross pay.

■ **EXPANSION: Numeracy practice for 2D**

1. Remind students that overtime pay is one and a half times your regular rate of pay.
   rate of pay x 1.5 = overtime rate
2. Tells students to look back at Exercise 1A. Ask: *What is Kim Martin's rate of pay?* ($12.25) Tell students to calculate her overtime rate. ($18.375)

Ⓔ GO ONLINE. Search for other common...

1. Read the directions. Ask students what they would search in English for information about common deductions on pay stubs.
2. Write the search string: *common pay stub deductions.* Have students search the internet and choose a specific deduction to read about.
3. Compare research as a class.

Digital Skills for 2E

1. Say: *State income tax rates vary in the U.S. from state to state. In fact, some states have no state income tax.* Tell students to go online and search for the state income tax rate in the state they are in and four other states.
2. Have students compare their research as a class.

 ActiveTeach: Review

Self-Directed Learning

Point out the blue bar. Ask students if they can do the lesson learning objective or if they need more practice. Tell them to check one of the boxes. Assign Extra Practice as needed.

Extra Practice

  pp. 137–138 Life Skills Writing

Workplace, Life, and Community Skills

2 UNDERSTAND PAYROLL DEDUCTIONS AND OVERTIME HOURS

A **MATCH. Look at the pay stub again. Match the deductions with the definitions.**

1. _e_ Federal tax
2. _a_ State tax
3. _b_ Social Security
4. _d_ Medicare
5. _c_ State Disability Insurance (SDI)

a. tax you pay the state government
b. money for older people not working now
c. money for workers who are disabled and can't work
d. money for health care for older people
e. tax you pay the U.S. government

B **INTERPRET. Read the excerpt from the employee handbook. Answer the questions.**

1. When does an employee get overtime pay?
   When he or she works more than 40 hours a week.
2. How many hours are in a standard work week? 40 hours a week.
3. What is the pay rate for overtime pay?
   One and a half times the regular hourly rate.

> *Overtime Policy*
> *When you are approved to work more than 40 hours a week, you earn overtime pay. Overtime pay is paid at one and a half times your regular hourly rate.*

C **DETERMINE. Read Alex's pay stub. Answer the questions.**

Name	Pay Date	Pay Period	Rate of Pay
Alex Smith	12/22	12/02–12/16	$12.00

Description	Hours	Earnings	Deduction		Amount
Regular	80	$960.00	Federal tax		$114.00
Overtime	10	$180.00	State tax		$57.00
			FICA	Social Security	$85.50
				Medicare	$20.50

Total Gross Pay	$1,140.00	**Total Deductions**	$277.00	**Net Pay**	$863.00

1. How many deductions were taken out of Alex's pay stub? Four.
2. Which deduction totaled $114? Federal tax
3. How many overtime hours did he work? Ten.
4. What two deductions are a part of FICA? Social security and Medicare.
5. How much money was taken out in deductions? $277.00.
6. How much money did he get after deductions? $863.00.

D **IDENTIFY. Look at Alex's pay stub. How much was Alex paid per hour for overtime?** $18 an hour

E **GO ONLINE. Search for other common deductions that can appear on a pay stub. Have you seen any of them before? Choose one deduction and explain it to your partner.**

I can understand payroll deductions and overtime hours. ■   I need more practice. ■

For more practice, go to MyEnglishLab.

Listening and Speaking

Ask a co-worker to cover your hours

1 BEFORE YOU LISTEN

DISCUSS. What should employees do if they are going to miss work?

2 LISTEN

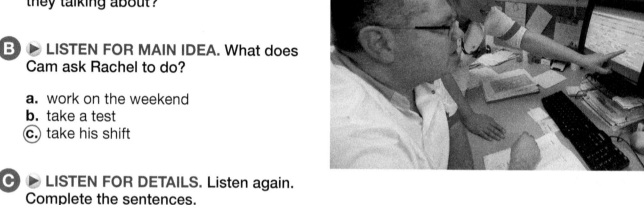

Cam   Rachel

A **PREDICT.** Look at the picture. What are they talking about?

B ▶ **LISTEN FOR MAIN IDEA.** What does Cam ask Rachel to do?

   a. work on the weekend
   b. take a test
   c. take his shift

C ▶ **LISTEN FOR DETAILS.** Listen again. Complete the sentences.

   1. Cam _____ work on Monday.
     a. wants to   **b.** can't   **c.** doesn't have to

   2. Rachel _____ take Cam's shift.
     a. is going to   **b.** can't   **c.** must not

D ▶ **EXPAND.** Listen to the whole conversation. Complete the sentences.

   1. Cam and Rachel check the schedule to see _____.
     a. who is working that day   **b.** what time the shift starts   **c.** what time the shift ends

   2. Rachel _____ work with Tim.
     a. doesn't want to   **b.** likes to   **c.** doesn't like to

Correlations

ELPS Level 2: 1, 2, 3, 4, 5, 6, 7, 8, 9, 10
CCRS Level A: SL.K.3
CASAS Reading: RDG 1.7, 2.3
CASAS Listening: L1.4, 2.1, 2.3, 4.2, 6.1, 6.2, 6.5
CASAS Competencies: 0.1.2, 0.1.4, 0.1.5, 0.1.6, 4.1.6, 4.6.5
Complete standards language available on the Pearson English Portal.

Self-Directed Learning

State the **lesson objective**. Say: *In this lesson, we will learn to ask a co-worker to cover our hours.*

1 BEFORE YOU LISTEN

DISCUSS. What should employees do if they...

1. Ask the question in the directions.
2. Form groups of 3. Tell groups to assign a recorder, listener, and reporter.
3. Tell groups to brainstorm and reporters to list their group's ideas (for example, *call as soon as they know they will miss work, ask another employee to work their shift, trade shifts with another employee, find another solution for a personal situation to avoid missing work*).
4. Ask: *What should employees do if they are going to miss work?* Call on the reporter from each group to say one idea. To avoid repetition, tell the listeners to look at the group's list and make checkmarks next to ideas other groups say.

2 LISTEN

A PREDICT. Look at the picture. What are...

1. Tell students to look at the picture. Ask: *Who do you see?* (two workers, Cam and Rachel) *Where are they?* (in an office at work) *What are they looking at?* (a schedule/calendar on the computer)
2. Ask: *What are they talking about?* Elicit ideas and write them. (the schedule, changing a shift)

B ▶ LISTEN FOR MAIN IDEA. What does Cam...

1. Tell students to read the directions and answer choices silently.
2. Play the audio. Students listen and choose the answer.
3. Students compare answers with a partner.

4. Ask: *Was your guess in Exercise 2A correct?* Ask for a show of hands.
5. Ask about **register**: *How does Cam ask Rachel to do something for him?* (Can I ask you a favor?) *What does Rachel say to show she is happy to do Cam a favor?* (Sure.)

C ▶ LISTEN FOR DETAILS. Listen again...

1. Read the directions. Tell students to read the sentences silently.
2. Play the audio. Students listen and choose the answers.
3. Play the audio again to aid comprehension. Students compare answers with a partner. Tell them to take turns reading the sentences.
4. Call on students to read the sentences.

Teaching Tip: Use the script

Optional: If students need additional support, tell them to read the Audio Script on page 275 as they listen to the conversations.

D ▶ EXPAND. Listen to the whole...

1. Read the directions. Tell students to read the answer choices silently.
2. Play the audio. Students choose the correct answers.
3. Ask: *Do you need to listen one more time?* If yes, play the audio again.
4. Call on students to read the completed sentences.
5. **Extend:** Ask: *Do you ever ask co-workers to cover your hours/shift? Do you ever cover hours for your co-workers? Are there some co-workers you prefer to work with? Why? What makes a good co-worker?*

Workplace Culture

1. Say: *In the U.S., in some jobs it is okay and even better if employees to find their own substitutes when they cannot work. They should check first with their supervisors to make sure it's okay to find a substitute. They should also check that their substitute is appropriate.*
2. Ask: *In your native country, is it okay for employees to find their own substitutes if they cannot work?*

Listening and Speaking

3 PRONUNCIATION

Ⓐ ▶ PRACTICE. Listen. Then listen and repeat.

1. Read the directions. Then read the **Pronunciation Note**.
2. *Optional:* Ask: *What kind of intonation do* yes/no *questions have?* (rising intonation) *What kind of intonation do information questions and statements have?* (falling intonation)
3. Tell students to look at the sentences. Say: *Point to the information questions. Point to the statements.*
4. Show the sentences on the board and mark the intonation. For each sentence, ask: *What's the most important word in the sentence?* (up, start, study, 9:30)
5. Read the directions. Say: *Listen for the voice to jump up on the most important word in each sentence and then go down at the end of each sentence.*
6. Play the audio. Students listen. Then students listen and repeat.

 ActiveTeach for 3A: Pronunciation Coach

Ⓑ ▶ APPLY. Listen. Use an arrow to mark…

1. Read the directions.
2. Play the audio. Students listen and mark the intonation with an arrow.
3. Write the sentences. Call on students to use an arrow to mark where the voice goes down. Ask: *What is the most important word in each sentence?*
4. Say each sentence and ask the class to repeat.

4 CONVERSATION

Ⓐ ▶ LISTEN AND READ. Then listen and repeat.

1. Note: This conversation is the same one students heard in Exercise 2B on page 234.
2. Tell students to read the conversation silently, find the *yes/no* questions, and mark the rising intonation. (*Can I ask you a favor? Can you take my shift for me?*) Tell them to find the information questions and mark the falling intonation.
(*What is it? What's up? What time do you start?*)
3. Write these statements: *I'm on the schedule for Monday, but I can't come in. I have to study for a test.* Mark the falling intonation and ask the class to repeat. Tell students to mark the intonation in the conversation.

4. Play the audio. Students read along silently. Then students listen and repeat. Walk around and make sure students are using the correct intonation.

Ⓑ WORK TOGETHER. Practice the…

1. Pair students and tell them to practice the conversation in Exercise 4A.
2. Tell students to take turns playing A and B. Walk around and help with intonation as needed.

Ⓒ CREATE. Make new conversations. Use the…

1. Read the directions.
2. Tell students to look at the information in the boxes. Write the blue questions on the board. Ask: *Rising or falling intonation?* Mark the falling intonation. Say the questions and ask the class to repeat.
3. Say the yellow phrases and ask the class to repeat.
4. Show the conversation on the board with blanks.
5. Erase the words in the blanks and ask two on-level students to make up a new conversation in front of the class.
6. Tell pairs to take turns playing A and B. Tell them to use their names and the information in the boxes to fill in the blanks. Walk around and check students' intonation.

Ⓓ ROLE-PLAY. Make your own conversations.

1. Read the directions.
2. Brainstorm and write different reasons for missing work. Begin each reason with the base form of a verb (for example, *go to my daughter's parent-teacher conference, go to the doctor, study for a test, stay home and wait for the plumber*). If possible, draw a yellow box around the list.
3. Pair students and tell them to practice the conversation, using information you wrote or their own information.
4. Walk around and remind students to switch roles. Check that students are using correct intonation.

Self-Directed Learning

Point out the blue bar. Ask students if they can do the lesson learning objective or if they need more practice. Tell them to check one of the boxes. Assign Extra Practice as needed.

Extra Practice

  pp. 139–140

Listening and Speaking

3 PRONUNCIATION

A ▶ PRACTICE. Listen. Then listen and repeat.

What's up?

What time do you start?

I have to study.

I start at 9:30.

Intonation in information questions and statements

In information questions and statements, the voice usually jumps up on the most important word in the sentence and then goes down at the end.

B ▶ APPLY. Listen. Use an arrow to mark where the voice goes down.

1. What's the favor?
2. I can take your shift.
3. I have to work.
4. Who is on the schedule?

4 CONVERSATION

A ▶ LISTEN AND READ. Then listen and repeat.

A: Hi, Rachel. Can I ask you a favor?
B: Sure. What is it?
A: I'm on the schedule for Monday, but I can't come in.
B: Oh, what's up?
A: I have to study for a test. Can you take my shift for me?
B: What time do you start?
A: 9:30.
B: No problem.

B WORK TOGETHER. Practice the conversation in Exercise A.

C CREATE. Make new conversations. Use the words in the boxes.

A: Hi, _____. Can I ask you a favor?
B: Sure. What is it?
A: I'm on the schedule for Monday, but I can't come in.
B: Oh. _____
A: I have to _____. Can you take my shift for me?
B: What time do you start?
A: 9:30.
B: No problem.

What's going on?	babysit my niece
What's happening?	go to the dentist
Why not?	pick up my in-laws at the airport

D ROLE-PLAY. Make your own conversations.

I can ask a co-worker to cover my hours. ■

I need more practice. ■

For more practice, go to MyEnglishLab.

Lesson 6 — Information questions with *Who / What / Which / When / Where*

Information questions with *Who*			Grammar Watch

Who = subject		Answer
Who	**works** on Monday? **collects** the timesheets?	**Cam** works on Monday. **Your supervisor** collects the timesheets.

Who = object			Answer
Who	**does** Cam **do** I	**work** with? **give** my timesheet to?	Cam works with **Rachel**. You give it to **your supervisor**.

Grammar Watch

- To ask about the subject, use *Who* + a verb.
- To ask about the object, use *Who* + a helping verb + a subject + a verb.

A APPLY. Put the words in order and write the questions. Capitalize the first word.

1. who / extra hours / needs — *Who needs extra hours?*
2. I / ask / who / do / about sick time — Who do I ask about sick time?
3. the schedule / makes up / who — Who makes up the schedule?
4. I / call / do / who / about trading shifts — Who do I call about trading shifts?
5. goes / on break / who / at 10:45 A.M. — Who goes on break at 10:45 A.M.?

B WRITE. Read the answer. Then write questions with *Who* to ask for the underlined information.

1. **A:** *Who needs a favor?*

   B: <u>Your co-worker</u> needs a favor.

2. **A:** Who do you usually work with?

   B: I usually work with <u>another associate</u>.

3. **A:** Who wants to talk to Jim?

   B: <u>The supervisor</u> wants to talk to Jim.

4. **A:** Who do they need to see?

   B: They need to see <u>their manager</u>.

5. **A:** Who helps you?

   B: <u>Someone</u> in the warehouse usually helps me.

Correlations

ELPS Level 2: 1, 2, 3, 4, 5, 6, 7, 8, 9, 10
CCRS Level A: L.1.1, L.1.2
CASAS Reading: RDG 1.7, 2.9, 3.4
CASAS Listening: L2.1, 2.3, 3.6
CASAS Competencies: 0.1.2, 0.1.5, 0.1.6
Complete standards language available on the Pearson English Portal.

Self-Directed Learning

State the **lesson objective**. Say: *In this lesson, we will learn to make information questions with* who / what / which / when / where.

Information questions with *Who*

 ActiveTeach: Grammar Discovery

1. Warm up. Write:
   • *By the way, who's working that day?*
   Underline *who's working*.
2. Tell students to look at the grammar charts. Read questions and answers and ask the class to repeat.
3. Point to the answer charts on the right. Read each answer and ask: *Who?* Underline: *Cam, Your supervisor, Rachel,* and *your supervisor.* Point to the underlined people in the first two answers and say: *They are subjects.* Point to the underlined people in the last two answers and say: *They are objects.* Tell students to circle the headings *Who = subject* and *Who = object* in their books.
4. Point to the question charts on the left. Read the questions in the bottom left chart. Say: *When* who *is the object of the question, use normal question word order.* Write: Who + does, do, *or* did + *subject + base form of verb.*
5. Read the questions in the top left chart. Say: *When* who *is the subject of the question, don't use* does, do, *or* did. *Don't change the verb, except to make third-person plural verbs singular.* Write: Who + verb. Then write: *Cam* works *on Mondays.* → *Who* works *on Mondays? / Cam and I* work *on Mondays* → *Who* works *on Mondays.*
6. Read the first point of the **Grammar Watch** note. Then read the questions and answers in the top grammar charts and ask the class to repeat.
7. Read the second point of the **Grammar Watch** note. Ask: *What are the helping verbs?* (*does, do,* and *did*) Then read the questions and answers in the bottom grammar charts. Ask the class to repeat.

 ActiveTeach: Grammar Coach

A APPLY. Put the words in order and write…
1. Read the directions.
2. Tell students to read the **Grammar Watch** note again and underline Who + *a verb* and Who + *a helping verb + a subject + a verb.*
3. Show the example on the board. Point to *Who* and *needs* in the answer and say: Who + *a verb.*
4. Tell students to find items in the exercise that have *do* and to mark those sentences *Object.* Tell them to review the grammar charts as they do the exercise.
5. Walk around and spot-check for capitalization. Remind students to use questions marks. If students have difficulty, suggest that they cross out the words as they use them.
6. Students compare answers with a partner. Tell them to take turns reading the questions.
7. Call on students to read the questions.

■ **EXPANSION: Grammar practice for A**
1. Tell pairs to write answers to the questions in Exercise A. Tell them to use classmates' names (for example, *Sergio needs extra hours. Ask Minh about sick time.*).
2. Call on pairs to read questions and answers.

B WRITE. Read the answer. Then write…
1. Read the directions. Show item 1 and point to the answer. Ask: *Why is the answer* Who needs a favor? (because *Your co-worker* is the subject) Ask two students to read the example.
2. Say: *Before you write a question, look at the underlined information in B's response. Decide if it's the subject or the object.* Tell students that if a noun follows a verb or a preposition it is an object. Read the **Grammar Watch** note again.
3. Students compare answers with a partner by reading the conversations. Walk around and spot-check for capitalization and question marks.
4. Call on pairs to read the conversations. Write the questions. Discuss any errors.

Information questions with *What / Which / When / Where*

 ActiveTeach: Grammar Discovery

1. Say: *Now we're going to study information questions with* What, Which, When, *and* Where.
2. Tell students to look at the grammar charts on page 237. Read the questions and answers and tell the class to repeat.
3. Tell students to look back at the **Grammar Watch** note on page 236. Ask the class: *Which pattern do these questions follow?* Write: *question word + a helping verb + a subject + a verb.* Ask: *What are the helping verbs?* List *does, do,* and *did* under *a helping verb.* Ask: *What form of the verb do you use?* Write *base form* under *a verb.* Tell students to underline the base forms of the verbs in the chart.
4. Tell students to close their books. Write: *What time, Which days, When,* and *Where.* Say: *at 3:00 p.m., Monday and Friday, in five minutes,* and *in a warehouse* and ask the class to call out the question word(s).

 ActiveTeach: Grammar Coach

C **WRITE. Make information questions. Use...**

1. Read the directions. Tell students to underline the question words in the directions.
2. Ask two students to read the example. Repeat the question. Point to *question word + a helping verb + a subject + a verb* on the board. Ask the class: *What are the question words?* (*Which day*) *What's the helping verb?* (*do*) *What's the subject?* (*you*) *What's the verb?* (*have off*) As students answer, write each word or phrase from the question under its corresponding label.
3. Tell students to first look at the responses and decide *what time, which, when,* or *where.*
4. Walk around and spot-check for capitalization and question marks.
5. Students compare answers with a partner by reading the conversations.
6. Call on pairs to read the conversations for the class. Write the questions. Discuss any errors.

Show what you know!

1. TALK ABOUT IT. Look at the employee work...

1. Tell students to look at the employee work schedule.
2. Give students time to study the schedule. Ask questions: *How many employees are there?* (six) *What are their names?* (Eduardo, Stan, Deng, Ivan, Marco, Will). *How long is the work schedule for?* (one week) *How many days off does each employee get this week?* (two)
3. Read the directions. Model the example with an above-level student.
4. Pair students. Tell them to take turns. Say: *Ask at least four questions.*
5. Students switch partners and repeat. They can ask the same questions or come up with new ones.

■ **EXPANSION: Speaking practice for 1**
Tell pairs to choose two employees with different hours from the work schedule and to role-play asking their partner to cover their hours. As a class, brainstorm ways to begin the conversation (for example, *Can you help me? I have to work on Friday, but...*)

2. WRITE ABOUT IT. Now write three questions...

1. Read the directions.
2. Tell students to use ideas from Steps 1 and 2 to write three questions on a sheet of notebook paper.
3. Students exchange papers with a partner and check each other's questions.
   - Questions should use the correct form of the helping verb.
   - Questions should begin with a capital letter.
   - Questions should end with a question mark.
4. Have students volunteer to write their questions on the board.

Self-Directed Learning
Point out the blue bar. Ask students if they can do the lesson learning objective or if they need more practice. Tell them to check one of the boxes. Assign Extra Practice as needed.

Extra Practice

  pp. 139–140

Grammar

Information questions with *What* / *Which* / *When* / *Where*

Questions				Answers
What time		my shift	**begin**?	At 3:00 p.m.
Which days	**do**	I	**have** off?	Monday and Friday.
When	**does**	you	**start** your break?	In five minutes.
Where		he	**work**?	In a warehouse.

C **WRITE. Make information questions. Use *What time*, *Which*, *When*, *Where* and the words in parentheses.**

1. **A:** (day / you / have off) _Which day do you have off?_

   B: Tuesday.

2. **A:** (your shift / start) _What time does your shift start?_

   B: At 3:00 P.M.

3. **A:** (I / get / a vacation) _When do I get a vacation?_

   B: After six months on the job.

4. **A:** (I / clock in) _Where do I you clock in?_

   B: Outside the employee break room. The time clock is on the wall.

5. **A:** (we / get / breaks) _What time do we get breaks?_

   B: At 10:15 A.M. and 2:30 P.M.

Show what you know!

1. **TALK ABOUT IT. Look at the employee work schedule. Take turns. Ask and answer questions. Use *What*, *Which*, *What time*, and *When*.**

   A: *What does Marco do?*
   B: *He's a cashier.*
   A: *What time does he start work?*
   B: *At 8:00.*

2. **WRITE ABOUT IT. Now write three questions that you asked.**

	Mon.	Tues.	Wed.	Thu.	Fri.	Sat.	Sun.
Eduardo, stock clerk	OFF	OFF	6–2 Break: 11–11:30	6–2 Break: 11–11:30	6–2 Break: 11–11:30	6–2 Break: 11–11:30	6–2 Break: 11–11:30
Stan, stock clerk	OFF	OFF	6–1 Break: 11–11:30	6–1 Break: 11–11:30	6–1 Break: 11–11:30	6–2 Break: 11–11:30	6–2 Break: 11–11:30
Deng, stock clerk	6–2 Break: 12–12:30	6–2 Break: 12–12:30	6–1 Break: 12–12:30	6–1 Break: 12–12:30	OFF	OFF	6–2 Break: 12–12:30
Ivan, cashier	OFF	OFF	8-2 Break: 11–11:30	8-2 Break: 11–11:30	8-2 Break: 11–11:30	8-2 Break: 11–11:30	8-2 Break: 11–11:30
Marco, cashier	8–2 Break: 12–12:30	8–2 Break: 12–12:30	8–2 Break: 12–12:30	8–2 Break: 12–12:30	OFF	OFF	8–2 Break: 12–12:30
Will, cashier	OFF	9–2 Break: 12–12:30	9–2 Break: 12–12:30	9–2 Break: 12–12:30	9–2 Break: 12–12:30	OFF	9–2 Break: 12–12:30

I can make information questions with *who* / *what* / *which* / *when* / *where*. ■   I need more practice. ■

For more practice, go to MyEnglishLab.

Read about the Social Security program

1 BEFORE YOU READ

A **COMPLETE. Use the words in the box to complete the sentences.**

disabled   earnings   qualify   retired   spouse

1. Your husband or wife is your _____spouse_____ .
2. Ann stopped working at age 66. Now she's _____retired_____ .
3. Ed was in a car accident. Now he can't walk. He's _____disabled_____ .
4. The money you get for the work you do is your _____earnings_____ .
5. If you _____qualify_____ for something (like a bank loan or free health insurance), then you can get it.

B **MAKE CONNECTIONS. What is Social Security? Who can have a Social Security card?**

2 READ

▶ **Listen and read.**

Academic Skill: Think about what you know
Before you read, think about what you already know about the topic.

Social Security Fact Sheet HOME | CONTACT US | HELP 🔍 Search

1 **What is Social Security?**
Social Security is a U.S. government program. It pays money, called *benefits*, to people. There are several ways a person can qualify for benefits. Most of the people who get them are age 62 or older. Often, they are retired. Some of the people are
5 disabled and can't work. Some are family members of workers who died.

How did it start?
The U.S. government created Social Security in 1935. It was during the Great Depression. Many people couldn't find jobs. Many were poor. Life was very hard for many older people. Social Security was created to help.

How does Social Security work?
10 Workers pay a Social Security tax. Employers take the money out of workers' paychecks and send it to the government. The government uses the money to pay benefits.

How much tax do people pay?
Workers pay 6.2 percent of their earnings. Their employers pay another 6.2 percent. Self-employed workers pay 12.4 percent of their earnings.

15 **Can everyone get Social Security benefits when they retire?**
No. You, or your spouse, have to work and pay Social Security taxes for ten years. Then you qualify to get retirement benefits.

Can a noncitizen get retirement benefits?
Yes. Any person who works legally in the U.S. and pays Social Security taxes for ten years can get them.

Does everyone get the same amount?
20 No. Some people pay more Social Security taxes than others. That's because they work longer or make more money. So they qualify for more money when they retire. The average benefit for a retired worker is now over $1,400 a month.

Lesson 7 | Reading

Correlations

ELPS Level 2: 1, 2, 3, 4, 5, 6, 7, 8, 9, 10
CCRS Level A: RI/RL.1.1, RI.1.2, RI.1.4, SL.K.2, SL.1.4
CASAS Reading: RDG 1.7, 1.8, 2.3, 3.2, 3.7, 3.11, 4.2
CASAS Listening: L2.1, 2.3, 4.2, 5.8, 6.1, 6.2
CASAS Competencies: 0.1.2, 0.1.5, 2.5.2
Complete standards language available on the Pearson English Portal.

Self-Directed Learning

1. State the **lesson objective**. Say: *In this lesson, we will learn to think about what we know before reading.*
2. Say: *We will read about the Social Security program.*

1 BEFORE YOU READ

A COMPLETE. Use the words in the box to...

1. Read the directions. Say the words in the box or call on a student to say them.
2. Read the first sentence. Ask: *What word means the same thing as a husband or a wife?* (spouse) Tell students to write *spouse* to complete the sentence.
3. Tell students to complete the sentences.
4. Call on students to read the completed sentences aloud.

B MAKE CONNECTIONS. What is Social...

1. Tell students to look at the picture. Ask: *What is she holding?* (a Social Security card)
2. Read the directions.
3. Tell students to look back at Exercise 2A on page 233. Ask: *What is Social Security?* (money for older people not working now) Ask: *Who can have a Social Security card?*
4. Elicit ideas and write them.

2 READ

▶ **Listen and read.**

1. Point to the **Academic Skill** and read it or ask a student to read it. Ask: *Why do you think it is helpful to think about what you already know before reading?* Elicit or point out that it may help you anticipate vocabulary, be better prepared for the content of the reading, and have a reason to find out more about a topic. Point out that Exercise 1B helped start the process of thinking about what they already know.
2. Say: *Let's think about what you already know about Social Security before you read about it.*

3. Draw a K-W-L chart (a three-column chart with the headings *Know, Want to Know,* and *Learned*). Under *Know,* list: *government program* and *money for older people not working now.* Ask: *What else do you know about Social Security?* Add students' ideas under *Know* (for example, *a U.S. government program, for retired people*).
4. Point to the second column in the chart and ask: *What do you want to know about Social Security?* Elicit a couple of questions and write them in the chart (for example, *How old do you have to be to get it? Do you have to be a U.S. citizen?*).
5. Introduce the visual. Ask: *What visual do you see?* (a photo of an older man with a child, maybe grandfather and grandson)
6. Introduce the reading. Tell the class to look at the reading. Ask: *Where can you find this information?* (online) *What is the title?* (Social Security Fact Sheet) Ask: *What is a fact sheet?* (a list of important information about a topic)
7. Ask: *What questions do you see about Social Security?* (What is Social Security? How did Social Security start? How does Social Security work? How much do people pay? etc.) Tell students to look at the K-W-L chart. Ask: *Are any of these questions the same as the questions in our chart?*

 ActiveTeach for 2: Anticipation Guide – *Before* Reading exercise

8. Read the text.
   a. Have an above-level student read the answer to the first question in the fact sheet. Ask: *Do you have to be 62 or older to receive Social Security benefits?* (no)
   b. Say: *Now we are going to read and listen to the information.*
   c. Play the audio as students listen and read along silently.
   d. Read your class's questions in the *Want to know* column of the chart. Play the audio again. Pause after each question and answer and ask if an answer was given to a question in the chart. Tell students to mark the text. Write answers under *Learned* in the chart. Ask: *What else did you learn?* For each question and answer in the reading, write one thing students learned in the chart. Tell students to underline the information listed in the *Learned* column.

 ActiveTeach for 2: Anticipation Guide – *After* Reading exercise

3 CLOSE READING

A IDENTIFY. What is the main idea?
1. Say: *Now we are going to identify the main idea.*
2. Read the directions. Have students circle the answer.
3. Elicit the answer from the class.

B CITE EVIDENCE. Complete the statements...
1. Say: *Now we are going to find information in the reading.*
2. Read the directions. Walk around as students work on the activity. If students are struggling, have them work in pairs or direct them to the text lines where they can find the information.
3. Call on students to read the sentence with the correct completion. Ask a different student: *Where is that information? What line number?*

4 SUMMARIZE

 ActiveTeach for 4: Vocabulary Practice

1. Read the directions. Ask students to read aloud the words in the box.
2. Tell students to complete the paragraph.
3. To check answers, call on students to read sentences in the summary with the blanks filled in. Ask other students to read the completed summary silently.

Culture Note
1. Say: *In the U.S., people who are over the age of 65 are called "seniors." In many communities, seniors can get benefits. For example, they pay less at the movies or pay less for transportation. They also can get free or almost free medical care.*
2. Ask: *At what age are people seniors in your native country? What benefits can seniors get?*

Show what you know!

1. THINK ABOUT IT. In your native country,...
1. Read the directions.
2. Model the activity. Ask an above-level student to talk about programs in his/her native country for older workers.
3. Tell students to take notes in answer to the questions.

2. WRITE ABOUT IT. Write your opinion of...
1. Read the directions.
2. Write the sentence frame. Call on an above-level student to say one thing about the Social Security program.
3. Give students time to complete the sentence frame with as many benefits as they can.
4. Call on students to read their sentences.

3. PRESENT IT. Compare retirement in your...
1. Read the directions.
2. Make a T-chart with the headings *U.S.* and *My Native Country*. Call on a student to say one thing about the U.S. and one thing about his/her native country. Write them in the chart.
3. Tell students to make T-charts and fill them in. If possible, tell students to compare their ideas with a partner from the same native country.
4. Form groups of students from different countries. Tell them to take turns giving short presentations.
5. Call on students to present to the class.

 ActiveTeach for 3: Academic Conversation Support

Self-Directed Learning
Point out the blue bar. Ask students if they can do the lesson learning objective or if they need more practice. Tell them to check one of the boxes. Assign Extra Practice as needed.

■ **EXPANSION: Self-directed learning**
Ask students to reflect: *What did you learn from this reading?* Call on students to share something they learned.

Extra Practice
 CCRS Plus   pp. 141–142

Reading

3 CLOSE READING

A IDENTIFY. What is the main idea?

Social Security is a U.S. government program that _____.
a. helps Americans who lose their jobs
b. takes money out of workers' paychecks
c. uses tax dollars to support retired or disabled people

B CITE EVIDENCE. Complete the statements. Where is the information? Write the line numbers.

Lines

1. The only way you can get Social Security benefits is to _____.
   a. be over age 62   b. be disabled   c. qualify   __2–3__
2. If a worker dies, his or her young children _____ Social Security benefits.
   a. can get   b. cannot get   c. have to pay for   __5__
3. Workers pay Social Security tax _____.
   a. in some states   b. out of every   c. on April 15   __10__
      but not others   paycheck   ("Tax Day")
4. To qualify for retirement benefits, you (or your spouse) have to pay Social Security taxes for _____ years.
   a. ten   b. twenty   c. forty   __16__
5. You _____ a U.S. citizen to get retirement benefits from Social Security.
   a. must be   b. don't have to be   c. can't be   __18__
6. Some retired people get a bigger Social Security check than others because _____.
   a. they need more   b. they paid the   c. they worked   __20__
      money to live on   higher 12.4% tax   longer

4 SUMMARIZE

Complete the summary with the words in the box.

benefits   disabled   retired   tax

Social Security is a U.S. government program that makes payments called
(1) ___benefits___ to people who qualify. Some of these people can't work because
they're (2) ___disabled___. Most of them are (3) ___retired___. The money to pay
benefits comes from a (4) ___tax___ on workers' earnings.

Show what you know!

1. **THINK ABOUT IT.** In your native country, what do older people do when they cannot work? Is there a program like Social Security?

2. **WRITE ABOUT IT.** Write your opinion of the Social Security program.

   In my opinion, Social Security is helpful because _____.

3. **PRESENT IT.** Compare retirement in your native country with retirement in the United States. Make a short presentation about government programs to support retired people.

I can think about what I know before reading. ■   I need more practice. ■

To read more, go to MyEnglishLab.

8 Request a schedule change

1 BEFORE YOU LISTEN

A **READ.** Look at some reasons that people change their work schedules.

My son is starting school.

I'm taking classes now.

My wife needs the car during the day.

My husband's work schedule changed.

B **DISCUSS.** What are some other reasons?

2 LISTEN

A **PREDICT.** Look at the picture. Who is Ron?

a. Linda's manager
b. Linda's customer
c. Linda's friend

Ron   Linda

B ▶ **LISTEN FOR MAIN IDEA.** What does Linda want to do?

a. work fewer hours
b. change her schedule
c. work in the morning

C ▶ **LISTEN FOR DETAILS.** Listen again. Answer the questions.

1. When does Linda work now?
   a. mornings   b. afternoons   c. evenings

2. Why does she ask for a schedule change?
   a. She wants to take classes.
   b. Her husband is taking classes.
   c. Her son's classes are in the mornings.

D ▶ **EXPAND.** Listen to the whole conversation. What kind of classes is Linda planning to take? She's planning to take business classes.

Correlations

ELPS Level 2: 2, 7
CCRS Level A: SL.1.1, SL.K.3, SL.K.6
CASAS Reading: RDG 1.7, 2.3
CASAS Listening: L1.4, 2.1, 2.3, 4.1, 4.2, 6.1, 6.2, 6.5
CASAS Competencies: 0.1.2, 0.1.4, 0.1.5, 0.1.6, 4.1.6, 4.6.5
Complete standards language available on the Pearson English Portal.

Self-Directed Learning

State the **lesson objective**. Say: *In this lesson, we will learn to request a schedule change.*

1 BEFORE YOU LISTEN

A READ. Look at some reasons that people…

1. Read the directions.
2. Call on students to read each reason.
3. Ask: *Which reasons do you think are the most common?*

Teaching Tip: Personalize

When students connect personally to the topic, they understand and remember better. Pair students to talk about which reasons they connect to the most.

B DISCUSS. What are some other reasons?

1. Ask: *What are some other reasons that people change their work schedules?* Write students' ideas (for example, *I want to work part-time/full-time. My child-care situation changed. I want to be home with my children after school. I need to get a ride with another employee.*).
2. *Optional:* Ask: *Have you ever asked to change your work schedule? What was the reason?*

2 LISTEN

A PREDICT. Look at the picture. Who is Ron?

1. Tell students to look at the picture. Ask: *Who do you see?* (Ron and Linda) *Where are they?* (at work, in a garage, at a car repair place) *What are they looking at?* (a schedule, some paperwork)
2. Tell students to read the answer choices silently. Ask: *Do you think Ron is Linda's manager?* Ask for a show of hands. Repeat with *Linda's customer* and *Linda's friend*.

B ▶ LISTEN FOR MAIN IDEA. What does…

1. Tell students to read the directions and answer choices silently.
2. Play the audio. Students listen and choose the answer.
3. Students compare answers with a partner.
4. Ask about **register**: *How does Linda interrupt Ron politely?* (Excuse me, Ron.) *How does she ask if she can talk to him?* (Can I speak to you for a minute?) *Is her language informal?* (No. It's formal—the sort of language used by an employee to a manager.)

C ▶ LISTEN FOR DETAILS. Listen again…

1. Read the directions. Tell students to read the questions and answer choices silently.
2. Play the audio. Students listen and answer the questions.
3. Tell students to ask and answer the questions with a partner.
4. Call on students to read the questions and answers.

Teaching Tip: Use the script

Optional: If students need additional support, tell them to read the Audio Script on page 275 as they listen to the conversations.

D ▶ EXPAND. Listen to the whole…

1. Read the directions.
2. Play the audio. Students listen for the answer.
3. Read the question again. Call on a student to say the answer.
4. **Extend:** Ask: *Why is Linda taking business classes?* (because she wants to be a manager) *What kinds of classes would help you get a better job?*

Workplace Culture

1. Say: *In the U.S., some employers will pay for their workers to take classes to increase their knowledge and improve their qualifications. This can be a benefit for both the employer and the worker.*
2. Ask: *In your native country, do employers ever pay for classes for their workers? Why or why not?*

Listening and Speaking

3 CONVERSATION

A ▶ LISTEN AND READ. Then listen and repeat.

1. Note: This conversation is the same one students heard in Exercise 2B on page 240.
2. Read the directions. Tell students to underline the questions in the conversation. Then tell students to mark where the voice goes up or down.
3. Play the audio. Students listen and read silently. Then students listen and repeat.

B WORK TOGETHER. Practice the...

1. Pair students and tell them to practice the conversation in Exercise 3A.
2. Tell students to take turns playing A and B. Walk around and help with pronunciation and intonation as needed.

C CREATE. Make new conversations. Use...

1. Read the directions. Tell students to look at the information in the boxes. Call on students to read each item.
2. Show the conversation on the board with blanks. Read through the conversation. When you come to a blank, fill it in with an on-level student's name or information from boxes.
3. Ask the two students whose names you used to read the conversation in front of the class.
4. Ask a pair of on-level students to make a new conversation.
5. Tell pairs to take turns playing A and B and to use information in the boxes to fill in the blanks.
6. Tell students to stand, mingle, and practice the conversation with several new partners.
7. Call on pairs to perform for the class.

D ROLE-PLAY. Make your own conversations.

1. Read the directions. Review the reasons for asking for a schedule change in Exercise 1 on page 240. Say the reasons and ask the class to repeat. Review the additional reasons the class brainstormed in Exercise 1B. Say the reasons and ask the class to repeat.
2. Say: *Pretend you need to ask for a schedule change at work.* Write: *When do you work now? Why do you need to change your schedule? What schedule do you want to change to?* (If possible, write the first question in blue, the second in green, and the third in yellow.) Tell students to write down their answers.
3. Model the activity. Write your own answers to the questions on the board. Play A and role-play a conversation with an above-level student. Substitute your answers into the conversation in Exercise 3C. At B's blue blank, prompt the student to use your first answer.
4. Pair students and tell them to practice the conversation, substituting the information they wrote into the conversation.
5. Walk around and remind students to switch roles.
6. Call on pairs to perform for the class.

Self-Directed Learning

Point out the blue bar. Ask students if they can do the lesson learning objective or if they need more practice. Tell them to check one of the boxes. Assign Extra Practice as needed.

Extra Practice
MyEnglishLab   Workbook p. 143

Listening and Speaking

3 CONVERSATION

A ▶ LISTEN AND READ. Then listen and repeat.

A: Excuse me, Ron. Can I speak to you for a minute?
B: Sure, Linda. What's up?
A: I need to talk to you about my schedule.
B: OK. Right now you work in the mornings, right?
A: Yes. But I'm planning to take classes now. Could I change to evenings?
B: Well, let me look at the schedule. I'll get back to you.
A: OK. Thanks.

B WORK TOGETHER. Practice the conversation in Exercise A.

C CREATE. Make new conversations. Use the words in the boxes.

A: Excuse me, _____. Can I speak to you for a minute?
B: Sure, _____. What's up?
A: I need to talk to you about my schedule.
B: OK. Right now you work   , right?
A: Yes. But   . Could I change to   ?
B: Well, let me look at the schedule. I'll get back to you.
A: OK. Thanks.

> the second shift
> Tuesdays and Thursdays
> full-time

> my daughter is starting school
> my hours changed at my other job
> my mom can't take care of my son anymore

> the first shift
> Mondays and Wednesdays
> part-time

D ROLE-PLAY. Make your own conversations.

I can request a schedule change. ■   I need more practice. ■

For more practice, go to MyEnglishLab.

Grammar

Can / Could to ask permission

Can / Could to ask permission			
Questions			**Answers**
Can **Could**	I	**speak** to you?	Sure.
		change to evenings?	Of course.
		have Friday off?	Yes, you **can**.

Grammar Watch

- *Could* is more formal than *can* to ask permission.
- Use *can* to answer questions. Do not use *could* in answers.

A **WRITE. Complete the conversations. Write questions with *can* or *could*.**

1. **A:** Can I take a break now?

   B: Sure, you can take a break. But please wait till Mara comes back.

2. **A:** Can/Could we trade shifts on Friday?

   B: Sure. No problem. We can trade shifts on Friday.

3. **A:** Can/Could I have Friday off?

   B: I'm sorry, but you can't have Friday off. We need you on Friday.

4. **A:** Can/could we talk about the schedule?

   B: Yes, we can talk about the schedule. Come into my office.

5. **A:** Can/could you cover my hours tomorrow?

   B: Sorry, I can't cover your hours tomorrow. I have plans.

6. **A:** Can/could I leave a little early tonight?

   B: Go ahead. You can leave a little early tonight. We're not that busy.

7. **A:** Can/could you give me more hours next week?

   B: OK. I think I can give you more hours next week. I'll see what I can do.

B **ROLE-PLAY. Ask permission to do something. Use the ideas in the box. Take turns.**

borrow your pen   copy your notes   have a piece of paper   use your dictionary

A: Could I use your dictionary, please?
B: Sure.

I can use *can / could* to ask permission. ■   I need more practice. ■

For more practice, go to MyEnglishLab.

Correlations

ELPS Level 2: 10
CCRS Level A: L.1.1
CASAS Reading: RDG 1.7, 2.9
CASAS Listening: L3.1
CASAS Competencies: 0.1.2
Complete standards language available on the Pearson English Portal.

Self-Directed Learning

State the **lesson objective**. Say: *In this lesson, we will learn to use* can / could *to ask permission.*

Can / Could to ask permission

 ActiveTeach: Grammar Discovery

1. Warm up. Say: *The conversation on page 241 used this grammar.* Turn back to page 241. Point to the sentences in Exercise 3A and then write:
   - *Can I speak to you for a minute?*
   - *Could I change to evenings?*
2. Underline *Can...speak* and *Could...change*.
3. Tell students to look at the grammar chart.
4. Read the **Grammar Watch** note aloud.
5. Write: *Can I speak to you?* and *Could I speak to you?* Ask: *Which one is more formal?* (Could I speak to you?) *Which one would you probably use with your manager?* (Could I speak to you?) *Which one would you probably use with a co-worker?* (Can I speak to you?) Point to the answer *Yes, you can* and ask: *Which one is this an answer for?* (both)
6. Read the questions and answers in the grammar chart and ask the class to repeat.

 ActiveTeach: Grammar Coach

A WRITE. Complete the conversations. Write...

1. Read the directions and the example. Ask: *What is the other possible question?* (Could I take a break now?) Point out that both *Can I take a break now?* and *Could I take a break now?* are correct.
2. *Optional:* Tell students to look at the responses. Say: *If it sounds like a manager, use* Could. *If it sounds like a co-worker, use* Can.
3. Students compare answers with a partner by reading the conversations.
4. Call on two pairs to read each conversation, one with *Can* and one with *Could*.

B ROLE-PLAY. Ask permission to do...

1. Read the directions.
2. Pair students. Say: *Look at the last idea in the box. What question can Student A ask?* Write:
   A: *Can / Could I use your dictionary?*
   B: _____
3. Tell students to study the grammar chart and Exercise A. Ask: *How can Student B answer?* List ideas on the board (for example, *Sure. Of course. Yes, you can... No problem... I'm sorry, but you can't... Go ahead...*). Say the responses and ask the class to repeat.
4. Tell students to take turns being Student A with the other ideas in the box. Walk around and check that students form questions with *Can / Could* correctly.
5. Call on pairs to perform for the class.

EXPANSION: Grammar and speaking practice for B

Tell students to take out their supplies, lunches, bags, etc., and lay out some objects so their partner can see what they have. Tell them to take turns asking each other's permission to use, borrow, and have these objects. For example, *Could I share your lunch? Can I borrow your scissors?*

EXPANSION: Grammar practice for B

1. Write the following list of people: *a manager, a co-worker, a police officer, a waiter or waitress, your child's teacher, a doctor, a sales associate, a family member, your teacher, a celebrity.*
2. Pair students. Say: *Copy the list of people. Ask each person for permission to do something. Write a question with* Can *or* Could.
3. Tell students to change partners and compare their questions.

Self-Directed Learning

Point out the blue bar. Ask students if they can do the lesson learning objective or if they need more practice. Tell them to check one of the boxes. Assign Extra Practice as needed.

Extra Practice		
MyEnglishLab	Workbook	p. 143

Correlations

ELPS Level 2: 3, 10
CCRS Level A: L.1.1, W.1.2, W.1.5
CASAS Reading: RDG 1.7, 1.8, 3.2
CASAS Listening: L2.1, 2.3, 3.11
CASAS Competencies: 0.1.2, 0.1.5, 0.1.6, 4.4.4
**Complete standards language available on the
Pearson English Portal.**

Self-Directed Learning

1. State the **lesson objective**. Say: *In this lesson, we will learn to give details to support an idea.*
2. Say: *You will write about job responsibilities.*

1 BEFORE YOU WRITE

1. Read the directions.
2. Point to the paragraph. Ask: *What is the title of the model?* (Food Service Job Responsibilities)
3. **Scaffold** the model. Write as a graphic organizer:

1	Job	
2	Clothing	
3	Health/safety rules	
4	Communicate with	

4. Point to the **Writing Skill**. Read it or call on an above-level student to read it while students listen. Tell students to read the model and underline the supporting details that use *this means* or *that is*.
5. Tell students to read the questions independently.
6. Call on students to answer the questions and mark the text.
7. Write the information into the graphic organizer.

2 PLAN YOUR WRITING

1. Erase the information in the graphic organizer on the board.
2. Read the directions.
3. Model with an above-level student. The student asks the teacher the questions.
4. Write the information into the graphic organizer.
5. Brainstorm and write different job titles. Students can use the vocabulary from the unit or other ideas.
6. Tell students to make their own graphic organizer on a piece of paper.
7. Have students work in pairs to ask and answer the questions and complete their own graphic organizers.

3 WRITE

1. Read the directions.
2. Use the information in the graphic organizer from Exercise 2 to write sentences in a paragraph. Leave out the health/safety rule. Ask: *What detail supports the idea that workers have to follow health and safety rules?* Elicit the rule and add it to the paragraph.
3. Tell students to write. Walk around to make sure students are writing in paragraph form and using *this means* or *that is* to give details.

 ActiveTeach for 3: Writing Support

4 CHECK YOUR WRITING

1. Read the directions. Point to the **Writing Checklist**. Call on students to read the checklist aloud.
2. Pair students to review their writings together. Say: *Read your sentences with a partner. Use the Writing Checklist.* For additional help, remind students that a correct sentence:
   • *begins with a capital letter*
   • *has a subject*
   • *has a verb*
   • *has a period*
   • *is a complete idea*
3. Walk around and verify that students are using the checklist. Collect the papers for review or put them in the students' writing portfolios.

Teaching Tip: Digital skills

Tell students to post their writing to a discussion board. Other students can comment on additional responsibilities for the job that they know about.

Self-Directed Learning

Point out the blue bar. Ask students if they can do the lesson learning objective or if they need more practice. Tell them to check one of the boxes. Assign Extra Practice as needed.

Extra Practice

 CCRS Plus   p. 144

Writing

Write about job responsibilities

1 BEFORE YOU WRITE

READ. Answer the questions.

Ardita Gega

Food Service Job Responsibilities

Food service workers have many responsibilities. For one thing, they need to wear the right clothing. That is, they have to wear clean uniforms. They also must follow health and safety rules. This means they have to wear latex gloves. Finally, they have to communicate well with co-workers. That is, they need to work as a team.

1. What job does Ardita know about? Food service.
2. What clothing do the workers need to wear? Clean uniforms.
3. What health and safety rule do they need to follow? They have to wear latex gloves.
4. Who do they have to communicate with? Co-workers.

2 PLAN YOUR WRITING

WORK TOGETHER. Ask and answer the questions.

1. What job do you know a lot about?
2. Do the workers need to wear the right clothing? Explain.
3. Do they need to follow rules? Explain.
4. Who do they need to communicate with?

3 WRITE

Now write about a job you know about. Use the model, the Writing Skill, and your ideas from Exercise 2 to help you.

4 CHECK YOUR WRITING

WORK TOGETHER. Read the checklist. Read your writing aloud. Revise your writing.

Writing Skill: Give details to support an idea

Give details to support each idea. Introduce the details with *This means* or *That is*.

For example:

For one thing, they need to wear the right clothing. That is, they have to wear clean uniforms.

WRITING CHECKLIST

☐ The paragraph answers the questions in Exercise 2.

☐ There is a topic sentence.

☐ There are supporting details introduced with the words *This means* or *That is*.

I can give details to support an idea. ■

I need more practice. ■

For more practice, go to MyEnglishLab.

11 Soft Skills at Work

Be a team player

1 MEET YURI

Read about one of his workplace skills.

I am a team player. When my co-workers can't finish important work, I help them. Sometimes that means I have to give up my personal time.

2 YURI'S PROBLEM

READ. Circle *True* or *False*.

Yuri is a mechanic. He had a busy workday today. He's tired and ready to go home. He says, "See you tomorrow!" His co-worker says, "Hey, Yuri, my customer needs his car today. I need to work on it for one more hour, but I have to leave. It's my mother's 70th birthday, and her party starts in 15 minutes. Can you help me out?"

1. Yuri just started work.   True   (False)
2. His co-worker wants to go to a party.   (True)   False
3. His co-worker wants Yuri to fix a car for him.   (True)   False

3 YURI'S SOLUTION

A WORK TOGETHER. Yuri is a team player. What does he say to Sam? Explain your answer.

(1.) Yuri says, "Sure. No problem."
2. Yuri says, "Sorry, no. That's your job."
3. Yuri says, "Maybe one of the other guys can help you."
4. Yuri says _____.

B ROLE-PLAY. Look at your answer to 3A. Role-play Yuri's conversation.

Show what you know!

1. **THINK ABOUT IT.** Are you a team player? Are you a team player in class? At work? At home? Give examples.

2. **WRITE ABOUT IT.** Write an example in your Skills Log.

   I'm a team player in class. When I do a group project with other students, I always help my partners.

I can give an example of how I am a team player. ▢

Unit Review: Go back to page 225. Which unit goals can you check off?

Correlations

CASAS Reading: RDG 1.7, 1.8, 3.2
CASAS Listening: L2.1, 2.3, 4.1, 4.2
CASAS Competencies: 0.1.2, 0.1.5, 0.1.6, 0.2.1, 4.6.4, 4.6.5
Complete standards language available on the Pearson English Portal.

Self-Directed Learning

State the **lesson objective**. Say: *In this lesson, we will give an example of how we are team players.*

1 MEET YURI

1. Ask: *What is the title of this lesson?* (Be a team player) Ask: *What does* team *mean?* (a group of people who work together to accomplish a goal).
2. Write: *Workplace Skill*. Read the directions. Say: *Listen as I read* Meet Yuri. Read the paragraph. Ask: *What is one of Yuri's workplace skills?* (He is a team player.) Next to *Workplace Skill*, write: *Be a team player*.
3. Under *Workplace Skill*, write: *Examples*. Ask: *How is Yuri a team player?* (He helps his co-workers. He gives up his personal time to help.) Write the examples. Elicit other ways to be a team player and write them under *Workplace Skill*.

2 YURI'S PROBLEM

1. Say: *Now we are going to read about Yuri at work. Listen while I read.* Read the first sentence. Use the photo and the **Career Awareness** information to help students understand his job.
2. Say: *Yuri has a problem at work. Listen while I read.* Read the rest of the paragraph. Explain any unfamiliar vocabulary as needed.
3. Students complete the questions after the reading. Call on students to answer. Ask them to **cite evidence:** *Where is that information?*
4. Ask: *What is Yuri's problem?* (He has finished work, but a co-worker asks him to work for him.)

Career Awareness: Auto mechanic

Auto mechanics check cars for problems, do regular maintenance like oil changes, and make repairs. They need to know how to use tools and special equipment. They mostly work in auto repair shops. They usually need on-the-job experience, some special training, and an associate's degree.

---

3 YURI'S SOLUTION

A WORK TOGETHER. Yuri is a team player...

1. Read the directions. Ask students to work together. Walk around and check that students understand that only one solution is correct.
2. Ask: *Is #1 being a team player?* (yes) *Why?* (He helps his co-worker.) Ask: *Is #2 being a team player?* (no) *Why not?* (He does not help his co-worker.) Ask: *Is #3 being a team player?* (no) *Why not?* (He does not help his co-worker.)
3. Ask students if they have any other ideas. Call on students to share item 4 with the class. Write their responses. Ask: *Is this being a team player? Why?*

 ActiveTeach for 3A: Academic Conversation Support

B ROLE-PLAY. Look at your answer to 3A...

1. Group students in pairs. Explain one person will be Yuri. The other person will be the co-worker. Model the activity with an above-level student. Have students practice the conversation with different partners.
2. Walk around and ask students to switch roles and continue practicing. If students aren't pronouncing their lines clearly, model correct pronunciation and ask them to repeat.

Show what you know!

1. THINK ABOUT IT. Are you a team player?...

Read the directions. Have students think about their answers for a few minutes. Then ask them to share with a partner. Call on students to share with the class.

2. WRITE ABOUT IT. Write an example in your...

Read the directions and the example. Have students write their examples in their **Skills Log** at the back of the book. Circulate and assist students as needed.

Self-Directed Learning

1. Point out the blue bar. Ask students if they can do the lesson learning objective or if they need more practice. Tell them to check one of the boxes. Assign Extra Practice as needed.
2. Ask students to turn to page 225. Go to the Unit Wrap-Up teaching notes on page T-225.

Extra Practice

 Workbook p. 145

MY SOFT SKILLS LOG

This is a list of my soft skills. They are skills I use every day. They are important for work, school, and home. In a job interview, I can talk about my soft skills. I can give these examples from my life.

Unit 1: I am inclusive.

For example, _____

_____

_____

_____

Unit 2: I separate work life from home life.

For example, _____

_____

_____

_____

Unit 3: I'm a good listener.

For example, _____

_____

_____

_____

Unit 4: I am professional.

For example, _____

_____

_____

_____

Unit 5: I take initiative.

For example, _____

_____

_____

_____

Unit 6: I am dependable.

For example, _____

_____

_____

_____

Unit 7: I show respect for others.

For example, _____

_____

_____

_____

Unit 8: I am honest.

For example, _____

_____

_____

_____

Unit 9: I plan well.

For example, _____

_____

_____

_____

Unit 10: I know when to ask for help.

For example, _____

_____

_____

_____

Unit 11: I follow safety procedures.

For example, _____

_____

_____

_____

Unit 12: I am a team player.

For example, _____

_____

_____

_____

UNIT 1 GRAMMAR REVIEW

A COMPLETE. Use the correct forms of the words in parentheses.

1. **A:** Excuse me. _____*Are you*_____ Tony Jones?

(you / be)

   B: No, I _____'m not_____. Tony _____is_____ the tall guy over there. He

(not / be)   (be)

   _____has_____ short, dark hair and a goatee.

(have)

   A: Oh, I see him. Thanks.

2. **A:** You look familiar. _____Are you_____ an employee at the county hospital?

(you / be)

   B: Yes, I _____am_____. I _____'m / am_____ a technician in the radiology

(be)   (be)

   department.

3. **A:** _____What is_____ your manager's name?

(what / be)

   B: Ted Chen. He 's / is _____ a really good supervisor.

(be)

B IDENTIFY. Cross out the incorrect words.

My name **has / is** Ellen. **I'm / I have**
21 years old. This is my sister, Isabel.
We're twins. As you can see, we
look alike. My hair **is / am** long and
brown, **and / but** my sister's hair is
similar. We both **have / are** brown
eyes. **I'm / I have** not tall, **but / and**
my sister is short.

We are very similar, **and / but** we're
not alike in every way. My sister
is / has talkative, **but / and** I'm quiet.

My sister **has / is** outgoing, **but / and** I'm shy. My sister is always cheerful, **and / but** I am
sometimes moody. Oh, and one more difference: I **am / are** laid-back, **but / and** my sister **is
/ are** bossy. Don't tell my sister I wrote that!

A COMPLETE. Write questions. Use the simple present and the verbs in parentheses.

1. _____Does_____ Rohan _____have_____ kids? (have) Yes, he does.

2. Where _____does_____ Ned _____work_____? (work) (He works) at a hospital

3. What _____do_____ Ned and Lan _____have_____ in common? (have) They live at their brother-in-law's house.

4. _____Does_____ Artur _____have_____ a child? (have) No, he doesn't.

5. Where _____does_____ Aki _____live_____? (live) (She lives) in an apartment.

6. How many children _____does_____ Lan _____have_____? (have) (He has) two (children).

7. Where _____do_____ Rohan and Lan _____work_____? (work) (They work) in an office.

8. _____Do_____ Lan and Aya _____have_____ something in common? (have) Yes, they do. (They have two children.)

9. What _____do_____ Aki, Artur, and Aya _____have_____ in common? (have) They live in apartr

10. _____Do_____ Rohan and Ned _____work_____ at the same place? (work) No, they don't.

B EXAMINE. Look at the chart. Answer the questions in Exercise A.

	Ned	Aki	Artur	Rohan	Lan	Aya
work	at a hospital	in a restaurant	in his uncle's store	in an office	in an office	at a hospital
live	at his brother-in-law's house	in an apartment	in an apartment	in a house	at her brother-in-law's house	in an apartment
children	1	2	0	3	2	2

UNIT 3 GRAMMAR REVIEW

A **COMPLETE.** Use the correct forms of the verbs. Use contractions if possible.

A: I _I'm going to run_ some errands this afternoon.
_____ **1. (be going to / run)**

B: Oh. What do you need to do?

A: First I _____ need to stop _____ at the bank. Then I _'m going to buy_ _____
_____ **2. (need / stop)** _____ **3. (be going to / buy)**

sweatpants. And you—what are your plans for today?

B: Well, I _'m going to relax_ at the swimming pool.
_____ **4. (be going to / relax)**

A: That sounds great. I _____ want to relax _____, too. Can I go with you? Maybe I really
_____ **5. (want / relax)**

_____ don't need to run _____ any errands today after all!
_____ **6. (not need / run)**

B **WRITE.** Look at the picture. Write the reason for each return. *(Answers will vary.)*

1. _It's too tight._
2. _The zipper is broken._
3. _They're too long._

4. _They're too small._
5. _A pocket is ripped._
6. _It's too big._

UNIT 4 GRAMMAR REVIEW

A IDENTIFY. Cross out the incorrect words.

A: Do you want to come over to watch the game?

B: Sorry, I can't. I ~~have~~ / **have to** go to the supermarket.
My sister is coming over tonight. I **like to** / ~~like~~ cook
a good dinner for her, so I **have to** / ~~have~~ get food.

A: OK. Maybe next week.

B: Sure. You know I love ~~watch~~ / **to watch** the games
on your big-screen TV.

A: Great. Make sure you ~~don't have~~ / **don't have to** run any errands next Saturday!

B COMPLETE. Write the sentences with adverbs.

1. I go to work on the weekends.
   (sometimes) _I sometimes go to work on the weekends._

2. Dave works on Tuesday and Thursday mornings.
   (usually) _Dave usually works on Tuesday and Thursday mornings._

3. Ted is late for meetings.
   (always) _Ted is always late for meetings._

4. Our supervisor brings coffee and doughnuts on Fridays.
   (often) _Our supervisor often brings coffee and doughnuts on Fridays._

5. Ralph eats meat or fish.
   (never) _Ralph never eats meat or fish._

6. We are at home during the week.
   (hardly ever) _We are hardly ever at home during the week._

UNIT 5 GRAMMAR REVIEW

A COMPLETE. Use the present continuous and the verbs in parentheses.

A: I _'m looking for_ Jon. Is he here today?
       1. (look for)

B: Yes, he _'s looking at_ the light in the lunchroom. It _'s not working_ , and he
       2. (look at)   **3. (not work)**

's trying to fix it. Bob is in there, too, and they _'re working_ it together.
4. (try)   **5. (work on)**

That's why May is on the phone right now. She _'s calling_ an electrician!
                                            6. (call)

B COMPLETE. Write questions and answers. Use *there is* and *there are*.

1. **A:** _____Are there_____ any restaurants nearby?

   B: Yes, _____there are_____.

2. **A:** _____Is there_____ a laundromat nearby?

   B: No, _____there isn't_____.

3. **A:** _____Are there_____ any stores nearby?

   B: No, _____there aren't_____.

C COMPLETE. Use the words in the box.

> Take   Don't use   Don't try   Tell   Call

1. There's no hot water. _____Tell / Call_____ the building manager.

2. The sink is clogged. _____Don't try_____ to fix it. _____Call / Tell_____ the landlord.

3. The washer is broken. _____Don't use_____ it. _____Take_____ the clothes to the laundromat.

UNIT 6 GRAMMAR REVIEW

A PRACTICE. Read the answers. Write questions about the underlined words.

1. **A:** _Did you work at Global Trading Company?_

   B: <u>Yes</u>, I did. I worked there for two years.

2. **A:** _When did Bo and Fang get married?_

   B: Bo and Fang got married <u>last year</u>.

3. **A:** _Where did Victor grow up?_

   B: Victor grew up <u>in Mexico</u>.

4. **A:** _Why did you move?_

   B: We moved <u>because we needed better jobs</u>.

5. **A:** _Did you know about the software problem?_

   B: <u>No</u>, we didn't. We didn't know about the software problem.

6. **A:** _When did Todd get that job?_

   B: Todd got that job <u>last year</u>.

B COMPLETE. Use the correct past forms of the verbs in parentheses.

A: ___Why did you decide___ to become a nurse?
  1. (why / you / decide)

B: My grandmother ___came___
  2. (come)

to live with us when I was young. When

she ___got___ older, she
  3. (get)

___had___ some health problems.
  4. (have)

My mom and dad both ___worked___,
  5. (work)

and they ___didn't have___ enough time
  6. (not have)

to do everything. So I ___took___
  7. (take)

care of my grandmother for many years, and I ___liked___ it. I
  8. (like)

___wanted___ to help other people, too. So I ___went___
  9. (want)   10. (go)

to nursing school.

A: ___Did you make___ the right decision?
  11. (you / make)

B: Yes, I ___did___. I ___grew___ to love nursing more
  12. (do)   13. (grow)

and more.

UNIT 7 GRAMMAR REVIEW

A COMPLETE. Use the simple past of a verb from the box.

break   cut   fall   get   ~~have~~

1. I ___had___ a cold for three weeks, but now I feel fine.
2. She ___fell___ down the stairs and hurt her back.
3. He had an accident at work and ___broke___ a bone in his foot.
4. Be careful with that knife. Jim ___cut___ his hand with it yesterday.
5. I went to the doctor's office, and I ___got___ a prescription.

B DECIDE. Complete the conversations with the words in the boxes.

at   by   for   ~~on~~

1. **A:** What are you doing _____ on _____ Wednesday afternoon?
   B: I'm going _____ for _____ a checkup.
   A: When is your appointment?
   B: It's _____ at _____ 4:30, but I need to go early. They want me to be there _____ by _____ 4:15.

at   because   by   from   in   to

2. **A:** I need to see a doctor _____ because _____ I think I have an infection.
   B: Can you be here _____ in _____ an hour?
   A: I'm sorry, I can't. I work _____ from _____ 3:00 _____ to _____ 11:00.
   B: How about tomorrow? We have an opening _____ at _____ 9:00.
   A: That's fine. Thank you.
   B: OK. Please be here _____ by _____ 8:45.

UNIT 8 GRAMMAR REVIEW

A COMPLETE. Use *can* and *can't* and the words in parentheses.

Manager: _____Can you use_____ a cash register?
              1. (you / use)

Terry: No, I _____ can't _____, but _____ I can learn _____.
               2.   **3. (I / learn)**

Manager: OK, well, maybe _____you can stock_____ shelves at first.
                    4. (you / stock)

Terry: Sure. _____ I can do _____ that.
           5. (I / do)

Manager: Do you prefer afternoons or evenings?

Terry: _____ I can work _____ in the afternoon or in the evening. I'm flexible.
        6. (I / work)

Manager: _____Can you work_____ on weekends?
         7. (you / work)

Terry: Sure. On the weekend, _____ I can work _____ mornings, afternoons, or evenings.
                  8. (I / work)

Manager: _____Can you start_____ tomorrow?
        9. (you / start)

Terry: Yes, _____ I can _____.
        10.

B DECIDE. Write *ago, and, in, last, later,* and *or.*

Ali Osman came to the U.S. _____in_____ 2015. One month _____later_____,
                                        1.   **2.**

he started school. He got his first job _____in_____ 2016. It was in a hospital, and he
          3.

worked nights. Ali didn't like his work schedule. A few weeks _____later_____, his boss
          4.

asked, "Ali, do you prefer days _____or_____ nights?" Ali said, "I prefer days." A week
          5.

_____later_____, he changed his hours.
   6.

Ali continued to go to school. _____Last_____ year, he had classes three nights a
          7.

week: on Monday, Tuesday, _____and_____ Thursday. This year, he's going to school
          8.

_____in_____ the morning. He changed jobs a few weeks _____ago_____. He has a
   9.   **10.**

better job at a different hospital. But now he works from 12:00 P.M. to 8:00 P.M., so he can't

go to class in the afternoon _____or_____ the evening.
          11.

UNIT 9 GRAMMAR REVIEW

A COMPLETE. Use *will* and the words in parentheses to talk about the future.

MARCH EVENTS
OAK GROVE MIDDLE SCHOOL

Bake Sale

The fourth grade __will have__ a bake sale
           1. (have)
on March 6 at 12:30 p.m. in the cafeteria.

Students __will sell__ cookies, cupcakes,
          2. (sell)
and other baked goods.

PTO Meeting

The Oak Grove PTO __will meet__
           3. (meet)
on March 9. Members __will discuss__
          4. (discuss)
new school programs for this year.

Please join us!

B APPLY. Write the possessive forms of the nouns. Change the adjectives to adverbs of manner.

1. **A:** How are my (son) _____son's_____ grades in math?

    B: Fine. He's doing very (good) _____well_____.

2. **A:** How were the (children) _____children's_____ grades?

    B: Great! They're working (hard) _____hard_____ in school.

3. A: I didn't hear the (woman) _____woman's_____ name.

  B: I think she said, "Mimi." She speaks (quiet) _____quietly_____.

4. A: I can't read the (student) _____student's_____ handwriting.

  B: I know. He writes (sloppy) _____sloppily_____.

C **DECIDE. Cross out the underlined nouns and write object pronouns.**

1. Do you know Mr. Jones? I like ~~Mr. Jones~~ *him* a lot.

2. My daughter Eliza is having a hard time. Can you help ~~Eliza~~ her?

3. Brad's homework is hard. He doesn't understand ~~his homework~~ it.

4. Asha's schoolbooks are heavy. It's hard for her to carry ~~her schoolbooks~~ them.

5. I want to meet my children's teachers. I want to talk to ~~the teachers~~ them.

UNIT 10 GRAMMAR REVIEW

A **IDENTIFY. Cross out the incorrect words.**

Cook: Do we have enough **meat** / ~~meats~~ for tomorrow?

Assistant: I think so. There's ~~much~~ / **a lot of** meat in the refrigerator. But there isn't **much** / ~~many~~ fish.

Cook: OK. Put it on the list. What about vegetables? Are there ~~much~~ / **any** potatoes?

Assistant: About 100 pounds. But there are only ~~a little~~ / **a few** carrots.

Cook: How ~~much~~ / **many** onions?

Assistant: Onions? There aren't **any** / ~~some~~.

Cook: OK. Then we need ~~any~~ / **some** carrots and onions. Put **rice** / ~~rices~~ on the list, too.

Assistant: OK. How ~~much~~ / **many** pounds of rice?

Cook: Fifty. And please get **some** / ~~any~~ fruit. I need ~~much~~ / **a lot of** apples for tomorrow's apple pies.

Assistant: I'll put them on the list. We have **some** / ~~any~~, but only ~~a little~~ / **a few**. I think we need some **sugar** / ~~sugars~~ for the pies, too.

B **WRITE.** Compare two food products. Make four sentences. Use the comparative forms of adjectives from the box or other adjectives.

| delicious | easy to cook | fattening | good for you | sweet | tasty |

Apples are better for you than candy bars.

1. _____
2. _____
3. _____
4. _____

UNIT 11 GRAMMAR REVIEW

A **COMPLETE.** Use the correct present continuous form of the verb in parentheses, or the correct form of *there be* in the past.

1. **A:** Hi, I *'m calling* _____ because I'm going to be late. I *'m sitting* _____ in my car.
   (call)   (sit)

   I'm stuck in a traffic jam. ___ *There was* ___ an accident near Lakeland.
   (there be)

   B: Oh, no! Was anyone hurt?

   A: I'm not sure. ___ *There was* ___ an ambulance here a few minutes ago.
   (there be)

   B: ___ *Are* ___ you ___ *moving* ___?
   (move)

   A: Actually, a police officer ___ *is directing* ___ traffic now. Got to go. I'll see you soon.
   (direct)

2. **A:** Hi, Rita. I hope I *'m not calling* _____ at a bad time?
   (not call)

   B: No, I *'m not working* _____ today. The factory is closed. ___ *There was* ___ an explosion
   (not work)   (there be)

   yesterday.

   A: You're kidding!

   B: No, it's true. Luckily, ___ *there were* ___ no injuries.
   (there be)

   A: That's amazing. ___ *Was there* ___ a fire?
   (there be)

   B: Yeah, a big one. ___ *There were* ___ ten or twelve fire trucks there.
   (there be)

   A: Wow.

UNIT 12 GRAMMAR REVIEW

A) **APPLY.** Use *have to, can, can't,* and *could* to complete the conversation. There may be more than one possible answer.

> **Safety Reminder**
> All employees must wear work boots. No sneakers or sandals allowed!

A: Excuse me. This is my first day. _____Can_____ I ask you something?

B: Sure. What do you want to know?

A: Well, do we have to wear these uniforms?

B: No, we don't. We _____can_____ wear our own shirts and pants if we want. But we _____have to_____ wear work boots. No sneakers or sandals. It's for safety.

A: OK. One more thing. _____Can / Could_____ I ask you a favor?

B: What is it?

A: I'm supposed to work Monday, but I _____can't_____. You're not on the schedule for Monday. _____Can/Could_____ you take my shift?

B: Sure. But ask the supervisor first. We _____have to_____ get permission.

B) **WRITE.** Make information questions. Use the words in parentheses.

1. **A:** (who) _Who do I give my vacation request form to?_
   B: Give your vacation request form to your supervisor.

2. **A:** (what time) _What time can Kevin take his break?_
   B: Kevin can take his break at 12:30.

3. **A:** (where) _Where do you store the floor cleaning equipment?_
   B: You store the floor cleaning equipment in the hall closet.

4. **A:** (which days) _Which days does Tam work this week?_
   B: Tam works on Thursday, Friday, and Saturday this week.

5. **A:** (when) _When did you work overtime?_
   B: I worked overtime on Thursday and Saturday.

UNIT 1, Lesson 3, page 10 and Lesson 9, page 22; UNIT 2, Lesson 3, page 30; UNIT 3, Lesson 6, page 56; UNIT 5, Lesson 3, page 90

Contractions are short forms. Contractions join two words together. In a contraction, an apostrophe (') replaces a letter. Use contractions in speaking and informal writing.

Contractions with *be*			
Affirmative		**Negative**	
I am	= I'm	I am not	= I'm not
you are	= you're	you are not	= you're not / you aren't
he is	= he's	he is not	= he's not / he isn't
she is	= she's	she is not	= she's not / she isn't
it is	= it's	it is not	= it's not / it isn't
we are	= we're	we are not	= we're not / we aren't
they are	= they're	they are not	= they're not / they aren't

Negative contractions with *do*	
I do not	= I don't
you do not	= you don't
he does not	= he doesn't
she does not	= she doesn't
it does not	= it doesn't
we do not	= we don't
they do not	= they don't

UNIT 5, Lesson 3, page 90

Spelling rules for *-ing* verbs

For most verbs, add *-ing* to the base form of the verb. For example:

work   ⟶   working
do   ⟶   doing

For verbs that end in *e,* drop the *e* and add *-ing.* For example:

change   ⟶   changing
leave   ⟶   leaving
make   ⟶   making

If the base form of a one-syllable verb ends with consonant, vowel, consonant, double the final consonant and add *-ing.* For example:

shop   ⟶   shopping
run   ⟶   running
cut   ⟶   cutting
begin   ⟶   beginning

UNIT 6, Lesson 6, page 116 and UNIT 7, Lesson 6, page 136

Simple past: irregular verbs

Base form	Past tense form	Base form	Past tense form	Base form	Past tense form
be	was/were	get	got	run	ran
begin	began	give	gave	say	said
bleed	bled	go	went	see	saw
break	broke	grow	grew	send	sent
bring	brought	have	had	sing	sang
buy	bought	hurt	hurt	sit	sat
come	came	keep	keep	sleep	slept
cost	cost	know	knew	speak	spoke
cut	cut	leave	left	spend	spent
do	did	lose	lost	swim	swam
drink	drank	make	made	take	took
drive	drove	meet	met	teach	taught
eat	ate	oversleep	overslept	tell	told
fall	fell	pay	paid	think	thought
feel	felt	put	put	understand	understood
find	found	quit	quit	wake up	woke up
forget	forgot	read	read	write	wrote

UNIT 9, Lesson 6, page 176

Spelling rules for adverbs of manner

We can make many adverbs of manner from adjectives.

For most adverbs of manner, add -ly to an adjective. For example:

nice	→	nicely
quiet	→	quietly
normal	→	normally

If an adjective ends in y, change y to i and add -ly. For example:

happy	→	happily
noisy	→	noisily
angry	→	angrily

UNIT 9, Lesson 9, page 182

Spelling rules for possessive nouns

A possessive noun shows that a person or thing owns something.
Add 's to most singular nouns and names. For example:

student	→	student's
girl	→	girl's
Ming	→	Ming's

Add 's to singular nouns and names that end in -s. For example:

boss	→	boss's
Mr. Jones	→	Mr. Jones's
James	→	James's

Add ' to plural nouns that end in -s. For example:

parents	→	parents'
classmates	→	classmates'
boys	→	boys'

Add 's to plural nouns that do not end in -s. For example:

children	→	children's
people	→	people's
women	→	women's

UNIT 10, Lesson 3, page 190

Spelling rules for plurals and irregular nouns

Add -s to make most nouns plural. For example:

1 student	→	2 students
1 pencil	→	5 pencils
1 house	→	10 houses

Add -es to nouns that end with s, z, x, sh, or ch. For example:

1 sandwich	→	3 sandwiches
1 bus	→	4 buses
1 dish	→	5 dishes

For most nouns that end in o, just add -s. For example:

1 avocado	→	2 avocados
1 radio	→	2 radios

For some nouns that end in a consonant and o, add -es. For example:

1 potato	→	2 potatoes
1 tomato	→	8 tomatoes
1 hero	→	4 heroes

When a noun ends in a consonant + y, change y to i and add -es. For example:

1 baby	→	3 babies
1 country	→	15 countries
1 berry	→	20 berries

When a noun ends in f, change f to v and add -es. When a noun ends in fe, change fe to v and add -es. For example:

1 wife	→	2 wives
1 knife	→	9 knives
1 loaf	→	7 loaves

Some nouns have irregular plural forms. For example:

1 foot	→	2 feet
1 tooth	→	10 teeth
1 man	→	5 men
1 woman	→	8 women
1 child	→	7 children
1 person	→	12 people

UNIT 10, Lesson 3, page 190

Non-count nouns

Drinks	Some food		Materials	Subjects	Activities	Other
coffee	beef	meat	corduroy	art	baseball	advice
juice	bread	pasta	cotton	language arts	basketball	equipment
milk	butter	rice	denim	math	exercise	furniture
soda	cheese	salad	fleece	music	hiking	homework
tea	chicken	salt	glass	physical	jogging	information
water	chocolate	soup	leather	education	running	mail
	fish	spinach	metal	science	soccer	money
	fruit	sugar	nylon	social studies	swimming	news
	ice cream	yogurt	silk	technology	tennis	paper
	lettuce		vinyl	world languages		traffic
			wood			weather
			wool			work

UNIT 10, Lesson 6, page 196

Spelling rules for comparatives and irregular comparatives

To make comparative adjectives from one-syllable adjectives, add -er. For example:

cheap ⟶ cheaper
tall ⟶ taller
cold ⟶ colder

If a one-syllable adjective ends in e, add -r. For example:

nice ⟶ nicer
late ⟶ later
large ⟶ larger

If an adjective ends in one vowel and one consonant, double the consonant and add -er. For example:

hot ⟶ hotter
big ⟶ bigger
sad ⟶ sadder
thin ⟶ thinner

For two-syllable adjectives that end with -y, change y to i and add -er. For example:

busy ⟶ busier
pretty ⟶ prettier
easy ⟶ easier

WORD LIST

UNIT 1

active learners, 18
address, 12
applicant, 12
application, 12
attractive, 8
average height, 7
average weight, 7
bald, 7
beard, 7
beautiful, 8
bossy, 14
break room, 16
cafeteria, 17
cheerful, 14
communication, 18
cook, 20
co-worker, 15
curly, 7

customer service
  representative, 16
demanding, 14
department head, 17
discussion, 18
DOB (date of birth), 12
e-mail address, 12
employer, 18
friendly, 15
funny, 15
gender, 12
goatee, 7
good-looking, 8
handsome, 8
heavy, 7
height, 7
hospital,
identification card (ID), 12

inclusive, 24
interesting, 15
interpersonal skills, 18
laid-back, 14
long hair, 7
manager, 22
medical assistant, 21
medium-length hair, 7
mobile phone, 13
moody, 14
mustache, 7
nurse, 20
office, 17
outgoing, 14
participate, 18
personality, 15
physical appearance, 7
practice, 18

quiet, 15
routine, 23
short hair, 7
shy, 14
slim, 7
small-group work, 18
social security, 12
straight hair, 7
supervisor, 14
supportive, 14
talkative, 14
tall, 7
thin, 7
ugly, 8
unattractive, 8
wavy, 7
weight, 7

UNIT 2

accountant, 40
advice, 32
apartment, 28
artist, 40
aunt, 27
balance, 32
bank, 34
book of stamps, 38
brother, 27
business, 36
Certificate of Mailing, 39
Certified Mail, 39
children, 27
Collect on Delivery (COD),
  39
cousin, 27
daughter, 27
Delivery Confirmation, 39
engineer, 40

envelope, 38
expert, 32
Express Mail, 38
family, 26
father, 27
father-in-law, 27
female, 26
fiancé, 27
fiancée, 27
First-Class Mail, 38
game show, 40
grandchildren, 27
granddaughter, 27
grandfather, 27
grandmother, 27
grandson, 27
handle, 32
hair salon, 30
have in common, 34

hazardous material, 39
husband, 27
Insurance, 39
job, 30
keep in touch, 43
letter, 38
mailing service, 38
male, 27
mother, 27
mother-in-law, 27
nephew, 27
niece, 27
package, 38
parents, 27
podcast, 40
pound, 38
prioritize, 32
Priority Mail, 38
Registered Mail, 39

relationship, 26
responsibility, 33
Retail Ground, 38
security guard, 41
sister, 27
sister-in-law, 27
son, 27
standard-sized, 38
take care of, 33
technician, 41
text, 43
tracking receipt, 38
uncle, 27
waiter, 44
wife, 27
work, 32
work/life balance, 32

UNIT 3

ad, 52
ATM, 54
bakery, 55
bank, 54
big, 58
bill, 58
blouse, 62
bookstore, 57
boots, 47
broken, 60
button, 60
buy, 48
cash, 58
change, 53
cheap, 62
cap, 47
check, 56
clearance sale, 48
clothing, 47
clothing store, 48
coat, 47

coffee shop, 62
cost, 58
credit card, 58
deli, 55
discount, 52
dress, 47
drugstore, 55
electronics, 64
errand, 55
exchange, 51
gas station, 55
gloves, 47
grocery store, 55
hardware store, 54
hat, 47
helmet, 47
high heels, 47
hole, 60
interest, 58
jacket, 47
jeans, 47

laptop, 64
laundromat, 54
library, 57
long, 61
loose, 60
mail room, 56
meeting, 56
minimum, 58
mistake, 53
missing, 60
online order, 52
on-the-job training, 56
order, 62
pair of pants, 48
payment, 58
post office, 55
purchase, 58
raincoat, 47
receipt, 48
rent-to-own, 58
return (a purchase), 48

return policy, 53
ripped, 60
sale, 52
sales receipt, 53
sales tax, 53
salesperson, 64
save (money), 63
scarf, 47
schedule, 56
seam, 60
shirt, 47
shoes, 62
shoppers, 48
shorts, 49
sneakers, 47
suit, 47
supermarket, 54
sweater, 47
sweat pants, 47
sweatshirt, 47
swimsuit, 53

swimwear, 53
tax, 52
team leader, 56

tie, 47
tight, 60
umbrella, 47

uniform, 47
windbreaker, 47
zipper, 60

UNIT 4

abbreviations, 78
adult, 72
auto mechanics class, 68
be busy, 80
business class, 68
calendar, 72
clean the office, 75
computer, 70
computer class, 70
computer programming, 70
cook, 74
digital, 72
do the dishes, 75
do laundry, 74
don't feel well, 80
email, 79
emoji, 78
employee, 76
exercise, 71
free-time, 67

get some coffee, 81
get up early, 75
go dancing, 67
go fishing, 67
go hiking, 67
go jogging, 71
go for a bike ride, 67
go for a walk, 67
go out to eat, 67
go running, 67
go shopping, 67
go swimming, 67
go to a meeting, 81
go to the beach, 67
go to the gym, 67
go to the movies, 70
go to the park, 67
go to the zoo, 67
guitar class, 68
hate, 76

have other plans, 80
indoor, 67
interview, 72
invitation, 80
invite, 81
iron, 74
lecture, 72
like, 76
love, 76
lunch, 81
make some calls, 81
message, 78
office, 75
outdoor, 67
polite, 79
professional, 84
punctuation, 78
read, 77
relaxing, 83
résumé, 72

run a business, 68
run some errands, 81
sales, 72
schedule, 73
shift, 76
sick, 76
spend time with family, 77
style, 79
take a walk, 81
take a break, 74
take the bus, 70
use a computer, 77
vacuum, 74
watch TV, 77
website, 72
weekend, 68
work outside, 75

UNIT 5

account, 93
ad, 92
air-conditioning, 92
balcony, 95
basement, 97
bathroom, 92
broken, 87
building manager, 88
bus stop, 95
ceiling, 87
charge, 93
cleaner, 104
clogged, 87
closet, 95
date of service, 93
dining room, 92
dishwasher, 90
door, 87
dryer, 92
eat-in kitchen, 92

electrician, 88
elevator, 96
faucet, 87
fee, 92
fix, 88
floor, 104
furnished, 97
give directions, 101
go straight, 100
go through (a light), 100
heat, 87
homeowner, 98
hot water, 87
investment, 98
kitchen, 95
laundry room, 94
laundromat, 95
leaking, 87
living room, 92
lock, 87

locksmith, 88
mailbox, 87
microwave, 95
own, 98
owner-occupied, 99
(not) working, 87
neighborhood, 96
paint, 90
parking, 97
parking lot, 95
pet, 92
plumber, 88
problem, 86
radiator, 88
rent, 92
rental agent, 94
rental apartment, 92
renter, 98
security deposit, 92
sell, 98

sink, 87
stove, 87
stuck, 87
subway stop, 95
supermarket, 95
take initiative, 104
toilet, 87
traffic, 99
transportation, 92
turn left , 100
turn right, 100
utilities, 92
utility bill, 93
vacuum cleaner, 104
value, 98
voice message, 104
washer, 92
washing machine, 87
window, 87

UNIT 6

anniversary party, 107
Barack Obama, 118
barbecue, 107
be born, 114
be late for work, 124
biography, 123
birthday party, 107
car keys, 121
celebrate, 113
Christmas Day, 112
college, 114
Columbus Day, 112
community, 118
dance all night, 108

dependable, 124
exhausted, 121
family reunion, 107
forget (your lunch), 120
funeral, 107
get a job, 114
get married, 114
get stuck in traffic, 120
gift, 107
government, 118
graduate from
school, 114
graduation, 107
grow up, 114

have car trouble, 120
have children, 114
health insurance, 119
holiday party, 107
holidays, 112
Independence Day, 112
Labor Day, 112
listen to family
stories, 108
look at old photos, 108
lose (your keys), 120
Martin Luther King Jr.
Day, 112
Memorial Day, 112

milestone, 114
miss (the bus), 121
national holiday, 113
New Year's Day, 112
oversleep, 120
parade, 112
politics, 119
president, 119
Presidents' Day, 112
register, 118
retirement party, 107
scan, 118
set an alarm, 124
stay up late, 108

surprise party, 107
take the wrong train, 120
Thanksgiving Day, 112

time line, 119
to-do list, 111
unhappy, 121

upset, 121
U.S. Holidays, 112
Veterans' Day, 112

vote, 118
wedding, 107

UNIT 7

accident, 134
appointment, 128
back, 135
break your arm, 134
break your tooth, 141
burn your hand, 134
call in sick/late, 144
caplets. 132
checkup, 140
chest pains, 126
clinic, 130
cold, 126
cold medicine, 142
cough, 126
cut your finger, 134
dentist, 130
dizzy, 128

dosage, 132
drug store, 132
earache, 126
emergency, 140
emergency room, 127
expiration date, 132
eye drops, 132
fall, 134
feel better, 140
fever, 126
flu, 126
flu shot, 140
get well soon, 141
good luck, 141
have a checkup, 140
have a cold, 132
headache, 126

health problem, 126
heartburn, 126
high blood pressure, 126
hospital, 140
hurt your head, 134
injury, 134
itchy, 128
loss of control, 138
manage stress, 138
medical assistant, 128
medicine, 132
medicine label, 132
miss work, 140
nauseous, 128
over-the-counter (OTC), 132
pharmacist, 133
pharmacy, 133

prescription, 133
rash, 126
refill, 133
respect, 144
shot, 140
sick, 129
sore throat, 126
sprain your ankle, 134
stress, 138
swollen, 128
symptom, 128
tablespoon, 133
take care of someone, 141
upset stomach, 126
wrist, 135

UNIT 8

agriculture, 158
assist customers, 147
availability, 160
candidate, 153
car service driver, 152
clean equipment, 149
computer application
    software, 152
cover letter, 152
computer system
    administrator, 147
customer experience, 149
employment, 159
experience, 152
flexible, 160
food service worker, 147
full-time, 152
gardener, 154
give notice at work, 160

greet visitors, 147
handle phone calls, 147
health benefits, 152
health care, 158
health insurance, 152
help wanted ad, 152
install computer
    systems, 147
job application, 151
job duties, 149
job history, 163
job interview, 148
job market, 159
job requirements, 152
job title, 146
manager, 147
manufacturing, 158
nursing assistant, 147
office assistant, 152

operate a forklift , 148
order supplies, 148
organize files,152
part-time, 152
plan work schedules, 147
prepare food, 147
problem solve, 147
receive shipments, 147
receptionist, 147
record patient
    information, 147
receptionist, 147
references, 152
résumé, 152
salesperson, 148
sales associate, 161
shift, 160
software, 159
software developer, 158

sort materials, 151
speak Spanish, 148
stock clerk, 147
stock shelves, 147
store manager, 148
supervise employees, 147
take care of patients, 147
technology, 158
truck driver, 155
unemployed, 154
unload materials, 147
use a cash register, 148
use a computer, 149
warehouse worker, 147
work as a team, 148
work history, 154

UNIT 9

art, 167
Associate's Degree, 178
Bachelor Degree, 178
be disrespectful, 180
behavior, 180
bully, 180
Certificate, 178
college, 178
college degree, 178
community college, 178
community service, 167
degree, 179
Doctor of Philosophy
    (Ph.D), 178
elementary school, 172

English language arts, 167
financial aid, 178
fool around, 180
for-profit, 178
get along with others, 180
get extra help, 174
grant, 178
guidance counselor, 182
high school, 178
loan, 179
Master's Degree, 178
math, 167
music, 167
non-profit, 178
notice from school, 168

parent-teacher
    conference, 168
P.E. (physical
    education), 167
phone message, 172
plan well, 184
principal, 171
private, 178
PTO (parent-teacher
    organization), 168
public, 178
report card, 182
scholarship, 179
school events, 169
school nurse, 182

school play, 169
school subject, 166
science, 167
science fair, 169
skip class, 180
social studies/history, 167
technology, 167
tuition, 178
university, 178
voicemail, 172
world languages, 167

UNIT 10

apple juice, 200
bag, 187
beans, 189
bottle, 187
bottled water, 200
box, 187 ·
bunch, 187
caffeine, 198
calories, 193
can, 187
carbohydrates, 192
cereal, 189
cholesterol, 192
coffee, 195
cola, 198
coleslaw, 200
commercial, 194
consume, 198
container, 187
convenience, 194
convenience store, 188

cucumber, 189
delicious, 196
dozen, 187
effect, 198
fat, 193
fattening, 197
fiber, 192
fish, 190
fish sandwich, 200
food labels, 192
French fries, 200
fresh, 197
gallon, 187
gram (g), 193
grocery store, 189
half-gallon, 187
hamburger, 200
head, 187
headache medicine, 198
healthy diet, 192
ice cream, 195

iced tea, 200
ingredient label, 192
jar, 187
lemon/lime soda, 198
low-fat, 195
macaroni and cheese, 200
mashed potatoes, 200
meatloaf, 200
menu, 200
milligram (mg), 193
mixed vegetables, 200
non-fat milk, 193
noodles, 200
nutrients, 192
nutrition label, 192
nutritious, 197
onion rings, 200
orange, 189
orange juice, 195
outdoor market, 188
picnic, 191

pint, 187
pork chop, 200
pound, 187
price, 194
protein, 192
quantity, 187
quart, 187
roast chicken, 200
salty, 196
serving, 193
shopping list, 191
soda, 200
sodium, 192
soup, 189
sugar, 192
supermarket, 188
taste, 194
tea, 198
tuna, 189
yogurt, 189

UNIT 11

allergic reaction, 207
ambulance, 208
bleed, 207
burn yourself, 207
call 911, 207
car accident, 214
choke, 207
construction accident, 214
distracted driving, 220
driver's license, 220
electric, 209
electrical cord, 212
electrical outlet, 212
electrical plug, 212
emergency, 206

employer, 219
escape plan, 212
exit, 212
explosion, 214
fall, 207
fall down, 207
fire escape, 212
fire extinguisher, 212
fire hazard, 212
have trouble
  breathing, 207
heart attack, 207
heater, 212
hurt, 215
injury, 215

inspector, 219
matches, 212
medical emergency, 207
OSHA (Occupational
  Safety and Health
  Administration, 218
police, 217
proof of insurance, 220
pull over, 220
registration, 220
report an accident, 220
robbery, 214
rug, 212
run a red light, 220
safety gear, 218

safety hazard, 218
safety procedure, 212
safety tip, 213
seat belt, 221
smoke alarm, 212
speed, 220
steering wheel, 220
swallow poison, 207
tailgate, 220
taxi, 208
toxic chemicals, 218
traffic jam, 217
traffic ticket, 220
unconscious, 207

UNIT 12

ask for a favor, 234
ask questions, 227
be a team player, 244
be on time, 226
call in late, 227
clock in/out, 227
cover someone's
  hours, 234
disabled, 238
earnings, 238
eat at my desk, 229
eat in the break room, 229
employee I.D. badge, 228
Federal tax, 233

first shift , 241
follow directions, 227
full-time, 241
gross pay, 232
health and safety rules, 243
latex gloves, 227
maintain equipment, 227
manager, 228
Medicare, 232
miss work, 234
net pay, 232
orientation meeting, 228
overtime hours, 233
part-time, 241

payroll deductions, 232
pay period, 232
pay stub, 232
rate of pay, 232
regular hour, 232
report a problem, 227
retired, 238
second shift, 241
sick-day policy, 228
Social Security, 232
Social Security benefits, 238
State Disability Insurance
  (SDI), 232
state tax, 232

store equipment, 227
talk to a manager, 229
uniform, 227
vacation-time policy, 228
wear a uniform, 227
wear safety gear, 227
work as a team, 227

UNIT 1

Page 8, Exercises 2A and 2B

Min: Hi, Eva.
Eva: Hi, Min. Are you coming to my party tonight?
Min: Of course. Are you inviting your friend?
Eva: Which friend?
Min: You know—he's handsome and he has short, black hair.

Page 8, Exercise 2C

Min: Hi, Eva.
Eva: Hi, Min. Are you coming to my party tonight?
Min: Of course. Are you inviting your friend?
Eva: Which friend?
Min: You know—he's handsome and he has short, black hair.
Eva: Does he have blue eyes?
Min: No, he has brown eyes.
Eva: Oh. You mean Victor. And he's not my friend. He's my brother! But of course I'll introduce you to him.

Page 14, Exercises 2A and 2B

Erica: Kay, tell me about your new supervisor. What's she like?
Kay: Well, she's outgoing and she's cheerful.
Erica: Yeah? What else?
Kay: She's demanding, but she's supportive too.

Page 14, Exercise 2C

Erica: Kay, tell me about your new supervisor. What's she like?
Kay: Well, she's outgoing and she's cheerful.
Erica: Yeah? What else?
Kay: She's demanding, but she's supportive, too.
Erica: That sounds good.
Kay: Yes, it is. And you know, I'm quiet. But she's talkative.
Erica: That's not a problem. You don't have to talk at all.

Page 20, Exercises 2B and 2C

Kara: Pia, I want to introduce you to my friend. Pia, this is Ron. Ron, this is Pia.
Pia: Nice to meet you, Ron.
Ron: Nice to meet you, too.
Pia: So, are you a nurse, like Kara?
Ron: No, I'm not. I work at the hospital, but I'm a cook in the cafeteria.

Page 20, Listen, Exercise 2D

Kara: Pia, I want to introduce you to my friend. Pia, this is Ron. Ron, this is Pia.
Pia: Nice to meet you, Ron.
Ron: Nice to meet you, too.
Pia: So, are you a nurse, like Kara?
Ron: No, I'm not. I work at the hospital, but I'm a cook in the cafeteria. How about you?
Pia: I work with Kara at the hospital, but I'm not a nurse. I'm a medical assistant.
Ron: Oh, how is it?
Pia: Good. I like it!

UNIT 2

Page 28, Exercises 2B and 2C

Amy: Tell me about your family.
Sam: Well, I don't have a very big family. I have a brother and two sisters.
Amy: Do they live here?
Sam: My sisters live in Senegal, but my brother lives here.

Page 28, Listen, Exercise 2D

Amy: Tell me about your family.
Sam: Well, I don't have a very big family. I have a brother and two sisters.
Amy: Do they live here?
Sam: My sisters live in Senegal, but my brother lives here.
Amy: Really? What does your brother do?
Sam: He works in a hospital. He's a medical assistant.
Amy: And does he live near you?
Sam: Yes. In fact, we live in the same apartment.
Amy: Wow, then he really lives near you!

Page 34, Exercises 2B and 2C

Ming: Tina, is this your sister?
Tina: Yes, it is. That's my sister, Lili. Do we look alike?
Ming: Yes, you do. You look a lot alike. Do you have a lot in common?
Tina: Actually, we do. She works in a bank, and I work in a bank, too.
She's really talkative and I'm really talkative.

Page 34, Exercise 2D

Ming: Tina, is that your sister?
Tina: Yes, it is. That's my sister, Lili. Do we look alike?
Ming: Yes, you do. You look a lot alike. Do you have a lot in common?
Tina: Actually, we do. She works in a bank, and I work in a bank, too.
She's really talkative and I'm really talkative.
But what about you, Ming? Do you have any brothers or sisters?
Ming: I have two sisters. And we have a lot in common, too.
Tina: Really?
Ming: Yeah. I have two sisters and my sisters have two sisters.
But I don't have any brothers and . . .
Tina: (chuckling) I know . . . and your sisters don't have any brothers! You do have a lot in common! (laughing)

Page 39, Exercise D

Customer: Hello. I'd like to mail this package.
Clerk: How do you want to send it?
Customer: How long does Retail Ground take?
Clerk: Two to eight days.
Customer: Okay. I'll send it Priority Mail.
Clerk: Do you want Delivery Confirmation or Insurance?
Customer: Yes. Insurance, please.
Clerk: Does it contain any hazardous materials?
Customer: No.

Page 40, Exercises 2B and 2C

Oliver: Hello, I'm Oliver Marley, and welcome to They're Your Family Now!—the game show where we ask people questions about their in-laws. Please welcome our first contestant, Mr. Trevor Scanlon.

Trevor: Hello.

Oliver: Now, Trevor, here are the rules of the game. Before the show, we asked your wife Ann ten questions about her family. Now, I'm going to ask you the same questions. You get $100 for every question you answer correctly.

Trevor: OK! I'm ready.

Page 40, Exercise 2D

Oliver: Hello, I'm Oliver Marley, and welcome to They're Your Family Now!, the game show where we ask people questions about their in-laws. Please welcome our first contestant, Mr. Trevor Scanlon.

Trevor: Hello.

Oliver: Now, Trevor. Here are the rules of the game. Before the show, we asked your wife Ann ten questions about her family. Now I'm going to ask you the same questions. You get $100 for every question you answer correctly.

Trevor: OK! I'm ready.

Oliver: Great. Trevor, here's your first question. Where do your wife's grandparents live?

Trevor: Oh! That's easy. They live in San Antonio with the rest of her family.

Oliver: Right! Good start. OK. Here's your next question. How many brothers and sisters does your mother-in-law have?

Trevor: My mother-in-law?! . . . Well, there's Martha, Paula, Henry, Charles, . . . and what's his name? . . . Paul! OK. My mother-in-law has two sisters and three brothers. So that's five in total.

Oliver: That's right! Good job. Next question. What does your brother-in-law Alex do?

Trevor: Oh, wow . . . I know he works in an office . . . Um, he's an engineer?

Oliver: No, he's an accountant!

Trevor: Oh!

Oliver: Better luck on the next one. Here it is . . . When does your sister-in-law Ella work?

Trevor: Oh, I know this one! Ella works at night because her husband works during the day. She watches the baby all day, and he watches him at night!

Oliver: Correct! Well, so far you have three points. We have to take a break, but we'll be right back with They're Your Family Now!

UNIT 3

Page 48, Exercise 2B

Lucy: Hi, this is Lucy Campbell for Eye Around Town, the podcast that tells you what's happening in town. So what's happening today? I'm here at the summer clearance at Big Deals, and the store is full of shoppers. Let's talk to a few of them . . . Excuse me. What's your name?

Erica: Erica.

Lucy: Hi, Erica. Tell us, why are you here at Big Deals today?

Page 48, Exercises 2C and 2D

Lucy: Hi, this is Lucy Campbell for Eye Around Town, the podcast that tells you what's happening in town. So what's happening today? I'm here at the summer clearance at Big Deals, and the store is full of shoppers. Let's talk to a few of them . . . Excuse me. What's your name?

Erica: Erica.

Lucy: Hi, Erica. Tell us, why are you here at Big Deals today?

Erica: Well, I shop here a lot. They have great prices on everything you need.

Lucy: And what do you need to buy today?

Erica: Well, I don't need to buy anything, but I want to buy a new pair of pants for work.

Lucy: Well, I hope you find some, Erica. Next . . . tell us your name, please.

Karen: Karen.

Lucy: Karen, why are you here today?

Karen: I'm here with my daughter. We don't need to buy anything today. We just need to return this dress. It's really easy to return things here if you have your receipt . . . Where is that receipt? I know it's here somewhere . . .

Lucy: Uh . . . OK. And you, sir. Who are you, and why are you here at Big Deals today?

Nick: My name's Nick. I need to buy some shorts for my son.

Lucy: Do you always shop here at Big Deals?

Nick: Yeah. It's so convenient. They have everything here, so I don't need to go to a lot of different stores. I really don't like to shop.

Lucy: OK, well, that's all for today, and I want to look for a jacket while I'm here! I'm Lucy Campbell, and this is the Eye Around Town podcast.

Page 50, Exercise B

1. **A:** I want to buy a few things after work today. Do you want to go to Shop Mart with me?
    B: Sure. I need to return a cap there.
    A: OK. What time do you want to leave here?
2. **A:** Do you want to go shopping during lunch today?
    B: Maybe. I need to get a present for my co-worker. But I don't want to spend a lot of money. I need to check the sales online.
    A: I understand. I need to be careful with my money, too.
3. **A:** All my uniforms for work are old. I need to buy some new ones.
    B: Oh, really? I don't need to wear a uniform to work—regular clothes like jeans are OK.

Page 54, 2A and 2B

Deb: So, what are your plans for tomorrow?

Max: Nothing. I'm going to relax.

Deb: Well, I have a lot to do. First, I need to go to the ATM. Then I need to go to the hardware store. Then I'm going to stop at the deli at the supermarket.

Max: Wow. You're going to be busy.

Page 54, Exercise 2C

Deb: So, what are your plans for tomorrow?

Max: Nothing. I'm going to relax.

Deb: Well, I have a lot to do. First, I need to go to the ATM. Then I need to go to the hardware store. Then I'm going to stop at the deli at the supermarket.

Max: Wow. You're going to be busy.

Deb: I know, And then I'm going to go to the drug store. And after that . . . hey . . . where are you going?

Max: [laughter as if he's joking] I'm going to take a nap. I'm tired just thinking about your errands tomorrow.

Page 60, Exercises 2B and 2C

Anna: Hi, Bessy. Are you going out at lunchtime?

Bessy: Yeah, I need to run an errand. I'm going to Kohn's. I need to return this jacket.

Anna: How come?

Bessy: The zipper is broken.

Anna: That's very annoying. . . . Actually, I need to go to Kohn's, too. I need to return a dress.

Page 60, Exercise 2D

Anna: Hi, Bessy. Are you going out at lunchtime?

Bessy: Yeah, I need to run an errand. I'm going to Kohn's. I need to return this jacket.

Anna: How come?

Bessy: The zipper is broken.

Anna: That's very annoying. . . . Actually, I need to go to Kohn's, too. I need to return a dress.

Bessy: Really? What's wrong with it?

Anna: It's too short. Here. . . . Look at it.

Bessy: Oh, no! Of course this is too short. It's a shirt, not a dress!

UNIT 4

Page 68, Exercises 2A and 2B

Mario: What are you doing this weekend?

Bi-Yun: I'm going to go to the beach with my family.

Mario: Really? Sounds like fun.

Bi-Yun: Yeah. We usually go to the beach on Sunday in the summer. What about you?

Mario: Well, I have class on Saturday. I have a business class every Saturday morning.

Page 68, Exercise 2C

Mario: What are you doing this weekend?

Bi-Yun: I'm going to go to the beach with my family.

Mario: Really? Sounds like fun.

Bi-Yun: Yeah. We usually go to the beach on Sunday in the summer. What about you?

Mario: Well, I have class on Saturday. I have a business class every Saturday morning.

Bi-Yun: You have a business? Wow. That's really neat.

Mario: No, I don't have a business . . .

Bi-Yun: But you're taking a business class, right?

Mario: Yeah. But I don't know how to run a business. That's why I'm taking a class!

Page 72, Exercise 1A

The City Library has several regular events.
The ESL Class for adults meets every Monday and Wednesday from 6 p.m. to 8 p.m.

There is a Job Fair on the fourth Saturday of the month from 9:00 am to 4:00 pm.

The special lecture is once a month, on the second Saturday of the month,

every Monday and Wednesday

from 6 p.m. to 8 p.m.

on the fourth Saturday of the month from 9:00 a.m. to 4:00 p.m.

once a month

on the second Saturday of the month

Page 73, Exercises 2A and 2B

Thank you for calling Atlas Community College's Library. Today is Monday, May 14th, and we are open from 8:00 a.m. to 9 p.m. Today's events:

The computer lab is open from 8:00 a.m. to 8:00 p.m. There is a special résumé writing workshop today. It meets in room 224 at 1:00 pm. There are two ESL Conversation Classes. The morning class meets from 9-11 am, and the evening class meets from 6:30 to 8:30 pm. The Job Interview Workshop series begins today. It meets from 4 to 6 pm.

Tomorrow, Tuesday, May 15th, the library is open from 8:00 am to 9 pm.

The computer lab is open from 8:00 am to 1:00 pm. Computer Skills for Adults meets from 1:00 to 3:00 pm. There is a special workshop on completing a Job Application. It meets at 5 pm.

Page 74, Exercise 2B

Katie: Welcome to the Talk Time podcast. I'm your host, Katie Martin. We all have things that we need to do, at home and at work. And here's the problem: A lot of times we don't like the things we need to do. So, what's the solution? Well, today we're talking to Dr. Collin Goldberg, and he has some ideas. Welcome to the podcast, Dr. Goldberg.

Page 74, Exercise 2C and 2D

Katie: Welcome to the Talk Time podcast. I'm your host, Katie Martin. We all have things that we need to do, at home and at work. And here's the problem: A lot of times we don't like the things we need to do. So, what's the solution? Well, today we're talking to Dr. Collin Goldberg, and he has some ideas. Welcome to the podcast, Dr. Goldberg.

Dr. Goldberg: Thanks, Katie. It's great to be here.

Katie: So, Dr. Goldberg, tell us about some of your ideas.

Dr. Goldberg: Sure. Here's the first one: When you need to do something you hate, do something you like at the same time. For example, if you hate to wash dishes, then do something you love while you wash the dishes. Wash the dishes and watch TV. Or wash the dishes and listen to a podcast. Or talk to a friend on the phone.

Katie: That way you're not thinking about the activity that you don't like.

Dr. Goldberg: Exactly.

Katie: That seems pretty easy. Do you have any other tips?

Dr. Goldberg:	Sure. Here's another idea: Put a time limit on the activities you hate to do.
Katie:	A time limit?
Dr. Goldberg:	Exactly. For example, say it's 1:00 and you need to clean up. Decide what time you're going to finish cleaning, say 3:00. When it's 3:00, you stop.
Katie:	That's it?
Dr. Goldberg:	Yes. It's an extremely simple idea, but it works. When you have a time limit, you know when the activity is going to end. And that can help a lot.
Katie:	That makes sense.
Dr. Goldberg:	Right. And here's one more: After you do something you hate, do something you like. For example, if you hate to answer email, but you love to read, then say to yourself, "I'm going to answer email. Then I'm going to take a break and read for half an hour."
Katie:	Dr. Goldberg, these sound like really good ideas.

Page 80, Exercise 2B and 2C

Meg:	Do you want to get some lunch?
Selda:	Sorry, I can't. I have to finish some work.
Meg:	Oh. Are you sure?
Selda:	Yes, I'm sorry. I'm really too busy.
Meg:	Well, how about a little later?
Selda:	Thanks, but I don't think so. Not today.

Page 80, Exercise 2D

Meg:	Do you want to get some lunch?
Selda:	Sorry, I can't. I have to finish some work.
Meg:	Oh. Are you sure?
Selda:	Yes, I'm sorry. I'm really too busy.
Meg:	Well, how about a little later?
Selda:	Thanks, but I don't think so. Not today. I have a big meeting this afternoon. Hold on a second. Hello? Oh, hi, Bob. OK. Great. Thanks for calling. Guess what? My meeting was canceled.
Meg:	That's great! So now you can go to lunch?
Selda:	Yes, I guess I can. Let me get my coat.

UNIT 5

Page 88, Exercises 2B and 2C

Harry:	Hello?
Joe:	Hi, Harry. It's Joe.
Harry:	Oh, hi, Joe. Can I call you back?
Joe:	Sure. No problem.
Harry:	Thanks. My radiator is broken and I'm trying to fix it.
Joe:	You should call the building manager for your apartment.

Page 88, Exercise 2D

Harry:	Hello?
Joe:	Hi, Harry. It's Joe.
Harry:	Oh, hi, Joe. Can I call you back?
Joe:	Sure. No problem.
Harry:	Thanks. My radiator is broken and I'm trying to fix it.
Joe:	You should call the building manager for your apartment.
Harry:	That's a good idea. There's just one problem.

| Joe: | What's that? |
| Harry: | Well, I just got a new job. Now I'm the building manager |

Page 94, Exercises 2B and 2C

Rental agent:	Hello?
Maria:	Hi, I'm calling about the apartment for rent. Can you tell me about it?
Rental agent:	Sure. There are two bedrooms and a large living room.
Maria:	Is there a laundry room?
Rental agent:	No, there isn't. But there's a laundromat down the street.
Maria:	I see. Is there a bus stop nearby?
Rental agent:	Yes, there is—just around the corner.

Page 94, Exercise 2D

Rental agent:	Hello?
Maria:	Hi, I'm calling about the apartment for rent. Can you tell me about it?
Rental agent:	Sure. There are two bedrooms and a large living room.
Maria:	Is there a laundry room?
Rental agent:	No, there isn't. But there's a laundromat down the street.
Maria:	I see. Is there a bus stop nearby?
Rental agent:	Yes, there is—just around the corner.
Maria:	Wow! And the ad says it's only $200 a month!
Rental agent:	Yes, sorry. That was a mistake. The rent is $2,000 a month, not $200.
Maria:	Oh, well, thanks. I guess I don't need any more information. I'm looking for something under $500 a month.

Page 100, Exercises 2B and 2C

Go straight on Warton Avenue for two blocks. Turn left onto Brice Road. Go straight for two blocks. Turn right onto Clarkson Street. Go through one traffic light.

Page 100, Exercise 2D

Go straight on Warton Avenue for two blocks. Turn left onto Brice Road. Go straight for two blocks. Turn right onto Clarkson Street. Go through one traffic light. Your destination is on the left.

Page 101, Exercise 2B

1.	there	4.	theater
2.	this	5.	the
3.	things	6.	third

UNIT 6

Page 108, Exercises 2B and 2C

Rose:	How was your weekend? How was the family reunion?
Sam:	It was really nice, thanks. My whole family showed up.
Rose:	Sounds great.
Sam:	Yeah, it was fun. We looked at old pictures and listened to family stories.

Page 108, Exercise 2D

| Rose: | How was your weekend? How was the family reunion? |
| Sam: | It was really nice, thanks. My whole family showed up. |

Rose: Sounds great.
Sam: Yeah, it was fun. We looked at old pictures and listened to family stories. How about you?
Rose: My weekend was pretty good. I had a surprise party on Saturday night.
Sam: Really? Was it someone's birthday?
Rose: No, it wasn't a birthday. I just invited some co-workers from my last job to come over. Then some other friends came over, and—surprise! It was a party!

Page 112, Exercise 1B

1.	New Year's Day	6.	Labor Day
2.	Martin Luther King, Jr. Day	7.	Columbus Day
3.	Presidents' Day	8.	Veterans' Day
4.	Memorial Day	9.	Thanksgiving Day
5.	Independence Day	10.	Christmas Day

Page 112, Exercise 1C

Welcome to our company. One of the many benefits we provide for our employees are days off on national holidays. You may not be familiar with the holidays we celebrate in the U.S., so I'll go over them quickly.

1 First of all, we have a free day to start off a year and get a good rest after parties the night before.

2 In May, there is a holiday that celebrates people who have died fighting for our country. It always falls on a Monday, so you get a longer weekend.

3 In the middle of summer, we like to stop and celebrate this country's birthday. You have the day off to go to your favorite parade, have a barbeque, and watch fireworks.

4 In September, there's a holiday to thank all working people. It usually falls on the first Monday of the month. This national holiday recognizes how hard everyone works.

5 There is also a holiday on the 4th Thursday of November. We even give our employees coupons so that they can buy their turkeys cheaper in a nearby store!

Page 114, Exercises 2B and 2C

Amber: Welcome to Star Talk, the podcast where we talk to today's biggest stars. I'm your host Amber Jenkins, and today I'm very excited to welcome actor Daniel Campos!
Daniel: Thanks. It's great to be here.
Amber: So, Daniel, tell us about yourself and your celebrity life.
Daniel: Uh—sure. But my life really isn't that interesting.
Amber: Your life? Not interesting? I don't believe it. I mean, you're a huge star. Now, let's start with your childhood. You were born in California?
Daniel: Yes, I was born in California, and that's where I grew up. I had a pretty normal childhood.
Amber: What about school?
Daniel: Uh, yeah. I went to school. I graduated from high school and went to college.
Amber: And you always wanted to be an actor?
Daniel: No, I didn't. Actually, I wanted to be a plumber when I was a kid. My dad was a plumber, and I wanted to be just like him. I started acting in college.

Page 114, Exercise 2D

Amber: Welcome to Star Talk, the podcast where we talk to today's biggest stars. I'm your host Amber Jenkins, and today I'm very excited to welcome actor Daniel Campos!
Daniel: Thanks. It's great to be here.
Amber: So, Daniel, tell us about yourself and your celebrity life.
Daniel: Uh—sure. But my life really isn't that interesting.
Amber: Your life? Not interesting? I don't believe it. I mean, you're a huge star. Now, let's start with your childhood. You were born in California?
Daniel: Yes, I was born in California, and that's where I grew up. I had a pretty normal childhood.
Amber: What about school?
Daniel: Uh, yeah. I went to school. I graduated from high school and went to college.
Amber: And you always wanted to be an actor?
Daniel: No, I didn't. Actually, I wanted to be a plumber when I was a kid. My dad was a plumber, and I wanted to be just like him. I started acting in college.
Amber: OK, so you had a normal childhood. You went to school. But now your life is very different, right? You probably do lots of interesting things.
Daniel: Uh, not really.
Amber: Oh, come on, tell us. What did you do last night? I'll bet you went to a big, fancy party.
Daniel: No, actually I stayed home. I watched some TV and went to bed early.
Amber: Went to bed early? That's not glamorous at all!
Daniel: I know, I'm telling you, I don't have a very glamorous life. I'm really just a regular guy.
Amber: Well, there you go, listeners—Daniel Campos is just a regular guy. . . .

Page 120 and 121, Exercises 2B and 2C

Maria: Is everything OK? You look stressed out.
Adam: Well, I had a rough morning.
Maria: Why? What happened?
Adam: First, I lost my car keys.
Maria: Oh, no!
Adam: Then I got stuck in traffic.
Maria: When did you get to work?
Adam: At 10:00. I was really late.

Page 121, Exercise 2D

Maria: Is everything OK? You look stressed out.
Adam: Well, I had a rough morning.
Maria: Why? What happened?
Adam: First, I lost my car keys.
Maria: Oh, no!
Adam: Then I got stuck in traffic.
Maria: When did you get to work?
Adam: At 10:00. I was really late.
Maria: That's too bad.
Adam: Wait—it gets worse.
Maria: Really? What happened?
Adam: When I finally got to work, I realized it was Tuesday.
Maria: So?
Adam: So, I don't work on Tuesdays! Tuesday is my day off!

UNIT 7

Page 127, Exercise C
1. I have a cold.
2. I have an earache.
3. I have the flu.
4. I have heartburn.

Page 128, Exercises 2B and 2C
Receptionist: Hello. Westview Clinic.
Roberto: Hi. This is Roberto Cruz. I'm sick, and I need to make an appointment, please.
Receptionist: All right. What's the matter?
Roberto: I have a fever and I'm nauseous.

Page 128, Exercise 2D
Receptionist: Hello. Westview Clinic.
Roberto: Hi. This is Roberto Cruz. I'm sick, and I need to make an appointment, please.
Receptionist: All right. What's the matter?
Roberto: I have a fever and I'm nauseous.
Receptionist: OK. How about Tuesday morning? At 9:00?
Roberto: Yes, that's fine.
Receptionist: All right. What's your name again?
Roberto: Roberto Cruz.
Receptionist: Roberto Cruz. OK, Mr. Cruz, we'll see you on Tuesday at 9:00.
Roberto: OK. Thank you.

Page 133, Exercise C
1. What is the name of the medicine? Milacam
2. How often do I take it? Once a day.
3. What is the dosage? Two tablespoons.
4. What is the expiration date? November 20, 2021
5. How many refills can I get? Two.

Page 134, Exercises 2B and 2C
Manolo: Hi, Val. What are you doing here?
Val: Oh, hi, Manolo. I had an accident. I broke my arm.
Manolo: Oh, no! I'm sorry to hear that.
Val: Thanks. What about you?
Manolo: I hurt my ankle at a soccer game. I think I sprained it.

Page 134, Exercise 2D
Manolo: Hi, Val. What are you doing here?
Val: Oh, hi, Manolo. I had an accident. I broke my arm.
Manolo: Oh, no! I'm sorry to hear that.
Val: Thanks. What about you?
Manolo: I hurt my ankle at a soccer game. I think I sprained it.
Val: That's too bad. I guess you can't play soccer for a while.
Manolo: Oh, I don't play soccer. I just watch.
Val: What? So how did you hurt your ankle?
Manolo: Well, I was at a soccer game. I was hungry, so I got some food. I had a drink and a sandwich in my hands, and I fell down the stairs on the way to my seat.

Page 140, Exercises 2B and 2C
Eva: Hello. Eva Perez speaking.
Sung: Hi, Eva. This is Sung. I can't come in today because I have to go to the doctor. I don't feel well.

Eva: Sorry to hear that. Thanks for calling, and take care of yourself.
Sung: Thanks.

Page 140, Exercise 2D
Eva: Hello. Eva Pérez speaking.
Sung: Hi, Eva. This is Sung. I can't come in today because I have to go to the doctor. I don't feel well.
Eva: Sorry to hear that. Thanks for calling, and take care of yourself.
Sung: Thanks.
Eva: Do you think you'll be in tomorrow?
Sung: I'm not sure. I can call you later after I go to the doctor.
Eva: All right. That sounds good.

UNIT 8

Page 148, Exercises 2B and 2C
Albert: Manny? Hi, I'm Albert Taylor, the store manager. Please have a seat.
Manny: Thank you. It's nice to meet you.
Albert: I have your application here. I see that you're working now. What are your job duties?
Manny: Well, I assist customers and stock shelves.

Page 148, Exercise 2D
Albert: Manny? Hi, I'm Albert Taylor, the store manager. Please have a seat.
Manny: Thank you. It's nice to meet you.
Albert: I have your application here. I see that you're working now. What are your job duties?
Manny: Well, I assist customers and stock shelves.
Albert: OK. Tell me about your skills. Can you use a cash register?
Manny: No, I can't, but I can learn.

Page 154, Exercises 2B and 2C
Albert: So, tell me more about your work experience.
Manny: Well, I came to the U.S. three years ago. First, I got a job as a gardener. Then last year, I got a job as a stock clerk.
Albert: OK. So now you're a stock clerk. Why are you looking for another job?
Manny: Things in my life have changed, and now I'd like to do something different.

Page 154, Exercises 2D
Albert: So, tell me more about your work experience.
Manny: Well, I came to the U.S. three years ago. First, I got a job as a gardener. Then last year, I got a job as a stock clerk.
Albert: OK. So now you're a stock clerk. Why are you looking for another job?
Manny: Things in my life have changed, and now I'd like to do something different.
Albert: I see. By the way, you wrote on your application that you were unemployed two years ago. Can you explain that?
Manny: Sure. I left my job because my mother was sick, and I had to take care of her for two months.

Page 160, Exercises 2B and 2C

Albert: Let me ask you a few questions about your availability. Do you prefer mornings or afternoons?
Manny: Well, I prefer mornings, but I'm flexible.
Albert: All right. Can you work on weekends?
Manny: Yes, I can.
Albert: Great. And when could you start?
Manny: In two weeks. I need to give two weeks' notice at my job.

Page 160, Listen, Exercise 2D

Albert: Let me ask you a few questions about your availability. Do you prefer mornings or afternoons?
Manny: Well, I prefer mornings, but I'm flexible.
Albert: All right. Can you work on weekends?
Manny: Yes, I can.
Albert: Great. And when could you start?
Manny: In two weeks. I need to give two weeks' notice at my job.
Albert: OK. Well, everything looks good. Do you have any questions for me?
Manny: Yes. When can I expect to hear from you?
Albert: Well, I have some other interviews this week. I can let you know next week.
Manny: OK. Thank you for the opportunity to talk with you. It was nice to meet you.
Albert: You, too.

UNIT 9

Page 168, Exercises 2B and 2C

Medi: Carlo brought a notice home from school today. There's a parent-teacher conference in two weeks.
David: Oh yeah? What day?
Medi: Thursday the 19th at 6:00. My mother will watch the kids. That way we can both go.
David: Oh, I have to work that day until 9:00, but I'll try to change my shift.

Page 168, Exercise 2D

Medi: Carlo brought a notice home from school today. There's a parent-teacher conference in two weeks.
David: Oh yeah? What day?
Medi: Thursday the 19th at 6:00. My mother will watch the kids. That way we can both go.
David: Oh, I have to work that day until 9:00, but I'll try to change my shift.
Medi: I hope you can.
David: Me, too. When is Carlo's band concert? I know it's coming up.
Medi: That's Monday the 23rd.
David: OK. I'll definitely go to that.

Page 172, Exercises 1B and 1C

Receptionist: Winter Hill Elementary School.
Elsa: Hello. This is Elsa Vega. May I speak to Mr. Taylor please?
Receptionist: I'm sorry. He's not available right now. May I take a message?
Elsa: Yes, please. I have a question about my daughter Maria's math homework. Please ask him to call me back.
Receptionist: Sure. What's your number?
Elsa: It's 718-555-4343.
Receptionist: OK. I'll give him the message.
Elsa: Thank you.

Page 172, Exercise 2A

Mobile voice mail: Hello. You have reached 718-555-4343. I am not available, but please leave a message after the beep.
Mr. Taylor: Ms. Vega. This is Mr. Taylor. I'm returning your call. Since Maria was home sick today, she won't need to complete next week's unit, but she will need to complete this week's unit. She'll take the quiz on Tuesday. Please call me or e-mail me at jtaylor@winterhill.edu. if you have questions.

Page 174, Exercises 2B and 2C

Mr. Thompson: Hi, I'm Harold Thompson, Carlo's teacher. Nice to meet you.
Medi: I'm Carlo's mother, Medi Duval. Nice to meet you, too. So, how's Carlo doing?
Mr. Thompson: Carlo's a good student. I enjoy having him in class.
Medi: That's good to hear.
Mr. Thompson: He does very well in math. He works carefully.
Medi: He likes math a lot. What about social studies?
Mr. Thompson: Well, he's having a little trouble in that class. He needs to do his homework.
Medi: OK. I'll talk to him.

Page 174, Listen, Exercise 2D

Mr. Thompson: Hi, I'm Harold Thompson, Carlo's teacher. Nice to meet you.
Medi: I'm Carlo's mother, Medi Duval. Nice to meet you, too. So, how's Carlo doing?
Mr. Thompson: Carlo's a good student. I enjoy having him in class.
Medi: That's good to hear.
Mr. Thompson: He does very well in math. He works carefully.
Medi: He likes math a lot. What about social studies?
Mr. Thompson: Well, he's having a little trouble in that class. He needs to do his homework.
Medi: OK. I'll talk to him.
Mr. Thompson: Have you thought about signing up Carlo for homework help after school?
Medi: Homework help? What's that?
Mr. Thompson: It's an after-school program. Older kids from the high school come and help students with their homework. The program is free, and students can get the extra help they need.

Page 180, Exercises 2B and 2C

Tito: Where's Luis?
Anna: He's at a friend's house. Why? What's up?
Tito: Well, his teacher called. He's having some trouble at school.
Anna: Uh-oh. What kind of trouble?
Tito: She said he's not paying attention and skipping class.

Anna: What? Well, we need to talk to him right away.
Tito: Definitely. Let's all talk tonight after dinner.

Page 180, Listen, Exercise 2D

Tito: Where's Luis?
Anna: He's at a friend's house. Why? What's up?
Tito: Well, his teacher called. He's having some trouble at school.
Anna: Uh-oh. What kind of trouble?
Tito: She said he's not paying attention and skipping class.
Anna: What? Well, we need to talk to him right away.
Tito: Definitely. Let's all talk tonight after dinner.
Anna: This is so strange. Luis never has problems at school.
Tito: I know. He's usually a great student.

UNIT 10

Page 186, Exercise C

1. a bag of potato chips
2. a box of cereal
3. a can of soup
4. a bottle of vinegar
5. a jar of mayonnaise
6. a container of yogurt
7. a bunch of bananas
8. a head of cauliflower
9. a pound of grapes
10. a pint of milk
11. a quart of orange juice
12. a half-gallon of ice cream
13. a gallon of water
14. a dozen eggs

Page 188, Exercises 2B and 2C

Agnes: Hi, Yuka. I'm going to the grocery store for some milk. Do you need anything?
Yuka: Uh, let me see. Could you get a can of tomatoes?
Agnes: A can of tomatoes? Sure, no problem.
Yuka: Oh, and I need some onions.
Agnes: How many onions?
Yuka: Two.
Agnes: All right. A can of tomatoes and two onions. I'll be back in a little while.

Page 188, Exercise 2D

Agnes: Hi, Yuka. I'm going to the grocery store for some milk. Do you need anything?
Yuka: Uh, let me see. Could you get a can of tomatoes?
Agnes: A can of tomatoes? Sure, no problem.
Yuka: Oh, and I need some onions.
Agnes: How many onions?
Yuka: Two.
Agnes: All right. A can of tomatoes and two onions. I'll be back in a little while.
Yuka: Wait a second, since you're going, we could use a jar of mayonnaise, a head of lettuce, and a box of cereal. Hey, what are you doing?
Agnes: I'm looking for a pen and paper. I need to write all this down!

Page 194, Exercises 2A and 2B

Your family is important to you. You want to take care of them. You want to give them food that tastes good and that's good for them. Better taste, healthier meals. That's what you get from Baker's Bread. With no added colors or flavors, Baker's Bread is better for you than any other brands. Never frozen, Baker's Bread is fresher than other bread. Try it. You'll taste the difference.

Page 195, Exercise B

A: Oh, you buy Franklin brand coffee. Is it good?
B: Yes, it's excellent. I think it's better than all the other brands.
A: Really? Why?
B: It tastes great and it's not expensive.

Page 200, Exercises 2B and 2C

Waitress: Here are your iced teas. Are you ready to order?
Edgar: Yes. I'd like the meatloaf.
Waitress: And what would you like with that?
Edgar: A side of mixed vegetables.
Waitress: OK. Meatloaf with mixed vegetables.
Edgar: And a hamburger with a side of onion rings.
Waitress: A hamburger with onion rings.

Page 200, Exercise D

Waitress: Here are your iced teas. Are you ready to order?
Edgar: Yes. I'd like the meatloaf.
Waitress: And what would you like with that?
Edgar: A side of mixed vegetables.
Waitress: OK. Meatloaf with mixed vegetables.
Edgar: And a hamburger with a side of onion rings.
Waitress: A hamburger with onion rings.
Edgar: Oh, and could we have some sugar?
Waitress: Sure. Here you go. I'll be right back with your order.
Lina: Excuse me. I want to order something, too.
Waitress: Oh! Aren't you having the hamburger?
Lina: Actually, no. The meatloaf and the hamburger are both for him.
Edgar: Yeah. I'm pretty hungry!

UNIT 11

Page 208, Exercises 2B and 2C

Operator: 9-1-1. What's your emergency?
Olivia: I think a man is having a heart attack.
Operator: OK. What's the location of the emergency?
Olivia: Dave's Sports Shop at 103 Elm Street.
Operator: What are the cross streets?
Olivia: 17th and 18th Avenues.
Operator: All right. What's your name?
Olivia: Olivia Ramos.

Page 208, Exercise 2D

Operator: 9-1-1. What's your emergency?
Olivia: I think a man is having a heart attack.
Operator: OK. What's the location of the emergency?
Olivia: Dave's Sports Shop at 103 Elm Street.
Operator: What are the cross streets?
Olivia: 17th and 18th Avenues.
Operator: All right. What's your name?
Olivia: Olivia Ramos.
Operator: All right, Ms. Ramos. An ambulance is on its way. But don't hang up. Stay on the line with me until the ambulance gets there.
Olivia: OK. I'll just tell the man that the ambulance is coming.

Page 212, Exercise 2B

a fire extinguisher
a smoke alarm
a fire escape
an escape plan
exits

Page 213, Exercise 2C

FIRE SAFETY TIPS for the Workplace
Get out! Stay out! Call 911
1 Leave your work area immediately. Do not take anything with you, but alert your co-workers.
2 Don't stop to call 911. Call from a safe location outside of the building.
3 Don't use an elevator to exit the building. Use the stairs.
4 Close any open doors. This will prevent the fire from spreading quickly.
5 Feel every closed door before opening it. Don't open a door that is hot. Try to find another exit.
6 If you smell smoke, stay close to the floor. Cover your mouth and nose with a wet cloth.
7 When you get outside, do not go back to your workplace for any reason. Tell firefighters about anyone still inside the building.

Page 214, Exercises 2B and 2C

Mr. Novak: Did you hear what happened yesterday?
Mrs. Novak: No. What happened?
Mr. Novak: There was a gas explosion downtown.
Mrs. Novak: Oh, my gosh. That's terrible. Was anybody hurt?
Mr. Novak: Yes. Two people went to the hospital.

Page 214, Exercise 2D

Mr. Novak: Did you hear what happened yesterday?
Mrs. Novak: No. What happened?
Mr. Novak: There was a gas explosion downtown.
Mrs. Novak: Oh my gosh. That's terrible. Was anybody hurt?
Mr. Novak: Yes. Two people went to the hospital.
Mrs. Novak: How did it happen? Do they know?
Mr. Novak: No, not yet. They're looking into the cause.
Mrs. Novak: I'll bet traffic is terrible around there.
Mr. Novak: Oh, yeah. It says here a lot of the streets are closed downtown.

Page 215, Exercise 2B

1. here, here
2. art, heart
3. high, I
4. Ow!, Ow!
5. ear, hear
6. high, high

Page 221, Exercises 2A and 2B

Hi, I'm Officer Ramirez, and I'm here today to talk to you about what to do if you're pulled over by a police officer.

So imagine: You're driving along, and everything's great. But suddenly you hear a siren, and behind you there's a police car with flashing lights. That can be really scary. But stay calm and follow this simple advice.

Anytime you see a police car with flashing lights or hear a siren, look for a place to pull over quickly. Always pull over to the right, even if you're in the left lane. Use your turn signal, and pull over to a safe spot.

After you stop your car, roll down your window. Wait for the police officer and stay in your car. Don't get out. If it's dark, turn on the light inside your car. Put your hands on the steering wheel where the officer can see them.

The officer will probably ask for your license, registration, and proof of insurance. Wait for the officer to ask for your documents. Then tell him what you're going to do. For example, say, "I'm going to get my wallet. It's in my purse."

Cooperate and be polite. Follow the officer's instructions. Do not argue with the officer. The officer will give you a warning or a ticket. If you get a ticket, there are instructions on the ticket about how to pay it. You don't pay the officer at that time. Never offer any money or other gifts to an officer.

Page 221, Exercise 2C

Hi, I'm Officer Ramirez, and I'm here today to talk to you about what to do if you're pulled over by a police officer.

So imagine: You're driving along, and everything's great. But suddenly you hear a siren, and behind you there's a police car with flashing lights. That can be really scary. But stay calm and follow this simple advice.

Anytime you see a police car with flashing lights or hear a siren, look for a place to pull over quickly. Always pull over to the right, even if you're in the left lane. Use your turn signal, and pull over to a safe spot.

After you stop your car, roll down your window. Wait for the police officer and stay in your car. Don't get out. If it's dark, turn on the light inside your car. Put your hands on the steering wheel where the officer can see them.

The officer will probably ask for your license, registration, and proof of insurance. Wait for the officer to ask for your documents. Then tell him what you're going to do. For example, say, "I'm going to get my wallet. It's in my purse."

Cooperate and be polite. Follow the officer's instructions. Do not argue with the officer. The officer will give you a warning or a ticket. If you get a ticket, there are instructions on the ticket about how to pay it. You don't pay the officer at that time. Never offer any money or other gifts to an officer.

Finally, don't start your car or leave until the officer gives you permission to go.

Remember, stay calm and listen to the police officer. Police officers want to help and protect you.

UNIT 12

Page 228, Exercises 2B and 2C

Hello, everybody. I'm Michelle Rivera from human resources. Welcome to the Greenville Hotel. I think that you will find this a great place to work. We're going to start our orientation meeting by talking about company policies, and then we'll take a tour of the building.

Let's start with employee responsibilities. We'll give you an employee ID badge at the end of this meeting. You must wear your employee ID badge during your work shift. This is very important.

Also, all employees must follow the dress code. Your manager will explain the dress code for your department. Employees in housekeeping and food service must wear a uniform. Please get your uniforms at the end of this orientation.

Here's another very important responsibility: You must clock in at the start of your shift and clock out at the end of the shift. Please be on time! And you must also clock in and out when you take your break. During your six-hour shift you must take a thirty-minute break. You must not clock in or clock out for another employee.

Page 228, Exercise D

Hello, everybody. I'm Michelle Rivera from human resources. Welcome to the Greenville Hotel. I think that you will find this a great place to work. We're going to start our orientation meeting by talking about company policies, and then we'll take a tour of the building.

Let's start with employee responsibilities. We'll give you an employee ID badge at the end of this meeting. You must wear your employee ID badge during your work shift. This is very important.

Also, all employees must follow the dress code. Your manager will explain the dress code for your department. Employees in housekeeping and food service must wear a uniform. Please get your uniforms at the end of this orientation.

Here's another very important responsibility: You must clock in at the start of your shift and clock out at the end of the shift. Please be on time! And you must also clock in and out when you take your break. During your six-hour shift you must take a thirty-minute break. You must not clock in or clock out for another employee.

Are there any questions? No? OK. Now, some information about our sick day policy. Please open your company policy booklet to page 5 . . .

Page 234, Exercises 2B and 2C

Cam: Hi, Rachel. Can I ask you a favor?
Rachel: Sure. What is it?
Cam: I'm on the schedule for Monday, but I can't come in.
Rachel: Oh, what's up?
Cam: I have to study for a test. Can you take my shift for me?
Rachel: What time do you start?
Cam: 9:30.
Rachel: No problem.

Page 234, Exercise 2D

Cam: Hi, Rachel. Can I ask you a favor?
Rachel: Sure. What is it?
Cam: I'm on the schedule for Monday, but I can't come in.
Rachel: Oh, what's up?
Cam: I have to study for a test. Can you take my shift for me?
Rachel: What time do you start?
Cam: 9:30.
Rachel: No problem. I can use the extra hours. By the way, who's working that day?
Cam: I don't know. Let's check the schedule . . . . Oh, Tim's working that day.
Rachel: Tim? Oh, definitely! I like working with him!

Page 240, Exercises 2B and 2C

Linda: Excuse me, Ron. Can I speak to you for a minute?
Ron: Sure, Linda. What's up?
Linda: I need to talk to you about my schedule.
Ron: OK. Right now you work in the mornings, right?

Linda: Yes. But I'm planning to take classes now. Could I change to evenings?
Ron: Well, let me look at the schedule. I'll get back to you.
Linda: OK. Thanks.

Page 240, Exercise 2D

Linda: Excuse me, Ron. Can I speak to you for a minute?
Ron: Sure, Linda. What's up?
Linda: I need to talk to you about my schedule.
Ron: OK. Right now you work in the mornings, right?
Linda: Yes. But I'm planning to take classes now. Could I change to evenings?
Ron: Well, let me look at the schedule. I'll get back to you.
Linda: OK. Thanks.
Ron: By the way, what classes are you planning to take?
Linda: Business classes. Someday I want to be a manager.
Ron: Oh, that's great. Let me know if I can help.

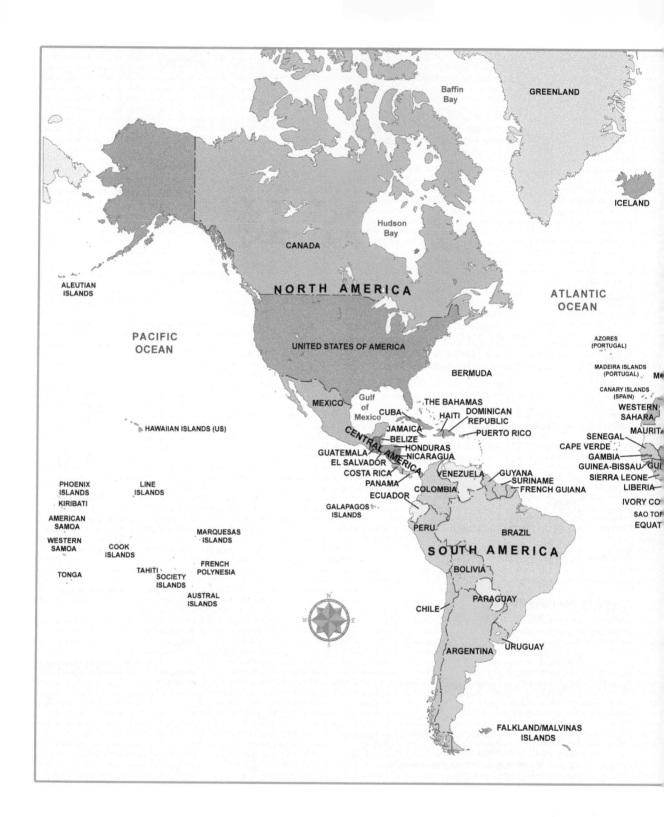

INDEX

CREDITS

Photos:

Front cover: (front, center): Hero Images/Getty Images; (back, upper left): Asiseeit/ E+/Getty; (back, lower left): Manuel Breva Colmeiro/Getty Images; (back, right): Hero Images/Getty Images.

Frontmatter
Page vi (cell phone): tele52/Shutterstock; vi (front cover images): Hero Images/Getty Images, Manuel Breva Colmeiro/Getty Images, Asiseeit/ E+/Getty, Hero Images/Getty Images; vi (ActiveTeach screenshot): Pearson; vi (MyEnglishLab screenshot): Pearson; vi (CCRS page, bottom, left): Wavebreakmedia/Shutterstock; vi (CCRS page, top, right): Illustration Forest/Shutterstock; vii: Dragon Images/Shutterstock; ix (left): Hill Street Studios/Blend Images/Getty Images; x (left): Nancy Honey/Cultura/Getty Images; x (Paco): Rolf Bruderer/Blend Images/Getty Images; x (Sandra): Fuse/Getty Images; x (Pablo): Kevin Dodge/Getty Images; x (Lola): Leung Cho Pan/123RF; x (Marcos): Sirtravelalot/Shutterstock; x (Ana): Jeff Cleveland/Shutterstock; x (Alba): Daniel Ernst/123RF; x (Sara): Arena Creative/Shutterstock; xii: Mandy Godbehear/Shutterstock; xiii: Eddie Gerald/ Alamy Stock Photo; xxii: Courtesy of Sarah Lynn; xxii: Courtesy of Ronna Magy; xxii: Courtesy of Federico Salas Isnardi.

Pre-unit: Welcome to Class
Page 2 (top, right): Daniel M Ernst/Shutterstock; 2 (center, left): StockLite/Shutterstock; 2 (center, center): Jim West/Alamy Stock Photo; 2 (center, right): Ashwin/Shutterstock; 2 (bottom, left): Geo Martinez/Shutterstock; 2 (bottom, right): Vario images GmbH & Co.KG/ Alamy Stock Photo.

Unit 1
Page 5: Ariel Skelley/Getty Images; 8: Paul Burns/Getty Images; 13 (top, right): Daniel Ernst/123RF; 13 (bottom, right): Daniel Ernst/Pavel L Photo and Video/Shutterstock; 14: Cathy Yeulet/123RF; 16 (left): MonicaNinker/E+/Getty Images; 16 (right): Olga Volodina/123RF; 18: Ammentorp/123RF; 20: Pearson/Original Photography by David Mager; 24: Photographee.eu/Shutterstock.

Unit 2
Page 25: Dragon Images/Shutterstock; 28: Rick Gomez/Corbis/Getty Images; 29: Hill Street Studios/Blend Images/Getty Images; 30: Nancy Honey/Cultura/Getty Images;31 (Paco): Rolf Bruderer/Blend Images/Getty Images; 31 (Sandra): Fuse/Getty Images; 31 (Pablo): Kevin Dodge/Getty Images; 31 (Lola): Leung Cho Pan/123RF; 31 (Marcos): Sirtravelalot/Shutterstock; 31 (Ana): Jeff Cleveland/Shutterstock; 31 (Alba): kadettmann/123RF; 31 (Sara): ARENA Creative/Shutterstock; 32: NinaViktoria/Shutterstock; 34: JGalione/E+/Getty Images; 38 (1): Lyroky/Alamy Stock Photo; 38 (2): Kari Marttila/Alamy Stock Photo; 38 (3): Alex Staroseltsev/Shutterstock; 38 (4): Jenny Schuck/Shutterstock; 38 (5): Mega Pixel/ Shutterstock; 39 (left): AshTproductions/Shutterstock; 39 (right): Iofoto/Shutterstock; 40: tele52/Shutterstock; 41: Maskot/Getty Images; 44: Eddie Gerald/Alamy Stock Photo.

Unit 3
Page 45: Monkey Business Images/Shutterstock; 46 (top, left): Jokic/Shutterstock; 46 (top, middle): Atstock Productions/Shutterstock; 46 (top, right): Alexandru Daniel Tantagoi/Alamy Stock Photo; 46 (bottom, left): Dmitry Kalinovsky/123RF; 46 (bottom, middle): LWA/Larry Williams/Blend Images/Getty Images; 46 (bottom, right): Klaus Mellenthin/Westend61 GmbH/ Alamy Stock Photo; 48 (top row, left): British Retail Photography/Alamy Stock Photo; 48 (top row, center left): Mega Pixel/Shutterstock; 48 (top row, center right): Erik Isakson/Blend Images/Brand X Pictures/Getty Images; 48 (top row, right): Olga Popova/123RF; 48 (center, right): Primagefactory/123RF; 48 (bottom row, left): Elenovsky/Shutterstock; 48 (bottom row, center): windu/Shutterstock; 48 (bottom row, right): Ruslan Kudrin/Zoonar GmbH/Alamy Stock Photo; 54: ERproductions Ltd/Blend Images/Getty Images; 56: Wavebreak Media Ltd/123RF; 58 (top, left): TatianaMara/Shutterstock; 58 (top, center): Gary Arbach/123RF; 58 (top, right): Sergey Ryzhov/123RF; 58 (Brian): Hill Street Studios/Blend Images/Getty Images; 58 (Cindy): Cosmonaut/iStock/Getty Images; 58 (Craig): Ginaellen/iStock/Getty Images; 60 (bottom, right): Mangostar/Shutterstock; 62: Maigi/Shutterstock; 64: Maskot/Getty Images.

Unit 4
Page 65: SVRSLYIMAGE/Shutterstock; 66 (1): Elena Elisseeva/Shutterstock; 66 (2): Jack Hollingsworth/Stockbyte/Getty Images; 66 (3): Melanie DeFazio/Shutterstock; 66 (4): Purestock/Getty Images; 66 (5): Comstock/Stockbyte/Getty Images; 66 (6): TongRo Images/ Alamy Stock Photo; 66 (7): Kzenon/123RF; 66 (8): Sarah Nicholl/123RF; 66 (9): Laurence Mouton/PhotoAlto Agency RF Collections/Getty Images; 66 (10): Monkey Business Images/ Shutterstock; 66 (11): Microstockasia/123RF; 66 (12): Cathy Yeulet/123RF; 68 (top, left): Cathy Yeulet/123RF; 68 (top, center): Monkey Business Images/Shutterstock; 68 (top, right): Goodluz/Shutterstock; 68 (center, right): Pearson/Original photography by David Mager; 68 (bottom, left): LawrenceSawyer/E+/Getty Images; 68 (bottom, center): Iakov Filimonov/123RF; 68 (bottom, right): Choi Ka Hin/123RF; 74: Nicolesy/iStock/Getty Images Plus/Getty Images; 75: Hero Images/Getty Images; 76: Tetra Images/Alamy Stock Photo; 76 (cell phone images): tele52/Shutterstock; 78 (Dan Brown): Luis Santos/Shutterstock; 80: Pearson/Original photography by David Mager; 84: Hongqi Zhang/123RF.

Unit 5
Page 85: Oscar Abrahams/Getty Images; 90: Lisa F. Young/Shutterstock; 91 (cell phone images): tele52/Shutterstock; 92 (top, right): All About Space/Shutterstock; 92 (bottom, left): Yury Stroykin/Shutterstock; 92 (bottom, right): Artazum/Shutterstock; 94 (cell phone images): tele52/Shutterstock; 94 (left): Hero Images/Getty Images; 94 (right): Bilderlounge/ Getty Images; 96: Sonya etchison/Shutterstock; 98 (left): Karen roach/123RF; 98 (left, left): Andy Dean Photography/Shutterstock; 98 (right, center): Blanscape/123RF; 98 (right): Andriy Popov/123RF; 104: Dmitry Kalinovsky/123RF.

Unit 6
Page 105: Hill Street Studios/Blend Images/Getty Images; 106 (1): Matka_Wariatka/ Shutterstock; 106 (2): Maximkabb/123RF; 106 (3): Image Source/Getty Images; 106 (4): RubberBall Productions/Brand X Pictures/Getty Images; 106 (5): Hill Street Studios/ Blend Images/Getty Images; 106 (6): Comstock/Stockbyte/Getty Images; 106 (7): Cathy Yeulet/123RF; 106 (8): AleksandarNakic/Getty Images; 106 (9): Comstock/Stockbyte/Getty Images; 106 (10): XiXinXing/Shutterstock; 108: PeopleImages/E+/Getty Images; 110 (cell phone image): tele52/Shutterstock; 116: AJR_photo/Shutterstock; 118: dpa picture allianc / Alamy Stock Photo; 120: Pearson/Original photography by David Mager; 121: Tyler Mabie/ Shutterstock; 124: Hadrian/Shutterstock.

Unit 7
Page 125: Perch Images/Stockbyte/Getty Images; 126 (1): Rene Jansa/Shutterstock; 126 (2): 9nong/123RF; 126 (3): Fuse/Corbis/Getty Images; 126 (4): DianaLundin/iStock/Getty Images

Plus/Getty Images; 126 (5): Antoniodiaz/Shutterstock; 126 (6): Pumatokoh/Shutterstock; 126 (7): Tatiana Gladskikh/123RF; 126 (8): SteveLuker/iStock/Getty Images Plus/Getty Images; 126 (9): Danilov1991xxx/Shutterstock; 126 (10): Alexander Raths/123RF; 126 (11): Custom Medical Stock Photo/Alamy Stock Photo; 126 (12): Mangostock/Shutterstock; 128 (left): Stock Asso/Shutterstock; 128 (right): Dmytro Zinkevych/123RF; 128 (cell phone image): tele52/Shutterstock; 130: Takayuki/Shutterstock; 131 (cell phone image): tele52/Shutterstock; 136: Litabit/Shutterstock; 138 (top, right): Cathy Yeulet/123RF; 138 (bottom): BananaStock/ Getty Images Plus/Getty Images; 140 (left): Ryuichi Sato/Taxi Japan/Getty Images; 140 (right): Angelicar/ iStock / Getty Images Plus/Getty Images; 142: Yakobchuk Viacheslav/ Shutterstock; 144: Hongqi Zhang/123RF.

Unit 8
Page 145: Jean Paul Chassenet/123RF; 146 (1A): GoGo Images Corporation/Alamy Stock Photo; 146 (1B): Comstock/Stockbyte/Getty Images; 146 (2A): Wendy Hope/Stockbyte/ Getty Images; 146 (2B): Pressmaster/Shutterstock; 146 (3A): Paul Bradbury/Caiaimage/Getty Images; 146 (3B): Andersen Ross/Stockbyte/Getty Images; 146 (4A): Cathy Yeulet/123RF; 146 (4B): Wavebreak Media Ltd/123RF; 146 (5A): Robert Kneschke/Shutterstock; 146 (5B): Diego Cervo/Shutterstock; 146 (6A): Dmitry Kalinovsky/123RF: 146 (6B): Carlos Davila/ Alamy Stock Photo; 146 (7A): Flairmicro/123RF;146 (7B): Phovoir/Shutterstock;148: Pearson/ Original Photography by David Mager; 154 (1): Ljansempoi/Shutterstock; 154 (2): ARENA Creative/Shutterstock; 154 (3): Diego Cervo/Shutterstock; 154 (4): Ana Bokan/Shutterstock; 154 (center, right): Pearson/Original Photography by David Mager; 158: Mandy Godbehear/ Shutterstock; 160: Pearson/Original Photography by David Mager; 164: Vgajic/E+/Getty Images.

Unit 9
Page 165: Monkey Business Images/Shutterstock; 166 (1): David Buffington/Blend Images/Getty Images; 166 (2): David Grossman/Alamy Stock Photo; 166 (3): SpeedKingz/ Shutterstock; 166 (4): Monkey Business Images/Shutterstock; 166 (5): AVAVA/Shutterstock; 166 (6): Wavebreak Media Ltd/123RF; 166 (7): Karelnoppe/Shutterstock; 166 (8): Fstop123/ E+/Getty Images; 166 (9): Rawpixel.com/Shutterstock; 166 (10): Frederic Cirou/PhotoAlto Agency RF Collections/Getty Images; 168: Pearson/Original Photography by David Mager; 170: Steve Debenport/E+/Getty Images; 172 (cell phone image): tele52/Shutterstock; 173 (cell phone image): tele52/Shutterstock; 174: Pearson/Original Photography by David Mager; 180: Tetra Images/Getty Images; 182: Fuse/Corbis/Getty Images; 184: Matimix/ Shutterstock.

Unit 10
Page 185: Rido/Shutterstock; 188 (1): Ariel Skelley/DigitalVision/Getty Images; 188 (2): DAJ/Getty Images; 188 (3): Kostic Dusan/123RF; 188 (center, right): Original Photography by David Mager/Pearson Education; 190: UltraOrto, S.A./Shutterstock; 191: Bluestocking/ E+/Getty Images; 192: Bluestocking/E+/Getty Images; 194 (1): Thodonal/123RF; 194 (2): Eurobanks/Shutterstock; 194 (3): Felix Mizioznikov/Shutterstock; 194 (4): Leungchopan/ Shutterstock; 194 (5): Noriko Cooper/123RF; 194 (a): Sergey Lapin/Shutterstock; 194 (b): Michael C. Gray/Shutterstock; 194 (c): Peter Cripps/123RF; 195: Pearson/Original Photography by David Mager; 196: AmorSt Photographer/Shutterstock; 197 (pizza): Nolie/ Shutterstock; 197 (salad): Robyn Mackenzie/Shutterstock; 197 (chips): AZ/istock/Getty Images; 197 (pretzels): Josh Brown/Shutterstock; 198 (left): Scott Rothstein/Shutterstock; 198 (left, center): Deepstock/Shutterstock; 198 (right, center): Mehmet can/123RF; 198 (right): Patryk Kosmider/Shutterstock; 200 (meatloaf): Jabiru/Shutterstock; 200 (chicken): Slawomir Fajer/Shutterstock; 200 (pork): Jeannette Lambert/Shutterstock; 200 (noodles): Peter Doomen/Shutterstock; 200 (hamburger): Pikselstock/Shutterstock; 200 (fish): Ciaran Griffin/Stockbyte/Getty Images; 200 (mac & cheese): Cathleen A Clapper/Shutterstock; 200 (coleslaw): Lorelyn Medina/Shutterstock; 200 (fries): Pikselstock/Shutterstock; 200 (vegetables): P Maxwell Photography/Shutterstock; 200 (onion rings): Shutterdandan/ Shutterstock; 200 (potatoes): Danny E Hooks/Shutterstock; 200 (bottom, right): Pearson/ Original Photography by David Mager; 204: Mint Images/Getty Images.

Unit 11
Page 205: Paul Burns/Blend Images/Getty Images; 208: Pearson/Original Photography by David Mager; 210: Terry Alexander/Shutterstock; 214: Racorn/123RF; 216: Loren Rodgers/ Shutterstock; 218 (left): Tribalium/Shutterstock; 218 (center): Photobac/Shutterstock; 218 (right): Paul Bradbury/Caiaimage/Getty Images; 220: Bibiphoto/Shutterstock; 224: Jabejon/ E+/Getty Images.

Unit 12
Page 225: Nightman1965/Shutterstock; 226 (1): Bilderbox/INSADCO Photography/ Alamy Stock Photo; 226 (2): Comstock Images/Stockbyte/Getty Images; 226 (3): Cathy Yeulet/123RF; 226 (4): Jupiterimages/Stockbyte/Getty Images; 226 (5): Maskot/Getty Images; 226 (6): Derek Meijer/Alamy Stock Photo; 226 (7): Hongqi Zhang/123RF; 226 (8): ndoeljindoel/123RF; 226 (9): Taylor Jorjorian/Alamy Stock Photo; 226 (10): Avava/ Shutterstock; 226 (11): Fuse/Corbis/Getty Images; 226 (12): Blend Images/ColorBlind Images/Brand X Pictures/Getty Images; 231 (cell phone image): tele52/Shutterstock; 234: Ton koene/Alamy Stock Photo; 238 (top): David Wasserman/Photolibrary/Getty Images; 238 (bottom): Monkey Business Images/Getty Images; 240 (top, left): Snowwhiteimages/123RF; 240 (top, left center): Elwynn/123RF; 240 (top, right center): Hongqi Zhang/123RF; 240 (top, right): Pixelheadphoto digitalskillet/Shutterstock; 240 (center, right): Hurst Photo/ Shutterstock; 244: Yoshiyoshi Hirokawa/DigitalVision/Getty Images.

Grammar Review
Page 247: Daniel M Ernst/Shutterstock; 248 (Ned): Felix Mizioznikov/Shutterstock; 248 (Aki): natu/Shutterstock; 248 (Artur): Avid_creative/Getty Images; 248 (Rohan): Ashwin/ Shutterstock; 248 (Lan): Shippee/Shutterstock; 248 (Aya): Flashpop/DigitalVision/Getty Images; 250: Motortion Films/Shutterstock;252: GagliardiImages/Shutterstock.

Illustrations: Laurie Conley, pp. 8, 37, 108, 114 (top), 128, 148 (top row, bottom row left, bottom row right), 157, 158, 171, 208, 249; ElectraGraphics, pp. 11, 44, 52, 53 (left), 64, 71, 72, 73, 74, 84, 91, 93, 100, 104, 113, 124, 132 (top a-f), 133 (center), 140, 144, 148 (bottom row center), 151, 152, 164, 184, 204, 212 (top), 213 (bottom), 214 (bottom), 220 (right, 224), 232, 233, 244, 279, 280-281; Brian Hughes, pp. 77, 189, 193; André Labrie, pp. 33, 34, 54, 88 (top), 120, 180, 228 (top); Paul McCuster, pp. 112, 212 (bottom); Marc Mones, pp. 57; Luis Montiel, pp. 6, 26, 27, 86, 89, 186, 214 (top), 228 (bottom); Allan Moon, pp. 53 (top, center, right); Neil Stewart/NSV Productions, pp. 12-13, 38-39, 132 (bottom), 133; Roberto Sadi, pp. 101; Steve Schulman, pp. 40, 49, 80, 206; Anna Veltfort, pp. 51, 88 (bottom), 111, 114 (bottom), 115, 134, 137, 150, 172, 211, 217